GREAT
AMERICAN
TRIALS

CONTRIBUTORS

Stephen G. Christianson

Kathryn Cullen-DuPont

Teddi DiCanio

Colin Evans

Elizabeth Gwillim

Bernard Ryan, Jr.

Thomas C. Smith

GREAT
AMERICAN
TRIALS

EDWARD W. KNAPPMAN,
EDITOR

Stephen G. Christianson and Lisa Paddock,
Consulting Legal Editors

A New England Publishing Associates Book

DETROIT • WASHINGTON, D.C. • LONDON

Great American Trials

Published by **Visible Ink Press**™
a division of Gale Research Inc.
835 Penobscot Bldg.
Detroit MI 48226-4094

Visible Ink Press is a trademark of Gale Research Inc.

ISBN 0-8103-9134-1

Front cover photo of Clarence Darrow at the Scopes "Monkey Trial" (1925): Bettman Archive.
Back cover photo of William Kennedy Smith (1991): AP/Wide World Photos.

Art Director: Cynthia Baldwin
Cover and Page Design: Mary Krzewinski

Printed in the United States of America

10 9 8 7 6 5

CONTENTS

In Chronological Order
(by date of trial)

1910–1919

1920–1929

1930–1939

CONTENTS

In Alphabetical Order
(by name of trial)

Y

CONTENTS

In Subject Order
(by the crime[s] charged)

Civil Suits

**Constitutional
Issues**

Education

Espionage

**Family &
Matrimonial
Issues**

Fraud

**Freedom of
Speech &
Press**

**Women's
Rights &
Issues**

**GREAT
AMERICAN
TRIALS**

PREFACE

Great American Trials provides readers and researchers with brief, accurate, and readable summaries of the most significant and celebrated trials in U.S. history.

As with any encyclopedic undertaking, the selection process was a complex one and inevitably involved some subjectivity given space limitations. Since the settlement of Jamestown in 1607, literally millions of civil and criminal trials have been conducted in American courts. Many thousands of these had some historic or legal significance or attracted wide public attention for one reason or another. From these, I have attempted to select the 200 I judged best met the following criteria:

Historic Significance: Did the trial have a major impact on the course of American history? Trials such as *Scott v. Sanford* (the Dred Scott case), which was a fateful step on the road to the Civil War, and the Boston Massacre Trial, which set the stage for the American Revolution, are included under this criterion.

Legal Significance: Did the trial result in an important legal precedent or a landmark Supreme Court decision? Examples of such trials include those of Dr. Sam Sheppard, which established a significant precedent concerning pre-trial publicity, *In Re Baby M*, which affected the validity of surrogate motherhood contracts, and *Gideon v. Wainwright*, which led the Supreme Court to rule that states had to provide free counsel to indigent defendants in criminal trials.

Political Controversy: Did the trial crystallize or generate a national political controversy? Among the trials included under this criterion are the Sacco–Vanzetti murder trial, which was tainted by hostility to radicals and immigrants; the Julius and Ethel Rosenberg treason trial; and the trial of the Chicago Seven for instigating disruptive anti-Vietnam War demonstrations.

Public Attention: Because of the fame of the participants or the nature of the alleged crime, many trials in our history have been national sensations. The trial of Bruno Hauptmann for kidnapping the Lindbergh baby falls under this category, as do the trials of Daniel Sickles, Lizzie Borden, Harry Thaw, Jean Harris, Patty Hearst, and Charles Manson.

Legal Ingenuity: Some trials earned a place in this book because the courtroom skills demonstrated by one or more of participating lawyers have become legendary. Among the trials included under this criteria are *Martinez v. Del Valle*, the occasion of Joseph Choate's most famous cross-examination; the Leopold and Loeb murder trial, featuring Clarence Darrow for the defense; and the Triangle Shirtwaist Fire trial, where Max Steuer won an acquittal few thought possible.

Literary Fame: Trials have inspired novelists, playwrights, screen-writers, non-fiction writers, and even songwriters. Their works have often left a greater impression on the public than the original trial. Among the trials that have been immortalized in literature are the Chester Gillette murder trial, the Salem Witchcraft trials, Joe Hill's murder trial, the Scopes "Monkey" trial, and the Richard Hickock/Perry Smith murder trial.

In my selection process, I have intentionally applied these criteria more leniently to recent trials than to those from the more distant past. This was done to serve the needs of readers who, I suspect, are far more likely to need or desire information on recent trials.

Because the important decisions of the Supreme Court are adequately covered in a host of other standard reference works, I have intentionally minimized the number of such decisions in **Great American Trials.** Only those that resulted from an actual courtroom trial (*Buck v. Bell*), had an impact on the way trials are conducted in this country (the *Miranda* decision), or marked critical turning points in American history (*Roe v. Wade*) have been included.

While another editor might have included some trials that I have not or omitted some that I included, the vast majority of trials would make any editor's list of the most important trials in our history. Several precautions were taken to avoid oversights and omissions. The legal editors of this volume—Lisa Paddock and Stephen Christianson— assisted me in compiling and evaluating the list of trials as did several members of the editorial staff at Gale Research. Although their assistance has been very helpful, the responsibility for any omissions is mine.

Each entry begins with a set of basic facts about the trial. This is followed by a narrative explaining the circumstances that led to the trial, pre-trial maneuvers, the trial itself, the judgment, and any subsequent appeals. We sought to entertain as well as inform. We have tried to provide the maximum amount of accurate information in the space available.

The extent of sources consulted varies considerably with the trial. Some trials, such as Lizzie Borden's and Sacco and Vanzetti's, have produced shelves of well-researched histories. Others are barely mentioned in secondary sources. Our contributors have dug as deep into the sources as necessary to establish the essential facts of each trial. However, for some 17th-, 18th-, and early 19th-century trials, the surviving records are sparse, failing even to note the full names of judges or lawyers.

All but a few entries end with suggestions for further readings. Contributors were asked to include their suggestions for further reading the most readily and widely available sources of additional information. As the intended audience for this book is general readers rather than legal researchers, we have excluded legal citations.

The trials are presented in chronological order. This was chosen as the most logical sequence for several reasons. First, the law evolves chronologically; today's cases apply yesterday's precedents. Second, many trials are emblematic of a particular historical period and are directly or indirectly connected (the various espionage and anti-Communist trials of the late 1940s and early 1950s, for example.) Third, there is no preferable alternative. Without a generally accepted convention for naming trials, an alphabetical arrangement would be of little benefit to readers. As *Great American Trials* contains three tables of contents—chronological, alphabetical, and category—plus a comprehensive index, readers will have little difficulty in locating any specific trial.

In editing this book, I have made a determined effort to translate legalese into plain English. Unfortunately, there are some legal terms that defy translation; the definition is so particular to the law that no plain English equivalent exists and any paraphrase would risk distorting the meaning. Such terms have been defined in the glossary found at the end of the volume.

Many people made vital contributions to the planning, writing, editing, and production of *Great American Trials:*

Chris Nasso of Gale Research provided indispensable support, encouragement, and wise counsel when this book was in its formative stages. Rebecca Nelson, with assistance from Jane Hoehner, gently but firmly kept the book on track and on deadline as we progressed through the editorial and production process. Charles A. Bayne and Alan Nichter deserve special recognition for their roles as advisors to the book.

Steve Christianson and Lisa Paddock, the book's legal editors, together scrutinized the entire manuscript and corrected many misinterpretations of trial procedures and misstatements about the intricacies of the American legal system.

The writers who contributed to *Great American Trials*—Steve Christianson, Teddi DiCanio, Kathryn Cullen-DuPont, Colin Evans, Elizabeth Gwillim, Bernie Ryan, and Tom Smith—were dogged researchers, skilled word smiths, and astonishingly conscientious about meeting their tight deadlines. Larry Hand copyedited this book with exceptional skill and diligence.

Susan Brainard helped me manage this project day-in, day-out, over two years with unfailing good humor and care. Jil Nelson Kaplan tracked down the illustrations, a task that proved far more difficult than either of us imagined when we began.

Finally I owe special thanks to my wife and partner, Elizabeth Frost Knappman, who has tolerated my foibles and helped me over the rough patches for 28 years, and to my daughter, Amanda, who brightens the days.

—*Edward W. Knappman*
August 1993

INTRODUCTION

Trials have been the ultimate means to resolve disputes in American society from Colonial times to the present. Many of the great turning points in the nation's history have occurred in courtrooms—from John Peter Zenger's trial for allegedly libeling the British governor of Colonial New York through *Roe v. Wade*, which barred states from prohibiting abortions in the early months of pregnancy.

Trials have been a prime source of popular entertainment, public ritual, and real-life human drama. In person and through the news media, Americans have flocked to courtrooms to be titillated, scandalized, uplifted, inspired, educated, and just plain amused. Before the age of mass communications, the local courthouse provided one of the few diversions available to a largely rural population. Indeed, judges, preachers, and editorial writers have so long and frequently denounced the "circus-like" atmosphere prevailing at many locally or nationally celebrated trials that the phrase has become a cliché of courtroom journalism. In more recent times, real and fictional trials have become a staple of movie producers and television programmers. Today, cable television's Court TV network enables trial junkies to perpetually indulge themselves without ever changing the channel.

As compelling as trials may be as drama, they fill a far more serious purpose in our society: they offer a mechanism for maintaining public order when one person, or other legal entity such as a corporation, violates the legally protected rights of another person or society at large. In this sense, a trial fulfills the human need for retribution, providing even the losing side with a sense that he or she at least has had an opportunity to air grievances, or has had his or her "day in court."

Trials, therefore, are the central focus of American jurisprudence. However, the process of resolving disputes through a trial of the facts— litigation—is only one area of legal practice. Only a fraction of those cases filed by litigators ever goes to trial. Indeed, most efforts of the vast majority of lawyers who are not litigators are devoted to avoiding trials by advising clients how to stay on the right side of the law and by drafting legal documents, such as contracts.

Fundamentals of the Law

To appreciate what made many of the trials described in **Great American Trials** "great" requires some familiarity with the branches of the law, the history and contours of the American system of jurisprudence, and the rules of procedure and evidence that govern the way trials are conducted. While the editors and contributors have attempted to translate legalese into plain English whenever possible, for some legal terms there is no common word or phrase with an identical meaning. Readers will find a glossary of such terms at the end of this book.

Perhaps the most important factor about a court is that it is a public body. In each case, a court must determine the facts, but in determining their legal significance, the court is performing a service not just to the litigants, but to the larger community as well. In deciding a particular controversy according to the law, courts provide guidance to others who may in the future confront similar issues, thereby ideally forestalling at least some potential litigation.

This evolutionary method of devising so-called judge-made law—as opposed to legislation—is a natural by-product of common-law systems of jurisprudence like ours, in which current cases are decided in accordance with precepts derived from earlier cases. This "common law" is a body of complex rules formulated out of thousands of decisions reached by generations of judges, beginning in England during the Middle Ages. As such, common law predates the creation of legislative bodies, whose primary function is drafting the rules interpreted and applied by modern courts to the cases tried before them.

"Civil law," by contrast, grew out of a written code of Roman laws and today is the system of laws prevailing in Western Europe (except for the United Kingdom, of course), as well as the state of Louisiana. Although today the number of statutes regulating both public, or criminal, law (in which the government has the most direct interest) and private, or civil, law (directly involving the interests of individuals) continues to grow, the common-law system predominates in the rest of our nation.

The Roots of the American Court System

The British judicial system was transplanted wholesale to the American colonies. In 17th-century America, lawmaking and judging were regarded as one and the same. As in England, Parliament was regarded as the highest court. The colonies, however, began to develop their own layered court systems. At the top of the hierarchy stood colonial legislatures, which served primarily as courts of appeals. Beneath them was a network of superior courts, which often included colonial governors among their presiding judges, and which mainly heard appeals in civil matters first tried in lower courts. Superior courts also tried criminal cases. The third level of local courts saw most of the trials in colonial America. These local courts performed governmental functions as well, such as levying and collecting taxes, and provided townspeople with an opportunity to socialize, conduct business, and discuss politics.

A modified version of this three-tier system remains the structure of the various state court systems today. Trials are held in the lowest level of courts; a level of appellate courts reviews all appeals from the trial courts; and a supreme court considers appeals on important issues of law.

As the population of the colonies grew, so did the length of court trial dockets. Courts dealt with increasing demand for their services largely by increasing the formality of their proceedings. When courts began to enforce procedural requirements, fewer cases were filed, and many of those were dismissed. This trend was reversed by the early 18th century with an increase in the number of trained lawyers.

Judges, by contrast, were often appointed lay persons unschooled in the law. This lack of a trained judiciary increased the importance of juries. At the trial of John Peter Zenger for seditious libel (1735), the jury found the defendant not guilty despite the clear import of the judge's instructions to the contrary. This helped establish the principle that juries could exercise considerable discretion in interpreting judicial instructions. Later in the 18th century, however, judges gained the power to order new trials in the face of verdicts that were, in their opinion, contrary to the weight of the evidence. Today, in trials conducted without a jury—so-called bench trials—judges settle questions of both law and fact. In jury trials the roles are apportioned so that jurors decide the facts of the case, while decisions about the law are left to judges.

The use of fictitious litigant names, a common practice by the time of *Roe v. Wade* (1973), first appeared in the late 1680s in a case involving "John Doe" and "Richard Roe." Obscuring the real names of the plaintiff and defendant meant the case would be decided on its specific merits rather than on the influence and connections of the contestants, which was a pattern that had encouraged many plaintiffs to hope that quick, rough justice would be administered in their favor.

The Courts under the Constitution

Article III of the United States Constitution, together with the first Judiciary Act (1789), established three types of federal courts, roughly modeled on the tripartite structure then operating in individual states. The two lower tiers, consisting of trial and appeals courts, are organized along regional lines, with the former vastly outnumbering the latter. District courts were and still are trial courts, each manned by a single district judge. Circuit courts, now federal appellate courts, employed three-judge panels then, as they do now. While circuit courts were then primarily trial courts, today the circuit courts of appeals are devoted to reviews of district court decisions. The Supreme Court was then mainly—and is now almost exclusively—devoted to reviewing decisions of lower appellate courts, both federal and state,[1] and consists of nine justices sitting *en banc,* or altogether.

The principles of Federalism recognized by the framers of the Constitution mandated that the states retain important rights. While the federal government concerned itself with national affairs, such as foreign relations and commerce among the states, states retained under their traditional police powers the right to govern matters of public health, safety, and morality.[2] Consequently, throughout the 19th century, development of many areas of the law was left to individual state legislatures and courts. To this day, important differences exist among states as to contract law, criminal law, and the law of torts, or non-criminal injuries.

In contrast, federal courts' jurisdiction, or power to hear and decide cases, was limited to hearing cases between citizens of different states, admiralty cases, and cases arising under federal law. This third area of empowerment led to the development of federal common-law doctrines and embraced the authority to interpret constitutional and statutory provisions, or even overturn them, as in *Marbury v. Madison* (1803), which established the principle of judicial review.[3] When federal courts hear cases between citizens of different states, known as diversity cases, they must apply the substantive law of whichever state has the strongest interest in the outcome.

Trial Procedures

Each state court system has its own set of procedural rules, but since 1938 and 1945, respectively, federal courts have followed their own rules of civil and criminal procedure, which often differ sharply from procedures observed by state courts.

Rules of procedure govern not just the trial itself, but also all the legally significant events leading up to it. They may, for example, govern the form in which the plaintiff in a civil case files his set of pleadings, customarily called a complaint, which initiates the lawsuit. These rules will ordinarily stipulate the time by which the defendant must respond to the plaintiff's charges in a formal answer. These rules are multitudinous and complex, as they must impose order on the vast array of legal weapons in a litigation attorney's arsenal, the majority of which are deployed before the trial ever begins. In fact, most litigators rarely see the inside of a courtroom. Instead, they spend their time negotiating with the opposing side (always, if that party is represented by counsel, through his or her attorney[4]) and drafting motion papers. Motions can pertain to such things as the pretrial testimony of potential witnesses and the exchange of documents and information that are a prelude to trial. Collectively, this is known as "discovery." Attempts to have an opponent's case dismissed on various grounds before trial also are made in the form of motions.

The purpose of discovery is to preserve evidence that might not be available at trial, such as the testimony of an infirm witness, to ascertain the issues actually in controversy, and to prevent either side from being taken off guard—by surprise evidence, for example. It seems fundamental that both sides should be in possession of all information relevant to the case before proceeding to trial, but the disclosure afforded by discovery is a relatively recent innovation. Discovery only became a vital part of the litigation process with the adoption of the Federal Rules of Civil Procedure. It has since become the focus of much of the debate about the delay and costs associated with modern-day litigation.

Once discovery is complete and rulings are made on motions by the two sides, more precautions are taken to ensure trials are conducted fairly. Both plaintiff's and defendant's counsels submit draft pretrial orders to the court. The pretrial order includes such items as lists of all witnesses the party intends to call and of all documentary evidence, or exhibits, the party intends to present at trial. The parties then proceed to select a jury if the trial is a criminal prosecution or if the plaintiff in a civil case has elected to have a jury trial. This selection process is called *voir dire* and, particularly in recent years, is a crucial stage of the trial, as each opposing counsel subtly maneuvers to get a trial (or *petit*) jury sympathetic to his or her case.

In some criminal prosecutions, a grand jury has already heard the case. Traditionally composed of 23 jurors (as opposed to the six- to 12-

person juries used in trials), the grand jury's purpose is to determine whether the facts and accusations presented by the prosecutor warrant an indictment and eventual trial of the accused. Others accused of criminal acts can face other types of juries convened before trial to hear only prosecution testimony. For example, although because of her age she did not herself appear, Cheryl Christina Crane, the 14-year-old daughter of film star Lana Turner, was the subject of a 1958 inquest by a coroner's jury into the murder of her mother's lover. Because the coroner's jury returned a verdict of justifiable homicide, criminal proceedings against Crane were discontinued.

The Sixth Amendment to the Constitution guarantees the accused the right to a trial by a jury of his or her peers, a concept as old as common law itself. The Sixth Amendment also guarantees the accused the right to be tried by an impartial jury, thus making the process of jury selection even more stringent in criminal trials. While voir dire always permits the attorneys for either side to excuse potential jurors for cause or for no cause at all (called a peremptory challenge), the Sixth Amendment mandates that this process result in a jury that represents a fair cross-section of the community and does not discriminate against any class of potential jurors. Disputes about a potential jury's racial balance can be central to the trial strategy of either side, as it was for the defendant's attorney in the 1968 murder trial of Black Panther activist Huey P. Newton. If excessive publicity surrounds the case, the court may take additional measures to make sure the jury remains impartial: sequestering the jury, delaying the trial, even granting a change of venue, as in the 1967 trial of mass murderer Richard Speck.

Trials begin with opening arguments delivered by attorneys for both sides, beginning with plaintiff's counsel—which in the case of most criminal prosecutions will be the government's attorney, such as a district attorney. (A defendant may reserve the right to present an opening statement until after the plaintiff's presentation of its case is complete.) These arguments present the judge and jury with an overview of the evidence each side intends to present and of their respective theories of the case. Plaintiff's counsel then presents his or her case. That starts with direct examination of the plaintiff's designated witnesses, which can include so-called expert witnesses who do not testify about the facts of the case, but about matters requiring specialized knowledge. Documentary or concrete evidence is introduced in the course of direct examination. Each side is permitted to ask open questions only of its own witnesses, unless that witness proves to be hostile, in which case he or she may be asked leading questions and even be cross-examined.

Cross-examination is generally reserved for counsel for the opposing side, who can question each witness before he or she steps down. The purpose of cross-examination is to discredit the witness or cast testimony already given in a light more favorable to the party represented by the cross-examiner. If cross-examination elicits testimony damaging to the party presenting its case, that party may seek to rebut or clarify it through redirect examination of the witness.

When the plaintiff has presented all of its evidence, the defense presents its case using the same process. After both sides have made their cases to the judge, or to judge and jury, plaintiff's counsel, then defendant's, delivers a closing statement summarizing his or her client's case. If it is a jury trial, the judge will then instruct the jurors on the applicable law, including which side has the burden of proof and what the measure of that burden is. There are three standards for the measure of proof that the party bearing the burden must meet to win the case. Most civil cases use the "preponderance of the evidence" standard, which means that the fact finder must be convinced that the fact at issue is more probably true than not. Some civil cases, such as those involving fraud, require proof by clear and convincing evidence, i.e., that there is a high probability that the fact at issue exists. The highest standard applies to criminal prosecutions, in which the defendant's guilt must be established beyond a reasonable doubt.

Juries deliberate, sometimes for weeks on end. Judges acting as finders of both law and fact sometimes deliberate or sometimes rule immediately from the bench. If the trial is criminal in nature, the verdict must be unanimous. Its delivery often is followed by a long delay before the trial court pronounces judgment and holds a sentencing hearing.

Rules of Evidence

Formal rules govern the introduction of both testimonial and documentary evidence. While not all states have codified their evidentiary rules, the Federal Rules of Evidence, which became effective in 1975, govern civil and criminal cases in most federal courts. As might be expected, additional rules apply in criminal cases. For example, if the state wishes to introduce the confession of a defendant at a criminal trial, the court must conduct an examination outside the presence and hearing of the jury (also called *voir dire*). This is done to determine if the statements were voluntarily obtained in compliance with the defendant's Miranda rights,[5] and therefore constitutionally admissible.

Attorneys can attempt at trial to introduce whatever new evidence—largely witness testimony—they feel will help their clients' cases; it is their opponents' job to object to and thus prevent the evidence from being admitted. The most common of these objections are relevance, hearsay, and privilege.

Relevance pertains to the link between the proposed evidence and the proposition it is supposed to support. Relevant evidence, whether direct or circumstantial, must tend to prove a fact that is material to the issue. Even relevant evidence may be excluded if its probative value is outweighed by the danger of unfair prejudice, confusion of the issues, or misleading of the jury.[6] Certain categories of relevant evidence, such as proof that a person was insured against liability in a case where his or her negligence is an issue, are never admissible.

The rule against hearsay is probably the most important—certainly the most complex—exclusionary rule of evidence. The Federal Rules define hearsay as "a statement, other than one made by the declarant while testifying at the trial or hearing, offered in evidence to prove the truth of the matter asserted." In other words, a witness's testimony about what someone else said or wrote or communicated nonverbally is not considered credible evidence of the content of that communication. The reason for the hearsay rule is that the witness's credibility is key to determining the truthfulness of his or her testimony. Without the adverse party's ability to cross-examine the communicant and without the jury's ability to scrutinize his or her demeanor, there is no adequate basis on which to judge the accuracy of the statement. An additional question arises in criminal cases in that the Sixth Amendment grants the accused the right to confront and cross-examine all the witnesses against him or her.

There are numerous exceptions to the hearsay rule, generally based on how trustworthy the statement at issue is and the necessity of making the exception. A witness's recital of a dying individual's declarations, for example, is generally admissible on the theory that a dying person has nothing to gain by lying,[7] and because this is the only method whereby such statements can be admitted as evidence after the speaker dies. As might be expected, exceptions in criminal trials are usually narrower to provide the defendant—who may have his or her life or liberty at stake—with additional safeguards. This is not always the case, however. One state-law exception permits statements made by one conspirator to be admitted against co-conspirators even if the statements are made after all conspirators are in custody. This has been ruled constitutional even though the usual rule is that this co-conspirator exception does not apply to any post-custody utterances.

The third common ground for objecting to admissibility is privilege, which applies to communications taking place in the context of legal or other confidential relationships, such as that between husband and wife, priest and penitent, physician and patient.

There is also, of course, a person's right under the Fifth Amendment to the Constitution to refuse to testify against himself or herself, the privilege against self-incrimination.

Appeals Procedures

The time in which an appeal from the trial court's decision is permitted begins to run after the verdict has been reached and, in a criminal case, the sentence pronounced. In a criminal case, the decision or the sentence can be appealed. The executions of Julius and Ethel Rosenberg after their 1951 espionage trial were delayed for two years, while both the conduct of their trial and the severity of their sentences were appealed.

There are two potential stages of appeal in federal and in most state court systems: from the trial court to the intermediate appellate court, then to the supreme court. While losing parties customarily have an automatic right to appeal to the intermediate courts, in most superior courts of appeal, appeals are usually heard only at the discretion of the court. (Appeals almost always reach the U.S. Supreme Court after a petition has been filed for a writ of *certiorari*.)

In the early stages of development of common law, both in England and in America, courts were divided into two types: courts of law and courts of equity. Courts of law ruled according to accepted common-law principles, but when injuries occurred for which law courts had no ready remedy, equity courts were able to address these issues according to general principles of fairness. An appeal in equity subjected both facts and law to review and retrial. Now, however, the two types of courts have been merged. Appeals seek a reversal of the lower court's opinion or a retrial, based almost exclusively on some misapplication of the law—such as in the judge's instructions to the jury regarding the law pertinent to the case—or on procedural error.

Criminal and civil appeals generally follow similar courses. One significant area of difference, however, falls under the rubric of double jeopardy. The principle of double jeopardy, applicable only in criminal prosecutions, is fundamental to common law and finds its expression in the Fifth Amendment, which provides that "No person . . . shall . . . be subject for the same offense to be twice put in jeopardy of life and limb." This principle operates at the federal and state levels. It prevents a second trial unless the first ended in a mistrial—one declared void prior to verdict, usually because the jury is deadlocked—or the defendant appeals a conviction, as Claus von Bülow did after being found guilty in 1982 of attempting to murder his wife. Von Bülow was acquitted of all charges after his second trial in 1985. For defendants less fortunate than von Bülow, double jeopardy also prevents double punishment and even makes the imposition of any higher penalty on retrial subject to increased judicial scrutiny.[8]

Legal Skills

Few, if any, attorneys are so versatile that they are equally adept in all facets of legal practice. Appellate practice often requires a keener grasp of legal technicalities than is required of a trial attorney. Often, a trial attorney's skill rests instead on keen intuitions about human nature. In the Triangle Shirtwaist Trial (1911), for example, defense attorney Max Steuer was able to secure a not-guilty verdict in the face of enormous odds because he understood the psychology of the jury.

Two manufacturers were on trial for the deaths by fire of 146 of their workers, owing to the fact that the doors to the New York City sweatshop where they worked were locked on the defendants' orders. As unsympathetic as these defendants' case appeared, however, Steuer was able to overcome the jury's emotions by appealing to their intellect. Steuer had the principal prosecution witness, a young female survivor of the fire, repeat her testimony three times. The first two recitals were identical; in the third she changed one word. Steuer won the case by making sure that the jury recognized that the witness had been rehearsed.

Other trial attorneys—Daniel Webster immediately comes to mind—succeed not so much on the basis of their examination technique, but on the eloquence and persuasiveness of their oratory. When great trial skills are combined with great issues, memorable trials result. Although the issue at stake in the 1925 Scopes "Monkey Trial," the teaching of evolution, was of great social significance, what made the trial most unforgettable was Clarence Darrow's clever examination of Fundamentalist politician William Jennings Bryan, whom the defense called to the stand as an expert on the Bible—an unorthodox maneuver, given that Bryan was also acting as plaintiff's counsel.

The Scopes trial was memorialized in a play and subsequent film, both entitled *Inherit the Wind*. Other trials, like the 1943 Errol Flynn rape trial, are famous because they featured an irresistible combination of celebrities and scandal. Some trials become infamous because the public perceives them to be a miscarriage of justice, like the 1979 Dan White case, where the accused was convicted of voluntary manslaughter rather than murder—in part because of the success of the unconventional

"Twinkies Defense," which argued that White's intake of junk food was the real culprit.

Some trials are celebrated, though, not because they feature notable parties, salacious facts, or incomparable trial tactics. As noted at the outset of this essay, what matters most about the American court system, ultimately, is its public nature. While spectacle certainly is one aspect of many great trials, perhaps the "greatest" one in American history, the one which arguably has had the most profound and lasting effect on our people, is *Brown v. Board of Education* (1954). *Brown v. Board of Education* was finally decided by the U.S. Supreme Court, and the attorney for the winning side, Thurgood Marshall, was himself later to become a Supreme Court justice. But the case revolved around a modest individual's attempt to gain recognition of his child's right to a good education. By overturning the "separate but equal" doctrine that had up to that time made ours a legally segregated society, *Brown v. Board of Education* fueled a social revolution that has changed the lives of every one of us.

—Lisa Paddock, Esq.
August 1993

[1] The Supreme Court, however, has been known to give state sovereignty great deference. For example, in *Buck v. Bell* (1927), the Court upheld the constitutionality of a Virginia statute permitting the forced sterilization of 18-year-old Carrie Buck, whose mother had been feebleminded.

[2] With increased emphasis on civil rights in the latter half of this century, many of the states' attempts to regulate morality were overturned. In *Griswold v. Connecticut* (1964), for example, the Supreme Court found unconstitutional an 1879 state statute prohibiting the use or distribution of or advisory services concerning contraceptives. While the justices found no basis in the Bill of Rights for voiding the statute, they explained their decision in terms of a newly explored right, the right of privacy, which was further expanded in such cases as *Roe v. Wade*.

[3] The only other instance before the Civil War in which the Supreme Court struck down a federal law occurred in the more infamous *Scott v. Sanford* (1856), in which the Court found the Missouri Compromise unconstitutional and the plaintiff, a slave, consequently not a citizen.

[4] Parties in civil actions—and even in some criminal cases—can appear *pro se*, that is, represent themselves. In *Gideon v. Wainwright* (1963), however, the Supreme Court ruled that every defendant in a felony trial had a right to counsel, and that if the defendant could not afford to hire his or her own lawyer, the state had to provide one. This decision makes impossible situations such as that prevailing during the second treason trial of John Fries in 1800, in which Justice Samuel Chase acted from the bench—much to the defendant's detriment—as Fries' counsel after the defendant's attorneys withdrew in the face of Chase's open hostility toward their client.

[5] Such rights are named for the landmark case of *Miranda v. Arizona* (1967), which ruled that at the time of their arrests, suspected criminals had to be read their rights to remain silent, to know that anything they said could be used against them, and that if they were indigent the state would provide them with counsel.

[6] The persuasiveness and prejudicial possibilities of circumstantial evidence are well illustrated by the 1955 kidnapping and murder trial of Burton Abbott, who was sentenced to death in the

gas chamber largely because the district attorney managed, despite the lack of any real foundation, to introduce the victim's unwashed undergarments and overwhelm the jury with their sight and smell.

[7]For an example of the questionableness of this rationale, one need turn no further than the Finch-Tregoff trial of 1960, in which one of the accused murderers was permitted to recite in open court his dying wife's apology for her own killing.

[8]Under the U.S. system of federalism, states and the national government are considered separate "sovereigns." Therefore, each can try a defendant for the same actions under different laws without violating the prohibition against double jeopardy. This principle permitted the federal government to prosecute four Los Angeles police officers in 1993 for violating the civil rights of Rodney King even though the defendants had been acquitted the prior year on state charges of using excessive force.

Anne Hutchinson Trials: 1637 and 1638

Defendant: Anne Hutchinson   **Crimes Charged:** "Traducing the ministers and their ministry" and heresy   **Chief Defense Lawyer:** None
Chief Prosecutors: Civil trial: John Winthrop; religious trial: the Reverend John Davenport   **Judges:** Civil trial: John Winthrop and the Magistrates of Massachusetts; religious trial: John Wilson and the ministers of the Church of Boston
Places: Civil trial: Newtown (Cambridge); religious trial: Boston
Dates of trials: Civil trial: November 7–8, 1637; Religious trial: March 22, 1638   **Verdicts:** Guilty   **Sentences:** Banishment from the colony and excommunication from the Church of Boston

SIGNIFICANCE

Anne Hutchinson was the defendant in the most famous of the trials intended to squelch religious dissent in the Massachusetts Bay Colony.

The Massachusetts Bay Colony had been founded so that the Puritans might perfectly practice their own faith. Religious liberty for others—a concept Americans would later take for granted—was not part of the Puritans' plan. Instead, founding Governor John Winthrop envisioned a model "Citty [*sic*] upon a hill," an example of Christian unity and order. Not incidentally, women were expected to play a submissive and supporting role in this society.

Anne Hutchinson, a skilled midwife and herbal healer with her own interpretation of Puritan doctrine, challenged the leaders of this "wilderness theocracy," as Barbara Ritter Dailey describes it. She arrived in the colony in 1634 and began holding religious meetings in her home. She quickly drew crowds of 60 to 80 men and women on a weekly basis. An alarmed assembly of church elders agreed that "women might meet [some few together] to pray and edify one another" but, without naming Hutchinson, denounced "one woman ... [who] took upon her the whole exercise ... [as] disorderly, and without rule."

Hutchinson continued to outline her views. Puritan doctrine emphasized the performance of "good works," which might be interpreted as evidence, or justification, that an individual had been elected for salvation. Hutchinson's favorite minister, John Cotton, stressed a "covenant of grace"—the idea that one's own spiritual consciousness of God's election might also be justification.

1

Hutchinson expanded this idea to include an in-dwelling Holy Ghost whose guidance replaced the self-will of the saved. She then denounced all of the colony's ministers except Cotton and her brother-in-law, John Wheelwright, for preaching only the "Covenant of Works."

Anne Hutchinson preaching. (Courtesy, Library of Congress)

General Court Summons Hutchinson

The General Court summoned Hutchinson in November 1637. She was put on trial for her theological views and for stepping outside the bounds assigned to women. Governor John Winthrop, acting as prosecutor, outlined the charges: "Mrs. Hutchinson, you are called here as one of those that have troubled the peace . . . you have spoken of divers[e] things . . . very prejudicial to the honour of the churches and ministers thereof, and you have maintained a meeting . . . that hath been condemned . . . as a thing not tolerable nor comely in the sight of God nor fitting for your sex."

Hutchinson responded haughtily, "I am called here to answer before you, but I hear no things laid to my charge."

Winthrop said, "I have told you some already and more I can tell you."

Finally, exasperated by Hutchinson's "What have I said or done?" stance, Winthrop exclaimed, "Why for your doings, this you did harbour and countenance those that are parties in this faction that you have heard of." He was referring to the fact that Hutchinson had encouraged others to sign a petition in support of Wheelwright, who, found guilty of sedition and contempt, had been banished.

Hutchinson simply stated, "That's a matter of conscience, Sir."

Winthrop replied: "Your conscience you must keep or it must be kept for you."

He then denounced her support for Wheelwright and his sympathizers. "What breach of law is that, Sir?" Hutchinson inquired.

"Why dishonoring of parents," Winthrop immediately replied, placing the commonwealth's governor and magistrates in that role.

Hutchinson asked sarcastically, "But put the case Sir that I do fear the Lord and my parents, may I not entertain them that fear the Lord because my parents will not give me leave?"

After some further discussion of the theological point, Winthrop directed his line of questioning toward a woman's right to hold religious meetings.

Hutchinson demanded, "[C]an you find a warrant [permission] for yourself and condemn me for the same thing?" Denying that men had attended, she cited a "clear rule in Titus, that the elder women should instruct the younger."

Winthrop told her to "take it in this sense that elder women must instruct the younger about their business and to love their husbands and not make them to clash." When Hutchinson objected, saying "it is meant for some publick times," Winthrop criticized her for drawing her students away from their house-work: "[I]t will not well stand with the commonwealth that families should be neglected for so many neighbours and dames and so much time spent, we see no rule of God for this . . . and so what hurt comes of this you will be guilty of and we for suffering you."

Seven ministers then testified in turn, as Winthrop summarized it, that Hutchinson "did say that they [the ministers] did preach a covenant of works and that they were not able ministers of the gospel." Shortly afterward, Hutchinson was ordered "to consider of it," and the court recessed until the following morning.

The next day, John Cotton's sympathetic testimony on theological points and the question of whether Hutchinson had "traduced the ministers" brought Hutchinson close to acquittal. Then, suddenly, she told the court that she knew through an immediate revelation from God that her inquisitors would be destroyed. This was proof enough of heresy, and Hutchinson was "banished from out of our jurisdiction as being a woman not fit for our society." The sentence was modified, however, to permit Hutchinson to remain "confined" in the colony until spring.

Church of Boston Enters Fray

Hutchinson continued to spread her views. Finally, as Winthrop recorded, "the Elders of Boston . . . declared their readinesse to deale with Mistris Hutchinson in a Church way."

At this trial, Cotton opposed Hutchinson and emphasized the dangers he thought a dissenting woman courted: "[T]hough I have not herd, nayther do I thinke, you have bine unfaythful to your Husband in his Marriage Covenant, yet that will follow upon it." He turned to the women present in the church and instructed them to ignore Hutchinson's teachings, saying "[Y]ou see she [Hutchinson] is but a Woman and many unsound and dayngerous principles are held by her."

The Reverend Thomas Shepard then testified that Hutchinson sought "to seduce and draw away many, Espetially simple Weomen of her owne sex." Her theological views were condemned, and the spiritual penalty of excommunication was then added to the earlier civil punishment of banishment. When the Reverend John Wilson ordered her "as a Leper to withdraw your selfe out of the Congregation," one woman—Mary Dyer—walked over to Hutchinson and joined hands with her. The two women walked together to the church door, where Hutchinson turned to deliver her own verdict to the ministers: "The Lord judgeth not as man judgeth, better to be cast out of the Church than to deny Christ."

The Aftermath: a Mixed Picture

Reaction to the trials was mixed. Hutchinson herself, as Winthrop recorded, "gloried in her sufferings, saying, that it [her excommunication] was the greatest happiness, next to Christ, that ever befel her." Hutchinson's husband William left the colony at her side; he later explained that "he was more nearly tied to his wife than to the church." Their son Francis later blasted the church as "a strumpet" and was excommunicated and fined 40 pounds. When he refused to pay the fine, he was jailed.

Finally, as Lyle Koehler points out, the church found it necessary to continue disciplining women for similar offenses, especially during the 18 months following Hutchinson's excommunication. Katherine Finch, for example, "spoke against the magistrates, against the Churches, and against the Elders" and was ordered whipped on October 10, 1638. Even after this punishment, Finch failed to conduct herself "dutifully to her husband." She was forced to make a public promise that she would, in the future, comply to his wishes. Phillip Hammond was excommunicated in 1639, in part for publicly declaring that "Mrs. Hutchinson neyther deserved the Censure which was putt upon her in the Church, nor in the Common Weale." In 1646, Sarah Keayne was excommunicated by the Boston church for holding her own mixed religious meetings and "irregular[ly] prophesying." Joan Hogg, found guilty of "disorderly singing and . . . saying she is commanded of Christ to do so," was also excommunicated.

To Hutchinson's detractors, however, the most stunning commentary on the controversy was when Mary Dyer and Anne Hutchinson became pregnant following Hutchinson's trials, and experienced what Boston clergy described as "monster births" and divine signs of guilt. (Hutchinson's modern diagnosis is of a hydatidiform mole.)

In 1643, when Hutchinson was killed by Indians in what would become New York state, the Reverend Peter Bulkeley delivered the ministers' final summation: "Let her damned heresies shee fell into . . . and the just vengeance of God, by which shee perished, terifie all her seduced followers from having any more to doe with her leaven."

—*Kathryn Cullen-DuPont*

Suggestions for Further Reading

Battis, Emery. "Anne Hutchinson," *Notable American Women, 1906–1950.* Edited by Edward T. James, Janet Wilson James, and Paul S. Boyer. Cambridge, Mass.: Belknap Press of Harvard University Press, 1971.

Dailey, Barbara Ritter. "Anne Hutchinson," *A Reader's Companion to American History.* Edited by Eric Foner and John A. Garraty. Boston: Houghton Mifflin, 1991.

Evans, Sara M. *Born for Liberty: A History of Women in America.* New York: The Free Press, A Division of Macmillan, Co. 1989.

Flexner, Eleanor. *Century of Struggle.* Cambridge, Mass.: Belknap Press of Harvard University Press, 1959.

Hutchinson, Thomas. *The History of the Colony and Province of Massachusetts Bay.* Edited from Hutchinson's copy of Vols. I and II and his manuscript of Vol. III by Lawrence Shaw Mayo, 1936. Volume II, Appendix II, pp. 366–391, reprint in Nancy Cott, ed. *Roots of Bitterness: Documents of the Social History of American Women.* New York: E. P. Dutton, 1972.

Koehler, Lyle. "The Case of the American Jezebels: Anne

Hutchinson and Female Agitation during the Years of the Antinomian Turmoil, 1636–1640." *William and Mary Quarterly,* 3d ser., 31 (1974): 55–78, reprint in Linda K. Kerber and Jane DeHart Mathews, eds. *Women's America: Refocusing the Past.* New York: Oxford University Press, 1972.

Morgan, Edmund S. *The Puritan Dilemma: The Story of John Winthrop.* Boston: Little, Brown and Company, 1958.

Stanton, Elizabeth Cady, Susan B. Anthony, and Matilda Joslyn Gage, eds. *History of Woman Suffrage, 1881.* Reprint Salem, N.H.: Ayer Co., 1985.

Winthrop, John. *Winthrop's Journal, "History of New England," 1630–1649* (2 vols.). New York: Charles Scribner's Sons, 1908.

Dorothy Talbye Trial: 1638

Defendant: Dorothy Talbye   **Crime Charged:** Murder
Chief Defense Lawyer: No Record   **Chief Prosecutor:** No Record
Judge: Governor John Winthrop   **Place:** Boston, Massachusetts Bay Colony
Date of Trial: October 4, 1638   **Verdict:** Guilty   **Sentence:** Death by hanging

SIGNIFICANCE

The Talbye case demonstrated that early American society and its legal system did not fully understand or acknowledge the concept that someone could commit a crime and yet be judged not guilty by reason of insanity. There was no practical alternative to treating the insane as ordinary criminals. Although England's officials had a few institutions, such as the Hospital of St. Mary of Bethlehem (known as Bedlam), to which they could send people, the American colonies had none.

A defense of not guilty by reason of insanity is a comparatively recent innovation. However, by 1641, the Massachusetts Bay Colony's "Body of Liberties" did state that:

> Children, Idiots, Distracted persons . . . shall have such allowances and dispensations in any Cause whether Criminall or other as religion and reason require.

Even if these words had been written three years earlier in 1638, they still might not have saved the "distracted" Dorothy Talbye from the gallows, for such "allowances" were limited. The 17th-century society could do little to either aid or restrain the severely mentally ill.

Over time, Dorothy Talbye changed from a respected member of the community, "of good esteem for godliness," into a melancholy woman given to fits of violence. She fought with family and neighbors. She experienced what she believed to be divine revelations, sometimes on a daily basis.

Talbye's husband and children were often the targets of her madness. Her revelations told her to starve her family and herself. According to her husband John, she tried to kill him. Prayers and admonitions of ecclesiastical authorities were useless. Finally, she was expelled from the church.

The expulsion seemed to aggravate her emotional state. Eventually her actions twice brought her before civil authorities. The second time a magistrate ordered her to be whipped. For a time, Talbye seemed to improve. But her condition worsened again. Dorothy's revelations convinced her that the only way to "free" Difficult, her daughter, "from future misery" such as Dorothy herself had suffered, was to kill the child. She took the 3-year-old to a secluded spot and broke her neck. When apprehended, Talbye confessed freely.

Talbye was charged in the Court of Assistants. Although she had earlier confessed to what she had done, in court Talbye "stood mute for a space" and would not enter a plea until Governor John Winthrop threatened she would be pressed (have stones piled on her chest). She pleaded guilty. The record states:

> When she was to receive judgment, she would not uncover her face, nor stand up, but as she was forced, nor give any testimony of her repentance, either then or at her execution.

Talbye was no stalwart martyr. As she had cursed her excommunication, so did she fight her execution. Talbye was dragged to the gallows where she refused to stand. She grabbed at the ladder. She may have been willing to "free" her daughter from "misery" but she was unwilling to be freed herself.

— Teddi DiCanio

Suggestions for Further Reading

Powers, Edwin. *Crime and Punishment in Early Massachusetts, 1620-1692, A Documentary History.* Boston: Beacon Press, 1966.

Winthrop, John. *Winthrop's Journal*, Vol. I. New York: Charles Scribner's Sons, 1908.

Judith Catchpole Trial: 1656

Defendant: Judith Catchpole   **Crimes Charged:** Infanticide and witchcraft
Chief Defense Lawyer: No Record   **Chief Prosecutor:** No Record
Judges: Michael Brook, William Fuller, Edward Lloyd, John Pott, and Richard
Preston   **Place:** Patuxent County, Maryland   **Date:** September 22, 1656
Verdict: Not Guilty

SIGNIFICANCE
While trying to adhere to common law, colonial judicial practices often arose from immediate practical needs, as had the common law itself. In this case, the practical need was for a woman's expertise, which led to an all-female jury.

Even after obtaining the vote with passage of the Nineteenth Amendment, for decades some states still prohibited women from serving on juries. Nevertheless, in 1656, an all-woman jury was impaneled to decide the case of Judith Catchpole. Although unusual, hers is not the only recorded case of a female jury.

Catchpole was an indentured servant, who had arrived in Maryland in January 1656 aboard the *Mary and Francis*. An unnamed fellow passenger, identified in court records only as the indentured servant of William Bramhall, told a bizarre story claiming Catchpole had given birth to a child that she subsequently murdered. The storyteller died before Catchpole could be tried, but not before telling his tale to other servants.

> Andrew Wilcox sworn and Examined Saith that William Bramhalls man Servant that dyed Said that when the Murther was done all the people and Seamen in the Ship were asleep and after it was done Judith Catchpole and the Said Servant of William Bramhall went up upon the Deck and walked a quarter of an hour afterward off they went to their lodging this being at Sea in the middle of the Night.

This trial was held eight months after Catchpole arrived. Others had not come forward to accuse her of infanticide. Nor was there any explanation of how Catchpole could hide a pregnancy and give birth aboard a cramped ship without anyone noticing.

According to additional hearsay evidence, the dead manservant also spoke of witchcraft. He claimed that she had "cut the Skinn of a maid's throat when She was a sleep," then sewn it up again without waking her. Catchpole was also supposed to have "prickt a Seaman in the back" with a knife the manservant had ground "Dutch fashion," following which she rubbed a little grease into the man's back "and he Stood up again." The manservant said that she was to kill several others.

In addition to weighing the evidence presented in testimony, the jury acted in an investigative capacity. The women examined Judith Catchpole for any physical signs of recent pregnancy and childbirth. They found none and gave an oath to that effect.

The court appeared to pay little attention to the charges of witchcraft. The decisions of the court seem to have hinged on the plausibility of the charges. Neither the judges nor the jury could give credence to the accusations made by the dead manservant. They declared Judith Catchpole's accuser to have been of unsound mind and released her.

— Teddi DiCanio

Suggestions for Further Reading

Browne, William Hand, ed. *Archives of Maryland*. Baltimore: Maryland Historical Society, 1883.

Rose, Lou. "A Memorable Trial in Seventeenth-Century Maryland." *Maryland Historical Magazine*, Vol. 83. (Winter, 1988).

Semmes, Raphael. *Crime and Punishment in Early Maryland*. Montclair, N.J.: Patterson Smith, 1970. [Reprint from Johns Hopkins Press, 1938.]

Mary Dyer Trials: 1659 and 1660

Defendant: Mary Dyer   **Crime Charged:** Quakerism
Chief Defense Lawyer: None   **Chief Prosecutor:** No Record
Judge: Governor John Endecott   **Place:** Boston, Massachusetts Bay Colony
Dates: October 19, 1659, and May 31, 1660   **Verdicts:** Guilty
Sentences: First trial: death by hanging, commuted to banishment from the colony and hanging should she return; second trial: death by hanging

SIGNIFICANCE

Quaker Mary Dyer's conviction and execution for practicing her faith in a manner other than the one approved by Massachusetts' colonial government was indicative of the draconian measures the puritan leaders of the colony were prepared to use to insure total theological conformity.

In 1638, when Anne Hutchinson was excommunicated from the Church of Boston, Mary Dyer walked to Hutchinson's side and offered her hand in solidarity. Accounts of Hutchinson's trials in the Massachusetts Bay Colony appear in every child's first American history text, while Mary Dyer's own trials—22 years later and with far more drastic consequences for the accused— are rarely examined.

The Puritan officials of the Massachusetts Bay Colony had struggled since the colony's founding to eliminate dissenters. In 1658, they found Quakers, or members of the Society of Friends, particularly alarming: The *Records of the Governor* states emphatically that "The doctrine of this sect of people . . . tends to overthrow the whole gospell [*sic*] & the very vitalls [*sic*] of Christianitie . . ." On October 19, 1558, the colony passed a law banishing Quakers "on pajne [*sic*] of death."

Two Quakers, William Robinson and Marmaduke Stephenson, were imprisoned in Boston in 1659; that summer, Dyer visited them and was thrown into prison as well. All three were ordered banished and threatened with execution should they ever return to the colony. They were released on September 12, 1659, but returned within a few weeks to "look [the] bloody laws in the face."

The three were thrown into jail for, as the governor's records describe it, "theire rebellion, sedition, & presumptuous obtruding themselves upon us," and "as underminers of this government." They stood trial before the General

Court on October 19, 1659. "[B]rought to the barre," they "acknowledged themselves to be the persons banished" and earlier "convicted for Quakers." Governor John Endecott declared the sentence to each of them in turn, using the same words: "You shall go from hence to the place from whence you came [jail], & from thence to the place of execution, & there hang till you be dead."

When Dyer heard her sentence, she said, "The will of the Lord be done." Her husband, William Dyer, accepted the situation with less equanimity. On August 30, 1659, he had written to the "Court . . . assembled at Boston" to object to the restriction of his wife's religious liberty. He likened the members of the General Court to the "Popish inquisitors" of the 13th century, since they served as "a judge and accuser both." He complained bitterly that the Puritans, who had left England to escape persecution, now persecuted others: "[S]urely you or some of you, if ever you had the courage to looke a bishop in the face, cannot but remember that the 1. 2 or third word from them was, You are a Puritane are you not, & is it not so in N. England, the magistracy having . . . assumed a coercive power of conscience, the first or next word After appearance is You are a Quaker."

Governor Thomas Temple of Nova Scotia, Governor John Winthrop, Jr., of Connecticut, and Dyer's son William added their objections, and Dyer received a dramatic suspension of her sentence. With Robinson and Stephenson, she was escorted by drum-beating soldiers to "the place of execution, & there [made] to stand upon the gallowes, with a rope about her necke." Robinson and Stephenson were both hanged but Dyer, to her surprise, was granted "liberty for forty eight howers . . . to depart out of this jurisdiction, after which time, being found therein, she is forthwith to be executed."

She remained outside the colony for only seven months before returning. Before Governor Endecott and the General Court on May 31, 1660, "she acknowledged herself to be Mary Dyer, . . . denied our lawe, [and said she] came to bear witness against it." Then "The whole court mett together voted, that the said Mary Dyer, for her rebelliously returning to this jurisdiction . . . shall . . . according to the sentence of the General Court in October last, be put to death."

Mary Dyer was hanged on June 1, 1660. In 1959, the Massachusetts General Court ordered a seven-foot statue of Dyer— which bears the inscription "Witness for Religious Freedom"—to be placed on the lawn of the Boston State House.

— Kathryn Cullen-DuPont

Suggestions for Further Reading

Chu, Jonathan M. *Neighbors, Friends, or Madmen: The Puritan Adjustment to Quakerism in Seventeenth-Century Massachusetts Bay.* Westport, Conn.: Greenwood Press, 1985.

Dyer, William. *Mary Dyer, Quaker: Two Letters of William Dyer of Rhode Island, 1659–1660.* Printed for Worthington C. Ford by the University Press, Cambridge, U.S.A., n.d.

McHenry, Robert, ed. *Famous American Women: A Biographical Dictionary from Colonial Times to the Present.* New York: Dover Publications, 1983.

Shurtleff, Nathaniel B., ed. *Records of the Governor and Company of the Massachusetts Bay in New England.* Boston: From the Press of William White, Printer to the Commonwealth, 1854.

Tolles, Frederick B. "Mary Dyer," *Notable American Women, 1906–1950.* Edward T. James, Janet Wilson James, and Paul S. Boyer, eds. Cambridge, Mass.: Belknap Press of Harvard University Press, 1971.

Nicholas More Impeachment: 1685

Defendant: Nicholas More   **Crimes Charged:** High crimes and misdemeanors   **Chief Defense Lawyer:** None   **Chief Prosecutor:** None
Place: Philadelphia, Colony of Pennsylvania
Date of Indictment: May 15, 1685   **Verdict:** None, although More was relieved of his judicial duties

SIGNIFICANCE

Like other early America impeachments, Pennsylvania's methods for impeaching a sitting judge were drawn from English precedents and from procedures improvised at the time due to immediate need. The Nicholas More case illustrated a potential area for conflict both between various branches of government and between the colonies and the distant mother country.

Most American colonies had no specific provision for impeachment in their charters. As needed, colonial legislatures appropriated to themselves the same right to impeach an official that England's House of Commons exercised. By the early 1700s, as American impeachments came to the attention of the Privy Council, crown lawyers repeatedly stated that colonial assemblies had no such right. Provincial legislators fashioned legal justifications for colonial impeachments during the decades-long quarrel between Mother England and her daughter colonies concerning parliamentary authority vs. colonial autonomy in local affairs.

William Penn, proprietor of the colony of Pennsylvania, appointed Nicholas More as chief justice in 1684. Like many of Penn's political appointments, More was a man of wealth. He had purchased 10,000 acres of land from Penn. Penn believed that men with a stake in the colony's future would serve Pennsylvania best, and he had faith in the abilities of men of business. Unfortunately, More, a physician with no legal training, was arrogant and contentious and thus temperamentally unsuited to the job.

Using a brief clause in Pennsylvania's Charter of Liberties, the Assembly impeached More. On May 15, 1685, an Assembly member introduced a formal complaint. More, a delegate that day, was asked to withdraw. After some discussion, the individual articles of impeachment were approved one by one. To name a few, the Assembly charged that More had: bullied a jury into rendering an unjust verdict; mistreated judges; harassed a witness; summoned juries unlawfully; altered a charge; and missed serving in several circuit courts. The articles were then presented to the colony's Council, which decided to hear evidence on the following day and ordered More to appear to answer the charges.

Furious, More refused to appear even when threatened with being "ejected as an unprofitable member of the House." Nor could the Assembly obtain records from the Provincial Court. The court's clerk, Patrick Robinson, made excuses for not turning over the records and continued to do so after his arrest on the Assembly's warrant.

After days of squabbling, the Assembly expelled More from the legislature and resolved that Robinson ought to be dismissed from his office. Even without court records, the Assembly presented enough evidence to the Council to substantiate several charges. John White, the Assembly's speaker, asked that both More and Robinson be removed from their offices.

The Council was inclined to do nothing. Although it finally deprived More of his bench, the Council avoided taking the impeachment matter further. Robinson remained in office one more year until impertinence to judges lost him his position.

After several months, the Assembly sent a petition to Penn. Penn's reaction was simply to appoint More to the five-member board that made up the Executive of the Province. More never served and he died in 1689.

— Teddi DiCanio

Suggestions for Further Reading:

Hoffer, Peter Charles, and N.E.H. Hull. *Impeachment in America, 1635–1805*. New Haven, Conn.: Yale University Press, 1984.

Lewis, Jr., Lawrence. "The Courts of Pennsylvania in the Seventeenth Century." *Pennsylvania Magazine of History and Biography*, Vol. V. Philadelphia: Historical Society of Pennsylvania, 1881.

Jacob Leisler Trial: 1691

Defendants: Jacob Leisler, Jacob Milborne, plus eight other men
Crimes Charged: The treasonable act of holding the king's fort by force against the royal governor, such action resulting in several deaths
Chief Defense Lawyer: None
Committee for Preparing the Prosecution: Nicholas Bayard, William Pinhorne, and Stephen Van Cortlandt **Chief Prosecutors:** James Emmott, George Farewell, and William Nichols
Judges for Court of Oyer and Terminer: Captain Isaac Arnold, Joseph Dudley, Captain Jasper Hickes, Major Richard Ingoldesby, Thomas Johnson, John Laurence, William Pinhorne, Sir Robert Robinson, William Smith and Colonel John Young **Place:** New York, N.Y. (Colony)
Dates of Trial: April 10–27, 1691 **Verdict:** Leisler, Milborne, and six others: guilty; two others acquitted; all eventually pardoned except Leisler and Milborne **Sentence:** Death by hanging, disembowelment, decapitation, and quartering

SIGNIFICANCE

The trial and the harsh sentence imposed reflected the extreme personal and political animosities that marked New York politics. The executions, applauded by many of the colony's Anglo-Dutch elite as an example to the Leislerians, exacerbated those animosities.

The American colonies were already restive when mother England created a Dominion of New England in an effort to obtain greater control of the region. Many measures adopted were disliked by colonists. Thus, when England's Glorious Revolution replaced Catholic James II with Protestant William and Mary (James' daughter) of Orange, the colonies overthrew some appointed royal officials, including the lieutenant governor for New York, Francis Nicholson.

On May 30, 1689, an argument between two officers at New York's Fort James sparked a rumor that Nicholson planned to burn the city. On May 31, a German immigrant merchant, Jacob Leisler, leading 500 men, seized the fort.

Two weeks later Nicholson sailed for England. He left his councillors in charge: Nicholas Bayard, Frederick Phillipse, and Stephen Van Cortlandt. They were unable to thwart Leisler's usurpation of civil authority, which was supported by members of the merchant, artisan, and laboring groups.

Leisler Assumes Control

In December 1689, John Riggs arrived from Britain bringing dispatches from the king for the lieutenant governor or "to such as for the time being take care to keep the peace and administer the laws of New York" in the governor's absence. The dispatches were clearly for the council, but Leisler interpreted the orders to declare himself lieutenant governor.

Some of Leisler's actions were laudable, such as strengthening the province's defenses. Others are subject to interpretation. Leisler held a convention of delegates from the counties and towns. (Not everyone came.) Later, based on writs he issued, an assembly was elected. Some historians praise this as the first representative body for the province. Others believe Leisler manipulated both convention and assembly, often by threat of arms.

In February 1691, Major Richard Ingoldesby arrived in New York, ahead of the new governor, Colonel Henry Sloughter. Ingoldesby demanded Leisler surrender. Leisler refused, saying Ingoldesby had no royal commission. Even when Sloughter arrived, Leisler delayed briefly before surrendering. His behavior gave his enemies justification for insisting on a criminal inquest, instead of the general inquiry ordered by the Crown.

Ten men were indicted. Leisler and Jacob Milborne, his son-in-law, refused to plead, insisting the judges must first rule on the legality of the authority by which they had held Fort James. That "authority" rested on the king's letter by which Leisler had declared himself lieutenant governor. After an unfavorable ruling, the two men still refused to plead. The jury acquitted two, but found Leisler, Milborne, and six others guilty. They were sentenced to death. In response to a petition, Sloughter wrote the king recommending a pardon for all except Leisler and Milborne.

A clamor arose to execute Leisler and Milborne without delay. Eventually Sloughter gave in. On May 16, 1691, from the scaffold, Leisler and Milborne insisted they had had no intent save "than to maintain against popery or any Schism or heresy" in the interests of the Crown. They begged forgiveness for any offenses and prayed that all hate be buried with them. They were then executed. Several years later, their estates, which had been seized, were restored to their heirs.

— Teddi DiCanio

Suggestions for Further Reading

Andrews, Charles M. *Narratives of the Insurrections, 1675–1690*. New York: Barnes & Noble, 1915. Reprinted 1967.

Balmer, Randall. "Traitors and Papists: The Religious Dimensions of Leisler's Rebellion." *New York History* (1989). Vol. 70.

Reich, Jerome R. *Leisler's Rebellion: A Study of Democracy in New York, 1664–1720*. Chicago: University of Chicago Press, 1953.

Salem Witchcraft Trials: 1692

Defendants: 200 accused, including: Bridget Bishop, Reverend George Burroughs, Martha Carrier, Giles Corey, Martha Corey, Mary Easty, Sarah Good, Elizabeth How, George Jacobs, Susannah Martin, Rebecca Nurse, Alice Parker, Mary Parker, John Procter, Ann Pudeator, Wilmot Reed, Margaret Scott, Samuel Wardwell, Sarah Wild, and John Willard.

Crimes Charged: Witchcraft   **Chief Examiners:** Jonathan Corwin and John Hathorne   **Place:** Salem Village (now Danvers, Massachusetts)

Dates of Hearings: March 1, 1692 through the spring

Chief Defense Lawyers: None   **Chief Prosecutors:** None

Judges for Court of Oyer and Terminer: Jonathan Corwin, Bartholomew Gedney, John Richards, Nathaniel Saltonstall, William Sergeant, Samuel Sewall, William Stoughton, and Wait Winthrop.   **Place:** Salem Town (present-day Salem, Massachusetts)

Dates of Trials: June 2, 1692–September 1692. The court was then suspended. A superior court, convened in January 1693, held trials in several cities.   **Verdicts:** 29 found guilty   **Sentences:** 19 hanged; remaining convicted and accused released over a period of years

SIGNIFICANCE

America's only massive witch-hunt resembled those that occurred in Europe over the centuries in that it transpired during a period of political unrest, but it was atypical in that it was localized and comparatively brief. However, the American witch-hunt remains singular in the effect it has exerted on the American imagination as historian and nonhistorian try to fathom the reasons for this frightening example of the perils of hysteria.

In the 17th century there was an almost universal belief in the effective power of witchcraft. English courts were specifically interested in maleficia, the performance of malicious acts against one's neighbors. Many mishaps, major and minor, were attributed to the malice of witches. Yet prior to the Salem Witch Trials, Massachusetts records indicate only about 100 people had ever been formally accused of witchcraft, 15 of whom were executed. In 1692, 200 were accused in a matter of months.

Over the centuries, witch-hunts generally occurred during times of anxiety or social upheaval. From the time the settlers first landed, they had enjoyed a nearly autonomous form of self-government. But in 1684 Massachusetts lost its charter. England then created the Dominion of New England combining several unwilling colonies. Not only was political autonomy threatened, but the dominion's new governor, Sir Edmond Andros, had declared that the revocation of the charter invalidated land titles. During the wake of England's Glorious Revolution of 1688, James II was deposed and Andros was overthrown. The colony was drifting in a legal limbo.

During the winter of 1691–92, in the kitchen of the Reverend Samuel Parris, Tituba, a Carib Indian slave entertained 9-year-old Betty, the minister's daughter, and 11-year-old Abigail Williams, his niece, with fortune-telling and magic. Eventually, the girls invited in eight more girls, ranging in age from 12 to 20. Key among them was Ann Putnam, Jr., the brilliant daughter of an embittered woman.

To Puritan eyes there was nothing innocent about flirting with magic spells for amusement. Moreover, Puritanism was unrelenting in its admonitions that the grace of God was man's only rescue from deserved damnation—a grace seemingly measured in droplets. However exciting their games, the girls were tense from the strain of their secret misdeeds. By January 1692, tension turned into what would now be termed hysteria.

Betty Parris and Abigail Williams began exhibiting strange symptoms. They fell into trances and, if addressed, made noises and gestures. Abigail suffered convulsions and screamed as if in pain. Other girls soon exhibited similar symptoms. Panic seized the village.

In February, Reverend Parris called in Dr. William Griggs, who, after extensive examination and treatment, concluded they were bewitched. Several ministers came to pray over the girls to no avail. The ministers insisted the girls must name those bewitching them.

An accepted maxim was that the Devil had to work through one person to affect another; in other words, he had to persuade someone to act as his agent. The Devil could then appear to his victims in the shape of his agent and harm them. The spectral shape was thought to be visible only to the afflicted. Such "spectral evidence," criticized by some, was accepted by the court.

Pressed, the girls finally named Tituba, the slave, Sarah Good, a near derelict, and the unpopular Sarah Osburn. On February 29, 1692, warrants were issued and they were arrested.

Magistrates Hold a Hearing

On March 1, two magistrates, Jonathan Corwin and John Hathorne opened a public hearing in the packed meeting house of the village. The examiners conducted themselves more like prosecutors than investigators. Pregnant, dressed in rags, the haggard Sarah Good stood before the magistrates and flatly denied tormenting the children. The girls fell into fits and blamed Good for their pains. Before being removed, Good shifted any possible blame onto Sarah Osburn.

Osburn, dragged from a sick bed when arrested, also denied tormenting the children. The girls again performed. Osburn said she "more like to be bewitched than that she was a witch." She reported a dream in which she was visited by something "like an Indian all black, which did pinch her in her neck" and drag her toward her door. Osburn died in jail awaiting trial. Others met the same fate.

Tituba told the magistrates what they wanted to hear. After briefly denying she had "familiarity" with the Devil, she said:

> [T]here is four women and one man, they hurt the children, and then they lay all upon me; and they tell me, if I will not hurt the children, they will hurt me.

She named Good and Osburn, but claimed she could not identify the other two. Following the magistrates' lead, Tituba wove into her testimony elements of spectral evidence such as talking cats, riding on sticks, and a tall, unidentified man of Boston.

One of the next two accused, Martha Corey, was vulnerable because she had unequivocally disbelieved the girls' claims. But Rebecca Nurse, a frail, elderly, pious matriarch, had never questioned the girls' condition. Few had a harsh word to say about her, except, perhaps, those engaged in a long land dispute with her family. Her sisters were subsequently accused of witchcraft. In the course of their investigations, the magistrates unearthed and recorded many old arguments and suspicious activities. Both women had to testify amidst the girls' fits and visions. The examiners made even less pretense of impartiality than they had with Good, Osburn, and Tituba, but they could not shake the two women in their denials.

Jails Fill with Accused

By May, the jails of Salem Town and Boston were filled with people awaiting trial. More women than men, the accused ranged from Dorcas Good, 5-year-old daughter of Sarah, to the Reverend George Burroughs, formerly the pastor of Salem Village. Ann Putnam claimed Burroughs was responsible for the deaths of his first two wives and of soldiers fighting Indians along the border. Reverend Cotton Mather believed Burroughs was the witches' master conspirator.

Also by May, Massachusetts had a new charter and a new governor, Sir William Phips. Phips convened the General Court, which appointed a special court to try the witches. He then left to tackle more pressing matters of skirmishes along the borders.

The first tried was Sarah Bishop, a tavern keeper. According to Samuel Gray, Bishop's specter appeared over the cradle of his child, bringing about the child's illness and death. Bishop was convicted and, on June 10, hanged.

Next, the judges consulted several ministers for guidance on witchcraft evidence. The ministers warned against heavy reliance on spectral evidence, saying the "demon may assume the shape of the innocent."

The court reconvened June 28. Of the five tried, one was briefly acquitted. The jury was impressed by Rebecca Nurse's demeanor and by a petition testifying to her character. Her daughter, Sarah Nurse, submitted a deposition:

> I saw Goody [term of address] Bibber pull pins out of her close [*sic*] and held them between her fingers and clasped her hands round her knees and then she cried out and said Goody Nurse Pinched her. This I can testify.

19th-century depiction of a witch trial. (Courtesy, Library of Congress)

After the verdict was read, the girls fell into howling fits, and Justice William Stoughton addressed the jury foreman:

> I will not impose on the jury, but I must ask you if you considered one statement made by the prisoner. When Deliverance Hobbs was brought into court to testify, the prisoner, turning her head to her said, 'What, do you bring her? She is one of us.' Has the jury weighed the implications of this statement?

Asked for an explanation, the half-deaf woman did not answer. After reconsideration, Rebecca Nurse was found guilty.

On July 19, the five women were hanged. Urged to confess by Reverend Nicholas Noyes, because "she knew she was a witch," Good retorted:

You're a liar. I am no more a witch than you are a wizard. If you take my life away, God will give you blood to drink.

Reports are that Noyes died bleeding from the mouth.

Six more were convicted in August. The execution of Elizabeth Proctor was delayed because she was pregnant. The delay saved her life. Her husband, John Proctor, an outspoken critic of the girls' visions, was hanged. His servant girl, Mary Warren, had tried to recant. Away from magistrates and the other girls, Warren would slowly return to a rational state of mind. Faced by them, she would dissolve into hysteria. Sarah Churchill, who also briefly recanted, said in private:

> If I told Mr. Noyes but once I had set my hand to the Book [witches book] he would believe me, but if I told him one hundred times I had not he would not believe me.

In September, 15 were convicted. Eight were hanged. These would be the last hangings. Trials were suspended and further executions postponed by Phips. Phips soon released into the custody of their families those against whom there was only spectral evidence.

Evidence Questioned

An independent opinion from New York clergy criticized almost every type of evidence accepted by the Massachusetts court. When the next court convened, spectral evidence was eliminated as a basis for conviction. Only three were convicted. Eventually Phips reprieved all the condemned.

But the reprieved still had legal and financial problems caused by the trials. The simplest was that jail residents had to pay their prison (lodging) fees before they were released.

As the emotional temper of the colony quieted, qualms about the witch trials grew. In January 1697, the General Court ordered a day of prayer and fasting. In 1703 and 1710, in response to petitions, the legislature reversed most of the convictions and voted compensation to the convicted or their families. Even Ann Putnam eventually repented in church. The convictions of seven, for whom no one submitted petitions, remain on record.

— *Teddi DiCanio*

Suggestions for Further Reading

Gragg, Larry. "Under an Evil Hand." *American History Illustrated* (March–April 1992): 54–59.

Starkey, Marion L. *The Devil in Massachusetts, A Modern Enquiry into the Salem Witch Trials.* Garden City, N.Y.: Doubleday & Co. 1949.

Upham, Charles W. *Salem Witchcraft.* Williamstown, Mass.: Corner House Publishers, 1971.

John Peter Zenger Trial: 1735

Name of Defendant: John Peter Zenger   **Crime Charged:** Seditious libel
Chief Defense Lawyers: Andrew Hamilton and John Chambers
Chief Prosecutor: Richard Bradley   **Judge:** James De Lancey   **Place:** New York, New York   **Date of Trial:** August 1735   **Verdict:** Not guilty

SIGNIFICANCE

By accepting truth as a legitimate defense in a libel case brought against a newspaper editor by a public official, the jury laid the foundations of freedom of the press in America later codified in the Bill of Rights.

Arguably the single most significant political trial ever held in an American courtroom took place in New York City in 1735, well before the colonies fought for and gained independence. The defendant was a printer charged with the crime of seditious libel for publishing items in the *New York Weekly Journal* that skewered and taunted the greedy royal governor of the colony of New York and his judicial appointees. John Peter Zenger's acquittal deeply and firmly planted the roots of freedom of the press in American soil by overthrowing the orthodox legal view that the publication of stinging criticism or ridicule of public officials was, at the very least, a threat to law and order and, at the worst, treason, and thus worthy of severe punishment as "seditious libel."

Fifty years later, American statesman and diplomat Gouverneur Morris described the verdict in this case as "the morning star of liberty which subsequently revolutionized America." Embedded in the Declaration of Independence and in the Bill of Rights of the U. S. Constitution, which Morris helped write, are the basic freedoms for which Zenger and his allies fought.

Zenger's Attack on the Royal Governor

Zenger hardly seemed destined to play a pivotal role in American history. He appeared an ordinary enough man, his career a struggling and undistinguished one until he reached his middle years. Born in the German Palatinate, Zenger emigrated to America in 1710 as a boy of 13. The following year he was accepted as an apprentice by William Bradford, the British colony's royal printer, who enjoyed a monopoly on government printing. By 1725, he became Bradford's partner in the colony's official newspaper, *New York Gazette,* but that year he decided to go into business for himself. Zenger eked out a living until 1733 printing religious pamphlets, supplementing his income by playing an organ in church.

What set Zenger's fate in motion was the arrival in New York from England of a new royal governor, William Cosby. While it is not certain that Cosby was a thief, he was unquestionably a grasping and tactless man who demanded huge sums in payment from the New York colonial council for his services. He even attempted to force the prior interim governor, Rip Van Dam, to turn over half the salary he had been paid. When Van Dam refused, Cosby instituted a claim against Van Dam, to whose cause rallied a sizable number of the colony's wealthier gentlemen.

To propagandize their contempt for Cosby—a sentiment as prevalent among the masses as among the rich—and knowing they could expect no help from Bradford's *Gazette* (not if Bradford wanted to continue to be royal printer), Cosby's enemies turned to Zenger, offering to finance a newspaper for which Zenger would act as editor-publisher. Zenger's *Weekly Journal* made its first appearance November 5, 1733, and, unlike the Bradford paper, was hardly dry reading. With many of the scorching editorials written by a Van Dam ally, attorney James Alexander, the *Journal* quickly got attention, particularly for its mock advertisements. In one of them, Francis Harrison, a Cosby lackey, was described as "a large Spaniel, of about 5 feet 5 inches high . . . lately strayed from his kennel with his mouth full of fulsome panegyrics," or lavish praise for his master. The sheriff found himself described as a "monkey . . . lately broke from his chain and run into the country." Song sheets stronger in their invective than their meter or rhyme followed. ("The petty-fogging knaves deny us rights as Englishmen. We'll make the scoundrel raskals fly, and ne'er return again.")

None of this set well with Cosby and his friends—one of whom threatened Alexander's wife—and, on November 2, 1734, Cosby ordered that four issues of Zenger's paper be burned by the common hangman. The hangman refused. The sheriff then "delivered the papers into the Hands of his own Negroe" who set the bonfire.

Cosby Strikes Back

Fifteen days later, Zenger was arrested, charged with "presenting and publishing several seditious libels . . . influencing [the people's] Minds with Contempt of his Majesty's Government." Zenger was confined to the dungeon of the old city hall, which housed the courts, on 400 pounds bail, an amount easily two or three times Zenger's annual revenue from the newspaper. (It was the bail placed on Zenger that later influenced the writing of the Eighth Amendment of the U.S. Constitution, forbidding excessive bails and fines.)

Cosby's next step was to disbar Zenger's lawyers, William Smith and James Alexander, when they argued against the bail and challenged the commission of Chief Justice James De Lancey, a Cosby appointee. Appointed to defend Zenger—who missed producing only one issue of his newspaper while in prison, dictating editorials to his wife through the dungeon door—was John Chambers, a conscientious enough fellow but one who belonged to the Cosby party.

Despite jury lists that seemed rigged in Cosby's favor, eventually a panel was obtained that contained seven New Yorkers of Dutch descent, among whom anti-British feeling was strong. Even so, the prosecution was confident of victory. Most legal opinion of the time held that defamatory words equaled libel, regardless of the truth or falsity of the words. Under the law, as interpreted by Cosby's attorney general, Richard Bradley, it was solely up to the judge, a Cosby appointee and crony, to decide if the articles were seditious and defamatory. The jury's role was limited to determining if Zenger was "guilty" of publishing the articles in question. Since the printer never denied this, the jury's verdict seemed a foregone conclusion.

Unknown to the Cosby forces, Zenger's friends had not been idle. As a result of their endeavors, a 59-year-old man was sitting in the audience as the trial began. Now he arose, and to the dismay of the judge and prosecutor, identified himself as Andrew Hamilton of Philadelphia, the most famous trial lawyer in the colonies. It was Hamilton's role in the Zenger trial that inspired the phrase, "When in trouble, get a Philadelphia lawyer."

Defense attorney Chambers, in a difficult spot, gladly deferred to Hamilton. From the start, Hamilton admitted Zenger had printed the papers, but observed that for a libel to be proved it must be both false and malicious. "It is a right," said Hamilton, "which all freemen claim, and are entitled to, to complain when they are hurt; they have a right publicly to remonstrate against abuses of power in the strongest terms, to put their neighbors upon their guard against the craft or open violence of men in authority"—a function for a newspaper to perform—"and to assert with courage the sense they have of the blessings of liberty."

Prosecutor Bradley vigorously contested Hamilton's argument, insisting on defining libel as words that were "scandalous, seditious, and tend to disquiet the people." To no one's surprise, Judge De Lancey sided with Bradley, declaring, "You cannot be admitted, Mr. Hamilton, to give the truth of a libel in evidence." Challenged by Hamilton, the chief justice, testily quoting from a British court ruling, declared, "The greater appearance there is of truth in any malicious invective, so much the more provoking it is." Although Hamilton quickly pointed out that the quote came from one of the notorious secret trials of religious dissenters held by the Star Chamber (a former oppressive English court), De Lancey was unmoved and the ruling stood, barring Hamilton from calling witnesses who would testify to the truth of the *Weekly Journal's* articles, testimony that Royal Governor Cosby very much wanted to avoid.

Hamilton's Appeal for Press Freedom

Since he was unable to present his evidence, Hamilton's only chance to acquit his client was through his summation to the jury. He began by pointing out that "the suppression of evidence ought always to be taken for the strongest

On November 2, 1734, Royal Governor Cosby ordered four issues of Zenger's *Weekly Journal* burned. (Courtesy, Library of Congress)

evidence." Warming to his subject, he denounced the inequities of "corrupt and wicked magistrates," the evils of the Star Chamber and its forbiddance of trial by jury. Liberty, he declared, is our "only bulwark against lawless power." Closing his argument, Hamilton declared:

> I am truly very unequal to such an undertaking on many accounts. And you see I labor under the weight of many years, and am borne down with great infirmities of body; yet old and weak as I am, I should think it my duty, if required, to go to the utmost part of the land where my service could be of any use in assisting to quench the flame of persecutions upon informations set on foot by the government to deprive a people of the right of remonstrating of the arbitrary attempts of men in power. Men who injure and oppress the people under their administration provoke them to cry out and complain; and then make that very complaint the foundation for new oppressions and prosecutions. . . . Gentlemen of the jury, . . . it is not the cause of a poor printer, nor of New York alone, which you are now trying. No! It may in its consequences affect every freeman that lives under a British government on the main of America. It is the best cause. It is the cause of liberty; and I make no doubt but your upright conduct this day will not only entitle you to the love and esteem of your fellow citizens, but every man who prefers freedom to a life of slavery will bless you and honor you, as men who have baffled the attempt of tyranny.

This spellbinding summation, one of the most famous and memorable in legal history, emboldened jurymen and spectators alike. As Zenger himself later noted: "The jury withdrew, and in a small time returned, being asked by the clerk whether they were agreed of their verdict, and whether John Peter Zenger was guilty of printing and publishing the libels in the information aforementioned, they answered by Thomas Hunt, their foreman: Not Guilty. Upon which there were three huzzas in the hall, which was crowded with people and the next day I was discharged from imprisonment."

Zenger Verdict's Legal Impact

Zenger quickly published the transcript of the trial, and his and other printings—one by Benjamin Franklin—soon spread the story of the trial throughout the American colonies and to England. While cheered by many people on both sides of the Atlantic, legal authorities and public officials were slow to accept the verdict as a binding legal precedent. It took the British Parliament until 1792, with the passage of the Fox Libel Act, to formally give juries the right to consider truth, not just publication, in seditious libel cases.

Although freedom of the press was enshrined in the American Bill of Rights, the bitter political battle between Federalists and Republicans after independence was won from Britain sparked seditious libel cases against newspapers in several states. In the 1803 prosecution of a scurrilous Federalist editor, Harry Croswell, for libeling President Thomas Jefferson, a devoutly Republican Justice Morgan Lewis ordered the jury to rule strictly on the fact of publication and banned evidence on the truth of the libel. Another Hamilton—Alexander— appealed to the New York Supreme Court to overturn the jury's guilty verdict and order a new trial, basing his argument on the Zenger case. Although the court split two-and-two on the issue, thus in effect denying the appeal, the eloquence of Hamilton's argument won over public opinion, and the prosecution dropped the proceedings against Croswell. The legal principles enunciated by Hamilton and repeated in the written opinion of Supreme Court Justice James Kent were incorporated into the New York Constitution of 1821.

Through the powerful oratory of both Hamiltons and the courage of Zenger's jurors, the right to free speech—to a free press—was established, and the importance of the right to trial by jury as a safeguard against oppressive government recognized.

—Edward W. Knappman

Suggestions for Further Reading

Buranelli, Vincent. *The Trial of John Peter Zenger*. Westport, Conn.: Greenwood Press, 1975.

Fleming, Thomas J. "A scandalous, malicious and seditious libel." *American Heritage* (December 1967): 22–27, 100–106.

Goebel, Julius and T.R. Naughton. *Law Enforcement in Colonial New York*. New York: Commonwealth Fund, 1944.

Hopkins, W. Wat. "John Peter Zenger." In *A Biographical Dictionary of American Journalism*, edited by Joseph P. McKerns. Westport, Conn.: Greenwood Press, 1989.

Konkle, B.A. *The Life of Andrew Hamilton, 1676–1741*. Philadelphia: National Publishing Co., 1941.

Morris, Richard. *Fair Trial*. New York: Alfred A. Knopf, 1952.

Rutherford, Livington. *John Peter Zenger, His Press, His Trial, and a Bibliography of Zenger Imprints*. New York: Arno Press, 1904.

Schuyler, L.R. *Liberty of The Press in The American Colonies Before The Revolutionary War*. New York: T. Whittaker, 1905.

The "Great Negro Plot" Trial: 1741

Defendants: More than 170 people, including: Caesar and Prince; John and Sarah Hughson, Sarah Hughson (daughter); Margaret Sorubiero, alias Kerry; Quack; Cuffee; and John Ury. **Crimes Charged:** Entering, theft (Caesar, Prince); receiving stolen goods, conspiracy to commit arson (John and Sarah Hughson, Sorubiero); conspiracy to commit arson (Sarah Hughson, daughter); arson, conspiracy to murder inhabitants of New York (Quack, Cuffee); conspiracy to commit arson and being a Catholic ecclesiastic (Ury)

Chief Defense Lawyer: None   **Chief Prosecutors:** James Alexander, Richard Bradley, John Chambers, Abraham Lodge, Joseph Murray, Richard Nicolls, and William Smith   **Judges:** James De Lancey, Daniel Horsmanden, and Frederick Philipse   **Dates of Trials:** 1741: May 1, (Caesar, Prince); May 6, (John and Sarah Hughson, and Sorubiero for receiving stolen goods); May 29, (Quack, Cuffee); June 4, (John and Sarah Hughson, Sarah Hughson, daughter, and Sorubiero, for conspiracy with Quack and Cuffee); July 29, (Ury). **Place of Trials:** New York, Colony of New York   **Verdicts:** Guilty   **Sentences:** 70 blacks, 7 whites banished from British North America; 16 blacks, four whites hanged; 13 blacks burned at the stake. Of the defendants named above: Hanging (Caesar, Prince, John and Sarah Hughson, Margaret Sorubiero, Ury); hanging, but pardoned in exchange for testimony, particularly against Ury (Sarah Hughson, daughter); burning at the stake (Quack, Cuffee)

SIGNIFICANCE

This series of cases served as a brutal example of the consequences of panic when legal procedures become dispensable.

The panic over the "Great Negro Plot" has been likened to the hysteria of the Salem Witchcraft Trials. The "plot" was thought to be a conspiracy to stage an uprising among slaves who would burn New York and murder the white citizens. A conspiracy is defined as an agreement to commit a crime. The crime of conspiracy exists separately from the crime or crimes agreed upon. The key question of the "Great Negro Plot" is the kind of conspiracy that existed, if any. That a few people conspired to burn and loot some buildings appears to be true.

That some slaves occasionally indulged in talk about revolt is plausible. Beyond that, the conspiracy was a delusion bred of fear.

In February 1741, Robert Hogg's tobacco shop was burglarized. An investigation led to the arrest of two slaves, Caesar and Prince, who frequented a tavern owned by John Hughson. Following the arrests, Mary Burton, a 16-year-old indentured servant in Hughson's tavern, dropped hints about the burglary. When questioned, Burton claimed that the Hughson family dealt in stolen property, assisted by a woman living at the tavern, Margaret (Peggy) Kelly or Sorubiero. (Caesar was rumored to be the father of her child.) Constables found the goods, arrested Hughson, and held the other three as accomplices.

Soon after the arrests, New York suffered several mysterious fires, starting with the city's fortress, Fort George. Subsequent fires, accompanied by theft, suggested arson. Indications that slaves were involved helped spark the conspiracy theories. Soon two slaves, Quack and Cuffee, were in custody.

They denied everything, even when convicted. Faced with the stake, they tried to save themselves with confessions. But the sheriff could not fight the mob that came to see them die.

By the time Mary Burton testified to the grand jury, the story she told was that John Hughson led a conspiracy that included Caesar, Prince, and Cuffee. They met at Hughson's to plan the fires and the massacre of the white population.

> Caesar should be governor, and Hughson . . . king . . . that she has seen twenty or thirty negroes at one time in her master's house . . . the three aforesaid negroes . . . were generally present . . . that the other negroes durst not refuse to do what they commanded them . . . That she never saw any white person . . . when they talked of burning the town, but her master, her mistress, and Peggy.

Mary Burton's testimony became wilder as the number of people she accused grew. Prosecutor Richard Bradley used the legally inadmissible testimony of convicted thief Arthur Price, who swore that several of the accused made damning admissions to him while in jail—admissions denied by defendants. Bradley also used hearsay evidence and testimony of frightened defendants trying to obtain mercy or to direct suspicion elsewhere. The court permitted Bradley's legal violations. Since no lawyer in New York would agree to defend any of the accused, no one objected. Next, Governor James Oglethorpe of Georgia wrote authorities in other colonies, warning them to beware of Spanish plots and spies. This led New York authorities to link this conspiracy to Spain and English schoolmaster John Ury.

Ury, skilled in Latin and theology, faced the flimsiest testimony "proving" he was a Catholic priest and the real head of the conspiracy. This contradicted earlier claims that Hughson was the leader. Ury produced witnesses to attest to his whereabouts during alleged plotting sessions. Nevertheless, he was hanged.

There were no more grand jury indictments, but Judge Daniel Horsmanden's obsession with the conspiracy led to one last death, a slave named Tom.

— Teddi DiCanio

Suggestions for Further Reading

Davis, T.J. *A Rumor of Revolt*. New York: The Free Press, 1985.

Horsmanden, Daniel. *The New York Conspiracy*. Boston: Beacon Press, 1971 [reprint].

Writs Of Assistance Trial: 1761

Petitioner for the Writ: James Cockle, a deputy customs official of Salem
Petitioners against the Writs: Merchants of Salem and Boston, Massachusetts Bay Colony **Attorney for the Customs Officials:** Jeremiah Gridley **Attorneys for the Merchants:** James Otis and Oxenbridge Thacher **Chief Judge:** Thomas Hutchinson **Place:** Boston, Massachusetts Bay Colony **Date:** February 24, 1761 **Verdict:** Deferred until a legal opinion could be obtained from England

SIGNIFICANCE

The case was the first major judicial confrontation over the extent and limits of English authority over colonial affairs. The argument highlighted the growing American notion of fundamental "constitutional" laws that included inalienable rights. The case helped lay the ideological foundations for the American Revolution and the Fourth Amendment of the Bill of Rights, which banned abusive search and seizure.

Under England's navigation laws, which governed the British Empire's commerce, the American colonies faced prohibitions and restrictions on trading and manufacturing certain goods within and without the empire. The British West Indies could not produce the amount of molasses needed by the colonists to make rum, a major product, and New England merchants were troubled by the substantial duty on molasses purchased from outside Britain's island colonies. Need, as well as greed, contributed to colonial smuggling.

During the French and Indian War, some smugglers continued to trade with French territories, supplying the enemy with essential goods. The smugglers faced weak opposition. Customs officials seldom bothered to search ships while they lay at anchor. Many customs appointees lived in England and assigned their duties to poorly paid colonial deputies, who often did not do the work. Great Britain spent an average of 8,000 pounds to collect 2,000 pounds in duties.

As the French and Indian War wound down, England moved to combat illegal trade. Merchants feared the crackdown would rely heavily on writs of assistance. Such writs had been issued in the past in the colonies, but they were seldom used. Writs of assistance were essentially general search warrants of tremendous scope.

The writs offered more latitude than ordinary search warrants. Usually a search warrant was based on a sworn statement of legitimate suspicion and permitted officials to examine a specific place for specific goods. Writs of assistance permitted customs officers (or anyone holding the writ), to search shops, ships, homes, and warehouses at will during the day. Once issued, they could be used again and again.

Writs of assistance expired within six months after the death of a reigning monarch. When George II died, a battle arose in Massachusetts over the legality of issuing new writs. Colonial merchants, represented by James Otis and Oxenbridge Thacher, petitioned Superior Court to refuse applications by customs officials for new writs. Otis had been the king's advocate general of Boston's Vice-Admiralty Court and had resigned rather than argue for customs officials.

Writs Versus Rights

The case turned on interpretation of the legal basis for the writs. Jeremiah Gridley, acting for the customs officials, maintained that necessities of state justified limitations on traditional English rights:

> It is true the common privileges of Englishmen are taken away in this Case, but even their privileges are not so in case of Crime and fine. 'Tis the necessity of the Case and the benefit of the Revenue that justifies this Writ. Is not the Revenue the sole support of Fleets & Armies abroad, & Ministers at home? without which the Nation could neither be preserved from the Invasion of her foes, nor the Tumults of her own Subjects. Is not this I say infinitely more important, that the imprisonment of Thieves, or even Murderers? yet in these Cases 'tis agreed Houses may be broken open.

Gridley included in his argument references to statutory precedents.

In rebuttal, Oxenbridge Thacher also referred to precedents. The colonial Superior Court's power was in the case of the writs being held comparable to that of the Court of Exchequer in England. Thacher reasoned there was no justification for such a comparison. He also criticized the longevity of the writs, stressing how their power could be abused by repeated use.

Following Thacher, James Otis spoke like "a flame of fire," according to John Adams. He, too, spoke of precedent. He built an elaborate argument that began with an individual's God-given natural rights and the birth of societal compacts. He continued through old Saxon laws, Magna Carta, and actions taken over time to secure and confirm rights and principals of England's unwritten constitution.

Otis repeatedly attacked the writs as directly contrary to basic English liberties:

It appears to me the worst instrument of arbitrary power, the most destructive of English liberty and the fundamental principles of law, that ever was found in an English law book.

Otis preferred "special warrants" which specified name, place, what was suspected, and by whom. Complaining of the unaccountability of those armed with writs of assistance, Otis said:

Every one with this writ may be a tyrant in a legal manner . . . Now one of the most essential branches of English liberty is the freedom of one's house. A man's house is his castle; and whilst he is quiet, he is as well guarded as a prince in his castle. This writ, if it should be declared legal, would totally annihilate this privilege.

Otis repeated a well-known story. A man named Ware held a writ which had been endorsed to him by a customs official. Ware was brought to court for swearing on the Sabbath. He took revenge on the judge and the constable who had arrested him. He used his writ to ransack their homes looking for smuggled goods.

Otis spoke for four hours. John Adams wrote:

Every man of an immense crowded audience appeared to me to go away as I did, ready to take arms against Writs of Assistance. . . . Then and there, the child Independence was born. In fifteen years, i.e. in 1776, he grew up to manhood and declared himself free.

The court did not immediately issue the writs, although it was known that Chief Justice Thomas Hutchinson favored them:

The Court has considered the subject of writs of assistance, and can see no foundation for such a writ; but as the practice in England is not known, it has been thought best to continue the question to the next term, that in the mean time opportunity may be given to know the result.

The query was sent to the colonial agent for Massachusetts in England. Legal authority to issue the writs was upheld and the court quietly did so. But apparently no customs official had the temerity to use them.

— *Teddi DiCanio*

Suggestions for Further Reading

Adams, John. Charles Francis Adams, ed. *Works.* Boston: 1856.

Gipson, Lawrence Henry. *The Coming of the Revolution, 1763–1775.* New York: Harper & Row, 1954.

Hart, Albert B. and Edward Channing, eds. *American History Leaflets.* New York: Simmons, 1892–1911.

Langguth, A.J. *Patriots, The Men Who Started the American Revolution.* New York: Simon & Schuster, 1988.

The Parsons' Cause Trial: 1763

Plaintiff: Reverend James Maury   **Defendants:** The collectors of the tax for Louisa County, Colony of Virginia   **Plaintiff Claim:** 300 Pounds in back pay
Chief Defense Lawyer: Patrick Henry, taking over from John Lewis
Chief Lawyer for Plaintiff: Peter Lyons   **Judge:** John Henry
Place: Hanover County, Colony of Virginia
Date of Hearing: December 1, 1763   **Verdict:** Damages awarded, one penny

SIGNIFICANCE

The case provided a forum for challenging the limits of England's power to control American colonial affairs.

The Parsons' Cause began as an argument over a piece of financial legislation and ended with an impassioned speech on a theory of government. That speech was one of the first signs of the schism occurring between England and her American colonies.

Because the Anglican Church was the established church of the colony of Virginia, its clergy were supported by taxes. By a 1748 statute, the salary of a parson was set at 16,000 pounds of tobacco a year. (Tobacco was a common form of tender during the colonial period.) In 1755 and again in 1758, due to shortages of tobacco brought on by drought, laws were enacted allowing tobacco obligations to be fulfilled with Virginia's paper money. Paper money, which generally depreciated in value, was blessed by debtors and loathed by creditors.

The 1758 law, the Two Penny Act, a temporary, one-year measure, allowed the ministers' salaries to be paid in currency at a fixed rate of twopence per pound of tobacco. The prevailing inflated market rate at the time was running at fourpence to sixpence per pound. Once depreciation was factored in, a clergyman was receiving about one-third of his normal, stipulated salary. The colony's council approved and, with the House of Burgesses, convinced Francis Fauquier, the royal governor, to allow the act to go into effect.

Virginia's revenue measures were supposed to be approved by the Privy Council back in London before being implemented. But Fauquier, in a letter to Great Britain's Board of Trade, argued that, given the economic need and the short-term duration of the measure, suspending the act until the Council could review was tantamount to rejecting it and, thus, eliminating all economic relief. Such a decision would repudiate the almost unanimous economic wisdom of experienced local legislators and to ignore the 1755 precedent for which the previous governor "incurred no Censure for having pass'd it."

The clergy objected. They argued that they should reap the benefit of high tobacco prices since they had had to accept whatever their tobacco would sell for when the price was low. But the Privy Council would probably have let the measure stand had it not been for the persistence of the Reverend John Camm of York County. Camm led a group of Anglican ministers determined to see the Two Penny Act nullified. When a war of pamphlets and lawsuits availed them nothing, Camm sailed for England.

In England he enlisted the help of the Archbishop of Canterbury and the Bishop of London. Camm argued that the Two Penny Act was a manifestation of the deliberate erosion of royal and Anglican authority in Virginia. Camm's narrow-minded focus on his own list of grievances ignored the act's purpose as a financial relief measure. (Some historians have questioned the need for the act and there were those in Virginia who were happy to see the ministers take a financial blow. But there is little evidence that the House of Burgesses deliberately set out to penalize the clergy.) The king and his council, on the recommendation of the Board of Trade, disallowed the measure and its predecessors.

Since the Two Penny Act of 1758 already had expired, the repeal of the law would have been moot had not several clergymen sued for back pay. Two cases were rejected on the grounds that the act was valid until it was actually disallowed by the Privy Council. One court awarded a parson double his salary in damages. But it was the case filed by Reverend James Maury of Louisa County that turned out to be the most significant.

Patrick Henry, above, served as counsel for the defense in the Parson's Cause Trial, despite the fact that his father was the presiding judge. (Courtesy, Library of Congress)

The Suit

Maury filed suit, in neighboring Hanover County to avoid the politically hostile climate in his home county. In November of 1763, the presiding judge, Colonel John Henry, ruled that the Two Penny Act had been rendered null from its beginning, contrary to the rulings in the earlier cases. Next came a hearing for damages in which the jury would determine what was due Maury.

At this point, the judge's son, young Patrick Henry, was requested to take over council for the defense. (Such conflicts of interest were common in colonial America.) On December 1, the hearing commenced and the Reverend Maury protested at the prospective jurors offered by the sheriff. Later, in a letter, Maury described them as "the vulgar herd." Maury had some justification for his protest. Three jurors were religious dissenters, and a fourth was a cousin of Patrick Henry's. Henry countered, "They were honest men, and, therefore, unexceptionable, they were immediately called to the book and sworn."

Next, Maury's gifted lawyer, Peter Lyons, rose, summed up the verdict of the previous month and called two tobacco dealers. They testified that the market price of tobacco averaged 50 shillings per 100 pounds in 1759. At 16,000 pounds of tobacco a year as salary, Lyons computed that Maury had been due 450 British pounds in cash, rather than the approximately 150 pounds he had received under the Two Penny Act. Thus Lyons, after praising the Anglican clergy at some length, asked the jury to award Maury 300 British pounds.

Patrick Henry rose. After a faltering start, the great oratorical gift that was to make him famous surfaced. Henry based his argument on an idea called the compact theory of government. According to Maury's letter, Henry stated:

> [The] act of 1758 had every characteristic of a good law, that it was a law of general utility, and could not, consistently with what he called the original compact between King and people, stipulating protection on the one hand and obedience on the other, be annuled.

Henry argued that by disallowing good laws, a king forfeited his right to the obedience of his subjects. Instead of being a father to his people, he "degenerates into a Tyrant." Lyons cried out that Henry had "spoken treason," a sentiment echoed by a few others in the courtroom.

Henry also attacked the Anglican clergy, accusing them of greed:

> Do they feed the hungry and clothe the naked? Oh, no, gentlemen! These rapacious harpies would, were their power equal to their will, snatch from the hearth of their honest parishioner his last hoe-cake, from the widow and her orphan children her last mich cow! the last bed-nay, the last blanket-from the lying-in woman!"

In conclusion, Patrick Henry suggested Reverend Maury be awarded one farthing. After five minutes of deliberation, the jury awarded four times that amount: one penny. This decision effectively put an end to any more suits.

Henry's spectacular performance gained him fame, good will, clients, and an entre into the political arena. More important, arguments over the compact theory of government and the limitations of royal and parliamentary authority would arise repeatedly as America pulled away from "Mother England." Indeed, its fullest and most eloquent expression would appear 13 years later in the Declaration of Independence.

— Teddi DiCanio

Suggestions for Further Reading

Beeman, Richard R. *Patrick Henry, A Biography*. New York: McGraw-Hill Book Co., 1974.

Languth, A.J. *Patriots: The Men Who Started the American Revolution*, New York: Simon & Schuster, 1988.

McCants, David A., "The Authenticity of James Maury's Account of Patrick Henry's Speech in the Parsons' Cause." *Southern Speech Communication Journal*, Vol. 42 (1976).

Nettels, Curtis P., *The Roots of American Civilization, A History of American Colonial Life*. New York: Appleton-Century Crofts, 1938.

Boston Massacre Trials: 1770

Defendants: Captain Thomas Preston; Corporal William Wemms; Privates Hugh White, John Carroll, William Warren, and Matthew Killroy, William McCauley, James Hartegan, and Hugh Montgomery

Crimes Charged: Murder and accessories to murder

Chief Defense Lawyers: Both trials: John Adams, Josiah Quincy, Jr.; First trial: Robert Auchmuty; Second trial: Sampson Salter Blowers

Chief Prosecutors (Attorneys for the Crown): Samuel Quincy and Robert Treat Paine   **Judges:** John Cushing, Peter Oliver, Benjamin Lynd, and Edmund Trowbridge   **Place:** Boston, Massachusetts Bay Colony

Dates of Trials: *Rex v. Preston:* October 24–30, 1770; *Rex v. Wemms et al.:* November 27–December 5, 1770   **Verdicts:** First trial: Captain Robert Preston, Not guilty; Second trial: Corporal Wemms, Privates White, Carroll, Warren, McCauley, and Hartegan, Not guilty; Privates Killroy and Montgomery, Not guilty of murder but guilty of manslaughter   **Sentences:** Branding on the thumbs for Killroy and Montgomery

SIGNIFICANCE

This case was a landmark on the road to the American Revolution. Despite a politically hostile atmosphere, two reasonably fair trials were conducted and the concept of the right of self-defense was upheld.

On the night of March 5, 1770, three men lay dead and two more were dying, following shots fired by British troops into an angry crowd outside of the Custom House in Boston, Massachusetts. This scene, known as the Boston Massacre, came after months of feuding between Bostonians and the soldiers sent to the city to protect newly appointed Customs commissioners. The British king and his cabinet viewed Boston as a hotbed of dissent in the colonies, where ill will blossomed in the years following the French and Indian War. Quarrels arose over Indian and frontier affairs, over customs regulations, over taxes, and particularly over how extensive was Parliament's right to tax the colonies. Boston, with its unusually stormy Stamp Act riots, seemed to be the focal point of the American political ferment.

Although some British troops had remained in the colonies following the war, the stationing of a large number of troops in a colonial city was a new and unwelcome phenomenon. In the 18th century, British citizens and colonists viewed the maintenance of a standing army in peace time as an abomination, much as Americans would regard a secret police force today. The ever-present troops in Boston seemed proof of the erosion of the colonists' rights as individuals and the usurpation of the powers of their cherished political institutions.

In such an atmosphere, trouble was inevitable. Snubs, shoving matches, loud arguments, and occasional fistfights occurred between Boston residents and the soldiers almost from the day the first contingent landed in the fall of 1768.

Snowballs, then Musket Balls Fly

The series of events that led to the confrontation on March 5, 1770, apparently began with a nasty exchange between Private Patrick Walker of the 29th Regiment and William Green, a local rope-maker.

Soldiers of low rank routinely augmented their meager salaries with odd jobs. As Walker passed Green on March 2, the rope-maker asked the soldier if he wanted work. When Walker said yes, Green replied, "Well, then go and clean my shithouse." Insulted, Walker swore revenge. He walked away and, in a few minutes, returned with several other soldiers.

A fight ensued between the soldiers and the rope-makers, who had rallied around Green. Clubs and sticks were used, as well as fists. The rope-makers routed the soldiers.

But the lull in the fighting was brief. Skirmishes popped up over the next two days. Rumors flew and tensions mounted. The commander of the 29th Regiment, Lieutenant Colonel Maurice Carr, wrote to Acting Governor Thomas Hutchinson to complain of the abuse his men were forced to endure from the citizens of Boston. On March 5, Hutchinson put the letter before the Governor's Council. The unanimous reply was that the people of the town would not be satisfied until the troops were removed.

The evening of the fifth was cold, and a foot of snow lay on the ground. When a wig-maker's apprentice named Edward Garrick insulted Private Hugh White, who was stationed at a sentry box near the Main Guard, the army's headquarters, White struck Garrick on the head with a musket. Nevertheless, other apprentices continued to bait White and throw snowballs at him.

Periodically, cries of "fire" could be heard in the streets, although no buildings were burning that night. Soldiers passed up and down Brattle Street carrying clubs, bayonets, and other weapons. In Boylston's Alley, a battle of snowballs and insults was quelled by a passing officer, who led the troops to nearby Murray's barracks and told their junior officers to confine them. Outside the barracks, a few more words were exchanged before Richard Palmes, a Boston merchant, persuaded many members of the crowd to go home. But some of the crowd shouted that they should go "away to the Main Guard."

At about the same time, some 200 people gathered in an area called Dock Square. More people joined them as groups flowed in from Boston's North End. Some came carrying cudgels. Others picked up whatever weapons they could find in the square. The crowd eventually gathered around a tall man whose words evidently sent the crowd to the Main Guard.

Meanwhile, Private Hugh White retreated from his sentry box near the Main Guard to the steps of the Custom House. From there, he threatened to fire on the approaching crowd and called for the assistance of other soldiers.

When word of the sentry's predicament reached Captain Thomas Preston, he led a small contingent from the 29th Regiment to White's rescue. With bayonets affixed, two columns of men managed to reach the beleaguered Private White. When the soldiers prepared to retrace their route, the prospect of retreating through the menacing crowd appeared more daunting. The soldiers positioned themselves in a rough semicircle, facing the crowd with their captain just in front of them. Their muskets were loaded. Some in the crowd flung angry words and taunts to fire. Finally, someone hurled a club, knocking down soldier Hugh Montgomery. He got to his feet, and a cry was heard to fire. Montgomery fired one shot. No one seemed to be hit and the crowd pulled away a little from the troops. There was a pause during which Captain Preston might have given an order to cease firing. The pause between the first and the subsequent shots could have been as little as six seconds or as much as two minutes, according to witnesses' accounts.

However long the pause, the troops commenced firing. Confusion ensued. Most people in the crowd believed the soldiers were firing only powder, not bullets. But two men were hit almost immediately. Samuel Gray fell with a hole in his head. A tall, burly sailor known as Michael Johnson (true name Crispus Attucks), variously described as black, mulatto, or Indian, took two bullets in the chest. As some members of the crowd surged forward to prevent further firing, another sailor, James Caldwell, was hit.

A ricocheting bullet struck 17-year-old Samuel Maverick as he ran toward the Town House. He died several hours later at his mother's boarding house. The fifth fatality was Patrick Carr. Struck in the hip by a bullet that "tore away part of the backbone," he lingered until the 14th of March. Carr's dying testimony later helped bolster the defense attorneys' claim that the soldiers fired in self-defense.

Captain Preston yelled at his men, demanding to know why they had fired. The reply was they thought he ordered them to shoot when they had heard the word "fire." As the crowd, which had fallen back, began to help those who had fallen, the troops again raised their muskets. Preston commanded them to cease fire and went down the line pushing up their musket barrels. The crowd dispersed, carrying the wounded, the dying, and the dead. Captain Preston and his men marched back to the Main Guard. The Boston Massacre was over. Although the city did not quiet, there were no more deadly altercations.

Following a brusque interview with Captain Preston, Royal Governor Hutchinson made his way to the council room of the town hall. Addressing the crowd from a balcony, Hutchinson promised a full inquiry and asked the townspeople to go home. He said, "The law shall have its course; I will live and die by the law." Thus, the Crown undertook an investigation into the Boston Massacre.

The Redcoats Are Indicted

That very night, two justices of the peace went to the council chamber and spent the next several hours calling witnesses to be examined. By morning, Captain Preston and his eight men had been incarcerated. A week later, a grand jury was sworn in, and, at the request of Attorney General Jonathan Sewall, indictments were promptly handed down.

But Sewall, a loyalist, busied himself with legal affairs out of town, leaving the prosecution of the soldiers to whomever the royal court appointed. The disappointing choice was another loyalist, Samuel Quincy, the colony's solicitor general. To strengthen the prosecution, at a town meeting, radicals led by Samuel Adams, persuaded Boston selectmen and citizens to pay prosecution expenses, bringing in the very successful lawyer Robert Treat Paine.

The choice of loyalist Robert Auchmuty to serve as the senior counsel for Captain Preston was no surprise, but the other two attorneys who agreed to act for the defense were: Josiah Quincy, Jr. (brother of the prosecutor Samuel Quincy), a fiery radical; John Adams, the cousin of Samuel Adams and just as offended as he by the presence of the king's troops in Boston. Both Quincy and Adams had participated in the funeral procession for four of the men the soldiers were accused of killing. For the trial of the soldiers, Auchmuty dropped out, and Adams became senior counsel, with Samuel Salter Blowers as junior counsel.

The trials were delayed more than once, providing a long period for tempers to cool. The radicals, thwarted in their efforts to obtain an immediate trial, tried to convict the troops in the press.

The decision on whether to hold one trial or two was not announced until the last minute. The troops wanted to be tried *with* Captain Preston. They believed separate trials would lessen their chances of acquittal, particularly if Preston were tried first and found not guilty, which would indicate that his men bore the responsibility for firing without orders.

Additionally, if the Captain and his men were tried together, the prosecution would have a difficult case in proving that a bullet from one specific gun, fired by one specific soldier had hit one specific victim. Furthermore, the troops knew that if the Crown *could* prove that Preston had given the order to fire, the greater share of responsibility and guilt would be his.

Probably to the disappointment of the troops, it was decided there would be two separate trials: the first for Captain Preston, the second for the troops.

Captain Preston's Trial

If a transcript of the trial of Captain Preston ever existed, it has disappeared. Summaries and notes of the testimony were made by various, sometimes partisan, individuals. The reconstruction from the available evidence is as follows.

The captain's trial began October 24, 1770, and was over October 30, 1770. It was the first criminal trial in Massachusetts to last longer than a day.

Samuel Quincy opened for the prosecution and called as its first witness Edward Garrick, the apprentice wig-maker whose taunts had ended with his being struck by Private Hugh White. After describing this incident, Garrick testified that he had seen soldiers in the streets carrying swords before Preston had led his men to the Custom House. The next witness, Thomas Marshall, supported that statement and added that Preston most certainly did have time to order his men to cease fire between the first and subsequent shots.

A fanciful engraving of the Boston Massacre. (Courtesy, Library of Congress)

Witnesses that followed also gave damning testimony. Peter Cunningham said that Preston had ordered his men to prime and load their muskets. Later, he qualified his statement by saying that the man who had ordered the troops to fire was definitely an officer by reason of the way he was dressed. Witnesses William Wyatt and John Cox both insisted that Preston had given the order to fire.

But on the following day, the Crown's testimony floundered. Witness Theodore Bliss said Preston had been standing in front of the guns. Bliss heard someone shouting "Fire" but did not think it was the captain. Henry Knox testified that the crowd was shouting, "Fire, damn your blood, fire." And Benjamin Burdick said he heard the word "Fire" come from behind the men.

The Crown regained some ground with witness Daniel Calef, who unequivocally stated that he had "looked the officer in the face when he gave the word" to fire. The next witness, Robert Goddard, also stated firmly that Preston, standing behind his men, had given the order to fire.

Samuel Quincy did not close the Crown's case with a summation of the evidence. Instead, he quoted from a few legal treatises:

> Not such killing only as proceeds from premeditated hatred or revenge against the person killed, but also in many other cases, such as is accompanied with those circumstances that shew the heart to be perversely wicked, is adjudged to be of malice prepense, and consequently murder.

The first three witnesses for the defense testified to the threats uttered against the soldiers by those in the street. According to one, Edward Hill, after the firing, he saw Preston push up a musket and say, "Fire no more. You have done mischief enough."

On the following day, a string of witnesses vividly described the confusion and anger that reigned March 5. The first witness for the defense, John Edwards, stated firmly that it was the corporal, William Wemms, who had given the men the order to prime and load their muskets. Another, Joseph Hilyer, said, "The soldiers seemed to act from pure nature, . . . I mean they acted and fired by themselves."

Reasonable Doubt

Richard Palmes testified that he had had his hand on Preston's shoulder just as the order to fire was given. At the time, the two men were in front of the troops. Even at that distance, Palmes could not be sure whether Preston or someone else had given the order. Palmes' testimony, even with its measure of ambiguity, threw a strong element of "reasonable doubt" on the Crown's case.

Another major witness for the defense was Andrew (no last name recorded). He was a slave, but he was always referred to as the "Negro servant" of merchant Oliver Wendell, a Son of Liberty, who testified emphatically to Andrew's integrity. In meticulous, coherent detail, Andrew described the explosive scene on March 5—the taunts, the threats, the objects thrown (mostly snowballs), the clash of stick against bayonet. Andrew also testified that the voice that gave the order to fire was different from the other voices calling out and he was sure the voice had come from beyond Preston.

When John Gillespie took the stand, he testified about an event that occurred at least two hours before the Massacre. He spoke of seeing a group of townspeople carrying swords, sticks, and clubs, coming from the South End. The tone of Gillespie's testimony implied a "plot" to expel the troops from Boston. Adams was opposed to such testimony and was angry with Josiah Quincy, who had prepared the witnesses. He feared attacking Boston's reputation would backfire on the defendant, angering a jury to a guilty verdict or inciting a mob to lynching. Adams threatened to withdraw from the case if any further evidence of that nature was introduced.

In making closing arguments, defense attorney Adams spoke first. He said, "Self-defence [*sic*] is the primary canon of the law of nature," and he explained how a homicide was justifiable under common law when an assaulted man had nowhere to retreat. Carefully reviewing the evidence, Adams ruthlessly demolished the Crown's weakly presented case. Instead of attacking the Crown's witnesses, he deftly wove parts of their testimony into his arguments and dismissed as honest mistakes those that he couldn't use.

In his summation for the prosecution, Paine, in an effort to dismiss the notion of self-defense introduced by Adams, pointed out that defense witness Palmes was standing in front of the soldiers' muskets. "Would he place himself before a party of soldiers and risque his life at the muzzles of their guns," Paine reasoned, "when he thought them under a necessity of firing to defend their life?"

In the judges' charge to the jury, the main points the jurors had to consider were: Whether the soldiers' party constituted an unlawful assembly? Whether that party was assaulted? Whether the crowd constituted an unlawful assembly? Whether Preston ordered the loading of the muskets and, if so, why? Was this a defensive action? And, most important, did Preston give the order to fire? Finally, in a move that favored the defense, the judges reminded the jury that self-defense was a law of nature.

The court adjourned at 5:00 P.M. on Monday. By 8:00 A.M. on Tuesday, the jury had reached a verdict. Preston was found not guilty.

The Soldiers' Trial

One month later in the trial of the soldiers, the Crown's first witnesses testified about the behavior of soldiers—who may or may not have been among those on trial—in the hours before the Massacre. Prosecution witnesses spoke of off-duty officers, armed with cutlasses, running through the streets and randomly assaulting citizens.

Apparently the prosecution wanted to broaden the court's scope of inquiry, a questionable move since testimony about other soldiers was irrelevant. The defense had little objection so long as it could introduce equally irrelevant testimony concerning the actions of citizens prior to the crucial events. The court permitted the lawyers to have their way.

Of the Crown's first witnesses, only one made a major point. The town watchman, Edward Langford, described the death of a citizen, John Gray. According to Langford, Gray had definitely been shot by Private Matthew Killroy.

The following day the Crown's witnesses faltered. James Brewer, who consistently denied that the crowd had uttered any threats against the soldiers, admitted that people all around were calling "Fire." Asked if he had thought the cry referred to a fire or if it was bidding the soldiers to fire, Brewer answered he could not "tell now what I thought then."

Another witness, James Bailey, was quite clear on the fact that boys in the street had pelted the soldiers with pieces of ice large enough to do injury. Bailey also stated that Private Montgomery had been knocked down and that he had seen Crispus Attucks (one of the men killed) carrying "a large cord-wood stick."

One of the prosecution's most effective witnesses was Samuel Hemmingway, who testified that Private Killroy had said, "He would never miss an opportunity, when he had one, to fire on the inhabitants, and that he had wanted to have an opportunity ever since he landed."

In his opening remarks for the defense, Josiah Quincy spoke about the widespread notion "that the life of a soldier was of very little value; of much less value, than others of the community. The law, gentlemen, knows no such distinction. . . . What will justify and mitigate the action of one, will do the same to the other." He dwelt on the bad feeling between the citizens and the soldiers and the fears of citizens that their liberties were threatened.

Like those for the prosecution, the first defense witnesses spoke of extreme behavior throughout the town. A picture emerged of a possible riot in the making. The testimony of William Hunter, an auctioneer who had seen the tall man addressing the crowd in Dock Square, suggested some of the crowd's activities may have been organized rather than spontaneous. But for the same reasons he had cited during the first trial, John Adams put a stop to further testimony of this sort. And again he threatened to withdraw from the case.

For two days, the defense presented solid evidence that the soldiers at the Custom House were jeopardized by a dangerous crowd. A stream of 40 witnesses appeared. One of the last witnesses was Dr. John Jeffries, who had cared for Patrick Carr, the fifth victim, as he lay dying. Jeffries said,

> I asked him if he thought the soldiers would have been hurt,, if they had not fired. He said he really thought they would, for he heard many voices cry out, kill them. I asked him then, meaning to close all, whether he thought they fired in self-defense, or on purpose to destroy the people. He said he really thought they did fire to defend themselves; that he did not blame the man whoever he was, that shot him.

In his closing remarks, Quincy pointed out that even a "moderate" person might impulsively seek to exact vengeance from the soldiers at the Custom House for the actions of soldiers elsewhere in the town that night. But the law did not permit this. The evidence demonstrated that the troops had acted in self-defense.

In his closing summation, a brilliant blend of law and politics, John Adams argued self-defense. He portrayed the wrath of the crowd, while subtly exonerating the city of Boston from blame and placing much of the blame on "Mother England." He pointed out, "At certain critical seasons, even in the mildest government, the people are liable to run into riots and tumults." The possibility of such events "is in direct proportion to the despotism of the government."

Adams turned his attention to a description of the crowd. "And why we should scruple to call such a set of people a mob?... Soldiers quartered in a populous town, will always occasion two mobs, where they prevent one. They are wretched conservators of the peace."

After 2½ hours of deliberation, the jury acquitted Corporal William Wemms, and Privates White, Warren, Carroll, McCauley, and Hartegan. Privates Killroy and Montgomery were found not guilty of murder but guilty of manslaughter. Sufficient evidence had shown that these two men had definitely shot their weapons. There was not enough evidence to prove which of the other soldiers had or had not fired.

On December 14, 1770, Killroy and Montgomery returned to court for sentencing. They pleaded "benefit of clergy." This legal technicality dated back centuries to a time when a member of a religious order could only be tried in an ecclesiastical court. By the 18th century, benefit of clergy had become a legal oddity, extended to those who could read and write, which enabled them to obtain a reduced sentence. The court granted the request to Killroy and Montgomery who were branded on the thumbs and released from custody.

The mystery of who actually gave the order to fire was solved after the trials. Shortly before he left Boston, Private Montgomery admitted to his lawyers that it was he who cried "Fire" after he had been knocked down by a thrown stick.

The massacre and the subsequent trials persuaded the British that troops quartered in Boston were more likely to spark than quench the flames of rebellion. Although British troops were soon withdrawn from Boston, patriots continued to use the massacre as evidence of British perfidy and to goad their fellow colonists toward insurrection.

— Teddi DiCanio

Suggestions for Further Reading

Adams, John. *The Adams Papers: The Legal Papers of John Adams*, 3 vols. Edited by L. Kinvin Wroth and Hiller B. Zobel. Cambridge, Mass.: Harvard University Press, 1965.

Calhoon, Robert McCluer. *The Loyalists in Revolutionary, America, 1760–1781*. New York : Harcourt Brace Jovanovich, 1973

Fleming, Thomas J. "The Boston Massacre." *American Heritage*. (December 1969): 6–11, 102–111.

Hansen, Harry. *The Boston Massacre: An Episode of Dissent and Violence*. New York: Hastings House, 1970.

Kidder, Frederic. *History of the Boston Massacre*. Albany, N.Y.: Munsell, 1870

Middlekauff, Robert. *The Glorious Cause, The American Revolution, 1763–1789*. New York: Oxford University Press, 1982.

Quincy, Josiah, Jr. *Reports of Cases Argued and Adjudged in the Superior Court of Judicature of the Province of Massachusetts Bay, between 1761 and 1772*. Edited by Samuel M. Quincy. Boston: 1885.

Zobel, Hiller B. *The Boston Massacre*. New York: W.W. Norton & Company, 1970.

Sergeant Thomas Hickey Court-Martial: 1776

Defendant: Sergeant Thomas Hickey   **Crimes Charged:** Mutiny and sedition
Chief Defense Lawyer: None   **Chief Prosecutor:** None
Court-Martial Board: Colonel Samuel Parsons, presiding officer
Place: Richmond Hill, New York   **Date of Court-Martial:** June 26, 1776
Verdict: Guilty   **Sentence:** Death by hanging

SIGNIFICANCE

The case reflected the uncertain, ill-defined state of American governmental affairs, particularly the chaotic state of the courts. Because New York's courts were "as yet held by authority derived from the Crown," the Provincial Congress handed soldiers accused of treasonous activities over to General George Washington, whose authority derived from the Continental Congress, the country's one unifying quasi-legal institution. The status of 13 civilian conspirators, although charged, seemed unsure. They were sent to Connecticut temporarily.

Expecting the British army to attack New York, George Washington's Revolutionary army prepared for battle in a city uneasily divided in its loyalties. In June 1776, a Tory conspiracy was discovered. Wild stories circulated. One said Washington was to be murdered. Stripped of exaggeration, the basic "plot" was to stage a combined uprising of Loyalists and secret turncoats in Washington's army timed to coincide with the landing of British forces.

William Collier, an alert waiter, notified a city official of a conspiracy involving Gilbert Forbes, a gunsmith, Royal Governor William Tryon, hiding in a warship anchored offshore, and David Mathews, the mayor. A businessman informed authorities that a former employee, James Mason, had said he was receiving money from the British. Mason, when questioned, implicated several soldiers, including members of Washington's guard. One of those named was Sergeant Thomas Hickey, then under arrest on suspicion of counterfeiting.

In jail, Hickey spoke too freely. According to fellow prisoner Israel Young, Hickey and prisoner Michael Lynch said they would never again fight for the American cause and boasted that "there were near seven hundred men inlisted [*sic*] for the King." Another prisoner, Isaac Ketchum, testified Hickey had tried to enlist him and that Hickey and Lynch had bragged of their involvement in a conspiracy against Washington.

A secret committee investigated the charges, then issued warrants for the arrest of several people, including the mayor. The soldiers involved were turned over to General Washington, who ordered a court-martial for Hickey.

William Greene, a soldier named by Mason, testified before the court-martial that he had bribed Hickey to enlist in the king's service after having himself been bribed by the mayor. Greene said that both his and Hickey's names were on a list in Tryon's possession. The gunsmith, Forbes, corroborated Greene's testimony, adding that Mayor Mathews had given him 100 pounds, supplied by Tryon, with which to bribe Continental soldiers. Ketchum reported Hickey had said American soldiers were ready to fire on their compatriots once British forces landed.

Hickey, pleading not guilty, defended his actions, saying he:

> engaged in the scheme at first for the sake of cheating the Tories, and getting some money from them, and afterwards consented to have his name sent on board the man-of-war, in order that, if the enemy should arrive and defeat the army here, and he should be taken prisoner, he might be safe.

Hickey, an Irishman, had deserted from the British army several years earlier.

Hickey was found guilty and sentenced to hang. Washington ordered that all men not on duty be present at Hickey's execution in the hopes that Hickey's "unhappy fate" would "be a warning to" all. On June 28, 20,000 people watched as Hickey, minus stripes and buttons, having refused a chaplain (he claimed clergy were all cutthroats), mounted the scaffold and died. The following day, British warships sailed into New York Harbor.

Hickey was the only conspirator executed. The 13 sent to Connecticut were never tried. Several conspirators, including Mayor Mathews, escaped. By fall the British had taken New York. The secret investigative committee had accused one man, James Clayford, of plotting to kidnap George Washington. But there seems to be no surviving record of what eventually happened to him.

— Teddi DiCanio

Suggestions for Further Reading

Fenwick, Ben C. "The Plot to Kill Washington." *American History Illustrated* (February 1987): 8–12.

Hughes, Rupert. *George Washington, The Rebel and the Patriot*. New York: William Morrow & Co., 1927.

Smith, Page. *A New Age Now Begins*, Vol. 1. New York: McGraw-Hill, 1976.

Van Doren, Carl. *The Secret History of the American Revolution*. New York: Augustus M. Kelley, 1973.

Wightman, William. *Minutes of a Conspiracy Against the Liberties of America*. New York: Arno Press, 1969.

Penhallow v. The Lusanna: 1777

Libelants: John Penhallow and Jacob Treadwell, representing 15 Portsmouth merchants who owned the privateer *McClary,* and George Wentworth, acting as agent for the ship's crew **Claimants:** Elisha Doane, owner of the *Lusanna,* Isaiah Doane (son), and James Shepherd **Lawyer for the Libelants:** Sewall (no other name listed) **Lawyers for the Claimants:** John Adams, John Lowell, and Oliver Whipple **Dates of Trial:** Circa December 16–20, 1777 **Place of Trial:** Portsmouth, New Hampshire **Judge of Admiralty:** Dr. Joshua Brackett **Verdict:** For the libelants

SIGNIFICANCE

Throughout its 18-year history, this case highlighted the controversy of federal vs. state jurisdiction.

Privateering was a kind of legal piracy by which warring countries preyed on each other's shipping. An authorized ship of Country A would capture a ship belonging to Country B, tow it to a port, then petition a court to "libel" the seized ship. If granted, the ship and cargo were auctioned and the proceeds divided, depriving Country A of resources.

When British authorities closed Boston's port, merchant Elisha Doane, with whale oil to sell and credits due him being held in London, moved to safeguard his financial affairs. Doane sent his son-in-law Shearjashub Bourne to England with the oil. Due to the volatile state of political affairs, Bourne had great discretion in making whatever decisions seemed necessary. Actions, taken to safeguard investors' interests, would be used in court as evidence of loyalist sympathies.

En route, Doane's ship, the *Lusanna,* was damaged by a storm. While in Halifax for repairs, the ship was seized twice by British authorities, then released. The second release was on condition the *Lusanna* be re-registered in Halifax. Later in London, Bourne would re-register the ship in his own name and sail for Gibraltar.

Upon returning to London, Bourne tried to reclaim a cargo of Doane's seized from the brigantine *Industry.* Bourne, in the guise of a loyal subject, submitted a memorial to the Treasury of England. His request was rejected when a former member of the Massachusetts Bar, Daniel Leonard, insisted Bourne had no true interest in the cargo and the owners probably planned to take military supplies to the rebels. The memorial, but not Leonard's refutation, would be used as evidence in the *Lusanna* trial.

Heading for Halifax on her return trip, the *Lusanna* was captured by the American privateer *McClary* on October 30, 1777. At Portsmouth, New Hampshire, the *Lusanna* was "libeled" in the state's Court Maritime on November 11. On December 1, attorney John Lowell filed claims on behalf of the owners to recover the ship and her cargo.

The libelants claimed that the ship and cargo belonged to inhabitants or subjects of Great Britain and the *Lusanna* was carrying supplies to the enemy's "Fleet or Army" in Halifax. The libelants also tried to claim:

> Cause of Condemnation viz. that the Brig made a Voyage to Gibralter with King's Stores in the Year 1776, tho this Cause is not set forth in the Libel.

Based on depositions, invoices, and the ship's register, the libelants maintained Bourne was a loyalist, and that Bourne, not Elisha Doane, owned the ship and much of the cargo. Records showed that government, possibly military, stores were part of *Lusanna*'s cargo to Gibralter. However, witnesses testified Bourne had refused to let the ship to the military transport service.

The claimants, too, had documents and depositions contradicting various allegations. But Bourne's testimony was needed. Under 18th-century rules of evidence, "interested" witnesses could not testify. Bourne conveyed to Isaiah Doane any interests he had in the cargo. His testimony was still barred.

It fell to the claimants' lawyers to argue that Bourne's actions were reasonable. John Adams pointed out that unless contradicted by law, a man could transport his property by whatever methods he chose. Moreover, a ship's registration did not convey property and the practice of altering registrations to protect property was common. Adams also insisted:

> there was no Law or Resolution of Congress that prohibited a Voyage to Gibralter, the Troops and Fleet not coming within the Meaning of the Law ie, Enemies acting against the United States of America.

Furthermore, Bourne would not have been cleared to leave London unless headed for a British, rather than an American, port.

The jury found for the libelants. The court decreed the *Lusanna* and her cargo forfeit. An appeal to Congress was denied on grounds the appeal could only be heard by the state's superior court. In September 1778, the claimants lost their appeal although they had amassed much evidence to justify Bourne's actions. This court, too, refused an appeal to Congress and on September 18, 1778, the *Lusanna* and her cargo were auctioned.

Elisha Doane petitioned Congress to review the case. Congress' Court of Congressional Commissioners of Appeals had recently reversed a decree of the Pennsylvania Admiralty Court. The Philadelphia court had refused to obey the reversal and suspended activities. After pondering the controversy, on March 6, 1779, Congress resolved that: its war powers enabled it to try prize appeals based on questions of fact and law; right of appeal could not be denied by state law; and the commissioners could make the final decree. New Hampshire voted for the resolution.

In June 1779, the commissioners ruled they had jurisdiction in the *Lusanna* affair, then delayed continuing the case until New Hampshire could react to Congress' March resolution. The case was heard September 11–13, 1783. (Elisha Doane was dead.) In 1780, the Congress had established a Court of Appeals in Cases of Capture which, on September 17, 1783, reversed the lower courts and ordered the claimants' property restored.

The libelants petitioned Congress, insisting the commissioners lacked jurisdiction. A congressional committee agreed. The Congress as a whole did not.

To have the court of appeals decree enforced, the claimants filed in Massachusetts where eventually its Supreme Judicial Court decided the court of appeals had no jurisdiction and declared the New Hampshire decree to be final. In March 1786, the claimants filed suit in Philadelphia's Court of Common Pleas to attach a ship belonging to a libelant. In 1787, that court decided it lacked jurisdiction in admiralty cases and discontinued the attachment.

The case languished until the Constitution was ratified and a federal court system established. In March 1792, administrators for Doane's estate asked the U.S. District Court in New Hampshire to execute the decree. Because the judge had once acted for the libelants, the case was moved to Circuit Court. There, Justice John Blair found for the administrators and asked for a report ascertaining damages. The report was submitted a year later. On October 24, 1794, Judge William Cushing awarded the claimants $38,518.69.

In 1795, the *McClary*'s owners appealed to the U.S. Supreme Court, on writ of error, to no avail. However, adjustments were made about damages.

— *Teddi DiCanio*

Suggestions for Further Reading

Adams, John. *Diary and Autobiography of John Adams.* Lyman H. Butterfield, ed., Cambridge, Mass.: Howard University Press, 1961.

——. *The Legal Papers of John Adams*, Vol. 2. L. Kinvin Roth & Hiller Zobel, eds. Cambridge, Mass.: Belknap Press, 1965.

Major John Andre Trial: 1780

Defendant: Major John Andre   **Crime Charged:** Espionage
Board of Enquiry: 14 generals of George Washington's staff headed by
Major General Nathanael Greene.   **Place:** Tappan, New York
Date of Trial: September 29, 1780   **Verdict:** Guilty   **Sentence:** Death by
hanging

SIGNIFICANCE

Major John Andre's trial for espionage sent shock waves through the American colonies by revealing the depth of a treason plot by General Benedict Arnold to hand over the American stronghold at West Point to the British. Had Andre not been captured and the conspiracy foiled, the American Revolution might well have been crushed.

On October 2, 1780, Major John Andre, a British officer, was hanged for espionage. His executioners would have preferred to hang the man with whom Andre consorted: the traitor, General Benedict Arnold.

Arnold was a talented field commander and one of that circle of men who were surrogate sons to General George Washington. Yet he was adept at making enemies. Appointed by Washington to command military forces in Philadelphia while he recovered from war wounds, Arnold's relentless ambition and greed eventually led to complaints to Congress that he was abusing his powers. Documents would later surface indicating Arnold was much more dishonest than local authorities ever suspected—documents unavailable when they lodged their complaints. After a list of eight charges wound its way first through Congress and then a haphazard court-martial (it was interrupted by wartime events), it was decided enough evidence existed to uphold two of the accusations. Arnold was found guilty of having used public wagons for private purposes and of having improperly issued a pass allowing a ship, the *Charming Nancy*, to leave port when all other vessels were quarantined. Arnold was sentenced to "receive a reprimand" from General Washington.

Arnold himself had asked—or more accurately, maneuvered—for a trial. "I ask only for justice," he wrote to Washington, complaining of his countrymen's treatment of him after all his sacrifices. He added, "I wish your Excellency for your long and eminent services, may not be paid in the same coin."

But, in the fall of 1779, at the same time he was trying to enlist Washington's help, Arnold opened a secret correspondence with Major John Andre, head of British intelligence. Arnold offered to either immediately enlist or "cooperate on some concealed plan with Sir Henry Clinton." Arnold sought at least 10,000 pounds for his "services." Negotiations were protracted and at one point the correspondence lapsed.

Eventually the persistent Arnold obtained command of the fort at West Point, on the Hudson River in New York, and the surrounding area. He agreed to deliver West Point to Clinton for the extraordinary sum of 20,000 pounds if the venture were completely successful and 10,000 pounds if it were not.

To plan the details of the surrender, Arnold and Andre wanted a meeting. Clinton reluctantly agreed but ordered that Andre: not go behind enemy lines; not carry any compromising papers; and never wear a disguise—he was to remain in uniform. If he were to be captured, this would protect Andre from any charge of spying (and execution).

On September 20, 1780, Joshua Smith, a loyalist friend of Arnold's, fetched Andre from the H.M.S. *Vulture*. The terms of the passes Smith carried allowed only one man to come. Thus, Colonel Beverly Robinson, who was to accompany Andre, was left behind.

Rather than going to Smith's house as originally planned, Andre and Arnold met six miles up river, at the foot of Long Clove Mountain. A British contingent was to attack West Point. The moves of the opposing forces had to be plotted in advance. Each order Arnold gave to his men had to appear reasonable at the time, yet still lead ultimately to the loss of the fort.

The two farmers who had been pressed into rowing the boat that had brought Andre, refused to take him back when he and Arnold were finished. As daylight broke, Arnold and Andre, his uniform covered by a cloak, rode to Smith's home on the Hudson River within sight of the *Vulture*. They passed an American sentry, which placed Andre behind American lines.

Several hours later, any hope of slipping Andre back aboard ship was blasted away by an American colonel at nearby Dobbs Ferry. Colonel James Livingston, with a small artillery battery, peppered the frigate, damaging her hull and driving her two miles away.

The simplest and safest action for Andre to have taken would have been to ride out in uniform carrying a flag of truce. Such actions were common as both sides made attempts to negotiate the exchange of prisoners. But Andre, a romantic who enjoyed amateur theatrics, yielded to Smith's insistence that he switch to civilian attire. Worse still, Andre carried a map and other incriminating documents, the contents of which he could have memorized.

Before leaving for West Point, Arnold wrote out three passes, one of which allowed Smith to transport Andre across the Hudson. But Smith was unwilling to venture again upon the water. Instead, the two rode toward White Plains. A day and a half later, as Andre entered a no-man's-land area, Smith left him.

Andre's Capture

A few miles later Andre encountered three Patriot "skinners." Andre mistook them for Loyalists and introduced himself as a British officer "on business of importance." He soon realized his mistake and showed them Arnold's pass made out to John Anderson, the name Andre had used in his correspondence. Andre tried to bluff them with threats that Arnold would be displeased if Andre were detained, implying that his first statement had been a ruse to protect himself from Loyalist "cow boys." Skinners and cow boys often relieved their respective enemies of worldly goods.

The men, John Paulding, David Williams, and Isaac Van Wert, of the New York militia, stripped and searched Andre. They found papers between his stocking and his English boot. Only Paulding could read. He realized Andre was a spy. After a brief conversation about the possibility of delivering Andre to British hands, for a consideration, the men took Andre to Lieutenant Colonel John Jameson at North Castle.

Jameson had received orders several days earlier to permit a John Anderson to pass through to West Point to visit Arnold. But this Anderson was headed in the wrong direction. The handwriting on all the papers, including the pass, was the same. However, Jameson was unfamiliar with Arnold's handwriting. Andre insisted he be taken to Arnold. Jameson reluctantly agreed. However, unbeknownst to Andre, Jameson sent the documents to General Washington.

Shortly after Andre left, under guard, Major Benjamin Tallmadge, the able head of Washington's secret service, arrived. Tallmadge convinced Jameson to recall this "John Anderson" but failed to convince him to recall the messenger sent to inform Arnold of Anderson's detention. Arnold escaped to the *Vulture* shortly before Washington reached West Point. The incriminating documents caught up with Washington there and he sent men in pursuit of Arnold. But it was too late.

An etching of Major John Andre from an English textbook. (Courtesy, Library of Congress)

Andre realized he could no longer carry on the pretense of being John Anderson. He wrote to Washington. "What I have as yet said concerning myself was in the justifiable attempt to be extricated." Without naming Arnold, Andre stated that he had come, in uniform, "to meet, upon ground not within posts of either army, a person who was to give me intelligence." Andre insisted that his presence behind American lines was unplanned and undesired. Andre's argument was that he was, in effect, a prisoner of war and as such had a right to attempt escape in civilian clothes. This would be his defense at his trial.

Washington also received a letter from Arnold:

I have ever acted from a principle of love to my country, since the commencement of the present unhappy contest between Great Britain and the colonies. The same principle of love to my country actuates my present conduct, however it may appear inconsistent to the world, who very seldom judge right of any man's actions.

He exonerated his wife (who had plotted with him) of any complicity and asked Washington to protect her.

Andre's Trial

At Washington's order, on September 29, 1780, a board was convened to examine and try Major John Andre. Andre's testimony conflicted on a major, damning point with evidence presented in letters from Arnold, Clinton, and Robinson. They all claimed that Andre had traveled to Arnold under a flag of truce. When asked the question directly, Andre, unaware of the letters, said:

that it was impossible for him to suppose he had come on shore under that sanction; and added that, if he had come ashore under that sanction, he might certainly have returned under it.

The board could not take seriously Andre's arguments about being made a prisoner of war, subject to Arnold's orders. Historian James Flexner pointed out, "Had Andre been acting legally, he would have had no need for an assumed name. An officer is not obligated to obey an enemy's orders." Flexner also wrote, "Flags do not cover suborning of treason." However, a flag would have given the board a semblance of an excuse to avoid a judgment of espionage, which it would have preferred to do. Andre's conduct brought him respect and sympathy. However, the evidence was overwhelming and the decision of the board was unanimous:

Major Andre, Adjutant General of the British Army, ought to be considered a spy from the enemy, and that, agreeable to the law and usage of nations, it is their opinion he ought to suffer death.

The next day Washington confirmed the verdict and ordered that Andre's execution take place the following day.

Sir Henry Clinton, under a flag of truce, sent a delegation to present arguments that Andre was not a spy, thus giving Washington an excuse to delay the execution. The British produced another letter from Arnold in which he took all blame upon himself. There were veiled threats that if Andre were executed, there might be a retaliation against American prisoners of war.

Hints reached Clinton that Andre could be exchanged for Arnold. Although Clinton despised Arnold, and Andre was his favorite aide, he rejected the idea, as members of the same side could not be exchanged as if prisoners of opposing sides. Moreover, returning Arnold to Washington would hardly encourage further defections from the revolutionary cause.

Eventually all negotiations fell through. Washington again set an execution date for Andre. He rejected an appeal from Andre for a soldier's death by firing squad over what was considered the less honorable mode of execution "on the gibbet." In the 18th century, spies were always hanged. To deviate from this practice would have thrown doubt on Andre's guilt. If Andre was not a spy, then he was a prisoner of war and should not be executed at all.

Until he saw the gallows, Andre was unaware that Washington had denied his request. He blanched briefly. Asked if he had any last words, Andre requested that those present "bear me witness that I meet my fate as a brave man." He, himself, adjusted his noose and the handkerchief over his eyes. He supplied the handkerchief with which his arms were tied. Andre, in uniform, was hanged about noon. As he died, many of those watching wept.

— Teddi DiCanio

Suggestions for Further Reading

Brown, Richard C. "Three Forgotten Heroes," *American Heritage* (August 1975): 25.

Flexner, James Thomas. *The Traitor And The Spy.* Boston: Little, Brown & Co., 1953.

Ford, Corey. *A Peculiar Service.* Boston: Little, Brown & Co., 1965.

Hatch, Robert McConnell and Don Higginbotham. *Major John Andre: A Gallant in Spy's Clothing.* Boston: Houghton Mifflin, 1986.

Smith, Page. *A New Age Now Begins*, Vol. II. New York: McGraw-Hill Book Co., 1976.

The Quock Walker Trials: 1781–83

Case 1: *Jennison v. Caldwell,* civil suit and appeal
Case 2: *Walker v. Jennison,* civil suit and appeal
Case 3: *Commonwealth v. Jennison,* criminal indictment
Plaintiffs: Nathaniel Jennison, (1); Quock Walker, (2)
Defendants: Nathaniel Jennison, (2,3); John and Seth Caldwell (2)
Charge: Assault and battery (1,3); deprivation of the benefit of his servant,
Walker (2) **Chief Prosecutor:** Robert Treat Paine (3)
Lawyers for Walker and the Caldwells: Levi Lincoln, Caleb Strong
Lawyers for Jennison: John Sprague, William Stearns **Judges:** Moses Gill,
Samuel Baker, Joseph Dorr, and Moses Gill (1,2); In appeals, Nathaniel P.
Sargent, presiding, David Sewall, James Sullivan (1,2); Chief Justice William
Cushing, Nathaniel Sargent, David Sewall, and Increase Sumner (3)
Dates of Trials: Circa June 12–16, 1781 (1); June 12–19, 1781 (2);
September 1781 (both appeals); April 20, 1783 (3)
Place of Trials: Worcester, Massachusetts **Verdict:** For the plaintiff, (1)
reversed on appeal; For the plaintiff (2), appeal dismissed; guilty (3)
Sentence: 25 pounds (1); 50 pounds (2); 40 shillings (3)

SIGNIFICANCE
These were the most famous cases concerning the abolition of slavery in
Massachusetts.

The exact point at which slavery ceased to exist in Massachusetts is unclear. Furthermore, whether slavery existed "legally" in Massachusetts is also questionable. The colony's *Body of Liberties* expressly forbade slavery except for war captives, indentured servants, and as punishment for a crime.

Slaves in colonial Massachusetts, from time to time, filed "freedom suits." Sketchy records are unclear as to whether slaves who succeeded were freed on legal or moral principles or because defects existed in masters' titles.

Massachusetts courts shut down during the Revolution. When they re-opened in 1781, a brand-new state constitution stated:

All men are born free and equal, and have certain natural, essential, and unalienable rights; among which may be reckoned the right of enjoying and defending their lives and liberty;

This clause would be invoked in court. In 1754, James Caldwell purchased a slave couple and their infant, Quock Walker. Caldwell died when Quock was 10. Caldwell's widow, who had inherited Quock, eventually married Nathaniel Jennison and ownership of Quock passed to him. Or did it? Quock Walker maintained Caldwell had promised he would be free at age 25 and Mrs. Caldwell had amended that promise to age 21. Isabell Caldwell Jennison died in 1773, when Walker was about 19.

Jennison would not set him free. At age 28, Walker ran away. Jennison found him working for John and Seth Caldwell, brothers of James. With help, Jennison beat Walker, dragged him back to his own farm, then locked Walker in a barn.

Quock Walker filed a civil suit against Nathaniel Jennison for assault and battery. Jennison filed suit against the Caldwell brothers for unlawfully enticing his servant—the word slave was not used—Walker "from the business & service of the said Nathaniel." Jennison asked for damages of 1,000 pounds.

Both cases came before Worcester County Court of Common Pleas on June 12, 1781. The *Jennison v. Caldwell* case appears to have been heard first. Jennison won and was awarded 25 pounds.

In *Walker v. Jennison*, Jennison's attorneys produced the bill of sale for Walker's purchase. Walker insisted his former master had promised him his freedom, while attorney Levi Lincoln attacked slavery on moral grounds. The jury found Quock Walker to be a free man and awarded him 50 pounds.

Both cases were appealed. In September 1781, the Massachusetts Supreme Judicial Court dismissed Jennison's appeal of *Walker v. Jennison* because his lawyers failed to submit the court records. In the Caldwell appeal, Lincoln insisted slavery was contrary to the law of God and to the Massachusetts Constitution's Declaration of Rights. Again, a jury decided Walker was a free man. As such, the Caldwells were within their rights to employ him.

In January 1782, Jennison asked the legislature that he be permitted to reenter his Walker appeal because he had "lost his law" through attorney negligence. In June 1782, he submitted a memorial claiming "he was deprived of ten Negro Servants" due to the court's interpretation of the Declaration of Rights clause, and claiming he should also be relieved of any obligation to support them. No final decision was made on either petition.

In April 1783, two years after a criminal indictment had been brought against Jennison, he was tried for assault, found guilty, and fined 40 shillings. A notion arose that this particular case abolished slavery in Massachusetts. The notion was born of the charge given to the jury by Chief Justice William Cushing, critical of "the right of Christians to hold Africans in perpetual servitude, and sell and treat them as we do horses and cattle," and voicing the opinion that slavery was inconsistent with the state constitution.

Actually, slavery was abolished by erosion. Each slave case won encouraged another. In the 1790 census, Massachusetts reported (probably erroneously) that it had no more slaves.

— Teddi DiCanio

Suggestions for Further Reading

Moore, George H., *Notes on the History of Slavery in Massachusetts*. New York: Negro Universities Press, 1968 [reprint].

O'Brien, S.J., William, "Did the Jennison Case Outlaw Slavery in Massachusetts?" *The William and Mary Quarterly*, Vol. XVII (April 1960).

Spector, Robert M., "The Quock Walker Cases (1781–83): The Abolition of Slavery and Negro Citizenship in Early Massachusetts." *The Journal of Negro History*, Vol. LIII (April 1968).

Alien and Sedition Acts: 1798

Defendants: 24 people, including: James Thompson Callender, Thomas Cooper, William Duane, Anthony Haswell, and Matthew Lyon.

Crime Charged: Seditious libel   **Chief Defense Lawyers:** Lyon acted for himself, advised by Israel Smith; David Fay and Israel Smith (Haswell); Thomas Cooper and Alexander Dallas, (Duane); Cooper acted for himself; and William B. Giles, George Hay and Philip Nicholas (Callender)

Chief Prosecutors: Charles Marsh (Lyon, Haswell); William Rawle (Duane, Cooper); and Thomas Nelson (Callender)   **Judges:** William Paterson and Samuel Hitchcock (Lyon, Haswell); Samuel Chase, and Richard Peters (Cooper); Bushrod Washington and Peters (Duane); and Samuel Chase (Callender)   **Dates of Trials:** October 8, 1799 (Lyon); May 5, 1800 (Haswell) April 16, 1800 (Cooper); June 3, 1800 (Callender); June 11, 1800 (Duane court appearance)   **Place:** Rutland, Vermont (Lyon); Windsor, Vermont (Haswell); Norristown, Pennsylvania (Duane); Philadelphia, Pennsylvania (Cooper); and Richmond, Virginia (Callender)   **Verdict:** Guilty (Lyon, Haswell, Cooper, and Callender)   **Sentences:** $1,000 fine, $60.96 court costs, 4 months in jail (Lyon); $200 fine, 2 months in jail (Haswell); $400 fine, 6 months in prison, a $2,000 surety bond upon leaving prison (Cooper); and $200 fine, 9 months in prison, a $1,200 bond for good behavior (Callender)

SIGNIFICANCE

On paper only, the terms of the Sedition Act were an improvement over traditional common law. But the fact that the federal government would enact a sedition law was a blow to freedom of the press.

Partisan politics contributed to the creation of the Alien and Sedition Acts. However, American perceptions and worries about European affairs, particularly realistic fears of a possible war with France, also contributed to their enactment. American attempts to maintain neutrality pleased no one at home or abroad.

The Naturalization and Alien Acts, which increased residency requirements for citizenship and gave extraordinary powers over aliens to the president, passed into oblivion unused. However, there were several prosecutions under the Sedition Act. The act's most pertinent provision allowed prosecutions against persons publishing "any false, scandalous and malicious writing" that brought the federal government, the Congress, or the president into disrepute.

Under common law, liberty of the press generally meant no prior restraint on publications. However, the publisher was responsible for what he (or she) wrote. If a court deemed the material to be libelous, the writer could be punished. Libel was a published statement that damaged a person's reputation, or in the case of seditious libel, the government or a government official. Truth was not a defense, nor did there need to be proof of malicious intent. Despite First Amendment prohibitions, most states had their own libel and sedition acts.

Satiric portrayal of the first fight in Congress—between Matthew Lyon and Roger Griswold. Lyon was later prosecuted under the Sedition Act. (Courtesy, Library of Congress)

The federal Sedition Act tried to strike a compromise between common law and new American freedoms. Truth was a defense under the new federal statute, proof of malicious intent was required, and the jury would decide whether a libel existed. Under common law, the judge decided if material was libelous and he was free to determine any sentence. The Sedition Act stipulated that those convicted could be fined not more than $2,000 and imprisoned for no more than two years.

In practice these changes availed nothing to those prosecuted. Federalist courts insisted on turning the truth-as-a-defense clause into a presumptive-guilt clause. The plaintiff, the government, did not have to prove that the statements made were false. The defendant had to prove they were true. And such attempts often were thwarted by the judge.

Benjamin Franklin Bache, the vitriolic publisher of the *Aurora*, spurred passage of the Sedition Act when he obtained and published a copy of a letter from France's foreign minister, Tallyrand. This action convinced many Federalists that connections existed between Republicans and the French government. Before the Sedition Act could be passed, Bache's intemperate remarks earned him a common law indictment for libeling President John Adams and his administration. Bache died of yellow fever before he could be tried.

The first man actually indicted under the new Sedition Act was a member of Congress, Matthew Lyon. Charges stemmed from publication of two letters. One, Lyon wrote to a newspaper in reply to an attack on him.

> When I shall see the efforts of that power bent on the promotion of the comfort . . . of the people, that executive shall have my zealous and uniform support: but whenever I shall . . . see . . . the public welfare swallowed up in a continual grasp for power . . . behold men of real merit daily turned out of office . . . men of meanness preferred for the ease with which they take up and advocate opinions . . . when I shall see the sacred name of religion employed as a state engine to make mankind hate . . . I shall not be their humble advocate.

The other letter, published by Lyon, was written by Joel Barlow. Commenting on a speech of Adams', Barlow wondered why Congress had not sent the president "to a mad house."

Lyon tried to defend himself on the grounds that the Sedition Law was unconstitutional. The court did not look kindly on this defense. Found guilty, Lyon wrote, published, and was re-elected from his cell.

Anthony Haswell, a supporter of Lyon's, was indicted because an advertisement to raise funds for Lyon's fine, described "the oppressive hand of usurped power" Lyon suffered and "the indignities . . . heaped upon him by a hard-hearted savage" [the jailer]. Also, reprinted from the *Aurora* was a charge Tories were holding government office. Haswell tried, unsuccessfully, to obtain testimony from the Secretary of War to prove the Tory charges. His lawyers argued just as unsuccessfully that the "oppressive hand of power" referred only to the marshal and the jailer.

The most elusive Republican was William Duane, who had married Bache's widow and taken over the *Aurora*. Duane charged that the British wielded great influence over administration politics and had spent a fortune in bribes. He claimed there was a secret alliance between England and America against France.

Duane appeared for trial, only to have the trial suspended for several months. A procedural reason was given, but the true reason rested with a letter Duane had obtained from Tench Coxe, one-time assistant to Alexander Hamilton in the Treasury. The letter, written years earlier to Coxe by John Adams, claimed the Pinckneys from South Carolina were enlisting help from the British to obtain federal appointments. Although this letter did not prove Duane's extravagant allegations, it showed some evidence of British influence.

While awaiting the new trial, Duane aggravated the Senate. He criticized a proposed, unpublished bill, to settle disputed presidential and vice presidential elections. Then, when summoned to answer questions, he refused to go because his lawyers refused to appear. They believed Senate rules precluded mounting an effective defense. Duane was arrested on a contempt warrant signed by Thomas Jefferson, president of the Senate.

Not until after the Congress adjourned did the administration indict Duane for libeling the Senate. When Jefferson became president, he dismissed that suit. To preserve the Senate's rights, Jefferson ordered a new suit instituted. The grand jury refused to indict.

Because he was one of Duane's lawyers, Thomas Cooper was indicted for a handbill published months prior to Duane's summons from the Senate. Prosecutor William Rawles treated the handbill as inflammatory:

> Error leads to discontent, discontent to a fancied idea of oppression, and that
> to insurrection.

Cooper maintained that his statements were true, he held no malicious motives, and had attributed none to Adams. The judge, Samuel Chase, blocked Cooper's defense at every turn.

When James Thompson Callender faced Judge Chase after being indicted for his savage writings about Adams, like met like. Callender had no regard for truth or decency. Chase had little regard for truth or law. Chase struck down every reasonable defense request made, harassing the defense lawyers until they withdrew from the case.

Callender's sentence expired the day the Act expired. The new Jefferson administration did not seek to renew the Sedition Act, although libel actions did continue under common law.

— *Teddi DiCanio*

Suggestions for Further Reading

Miller, John C. *Crisis in Freedom.* Boston: Little, Brown & Co., 1951.

Smith, James Morton. *Freedom's Fetters, The Alien and Sedition Laws and American Civil Liberties.* Ithaca, N.Y.: Cornell University Press, 1956.

John Fries Trials: 1799

Defendant: John Fries   **Crime Charged:** Treason
Chief Defense Lawyers: First trial: Alexander Dallas, James Ewing, and
William Lewis; second trial: none   **Chief Prosecutors:** First trial: William
Rawle and Samuel Sitgreaves; second trial: Jared Ingersoll and Rawle
Judges: First trial: James Iredell and Richard Peters; second trial: Samuel
Chase and Peters   **Dates of Trials:** First trial: April 30–May 9, 1799;
second trial: April 24–25, 1800   **Place:** Philadelphia, Pennsylvania
Verdict: Guilty, both trials   **Sentence:** Hanging. However, President John
Adams pardoned Fries.

SIGNIFICANCE
John Fries' fate hinged on the interpretation of his actions, whether they
constituted riot or levying war, i.e., treason.

In 1798, the U.S. Congress, anticipating a possible war with France, passed a tax to be laid according to assessed values on slaves, lands, and houses. The legislation, well publicized in urban areas, was little known or understood in some rural areas. This lack of understanding, particularly in northeastern Pennsylvania where many residents knew only German, led to confrontations with excise officers as they tried to examine property. One series of incidents led to a charge of treason after a band of armed men from Bucks County, led by John Fries, a former Continental Army officer, forced U.S. Marshal William Nichols to release 23 men being held on charges of insurrection. No one was hurt.

As comprehension about the tax legislation grew and affairs quieted down in Bucks and neighboring Northampton counties, rumors grew in Washington that the disturbances constituted a "plot." Members of both the Federalist and Republican "parties" fantasized reasons as to why the other group would create trouble. President John Adams dispatched troops to the area.

Upon their arrival were no disturbances to quell. Instead the military sought the ringleaders of the "insurrection." At an auction, troops grabbed John Fries and others who did not scramble away quickly enough. Of these, 15, including Fries, were charged with treason and taken to Philadelphia. The only ones tried were Fries, Anthony Stahler, and Frederic Hearny.

At Fries' first trial, prosecutor William Rawle stated that an action taken to prevent the execution of a public officer's duties was "an act of levying war," i.e., treason. Fries' fears about his rights and property were insufficient reasons to justify resistance. The defense argued that Fries' action constituted riot, which was a high misdemeanor, rather than treason. Alexander Dallas spent hours weaving points of English common law into an argument that the jury had the power to decide whether actions taken constituted treason as well as whether the defendant had committed said actions. Moreover, Fries' inability to read English had left him ignorant of the excise officers' purposes. But, in his charge to the jury, Judge James Iredell made it clear that armed resistance constituted treason.

The jury found Fries guilty. However, the judges agreed to a request for a new trial since apparently one juror had formed an opinion before the trial.

But the second trial promised to be worse than the first when Judge Samuel Chase issued a written opinion prior to the trial. It was this action which brought the trial so much attention. Chase maintained English common law had no bearing on the case and that:

> Any insurrection . . . for the purpose of resisting or preventing by force . . . the execution of any statute of the United States . . . is levying war against the United States, within the . . . true meaning of the Constitution.

Although prosecutor Rawle persuaded Chase to withdraw his opinion, the defense lawyers withdrew from the case. Given the mind of the court, it would be impossible to mount an adequate defense. Fries declined to obtain other counsel, and the judge advised the defendant throughout the trial, which was an old common law practice. Fries was found guilty and sentenced to hang. He appealed to President Adams for a pardon, a step he also had taken after the first trial.

Adams sent his son Thomas to ask the defense lawyers for their briefs. He did not ask for the judges' notes—an unusual move. After consulting his cabinet members, who were opposed to much leniency, Adams first granted amnesty to

THE

TWO TRIALS

OF

· JOHN FRIES,*

on an Indictment for

TREASON;

TOGETHER WITH A BRIEF REPORT OF THE TRIALS OF SEVERAL OTHER PERSONS, FOR

Treason and Insurrection,

In the Counties of Bucks, Northampton and Montgomery,

IN THE *CIRCUIT COURT* OF THE *UNITED STATES,*

Begun at the City of Philadelphia, April 11, 1799; continued at Norristown, October 11, 1799;—and concluded at Philadelphia, April 11, 1800; before the Hon. Judges, IREDELL, PETERS, WASHINGTON and CHASE.

TO WHICH IS ADDED,

A copious Appendix, containing the evidences and arguments of the counsel on both sides, on the motion for a new trial; the arguments on the motion for removing the case to the county where the crime was committed, and the arguments against holding the jurisdiction at Norristown.

TAKEN IN SHORT HAND BY THOMAS CARPENTER.

[COPY-RIGHT SECURED.]

PHILADELPHIA:

Printed and sold by WILLIAM W. WOODWARD, No. 17 Chesnut, near Front street.

1800.

A facsimile of a published account of the trial of John Fries. (Courtesy, The Library Company of Philadelphia)

all those awaiting trial, then pardoned those already convicted: Fries, Stahler, and Hearny.

— Teddi DiCanio

Suggestions for Further Reading

Davis, W.W.H. *The Fries Rebellion, 1798–99*. Doylestown, Pa.: 1899.

Dos Passos, John. *The Men Who Made the Nation*. Garden City, N.Y.: Doubleday & Co., 1957.

Elsmere, Jane Shaffer. "The Trials of John Fries." *The Pennsylvania Magazine of History and Biography* (October, 1979): Vol. CIII, No.4.

Wharton, Francis. *State Trials of the United States*. Philadelphia: 1849.

Marbury v. Madison: 1803

Plaintiffs: William Marbury, William Harper, Robert R. Hooe, and Dennis Ramsay   **Defendant:** Secretary of State James Madison
Plaintiff Claim: That Madison had illegally refused to deliver judicial commissions to their rightful recipients   **Chief Defense Lawyer:** U.S. Attorney General Levi Lincoln   **Chief Lawyer for Plaintiffs:** Charles Lee
Justices: Samuel Chase, William Cushing, John Marshall, Alfred Moore, William Paterson, and Bushrod Washington   **Place:** Washington, D.C.
Dates of Trial: February 10–11, 1803   **Verdict:** Plaintiffs could not force Madison to deliver the commissions, because the Judiciary Act of 1789 was unconstitutional.

SIGNIFICANCE

Marbury v. Madison may be the most important case in American history, because it established the principle of judicial review.

In the late 18th century and early 19th century, the two parties dominating the American political scene were the Federalists and the Democratic-Republicans. In the presidential election of 1800, the Electoral College had a tie vote, and it fell to the House of Representatives to decide the outcome. After a bitter battle and 36 ballots, the House voted February 17, 1801 for Democratic-Republican candidate Thomas Jefferson.

The outgoing president, Federalist John Adams, had as his secretary of state the distinguished lawyer John Marshall. In January 1801, Adams secured Marshall's nomination as chief justice of the United States. Marshall was sworn in February 4 but continued to serve as Adams' secretary of state until March 3, when Adams' term ended. Meanwhile, Adams and the Federalists in Congress had been moving to pack the federal judiciary with as many new Federalist judges as possible before the Jefferson administration took power.

As part of the Federalists' efforts to preserve their control over the judiciary, on February 27, 1801, Congress gave Adams the power to appoint justices of the peace for the District of Columbia. On March 2, one day before the end of his term, Adams appointed 42 justices of the peace, and Congress approved their appointments the next day. As secretary of state, Marshall signed and sealed the necessary judicial commissions, but the commissions were not delivered by the end of March 3. Thomas Jefferson's term began March 4, and he ordered his new secretary of state, James Madison, not to deliver the commissions. Jefferson decided to view the commissions as invalid unless delivered.

Marbury Goes to Court

Having demonstrated his power, Jefferson ultimately allowed most of the Adams appointees to take their offices. One of the appointees that Jefferson did not allow to take office, William Marbury, filed a petition with the Supreme Court December 16, 1801 requesting that the Supreme Court order Madison to deliver Marbury's commission. Marbury was joined by three other disappointed appointees, William Harper, Robert R. Hooe, and Dennis Ramsay. Of course, by now Marshall had been the chief justice for over nine months. Under the Judiciary Act of 1789, the Supreme Court had the power to issue the order Marbury requested, called a "writ of mandamus."

On December 18, 1801, Marshall ordered a hearing on Marbury's petition, to take place at the Court's next session, the February Term of 1803. The hearing began February 10, 1803. Charles Lee, a Federalist and former attorney general, represented Marbury and the others. Jefferson's attorney general, Levi Lincoln, was present in court as a witness, but not as Madison's lawyer.

Lee argued that Madison, as secretary of state, was not only an official of the executive branch, bound to obey the president, but a public servant obligated to perform his duty and deliver Marbury's lawful commission. Therefore, the Court must exercise its authority under the Judiciary Act to issue a writ of mandamus against Madison. Attorney General Lincoln said practically nothing, except that the issue of the commissions was purely political and thus not subject to the judiciary.

Secretary of State James Madison, defendant in *Marbury v. Madison*, which established the principle of judicial review. (Courtesy, Library of Congress)

Marshall Proclaims the Doctrine of Judicial Review

On February 24, 1803, Chief Justice Marshall issued the Court's opinion. He proceeded in three steps.

First, he reviewed the facts of the case. He stated that Marbury had the right to receive his commission:

> To withhold his commission, therefore, is an act deemed by the court not warranted by law, but violative of a vested right.

Second, Marshall analyzed Marbury's legal remedies. He concluded that the Judiciary Act clearly entitled Marbury to the writ of mandamus he requested.

Portrait of Chief Justice John Marshall by St. Memin. (Courtesy, Library of Congress)

Marshall's third and final question, therefore, was whether the writ of mandamus could be issued by the Supreme Court. Although the Judiciary Act would allow the Court to issue the writ, Marshall was concerned about the Court's authority under Article III, Section 2, Paragraph 2 of the U.S. Constitution, which states:

> In all cases affecting ambassadors, other public ministers and consuls, and those in which a State shall be a Party, the Supreme Court shall have original jurisdiction. In all other cases . . . the Supreme Court shall have appellate jurisdiction . . . .

If the Court didn't have original jurisdiction—the responsibility for hearing the evidence and making an initial decision—then under the Constitution, Marbury couldn't go directly to it to get his requested writ of mandamus. He would have to go to a federal District Court, and only if he lost there could he then appeal to the Supreme Court under its *appellate* jurisdiction. As Marshall stated:

> To enable this court, then, to issue a mandamus, it must be shown to be an exercise of appellate jurisdiction . . . .

Marshall now addressed the critical question: Would the court use the authority that the Judiciary Act granted it, but that the Constitution denied it, to issue Marbury's writ of mandamus?

Marshall said no, it would not. No act of Congress, including the Judiciary Act, could do something forbidden by the Constitution:

> Certainly all those who have framed written constitutions contemplate them as forming the fundamental and paramount law of the nation, and consequently, the theory of every such government must be, that an act of the legislature, repugnant to the constitution, is void.

Therefore, because the Judiciary Act violated the Constitution, it was unenforceable. Marbury and the others could not get their writ of mandamus from the Court because their petition had been sent to the Court directly, not on appeal. In declaring the Judiciary Act unconstitutional, Marshall set forth for the first time the doctrine of judicial review. Judicial review means that the federal courts, above all the Supreme Court, have the power to declare laws unenforceable if they violate the Constitution:

> It is emphatically the province and duty of the judicial department to say what the law is. Those who apply the rule to particular cases must of necessity expound and interpret the rule. If two laws conflict with each other, the courts must decide on the operation of each.

Marshall's decision meant that the Court would not give his fellow Federalist Marbury the writ of mandamus. Nevertheless, it was a brilliant move. In refusing to confront Jefferson, Marshall had asserted a new and potent power for the judiciary, namely the doctrine of judicial review. Despite various issues, such as whether Marshall should have removed himself from the case because of his role as Adams' secretary of state, *Marbury v. Madison* permanently established the principle of judicial review. This power to overturn unconstitutional laws is the basis for the courts' power today to prevent such evils as civil rights violations.

—Stephen G. Christianson

Suggestions for Further Reading

Baker, Leonard. *John Marshall: A Life in Law.* New York: Macmillan Co., 1974.

Berger, Raoul. *Congress v. the Supreme Court.* Cambridge: Harvard University Press, 1969.

Beveridge, Albert J. *The Life of John Marshall.* Marietta, Ga.: Cherokee Publishing, 1990.

Bickel, Alexander M. *The Least Dangerous Branch: the Supreme Court at the Bar of Politics.* New Haven: Yale University Press, 1986.

Cusack, Michael. "America's Greatest Justice?" *Scholastic Update* (January 1990): 11.

Ellis, Richard E. *The Jeffersonian Crisis: Courts and Politics in the Young Republic.* New York: Oxford University Press, 1971.

Levy, Leonard Williams. *Judicial Review and the Supreme Court.* New York: Harper & Row, 1967.

McHugh, Clare. "The Story of the Constitution: Conflict and Promise." *Scholastic Update* (September 1987): 8–11.

Warren, Charles. *The Supreme Court in United States History.* Littleton, Colo.: F.B. Rothman, 1987.

Samuel Chase Impeachment: 1805

Defendant: Associate Supreme Court Justice Samuel Chase
Crime Charged: "High Crimes and Misdemeanors" within the meaning of
Article II, Section 4 of the Constitution   **Chief Defense Lawyers:** Robert
Goodloe Harper, Joseph Hopkinson, and Luther Martin
Chief Prosecutor: Trial Managers John Randolph and Caesar Rodney
Judges: The U.S. Senate, with Vice President Aaron Burr presiding
Place: Washington, D.C.   **Dates of Trial:** February 4–March 1, 1805
Verdict: Not guilty

SIGNIFICANCE

Congress for the first and only time exercised its constitutional prerogative to try a
justice of the U.S. Supreme Court.

Samuel Chase was born in Somerset County, Maryland in April of 1741. During the next 70 years, until his death in 1811, he would become one of America's most famous and controversial founding fathers.

Chase was active in politics from an early age and was elected to colonial Maryland's Assembly on the strength of his anti-English platform. He was Maryland's delegate to the Continental Congress of 1774 in Philadelphia, Pennsylvania and was one of the signers of the 1776 Declaration of Independence. After fighting in the Revolutionary War, during which he became friends with George Washington, Chase returned to Maryland. Chase used his influence in the Federalist Party to further his judicial career, and he swiftly rose through a succession of ever more prestigious posts. Chase was appointed presiding justice of the Baltimore Criminal Court, then in 1791 he was appointed chief justice of the Maryland Court of Appeals, and finally in 1796 he was appointed to the U.S. Supreme Court. Chase's Supreme Court nomination had Washington's personal backing.

From the Maryland courts to the Supreme Court, Chase was an openly Federalist judge, and he never hid his political loyalties. He zealously enforced the Federalist-sponsored Alien and Sedition Acts, and he supported the strict prosecution of persons involved in antigovernment demonstrations and allegedly treasonous activities. Chase presided at several trials involving supporters of his fellow founding father and presidential contender Thomas Jefferson.

Jefferson was the candidate of the opposition Democratic-Republican Party and won the hotly contested election of 1800.

Jefferson had a series of political struggles with the Federalists, whose supporters such as Chase and Supreme Court Chief Justice John Marshall dominated the federal judiciary. For several years, Jefferson's energies were focused on the legal issues in *Marbury v. Madison* (see separate entry), which ended on February 24, 1803 with Marshall's famous opinion proclaiming the doctrine of judicial review.

Congress Impeaches Chase

After *Marbury*, Jefferson adopted a different tactic in attacking the Federalist judiciary. He decided to exploit his party's domination of the Senate, where 25 of the 34 senators were Democratic-Republicans and only nine were Federalists. Under Article II, Section 4 of the Constitution, federal judges can be impeached for "High Crimes and Misdemeanors," and under Article I, Section 3, the trial must be conducted before the Senate. Jefferson's allies in the House of Representatives passed Articles of Impeachment against Chase, which were duly received by the Senate.

The Senate's High Court of Impeachment, presided over by Vice President Aaron Burr, opened on February 4, 1805. The "trial managers," or prosecutors, were John Randolph and Caesar Rodney. Chase's lawyers were Robert Goodloe Harper, Joseph Hopkinson, and Luther Martin. There were eight Articles, or charges, which named a variety of Democratic-Republican grievances against Chase concerning the trials over which he had presided. The charges ranged from giving a false legal definition of treason during the trial of one John Fries (see separate entry) in Article One to making very political comments to a Baltimore grand jury in Article Eight.

There was certainly plenty of evidence that Chase was a highly opinionated Federalist judge, who had perhaps acted with little regard for courtroom niceties, but there was very little proof that his actions were serious enough to be deemed constitutional violations. Even the Democratic-Republican senators felt uncomfortable. Trial manager Rodney in his closing argument lamely begged the Senate:

> Remember, if this honorable court acquit the defendant, they declare in the most solemn manner, . . . that he has . . . behaved himself well, in a manner becoming the character of a judge worthy of his situation.

On March 1, 1805, the Senate voted on Chase's impeachment. On each of the eight Articles, enough Democratic-Republican senators joined the Federalists in voting "not guilty" so that Chase was acquitted of all the charges against him. Chase continued to serve on the Supreme Court until he died in June 1811.

Samuel Chase's acquittal was a defeat for Thomas Jefferson, who may have planned to impeach Chief Justice John Marshall if Chase had been found guilty. The Samuel Chase impeachment was the first and only time Congress impeached a justice of the U.S. Supreme Court.

—Stephen G. Christianson

Suggestions for Further Reading

Elsmere, Jane Shaffer. *Justice Samuel Chase.* Muncie, Ind.: Janevar Publishing, 1980.

Haw, James. *Stormy Patriot: the Life of Samuel Chase.* Baltimore: Maryland Historical Society, 1980.

Rehnquist, William H. *Grand Inquests: the Historic Impeachments of Justice Samuel Chase and President Andrew Johnson.* New York: William Morrow & Co., 1992.

George Sweeney Trial: 1806

Defendant: George Wythe Sweeney **Crime Charged:** Murder
Chief Defense Lawyers: Edmund Randolph and William Wirt
Chief Prosecutor: Philip Norborne Nicholas **Judges:** Joseph Prentes and
John Tyler, Sr. **Place:** Richmond, Virginia
Dates of Trial: September 2–8, 1806 **Verdict:** Not guilty

SIGNIFICANCE

Because the law forbade blacks from testifying in the criminal trial of a white man, George Wythe Sweeney was acquitted of the murder of his distinguished granduncle, George Wythe.

George Wythe was born in 1726 in Elizabeth City County, Virginia. He had a long and distinguished career as one of America's founding fathers. Wythe was admitted to practice law before the bar of Virginia's General Court at the early age of 20. In addition to becoming one of Virginia's preeminent lawyers, Wythe was a successful politician. He was elected to Virginia's House of Burgesses several times before the American Revolution and was a member of the 1775 Continental Congress. In 1776, he signed the Declaration of Independence on behalf of the Commonwealth of Virginia.

After the Revolution, Wythe served as a judge on Virginia's High Court of Chancery and as the first professor of law at the College of William and Mary. In 1789 he moved to Richmond to live out his final years. Wythe continued to serve on the High Court of Chancery after the turn of the 19th century and was strong and healthy until the age of 80, well past the average life expectancy of the times.

Unfortunately for Wythe, his young grandnephew, George Wythe Sweeney, came to live with him in Richmond. Sweeney had inherited none of Wythe's character. Sweeney lived off Wythe's fortune, and he lost considerable sums of money drinking and gambling. In 1805, Sweeney stole some books from Wythe's personal library and tried to sell them at a public auction. In April 1806, Sweeney forged Wythe's name on six bank checks. The next month, Sweeney became afraid that the forgeries would be discovered. Further, Sweeney knew that he was a beneficiary in Wythe's will, and he was too greedy for his inheritance to let Wythe die naturally. Therefore, Sweeney decided to murder Wythe.

Sweeney Poisons Wythe and Is Tried for Murder

In late May 1806, Sweeney bought a large quantity of yellow arsenic. Early in the morning of Sunday, May 25, Sweeney laced the household's kitchen coffee pot with some of the poison. Wythe and a servant, a free black servant boy named Michael Brown, drank some of the coffee. After days of slow, agonizing illness, Brown died on June 1 and Wythe on June 8. Wythe's last words were typical of the way he had lived his life: "Let me die righteous."

Suspicion immediately fell on Sweeney, and on June 18 he was arrested. Prosecutor Philip Norborne Nicholas charged Sweeney with murdering Wythe and Brown. The judges were Joseph Prentes and John Tyler, Sr. Sweeney was represented by Edmund Randolph and William Wirt. The trial began September 2, 1806 in the District Court of Richmond.

Lydia Broadnax, a free black woman who had been Wythe's cook for several decades, testified that suspicious circumstances indicated Sweeney put something into the coffee on the morning of May 25. Broadnax had drunk some of the coffee, but not enough to die:

He went to the fire, and took the coffee-pot to the table, while I was toasting the bread. He poured out a cupful for himself and then set the pot down. I saw him throw a little white paper in the fire. . . . I didn't think there was anything wrong then.

Broadnax's suspicions became aroused, however, when she, Wythe, and Michael Brown fell ill after drinking the coffee:

I gave Michael as much coffee as he wanted, and then I drank a cup myself. After that, with the hot water in the kettle I washed the plates, emptied the coffee-grounds out and scrubbed the coffee-pot bright, and by that time I became so sick I could hardly see, and had a violent cramp. Michael was sick, too; and old master [Wythe] was as sick as he could be. He told me to send for the doctor. All these things makes [sic] me think Mass [sic] George must have put something in the coffee-pot.

Judges Prentes and Tyler, however, refused to allow Broadnax's testimony, and that of other black servants who had seen suspicious behavior by Sweeney, into evidence. The judges were bound by a principle of law that prevented blacks from testifying against whites in criminal trials: "It was gleaned from negroes, which is not permitted by our laws to go against a white man."

Therefore, prosecutor Nicholas was forced to rely on such white witnesses as he could produce. Nicholas did his best under the circumstances and was able to come up with some evidence. William Rose, the Richmond city jail warden, testified that Sweeney was not searched after he was arrested and soon thereafter a packet of arsenic was found in the prison yard, as if thrown from Sweeney's cell window. Samuel McCraw, a friend of Wythe's, testified that when he visited Wythe on his deathbed, Wythe asked McCraw to search Sweeney's room. McCraw stated that he found arsenic in a glass container in Sweeney's room.

In addition to these witnesses, there was the fact that Wythe amended his will before he died to exclude Sweeney from any inheritance. On June 1, 1806 Wythe executed a codicil to his will which revoked:

> The said will and codicils in all the devises and legacies in them or either of them, contained, relating to, or in any manner concerning George Wythe Sweeney, the grandson of my sister: but I confirm the said will and codicils in all other parts except as to the devise and bequest to Michael Brown, . . . who, I am told, died this morning.

Nicholas' witnesses, however, could give only hearsay testimony. Under the law, this wasn't enough to convict Sweeney. On September 8, 1806, the jury returned a verdict of not guilty after deliberating for only a few minutes.

Sweeney was acquitted because traditional legal principles prevented blacks from testifying against whites in criminal trials. This rule of law was not changed in Virginia until 1867. As for Sweeney, there are only rumors about what happened to him after his acquittal. According to the most reliable accounts, however, he went to Tennessee, where he was eventually arrested and convicted for stealing horses.

—Stephen G. Christianson

Suggestions for Further Reading

Blackburn, Joyce. *George Wythe of Williamsburg*. New York: Harper & Row, 1975.

Boyd, Julian P. *The Murder of George Wythe*. Philadelphia: Philobiblon Club, 1949.

Brown, Imogene E. *American Aristides: a Biography of George Wythe*. Rutherford, N.J.: Fairleigh Dickinson University Press, 1981.

Clarkin, William. *Serene Patriot: a Life of George Wythe*. Albany N.Y.: Alan Publications, 1970.

Kirtland, Robert B. *George Wythe: Lawyer, Revolutionary, Judge*. New York: Garland, 1986.

Aaron Burr Trial: 1807

Defendant: Former Vice President Aaron Burr   **Crime Charged:** "Treason" within the meaning of Article III, Section 3 of the U.S. Constitution
Chief Defense Lawyers: Benjamin Botts, Luther Martin, Edmund Randolph, and John Wickham.   **Chief Prosecutors:** George Hay, Gordon MacRae, and William Wirt   **Judges:** Cyrus Griffin and John Marshall   **Place:** Richmond, Virginia   **Dates of Trial:** August 3–September 1, 1807   **Verdict:** Not guilty

SIGNIFICANCE

The Aaron Burr treason trial was the only time in American history that a court tried such a high-level official of the United States for treason. Although Burr was acquitted, his political career was destroyed.

With the exception of scholars of American history, most people are oblivious to how unstable the political situation in the United States was in the early decades of the 1800s. In the years immediately following the Revolutionary War, the country suffered under the disastrous Articles of Confederation of 1781 until the states adopted the Constitution in 1789. However, even after the Constitutional Convention, there were serious differences among the political elite. The two main political camps were the Federalists and the Democratic-Republicans, and they had fundamentally different notions over what direction the new United States should take in its foreign policy.

The Federalists believed that, since the United States had been shaped by the cultural and economic influence of Great Britain, the Revolutionary War should not prevent the reestablishment of ties with the "Mother Country." The Democratic-Republicans believed that the United States should ally itself with France instead. Not only had France provided critical assistance to the colonies during the Revolutionary War, but the French Revolution had installed a government in France that professed belief in democratic ideals. Further, an alliance with France, a European great power, represented the only viable opportunity for the fledgling United States to oppose the might of the British Empire. Aaron Burr's political career put him squarely in the center of this schism.

Aaron Burr's Roller-Coaster Career

Burr's impeccable credentials as an American patriot made him an unlikely candidate to be charged with treason. Born in Newark, New Jersey, and educated at what became Princeton University, he was commissioned as an officer in the American army during the Revolution-

ary War. Burr distinguished himself in combat, and by the end of the war had risen to the rank of lieutenant colonel. After the war, Burr turned his energies to the legal profession. He did not graduate from a law school but instead studied law under an attorney's supervision, a practice which today is permitted by only one state (Virginia) but was then common. Burr was successful in his studies, and in 1782 was admitted to the New York state bar.

Burr capitalized on his successful career and entered into politics. He joined the pro-French Democratic-Republicans and became their candidate for vice president in the elections of 1800. At the time, members of the electoral college cast two votes each: one for the presidential candidate and one for the vice presidential candidate. Each Democratic-Republican elector had cast a vote for Burr and a vote for the party's presidential candidate, Thomas Jefferson. The result was a tie, and it fell to the House of Representatives to decide the outcome of the election. After a bitter battle and 36 ballots, the House voted for Jefferson, and Burr became vice president. Understandably, Jefferson suspected Burr of disloyalty and in 1804 managed to arrange his rejection by the Democratic-Republicans for a second vice presidential nomination.

Aaron Burr's political career was destroyed by his "imperial ambitions." (Courtesy, Library of Congress)

Burr and Alexander Hamilton, one of the principal Federalists, became intense adversaries and quarreled at every opportunity. In 1804, with Burr seeking the governorship of New York, Hamilton publicly denounced him and expressed his opinion that Burr was unfit for public office. Furious, Burr challenged Hamilton to a duel. Hamilton accepted. On July 11, 1804, at Weehawken, New Jersey, Burr shot Hamilton in the chest. Hamilton died soon thereafter.

Although he won the duel, Burr lost in the ensuing political uproar. State authorities in both New York and New Jersey sought to prosecute Burr for Hamilton's death, and Hamilton's supporters made Burr a political outcast in Washington.

In March 1805, Burr left the increasingly hostile capital for the frontier lands of the recently acquired Louisiana Purchase. Burr abandoned his allegiance to the Democratic-Republicans, and concocted a grandiose plan to lead a revolt with British assistance in these western lands. Burr hoped to establish a "Western Empire" with himself as ruler.

Burr's imperial ambitions were supported by Anthony Merry, the British envoy to the United States. Burr had other powerful allies for his scheme. Senator Jonathan Dayton of New Jersey and a wealthy Ohioan named Harman Blennerhassett joined Burr and extended financial support for the planned revolt. Finally, Burr had the support of General-in-Chief of the Army James Wilkinson, who was also one of the joint commissioners for the Territory of Louisiana.

The conspirators' procrastination, however, proved to be their undoing. By the fall of 1806, still they had not moved. Great Britain's new foreign minister, Charles James Fox, recalled Anthony Merry and terminated British support for Burr's plan. Wilkinson grew nervous, and went to President Jefferson with the details of Burr's conspiracy. When Burr finally decided to act in November 1806, he used Blennerhassett's Ohio estates and private island as the base of operations for the revolt. Jefferson arranged for Ohio Governor Edward Tiffin to send in the local militia and the conspiracy was crushed. Burr went into hiding but was arrested within a few months.

Burr Tried Before Chief Justice Marshall

On March 26, 1807, Burr was taken by his captors to Richmond, Virginia, for trial before the federal court. Normally, Judge Cyrus Griffin of the District of Virginia would have presided over the trial. At the time, however, Supreme Court Chief Justice John Marshall was present in Richmond to hear appeals from the circuit that encompassed Virginia. Griffin soon found himself playing second fiddle to the eminent Marshall, who took control over the widely publicized trial.

The principal charge against Burr was treason against the United States. The prosecutors also made a related charge of "high misdemeanors" against Burr. George Hay, William Wirt, and Gordon MacRae formed the team of prosecutors for the government. Hay was a prominent attorney, thanks largely to his political connections as James Monroe's son-in-law. Wirt, a tall blond man, had a reputation for having an excellent courtroom presence. MacRae was primarily a politician and, in addition to being a prosecutor, was also Virginia's lieutenant governor.

Burr's defense attorneys were Edmund Randolph, John Wickham, Luther Martin, and Benjamin Botts. The distinguished Randolph was not only a former attorney general, but had served as George Washington's Secretary of State and as Governor of Virginia as well. Wickham, Martin and Botts were also widely respected and prominent attorneys.

Their task was also much easier than that of the prosecution, due to the particular requirements of Article III, Section 3 of the Constitution.

Article III, Section 3 states:

Treason against the United States, shall consist only in levying War against them, or in adhering to their Enemies, giving them Aid and Comfort. No Person shall be convicted of Treason unless on the Testimony of two Witnesses to the same overt Act, or on Confession in open Court.

Thus, the prosecution not only had to produce two witnesses, but those witnesses had to have seen some overt act by Burr in "levying war" or leading the planned revolt against the United States. Luckily for Burr, he had not been present in Ohio when Governor Tiffin's militia stormed Blennerhassett's island compound. As Burr himself stated, Jefferson's prompt action based on General Wilkinson's confession led to the destruction of the plot before the procrastinating Burr had taken much action: "Mr. Wilkinson alarmed the President and the President alarmed the people of Ohio."

Marshall's concern over whether the prosecution could bear the heavy burden of proof demanded by the Constitution caused the trial to be delayed until August 3, 1807. In the interim, the prosecution presented a series of witnesses, including General Wilkinson. These witnesses testified as to treasonous statements made by Burr and on the military preparations made on Blennerhassett's island. The evidence presented convinced a grand jury that Burr should be tried on the charges filed against him, and Marshall finally opened the trial.

The prosecution, led by Wirt, argued that Burr's involvement in the conspiracy made him "constructively present" on the island and thus involved in an overt act. Referring to the mercenaries arrested during the Blennerhassett raid, Wirt said:

What must be the guilt of [Burr], to that of the poor ignorant man who was enlisted into his services with some prospect of benefitting himself and family?

Definition of an Overt Act Debated

Burr's defense counsel countered Wirt's impressive oratory by keeping the focus of attention on the prosecution's strained interpretation on what constituted an "overt act." After all, the only act of the revolt remotely "overt" had been the preparations at Blennerhassett's island during which Burr had not been present. Therefore, Botts retorted:

Acts on the island were not acts of war; no war could be found in Mississippi or Kentucky. There was no bloody battle. There was no bloody war. The energy of . . . [the] government prevented that tragical consequence.

On August 31, Marshall made a lengthy ruling on the arguments presented by both sides, later turning the tide in favor of Burr. Marshall held that if the prosecution had proven with two witnesses that Burr had "procured" or caused the men and material to assemble on the island to launch a revolt, then the necessary overt act could be established. The prosecution had not done this, however. All they had presented at trial was testimony that would "confirm" or "corroborate" such eyewitnesses, but not any eyewitnesses themselves. Therefore, the prosecution's evidence was inadmissible and the jury had to ignore it.

Faced with Marshall's ruling, the jury had no choice. On September 1, the jury acquitted Burr when it gave its somewhat left-handed verdict: "We of the jury say that Aaron Burr is not proved to be guilty under this indictment by any evidence submitted to us."

Although he was acquitted, the press and public still considered Burr a traitor, and his political career was ruined. Burr went to Europe for several years, staying one step ahead of money lenders who financed his lifestyle, and finally returned to the United States in 1812. He lived out the rest of his life in obscurity, dying a broken man in 1836.

—Stephen G. Christianson

Suggestions for Further Reading

Burr, Aaron. *Reports of the Trials of Colonel Aaron Burr*. New York: Da Capo Press., 1969 (repr. of 1808 ed.).

Lomask, Milton. *Aaron Burr*, Vols. 1 and 2. New York: Farrar, Straus & Giroux, 1979 and 1982.

Nolan, Charles J., Jr. *Aaron Burr and the American Literary Imagination*. Westport, Conn.: Greenwood Press, 1980.

Parmet, Herbert S. and Marie B. Hecht. *Aaron Burr: Portrait of an Ambitious Man*. New York: Macmillan Co., 1967.

Wilson, R.J. "The Founding Father." *New Republic* (June 1983): 25–31.

John Francis Knapp and Joseph Jenkins Knapp Trials: 1830

Defendants: John Francis Knapp and Joseph Jenkins Knapp
Crimes Charged: Accessories to murder
Chief Defense Lawyers: F. Dexter and W.H. Gardiner
Chief Prosecutor: Daniel Webster   **Judges:** Marcus Morton, Samuel Putnam, and Samuel S. Wilde   **Place:** Salem, Massachusetts
Dates of Trials: July Term, 1830 for John Francis Knapp; November Term, 1830 for Joseph Jenkins Knapp   **Verdicts:** Guilty, both trials
Sentences: Death by hanging, both trials

SIGNIFICANCE

In this prosecution of the Knapps by the famous lawyer Daniel Webster, the actual murderer was a hired assassin named Richard Crowninshield, who committed suicide before the Knapps went to trial. Due to Webster's eloquence, this became one of the first cases in which accessories to murder were tried, convicted and executed even though the actual murderer was never convicted.

Brothers John Francis Knapp (who went by his middle name) and Joseph Jenkins Knapp had a wealthy uncle, Captain Joseph White, who lived in Salem, Massachusetts. Captain White was 82 years old, an extraordinary age for that time, but the Knapps were impatient to receive their anticipated inheritance and decided that they couldn't wait for the old man to die naturally. The Knapps hired a hit man, 28-year-old Richard Crowninshield, to murder Captain White.

On the night of April 6, 1830, Crowninshield quietly broke into Captain White's house and went into the bedroom where the old man was asleep. While Francis and Joseph Knapp waited in the street outside, approximately 300 feet away, Crowninshield clubbed and stabbed Captain White to death. With the Knapp brothers' help, Crowninshield fled the house without being seen.

For a while it seemed as if the Knapps' scheme had succeeded. The citizens of Salem were outraged by the brutal murder of the prominent Captain White and formed a Committee of Vigilance to search for the killer. After two months of searching, however, the Committee had gotten nowhere. Then, the police in New Bedford arrested a pickpocket, who testified before a grand jury that he was a friend of Crowninshield and that Crowninshield had told him that he killed Captain White.

Trail Leads to Knapps

Crowninshield was promptly arrested, but he kept quiet since he could not implicate Francis or Joseph Knapp without confessing to his role in the murder. Unfortunately, Crowninshield had told another one of his criminal acquaintances, John Palmer, about the Knapps' involvement. Palmer wrote a blackmail letter to the Knapps, but it was received instead by the Knapps' father. The elder Knapp turned the letter over to the police, who arrested the Knapp brothers. After Joseph Knapp confessed, Crowninshield realized that no hope was left and hung himself in his prison cell.

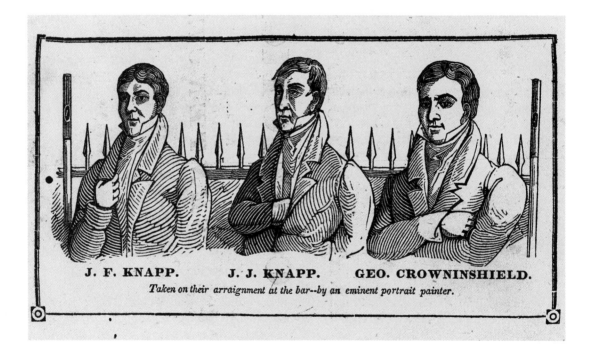

J. F. KNAPP.   J. J. KNAPP.   GEO. CROWNINSHIELD.

Taken on their arraignment at the bar--by an eminent portrait painter.

The Knapp brothers and Richard Crowninshield at their arraignment. (Courtesy, Peabody & Essex Museum)

To prosecute the Knapps, the Massachusetts attorney general used the distinguished Daniel Webster. Born in 1782, Webster had practiced law in New Hampshire for a while before coming to Boston, which he would eventually leave for service in the federal government. Like many attorneys in private practice at the time, Webster occasionally worked for the state as a prosecutor.

The Knapps were charged with being accessories to murder. Both Francis and Joseph Knapp were to be tried before the Salem division of the Massachusetts Supreme Judicial Court. The judges were Marcus Morton, Samuel Putnam, and Samuel S. Wilde. For their defense, the Knapps were represented by F. Dexter and W.H. Gardiner. Francis Knapp was to be tried first, and the most important issues would be addressed in his trial.

Francis Knapp's trial was set for the court's 1830 July Term. Webster knew that his biggest difficulty lay in the fact that Richard Crowninshield, the actual murderer, had committed suicide before he could be tried and convicted. Under the ancient common law of England, which was the primary influence on the legal principles of all American states, accessories to murder could not be convicted unless (1) the actual murderer had been convicted, or (2) the accessories had been present at the time of the murder. Crowninshield was dead, and the Knapps had been 300 feet away in the street at the time of the murder.

Like every good prosecutor, Webster laid the foundation for his case by appealing to the jury's emotions. He described Captain White, who had gone to sleep on the night of the murder unaware of his nephews' plot:

> A healthful old man to whom sleep was sweet, the first sound slumbers of the night held him in their strong embrace.

Webster went on to portray Crowninshield's stolen entry into White's home:

> With noiseless feet he paces the lonely hall half lighted by the moon; he winds up the ascent of the stairs . . . beholds his victim before him . . . the moon resting on the grey locks of this aged victim shows him where to strike.

As to Crowninshield's suicide, Webster assured the jury that divine justice was punishing Crowninshield's soul:

> A vulture is devouring it . . . . It can ask no sympathy from Heaven or Earth.

Dexter and Gardiner tried to keep the focus of the trial on the fact that Webster had not satisfied the legal requirements for conviction:

> Upon this evidence the prisoner cannot be convicted as a principal in the murder. A principal in the second degree, according to the law of England, is by our statutes an accessory before the fact, and cannot be tried until there has been a conviction of the principal.

Verdict Hangs on Legal Definition

Webster, however, raised the question of whether Francis and Joseph Knapp could be legally considered as "present" during the murder so that they could be convicted. True, the Knapps had been 300 feet away in the street, but they had been there to help Crowninshield:

> To constitute a presence, it is sufficient if the accomplice is in a place, either where he may render aid to the perpetrator of the felony, or where the perpetrator supposes he may render aid. If they selected the place to afford assistance, whether it was well or ill chosen for that purpose is immaterial. The perpetrator would derive courage and confidence from the knowledge that his associate was in the place appointed.

Webster's definition of presence would include Francis Knapp and, by implication, ultimately anyone involved in a murder who had come near enough to the scene of the crime to be considered "aiding and abetting" the actual murderer. Dexter argued strenuously for a conservative approach, that only physical presence at a murder could mean legal presence. According to Dexter, Francis Knapp would have to have been in Captain White's bedroom with Crowninshield to be considered present and found guilty:

> To make a man a principal by aiding and abetting in a felony, he must be in such a situation at the moment when the crime is committed, that he can render actual and immediate assistance to the perpetrator; and that he must be there by agreement, and with the intent to render such assistance.

Faced with these powerful but opposing legal arguments, the jury at first could not reach a verdict, but ultimately it found Francis Knapp guilty by the close of the July Term. Knapp was going to hang, and now it was his brother Joseph's turn to be tried.

Joseph Knapp's trial took place during the Court's November Term of 1830. Joseph Knapp had testified against Crowninshield at the arraignment, but he refused to testify against his brother Francis at his trial. Therefore, the state dropped its earlier promise to give Joseph Knapp immunity and put him before Webster to be prosecuted. Dexter and Gardiner had lost the debate over the legal definition of presence at Francis Knapp's trial, so in Joseph Knapp's trial, they shifted their attack to whether the Knapps had been close enough to aid and abet Crowninshield. The trial record states:

> The prisoner's counsel now offered evidence in regard to the place at which the principal . . . was stationed during the perpetration of the murder, their object being to show that in that situation it was impossible for him to aid and abet the person who was actually striking the blow.

The jury rejected Dexter and Gardiner's last-ditch attempt to save Joseph Knapp, however, and by the close of the November Term found him guilty.

Francis and Joseph Knapp went to the gallows. Having successfully convicted them of murder, the state of Massachusetts also tried and convicted George Crowninshield, a brother of Richard's who had a minor role in the whole affair, of aiding and abetting Captain White's murder.

The whole Francis and Joseph Knapp affair would have gone down in history as a typical sordid murder if it had not been for Daniel Webster's eloquence. Webster persuaded the judges and the jury to expand the boundaries of an accessory's liability for murder. Once thus expanded, the old common law restrictions that would have prevented guilty men such as Francis and Joseph Knapp from being brought to justice were, over time, eventually swept away.

—Stephen G. Christianson

Suggestions for Further Reading

Bartlett, Irving H. *Daniel Webster*. New York: W.W. Norton & Co., 1978.

A Biographical Sketch of the Celebrated Salem Murderer. Boston: Unknown publisher, 1830.

Wilson, Colin. *Encyclopedia of Murder*. New York: G.P. Putnam's Sons, 1962.

Wiltse, Charles M. and Harold D. Moser, editors. *The Papers of Daniel Webster*. Hanover, Mass.: Published for Dartmouth College by the University Press of New England, 1974–1989.

Cherokee Nation v. Georgia: 1831

Plaintiffs: Cherokee Indian Nation   **Defendant:** State of Georgia
Plaintiffs Claim: That under the Supreme Court's power to resolve disputes
between states and foreign nations, the Court could forbid Georgia from
unlawfully attempting to move the Cherokees from their lands
Chief Defense Lawyer: None   **Chief Lawyer for Plaintiffs:** William Wirt
Justices: Henry Baldwin, Gabriel Duvalt, William Johnson, John Marshall,
John McLean, Joseph Story, and Smith Thompson   **Place:** Washington, D.C.
Date of Decision: March 5, 1831   **Decision:** That the Court had no power
to hear the dispute, because Indian tribes are not foreign nations

SIGNIFICANCE

By refusing to help the Cherokees, the U.S. Supreme Court left the Indians at the
mercy of land-hungry settlers. The Cherokees ultimately were forced to move to
Oklahoma along the famous "Trail of Tears."

The Cherokee Indians originally inhabited much of America's southeastern seaboard. In the 17th and 18th centuries, European settlers pushed the Cherokees from many of their lands. Unlike most Indians, however, the Cherokees were able to resist white encroachment by adapting to white ways. After the American Revolution, the Cherokees copied white farming methods and other aspects of the white economy. The Cherokees sent some of their children to American schools and permitted mixed marriages. Further, they signed a series of treaties with the federal government that seemed to protect what remained of their lands.

The Cherokee presence was particularly strong in Georgia, where they prospered under the new ways. Cherokee plantations even had Negro slaves. However, in 1828, prospectors discovered gold in Cherokee territory. Georgia wanted to give the land to whites, and enacted laws to force the Cherokees to leave. The Cherokees fought back, hiring white lawyers to represent them.

The Cherokees' chief lawyer was William Wirt. He went directly to the Supreme Court and asked for an injunction forbidding Georgia from removing the Cherokees. Because Article III, Section 2 of the U.S. Constitution gives the Court original jurisdiction in cases to which a state is a party, Wirt didn't have to go through the Georgia state courts and couldn't go through the lower federal courts. Unfortunately, Article III, Section 2 generally limits the Court's jurisdiction to cases involving American citizens, and Indians were not yet recognized as citizens. The only arguable basis for jurisdiction was the Court's power to hear disputes "between a State, or the Citizens thereof, and foreign States, Citizens or Subjects."

Therefore, Wirt had to convince the Court that the Cherokees were a foreign nation or the Court would refuse to act. On March 5, 1831, in Washington, D.C., he pleaded the Cherokees' case before Supreme Court Justices Henry Baldwin, Gabriel Duvalt, William Johnson, John Marshall, John McLean, Joseph Story, and Smith Thompson. Georgia, an ardent supporter of states' rights, denied that the federal courts had jurisdiction and refused to send a defense lawyer.

Wirt reminded the Court that the Cherokees had uncontestable rights to the lands in Georgia:

> The boundaries were fixed by treaty, and what was within them was acknowledged to be the land of the Cherokees. This was the scope of all the treaties.

Next, Wirt begged the Court to prevent what was about to happen to the Cherokees:

> The legislation of Georgia proposes to annihilate them, as its very end and aim. . . . If those laws be fully executed, there will be no Cherokee boundary, no Cherokee nation, no Cherokee lands, no Cherokee treaties. . . . They will all be swept out of existence together, leaving nothing but the monuments in our history of the enormous injustice that has been practised towards a friendly nation.

Associate Justice Story did not vote with the majority in the 1831 *Cherokee Nation v. Georgia* decision that led to the "Trail of Tears." (Courtesy, Library of Congress)

That same day, the Supreme Court denied Wirt's petition, holding that the Cherokees and other Indian tribes were only "domestic dependent nations," not foreign nations, and thus the Court had no authority to help them. A year later, in the 1832 case of *Worcester v. Georgia*, the Court freed some missionaries who were sympathetic to the Cherokee cause and had been arrested by Georgia authorities, but only because the missionaries were white citizens.

Powerless to resist, the Cherokees were stripped of all their lands by 1838. In that year, over 7,000 soldiers forced the Cherokees to leave what was left of their territory for relocation in Oklahoma. Over 4,000 Cherokees died during the journey of thousands of miles to the west, which became known as the Trail of Tears.

—*Stephen G. Christianson*

Suggestions for Further Reading

Guttmann, Allen. *States' Rights and Indian Removal: the Cherokee Nation v. the State of Georgia.* Boston: D.C. Heath, 1965.

Lumpkin, Wilson. *The Removal of the Cherokee Indians from Georgia.* New York: Arno Press, 1969.

Peck, Ira. "Worcester v. Georgia: the Campaign to Move the Cherokee Nation." *Senior Scholastic* (November 1982): 17–20.

Warren, Mary Bondurant. *Whites Among the Cherokees.* Danielsville, Ga.: Heritage Papers, 1987.

Wilkins, Thurman. *Cherokee Tragedy.* Norman: University of Oklahoma Press, 1986.

U.S. v. Cinque: 1839

Defendants: Joseph Cinque and others   **Crimes Charged:** Murder and
piracy   **Chief Defense Lawyers:** John Quincy Adams, Roger S. Baldwin,
Joshua Leavitt, and Seth Staples   **Chief Prosecutor:** William S. Holabird
Judges: Andrew T. Judson and Smith Thompson   **Place:** New Haven,
Connecticut   **Dates of Trial:** November 19, 1839–January 13, 1840
Verdict: Not guilty

SIGNIFICANCE

When the courts refused to convict slaves from the schooner *Amistad* after they
killed their captors to free themselves, the decision was widely hailed as a victory
for the cause of abolition.

By the 1830s, many countries were beginning to take steps to limit the age-old
institution of slavery. Although slavery was still legal in the United States, it
was illegal to bring new slaves into the country. Further, the abolitionist
movement, which sought to do away with slavery altogether, was gaining more
and more support. Great Britain was strongly in favor of abolition, and had used
its naval power to pressure Spain, whose colonies were dominated by slave
owners, to also make it illegal to bring new slaves into any Spanish possessions.

Spanish power in the New World was declining, however, and the government in Madrid lacked the power to enforce its will. The wealthy landowners in
Cuba and elsewhere throughout the Spanish New World needed slaves to work
their estates, and obeying the import restriction meant waiting for the children
of existing slaves to mature. With slave owner demand strong and central
authority weak, a flourishing illegal slave trade soon emerged. Slavers went to
the west coast of Africa, captured healthy young black men and women, and
brought them back to Cuba for sale. The colonial authorities did nothing to stop
this trade. In 1839, slavers brought back a cargo of slaves from what is now Sierra
Leone. Among the slaves was a young man they named Joseph Cinque.

In June of 1839, Jose Ruiz and Pedro Montes purchased 49 captured
Africans, including Cinque, in Havana for their estates in the Cuban town of
Puerto Principe. Ruiz and Montes put the slaves aboard the schooner *Amistad*,
intending to sail from Havana up the Cuban coast to Puerto Principe. The
Spanish crew taunted the ignorant slaves, telling them wild stories, such as that

their new owners intended to kill and eat them when they arrived. On the night of July 1, Cinque led the blacks in a successful rebellion and seized control of the ship. The blacks killed several members of the crew in the struggle, but let Ruiz and Montes live. Cinque ordered Ruiz and Montes to take the ship to Sierra Leone so the blacks could go home.

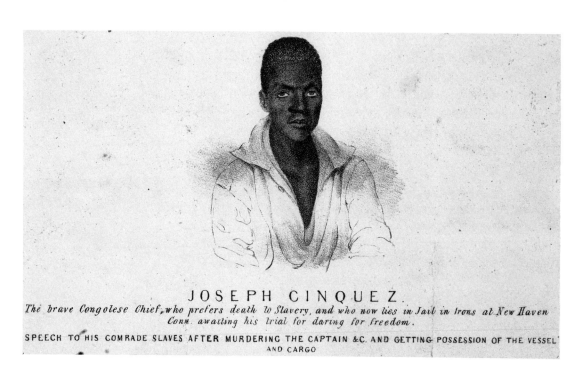

JOSEPH CINQUEZ.

The brave Congolese Chief, who prefers death to Slavery, and who now lies in Jail in Irons at New Haven Conn. awaiting his trial for daring for freedom.

SPEECH TO HIS COMRADE SLAVES AFTER MURDERING THE CAPTAIN &C. AND GETTING POSSESSION OF THE VESSEL AND CARGO

It was ruled that Joseph Cinque, leader of the *Amistad* rebellion, and his comrades "were born free, and ... of right are free and not slaves." (Courtesy, Library of Congress)

The Spaniards sailed east for Africa by day, but secretly reversed course by night. For nearly two months, the *Amistad* meandered back and forth, but eventually winds and currents drove it north to the coast of the United States. On August 26, the U.S.S. *Washington* spotted the *Amistad* off the coast of New York, seized the ship, and brought it into New London, Connecticut.

Cinque Goes on Trial

In New London, Ruiz and Montes described the slave rebellion to the American authorities, and pressed their claim for the return of the *Amistad* with its cargo of slaves. Despite the slaves' illegal capture, the Spanish government backed Ruiz's and Montes' claim. With the blessing of President Martin Van Buren's administration, District Attorney William S. Holabird charged Cinque and the other blacks with committing murder and piracy aboard the *Amistad*.

The trial was held in the U.S. District Court for Connecticut. The judge was District Court Judge Andrew T. Judson, assisted by Associate Supreme

Court Justice Smith Thompson. The abolitionists hired a team of defense lawyers to represent the blacks, comprised of Roger S. Baldwin, Joshua Leavitt, Seth Staples, and an ex-president of the United States, John Quincy Adams.

The trial began November 19, 1839. The defense lawyers asserted that the blacks had the right to free themselves from the horrible conditions of slavery. In support of their position, they introduced Dr. Richard R. Madden, who had traveled extensively in Cuba and was an expert on slave conditions:

> [S]o terrible were these atrocities, so murderous the system of slavery, so transcendent the evils I witnessed, over all I have ever heard or seen of the rigour of slavery elsewhere, that at first I could hardly believe the evidence of my senses.

Further, as the testimony of Madden and various witnesses made clear, returning Cinque and the others to Cuba meant certain death at the hands of the pro-slavery colonial authorities. In addition, since the blacks had originally been captured in Africa in violation of Spanish law, the abolitionists argued that the blacks were not legally slaves and therefore were not "property" belonging to Ruiz and Montes.

Despite pressure from the Van Buren administration, which wanted to avoid diplomatic tension with Spain, on January 13, 1840, Judge Judson ruled in favor of the blacks. Although the *Amistad* with its goods would be returned to Ruiz and Montes, subject to salvage costs, Cinque and the others:

> were born free, and ever since have been and still of right are free and not slaves.

Further, because they had been illegally enslaved, the blacks were innocent of murder and piracy since they had only acted to free themselves.

The prosecution appealed Judson's decision to the Supreme Court. The abolitionists had anticipated this move, since five Supreme Court justices, including Chief Justice Roger B. Taney, were Southerners and had owned slaves. The defense relied on John Quincy Adams to present its case, banking on his prestige as much as on his legal ability. On February 22, 1840, the Supreme Court heard both sides' arguments, and on March 9 issued its opinion. The Court upheld Judson's decision, and so the blacks were finally free. Cinque and the other blacks were returned to Africa.

Technically, the *Amistad* decision did not condemn slavery, it only held that blacks not legally slaves were also not property. Still, the courts could have just as easily turned the blacks over to Spanish authorities or returned them to Cuba if they wished. The case was seen as a victory for the abolitionist cause, and was a milestone in the movement's quest for the total elimination of slavery.

—*Stephen G. Christianson*

Suggestions for Further Reading

Adams, John Quincy. *Argument in the Case of U.S. v. Cinque.* New York: Arno Press, 1969.

Cable, Mary. *Black Odyssey: the Case of the Slave Ship Amistad.* New York: Penguin Books, 1977.

"Cinque." *Jet* (March 1984): 21.

Jones, Howard. *Mutiny on the Amistad: The Saga of a Slave Revolt and its Impact on American Abolition, Law, and Diplomacy.* New York: Oxford University Press, 1987.

Owens, William A. *Slave Mutiny: the Revolt on the Schooner Amistad.* New York: J. Day Co., 1953.

Alexander Holmes Trial: 1842

Defendant: Alexander William Holmes   **Crime Charged:** Manslaughter
Chief Defense Lawyer: David Paul Brown   **Chief Prosecutor:** William M. Meredith   **Judge:** Baldwin (historical records do not indicate his first name)
Place: Philadelphia, Pennsylvania   **Dates of Trial:** April 13–23, 1842
Verdict: Guilty   **Sentence:** 6 months in prison and a $20 fine

SIGNIFICANCE

In the Alexander Holmes trial, the court held that self-preservation was not always a defense to homicide.

O n March 13, 1841, an American ship, the *William Brown*, left Liverpool, England for Philadelphia, Pennsylvania. In addition to her cargo, she carried 17 crewmen and 65 passengers, who were mostly Scots and Irish emigrants. On the night of April 19, 250 miles from Newfoundland, the *William Brown* struck an iceberg and began to sink rapidly. There were two lifeboats, one small and one large. The captain and most of the crew took the small lifeboat, and the passengers crowded aboard the large lifeboat. There was not enough space on the large lifeboat for all the passengers, and 31 died on board the *William Brown* when it sank.

First Mate Francis Rhodes, Alexander William Holmes, and another seaman commanded the large lifeboat. The passengers were still dressed in their night clothes and suffered terribly in the cold Atlantic weather, which was made worse by a pelting rain. The two lifeboats stayed together through the night but separated the morning of the 20th because the captain, George L. Harris, thought there was a better chance of rescue if the two boats took different directions. Rhodes said that his boat was overcrowded and that some people would have to be thrown overboard to keep it from capsizing. Captain Harris said, "I know what you'll have to do. Don't speak of that now. Let it be the last resort." Throughout the day of the 20th and into the night, the rain and the waves worsened. The boat began to leak and fill with water, despite constant bailing. Around ten o'clock that night, Rhodes cried out in despair, "This work won't do. Help me, God. Men, go to work." Holmes and the other seaman began throwing people overboard. They threw 14 men and two women into the freezing water. They chose single men only, spared the married men on board, and threw the two women overboard only because they were sisters of a man already thus ejected and had demanded to be sacrificed with their kin. None of the crew was thrown out.

Holmes Tried for Manslaughter

The next day, on the morning of the 21st, Holmes' lifeboat was spotted by a ship and rescued. Captain Harris' lifeboat was rescued by another ship six days later. Upon reaching Philadelphia, the news of the fate of the *William Brown* was an instant sensation, generating a great deal of public outrage against the crew. U.S. District Attorney William M. Meredith charged Holmes and Rhodes with manslaughter, which is a lesser degree of homicide than murder because it means killing without malice. Rhodes fled the city, never to be found, so Holmes was tried alone.

Holmes' chief defense lawyer was David Paul Brown, and the trial began on April 13, 1842. One of Meredith's assistants, Mr. Dallas (historical records do not indicate his first name) opened for the prosecution:

> [Holmes'] defense is that the homicide was necessary to self-preservation. First, then, we ask: was the homicide thus necessary? That is to say, was the danger instant, overwhelming, leaving no choice or means, no moment for deliberation? For, unless the danger were of this sort, the prisoner, under any admission, had no right, without notice or consultation, or lot, to sacrifice the lives of 16 fellow beings.

Holmes' defense lawyers countered that, in the dangerous circumstances Holmes was placed in, he was not required to wait until the last second to act in self-preservation:

> In other words, he need not wait until the certainty of the danger has been proved, past doubt, by its result. Yet this is the doctrine of the prosecution. They ask us to wait until the boat has sunk. . . . They tell us to wait until all are drowned.

After the prosecution and the defense had rested, Judge Baldwin (historical records do not indicate his first name) gave his instructions to the jury. Although he recognized the principle that self-preservation was a defense to homicide, he stated that there were some important exceptions. One of these exceptions was when someone had accepted a duty to others that implied that he or she would put his or her life at risk before risking the lives of the others. Judge Baldwin held that seamen like Holmes had accepted such a duty, and that therefore self-preservation was not an adequate defense to the charge of manslaughter:

> [W]e must look, not only to the jeopardy in which the parties are, but also to the relations in which they stand. The slayer must be under no obligation to make his own safety secondary to the safety of others. . . . Such . . . is the relation which exists on shipboard. The passenger stands in a position different from that of the officers and seamen. . . . The sailor . . . is bound to set a greater value on the life of others than on his own.

After 16 hours of deliberation, the jury found Holmes guilty on April 23, 1842. As the official court report notes, the verdict was given "with some difficulty," and was accompanied by the jury's recommendation for mercy. Judge Baldwin sentenced Holmes to six months in prison and a $20 fine. There was some public sympathy for Holmes, but a movement by the Seamen's Friend Society for a presidential pardon came to nothing.

The Alexander Holmes trial dictated that seamen have a duty to their passengers that is superior even to their own lives. Further, it held that the ancient defense of self-preservation was not always adequate in a homicide prosecution if the accused was under a special obligation to the deceased.

—Stephen G. Christianson

Suggestions for Further Reading

Duke, Thomas Samuel. *Celebrated Criminal Cases of America*. San Francisco: James H. Barry Co., 1910.

Hicks, Frederick Charles. *Human Jettison: a Sea Tale From the Law*. St. Paul, Minn.: West Publishing Co., 1927.

Mackenzie Court-Martial: 1843

Defendant: Commander Alexander Slidell Mackenzie **Crimes Charged:** 5 criminal offenses, including murder, for having executed 3 seamen suspected of mutiny **Chief Defense Lawyer:** None **Chief Prosecutor:** Judge Advocate William H. Norris **Judges:** Captains William C. Bolton, John Downes, John Gwinn, Isaac McKeever, Benjamin Page, George C. Read, John D. Sloat, Joseph Smith, George W. Storer, Daniel Turner, and Thomas W. Wyman, and Commanders Henry W. Ogden and Irvine Shubrick **Place:** New York, New York **Dates of Trial:** January 28–March 31, 1843 **Verdict:** Not guilty

SIGNIFICANCE

The alleged mutiny aboard Commander Alexander Slidell Mackenzie's ship, the U.S.S. *Somers,* was the first such incident in the history of the U.S. Navy. It was also the inspiration behind Herman Melville's novel *Billy Budd.*

On December 14, 1842, a warship of the U.S. Navy, the brig U.S.S. *Somers,* came into New York City harbor after a voyage to the African coast. The captain, Commander Alexander Slidell Mackenzie, reported to the astonished naval authorities that the vessel contained the bodies of three men hung for mutiny, the first such instance in American naval history.

The dead men were Samuel Cromwell, Elisha Small, and Philip Spencer. According to Mackenzie, they had been the ringleaders behind a plot to mutiny, murder Mackenzie and take the ship for themselves. Then, they would use the ship for piracy, preying on Atlantic shipping. Supposedly, two-thirds of the crew were prepared to join the mutiny, so Mackenzie was forced to act quickly by eliminating the leaders. Cromwell and Small were common sailors, but Spencer was the son of John C. Spencer, the powerful secretary of war for President John Tyler.

Mackenzie requested a court-martial to clear his name. It is probable that Secretary Spencer would have demanded a court-martial anyway: In addition to losing his son, he wanted to investigate America's first naval mutiny. The prosecutor, Judge Advocate William H. Norris, charged Mackenzie with five criminal offenses, the most significant of which was murdering the three seamen. Mackenzie had no lawyer; he represented himself. The judges were

Captains William C. Bolton, John Downes, John Gwinn, Isaac McKeever, Benjamin Page, George C. Read, John D. Sloat, Joseph Smith, George W. Storer, Daniel Turner, and Thomas W. Wyman, and Commanders Henry W. Ogden and Irvine Shubrick.

The trial began January 28, 1843. Under Norris' questioning, Mackenzie steadfastly maintained that imminent mutiny among the ship's crew made it imperative that he execute the three ringleaders. Apparently Mackenzie made this decision when quite a few disloyal sailors were discovered and a shipboard investigation was begun:

Question: When did you first suppose it would be necessary to execute Mr. Spencer, Cromwell, and Small, for the safety of the vessel, officers, and crew?

Answer: When we made more prisoners [from the crew] than we had the force to take care of, and I was more fully convinced after the examination in the wardroom before the council of officers.

The USS *Somers* with the bodies of three alleged mutineers hanging from the yardarm. (Courtesy, Rear Admiral Elliot Snow, USN, U.S. Naval Historical Center)

Norris introduced other personnel from the *Somers* as witnesses, but their testimony failed to contradict Mackenzie's tale. On March 31, the judges pronounced Mackenzie innocent:

The court . . . do acquit Commander Alexander Slidell Mackenzie of the charges and specifications preferred by the secretary of the navy against him.

There is no direct evidence that Secretary Spencer had attempted to influence the proceedings. Still, the judges must certainly have been aware of Spencer's reputation as a vindictive man, and of his unsuccessful effort to bring Mackenzie to trial in the civil courts as well. The court's verdict had been made without the customary statement of confidence in the accused's innocence, probably to placate Spencer:

> As these charges involved the life of the accused, and as the finding is in his favor, he is entitled to the benefit of it, as in the analogous case of a verdict before a civil court; and there is no power which can constitutionally deprive him of that benefit. The finding, therefore, is simply confirmed and carried into effect, without any expression of approbation.

Mackenzie labored under the left-handed acquittal until he died in 1848. Meanwhile, the story of America's first naval mutiny had captured national attention in the press, and was the inspiration for Herman Melville's novel about struggle and life at sea, *Billy Budd*.

It also led to more concern within the U.S. Navy for the proper training and military discipline of American seamen, concerns vital to the emergence of the United States as a naval power in future years. For example, the *Somers* incident was the primary reason for the founding of the United States Naval Academy at Annapolis, Maryland in 1845.

—Stephen G. Christianson

Suggestions for Further Reading

Hayford, Harrison. *The Somers Mutiny Affair*. Englewood Cliffs, N.J.: Prentice Hall, 1959.

McFarland, Philip James. *Sea Dangers: the Affair of the Somers*. New York: Schocken Books, 1985.

Melville, Herman. *Billy Budd*. New York: F. Watts, 1968.

Van de Water, Frederic F. *The Captain Called it Mutiny*. New York: Washburn, 1954.

Albert Tirrell Trial: 1846

Defendant: Albert J. Tirrell   **Crime Charged:** Murder
Chief Defense Lawyer: Rufus Choate   **Chief Prosecutor:** Samuel D. Parker
Judges: Dewey, Hubbard, and Wilde (No record of first names)
Place: Boston, Massachusetts   **Dates of Trial:** March 26–30, 1846
Verdict: Not guilty

SIGNIFICANCE

Albert Tirrell's trial was the first time in American history that sleepwalking was successfully used as a defense to a murder prosecution.

Not much is known about Albert Tirrell's life prior to his sensational murder trial. He came from a moderately prosperous family and had a wife and two children in Weymouth, Massachusetts. Tirrell had a reputation for wild and reckless behavior; he left his family in 1845 for a young prostitute named Maria Ann Bickford.

Bickford was very beautiful and lived in a Boston brothel, where she catered only to the richest customers. Tirrell had met her and fallen in love. He moved to Boston to be near her, and apparently she returned his affections but did not give up her profession. Bickford's patrons enabled her to live well; she had a maid and an expensive wardrobe.

The details are sketchy, but apparently on October 27, 1845, Tirrell came into Bickford's bedroom after she had spent an evening with a customer. Tirrell cut her throat from ear to ear with a razor and set three fires in the brothel before leaving. Brothel owner Joel Lawrence lived in the building and woke up in time to put out the fires. He discovered Bickford's body and alerted the police. Several people had seen Tirrell enter and leave the brothel, and the police began a search for him.

Tirrell fled Boston in the early hours of October 28. He took a carriage back to Weymouth, then went on to New York and finally New Orleans, Louisiana. The authorities caught up with Tirrell December 6, arrested him, and returned him to Boston for trial.

Rufus Choate Defends Tirrell

The state prosecutor was Samuel D. Parker and the judges assigned to oversee the trial were Justices Dewey, Hubbard, and Wilde (no record survives of the judges' first names). Tirrell's parents hired a famous lawyer, Rufus Choate, to defend him. Choate had a reputation for successfully using unusual legal defenses to acquit his clients. Tirrell's trial opened March 26, 1846.

Although Parker had plenty of witnesses as to Tirrell's affair with Bickford and his presence in the brothel on the night of Bickford's murder, no one had actually seen Tirrell kill her. No matter how overwhelming, the evidence was circumstantial. Choate argued to the jury that Tirrell had no motive to kill the woman he loved:

> [Tirrell] was fascinated by the wiles of the unhappy female whose death was so awful; he loved her with the love of forty thousand brothers, though alas, it was not as pure as it was passionate.

Choate laid two possible alternatives before the jury. First, Bickford could have committed suicide:

> What proof is there that she did not rise from her bed, set fire to the house, and in the frenzy of the moment, with giant strength, let out the stream of life. . . . Suicide is the natural death of the prostitute.

This was not a strong argument, however, for Choate knew that it was very hard to imagine Bickford cutting her own throat so savagely that her head was nearly severed from her body. Therefore, Choate relied more on his second alternative, namely that Tirrell was a habitual sleepwalker and thus must have murdered Bickford while in an unconscious trance or under the influence of a nightmare. In the 1840s, doctors could only guess at the causes of sleepwalking, and they differed over whether it was caused by disease, mental disorders, or insanity. Whatever the cause, however, Tirrell's sleepwalking gave Choate a means to influence the jury. Choate read descriptions of violence attributed to sleepwalking from popular treatises:

> This I mention as a proof that nothing hinders us, even from being assassins of others or murderers of ourselves, amid the mad follies of sleep, only the protecting care of our Heavenly Father!

Having thus introduced some doubt to the jury as to the prosecutions case against Tirrell, Choate cleverly reminded them that their guilty verdict meant certain execution for Tirrell. If Tirrell was executed while there was even the remotest chance that the crime had been committed by someone else, the jurors would be responsible:

> Every juror when he puts into the urn the verdict of Guilty, writes upon it also, "Let him die!" . . . Under the iron law of Rome, it was the custom to bestow a civic wreath upon him who should save the life of a citizen. Do your duty this day, gentlemen, and you too may deserve the civic crown.

Choates oratory was impressive, but it was far from certain that he would win. Not only had the Boston papers turned Bickford's murder into a popular sensation with the public being firmly convinced of Tirrell's guilt, but Choate had been criticized before for actions on behalf of clients that bordered on the unethical. Choate himself had admitted that the m rder was particularly horrible—"murder and arson committed in a low brothel." While there was widespread respect for Choate's legal ability, there were also critics who said:

> [T]he lightnings of his genius were brandished with litt e regard to consequences, and that it was comparatively a matter of indifference to the great actor of the scene whether they purified the moral atmosphere by vindicating the cause of truth and justice, or struck down the fair fabrics of public virtue and public integrity.

The Jury Acquits Tirrell

On March 30, 1846, the jury announced its verdict after less than two hours of deliberation. The jurors pronounced Albert Tirrell innocent. Despite the questions about his conduct and the evidence against his client, Rufus Choate had successfully defended Tirrell on the grounds that Tirrell could have killed Bickford while sleepwalking and was thus not responsible for his behavior. Tirrell left the courtroom a free man, but it was not long before he was in trouble again.

In January 1847, the prosecution initiated new charges against Tirrell, this time charging him with arson relating to the fires he set in Bickford's brothel on the night of her murder. Choate represented Tirrell again. This time, the trial was presided over by Massachusetts Chief Justice and distinguished jurist Lemuel Shaw. The prosecution presented essentially the same witnesses as in the first trial concerning Tirrell's presence in the brothel on the night the fires were set. Once again, Choate was able to attack the prosecution's case for its reliance on solely circumstantial evidence.

The jury found Tirrell not guilty, and for the second and final time, he left the courtroom a free man. In addition to Choate's expertise, Tirrell was assisted by Judge Shaw's instructions to the jury. Shaw's instructions criticized the prosecution's witnesses, saying that they were of "disreputable character" and pointing out discrepancies in their testimony.

Tirrell had little gratitude for Choate's extraordinary accomplishments. In fact, Tirrell even demanded that Choate refund half his legal fees since Tirrell's innocence had been so "obvious" in two trials. Of course, Choate refused. Tirrell spent the rest of his life in obscurity, but his trials became famous for Choate's successful use of a sleepwalking defense to charges of murder and arson.

—Stephen G. Christianson

Suggestions for Further Reading

Bickford, James. *The Authentic Life of Mrs. Mary Ann Bickford*. Boston: The Compiler, 1846.

Brown, Samuel Gilman. *The Life of Rufus Choate*. Boston: Little, Brown & Co., 1898.

Fuess, Claude Moore. *Rufus Choate, the Wizard of the Law*. Hamden, Conn.: Archon Books, 1970.

"A Lady of Weymouth." *Eccentricities & Anecdotes of Albert John Tirrell*. Boston: Unknown publisher, 1846.

Matthews, Jean V. *Rufus Choate, the Law and Civic Virtue*. Philadelphia: Temple University Press, 1980.

Neilson, Joseph. *Memories of Rufus Choate*. Littleton, Colo.: F.B. Rothman, 1985.

Dr. John Webster Trial: 1850

Defendant: Harvard Professor Dr. John Webster   **Crime Charged:** Murder
Chief Defense Lawyers: Pliny Merrick and Edward D. Sohier
Chief Prosecutors: George Bemis and John H. Clifford   **Judges:** Lemuel
Shaw, Charles A. Dewey, Thomas Metcalf, and Samuel Wilde
Place: Boston, Massachusetts   **Dates of Trial:** March 19–April 1, 1850
Verdict: Guilty   **Sentence:** Death by hanging

SIGNIFICANCE

Because Dr. John Webster had dismembered his victim's body and disposed of most of the parts, the prosecution had to try Webster without showing the *corpus delicti,* or proof of the murder, namely the body. Webster's trial was one of the first murder convictions based on the testimony of the medical experts and other evidence produced by the prosecution that established guilt beyond a reasonable doubt.

By the 1840s Boston, one of America's oldest cities, had become home to many wealthy families with preeminent positions in American society, business, and politics. This East Coast elite were often referred to as "blue bloods." They were active in charitable and social causes, including supporting leading educational institutions such as the venerable Harvard University in nearby Cambridge.

Dr. John Webster, a professor of chemistry and mineralogy at Harvard's Medical College, had also earned his medical degree from Harvard. His fellow professors included Oliver Wendell Holmes, Sr. Webster, an educated and intelligent man, soon established a place for himself in Boston society. He socialized with some of America's great cultural and literary figures, including poet Henry Wadsworth Longfellow. However, Webster found his new social prominence expensive to support.

Webster lacked personal wealth. Unlike his peers, he had not inherited a family fortune. Nor did his modest Harvard salary allow for lavish entertaining. He could support his social ambitions only by going into debt. One of his many creditors included Dr. George Parkman, whose family was one of Boston's most prominent. Webster borrowed more than $400 from Parkman, which in the

1840s was a sizable sum. Webster could not repay the debt, and in the fall of 1849 Parkman began to hound Webster to repay him.

Webster Kills Dr. Parkman

Shortly before Thanksgiving Day, 1849, Parkman confronted Webster in person at Webster's laboratory on the Harvard Medical College grounds. Parkman demanded that Webster pay his debt and threatened to use his influence to have Webster removed from the faculty. What must have gone through Webster's mind is still an open question and is colored by his post-trial confession that suggests temporary insanity. Whether Webster developed an uncontrollable temper or was carrying out a plan of premeditated murder, the fact remains that he savagely struck Parkman on the head with a piece of firewood from the nearby fireplace.

The blow fractured Parkman's skull, and he fell to the floor. Webster's homicidal fury subsided, and he unsuccessfully attempted to revive Parkman. When this effort failed, Webster bolted his lab door shut and used his medical instruments to dismember Parkman's body. He burnt most of Parkman's body in the lab furnace, but the process went slowly.

Ephraim Littlefield, the Medical College's janitor, had seen an earlier confrontation between Webster and Parkman. Littlefield became suspicious when on the day of Parkman's fatal visit to Webster, Littlefield found the lab door bolted shut and the wall by the furnace red-hot. Several days later, the Parkman family began advertising rewards for information leading to the where-abouts of the missing doctor. Littlefield's suspicions deepened, and he took it upon himself to break into Webster's laboratory by patiently chiseling his way through one of the lab's brick walls. After a couple of days Littlefield broke through, and to his horror saw the partial remains of a human body, including portions of the legs and pelvis of a man.

Littlefield quickly informed the police, who searched Webster's lab and found more remains, charred and half-destroyed, in the furnace. The police arrested Webster, who unsuccessfully tried to commit suicide by swallowing a poison pill. The authorities charged Webster with Parkman's murder, to which he pleaded not guilty. Webster's well-heeled friends attempted to hire counsel on his behalf, but they were unable to find lawyers willing to represent someone who seemed guilty of a heinous crime. Webster was forced to rely on two court-appointed attorneys, Pliny Merrick and Edward D. Sohier, for his defense.

Webster's Trial Rocks Boston Society

The trial opened March 19, 1850. The principal judge was state Supreme Judicial Court Chief Justice Lemuel Shaw. Associate Justices Charles A. Dewey, Thomas Metcalf, and Samuel Wilde also sat on the bench. The state's case was handled by Attorney General John H. Clifford, with the assistance of George Bemis. The prosecution, aware of the problem of the missing *corpus delicti*, wasted no time in bringing forward a series of medical experts to testify that the remains discovered in Webster's lab were those of Dr. Parkman.

The prosecution's medical experts included Dr. Nathan C. Keep, Parkman's dentist. Keep testified that he recognized certain false teeth found among the human remains in Webster's lab as the very ones that Keep had made for Parkman years before. To establish the necessary connection between the experts' identification of Parkman's remains and their presence in Webster's lab, the prosecutors brought in Littlefield.

By this time, the spectators' gallery was packed. By the end of the trial, more than 50,000 people had been present at one time or another. The prosecution knew that Littlefield would make or break their case, and they brought out his testimony slowly but surely, leading eventually to Littlefield's climactic discovery of Parkman's remains in Webster's lab:

> I took the crowbar and knocked the bigness of a hole right through. . . . There are five courses of brick in the wall. I had trouble with my light, as the air drew strongly through the hole. I managed to get the light and my head into the hole, and then I was not disturbed with the draft. I held my light forward. The first thing which I saw was the pelvis of a man and two parts of a leg. The water was running down on these remains from the sink.

Littlefield's next comment was an understatement, to say the least:

> I knew that it was no place for these things.

Clifford had put on an excellent case, and Webster's attorneys were hard-pressed. They tried to attack the janitor Littlefield's testimony by questioning his motives, including his desire to collect the reward offered by Parkman's family. Unable to succeed with this tack, Merrick and Sohier then presented a series of character witnesses. Although the retinue of socialites who testified on Webster's behalf was impressive, they could not shake the facts set forth by Littlefield's and the medical experts' testimony.

Corpus Delicti Issue Decides Webster's Fate

Webster's lawyers still had one ace in the hole, however. The law required that the prosecutors prove the existence of a crime, or the *corpus delicti*. In a murder case, this had always been assumed to mean that the prosecutors must physically produce the corpse of the person allegedly murdered. Therefore, Merrick's closing argument for the defense rested on the assertion that, in the eyes of the law, the state had not proven that the remains found in the lab were Parkman's. Even if the remains were Parkman's, Merrick continued, the state hadn't shown how he was killed.

After the lawyers made their closing arguments, Judge Shaw spoke to the jury on the issue of whether circumstantial evidence could establish the existence of a crime. If so, then the prosecution's evidence would be enough to prove the *corpus delicti* and convict Webster of murder. Shaw's ruling destroyed the defense's chances for victory:

It has sometimes been said by judges that a jury never ought to convict in a capital case unless the dead body is found. That, as a general proposition, is true. It sometimes happens, however, that it cannot be found, where the proof of death is clear. Sometimes, in a case of murder at sea, the body is thrown overboard on a stormy night. Because the body is not found, can anybody deny that the author of that crime is a murderer?

Therefore, Shaw made it possible for the jury to conclude from the overwhelming evidence presented by the prosecution that Webster had murdered Parkman. The jury took less than three hours of deliberation to find Webster guilty. On April 1, 1850, Shaw sentenced Webster to death by hanging. After an unsuccessful appeal and an equally fruitless petition for leniency from the governor, Webster confessed. Webster admitted that Parkman had visited him in his lab and that when Parkman pressed him for payment of his debts he had killed him, dismembered his body, and attempted to destroy the parts.

Webster's version of the events was that Parkman had provoked him to the point of blind fury, thus causing him to kill Parkman. After seeing what he had done, Webster said he panicked and butchered Parkman's body to conceal the evidence. Webster's confession, if made at trial and believed by the jury, could have led to his receiving a lighter sentence based on a plea of temporary insanity.

But it was too late for Webster to escape the hangman. His confession did not persuade the governor to commute his sentence. On August 30, Webster was executed. Webster's hanging put an end to one of the most sensational scandals to rock Boston society and Victorian America.

—Stephen G. Christianson

Suggestions for Further Reading

Cozzens, James Gould. *A Rope for Dr. Webster*. Columbia, S.C.: Bruccoli Clark, 1976.

Morris, Richard. *Fair Trial*. New York: Alfred A. Knopf, 1952.

Schama, Simon. *Dead Certainties*. New York: Alfred A. Knopf, 1991.

Sullivan, Robert. *The Disappearance of Dr. Parkman*. Boston: Little, Brown, & Co. 1971.

Thomson, Helen. *Murder at Harvard*. Boston: Houghton Mifflin, 1971.

State of Missouri v. Celia, a Slave: 1855

Defendant: Celia, a Slave   **Charge:** Murder
Chief Defense Lawyers: Isaac M. Boulware, John Jameson, and Nathan Chapman Kouns   **Chief Prosecutor:** Robert Prewitt   **Judge:** William Hall
Place: Calloway County, Missouri   **Dates of Trial:** October 9–10, 1855
Verdict: Guilty   **Sentence:** Hanging

SIGNIFICANCE
This case graphically illustrates that enslaved women had no legal recourse when raped by their masters. Although the second article of Section 29 of the Missouri statutes of 1845 forbade anyone "to take any woman unlawfully against her will and by force, menace or duress, compel her to be defiled," Judge William Hall refused to instruct the jury that the enslaved Celia fell within the meaning of "any woman"—giving the jury no latitude to consider Celia's murder of her sexually abusive master a justifiable act of self-defense.

In 1850, the recently widowed Robert Newsom purchased the 14-year-old Celia, ostensibly to help his daughters with the housework. En route from Audrain County, the site of the transaction, to his own home in neighboring Calloway County, Missouri, Newsom raped the young girl. Back at his farm, Newsom ensconced her in a small cabin 150 feet from his home. Between 1850 and 1855, Celia bore two of Newsom's children, both of whom became her master's property. She also began a relationship with a fellow slave named George. When she became pregnant in 1855, she was unsure which of the men was the father. At that point, George told Celia that "he would have nothing more to do with her if she did not quit the old man."

Celia first asked Newsom's daughters to intercede. She told Mary (19 years old, as was Celia in 1855) and Virginia (36 and returned to her father's home with her own three children) that her pregnancy was making her feel unwell and that she wished Robert Newsom to respect her condition and leave her alone. There is no indication that either Newsom daughter challenged her father.

Celia herself pleaded with Newsom on June 23, but he brushed aside her objections and said "he was coming to her cabin that night." That afternoon, Celia brought a heavy stick, "about as large as the upper part of a Windsor chair, but not so long," into her cabin. When Newsom arrived and refused to back off, she killed him with two blows to the head. She spent the night burning his corpse in her fireplace. As morning approached, she ground the smaller bones into pieces with a rock; the larger bones, she hid "under the hearth, and under the floor between a sleeper and the fireplace." Later that day, she gave Newsom's unwitting grandson, Virginia's son Coffee Waynescot, "two dozen walnuts [to] carry the ashes out." Coffee disposed of his grandfather's remains on the ground beside "a beat down like" path on the property.

Celia Speaks

By Sunday, June 24, Newsom's family and neighbors had become concerned. They first questioned George, who quickly implicated Celia. (George afterward ran away.) Harry and David Newsom, Robert's sons, had come from their own homes to investigate; with Robert's neighbor William Powell, they demanded a confession from Celia. She at first denied any involvement. Then, afraid of Harry's and David's reactions, she told Powell she would confess if he would "send the two men out of the room." They left, and Celia told her story to Powell. Powell and the Newsom family then examined the fireplace, where Virginia located "buttons my sister [Mary] sewed on my father's breeches a few days before his death," and various splinters of bone. Newsom's larger bones were then recovered from the hiding space beneath the hearth.

On June 25, David Newsom delivered his affidavit to two local justices of the peace, D.M. Whyte and Isaac P. Howe. The affidavit stated that David Newsom "has cause to suspect and believe that one Negro woman named Celia a Slave of the said Robert Newsom did at the county aforesaid feloniously, willfully, and with malice aforethought with a club or some other weapon strike and mortally wound the said Robert Newsom, of which wound or wounds the said Robert Newsom instantly died." Celia was arrested and "deliver[ed] . . . forthwith to the keeper of the common jail of said County to await her trial."

Because white Calloway County residents were afraid Celia might have had help from another slave or slaves still at large, county Sheriff William T. Snell permitted two men, Thomas Shoatman and Jefferson Jones, to interrogate Celia. All of the above information about Celia's life on the Newsom farm comes from her interviews with William Powell, Jefferson Jones, and Thomas Shoatman. It does not come from Celia's trial testimony because she gave none. In the 19th century, blacks generally were not allowed to testify in criminal trials.

The Trial Begins

Celia's trial began on October 9, 1855. Her court-appointed attorneys, Isaac M. Boulware, John Jameson, and Nathan Chapman Kouns, seem to have given the most vigorous defense possible. On her behalf, they pleaded not guilty and described Celia as one who was "ready for trial, and prayed herself upon her God and her Country."

On October 10, prosecutor Robert Prewitt called Jefferson Jones to the stand. Jones recited for the court the account that Celia had given to him several months earlier. He said that Celia said she "had been having sexual intercourse" with her master and that George had threatened to leave her if these relations continued. When Jameson cross-examined Jones about Celia's account of the rape on the day of Newsom's purchase, Newsom's sexual demands during the following five years, and the birth of her two children fathered by Newsom, Jones said that he couldn't "say positively whether Celia said the accused had forced her on the way home" and couldn't "know with certainty whether she told me so."

Robert Newsom's daughter, Virginia Waynescot, was called by the prosecutor, and she described the discovery of some of her father's remains. Jameson then cross-examined her and tried tactfully and not very successfully to examine the relationship between her father and the enslaved Celia. Asked where her father customarily slept, Virginia replied: "[I] did not notice the [Newsom's] bed. Sister made the bed up." Virginia did, however, disclose that Celia "took sick in February. Had been sick ever since." Virginia's son, Coffee Waynescot, then testified about his disposal of his grandfather's ashes. On cross-examination, Jameson tried—again, with tact and with little success—to elicit information about the sexual relationship between Newsom and Celia.

William Powell was the next witness. For the prosecution, he related Celia's detailed confession that she had killed Newsom. During his cross-examination of Powell, Jameson abandoned the reticence he had shown to Newsom's daughter and grandson. Powell testified that Celia had told him of Newsom's misconduct and of her pleas to Newsom's daughters for intercession. He also testified that Celia had claimed to act only from a desperate wish to end Newsom's sexual demands.

Jameson called Dr. James M. Martin, a Fulton doctor, to testify. All of Jameson's questions to Dr. Martin concerning how long it would take to burn an adult human body brought objections from the prosecutor, which were sustained by Judge William Hall. Thomas Shoatman then testified for the defense, saying "the reason she gave for striking him the second blow was that he threw up his hands to catch her" and "only to hurt him, to keep him from having sexual intercourse with her." Judge Hall ordered both of these statements stricken from the record.

Jameson had valiantly tried to bring Celia's motives before the jury, and the prosecutor had fought to keep her motives from consideration. Slaves had the legal right to preserve their lives, even if the use of deadly force was required. Moreover, according Missouri law, it was a crime "to take any woman unlawfully against her will and by force, menace, or duress, compel her to be defiled." A homicide committed while warding off such a crime against one's person was justifiable. Therefore, when it was time for both the prosecuting and defending attorneys to present Judge Hall with proposed instructions for the jury, Jameson asked that the jury be instructed that "if they . . . believe from the testimony, that the said Newsom at the time of said killing, attempted to compel her against her will to sexual intercourse with him, they will not find her guilty of murder in the first degree." He also asked that "the words 'any woman'" in the Missouri rape statute quoted above, "embrace slave women, as well as free white women."

Jameson's proposed instructions challenged Missouri slave law, which held that since the owned woman was *property*, what we would view as the rape of an enslaved woman by someone other than her master was actually considered *trespass*. And, as Melton McLaurin summarizes the legal quandary posed by this definition, "an owner could hardly be charged with trespassing upon his own property."

Judge Hall refused to present Jameson's self-defense arguments to the jury. On October 10, 1855, Celia was found guilty and ordered "hanged by the neck until dead on the sixteenth day of November 1855." In the meantime, either during or shortly after her trial, Celia's pregnancy ended in a stillbirth.

On to the Missouri Supreme Court

Jameson appealed to the Missouri Supreme Court. He asked for, and expected, a stay of execution until such time as that court ruled.

The court agreed to hear the case but refused a stay of execution. Some unidentified but presumably outraged Calloway County residents "kidnapped" Celia from jail just before her scheduled execution and returned her once the date had passed. Jameson wrote a personal letter to one of the three Missouri Supreme Court justices. Two of the justices sitting in 1855—Judge William Scott and John F. Ryland—had participated in issuing the infamous, proslavery *Dred Scott* decision, which would be upheld by the U.S. Supreme Court in 1857. Jameson wrote to the third justice, Judge Abiel Leonard, saying Judge Hall had "cut out all means of defense," begging for a stay of execution, and pleading with the justices to "please give the matter your earliest attention."

The Supreme Court rendered its decision on December 14, 1855:

> Upon an examination of the record and proceedings of the Circuit Court of Calloway County in the above case, it is thought proper to refuse the prayer of the petitioner—there being seen upon inspection of the record aforesaid no probable cause for such appeal; nor so much doubt as to render it expedient to take the judgment of the Supreme Court thereon. It is thereby ordered by the Court, that an order for the stay of the execution in this case be refused.

Celia was interviewed by a *Fulton Telegraph* reporter on December 20. She said, "As soon as I struck him the Devil got into me, and I struck him with the stick until he was dead, and then rolled him in the fire and burnt him up." She was hanged on December 21, 1855.

—Kathryn Cullen-DuPont

Suggestions for Further Reading

Brownmiller, Susan. *Against Our Will: Men, Women, and Rape.* New York: Simon & Schuster, 1975.

Fox-Genovese, Elizabeth. *Within the Plantation Household: Black and White Women of the Old South.* Chapel Hill, N.C.: University of North Carolina Press, 1988.

McLaurin, Melton A. *Celia: A Slave: A true story of violence and retribution in antebellum Missouri.* Athens, Ga.: University of Georgia Press, 1991.

Sterling, Dorothy. *We Are Your Sisters: Black Women in the Nineteenth Century.* New York: W.W. Norton & Co., 1984.

Dred Scott Decision: 1856

Appellant: Dred Scott **Defendant:** John F.A. Sanford
Plaintiff Claim: That Scott, who was a slave, had become a free man when
his owner had taken him to a state designated as "free" under the 1820
Missouri Compromise **Chief Defense Lawyers:** Hugh A. Garland, H.S.
Geyer, George W. Goode, Reverdy Johnson, and Lyman D Norris
Chief Lawyers for Appellant: Samuel M. Bay, Montgomery Blair, George
Ticknor Curtis, Alexander P. Field, Roswell M. Field, and David N. Hall
Justices: John A. Campbell, John Catron, Benjamin R. Curtis, Peter Daniel,
Robert Cooper Grier, John McLean, Samuel Nelson, Roger B. Taney, and
James M. Wayne. **Place:** Washington, D.C. **Date of Decision:** 1856
December Term **Decision:** That Dred Scott was still a slave, regardless of
where his owner took him.

SIGNIFICANCE

The Dred Scott decision effectively ended the Missouri Compromise, hardening
the political rivalry between North and South and paving the way for the Civil War.

Dred Scott was born in Virginia sometime in the late 1790s, although historical records concerning the exact time and place are incomplete. Because Scott was black and born into slavery, no one at the time would have taken much interest in such details, other than to note the arrival of another piece of property.

Scott's owner was Peter Blow, who owned a reasonably successful plantation. In 1819, Blow took his family and several slaves, including Scott, to Alabama to start a new plantation. Blow grew tired of farming, and in 1830 moved to St. Louis, Missouri. St. Louis was then a booming frontier town, and Blow opened a hotel. Both Blow and his wife became seriously ill, and were dead by 1832.

Scott's travels westward in a sense mirrored the expansion of the United States during this time period. From the original 13 states on the Atlantic Seaboard, American colonists had pushed to the Mississippi River and beyond. This expansion gave rise to serious political problems, however. Southern states wanted to bring slavery and the plantation lifestyle into the new territories, whereas the Northern states wanted to keep the territories free. Both sides were afraid that, when portions of the territories were eventually admitted as states, the other side would gain political supremacy in Congress owing to the new states' senators and representatives. In 1820, the North and the South struck a deal called the Missouri Compromise. Missouri was admitted to the union as a slave state and Maine was admitted as a free state, preserving the political balance in Congress. Further, slavery was forbidden in any territory north of, but permitted in any territory south of, Missouri's northern border at approximately 36 degrees latitude north.

After the Blows' deaths, their estate sold Scott to an army doctor named John Emerson. Emerson took Scott with him during tours of duty in Illinois and in that part of the Wisconsin and Iowa Territories which would become Minnesota. Both Illinois and Minnesota were within the free territory of the Missouri Compromise. Emerson returned to St. Louis and died December 29, 1843. He left everything, including Scott, to his wife and appointed as executor his wife's brother, John F.A. Sanford.

Scott Sues for Freedom

Tired of a lifetime of slavery, Scott tried to buy his freedom from the widow Emerson, without success. Scott had acquired more education than most slaves and realized that his travels into free territory might give him a claim to freedom. Represented by former Missouri Attorney General Samuel M. Bay, on April 6, 1846, Scott sued for his freedom in the Missouri Circuit Court for the City of St. Louis. Sanford and the widow Emerson were represented by George W. Goode. Because Sanford was the estate executor for Scott's former master, the official reports bear his name as the primary defendant, misspelled to read "*Scott v. Sandford.*"

Legally, Scott's suit was for assault and false imprisonment. A slave could be punished and kept as property, but a free person could not, so the legal charges were in fact window dressing for the issue of Scott's freedom. On June 30, 1847 the case came to trial before Judge Alexander Hamilton. Bay committed a technical error in presenting the plaintiff's evidence, and the jury returned a verdict that same day in Emerson and Sanford's favor. Hamilton granted Bay's motion for a new trial, which was held on January 12, 1850, again before Judge Hamilton. This time, Scott's lawyers were Alexander P. Field and David N. Hall. Sanford had by this time completely taken over the widow Emerson's affairs and retained Hugh A. Garland and Lyman D. Norris for the defense.

At the second trial, the jury held that Scott was a free man, based on certain Missouri state court precedents that held that even though Missouri was a slave state, residence in a free state or territory resulted in a slave's emancipation. Scott's freedom was short-lived, however.

Sanford appealed to the Missouri Supreme Court. After more than two years, Judge William Scott announced that court's decision on March 22, 1852.

Scott reversed the jury verdict of the second trial, stating that Dred Scott was still a slave. Although Judge Scott's decision was couched in legal terms concerning states' rights and the legality of slavery within Missouri's borders, in fact the real basis for the decision was the rise to power of pro-slavery Democrats on the court. Judge Scott justified the court's decision to reverse those legal precedents that supported Dred Scott's freedom by stating that blacks were destined to be slaves:

> We are almost persuaded that the introduction of slavery amongst [Americans] was, in the providence of God, who makes the evil passions of men subservient to His own glory, a means of placing that unhappy race within the pale of civilized nations.

Scott Tries Federal Courts

Following the Missouri Supreme Court's decision, the case was sent back to Judge Hamilton in St. Louis, who was supposed to issue the final order dismissing the case and returning Scott to slavery. Hamilton procrastinated, however, which gave Scott time to hire a new lawyer and get his case into the federal courts. Scott replaced Field and Hall. His new lawyer was Roswell M. Field, who was unrelated to the previous Field. The new Field realized that Sanford had moved to New York City, and was therefore no longer a resident of Missouri. Therefore, Field initiated new proceedings on November 2, 1853, in federal court, under legal provisions that give federal courts jurisdiction over cases between citizens of different states. This principle is called "diversity jurisdiction," and is still valid today. Diversity jurisdiction enabled Scott, as a citizen of Missouri, to sue Sanford, as a citizen of New York, in federal court. The issue of Scott's freedom was now before Judge Robert W. Wells of the U.S. Court for the District of Missouri, located in St. Louis.

At the circuit court's 1854 April Term, Wells held that Scott was a Missouri "citizen" for diversity jurisdiction purposes, despite the fact of Scott's slavery. The case then went to trial, which was held on May 15, 1854. In this, Scott's third freedom trial, the jury ruled in Sanford's favor and held that Scott was still a slave. This was despite the fact that Wells, who was a Southerner, was sympathetic to Scott's cause. Field promptly appealed to the U.S. Supreme Court in Washington, D.C. He convinced the distinguished lawyer Montgomery Blair to represent Scott before the Supreme Court, although Scott was virtually penniless.

Blair, who also was originally from Missouri, had successfully pursued political and legal ambitions in Washington. His residence was the now-famous Blair House on Pennsylvania Avenue. Blair was assisted by George Ticknor Curtis. With the assistance of Southern pro-slavery interests, who recognized the potential importance of the Scott case, Sanford also retained some very eminent lawyers. Sanford was represented before the Supreme Court by former Senator Henry S. Geyer, who like Blair had come from Missouri and made a name for himself as a Washington lawyer. Geyer was assisted by former Senator and U.S.

FRANK LESLIE'S ILLUSTRATED NEWSPAPER

Entered according to Act of Congress, in the year 1857, by FRANK LESLIE, in the Clerk's Office of the District Court for the Southern District of New York. (Copyrighted June 22, 1857.)

No. 82.—VOL. IV.]　　　NEW YORK, SATURDAY, JUNE 27, 1857.　　　[PRICE 6 CENTS.

TO TOURISTS AND TRAVELLERS.

We shall be happy to receive personal narratives, of land or sea, including adventures and incidents, from every person who pleases to correspond with our paper.

We take this opportunity of returning our thanks to our numerous artistic correspondents throughout the country, for the many sketches we are constantly receiving from them of the news of the day. We trust they will spare no pains to furnish us with drawings of events as they may occur. We would also remind them that it is necessary to send all sketches, if possible, by the earliest conveyance.

VISIT TO DRED SCOTT—HIS FAMILY—INCIDENTS OF HIS LIFE—DECISION OF THE SUPREME COURT.

WHILE standing in the Fair grounds at St. Louis, and engaged in conversation with a prominent citizen of that enterprising city, he suddenly asked us if we would not like to be introduced to Dred Scott. Upon expressing a desire to be thus honored, the gentleman called to an old negro who was standing near by, and our wish was gratified. Dred made a rude obeisance to our recognition, and seemed to enjoy the notice we expended upon him. We found him on examination to be a pure-blooded African, perhaps fifty years of age, with a shrewd, intelligent, good-natured face, of rather light frame, being not more than five feet six inches high. After some general remarks we expressed a wish to get his portrait (we had made

efforts before, through correspondents, and failed), and asked him if he would not go to Fitzgibbon's gallery and

have it taken. The gentleman present explained to Dred that it was proper he should have his likeness in the "great illustrated paper of the country," overruled his many objections, which seemed to grow out of a superstitious feeling, and he promised to be at the gallery the next day. This appointment Dred did not keep. Determined not to be foiled, we sought an interview with Mr. Crane, Dred's lawyer, who promptly gave us a letter of introduction, explaining to Dred that it was to his advantage to have his picture taken to be engraved for our paper, and also directions where we could find his domicile. We found the place with difficulty, the streets in Dred's neighborhood being more clearly defined in the plan of the city than on the mother earth; we finally reached a wooden house, however, protected by a balcony that answered the description. Approaching the door, we saw a smart, tidy-looking negress, perhaps thirty years of age, who, with two female assistants, was busy ironing. To our question, "Is this where Dred Scott lives?" we received, rather hesitatingly, the answer, "Yes." Upon our asking if he was home, she said,

"What white man arter dad nigger for?—why don't white man 'tend to his own business, and let dat nigger 'lone? Some of dese days dey'll steal dat nigger—dat are a fact."

ELIRA AND LIZZIE, CHILDREN OF DRED SCOTT.

DRED SCOTT. PHOTOGRAPHED BY FITZGIBBON, OF ST. LOUIS.

HIS WIFE, HARRIET. PHOTOGRAPHED BY FITZGIBBON, OF ST. LOUIS.

The Supreme Court held that Dred Scott, above, was his owner's property and the only "rights" at issue were those of the owner.
(Courtesy, Library of Congress)

Attorney General Reverdy Johnson, who was a personal friend of Chief Justice Roger B. Taney.

Victory for Slavery, Defeat for Scott

The Scott case was filed with the Supreme Court on December 30, 1854, and set for oral argument on the Court's February 1856 Term before Justices John A. Campbell, John Catron, Benjamin R. Curtis, Peter Daniel, Robert Cooper Grier, John McLean, Samuel Nelson, Roger Brooke Taney, and James M. Wayne.

The political makeup of the Court would weigh heavily in its eventual decision. Southern and pro-slavery justices had a clear majority. Campbell was from Alabama. Catron was from Tennessee. Curtis was from Massachusetts, but was sympathetic to the South. Daniel was from Virginia. Grier was from Pennsylvania, but he was a conservative states' rights advocate. McLean, from Ohio, was the only openly anti-slavery justice on the Court. Nelson was from New York, but like Grier he was a defender of states' rights and lukewarm to the anti-slavery cause. Taney, the chief justice, was from Maryland and the leader of the Court's Southern majority. Finally, Wayne was from Georgia. The justices also were conscious of the fact that 1856 was an election year, and that the Scott decision would have important political consequences.

During the 1856 February Term, the justices listened to the parties' arguments for three days. Scott's attorneys presented the "free soil" argument, one favored by Northern abolitionists: once a slave stepped into a free state or territory, he or she was emancipated, or else the power to prohibit slavery was meaningless. Sanford's attorneys presented the states' rights argument, which favored the institution of slavery: Scott had been a slave in Missouri, he had returned to Missouri, and had subjected himself to the jurisdiction of Missouri law and Missouri courts. Therefore, Missouri was entitled to declare Scott a slave, and ignore the fact that Scott would not be a slave elsewhere.

Not surprisingly, most of the justices were in favor of rejecting Scott's freedom plea. However, they could not agree on the proper legal grounds. Some justices wanted to hold that a slave couldn't sue in federal court, other justices wanted to discuss congressional power to prohibit slavery in the territories and the constitutionality of the Missouri Compromise. The justices decided to postpone their decision until after the presidential election and ordered Scott's and Sanford's lawyers to re-argue the case during the Court's 1856 December Term.

In November 1856, Democrat James Buchanan was elected president. Buchanan, indifferent to the slavery issue, would sit idly by over the next four years while the country was split into North and South and headed toward civil war. After the second round of oral argument in December, during which the parties reiterated the same basic positions, Chief Justice Taney announced the decision of the majority of the Court. Taney and six other justices voted to hold that Scott was still a slave. Taney refused to recognize any rights for blacks as citizens under the U.S. Constitution:

> We think they are not, and that they are not included, and were not intended to be included, under the word "citizens" in the Constitution, and can therefore claim none of the rights and privileges which that instrument provides for and secures to citizens of the United States. On the contrary, they were at that time considered as a subordinate and inferior class of beings, who had been subjugated by the dominant race, and, whether emancipated or not, yet remained subject to their authority, and had no rights or privileges but such as those who held the power and the Government might choose to grant them.

From this holding, Taney went on to state that Scott was a slave wherever he went, and could be reclaimed at any time by his lawful owner under that provision of the Constitution that forbids Congress from depriving Americans of life, liberty, and property without due process of law. Taney held that Scott was "property" and therefore the Missouri Compromise was unconstitutional:

> An Act of Congress which deprives a citizen of the United States of his property, merely because he came himself or brought his property into a particular Territory of the United States, and who had committed no offense against the laws, could hardly be dignified with the name of due process of law.

Scott was a slave once again, and the South had won an important victory. The Missouri Compromise, which had preserved the political status quo for nearly 40 years, was swept away. The North would eventually prevail and abolish slavery, but it would do so only after many battles of a much different and bloodier nature during the Civil War.

—Stephen G. Christianson

Suggestions for Further Reading

Ehrlich, Walter. *They Have No Rights: Dred Scott's Struggle for Freedom.* Westport, Conn.: Greenwood Press, 1979.

Fehrenbacher, Don Edward. *Slavery, Law, and Politics: The Dred Scott Case in Historical Perspective.* New York: Oxford University Press, 1981.

Kutler, Stanley I. *The Dred Scott Decision: Law or Politics?* Boston: Houghton Mifflin, 1967.

McGinty, Brian. "Dred Scott's Fight for Freedom Brought Him a Heap O' Trouble." *American History Illustrated* (May 1981): 34–39.

Sudo, Phil. "Five Little People Who Changed U.S. History." *Scholastic Update* (January 26, 1990): 8–10.

Emma Cunningham Trial: 1857

Defendant: Emma Augusta Cunningham   **Crime Charged:** Murder
Chief Defense Lawyer: Henry L. Clinton   **Chief Prosecutor:** A. Oakley Hall
Judge: Recorder Smith (historical records do not indicate first name)
Place: New York, New York   **Dates of Trial:** May 6–May 9, 1857
Verdict: Not guilty

SIGNIFICANCE

Emma Augusta Cunningham was acquitted of Dr. Harvey Burdell's murder, and nearly succeeded in her attempt to collect Burdell's estate on the basis of a forged marriage certificate and a fake pregnancy. Victorian attitudes toward women prevented the authorities from bringing Cunningham to justice.

Emma Augusta Hempstead was born in New York City in 1816. She grew up to be an attractive and intelligent woman. She was also ambitious to make her fortune, and did so through one of the few means open to women of that era: by marrying wealthy men.

She became Emma Cunningham in 1835 when she married George Cunningham, whose life insurance policy left her with $10,000 (a sizable amount in those days) when he died in 1852. Cunningham was a widow but still attractive and only in her 30s when she met Dr. Harvey Burdell, a New York dentist.

Burdell was born in Herkimer, New York, in 1811. He learned dentistry and moved to New York City, where his practice prospered and he accumulated a personal fortune estimated to exceed $100,000. Despite his wealth and professional standing, however, Burdell was far from being a pillar of the community. He was constantly being accused by his creditors of reneging on debts. In 1835, Burdell caused a scandal when on his wedding day he demanded $20,000 from the wealthy father of the bride-to-be to go through with the marriage. Furious, the bride's father refused, threw Burdell out of his house, and canceled the wedding.

In the early 1850s, Cunningham met Burdell, and in 1855 rented a suite of rooms at Burdell's 31 Bond Street mansion. Burdell's mansion was so large that Burdell not only lived there, he also ran his dental practice there, in addition to keeping several tenants such as Cunningham. Cunningham soon developed an intimate relationship not only with Burdell, but also with another tenant, John J. Eckel.

On the night of January 30, 1857, a neighbor heard a scream from Burdell's house that sounded like, "Murder!" The next morning, one of Burdell's servants discovered the doctor's body in his office, covered with multiple stab wounds. Police medical experts examined the body, and determined that Burdell had been stabbed 15 times with a knife wielded by a left-handed assailant. The police suspected that Cunningham, who was left-handed, had murdered Burdell with Eckel's help. The police arrested Cunningham for Burdell's murder, and she was imprisoned until trial.

The crowded courtroom where the jury returned a verdict of not guilty. (*Harper's Weekly*)

Cunningham Makes Startling Announcement

From her prison cell Cunningham announced that she had been Burdell's wife and revealed a marriage certificate, which stated that the marriage took place on October 28, 1856. Eckel's physical appearance resembled Burdell's, however, and the police suspected that Cunningham had had Eckel impersonate Burdell to obtain the certificate. Further, Cunningham said she was pregnant with Burdell's baby. If Cunningham was Burdell's wife and the mother of his child, not only would it be harder for the prosecution to show motive for the murder but, if acquitted, Cunningham would be entitled to all of Burdell's $100,000 estate.

Cunningham's trial began May 6, 1857. Her lawyer was Henry L. Clinton. The prosecutor was District Attorney A. Oakley Hall and the judge was Recorder Smith. Very little of the actual trial testimony has survived, but according to several accounts, Cunningham testified that her marriage with Burdell was a happy one and she denied murdering her supposed husband. One of Burdell's maids, however, testified that Cunningham had once stated that Burdell was "not fit to live" and that it was time he "was out of this world." Further, according to the maid, Cunningham had called Burdell "a bad man."

Prosecutor Hall also introduced Mary Crane, an old friend of Dr. Burdell's, as a witness. Crane testified that shortly before his death Burdell told her "that he had let his house to a lady and that she was the most horrible woman he ever met." Further, according to Crane, Burdell suspected that Cunningham was involved with Eckel and had claimed that the two were "prowling about" at night.

Victorian morality prevented doctors from examining Emma Cunningham and proving her pregnancy false. (*Harper's Weekly*)

Unfortunately for Hall, Burdell's own reputation made it difficult to make anything stick against Cunningham. Further, Clinton introduced witnesses such as Dr. Roberts, (no first name available) a colleague of Burdell's who testified that the relationship between Burdell and Cunningham had been to all appearances peaceful and loving. Finally, Cunningham's alleged pregnancy was now well advanced, and her abdomen was appropriately swollen whenever she appeared in public. On May 9, 1857, the jury returned a verdict of not guilty. Cunningham left the courtroom a free woman.

The affair was not over yet, however. Dr. Uhl, (no first name available) who was attending to Cunningham during her supposed pregnancy, went to Hall and stated that he was suspicious. Uhl thought that Cunningham was simply stuffing her dress with cushions. Unfortunately, Cunningham had refused to let Uhl physically examine her, and Uhl's treatment had been limited to minor matters such as prescribing bed rest in response to Cunningham's verbal descriptions of her symptoms. At the time, however, it was not unusual for a woman to refuse physical examination during pregnancy on the grounds that it was immoral for any man not her husband to touch her.

Further, Victorian morality made it impossible for Hall to order Cunningham to submit to a proper medical examination. However, Hall ordered a stakeout of 31 Bond Street, where Cunningham still lived. On July 27, 1857, the police stopped a nun who was bringing a basket to the door. The basket contained a baby, which Cunningham had paid $1,000 to adopt.

Caught red-handed, Cunningham dropped her claims to Burdell's estate, thus implicitly admitting that she had never been married to Burdell nor been pregnant with his child. Hall didn't have any medical evidence to prove that Cunningham had faked her pregnancy, however, and since she had already been acquitted of Burdell's murder, the legal obstacles to bringing her to justice were practically insurmountable. Therefore, Hall was forced to let Cunningham go. Cunningham was smart enough to realize that she would always be under a cloud of suspicion in New York City, and she moved to California. Apparently she spent her final years running a moderately prosperous vineyard.

No one was ever convicted of Burdell's murder. If he had been able to get the proper medical evidence, Hall might have been able to prove that Cunningham was guilty. Victorian morality, however, prevented this. The real mother of the "market-basket" baby Cunningham had tried to purchase for $1,000 stayed in New York City, and rented her baby to P.T. Barnum's circus for $25 a week for the public to view.

—Stephen G. Christianson

Suggestions for Further Reading

Clinton, Henry Lauren. *Celebrated Trials*. New York: Harper & Brothers, 1897.

Duke, Thomas Samuel. *Celebrated Criminal Cases of America*. San Francisco: James H. Barry Co., 1910.

Lewis, Alfred Henry. *Nation-Famous New York Murders*. New York: G.W. Dillingham Co., 1914.

Paul, Raymond. *The Bond Street Burlesque: a Historical Novel of Murder*. New York: W.W. Norton & Co., 1987.

Pearson, Edmund Lester. *Murder at Smutty Nose, and Other Murders*. Garden City, N.Y.: Dolphin Books, 1965.

"Duff" Armstrong Trial: 1858

Defendant: William Armstrong **Crime Charged:** Murder
Chief Defense Lawyer: Abraham Lincoln **Chief Prosecutors:** Hugh
Fullerton and J. Henry Shaw **Judge:** James Harriot **Place:** Beardstown,
Illinois **Date of Trial:** May 8, 1858 **Verdict:** Not guilty

SIGNIFICANCE

William Armstrong's trial is considered to be Lincoln's most famous case. By
introducing an almanac into evidence, Lincoln proved that the witness who swore
that he saw Armstrong kill a man at night under a full moon was lying.

When he was nothing more than a young backwoods man struggling to make his way in the world, Abraham Lincoln lived for a while in the little town of New Salem, Illinois. He studied law while working in the local grocery store. One day, a local bully named Jack Armstrong challenged Lincoln to a wrestling match. Lincoln won the match, and earned Armstrong's respect. Soon, Lincoln was a close friend of Armstrong and his wife Hannah. When the Armstrongs had a baby, William, Lincoln used to rock the infant to sleep whenever he paid a visit.

Lincoln eventually left New Salem for Springfield, Illinois and an eminently successful career in law and politics. Over 20 years later, in 1857, Lincoln learned that William Armstrong, nicknamed "Duff" and now a grown man, had been charged with murder. According to the authorities, an intoxicated "Duff" Armstrong murdered James Preston Metzker on the night of August 29, 1857. Jack Armstrong, the father, was dead, and Hannah Armstrong was a widow. Lincoln wrote Mrs. Armstrong and asked to defend her son:

> I have just heard of your deep affliction, and the arrest of your son for murder. I can hardly believe that he can be capable of the crime alleged against him. It does not seem possible. I am anxious that he should be given a fair trial at any rate; and the gratitude for your long continued kindness to me in adverse circumstances prompts me to offer my humble service gratuitously in his behalf.

Lincoln went to the town of Beardstown, Illinois, where Armstrong was being tried. The trial was held May 8, 1858. Lincoln was the defense lawyer, and the prosecutors were Hugh Fullerton and J. Henry Shaw. The judge was James Harriot.

The prosecution's case rested on the testimony of key witness Charles Allen, who said that on the night of the murder he saw "Duff" Armstrong strike Metzker under the light of a full moon. According to the notes of an eyewitness, Lincoln was calm, almost bored while the prosecution made its case:

> Lincoln sat with his head thrown back, his steady gaze apparently fixed upon one spot of the blank ceiling, entirely oblivious to what was happening about him, and without a single variation of feature or noticeable movement. . . .

When it was his turn to cross-examine Allen, Lincoln asked Allen about the precise details of the night in question. Allen testified that on the night of August 29, 1857, there was a full moon and that from a distance of about 150 feet he saw Armstrong kill Metzker. Allen further stated that the incident occurred about 11:00 o'clock.

With dramatic suddenness, Lincoln dropped his bored veneer and asked Judge Harriot for permission to enter an 1857 almanac into evidence. Judge Harriot granted Lincoln's motion, and Lincoln had Allen read the almanac entry for August 29, 1857. There was no full moon that night; in fact, there had been no moon at all by 11:00 o'clock. Therefore, it would have been impossible for Allen to see anything from a distance of 150 feet. Allen had obviously lied under oath.

Armstrong's trial closed by the end of the day. Judge Harriot had allowed the jury to look at the almanac and confirm their opinion that Allen had perjured himself. After a passionate plea to the jury for Armstrong's freedom, Lincoln rested the defense. While the jury deliberated, Lincoln confidently predicted that they would acquit Armstrong by sunset. He was right: after only one ballot, the jury's verdict was not guilty.

Lincoln won Duff's acquittal by convincing Judge Harriot to allow into evidence scientific data in the form of the almanac as to what the actual lunar conditions had been. This procedure is called judicial notice, and is a common occurrence today. In the 1850s, however, it was a novelty because the judicial system relied almost entirely on witness testimony.

For what eventually would be regarded as his most famous case, Lincoln didn't charge "Duff" or Hannah Armstrong one cent. Illinois' most famous lawyer, and ultimately one of America's greatest presidents, did the case for free.

—*Stephen G. Christianson*

Suggestions for Further Reading

Fleming, Thomas. "Lincoln's Favorite Case." *Boys' Life* (September 1985): 20.

Frank, John Paul. *Lincoln as a Lawyer.* Urbana: University of Illinois Press, 1961.

Hill, Frederick Trevor. *Lincoln, the Lawyer.* New York: Century Co., 1906.

Whitney, Henry Clay. *Life on the Circuit with Lincoln.* Caldwell, Idaho: Caxton Printers, 1940.

Woldman, Albert A. *Lawyer Lincoln.* Boston & New York: Houghton Mifflin Co., 1936.

Daniel Sickles Trial: 1859

Defendant: Daniel Sickles   **Crime Charged:** Murder
Chief Defense Lawyers: James T. Brady, John Graham, and Edwin M.
Stanton   **Chief Prosecutor:** Robert Ould   **Judge:** Crawford (First name
unavailable)   **Place:** Washington, D.C.   **Dates of Trial:** April 4–26, 1859
Verdict: Not guilty

SIGNIFICANCE

The first use of a plea of temporary insanity by a criminal defendant and the
unabashed appeal to the "unwritten law" to justify homicide made the Daniel
Sickles case noteworthy in American legal history. It was equally significant for
the irreparable damage done to Sickles' promising career as a leader of the
Democratic Party.

Daniel Sickles' murder of Philip Barton Key was the kind of crime that piques
the interest of all but the most austere newspaper editors. The lurid trial
captivated the nation's press.

The menu for the trial was perfect: glamorous celebrities, political in-
trigue, spellbinding lawyers, the plot of an Italian opera, and an adulterous affair.
The accused, Dan Sickles, was a prominent and well-connected 39-year-old
Congressman from New York with a hair-trigger temper and a reputation as a
ladies' man; the victim, Barton Key, was not only a close friend of his killer,
whose political clout with President James Buchanan had secured Key's appointment as Washington's district attorney, but he also was the son of Francis
Scott Key, author of "The Star Spangled Banner." He was described as "the
handsomest man in all Washington society" by the city's most prominent
hostess and biggest gossip, Mrs. Clement Clay.

The very time and scene of the crime commanded the public's attention
and sparked courtroom and editorial fireworks. Not even the most highbrowed
Victorian could ignore a killing that occurred in broad daylight on a Sunday
afternoon on the sidewalk surrounding Lafayette Park, literally so near the
White House it could have been witnessed from its front windows.

But it was the motive that added the most spice to the story. Sickles
gunned Key down after discovering that he and the beautiful 22-year-old Mrs.

Sickles had been having an affair, at times carrying on in the front library of the Sickles home.

Lafayette Park Killing

By the time Sickles was tipped off by an anonymous letter, dated February 24, 1859, the relationship between Teresa Sickles and Key was certainly the primary topic of conversation in the family's servant quarters and had started tongues wagging in Washington society. Confronting his wife with the evidence that he and a close friend collected, Dan Sickles extracted a detailed written confession from her and then, in state of near hysteria, called two of his political cronies to his home to ask for their advice.

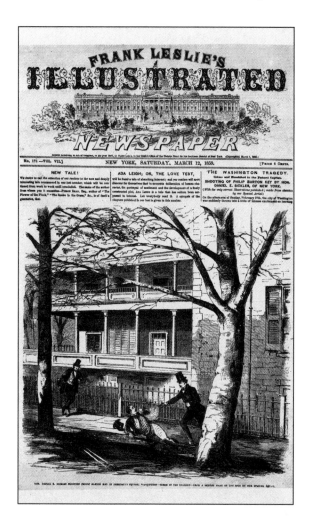

Meanwhile, upset because he had not heard from Teresa Sickles for several days, Key rented a front room in the Cosmos Club across Lafayette Park from the Sickles home. From there, peering through his opera glasses, he tried to spot a signal from Mrs. Sickles. Impatient and unaware that her husband knew all, Key twice passed in front of the Sickles' home on February 27, brazenly signaling Teresa Sickles with his white pocket handkerchief.

At home and pacing the floor, Dan Sickles abruptly stopped, looked out a front window, and cried out, "That villain is out there now making signs." One of the advisors consoling him, the Tammany politician Samuel F. Butterworth, agreed to go across the park to check whether Key had a room at the club. A few moments later, Butterworth recollected, Sickles stormed out of the house, whereupon he saw Key mingling with the Sunday afternoon strollers promenading around Lafayette Park.

Congressman Daniel Sickles' promising political future was doomed after he shot his friend Barton Key. (Courtesy, Library of Congress)

Pounding up to Key, Sickles raged, "Key, you scoundrel, you have dishonored my house—you must die!"

Sickles pulled out a pistol and fired. The two men grappled momentarily before Sickles pulled himself away and fired again. Hurling his opera glasses at his attacker, the wounded Key ducked behind a tree where Sickles' next bullet lodged. Ignoring Key's cries for mercy, Sickles shot again and Key staggered and fell into the gutter. Standing over Key, Sickles aimed at his head, but the gun misfired. Finally, a passerby became involved, pinning Sickles' arms and subduing him.

While Key was dying inside the club, Sickles took a carriage to the home of Attorney General Jeremiah S. Black and surrendered.

Mobilizing the Defense

Refusing bail, Sickles awaited trial in Washington's vermin-infested jail as the press, fed juicy tidbits by the defense, rehashed the details of the case daily until the editors, bored with facts, filled their columns with malicious gossip and preposterous speculation, including a rumor that Teresa Sickles was pregnant with Key's child.

Washington and the nation anticipated a hugely entertaining trial. A reinforced police contingent barely contained the mobs demanding admission to the old City Hall where the court convened on April 4, 1859 to select a jury.

Inside the cramped courtroom, eight renowned lawyers assembled to defend Sickles. Led by the suave James T. Brady, a New York criminal lawyer famed for his ability to manipulate witnesses, the team included Edwin M. Stanton, a Constitutional expert and an emotional orator of unsurpassed decibel power, and John Graham, a defense lawyer famed for his ability to draw tears from the most hard-hearted juror. The prosecution was badly out-classed. U.S. District Attorney Robert Ould, Key's meek and untalented former assistant, had little heart for his arduous and unpopular task. Ould inspired so little confidence in Key's relatives that they insisted he take on James Carlisle as assistant counsel, paying his fee out of their own pockets.

If Ould and Carlisle had any illusions about their prospects, these were quickly dispelled during the three days it took to select a jury. Of the first 75 potential jurors called, 72 openly sympathized with Sickles. Some 200 were excused for pro-Sickles bias before a jury of tradesmen and farmers could be impaneled.

Cold-Blooded Murder or Justifiable Homicide?

Ould opened with a sarcastic attack on Sickles' desecration of the Sabbath by a "deed of blood" against an "unarmed and defenseless victim." Noting that Sickles "bravely" and "fully prepared" himself with three guns, Ould portrayed the slaying as deliberate, premeditated, and merciless—a clear case of murder "no matter what may be the antecedent provocations in the case." Of course, it was precisely these "antecedent provocations," or Teresa Sickles' adultery, that everyone, including the jurors, were most interested in and exactly what the defense planned to spotlight in its case.

The defense's version of the slaying was distilled to its essence in John Graham's opening statement: "The injured husband and father rushes upon" the "confirmed and habitual" adulterer "in the moment of his guilt, and under the influence of a frenzy executes upon him a judgment which was as just as it was summary." Generously sprinkling his statement with Biblical quotations, Graham described Sickles' action as no less than the execution of "the will of Heaven."

Just in case the jury didn't accept Dan Sickles as one of the Lord's avenging angels, defense attorney Graham argued with equal fervor that the provocation had so unbalanced the defendant's mind that he could not be held accountable for his actions: "If he was in a state of white heat, was that too great a state of passion for a man to be in who saw before him the hardened, the unrelenting seducer of his wife?"

By the end of Graham's three-day statement, it was obvious Key would be the real defendant in the trial. Sickles' lawyers clearly planned to paint the victim as a lecher who richly deserved his fate at the hands of the accused. Despite this unveiling of the defense strategy, Ould did nothing to expose the hypocrisy of Sickles, who himself was vulnerable as a notorious philanderer. Instead, Ould contented himself with calling a series of eyewitnesses to the slaying who merely repeated the same tale in slightly different words.

The defense called numerous witnesses who attested to Sickles' mental anguish at the time of the slaying. Former Secretary of the Treasury Robert J. Walker declared Sickles was in "an agony of despair, the most terrible thing I ever saw in my life. . . . I feared if it continued he would become permanently insane." Sickles was so racked with sobs during Walker's testimony that he had to be ushered from the courtroom to compose himself. As he left, many in the audience wept.

When the defense attempted to introduce Teresa Sickles' confession into evidence, Ould leapt to his feet objecting that it was inadmissible as both hearsay and a privileged communication between husband and wife. Judge Crawford sustained him on the common law principle that putting such a document into the public record might do irreparable harm to the marriage. Judge Crawford's instruction to the jury to ignore the confession was so much wasted breath. The confession was reproduced in full on the front page of the April 23, 1859 issue of *Harper's Weekly*.

Time and again as the defense tried to introduce evidence of the adultery, prosecutor Ould furiously objected and Stanton responded with withering sarcasm. Trapped by the precedent of his own ruling in a similar case, Judge Crawford was forced in the end to permit the defense to present some evidence proving the adultery. However, the real damage was done in the uneven exchanges between Ould and Stanton, who skillfully maneuvered the prosecutor into seeming to conceal, if not excuse, infidelity and debauchery.

Assistant prosecutor Carlisle did his best to refute the defense claims of justifiable homicide and/or temporary insanity in his final statement before the jury. But, he couldn't compete with defense attorney Stanton's soaring and thunderous expression of indignation over the sanctity of the American family and the rights of the betrayed American husband. Wrapping himself and his client in the cloak of virtue, Stanton declaimed that a "higher law" than those enacted by human legislators "was written in the heart of man in the Garden of Eden" and that this law and even the laws of self-preservation set death as the penalty for seducing another man's wife. Inevitably, Stanton proclaimed, once a wife has "surrendered to the adulterer, she longs for the death of her husband, whose life is often sacrificed by the cup of the poisoner or the dagger or pistol of the assassin."

Before the case went to the jury April 26, Judge Crawford pointedly instructed the jurors that, in the eyes of earthly law, any delay between becoming aware of an adultery and the slaying of the adulterer by an enraged husband made the killing deliberate murder, or at the very least manslaughter.

When the jury returned in a little over an hour and, to no one's surprise, delivered a verdict of "Not Guilty," it was greeted by three cheers and sparked a spirited celebration among spectators and the defense team. The usually dour Stanton performed a jig on the spot. That evening 1,500 people joined Sickles in a victory party.

Sickles' defense team successfully portrayed their client as temporarily insane. The jury returned a verdict of "not guilty" in less than one hour. (Courtesy, Library of Congress)

Public Opinion Turns Against Sickles

Some segments of society and the legal profession were sickened by the verdict and even more by the way the defense had secured it. The mud thrown at the deceased's name, the public humiliation of Teresa Sickles, the manipulation of the press and, perhaps most of all, the cynical appeal to Old Testament morality in defense of a notorious Don Juan made the trial a farce and a travesty of justice in the eyes of many.

What little social standing and political aspirations Sickles retained were utterly destroyed when he and Teresa effected a public reconciliation only three months after the acquittal. The move flabbergasted his political cronies, scandalized society, and called down upon the couple the wrath and ridicule of the press.

Although Sickles partially redeemed his reputation in 1863 by losing a leg to a Confederate cannonball at the Battle of Gettysburg, public distrust was too deep for his political career to regain its early momentum. When Sickles died in 1914, he was remembered as the first accused murderer to escape punishment by pleading temporary insanity.

—Edward W. Knappman

Suggestions for Further Reading

Balderston, Thomas. "The Shattered Life of Teresa Sickles." *American History Illustrated* (September 1982): 41–45.

Cooney, Charles F. "The General's Badge of Honor." *American History Illustrated* (April 1985): 16–17.

Morris, Richard B. *Fair Trial.* New York: Alfred A. Knopf, 1952.

Pinchon, Edgcumb. *Dan Sickles, Hero of Gettysburg and "Yankee King of Spain."* Garden City, N.Y.: Doubleday & Co., 1945.

Swanburg, W.A. *Sickles the Incredible.* New York: Charles Scribner's Sons, 1956.

John Brown Trial: 1859

Defendant: John Brown   **Crime Charged:** Insurrection and murder
Chief Defense Lawyers: Lawson Botts, Thomas C. Green, Samuel Chilton, and Hiram Griswold   **Chief Prosecutor:** Andrew Hunter   **Judge:** Richard Parker   **Place:** Charles Town, Virginia
Dates of Trial: October 27–November 2, 1859   **Verdict:** Guilty
Sentence: Death by hanging

SIGNIFICANCE

Tried for leading a famous but unsuccessful raid on the federal arsenal in Harpers Ferry, Virginia, with the object of arming Southern slaves, John Brown's trial and execution by the Commonwealth of Virginia made him a martyr to Northerners determined to abolish slavery.

"A house divided cannot stand." These five words have been used by statesmen and historians alike to describe the condition of the United States in the years leading up to the Civil War. The tension between the Southern slave states and the Northern free states, which had never been resolved by the founding fathers, grew steadily worse after 1800 as the economic importance of cotton and slavery to the South increased. Despite repeated attempts at compromise, no satisfactory political formula could be found to reconcile North and South.

The schism widened as the newly settled territories of the West applied for admission to the Union in the early and middle decades of the 19th Century. Northerners wanted new states to be Free, and thus off limits to slavery. Southerners wanted new states to be Slave, and thus potential areas of expansion for the plantation economy of the South. Both sides wanted to have the votes of the representatives that a new state would send to Washington, particularly in the U.S. Senate, where every state, large or small, has two votes. As pro-slavery and anti-slavery forces from inside and outside the territories contested bitterly for control of these soon-to-be states, they turned to violence to resolve the issue.

Brown Raises Sword of Abolition

Sometimes great events thrust ordinary and obscure people into the limelight. Certainly this was true of John Brown, born in 1800 to Yankee farmers Owen Brown and Ruth Mills Brown. The Browns made a modest living from the family farm near Torrington, Connecticut, enough to permit their son to enter school for training as a minister. John Brown was a poor student, however, and shortly returned to the family farm after failing his classes. This failure was to be the first of many. John Brown went on to try and fail at earning a living as a farmer, surveyor, real estate investor, postmaster, teacher, racehorse breeder, tanner, and wool merchant.

Unsuccessful in business throughout his life, Brown was already past 50 when he took up the cause of abolition. Some wealthy east coast businessmen and philanthropists gave Brown the support and financing necessary to set up a farm in North Elba, New York, where runaway slaves would be taught how to become independent farmers. Brown soon lost interest in the project, however, and set out for the "front lines" of the abolitionist struggle. In the mid-1850s, Brown took his wife and some of his many sons to the little hamlet of Osawatomie, Kansas.

Kansas at the time was a battleground, known as "Bleeding Kansas" for the undeclared war raging then between the Free and Slave state forces. Brown lost no time in joining the fray. From Osawatomie, Brown led his sons and several followers in a raid on the neighboring pro-slavery settlement of Pottawatomie that left five dead. After this massacre, Brown and his followers became fugitives, engaging in hit-and-run raids against pro-slavery forces in Kansas and elsewhere.

Despite his unabashed use of violence, Brown continued to attract wealthy and influential backers. Of his backers, the most important were the "Secret Six": Gerrit Smith, heir to a large fortune who had financed temperance and prison reform movements before turning to abolition; Franklin B. Sanborn, a young Massachusetts patrician with a Harvard education; George Luther Stearns, who financed Brown's activities with the profits from Stearns' thriving business; Samuel Gridley Howe, a prominent abolitionist who preached violence in the cause of ending slavery and looked to Brown to practice it; Thomas Wentworth Higginson, a liberal minister; and Ralph Waldo Emerson, the famous poet. In 1859, Brown obtained support from these men for a proposed raid on the federal arsenal at Harpers Ferry, Virginia. The plan was to seize the arsenal, arm the hordes of slaves who would supposedly flock to Brown's cause, and march on Southern state capitals to end slavery forever.

On October 16, 1859, Brown and 21 raiders succeeded in seizing the Harpers Ferry arsenal by surprise. Instead of attracting black followers, however, the raid only succeeded in bringing out the armed and angry local white residents, who surrounded the arsenal until federal troops arrived. Ironically, the soldiers sent to protect federal property were commanded by Colonel Robert E. Lee, the famous general of the Confederacy during the Civil War. After a brief siege, the arsenal was stormed. Brown, together with his few surviving followers, was captured and taken under guard to nearby Charles Town, Virginia. (Harpers Ferry and Charles Town later became part of West Virginia.)

Virginia Tries Brown for Treason

When news of Harpers Ferry reached Richmond, Henry A. Wise, the politically ambitious governor, had an important decision to make. Under the division of power that existed between state and federal governments before the Civil War, it was Wise's prerogative to decide whether Brown would be tried in a Virginia court for violating the laws of the commonwealth or turned over to the national authorities for prosecution in the federal courts. The Virginia court at Charles Town, where a grand jury was already in session, would be quicker. A federal court, however, would not be as open to charges of Southern bias. Whether out of fear that a mob would lynch Brown if he were not tried quickly, or out of a desire to score political prestige for himself and Virginia, Governor Wise decided to proceed with a state trial.

It fell to Andrew Hunter, the district attorney for Charles Town, to be the prosecutor. Hunter shared Governor Wise's desire to prosecute Brown quickly. To defend Brown, a magistrate appointed Lawson Botts, a local Virginia attorney, and Thomas C. Green, an attorney who was also the mayor of Charles Town. From his prison cell, Brown wrote his abolitionist allies for outside legal counsel.

Judge Richard Parker, justice of the circuit court for the town of Charles Town, was also an advocate of speedy justice. Judge Parker's grand jury returned an indictment against Brown within 24 hours. Further, Judge Parker denied Botts' and Green's request that the trial be delayed until Brown could recover from injuries sustained when the troops stormed the arsenal. As a result, when Brown's trial began on October 27, he attended the proceedings lying in a cot, nursing his wounds.

Brown's Lawyers Search for a Defense

Brown's attorneys had to put together a defense in the face of opposition not only from Judge Parker and prosecutor Hunter, but from Brown himself. When the trial began, Botts made a critical motion to Judge Parker. Botts asked him to declare Brown insane, using a telegram from a certain A.H. Lewis of Akron, Ohio, to support this plea. Lewis, who apparently had known Brown from when the family lived in Akron, wrote, "Insanity is hereditary in that family. . . . These facts can be conclusively proven by witnesses residing here, who will doubtless attend the trial if desired."

A successful insanity defense could have saved Brown from the gallows, leaving him to live out his life in an asylum. Brown himself, however, closed the door on the issue. Protesting from his cot, he said angrily: "I look upon this as a miserable pretext of those who ought to take a different course in regard to me, if they took any at all. . . . I am perfectly unconscious of insanity, and I reject, so far as I am capable, any attempt to interfere on my behalf on that score." This outburst effectively destroyed the chances for any insanity defense, despite some later attempts to revive the issue.

Despite their Virginia roots and the weight of Southern opinion, Botts and Green had gone out on a limb for Brown by asserting "hereditary insanity" and were soon out of the case. They were replaced by Hiram Griswold, a lawyer from Cleveland, Ohio, and Samuel Chilton, a lawyer from Washington, D.C. Judge Parker would not permit the momentum of Hunter's prosecution to slacken for one instant, however, and refused to give Griswold and Chilton any extra time to organize their defense. Hunter had more than enough witnesses ready to testify.

To support the charge of murder, witnesses described the killings by Brown and his men during the Harpers Ferry raid. The charge of insurrection was supported by the testimony of witnesses who had overheard Brown talk of arming runaway slaves to fight their masters.

Despite the disadvantages he labored under, Griswold put together an aggressive closing statement. He attacked the charge of insurrection, claiming that as a non-Virginian Brown didn't owe the commonwealth any duty of loyalty. This last line of defense fared no better than the insanity argument. After less than an hour of deliberation, the jury returned a guilty verdict. Judge Parker then held the trial in recess for a few days while one of Brown's fellow raiders was tried in the same courtroom. On November 2, the trial was reconvened and Judge Parker sentenced Brown to hang on December 2, 1859.

John Brown's photograph was taken shortly before his death. (Courtesy, Library of Congress)

Brown's Martyrdom Secures Victory in Death

When he stood before Judge Parker on November 2, 1859, to receive his sentence, John Brown must have known he faced certain execution. Affirmation of the sentence by the Virginia Court of Appeals would be a formality. Brown used the occasion, however, to make a stirring statement that would galvanize Northern public opinion against slavery and the South:

This court acknowledges, as I suppose, the validity of the law of God. I see a book kissed here which I suppose to be the Bible, or at least the New Testament. That teaches me that all things whatsoever I would that men should do to me, I should do even so to them. It teaches me, further, to "remember them that are in bonds, as bound with them." I endeavored to act up to that instruction. I say, I am yet too young to understand that God is any respecter of persons. I believe that to have interfered as I have done—in behalf of His despised poor, was not wrong, but right. Now, if it is deemed necessary that I should forfeit my life for the furtherance of the ends of justice, and mingle my blood further with the blood of my children and with the blood of millions in this slave country whose rights are disregarded by wicked, cruel, and unjust enactments, I submit, so let it be done!

In the month following Brown's sentencing, Governor Wise received thousands of letters and petitions pleading for mercy. Some came from astute Southerners, who realized that Brown's execution would rally anti-slavery forces. Nevertheless, Wise let the sentence stand. On December 2, 1859, before he went to the gallows, Brown delivered his final message to North and South alike, one that predicted and sealed in the minds of many Americans the inevitability of the Civil War:

> I John Brown am now quite certain that the crimes of this guilty land will never be purged away but with Blood. I had, as I now think, vainly flattered myself that without very much bloodshed it might be done.

—Stephen G. Chrisrianson

Suggestions for Further Reading

Ansley, Delight. *The Sword and the Spirit: A Life of John Brown.* New York: Thomas Y. Crowell Co., 1955.

Emerson, Ralph Waldo. "John Brown," *Emerson's Complete Works.* Boston and New York: Houghton Mifflin, 1878 and 1883.

"The Ghost at Harpers Ferry." *American Heritage* (November 1988): 30–31.

McGlone, Robert E. "Rescripting a Troubled Past: John Brown's Family and the Harpers Ferry Conspiracy." *Journal of American History* (March 1989): 1179–1200.

Oates, Stephen B. *To Purge This Land With Blood: A Biography of John Brown.* New York: Harper & Row, 1970.

Ruchames, Louis. *John Brown: The Making of a Revolutionary.* New York: Grossett & Dunlap, 1969.

Sanborn, Franklin B. *The Life and Letters of John Brown.* Boston: Roberts Brothers, 1885.

Packard v. Packard: 1864

Plaintiff: Reverend Theophilus Packard, Jr.   **Defendant:** Elizabeth Parsons Ware Packard   **Plaintiff Claim:** That his wife was insane and that he was therefore entitled to confine her at home   **Chief Defense Lawyers:** Stephen Moore and John W. Orr   **Chief Lawyer for Plaintiff:** No record
Judge: Charles R. Starr   **Place:** Kankakee, Illinois
Dates of Trial: January 13–18, 1864   **Verdict:** Elizabeth Packard declared sane and restored to liberty

SIGNIFICANCE

In 1864, Illinois law permitted a man to institutionalize his wife "without the evidence of insanity required in other cases." After her own court-ordered release, Elizabeth Packard campaigned to change the law in Illinois and similar laws in 30 other states; during her lifetime, four states revised their laws.

Near the end of 1863, the Reverend Theophilus Packard locked his wife Elizabeth in the nursery and nailed the windows shut. Earlier, he had committed her for three years to the Illinois State Hospital for the Insane, based only on his own observation that she was "slightly insane," a condition he attributed to "excessive application of body and mind." In many states in the 19th century, it was a husband's legal prerogative to so institutionalize his wife, and Elizabeth Packard had no recourse against that earlier confinement. Now, however, she had a valid argument: the law did not permit a husband to "put away" a wife *in her own home.* Elizabeth Packard dropped a letter of complaint out her window, which was delivered to her friend, Sarah Haslett. Haslett immediately appealed to Judge Charles R. Starr.

Judge Starr issued a writ of *habeas corpus* and ordered Reverend Packard to bring Elizabeth to his chambers on January 12, 1864. Packard produced Elizabeth and a written statement explaining that she "was discharged from [the Illinois State] Asylum without being cured and is incurably insane . . . [and] the undersigned has allowed her all the liberty compatible with her welfare and safety." Unimpressed, the judge scheduled a jury trial to determine whether Elizabeth Packard was insane.

Reverend Packard Presents His Case

Reverend Packard was a Calvinist minister with an austere interpretation of his faith, and he claimed his wife's religious views had convinced him of her insanity. Dr. Christopher Knott, who had spoken with Elizabeth prior to her commitment to Illinois State, testified, "Her mind appeared to be excited on the subject of religion. On all other subjects she was perfectly rational. . . . I take her to be a lady of fine mental abilities. . . . I would say she was insane," he concluded, "the same as I would say Henry Ward Beecher, Spurgeon, Horace Greeley, and like persons are insane."

Dr. J.W. Brown had been falsely introduced to Elizabeth as a sewing machine salesman several weeks before, and had surreptitiously interviewed her during what she thought was a sales pitch. She had described her husband, Dr. Brown testified, as wishing that "the despotism of man may prevail over the wife," but it was during their discussion of religion that he "had not the slightest difficulty in concluding that she was hopelessly insane." Elizabeth Packard, Dr. Brown said, had claimed to be "the personification of the Ghost." Moreover, "She found fault that Mr. Packard would not discuss their points of difference in religion in an open manly way instead of going around and denouncing her as crazy to her friends and to the church. She had a great aversion to being called insane. Before I got through the conversation she exhibited a great dislike to me."

Abijah Dole, the husband of Reverend Packard's sister Sybil, testified that he knew Elizabeth had become disoriented because she told him that she no longer wished to live with Reverend Packard. Dole also testified that Elizabeth had requested a letter terminating her membership in her husband's church. "Was that an indication of insanity?" Elizabeth's lawyer, John W. Orr, inquired. Dole replied: "She would not leave the church unless she was insane."

Sybil Dole also testified against Elizabeth, stating, "She accused Dr. Packard very strangely of depriving her of her rights of conscience—that he would not allow her to think for herself on religious questions because they differed on these topics."

Sarah Rumsey, a young woman who had briefly served as a mother's helper for the Packards, also gave evidence of what she considered Elizabeth Packard's insanity: "She wanted the flower beds in the front yard cleaned out and tried to get Mr. Packard to do it. He would not. She put on an old dress and went to work and cleaned out the weeds . . . until she was almost melted down with the heat. . . . Then she went to her room and took a bath and dressed herself and lay down exhausted. . . . She was angry and excited and showed ill-will."

Finally, a certificate concerning Elizabeth's discharge from the Illinois State Hospital, issued by the superintendent, Dr. Andrew McFarland, was read. It said that Elizabeth Packard was discharged because she could not be cured. Reverend Packard's lawyers rested their case.

Elizabeth Packard Defends Her Sanity

Elizabeth Packard's lawyers, Stephen Moore and J.W. Orr, asked her to read aloud an essay which she had written for a Bible class. It contained statements such as ". . . the Christian farmer has no more reason to expect success in his farming operations than the impenitent sinner." Then Mr. and Mrs. Blessing, Methodist neighbors of the Packards, testified in turn as to Mrs. Packard's sanity.

Sarah Haslett described Elizabeth's housekeeping efforts after her release from the Illinois State Hospital: "I called to see her a few days after she returned from Jacksonville. She was in the yard cleaning feather beds. . . . The house needed cleaning. And when I called again it looked as if the mistress of the house was *home*." Haslett then testified about her friend's in-home confinement and described the sealed window, "fastened with nails on the inside and two screws passing through the lower part of the upper sash and the upper part of the lower sash from the outside."

The last person to testify on Mrs. Packard's behalf was a Dr. Duncanson, who was both a physician and theologian. He testified that he had conversed with Mrs. Packard for three hours, and he disagreed with Dr. Brown's understanding of Mrs. Packard's thoughts concerning her relationship to the Holy Ghost. Mrs. Packard later wrote, "A spiritual woman is a living temple of the Holy Ghost." At her trial, Dr. Duncanson located this belief in a neglected 16th century doctrine expounded by Socinus of Italy. "I did not agree with . . . her on many things," Duncanson testified, "but I do not call people insane because they differ with me. . . . You might with as much propriety call Christ insane . . . or Luther, or Robert Fuller. . . . I pronounce her a sane woman and wish we had a nation of such women."

Verdict Takes Seven Minutes

On January 18, the jury reached its verdict in seven minutes. "We, the undersigned, Jurors in the case of Mrs. Elizabeth P.W. Packard, alleged to be insane, having heard the evidence . . . are satisfied that [she] is sane." Judge Starr ordered "that Mrs. Elizabeth P.W. Packard be relieved of all restraints incompatible with her condition as a sane woman." Neither the judge nor jury addressed the question of whether, had Mrs. Packard been found insane, Mr. Packard had the right to confine her at home rather than in an asylum.

The Packards remained married but estranged for the remainder of their lives. Elizabeth Packard wrote, lectured, and lobbied on behalf of the rights of women and those alleged to be insane; she was instrumental in changing the commitment laws in four states and in passing a married women's property law in Illinois.

—Kathryn Cullen-DuPont

Suggestions for Further Reading

Burnham, John Chynoweth. "Elizabeth Parsons Ware Packard," in *Notable American Women, 1906–1950*. Edward T. James, Janet Wilson James and Paul S. Boyer, eds. Cambridge, Mass.: Belknap Press of Harvard University Press, 1971.

Packard, Elizabeth Parsons Ware. *Great Disclosure of Spiritual Wickedness!! in high places. With an appeal to the government to protect the inalienable rights of married women*. Written under the inspection of Dr. M'Farland, Superintendent of Insane Asylum, Jacksonville, Illinois, 4th ed. Boston: Published by the authoress, 1865.

——. *Marital Power Exemplified in Mrs. Packard's Trial and self-defense from the charge of insanity, or, Three years imprisonment for religious belief, by the arbitrary will of a husband, with an appeal to the government to so change the laws as to afford legal protection to married women*. Hartford, Conn.: Case, Lockwood & Co., 1866.

——. *The Mystic Key; or, The Asylum Secret Unlocked*. Hartford, Conn.: Case, Lockwood & Brainard Co., 1886.

——. *The prisoners' hidden life, or Insane asylums unveiled: as demonstrated by the Report of the Investigating Committee of the Legislature of Illinois, together with Mrs. Packard's coadjustors' testimony*. Chicago: The Author; A. B. Case, Printer, 1868.

Sapinsley, Barbara. *The Private War of Mrs. Packard*. New York: Paragon House, 1991.

Dr. Samuel Mudd Trial: 1865

Defendant: Dr. Samuel A. Mudd   **Crimes Charged:** Treason and conspiracy
Chief Defense Lawyer: General Thomas Ewing   **Chief Prosecutor:** Judge
Advocate Joseph Holt   **Judges:** Military commission officers Lieutenant
Colonel David Clendenim, Brevet Brigadier General James Ekin, Brigadier
General Robert Foster, Brigadier General T. M. Harris, Major General David
Hunter, Brigadier General Alvin Howe, Brevet Major General August Kautz,
Brevet Colonel C. H. Tompkins, and Major General Lew Wallace
Place: Washington, D.C.   **Dates of Trial:** May 9–June 30, 1865
Verdict: Guilty   **Sentence:** Life imprisonment, pardoned in 1868

SIGNIFICANCE

During his flight after assassinating President Abraham Lincoln, John Wilkes
Booth visited Dr. Samuel A. Mudd for treatment of his broken ankle. Although
there was little evidence linking him to Booth's crime, Mudd was convicted by a
military commission interested more in vengeance than justice. The military's
assertion of its authority over that of civilian courts represented the post-Civil War
Union's thirst for retribution at the expense of justice.

By spring 1865, the Civil War was all but over. General Robert E. Lee
surrendered his army at Appomattox, Virginia, effectively ending the
Confederacy. Although the North resounded with triumph, Southerners and
their sympathizers were bitter and resentful. Particularly bitter was a minor actor
from Maryland named John Wilkes Booth.

After Appomattox, Booth, long a Confederate sympathizer, vowed to kill
President Abraham Lincoln. On April 14, 1865, Booth had his chance. Lincoln
went to see the play *Our American Cousin* at Ford's Theater in Washington D.C.
The lone security guard assigned to protect Lincoln had gone to a nearby bar for
a drink. Unimpeded, Booth sneaked into the theater. From behind the presidential party's box seats, Booth pulled out his pistol and shot Lincoln in the
head. Booth leapt from the box to the stage, 12 feet below, breaking his left
ankle in the process. After shouting "Sic Semper Tyrannis!" ("thus shall it ever
be for tyrants," the state motto of Virginia), Booth ran from the theater and fled
Washington on horseback.

Troops Search for Booth and His Co-Conspirators

Lincoln died within hours. On the same night, two of Booth's accomplices, David Herold and Lewis Payne, tried unsuccessfully to assassinate Secretary of State William H. Seward. Payne was arrested at the boarding house where he lived, as was Mary Surratt, the owner of the house. Herold was able to join Booth across the Anacostia River in Maryland and the two rode south. Meanwhile, the authorities continued to round up others suspected of assisting Booth.

As Booth rode through southern Maryland, his ankle worsened. On April 15, shortly before dawn, he stopped at Dr. Samuel Mudd's house outside Bryantown and asked for help. Mudd did what he could for Booth's ankle, provided Booth with crutches, and collected $25 as his fee. Booth then continued to ride south, eventually crossing into Virginia and eluding the authorities. On April 26, federal troops caught up with Booth outside the town of Port Royal, Virginia. A soldier shot Booth, who had barricaded himself in a barn.

Secretary of War Edwin M. Stanton had anyone suspected of conspiring with Booth arrested. In addition to Herold, Payne, and Surratt, the authorities arrested Samuel Arnold, George A. Atzerodt, Michael O'Loughlin, Edward Spangler, and the unfortunate Dr. Mudd. Each of the first four men had had some degree of contact with Booth. Although there was no proof that Mudd was involved in the conspiracy, he had met Booth at least once before the assassination.

Mudd and Conspirators Tried

Nine officers—Major General David Hunter, Major General Lew Wallace, Brevet Major General August Kautz, Brigadier General Alvin Howe, Brigadier General T. M. Harris, Brigadier General Robert Foster, Brevet Brigadier General James Ekin, Brevet Colonel C.H. Tompkins, and Lieutenant Colonel David Clendenim—comprised the military commission formed to try Dr. Mudd and the others. The trial began May 9, 1865, with Judge Advocate Joseph Holt as prosecutor and General Thomas Ewing as Mudd's defense counsel.

From May 9 until June 30, the military commission listened to the evidence Holt presented. Although Mudd was entitled to a presumption of innocence until proven guilty, the trial was conducted under military jurisdiction, making the rules of the game favor the prosecution. Further, the public was clamoring for convictions. Nevertheless, Ewing showed with remorseless logic how the prosecution had failed to prove that Mudd was guilty of treason in tending to Booth's broken ankle:

> I will show, first, that Dr. Mudd is not, and cannot possibly be, guilty of any offense known to the law.
>
> One. Not of treason. The overt act attempted to be alleged is the murder of the President. The proof is conclusive, that at the time the tragedy was enacted Dr. Mudd was at his residence in the country, thirty miles from the place of the crime. Those who committed it are shown to have acted for themselves, not as the instruments of Dr. Mudd. He, therefore, cannot be

charged, according to law, and upon the evidence, with the commission of this overt act. There are not two witnesses to prove that he did commit it, but abundant evidence to show negatively that he did not.

Ewing went on to show that, since the prosecution had not proven that Mudd was a member of Booth's conspiracy, Mudd could not be convicted of being an "accessory after the fact" in tending to Booth's ankle. Under the law, Mudd could only be convicted of being an accessory after the fact if the prosecution proved that he knew Booth was trying to escape the authorities because of Lincoln's murder:

> If a man receives, harbors, or otherwise assists to elude justice, one whom he knows to be guilty of felony, he becomes thereby an accessory after the fact in the felony. . . . Now, let us apply the facts to the law, and see whether Dr. Mudd falls within the rule. On the morning after the assassination, about daybreak, Booth arrived at his house. He did not find the Doctor on watch for him, as a guilty accomplice, expecting his arrival, would have been, but he and all his household were in profound sleep. . . . The Doctor rose from his bed, assisted Booth into the house, laid him upon a sofa, took him up stairs to a bed, set the fractured bone. . . . But he did not know, and had no reason to suspect, that his patient was a fugitive murderer.

Despite Ewing's eloquence, the military commission focused on any circumstance that tended to implicate Mudd, including the fact that Mudd had met Booth on at least one occasion prior to Lincoln's assassination. On June 30, 1865, the commission pronounced Mudd guilty and sentenced him to life imprisonment. Of the other defendants, Atzerodt, Herold, Payne, and Surratt were sentenced to death by hanging. Arnold and O'Loughlin were also given life sentences, and Spangler was sentenced to imprisonment for six years.

Was Mudd Really Guilty?

The government first sent Mudd to serve his sentence in an Albany, New York penitentiary. Later the government sent Mudd to a prison on Dry Tortugas Island in Florida. Poor prison conditions, low 19th-century standards of hygiene, and the tropical climate led to an epidemic of disease on the island. Mudd used his professional training to save the lives of many fellow inmates. President Andrew Johnson pardoned Mudd for his humanitarian work in 1868.

Although Mudd was a free man after 1868, he was tainted by the military commission's guilty verdict until he died in 1883. While there were certainly some guilty individuals among the convicted conspirators, Mudd's involvement seemed so innocent that many historians as well as Mudd's descendants have challenged the commission's guilty verdict as being politically motivated. These believers in Mudd's innocence kept his cause alive. In the late 1970s, President Jimmy Carter wrote Mudd's descendants to express his belief in Mudd's innocence and effectively extended Johnson's pardon to cover any implication that Mudd had been involved in Booth's conspiracy.

—Stephen G. Christianson

Suggestions for Further Reading

Carter, Samuel. *The Riddle of Dr. Mudd.* New York: Putnam, 1974.

Herold, David E. *The Assassination of President Lincoln and the Trial of the Conspirators.* Westport, Conn.: Greenwood Press, 1974.

———. *The Conspiracy Trial for the Murder of the President.* New York: Arno Press, 1972.

Mudd, Samuel Alexander. *The Life of Dr. Samuel A. Mudd.* Linden, Tenn.: Continental Book Co., 1975.

Weckesser, Elden C. *His Name Was Mudd.* Jefferson, N.C.: McFarland & Co., 1991.

Henry Wirz Trial: 1865

Defendant: Captain Henry Wirz   **Crimes Charged:** 13 counts of murder, assault, battery, torture and other offenses against Union prisoners
Chief Defense Lawyer: Louis Schade   **Chief Prosecutor:** Judge Advocate Colonel N. P. Chipman   **Judges:** Military Commission officers Brevet Colonel T. Allcock, Brevet Brigadier General John F. Ballior, Brigadier General A. S. Bragg, Brigadier General Francis Fessenden, Brevet Major General G. Mott, Lieutenant Colonel J. H. Stibbs, Brevet Major General L. Thomas, and Major General Lew Wallace   **Place:** Washington, D.C.
Dates of Trial: August 23–October 18, 1865   **Verdict:** Guilty
Sentence: Death by hanging

SIGNIFICANCE

After the Civil War, the Union tried Confederate Captain Henry Wirz for war crimes resulting from his command of a prison camp for Union captives at Andersonville, Georgia. Henry Wirz's trial was the first war-crimes trial in U.S. history and the only trial for war crimes of a Confederate after the Civil War.

Toward the end of the Civil War, General William T. Sherman launched his famous March to the Sea through Georgia. Sherman's troops stripped the land of food and destroyed every plantation, railroad track, and other things of military importance in their path. As they cut a swath 60 miles wide through the heart of the crumbling Confederacy, Sherman's troops encountered some men, nearly starved to death and in tattered clothing, who claimed that they had escaped from a Confederate prison camp at Andersonville, Georgia, where thousands more like them were still captive. When Union troops took Andersonville, they found these reports were true.

Like the Allied troops in 1945 advancing deep into the Nazi heartland and coming upon Auschwitz or Treblinka decades later, Union soldiers saw how in modern warfare a civilized country could treat its enemies with barbarism. In the middle of some of the South's richest farm land, Union prisoners starved to death. Captain Henry Wirz kept them under heavy guard on a small patch of land, through which a little creek flowed and provided the only source of drinking water and sanitation. The creek was soon fouled with excrement, causing disease to spread like wildfire among the prisoners penned up in

Andersonville. Wirz did nothing to ensure that adequate food, clothing, or medical care reached the men under his care.

In his Andersonville diary, John Ransom wrote that in particularly bad months, one-third to one-half of the prisoners in Andersonville died from the terrible conditions there. Although these tragedies were taking place every month, Andersonville's population continued to swell due to fresh battles and Confederate captures of Union troops. For example, in August 1864, there were nearly 40,000 men in Andersonville, which was designed to hold only 10,000.

After Union troops arrived, the liberated prisoners spoke of atrocities Wirz personally committed. According to the prisoners, Wirz had on several occasions shot, tortured, and otherwise mistreated Union prisoners for no reason.

Captain Wirz, reclining, the only person tried by the Union for war crimes following the Civil War. (Courtesy, Library of Congress)

Wirz Tried for War Crimes

General James H. Wilson arrested Wirz and kept him imprisoned at Wilson's headquarters. In May 1865 Wirz was taken under heavy guard to Washington, D.C., for trial. The escort was not so much to prevent Wirz from escaping, but to protect him from being killed en route by his ex-prisoners. To try Wirz, the military authorities in Washington formed a commission, comprised of Major General Lew Wallace, Brevet Major General L. Thomas, Brevet Major General G. Mott, Brigadier General Francis Fessenden, Brigadier General A. S. Bragg, Brevet Brigadier General John F. Ballior, Brevet Colonel T. Allcock, and Lieutenant Colonel J. H. Stibbs. The prosecutor was Judge Advocate Colonel N. P. Chipman.

Wirz's trial began August 23, 1865. His chief defense lawyer was Louis Schade. The prosecution opened the case with witnesses on Wirz's authority as commandant of Andersonville. Ex-Confederate officers' testimony quickly established that Confederate authorities had given Wirz supreme authority over the prison camp. The prosecution could now make its case that, having had the power to alleviate conditions at the prison camp, by not doing so Wirz was responsible for the prisoners' suffering.

Union Prisoners' Testimony Destroys Wirz

First, witnesses testified that Wirz had established a "Dead Line," or boundary about the prison camp, which prisoners could not cross without being shot by guards or attacked by vicious dogs. Then, the prosecution introduced as witnesses several Confederate doctors stationed in Andersonville, such as Chief Surgeon Dr. R. Randolph Stevenson. Stevenson testified to the abysmal medical and psychological condition of the prisoners:

> The mental condition connected with long confinement, with the most miserable surroundings, and with no hope for the future, also depressed all the nervous and vital actions, and was especially active in destroying the appetite. The effects of mental depression, and of defective nutrition, were manifested not only in the slow, feeble motions of the wasted, skeleton-like forms, but also in such lethargy, listlessness, and torpor of the mental faculties as rendered these unfortunate men oblivious and indifferent to their afflicted condition.

One of the prosecution's charges was that Wirz and General John H. Winder, one-time commander of Confederate prisons, had conspired to kill as many Union prisoners as possible. Perhaps the prosecution suspected that Wirz and Winder hoped to weaken Union armies by reducing the number of men returned in any prisoner exchange between the Union and the Confederacy. There was testimony that Wirz had boasted he was killing more Union soldiers than the Confederate armies in the field. At any rate, the prosecution went on to argue that not only had Wirz been responsible for the prisoners' suffering in general, but that he had inflicted suffering and death on individual prisoners. Of the Union soldiers' testimony, the following was typical:

> On the 8th of July I arrived at Andersonville, with 300 or 400 other prisoners, most of them sick and wounded. We were brought up to Captain Wirz' headquarters; were drawn up in line, four ranks deep, and kept there for a considerable length of time, without any business being transacted. The guards had orders to let none of us go to the water. One of the prisoners was attacked with epilepsy or fits; he fell down; some of his friends or neighbors standing near him ran down to the creek after water.

Question by the prosecution: By permission of the guard?

I don't know; I suppose so; because the guard was tied up by the thumbs for permitting them to do so. First I heard a shot fired, without seeing who fired it. After hearing that shot fired, I looked down to the left, and I saw Captain Wirz fire two more shots, wounding two men. . . .

He asked the lieutenant of the guard, "Where is the guard who allowed this [Union prisoner] to fall out of ranks?" The guard was pointed out, and Captain Wirz ordered him to be tied up by the thumbs for two hours. After this, Captain Wirz pointed out [the Union prisoner], and said, "That is the way I get rid of you damned sons of bitches."

More than 100 witnesses testified at Wirz's trial, and the trial record ran into thousands of pages. In addition to testimony such as the above, Union soldiers related how any prisoner who went near or beyond the Dead Line was either immediately shot or cruelly ripped apart by guard dogs. Given the prosecution's parade of witnesses, defense counsel Louis Schade never really had a chance, despite his various pleas that Wirz should be tried before a civil court and that Wirz was immune from prosecution under the terms of surrender given to former Confederates.

On October 18, 1865, the prosecution ended its case. The military commission declared Henry Wirz guilty and sentenced him to death by hanging. President Andrew Johnson approved Wirz's sentence, and on November 10, 1865, Wirz went to the scaffold. Wirz was the only person tried by the Union for war crimes after the Civil War, and he has the dubious distinction of being the first person in history to be judged a war criminal.

—Stephen G. Christianson

Suggestions for Further Reading

The Andersonville Diary & Memoirs of Charles Hopkins. Kearny, N.J.: Belle Grove Publishing Co., 1988.

Foote, Shelby. *The Civil War: A Narrative.* New York: Vintage Books, 1986.

Hopkins, Charles. "Hell and the Survivor." *American Heritage* (October–November 1982): 78–93 (a portion of the book listed below).

McElroy, John. *This Was Andersonville.* New York: McDowell, Obolensky, 1957.

Ransom, John L. *John Ransom's Andersonville Diary.* Middlebury, Vt.: Paul S. Eriksson, 1986.

Rutherford, Mildred Lewis. *Andersonville Prison and Captain Henry Wirz' Trial.* Plains, Ga.: United Daughters of the Confederacy, 1983.

Stearns, Amos Edward. *The Civil War Diary of Amos E. Stearns, a Prisoner at Andersonville.* London: Associated University Presses, 1981.

President Andrew Johnson Impeachment Trial: 1868

Defendant: President Andrew Johnson   **Crime Charged:** "High Crimes and Misdemeanors" within the meaning of Article II, Section 4 of the Constitution   **Chief Defense Lawyers:** William Maxwell Evarts and Benjamin R. Curtis   **Chief Prosecutors:** Seven "trial managers" from the House of Representatives   **Judges:** U.S. Senate, with Chief Justice Salmon P. Chase presiding   **Place:** Washington, D.C.   **Dates of Trial:** March 30–May 26, 1868   **Verdict:** No impeachment

SIGNIFICANCE

The U.S. Congress for the first time exercised its Constitutional prerogative to try a president of the United States for impeachable offenses. Johnson survived the Senate impeachment trial by one vote, but his hopes for re-election in 1868 were destroyed. Johnson was succeeded by the corrupt administration of Ulysses S. Grant.

After five years of bloody Civil War, the Union emerged victorious. President Abraham Lincoln and his Republican administration were vindicated. On April 14, 1865, to the shock and horror of the Union, while attending a performance at Ford's Theatre, Lincoln was assassinated by John Wilkes Booth. The next day, Vice President Andrew Johnson was sworn in as president of the United States. Ironically, the man who would lead the United States into the Reconstruction era was a Southerner.

Born in North Carolina and raised in Tennessee, Johnson entered into politics and had enjoyed a successful career with the Democratic Party. He was chosen to represent Tennessee in the U.S. Senate. When the Southern states left the Union to form the Confederacy, Johnson was widely admired in the North for being the only Southern senator to remain loyal while his state seceded.

Johnson's loyalty and newfound fame caught the attention of President Abraham Lincoln. First, Lincoln appointed Johnson the Union's military governor of Tennessee. When Lincoln was up for re-election in 1864 against General George McClellan, Lincoln chose Johnson as his running mate. As a Southern

Democrat and loyalist, Johnson would attract moderate voters in addition to the abolitionist and radical Republican forces already in Lincoln's camp.

Lincoln won the election of 1864. Although his assassination makes it impossible to know for certain how his Reconstruction administration would have proceeded, he had chosen Johnson as vice-president and had used the phrase "with malice toward none, with charity for all" in advocating leniency toward the South. Thus, many historians have concluded that Lincoln would have pursued a moderate and conciliatory approach toward the reunited Confederate states.

Johnson Becomes an Unpopular President

Johnson lacked the stature that Lincoln had gained as the president who held the Union together. Although Lincoln would probably have approved of Johnson's moderate policies toward Reconstruction, Johnson did not have the prestige necessary to convince Congress or the American people that he was suited to the job. The electorate of the victorious Union, having undergone the bloodiest war in American history, sent mostly Republicans to Congress because the Republicans had been Lincoln's party. Within Congress, the Republican majority became Johnson's enemy.

The political antagonism between Johnson and Congress was further aggravated by Johnson's opposition to the Fourteenth Amendment, which expanded Constitutional protection of basic civil liberties, and such Congressional initiatives as establishment of the Freedmen's Bureau to assist freed slaves. Johnson went on a nationwide speaking tour, known as the "Swing Around the Circle," in which he made a series of abrasive and blunt speeches full of accusations against his political enemies in Congress. The Swing Around the Circle only served to erode further Johnson's public support.

Sensing vulnerability, Congress moved against Johnson by passing the Tenure of Office Act, which limited Johnson's ability to remove cabinet officials without Congressional approval. Predictably, Johnson fought the act, particularly because he wished to rid his cabinet of Secretary of War Edwin M. Stanton, who was now allied with the opposition. When Johnson attempted to fire Stanton, Congress retaliated. Thaddeus Stevens, a Representative from Pennsylvania who spoke for radical Republicans in favor of harsh treatment for the South as "conquered territory," led the House of Representatives to a 126–47 vote in favor of a short but historic resolution: "Resolved, that Andrew Johnson, President of the United States, be impeached of high crimes and misdemeanors in office."

Senate Tries President Johnson

Although the House of Representatives had adopted the resolution to impeach Johnson, Article I, Section 3 of the Constitution mandates that the Senate must conduct the impeachment trial. This provision further states that at least two-thirds of the Senate must vote in favor of impeachment and, because a presidential impeachment was at issue, that Chief Justice Salmon P. Chase of the Supreme Court must preside.

Therefore, the House appointed seven congressmen as "trial managers," or prosecutors for the impeachment. These congressmen were John A. Bingham, George Boutwell, Benjamin F. Butler, John A. Logan, Thaddeus Stevens, Thomas Williams and James F. Wilson. Although Stevens had been the House leader, illness forced him to relinquish most of his authority to Benjamin Butler.

The Senate impeachment trial of President Andrew Johnson. (Courtesy, Library of Congress)

Butler was a colorful character. A general in the Union army during the Civil War, he was the military governor of New Orleans after the city was taken. During his governorship, he tolerated no pro-Southern dissent. One day when Butler perceived that he had been slighted by a group of New Orleans women, he issued an order that any woman showing "contempt for a United States officer" should be considered a "woman of the town plying her avocation" and thus implicitly subject to prosecution for prostitution. After the war, Butler returned to Massachusetts and was elected to the House. Butler lost no time in launching the House's case against Johnson. From the beginning, however, it was clear that the proceedings would be dominated by the political struggle between Johnson and Butler. Legal niceties were secondary.

Under Butler's direction, the trial managers presented the House's articles of impeachment. These eleven articles consisted of various nonspecific charges of "high crimes and misdemeanors" against Johnson. For example, Johnson was accused of making "intemperate, inflammatory, and scandalous harangues" against Congress during the Swing Around the Circle. Johnson's response to these vague charges was quick and furious:

> Impeach me for violating the Constitution! Damn them! I have been struggling and working ever since I have been in this chair to uphold the Constitution they trample underfoot! I don't care what becomes of me, but I'll fight them until they rot! I shall not allow the Constitution of the United States to be destroyed by evil men who are trying to ruin this government and this nation!

The trial began March 30, 1868. After some initial confusion, the trial managers decided to pursue a two-pronged attack. They would attempt to prove that Johnson's opposition to the Tenure of Office Act was unconstitutional and that Johnson had flagrantly abused his office with his comments about Congress. The testimony of witnesses the trial managers produced was not limited to these issues, however. There was testimony on practically any matter that could serve to discredit Johnson, such as Johnson's alleged excessive drinking habits.

Johnson's defense rested with William Maxwell Evarts, a New York attorney highly regarded throughout the North, and Benjamin R. Curtis, a former Supreme Court justice. Other lawyers, such as former Attorney General Henry Stanbery, assisted with the defense. All of Johnson's counsel felt strongly enough about the importance of the case that they worked free of charge.

Senate Republicans Thwart Johnson's Defense

Johnson's lawyers attempted to introduce evidence showing that Johnson's opposition to the Tenure of Office Act was no more than a legitimate desire to test the constitutional validity of the act in the federal courts. The defense offered to produce witnesses who could testify that Johnson's opposition to the act on constitutional grounds had long preceded his quarrel with Secretary of War Stanton. Chief Justice Chase ruled that this evidence was admissible. Although a two-thirds vote of the Senate was necessary for a conviction of impeachment, it took only a simple majority vote to decide procedural matters. Therefore, despite Chase's rulings, the Senate repeatedly voted to prevent the defense from producing its witnesses concerning Johnson's legitimate opposition to the act.

The second prong of the trial managers' attack concerned Johnson's public statements. But the defense argued that the Senate could hardly impeach Johnson for exercising the right of freedom of speech that the Constitution gave to every American. Butler's retort made little legal sense but was good rhetoric and played well with the anti-Johnson public of the North:

> Is it, indeed, to be seriously argued here that there is a constitutional right in the President of the United States, who, during his official life, can never lay aside his official life, can never lay aside his official character, to denounce, malign, abuse, ridicule, and condemn, openly and publicly, the Congress of the United States: a coordinate branch of the government?

Consciences of Seven Republicans Save Johnson

Throughout the two-month-long trial, Johnson's defense lawyers repeatedly saw their sound legal arguments thwarted by purely political forces. However, seven Republican senators were disturbed by how the proceedings had been manipulated to permit a one-sided presentation of the evidence. Senators William Pitt Fessenden, Joseph S. Fowler, James W. Grimes, John B. Henderson, Edmund G. Ross, Lyman Trumbull, and Peter G. Van Winkle defied their party and public opinion and voted against impeachment.

The Senate met on May 26, 1868, for the final vote. The shift by the seven Republicans proved critical: the tally was 35 to 19 in favor of impeachment, one vote short of the two-thirds majority necessary to impeach Johnson. Johnson was acquitted. But his political career never recovered. Later in 1868 the war hero General Ulysses S. Grant was elected the next president of the United States.

—Stephen G. Christianson

Suggestions for Further Reading

Aymar, Brandt and Edward Sagarin. *Laws and Trials That Created History.* New York: Crown Publishers, 1974.

Dorris, Jonathan Truman. *Pardon and Amnesty Under Lincoln and Johnson.* Chapel Hill: University of North Carolina Press, 1953.

Gerson, Noel B. *The Trial of Andrew Johnson.* Nashville and New York: Thomas Nelson, 1977.

Paul, M. "Was Andrew Johnson Right?" *Senior Scholastic* (Teachers' Edition). (November 1982): 26.

Simpson, Brooks D., Leroy F. Graf, and John Muldowny. *Advice After Appomattox: Letters to Andrew Johnson.* Knoxville: University of Tennessee Press, 1987.

Smith, Gene. *High Crimes & Misdemeanors: The Impeachment and Trial of Andrew Johnson.* New York: William Morrow & Co., 1977.

Strong, George Templeton. *Diary.* New York: Macmillan Co., 1952.

Trefousse, Hans L. *Andrew Johnson, a Biography.* New York and London: W.W. Norton & Co., 1989.

Hester Vaughan Trial: 1868

Defendant: Hester Vaughan **Crime Charged:** First-degree murder
Chief Defense Lawyer: Guforth (No first name listed.)
Chief Prosecutor: No record **Judge:** Ludlow (No first name listed)
Place: Philadelphia, Pennsylvania **Dates of Trial:** June 10–July 2, 1868
Verdict: Guilty **Sentence:** Death

SIGNIFICANCE

When the teenaged Hester Vaughan allegedly murdered her newborn infant, she was prosecuted by a male district attorney, defended by a male attorney, found guilty by an all-male jury and sentenced to death by a male judge. Women's rights leaders, protesting that Vaughan had not had "a trial by a jury of her peers," promptly organized their followers. The women's outcry gained much attention in the press and persuaded Pennsylvania Governor John Geary to exile Vaughan to her native England rather than sign her death warrant.

According to Hester Vaughan's report to her female sympathizers, she had traveled to the United States from her native England to marry her American fiancé. After one and a half years—and upon Vaughan's discovery that her "husband" had another wife and family—Vaughan was deserted. Too ashamed to return home, she accepted a housekeeper's position in Philadelphia, Pennsylvania. She was raped by a member of her employer's household and became pregnant. She left that household, rented a small room, and took in odd sewing jobs while awaiting her baby's birth.

The press and other historical accounts of the trial are sketchy and riddled with gaps. It is clear that on February 8 or 9, 1868, Hester Vaughan, malnourished and living alone in an unheated room at 703 Girard Avenue, Philadelphia, gave birth. Two days later, she asked another resident of the building for a box in which to place a dead baby. She also asked that the matter be kept secret.

Instead, the police were notified. Vaughan was arrested and brought to trial on murder charges on June 30, 1868. The prosecution presented several witnesses, whose testimony was summarized by the *Philadelphia Inquirer*:

> [Vaughan] explained [to the resident from whom she had requested a box] that she had been frightened by a lady going into the room with a cup of coffee, and fallen back upon her child, thus killing it. . . . Dr. Shapleigh [of

the Coroner's office], who examined the body, found several fractures of the skull, made apparently with some blunt instrument, and also clots of blood between the brain and skull. The lady who took the coffee to the prisoner heard the child give one or two faint cries.

The commonwealth rested its case, and Judge Ludlow ordered Vaughan's lawyer, a Mr. Guforth, to present the defense's witnesses the next morning. According to reports later published by women's rights leaders Elizabeth Cady Stanton and Susan B. Anthony, Vaughan had paid Guforth her last few dollars to retain him as her lawyer, but Guforth, after taking her money, never saw her again until the first day of trial.

On the morning of July 1, Guforth presented a witness or witnesses who testified as to Vaughan's good character. He then offered his own arguments against her conviction: First, "the prisoner should not be convicted of murder in the first degree, because in the agony and pain she must have suffered, she may have been bereft of all reason," and second, "the death may have been caused by accident, for the prisoner was the only human being who saw the death, and her lips were sealed by law." Presumably, this latter argument may have referred to the 19th-century belief that women were incompetent witnesses.

Sentenced to Die

Vaughan was found guilty and sentenced to die. Susan A. Smith, M.D., one of the country's first women doctors, learned of the case and visited Vaughan in Moyamensing prison. Upon medical examination and after repeated interviews, Dr. Smith wrote to Pennsylvania Governor John W. Geary concerning the circumstances of Vaughan's pregnancy, labor and delivery:

> [Vaughan] rented a third story room . . . from a family who understood very little English. She furnished this room, found herself in food and fuel for three months on twenty dollars. She was taken sick in this room at midnight on the 6th of February and lingered until Saturday morning, the eighth, when her child was born, she told me she was nearly frozen and fainted or went to sleep for a long time.

> You will please remember, sir, throughout this period of agony she was alone, without nourishment or fire, with her door unfastened.

> My professional opinion in Hester Vaughan's case is that cold and want of attention produced painful and protracted labor—that the mother, in endeavoring to assist herself, injured the head of her child in its birth—that she either fainted or had a convulsion, and was insensible for a long time.

Despite court testimony that the baby had cried, Dr. Smith and another woman doctor, Clemence Lozier, later questioned whether the child had even been born alive.

When Governor Geary failed to respond to Dr. Smith's request for Hester Vaughan's pardon, the case was brought to the attention of Elizabeth Cady Stanton, Susan B. Anthony, and other members of the Working Women's National Association. They promptly scheduled a protest meeting in New York City's Cooper Institute. Cady Stanton and Anthony decried what they called

Vaughan's "condemn[ation] on insufficient evidence and with inadequate defense." However, their protest was based primarily on 19th-century women's exclusion from the ballot and jury boxes. The crowd in attendance voted unanimously to petition Governor Geary for either a new trial or an unconditional pardon for Hester Vaughan. They sent the governor—and several major newspapers—the following resolution:

> Whereas, The right of trial by a jury of one's peers is recognized by the governments of all civilized nations as the great palladium of rights, of justice, and equality to the citizen: therefore, Resolved, That this [Working Women's National] Association demand that in all civil and criminal cases, woman shall be tried by a jury of her peers; shall have a voice in making the law, in electing the judge who pronounces her sentence, and the sheriff who, in case of execution, performs for her that last dread act.

In their travels across the country and in their own newspaper, the *Revolution*, Cady Stanton and Anthony kept up a campaign of condemnation against a male dominated society that would sentence to death a "young, artless, and inexperienced girl." Women, exhorted by Cady Stanton and Anthony to view the case with a "sense of . . . responsibility in making and executing the laws under which [our] daughters are to live or perish," responded: they continued to petition the governor and even wrote poems about the case of Hester Vaughan.

Finally, in the summer of 1869, Governor Geary pardoned Vaughan—but with the condition that private funds be raised to pay her passage back to England. Cady Stanton and Anthony raised the money and triumphantly published Vaughan's thank-you letter in the *Revolution* on August 19, 1869.

—Kathryn Cullen-DuPont

Suggestions for Further Reading

Barry, Kathleen. *Susan B. Anthony.* New York: New York University Press, 1988.

Harper, Ida Husted. *Life and Work of Susan B. Anthony,* Vol. 1. 1898, reprint, Salem, NH: Ayer Co., Publishers, 1983.

New York Times, December 4, 1868.

Philadelphia Inquirer, July 1–2 and December 3–4, 1868.

Revolution, December 10, 1868–August 19, 1869.

Ex Parte McCardle: 1868

Defendant: William H. McCardle **Crimes Charged:** Inciting insurrection and impeding post-Civil War Reconstruction **Chief Defense Lawyers:** Jeremiah S. Black, David Dudley Field, Charles O'Conor, W. L. Sharkey, and Robert J. Walker **Chief Prosecutors:** Mathew H. Carpenter and Lyman Trumbull **Justices:** Salmon P. Chase, Nathan Clifford, David Davis, Robert Cooper Grier, Stephen, J. Field, Samuel F. Miller, Samuel Nelson, and Noah H. Swayne. **Place:** Washington, D.C. **Date of Decision:** 1868 December Term **Decision:** That the Supreme Court was without jurisdiction to render a decision, because Congress had repealed certain appeals legislation

SIGNIFICANCE

For the first and only time in American history, Congress exercised its authority to prevent the Supreme Court from hearing certain types of politically sensitive cases.

After the Civil War, the victorious Union army occupied the defeated Confederacy and the period known as Reconstruction began. On March 2, 1867, Congress passed a law entitled "An Act to Provide for the More Efficient Government of the Rebel States," which officially provided for the military administration of the South. The act abolished the legal existence of the Southern states, and divided the Confederacy into a series of military districts, each commanded by a General who possessed extensive powers to suppress any act of defiance.

In the city of Vicksburg, Mississippi, public resentment against the Union was particularly high. The city was strategically located on the Mississippi River and had fallen to the Union after a long and bloody siege by General Ulysses S. Grant. After the Civil War, the Fourth of July was not celebrated in Vicksburg for 75 years.

William H. McCardle was the editor of a local newspaper, the *Vicksburg Times*. McCardle published various articles criticizing Reconstruction in general and Major General Edward O.C. Ord in particular. Ord was the Commanding General of the Fourth Military District, which included Vicksburg. General Ord was not amused. He had McCardle arrested in November 1867 for various offenses relating to inciting insurrection and impeding Reconstruction. On

November 11, 1867, McCardle sent a petition to the Circuit Court of the United States for the Southern District of Mississippi, asking for a writ of *habeas corpus*, meaning a court order to free McCardle from illegal imprisonment. The circuit court refused McCardle's request, and McCardle appealed to the Supreme Court.

Congress Denies McCardle Access to Supreme Court

The Supreme Court is the only federal court specifically provided for by the Constitution. Under Article III, Section 2, the Supreme Court has original jurisdiction, meaning sole authority, only in "Cases affecting Ambassadors, other public Ministers and Consuls, and those in which a State shall be Party." In all other cases, the Supreme Court has jurisdiction only on appeal from such federal courts as Congress may decide to create and from state supreme courts. This appellate jurisdiction is expressly subject to "such Exceptions, and under such Regulations as the Congress shall make."

On September 24, 1789 Congress passed the Judiciary Act, which is the basis for the federal court system and gave the Supreme Court various appellate powers. On February 5, 1867 Congress amended the Judiciary Act to enable the Supreme Court to hear appeals in *habeas corpus* cases. It was precisely this amendment, called the Habeas Corpus Act of 1867, that enabled the Court to hear the McCardle case.

The Radical Republicans who controlled Congress feared that the McCardle case would give the Court an excuse to overturn Reconstruction legislation and end martial law in the South. Therefore, on March 27, 1868, Congress passed a law repealing the appeal provisions of the Habeas Corpus Act of 1867:

> And be it further enacted, That so much of the act approved February 5, 1867, entitled 'An act to amend an act to establish the judicial courts of the United States, approved September 24, 1789,' as authorized an appeal from the judgment of the Circuit Court to the Supreme Court of the United States, or the exercise of any such jurisdiction by said Supreme Court, on appeals which have been, or may hereafter be taken, be, and the same is hereby repealed.

The case came before the Supreme Court during the 1868 December Term. McCardle was represented by Jeremiah S. Black, David Dudley Field, Charles O'Conor, W.L. Sharkey and Robert J. Walker. The government was represented by Mathew H. Carpenter and Lyman Trumbull.

The hearing focused on the effect of Congress' repeal of the Court's jurisdiction. If the Court didn't have jurisdiction, the validity or invalidity of McCardle's imprisonment was irrelevant. Sharkey argued that Congress' action was unconstitutional because it was designed solely to affect the McCardle case:

> Its language is general, but, as was universally known, its purpose was specific. If Congress had specifically enacted 'that the Supreme Court of the United States shall never publicly give judgment in the case of McCardle, already argued, and on which we anticipate that it will soon deliver judgment, contrary to the views of the majority in Congress, of what it ought to

decide,' its purpose to interfere specifically with and prevent the judgment in this very case would not have been more real or, as a fact, more universally known.

Congress Could Not Be Denied

Carpenter and Trumbull responded by citing the plain language of Article III, Section 2 of the Constitution, under which Congress' authority to restrict the Court's appellate jurisdiction could not be denied. Further, Carpenter and

Chief Justice Salmon Chase (center) announced the Court's unanimous decision in *Ex parte McCardle.* (Courtesy, Library of Congress)

Trumbull pointed out that the language of Congress' repeal of the Court's authority "embraces all cases in all time." Although Sharkey was certainly accurate in describing Congress' real motivations, Carpenter and Trumbull correctly pointed out that legally, any assumption that the repeal was aimed specifically at McCardle couldn't be proven and therefore was "gratuitous and unwarrantable."

By the end of the 1868 December Term, Chief Justice Salmon P. Chase announced the Court's unanimous decision. Chase held that McCardle's appeal was dismissed for lack of jurisdiction, because of Congress' repeal of the Court's authority. Chase stated in blunt terms that Congress had undeniably exercised its power to create exceptions to the Court's authority:

The provision of the act of 1867 affirming the appellate jurisdiction of this court in cases of *habeas corpus* is expressly repealed. It is hardly possible to imagine a plainer instance of positive exception.

The McCardle case is the only time in American history that Congress used its power under the Constitution to prevent the Supreme Court from hearing certain types of politically sensitive cases. There have been periodic movements in Congress to restrict the Court's authority to hear school desegregation cases, school prayer cases, abortion cases and other politically sensitive cases, but nothing has ever happened. However the Court did not completely surrender to Congress actions. Only one year later, in 1869, the Court agreed to hear a case very similar to McCardle's called Ex Parte Yerger, and side-stepped Congress' repeal of the Court's authority. Yerger was released from custody before the Court could hear the case and get into any confrontation with Congress. As more than one legal commentator has opined, given the need for the different branches of government to work peacefully with each other, it may be politically healthy that the limits of congressional power under the Constitution have never been completely clarified.

—Stephen G. Christianson

Suggestions for Further Reading

Franklin, John Hope. *Reconstruction: After the Civil War.* Chicago: University of Chicago Press, 1961.

Morris, Richard B. *Encyclopedia of American History.* New York: Harper & Row, 1982.

Tortora, Anthony. "Ex parte McCardle." *National Review* (September 19, 1980): 1140–1141, 1157.

Trefousse, Hans L. *Historical Dictionary of Reconstruction.* Westport, Conn: Greenwood Press, 1991.

Boss Tweed Trials: 1873

Defendant: William Marcy Tweed   **Crimes Charged:** 55 criminal offenses relating to embezzlement of public funds   **Chief Defense Lawyers:** David Dudley Field, John Graham, and Elihu Root   **Chief Prosecutors:** Wheeler H. Peckham, Benjamin K. Phelps, and Lyman Tremain   **Judge:** Noah Davis   **Place:** New York, New York   **Dates of Trials:** January 7–November 19, 1873   **Verdict:** Guilty   **Sentence:** 1 year in prison and a $250 fine

SIGNIFICANCE

After decades of committing blatant embezzlement of New York City municipal funds with the connivance of Tammany Hall and public officials, Boss Tweed's power was broken. Tweed's fall from power marked the beginning of a new demand by the public and by the press for efficient and honest urban administration.

Descended from hard-working Scottish immigrants, William Marcy Tweed was born in 1823 in New York City. He was a brawling bully from his early youth, heavyset and strong, and as a boy he enjoyed beating the other children in his neighborhood. As an adult he weighed nearly 300 pounds. Tweed bullied and fought his way to a position of leadership among New York's criminal elements, notably the "Forty Thieves" gang. In the 1851 elections Tweed used threats and intimidation of the voters in his precinct to force his way onto New York City's Board of Aldermen.

Tweed was an alderman for two years, and he used the position as a stepping stone for his political career. He served on the Board of Education, and even finagled his election to the U.S. House of Representatives. In 1857, Tweed was elected to New York City's Board of Supervisors, which ran the city's municipal government and controlled its finances. The position was ideal for the greedy Tweed, who promptly installed his cronies as "assistants" and raised the level of city corruption to new heights.

Tweed and his gang were called the Tweed Ring, and they stole enormous sums from the city treasury by falsifying municipal accounts and by creating false or grossly exaggerated expense records. Anyone who opposed them was beaten or killed. In the 1860s, Tweed extended his power to include control over the city's courts. Tweed had George G. Barnard appointed chief judge, although Barnard had practically no legal experience and his only qualification for the post was his allegiance to Tweed. Other judges were on Tweed's payroll as well, including the father of future Supreme Court Justice Benjamin Cardozo.

Tweed's control of the city was buttressed by the support of the Tammany Hall political organization. To control the elections, Tammany Hall sold citizenship documents to practically any immigrant who promised to vote for the Tweed slate. Since New York was teeming with millions of new immigrants, most of whom had fled poverty and were desperate to stay in America, Tweed and Tammany Hall not only were able to control the elections but made hundreds of thousands of dollars as well.

Reformers Fight Back

By the early 1870s, reform politicians determined to end urban corruption had risen to power. New York State Governor Samuel Tilden and state Attorney General Charles Fairchild went after Tweed. They were supported by influential elements of the New York City press, led by political commentator and cartoonist Thomas Nast of the *New York Times*. Nast had grown up in Tweed's neighborhood, and as a child lived with the fear of Tweed's random beatings. Nast's personal vendetta against Tweed took the form of scathing cartoons depicting Tweed as a fat and corrupt Tammany boss. Other papers, such as *Harper's Weekly*, joined the *Times* in exposing Tweed's abuse of power and in calling for his prosecution.

Cartoonist Thomas Nast recalled growing up in fear of the random beatings meted out by Tweed's gang. In the above cartoon he shows relief that justice has been served. (*Harper's Weekly*)

Nast's *Times* and the other papers successfully stirred New Yorkers out of their apathy toward Tweed. On September 4, 1871, an enormous crowd went to hear various influential reformers speak out against Tweed. Bolstered by the crowd's enthusiasm for their cause, the reformers, led by Tilden and Fairchild, sought an injunction against Tweed and his Ring preventing them from using any more public funds. Probably because Tilden promised him protection, Judge Barnard turned against Tweed and granted the injunction on September 7.

Once Tweed was prevented from plundering the city treasury, his organization began to fall apart. On October 27, 1871, Tilden had Tweed arrested and charged with 55 criminal offenses relating to embezzlement of public funds. Because each alleged offense involved several counts, or multiple incidents,

Tweed was actually prosecuted for several hundred crimes. Tweed's lawyers were David Dudley Field, John Graham and Elihu Root. The chief prosecutors were Wheeler H. Peckham, Benjamin K. Phelps and Lyman Tremain. On January 7, 1873, the trial began before Judge Noah Davis.

The proceedings began badly for the prosecution when their poor choice of witnesses caused a mistrial. Tweed bragged that no jury could ever convict him and took a vacation in California. Tweed's second trial began November 5, 1873. This time, the prosecution conducted its case more carefully, and after only a minimal amount of evidence was presented the jury found Tweed guilty on November 19,1873.

Tweed Fights Verdict

Of the several hundred counts contained within the 55 charges against Tweed, the jury found him guilty of 102 crimes. Each crime was punishable by a year in prison and a nominal $250 fine, and so the prosecutors sought a conviction totaling 102 years and a fine of $25,500. On Tweed's behalf, Graham pleaded for mercy:

> Your honor, we are taught, from the time we enter this world, to ask for mercy; and those prayers which we put up in our own behalf must teach us to render deeds of mercy to. . . .

Graham, either genuinely upset or putting on a superb act, could not continue and broke down in tears. Prosecutor Tremain retorted:

> I cannot but feel, and I am sure my associates feel with me, indeed, all must feel, how terrible is the position of this man, who has been so high and who has fallen so low. He is now drinking the bitter waters of humiliation. The spell is broken.

Tremain turned to Judge Davis, and reminded him of the notoriety of the case:

> The law has placed in your hands the responsibility of the matter. The case is one of international interest and attracts the attention of the whole world. We now leave to you the question of what shall be meted out to the prisoner as an impartial and just penalty.

Judge Davis sentenced Tweed to 12 years in prison and a $12,750 fine. Tweed's attorneys appealed the verdict to the New York Court of Appeals, which ruled that despite the multiple offenses Tweed could not be sentenced for more than the punishment applicable to just one crime. Therefore, Tweed served just one year in prison, paid his $250 fine, and on January 15, 1875, was released from prison.

However, Tilden had anticipated Tweed's release. Tilden had Tweed arrested again, this time to recover the millions Tweed stole from the treasury. Unable to make the $3,000,000 bail, Tweed sat in prison awaiting his next trial. Although greatly diminished, Tweed's influence was still strong enough to enable him to circumvent most of the restrictions of his confinement. The prison warden allowed him to take carriage drives throughout the city, and dine at

Tweed's own home if he wished. On December 4, 1875, Tweed took advantage of the warden's laxity and never returned from one of his afternoon drives.

Tweed stayed in various hideouts in Staten Island and New Jersey until he was able to obtain a boat to take him to Florida. From Florida he fled to Cuba and from there on to Spain, which was then a notorious haven for refugees. The Spanish authorities, however, would not tolerate Tweed's presence, and arrested him when he arrived in Vigo, Spain. Spain turned Tweed over to the United States and the naval vessel U.S.S. *Franklin* brought Tweed back to New York.

Tweed returned to prison, having now committed the additional offense of attempted escape. He confessed to the charges against him, and what was left of the Tweed Ring was either arrested or, if they returned their share of the stolen money, allowed to fade into obscurity. Of the tens of millions of dollars embezzled over the decades, however, the city recovered only a fraction. The rest had been frittered away in high living by Tweed and his cronies, spent in maintaining the Tammany Hall organization, or lost to the gangs and criminals affiliated with the Ring.

In 1871, when Tweed was still firmly in power and the public and press had just begun to challenge him, a reporter confronted Tweed and asked him about the charges against him. Tweed answered arrogantly, "Well, what are you going to do about it?" Thanks to the efforts of a new breed of reform politicians, supported by the demands of the public and the press for efficient and honest urban administration, Tweed found out just what could be done about it. Tweed's power was forever broken, and he died in prison on April 12, 1878.

—Stephen G. Christianson

Suggestions for Further Reading

Bales, William Alan. *Tiger in the Streets*. New York: Dodd, Mead & Co., 1962.

Clinton, Henry Lauren. *Celebrated Trials*. New York: Harper & Brothers, 1897.

Gustaitis, Joseph. " 'Boss' Tweed: Colossus of Corruption?" *American History Illustrated* (November 1988): 34–35.

Lynch, Denis Tilden. *Boss Tweed: The Story of a Grim Generation*. New York: Boni and Liveright, 1927.

Mandelbaum, Seymour J. *Boss Tweed's New York*. Chicago: I.R. Dee, 1990.

U.S. v. Susan B. Anthony: 1873

Defendant: Susan B. Anthony **Crime Charged:** Unlawful Voting
Chief Defense Lawyers: Henry R. Selden and John Van Voorhis
Chief Prosecutor: Richard Crowley **Judge:** Ward Hunt
Place: Canandaigua, New York **Dates of Trial:** June 17–18, 1873
Verdict: Guilty

SIGNIFICANCE

This was one of the first in a series of decisions—including two rendered by the Supreme Court—which found that Section 1 of the Fourteenth Amendment to the U.S. Constitution did not expand or protect women's rights, an interpretation which remained unchanged for almost 100 years.

Several cases in the 1870s, including *U.S. v. Susan B. Anthony*, grew out of women's attempts to gain full rights of citizenship through the judicial system. Had this strategy worked, women would have been spared what followed: a 60-year-long, state-by-state legislative campaign for suffrage and 100 years in which the Fourteenth Amendment's equal protection clause was not applied to sex discrimination cases.

In July 1868, exactly 20 years after the Seneca Falls Convention and American women's first public demand for suffrage, the Fourteenth Amendment was adopted. Section 2, intended to encourage states to grant suffrage to African-American men, angered women's rights leaders because it introduced the word "male" into the Constitution and, some thought, called into question the citizenship of females. Francis Minor, an attorney and husband of Virginia Minor, the Woman Suffrage Association of Missouri's president, thought women were looking at the wrong clause. Section 1, he pointed out in 1869, declared:

> All persons born or naturalized in the United States, and subject to the jurisdiction thereof, are citizens of the United States and of the State wherein they reside. No State shall make or enforce any law which shall abridge the privileges or immunities of citizens of the United States.

Minor wrote that this clause *confirmed* the citizenship of women and concluded, "provisions of the several State Constitutions that exclude women from the franchise on account of sex, are violative alike of the spirit and letter of the Federal Constitution."

Susan B. Anthony and Elizabeth Cady Stanton published Minor's analysis in their newspaper, the *Revolution*, and urged women to go to the polls. In 1871 and 1872, in at least 10 states, women did so. Most were turned away, but a few actually managed to vote.

"I Have Been & Gone & Done it!!"

One of those who voted in 1872 was Susan B. Anthony. Before registering in Rochester, New York, she had consulted Judge Henry R. Selden, who agreed that Section 1 of the Fourteenth Amendment should entitle women to suffrage; she carried his written opinion with her and threatened to sue the registrars if they failed to take her oath. They complied. Anthony and 14 female companions were registered and, on November 5, they voted. On November 28, Susan B. Anthony, the other 14 women, and the inspectors who had registered them were arrested.

All parties were offered release upon payment of $500 bail; Anthony alone refused to pay. Henry Selden, acting as her attorney, applied for a writ of *habeas corpus*, and Anthony was temporarily released. A U.S. district judge denied the writ and reset her bail at $1,000 on January 21, 1873. Anthony refused to pay, but Selden—who would later explain that he "could not see a lady I respected put in jail"—paid the bail. Anthony was released and immediately lost her right to appeal to the Supreme Court on the basis of the writ of *habeas corpus*.

Stumping Before the Trial

Anthony tried to present her side of the story to prospective jurors before the scheduled May 13 trial began. She gave the same speech in all 29 postal districts of her county:

"Friends and Fellow-Citizens, I stand before you under indictment for the alleged crime of having voted at the last presidential election, without having a lawful right to vote. . . . We no longer petition legislature or Congress to give of the right to vote, but appeal to women everywhere to exercise their too long neglected 'citizen's right'. . . . we throw to the wind the old dogma that governments can give rights. The Declaration of Independence, the United States Constitution the constitutions of the several states . . . propose to *protect* the people in the exercise of their God-given rights. Not one of them pretends to bestow rights. . . . One half of the people of this Nation today are utterly powerless to blot from the statute books an unjust law, or to write a new and just one. The women, dissatisfied as they are with this form of government, that enforces taxation without representation—that compels them to obey laws to which they have never given their consent—that imprisons and hangs them without a trial by a jury of their peers—that robs them, in marriage of the custody of their own persons, wages, and children—are this half of the people left wholly at the mercy of the other half."

Because Anthony had "prejudiced any possible jury," her trial was moved out of her own Monroe County to Canandaigua, a town in Ontario County, New

York, and rescheduled for June 17. By June 16, Anthony had spoken in every Ontario village.

Trial Begins June 17

The trial opened before Judge Ward Hunt on June 17, 1873. U.S. District Attorney Richard Crowley presented the government's case: "Miss Susan B. Anthony . . . upon the 5th day of November, 1872, . . . voted . . . At that time she was a woman."

Beverly W. Jones, one of the inspectors under indictment for registering Anthony, testified that he had indeed registered her and that he had received ballots from her on November 5.

Crowley introduced the poll list bearing the name of Susan B. Anthony as proof that the woman voted, and the government rested its case.

Henry Selden then tried to call Anthony to the stand. Crowley objected: "She is not competent as a witness in her own behalf." (Women were not permitted to testify in federal court in the 19th century.)

The judge "so held" that Anthony could not testify.

Selden then took the stand and testified that he concurred with Anthony's reading of the Fourteenth Amendment and that he had advised her to cast her ballot. Selden argued: "The only alleged ground of illegality of the defendant's vote is that she is a woman. If the same act has been done by her brother under the same circumstances, the act would have been not only innocent, but honorable and laudable; but having been done by a woman it is said to be a crime. The crime, therefore, consists not in the act done, but in the simple fact that the person doing it was a woman and not a man."

Susan B. Anthony's response to Judge Hunt's fine: "May it please your honor, I will never pay a dollar of your unjust penalty. . . ." (Courtesy, Library of Congress)

At the conclusion of argument, Judge Hunt read a statement—prepared before he had heard testimony—to the "Gentlemen of the Jury":

> The right of voting, or the privilege of voting, is a right or privilege arising under the Constitution of the State, and not of the United States. . . If the State of New York should provide that no person should vote until he had reached the age of thirty-one years, or after he had reached the age of fifty, or that no person having gray hair, or who had not the use of all his limbs, should be entitled to vote, I do not see how it could be held to be a violation of any right derived or held under the Constitution of the United States.

Judge Hunt directed the jury to deliver a guilty verdict.

Selden objected, saying, "it is for the jury [to decide]."

Hunt addressed the jury again: "I have decided as a question of law . . . that under the Fourteenth Amendment, which Miss Anthony claims protects her, she was not protected in a right to vote. . . . I therefore direct you to find a verdict of guilty."

Hunt then asked the clerk to record the jury's verdict. The next day, Selden presented a motion and arguments for a new trial, which Hunt denied. Hunt then asked Anthony to stand. "The sentence of the Court is that you pay a fine of $100.00 and the costs of prosecution."

Anthony replied: "May it please your honor, I will never pay a dollar of your unjust penalty. . . . 'Resistance to tyranny is obedience to God.'"

Hunt released her, saying, "Madam, the Court will not order to stand committed until the fine is paid."

Anthony never paid the fine.

Supreme Court Reviews Women and the Fourteenth Amendment

In 1873, the Supreme Court heard the case of Myra Bradwell, who claimed that her Fourteenth Amendment rights were abridged by Illinois' law prohibiting women from the practice of law. The Court found that her rights had not been violated since "the right of females to pursue any lawful employment for a livelihood [the practice of law included]" was not "one of the privileges and immunities of women as citizens." Justice Samuel F. Miller, writing for the majority, explained: "The paramount destiny and mission of woman are to fulfill the noble and benign offices of wife and mother. This is the law of the Creator. And the rules of civil society must be adapted to the general constitution of things."

In its decision on *Minor v. Happersett*, the Supreme Court's unanimous opinion was that the right of suffrage was not one of the privileges and immunities of citizenship, and women—although citizens of the United States—could be denied the vote by their respective states.

The first successful Fourteenth Amendment challenge to a sex-biased law was brought by Sally Reed in 1971. Reed's son died intestate (having made no valid will), and the Idaho court automatically appointed Reed's estranged husband Cecil as administrator of the estate, because of his sex, and denied Reed's own petition, because of hers. More than 100 years after the adoption of the Fourteenth Amendment, Chief Justice Warren E. Burger delivered the following opinion for the court: "We have concluded that the arbitrary preference established in favor of males by the Idaho Code cannot stand in the face of the Fourteenth Amendment's command that no State deny the equal protection of the laws to any person within its jurisdiction."

—Kathryn Cullen-DuPont

Suggestions for Further Reading

Barry, Kathleen. *Susan B. Anthony: A Biography.* New York: New York University Press, 1988.

Flexner, Eleanor. *Century of Struggle.* Cambridge, Mass.: Belknap Press of Harvard University Press, 1959, revised 1975.

Frost, Elizabeth and Kathryn Cullen-DuPont. *Women's Suffrage in America: An Eyewitness History.* New York: Facts On File, 1992.

Harper, Ida Husted. *Life and Work of Susan B. Anthony.* 1898. Reprint. Salem, N.H.: Ayer Co., 1983.

Stanton, Elizabeth Cady, Susan B. Anthony, and Matilda Joslyn Gage. *History of Woman Suffrage*, Vol. II. 1882. Reprint. Salem, N.H.: Ayer Co., 1985.

Tilton v. Beecher: 1875

Plaintiff: Theodore Tilton   **Defendant:** Henry Ward Beecher
Plaintiff Claim: That Beecher had committed adultery with Tilton's wife
Chief Defense Lawyers: William M. Evarts, John L. Hill, John K. Porter,
Thomas G. Shearman, and Benjamin F. Tracy
Chief Lawyers for Plaintiff: W. Fullerton, Samuel D. Morris, and Roger A.
Pryor   **Judge:** Neilson (historical records do not indicate first name)
Place: Brooklyn, New York   **Dates of Trial:** January 4–July 1, 1875
Decision: Verdict for Beecher

SIGNIFICANCE

This was one of the most celebrated and emblematic cases of the Victorian era. Despite its notoriety and Beecher's public stature, the woman he allegedly committed adultery with never testified. This was due to the common-law rule of interspousal witness immunity: Because her husband was the plaintiff, she could not testify. This case aptly illustrates the burden this old rule placed on the judicial system's effort to discover the truth.

Reverend Henry Ward Beecher had a long and prestigious career as one of 19th-century America's foremost preachers. Not only was he popular with the faithful at his Plymouth Congregational Church in Brooklyn, New York, he was also well-known for his advocacy of social reform. Beecher spoke out on behalf of abolition before the Civil War freed the slaves, in favor of women's suffrage long before women got the right to vote, and expressed his belief in Charles Darwin's theory of natural selection decades before evolution gained popular acceptance.

Beecher often used a local newspaper called the *New York Independent* as a forum to express his views. The *Independent* was operated by Congregational ministers sympathetic to Beecher's views, and his sermons and letters were routinely published. Beecher's influence over the paper was such that, when in 1861 the *Independent* needed a new editor, he was able to arrange the appointment of his young protege Theodore Tilton. Tilton was a member of the Plymouth Church congregation and had become Beecher's friend. Although in theory Beecher himself became the chief editor of the *Independent* and Tilton was only his assistant, Tilton in fact ran the paper.

Beecher and Tilton remained friends through the 1860s. Beecher regularly visited Tilton, his wife Elizabeth and their family at home. In the late 1860s, however, Tilton's editorials in the *Independent* began to take a very radical turn. He began to espouse the doctrine of "free love," which challenged the institution of marriage and traditional morality. Further, beginning in 1868, Elizabeth Tilton began to see Beecher regularly and privately for what Beecher later claimed was religious guidance and consolation regarding Tilton's unorthodox beliefs.

In July of 1870, however, Elizabeth Tilton went to her husband with an entirely different story. She claimed that Beecher had made "improper advances" to her and implied that Beecher had tried to seduce her, but she didn't expressly admit to adultery. For some reason, Tilton waited nearly four years until June of 1874 to make his wife's claims public. When he did, New York and the entire nation were shocked. Tilton had long since been removed as editor of the *Independent*, and Beecher now saw to it that Tilton was expelled from the Plymouth Church.

Plymouth Church Clears Beecher

When the scandal became public, Beecher asked for an investigation to clear his name. He turned to the membership of the Plymouth Church, and asked its most distinguished members to form an investigating committee. This committee investigated the scandal beginning on June 27, 1874 and issued its report on August 27. The committee's investigation was reputed to be thorough but naturally somewhat suspect since Beecher was their preacher. The committee reported:

> The Committee have given the evidence their most useful consideration, and find therefore that in 1861 Mr. Beecher became editor and Mr. Tilton assistant editor of the *Independent*, and that during this relation they became warm and intimate friends. On or about 1863 Mr. Tilton began to urge Mr. Beecher to visit his [Tilton's] house, and he became more intimately acquainted with Tilton's family. . . .

> The friendly relations existing between Mr. Beecher and Mrs. Tilton were always well known and understood, and met with Mr. Tilton's cordial approval. . . .

> [Tilton's] social views [around 1870] underwent a radical change in the direction of free love. This marked change in the religious and social views of Mr. Tilton was a source of great grief and sorrow to Mrs. Tilton. Mrs. Tilton seemed to be a very religious woman, amounting almost to enthusiasm, and when this change occurred in her husband she naturally sought her pastor for counsel and sympathy. . . . It now appears that during these years Mrs. Tilton became strongly attached to Mr. Beecher and in July, 1870, confessed to her husband an overshadowing affection for her Pastor.

The committee found Beecher innocent, and issued a ringing endorsement of his character:

This man has been living in the clear light of noonday, before his people and before all men, a life of great Christian usefulness and incessant work. None have known him but to admire and love him. . . . Upon a review of all the evidence, made with an earnest desire to find the truth, and to advise what truth and justice shall require, we feel bound to state that, in our judgment, the evidence relied on by the accuser utterly fails to sustain the charges made.

Tilton was not satisfied with the committee's findings, however, and filed a lawsuit against Beecher. Beecher's lawyers were William M. Evarts, John L. Hill, John K. Porter, Thomas G. Shearman, and Benjamin F. Tracy. Tilton's lawyers were ex-Judge W. Fullerton, Samuel D. Morris, and Roger A. Pryor. The judge was Judge Neilson. The trial began January 4, 1875 and was to titillate the public for nearly six long months.

Mrs. Tilton Never Testifies

Although Tilton and Beecher both testified during the trial, Elizabeth Tilton never took the witness stand. This was because of the common-law principle of interspousal immunity. When Tilton's attorneys attempted to put Tilton on the witness stand, Evarts objected on Beecher's behalf that the same interspousal immunity rule prevented him from testifying as well:

Neither in a civil action nor in a criminal prosecution are they [spouses] permitted to give any evidence which, in its future effects, may incriminate each other, and this rule is so inviolable that no consent of the other party may authorize the breach of it.

This rule, accurately expressed by Evarts, meant that spouses couldn't testify for or against each other in court for fear that, if the testifying spouse committed perjury or revealed something adverse under cross-examination, the marriage would be hurt and possibly result in divorce. Marriage was sacred to the common law, which held that "two souls are joined as one."

Although Elizabeth Tilton couldn't testify, Judge Neilson allowed Tilton to take the stand but stated that Tilton couldn't testify concerning any "confidential communications" with his wife. This was an accepted exception to the interspousal testimony rule, but it meant that the courtroom testimony about the alleged adultery took place in very elliptical terms. Further, much of Tilton's testimony suggested that there had been no adultery. An example is the following cross-examination of Tilton by Evarts:

Question: Now, up to the time of [Mrs. Tilton's alleged confession] had you observed in the demeanor of Mr. Beecher toward your wife, or of your wife toward Mr. Beecher, any variance from that ordinary relation which you had been familiar with?

Answer: No sir; one or two little incidents happened a number of years before that, which Mrs. Tilton explained away, and which left no impression.

Beecher's testimony was equally unimpressive. He contradicted himself and his supporting witnesses many times and repeatedly claimed that he couldn't remember the specifics of certain events. The trial dragged on for nearly six months, as Beecher's attorneys brought in nearly 100 supporting witnesses. These witnesses' testimony was often repetitive, and frequently consisted merely of vouching for Beecher's character.

The jury deliberated for several days, and on July 1 reported to Judge Neilson that it couldn't reach a verdict. Nine jurors believed that Beecher was innocent, the other three that he was guilty. There was no retrial. Beecher was vindicated, and Judge Neilson even expressed his belief in Beecher's innocence when he spoke eight years later at a party given by the Brooklyn Academy of Music to celebrate Beecher's 70th birthday:

> By the integrity of his life and the purity of his character he has vanquished misrepresentation and abuse.

Beecher never quite regained his previous stature as a spokesman on social issues, however, because of the scandal.

In addition to its notoriety, *Tilton v. Beecher* demonstrated the severe limitations of the interspousal immunity rule concerning testimony. The woman Beecher allegedly committed adultery with never testified, because her husband was the plaintiff. The judicial system was thus unable to get at the complete truth. Although Beecher may well have been innocent, there is no way to determine what additional facts would have been brought out by Elizabeth Tilton's testimony. In the 20th century, courts and legislatures began to recognize the problems that the rule imposed on the judicial system, and today it has been virtually abolished.

—*Stephen G. Christianson*

Suggestions for Further Reading

Abbott, Lyman. *Henry Ward Beecher*. New York: Chelsea House, 1980.

Kohn, George C. *Encyclopedia of American Scandal*. New York: Facts On File, 1989.

Marshall, Charles F. *The True History of the Brooklyn Scandal*. Philadelphia: National Publishing Co., 1874.

Ryan, Halford Ross. *Henry Ward Beecher: Peripatetic Preacher*. Westport, Conn.: Greenwood Press, 1990.

Shaplen, Robert. *Free Love and Heavenly Sinners*. New York: Alfred A. Knopf, 1954.

Waller, Altina L. *Reverend Beecher and Mrs. Tilton: Sex and Class in Victorian America*. Amherst: University of Massachusetts Press, 1982.

U.S. v. Cruikshank: 1875

Defendants: William J. Cruikshank and others   **Crimes Charged:** 16
violations of federal law relating to the defendants' involvement in lynching
two black men, including violating the victims' "right and privilege peaceably
to assemble together."   **Chief Defense Lawyers:** E. John Ellis, David Dudley
Field, Reverdy Johnson, R.H. Marr, Philip Phillips, and W.R. Whitaker
Chief Prosecutors: J.R. Beckwith, Edward Pierrepont, and Samuel F. Phillips
Judge: William B. Woods   **Place:** New Orleans, Louisiana
Date of Trial: 1874 April Term   **Verdict:** Guilty, overturned by U.S. Supreme
Court   **Sentence:** None.

SIGNIFICANCE

The Supreme Court in *Cruikshank* severely limited the ability of the federal
government to protect the civil rights of newly freed African-Americans. The
federal government would not achieve the power to effectively protect civil rights
until well into the 20th century.

In many ways, the Civil War began as a simple struggle between North and
South over whether the Union would survive. Abolishing slavery became its
primary purpose only after nearly two years of combat. President Abraham
Lincoln was initially hesitant about freeing the slaves, and many leading
Northerners, such as General George McClellan, were openly against abolition.
After Lincoln finally decided to side with the abolitionists and issued the
Emancipation Proclamation, however, the Civil War became almost a crusade
against slavery for the people of the North. Renewed popular enthusiasm for the
war, plus the addition of black regiments to Union forces, contributed to victory
for the North in 1865.

African-Americans were finally freed, but their hold on liberty was precarious. The former slaves were uneducated, poor, and dependent on white landowners for their living. Many left the land for the industrial cities of the North,
but most stayed home because they had no skills other than as agricultural
laborers. During the early years of Reconstruction, the South was under military
occupation and ex-slaves in the states of the former Confederacy were protected
from their former masters. Further, it seemed as if the abolitionists had suc-

ceeded in obtaining permanent and meaningful legal recognition of African-Americans' civil rights through a series of amendments to the Constitution.

The Thirteenth Amendment, forbidding slavery, was ratified in 1865. The Fourteenth Amendment, providing for equal protection and due process under the law, was ratified in 1868. The Fifteenth Amendment, protecting the right to vote, was ratified in 1870. The Fourteenth Amendment is the most extensive of these three amendments, and based on it, Congress enacted legislation May 31, 1870 that made it a felony if two or more people conspired to deprive anyone of his federal civil rights.

Southern Racism Makes a Comeback

Despite the new legal protection for ex-slaves, as Southern states were re-admitted to the Union and the occupation forces went home, the old ways returned in new guises. Landowners no longer owned slaves, but the practice of sharecropping effectively kept blacks tied to the land and subservient to whites. Southern states passed "Jim Crow" laws enforcing the separation of blacks from whites in public accommodations. What states couldn't do in public, Southern whites did in private. The Ku Klux Klan developed as an instrument of terror to enforce white supremacy. Hard-won black liberties began to slip away.

As Congress' act of 1870 demonstrated, however, the North would not give up without a fight. Three years later, matters came to a head. On April 13, 1873, a Southern mob in Grant Parish, Louisiana numbering nearly 100 people lynched two African-American men, Levi Nelson and Alexander Tillman. Apparently Nelson and Tillman had tried to vote in a local election against the wishes of white residents. Approximately 80 people in the lynch mob were indicted for violations of federal law and 17 were eventually brought to trial, including one William J. Cruikshank. The U.S. attorney in charge, J.R. Beckwith, charged each of them with 16 violations of the 1870 law. The most important charge was violating the victims' "right and privilege peaceably to assemble together."

Cruikshank and the others, however, were not charged with murder. Nelson and Tillman's murder was a Louisiana state offense, not a violation of the federal law, and the Louisiana authorities didn't prosecute. The defendants were brought to trial in New Orleans before a judge of the federal Circuit Court for the District of Louisiana, William B. Woods, E. John Ellis, R.H. Marr, and W.R. Whitaker represented the defendants at the trial, which took place during the Circuit Court's 1874 April Term.

Little is known about the actual trial, as the real action was yet to come. Cruikshank and the others were found guilty. The defense lawyers promptly appealed for a stay to Joseph P. Bradley, an associate justice of the U.S. Supreme Court. In that day and age, individual justices of the Supreme Court were charged with hearing appeals in various parts of the country before the appeals went to the full Court in Washington, D.C. The District of Louisiana had been assigned to Bradley.

Justice Bradley granted the defense's motion to stay the guilty verdicts, and Cruikshank's case was sent to the Supreme Court for a final decision. David Dudley Field, Reverdy Johnson, and Philip Phillips joined the defense team, while Attorney-General Edward Pierrepont and Solicitor-General Samuel F. Phillips personally assisted the prosecution as both sides prepared for their arguments before the Court.

At the Court's 1874 October Term, the prosecution argued that the 1870 act and the Fourteenth Amendment gave the government the power to try and convict offenders like Cruikshank. The defense argued that the Fourteenth Amendment gave the federal government authority to act only against state government violations of civil rights, but not against one citizen's violation of another's civil rights, like Cruikshank's violation of Nelson and Tillman's rights. The defense's argument, that Congress could legislate against only "state action," would have the effect of leaving the federal government powerless to prosecute lynch mobs and groups such as the KKK. African-Americans would be protected only by their state courts against white violence, which in the South, of course, meant no protection at all.

Justice Joseph Bradley granted the defense's motion to stay the guilty verdicts, paving the way for a Supreme Court decision in *Cruikshank*. (Courtesy, Library of Congress)

Supreme Court Delivers a Crushing Blow

After hearing both sides' arguments, the Court took a year to render its decision. Chief Justice Morrison R. Waite wrote the Court's ruling, issued in the 1875 October Term. Waite's opinion would stymie the federal government's ability to protect African-American civil rights for 90 years.

Waite began by reiterating the dual nature of American government:

We have in our political system a government of the United States and a government of each of the several States. Each one of these governments is distinct from the others, and each has citizens of its own who owe it allegiance, and whose rights, within its jurisdiction, it must protect. The same person may be at the same time a citizen of the United States and a citizen of a State, but his rights of citizenship under one of these governments will be different from those he has under the other.

Waite then stated that the 16 violations of the 1870 act charged against Cruikshank and the others were really simple state conspiracy charges. The federal prosecution was thus unconstitutional. Even the most important charge, violating the victims' "right and privilege peaceably to assemble together," was really a violation of state rights. If the victims had assembled to "petition for a redress of grievances," or some other right specifically granted by the Constitution, then perhaps a federal prosecution would be permissible. Waite refused, however, to give the federal government jurisdiction over any civil rights violation not specifically covered by the Constitution:

> This [case] is nothing else than [an allegation of] a conspiracy to falsely imprison or murder citizens of the United States, being within the territorial jurisdiction of the State of Louisiana. . . . Sovereignty, for this purpose, rests alone with the State. It is no more the duty or within the power of the United States to punish for a conspiracy to falsely imprison or murder within a State, than it would be to punish for false imprisonment or murder itself.

Cruikshank and the others would thus go free. Through Waite, the Supreme Court had firmly endorsed the defendants' "state action" argument:

> The Fourteenth Amendment prohibits a State from depriving any person of life, liberty, or property, without due process of law; but this adds nothing to the rights of one citizen as against another.

Because the Court had essentially told people to go to their state governments and courts for protection, African-American civil liberties underwent a long eclipse, particularly in the South, from which they would not recover until the 1960s. The Court had turned a blind eye to the fact that in the South, state governments were *de facto* supporters of "private" racism such as the Ku Klux Klan and the lynch mobs. For African-Americans, state protection was no protection at all.

In the 1960s, the federal government enacted new civil rights laws and moved aggressively to enforce them. This time, in dozens of cases the Court consistently upheld the constitutionality of federal measures. The Court's change in attitude was due to the political upheavals of the time and the new majority of liberal justices. Obstacles such as the "state action" requirement of the Fourteenth Amendment were substantially reduced. Further, the Court allowed the federal government broad civil rights enforcement powers under other sections of the Constitution as well, such as the federal authority to regulate any conduct that even remotely affects interstate commerce. Cases like *Cruikshank*, however, had prevented the federal government from protecting civil rights 90 years earlier.

—Stephen G. Christianson

Suggestions for Further Reading

Burns, James MacGregor. *A People's Charter: the Pursuit of Rights in America*. New York: Alfred A. Knopf, 1991.

Emerson, Thomas Irwin. *Political and Civil Rights in the United States: A Collection of Legal and Related Materials*. Boston: Little, Brown & Co., 1967.

Foner, Eric. "The New View of Reconstruction." *American Heritage* (October 1983): 10–16.

Franklin, John Hope. "Mirror for Americans: a Century of Reconstruction History." *The American Historical Review* (February 1980): 1–14.

Neely, Mark E. *The Fate of Liberty: Abraham Lincoln and Civil Liberties.* New York: Oxford University Press, 1991.

Nieman, Donald G. *Promises to Keep: African-Americans and the Constitutional Order, 1776 to the Present.* New York: Oxford University Press, 1991.

1875

U.S. v. Cruikshank

Martinez v. Del Valle: 1877

Plaintiff: Eugenie Martinez   **Defendant:** Juan Del Valle
Plaintiff Claim: That Del Valle broke his promise to marry the plaintiff
Chief Defense Lawyer: Joseph H. Choate
Chief Lawyer for Plaintiff: William H. Beach   **Judge:** Donohue (historical
records do not indicate first name)   **Place:** New York, New York
Date of Trial: 1877 January Term   **Decision:** Jury verdict in favor of the
plaintiff for damages of $50

SIGNIFICANCE

The famous lawyer Joseph Choate represented Juan Del Valle, and his handling of
Eugenie Martinez on the witness stand has been hailed as a model of the art of
cross-examination.

Juan Del Valle was a wealthy businessman from Cuba who had established himself in New York City. He had divorced his first wife and was well into middle age when he met a dark-haired Spanish beauty in her early 20s named Eugenie Martinez. On January 14, 1875, Martinez slipped while walking on an icy sidewalk and sprained her ankle. Del Valle happened to be nearby, and he helped her up and took her home.

According to Martinez, Del Valle visited her the next day to see how she was recovering. Del Valle became her regular suitor and, after only three weeks of courtship, allegedly promised to marry Martinez but reneged after an "engagement" of several months. Martinez sued Del Valle for $50,000 in damages for breach of promise of marriage.

It was rumored that Del Valle offered Martinez $20,000 to settle out of court and avoid a scandal, but she refused. Martinez was represented by William H. Beach, and Del Valle was represented by Joseph H. Choate. With Judge Donohue presiding, the case was tried in the New York City Court's 1877 January Term. Because Del Valle was a rich man and Martinez's family was poor, the press labeled Martinez a "golddigger" and the case attracted considerable publicity.

Choate was a famous lawyer, known for his verbal skills and scathing comments. From start to finish he stole the show. Choate encouraged the public's low opinion of Martinez when he referred to her case:

Never did a privateer upon the *Spanish Main* give chase to and board a homeward bound [ship] with more avidity and vigor than this family proposed to board this rich Cuban and make a capture of him.

Choate Cross-Examines Martinez

Beach's principal witness was Martinez herself, and he had her relate the entire story to the jury. A key element of Martinez's case was her claim that, when Del Valle proposed to her three weeks after they met, he took her to a jewelry shop and bought her a ring as a token of his sincerity. Del Valle claimed he bought Martinez the ring the day after they met, and not as a promise of marriage but merely out of affection for a young lady in distress that he had helped. As proof that Del Valle's version of the story was the true one, Choate had arranged for the jeweler to be available to testify that the ring was purchased on January 15. First, however, Choate would let Martinez perjure herself under oath.

Choate began by allowing Martinez to claim that, because of her sprained ankle, she didn't leave her house for five days after her fall.

Question: How long was it before you got entirely over it so as to be able to go out of doors?

Answer: Well, I went out the fifth day.

Question: And not before?

Answer: And not before.

Question: So that because of the injuries that you sustained, you were confined to the house for five days?

Answer: I was.

Next, Choate got Martinez to commit herself to her claim that she went to the jewelry store with Del Valle three weeks after they met.

Question: Some considerable number of weeks, you say, intervened between your first acquaintance [with Del Valle] and . . . the giving of the ring?

Answer: About three weeks as nearly as I can fix the time.

Choate now had Martinez on record as testifying that she did not leave her house for five days following her January 14 fall and that Del Valle bought her the ring three weeks after they met. Choate continued to cross-examine Martinez at length on some other issues to raise skepticism in the minds of the jurors about her story, so that once he revealed her lies her credibility would be completely destroyed. For example, Choate questioned Martinez about her claim that Del Valle's courtship included many long, intimate meals at a popular restaurant called Solari's.

Question: How long were these [meetings] at Solari's: these meetings when you went there and had a private room generally?

Answer: They varied in length. Sometimes we arrived there at 2:00 and remained until 4:00, sometimes we arrived there a little earlier.

Question: About a couple of hours?

Answer: Two or three hours.

Question: What were you doing all that time?

Answer: We were eating.

Question: What, not eating all the time?

Answer: Eating all the time.

Question: Two hours eating! Well, you must have grown fat during that period!

Answer: Well, perhaps you eat much quicker than I do.

After Martinez's cross-examination, Choate put the jeweler on the witness stand. The jeweler testified that Martinez and Del Valle were in his shop on January 15, the day after the fall. Further, the jeweler had made an entry in his account books showing that the purchase was made on the 15th.

The jeweler's testimony proved that Eugenie Martinez had lied about being unable to leave her house for five days and about the purchase date of the ring. Her credibility was further shaken by Choate's expert cross-examination, which brought every weakness and hard-to-believe aspect of her story to light. If it hadn't been for Choate's skill, the jury might have taken the obvious signs of Del Valle's affection for Martinez as evidence of a promise of marriage regardless of when the ring was bought. Instead, while the jury returned a verdict in Martinez's favor, it gave her only $50 in damages, far short of the $20,000 Juan Del Valle had been willing to pay to avoid a scandal.

—Stephen G. Christianson

Suggestions for Further Reading

Choate, Joseph Hodges. *The Choate Story Book*. New York: Cameron, Blake & Co., 1903.

Strong, Theron George. *Joseph H. Choate: New Englander, New Yorker, Lawyer, Ambassador*. New York: Dodd, Mead and Co., 1917.

Wellman, Francis Lewis. *The Art of Cross-Examination*. New York: Collier Books, 1986.

Reynolds v. U.S.: 1879

Defendant: George Reynolds   **Crime Charged:** Bigamy
Chief Defense Lawyers: George W. Biddle and Ben Sheeks
Chief Prosecutor: William Carey   **Judge:** Alexander White   **Place:** Salt
Lake City, Utah   **Dates of Trial:** October 30–December 10, 1875
Verdict: Guilty   **Sentence:** Two years imprisonment and a $500 fine

SIGNIFICANCE

The Mormons, who settled Utah, permitted members of their religion to practice polygamy. In *Reynolds,* the Supreme Court held that federal legislation banning polygamy was constitutional and did not violate the Mormons' First Amendment right to free exercise of their religion. The *Reynolds* case still remains the leading Supreme Court decision that the First Amendment does not protect polygamy.

After a somewhat checkered history and a long trek westward, in the mid-19th century the followers of a religious prophet named Joseph Smith settled the western lands that became the state of Utah. Their religion was called the Church of Jesus Christ of Latter-Day Saints, but most people called them the Mormons. They held a variety of novel beliefs, ranging from their conviction that Jesus Christ visited the American Indians to a prohibition against caffeine drinks such as coffee and tea. Their most controversial belief, however, was that a man could have more than one wife.

Most of the United States knew about the Mormon practice of polygamy since 1852. Most Americans were traditional Christians and believed in monogamy, or having only one spouse. Until the Mormons arrived, however, there were no federal laws against bigamy (legal term for marrying a second spouse while still married to a first spouse) or polygamy (practice of having several spouses). The government left the Mormons alone for many years, but in 1862 President Abraham Lincoln signed the Morrill Anti-Bigamy Act into law. The Morrill Act outlawed polygamy throughout the United States in general and in Utah in particular. The government did not do much to enforce the law, however, because it was preoccupied with the Civil War.

Congress Strengthens Anti-Bigamy Law

After the Civil War, Congress regained interest in the question of Mormon polygamy. Congress strengthened the Morrill Act by passing the Poland Law in 1874. The Poland Law increased the powers of the federal judiciary within the territory of Utah. Because federal judges were federally appointed, they were more likely to be non-Mormons and thus more aggressive about enforcing the law.

Mormon leader Brigham Young and George Q. Cannon, territorial delegate to Congress and advisor to Young, decided to challenge the federal government in court. They were confident that if the government tried any Mormons for bigamy, the United States Supreme Court would throw out the convictions, based on the First Amendment right to free exercise of their religion. Therefore, they planned to arrange for a "test case" to be brought to court. Young and Cannon chose Young's personal secretary, a devout Mormon and practicing polygamist, George Reynolds.

Young and Cannon were successful: the government indicted Reynolds for bigamy in October 1874. Reynolds had to be re-tried, however, due to jury-selection problems. The government indicted Reynolds again in October 1875. The judge was territorial Supreme Court Chief Justice Alexander White, and the prosecutor was William Carey. George W. Biddle and Ben Sheeks represented Reynolds.

The government charged that Reynolds was currently married to both Mary Ann Tuddenham and Amelia Jane Schofield. The prosecution had little difficulty in proving that Reynolds lived with both women, despite some trouble in serving Schofield with her subpoena. The following dialogue is an excerpt from the prosecution's questioning of Arthur Pratt, a deputy marshal sent to serve a subpoena on Schofield:

George Reynolds surrounded by his 12 sons. (Courtesy, Utah State Historical Society)

Question: State to the court what efforts you have made to serve it.

Answer: I went to the residence of Mr. Reynolds, and a lady was there, his first wife, and she told me that this woman was not there; that that was the only home that she had, but that she hadn't been there for two or three weeks. I went again this morning, and she was not there.

Question: Do you know anything about her home, where she resides?

Answer: I know where I found her before.

Question: Where?

Answer: At the same place.

Following more evidence of Reynolds' two marriages, which the defense had no chance of refuting, Judge White gave instructions to the jury. White's instructions smashed Reynolds' defense that by virtue of the First Amendment he was innocent because of his Mormon religious beliefs:

> [If you find that Reynolds] deliberately married a second time, having a first wife living, the want of consciousness of evil intent, the want of understanding on his part that he was committing crime, did not excuse him, but the law inexorably, in such cases, implies criminal intent. . . .

The jury found Reynolds guilty on December 10, 1875. On July 6, 1876, the territorial Supreme Court affirmed his sentence. Reynolds appealed to the U.S. Supreme Court. On November 14 and 15, 1878, Biddle and Sheeks argued to the Supreme Court that it must overturn Reynolds' conviction on the basis of the First Amendment.

The Supreme Court Destroys Mormons' Hopes

On January 6, 1879, the Supreme Court upheld the trial court's decision. The Supreme Court said that the First Amendment did not protect polygamy, and based its decision on historic American cultural values:

> Polygamy has always been odious among the northern and western nations of Europe, and, until the establishment of the Mormon Church, was almost exclusively a feature of the life of Asiatic and of African people. At common law, the second marriage was always void, and from the earliest history of England polygamy has been treated as an offence against society. . . . In the face of all this evidence, it is impossible to believe that the constitutional guaranty of religious freedom was intended to prohibit legislation in respect to this most important feature of social life. Marriage, while from its very nature a sacred obligation, is nevertheless, in most civilized nations, a civil contract, and usually regulated by law.

Therefore, the Supreme Court upheld Reynolds' sentence of two years imprisonment and a $500 fine. The Supreme Court's decision rocked the Mormons, who initially vowed to defy the Court but later seemed to accept the inevitable. In 1890, Mormon leader Wilford Woodruff issued a document called the Manifesto, which terminated "any marriages forbidden by the law of the land." After 1890, most Mormons abandoned polygamy.

The *Reynolds* case is still the leading Supreme Court decision that the First Amendment does not protect polygamy. In 1984, a U.S. District Court considered the case of Utah policeman Royston Potter, who was fired for bigamy. District Court Judge Sherman Christensen rejected Potter's First Amendment defense, and the U.S. 10th Circuit Court of Appeals upheld Christensen's ruling. In October of 1985 the Supreme Court refused to hear Potter's appeal. By refusing to consider cases like Potter's, the Supreme Court has effectively decided to keep *Reynolds* as the law of the land.

Many legal scholars have criticized the Supreme Court for not modifying or overturning *Reynolds*. It has been over 100 years since 1879, and in many subsequent cases the Supreme Court has greatly expanded the First Amendment's legal protection for free exercise of religion. Further, in the 1960s and early 1970s the Supreme Court increased the Constitution's protection for the civil rights of women, minorities and other persons whose equality under the law had never been a part of the old common law cited in *Reynolds*. Logically, therefore, one could expect the Supreme Court to reconsider its position on the constitutionality of polygamy. To date, however, the Supreme Court has not reversed its decision.

—Stephen G. Christianson

Suggestions for Further Reading

Cannon, George Quayle. *A Review of the Decision of the Supreme Court of the United States, in the Case of Geo. Reynolds vs. the United States.* Salt Lake City, Utah: Deseret News Printing, 1879.

Casey, Kathryn. "An American Harem." *Ladies Home Journal.* (February 1990): 116–121.

Embry, Jessie L. *Mormon Polygamous Families: Life in the Principle.* Salt Lake City, Utah: University of Utah Press, 1987.

Firmage, Edwin Brown. *Zion in the Courts: A Legal History of the Church of Jesus Christ of Latter-day Saints, 1830–1900.* Urbana: University of Illinois Press, 1988.

Foster, Lawrence. *Religion and Sexuality: The Shakers, the Mormons, and the Oneida Community.* Urbana: University of Illinois Press, 1984.

Wagoner, Richard S. *Mormon Polygamy: A History.* Salt Lake City, Utah: Signature Books, 1989.

Charles Guiteau Trial: 1881

Defendant: Charles J. Guiteau   **Crime Charged:** Assassinating President James A. Garfield   **Chief Defense Lawyers:** Leigh Robinson and George Scoville   **Chief Prosecutors:** George Corkhill, Walter Davidge, John K. Porter, Elihu Root, and E.B. Smith   **Judge:** Walter Cox   **Place:** Washington, D.C.   **Dates of Trial:** November 14, 1881–January 13, 1882   **Verdict:** Guilty   **Sentence:** Death by hanging

SIGNIFICANCE

Charles Guiteau's trial was one of the first murder trials in which the defendant's claim of insanity was subjected to the modern legal test: namely, whether or not Guiteau understood that his actions were wrong.

Less than 20 years after Abraham Lincoln was shot by John Wilkes Booth, the United States would see another president assassinated. James A. Garfield, a Union major general, had a distinguished military career, on which he capitalized even before the war ended by getting elected to the House of Representatives in 1863. Garfield was a successful politician, becoming the House Republican leader in 1876. Garfield was known for his opposition to President Ulysses S. Grant, a Republican whose scandal-ridden administration and flawed policies had alienated many of his fellow party members such as Garfield. In 1880, Garfield was the Republican candidate for president and won the election.

Unfortunately for Garfield, his presidency had attracted the obsessive interest of one Charles Guiteau. Guiteau claimed to be a lawyer and specialized in taking small-claims court cases for an unheard-of 75 percent contingency fee. Guiteau's legal career never amounted to much, and he was frequently on the run from creditors seeking payment on overdue bills. He also toyed with various political causes, joining the Oneida Community and other experimental religious communities springing up in the 1860s and 1870s. Guiteau tired of the communal life and moved to Washington, D.C., where he joined the Garfield election campaign as a lowly staff member.

Imaginary Insult Prompts Revenge

Guiteau never had any position of importance in the Garfield campaign except in his own mind. Guiteau's behavior had always been erratic, and it is possible that he contracted venereal diseases that further aggravated his mental problems. He was inspired to write a speech, which he hoped that Garfield would use in a debate with the Democratic presidential candidate, W.S. Hancock. Garfield never even read the speech, much less used it in the debate, but Guiteau was convinced that Garfield won the election thanks to his speech. Guiteau demanded to be appointed ambassador to France, and he even personally accosted Secretary of State James G. Blaine several times. Blaine tried to put Guiteau off politely, but be eventually lost patience and, on their final encounter, pushed Guiteau away and told him never to bother him again.

Bitter with resentment, Guiteau decided to take revenge against Garfield. Guiteau trailed Garfield throughout the month of June 1881, waiting for the right opportunity. On July 2, Guiteau got his chance. The Washington newspapers had reported Garfield's plans to go on a trip with his family, and Guiteau waited for the president at the train station, from where he was to leave. In the station's lobby, Guiteau came from behind Garfield and shot the president in the back. Station police rushed to arrest Guiteau, who offered no resistance. Meanwhile, Garfield was taken away for medical attention.

Guiteau's shot didn't kill Garfield outright. The president survived only to be diagnosed as having a fatal wound. The bullet had grazed Garfield's spine and lodged in his stomach, where it came to rest in such a position that blood continued to circulate but the bullet could not be removed without killing Garfield. The doctors therefore didn't operate, and they could do nothing for Garfield except try to make him comfortable until the inevitable happened. Garfield was a strong man, and he lived for almost three months until September 19, 1881. The American public was outraged by the murder, and one of the soldiers that guarded Guiteau's prison even tried unsuccessfully to shoot him before trial.

Was Guiteau Insane?

Once Garfield was dead, the government could finally try Charles Guiteau for murder. The trial opened November 14, 1881, in the District of Columbia. The judge was Walter Cox. Guiteau's lawyers were Leigh Robinson and George Scoville, although Guiteau would insist on trying to represent himself during the trial. U.S. Attorney General Wayne MacVeagh, determined to secure a conviction, named five lawyers to the prosecution team: George Corkhill, Walter Davidge, John K. Porter, Elihu Root, and E.B. Smith. Corkhill, who was also the District of Columbia's district attorney, summed up the prosecution's opinion of Guiteau's insanity defense in a pre-trial press statement that also mirrored public opinion on the issue:

> He's no more insane than I am. . . . There's nothing of the madman about
> Guiteau: he's a cool calculating blackguard, a polished ruffian, who has

gradually prepared himself to pose in this way before the world . . . he was a dead-beat, pure and simple. . . . Finally he got tired of the monotony of dead-beating. He wanted excitement of some other kind and notoriety, and he's got it.

Unfortunately for his attorneys, Guiteau not only fought their attempt to assert an insanity defense, but insisted on asserting some bizarre legal defenses of his own. For example, he wrote a plea to Judge Cox arguing that the cause of Garfield's death was the doctors' failure to properly treat the bullet wound and

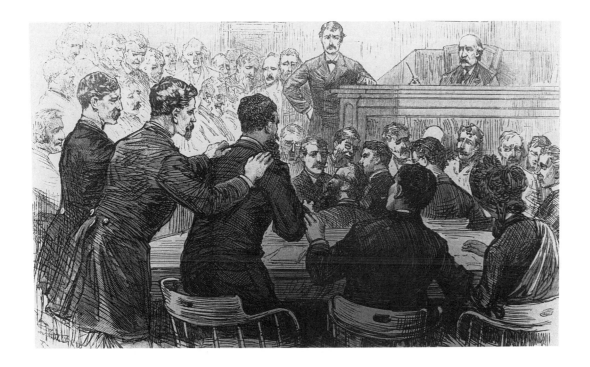

An angry Guiteau being restrained during his sensational trial for the killing of President Garfield. (*Harper's Weekly*)

therefore Guiteau was not guilty of murder. Of course, Guiteau's argument had no legal support. Any chance of acquitting Guiteau rested with his attorneys' efforts to prove that he was insane.

There is still some debate over what constitutes legal insanity, but most authorities generally agree that the basic test is whether the defendant knew that his actions were wrong. At the time of the Guiteau trial, however, the prevailing test of legal insanity was whether defendant knew that his actions were criminal. Therefore, even though someone like Guiteau might be considered insane because he didn't think it was wrong to shoot the president, he could be convicted if the judge determined that he understood that the law made it illegal to shoot people. By the 1880s, courts were beginning to apply the less harsh "was it wrong" test, which also gave the jury rather than the judge the task of determining insanity.

Influenced by this trend in the law, Judge Cox allowed both sides to argue their case directly to the jury, and intervened only occasionally. Despite strong evidence of his insanity, Guiteau insisted he was sane, so his attorneys simply let him ramble on and hoped that the jury drew the right conclusion. For example, they let Guiteau explain that he shot Garfield not only out of revenge, but also because God had told him that Garfield was ruining the Republican Party and must be killed to save the country from the Democrats. Guiteau testified that God had promised to protect him if he shot Garfield:

> I want to say right here in reference to protection, that the Deity himself will protect me; that He has used all these soldiers, and these experts, and this honorable court, and these counsel, to serve Him and protect me. That is my theory about protection. The Lord is no fool, and when He has got anything to do He uses the best means He can to carry out His purposes.

Judge Cox and the prosecutors agreed that Guiteau's sanity or insanity had to be measured by whether he knew his actions were wrong, but they were also determined not to let Guiteau escape the hangman. Cox instructed the jury that any minimal amount of understanding on Guiteau's part would be enough to support a guilty verdict:

> When you come . . . to consider . . . such a crime as we have here, murder most foul and unnatural, the law requires a very slight degree of intelligence indeed.

The way was thus paved for the prosecutors, led by Davidge, to make an emotional appeal to the jurors in their closing argument for Guiteau's conviction:

> A man may not have intelligence enough to be made responsible, even for a less crime; but it is hard, it is very hard to conceive of the individual with any degree of intelligence at all, incapable of comprehending that the head of a great constitutional republic is not to be shot down like a dog.

The defense was paralyzed, and their efforts to portray Guiteau as not guilty by reason of insanity were brushed aside. Davidge asserted that Guiteau's erratic behavior could be explained by his overweening ego:

> Such is the indescribable egotism of this man that he put himself on the same plane as the Savior of mankind and the prophets. There you have the explanation of his applying for the mission at Paris. For this man, in his indescribable egotism, seems to have thought all along that there was nothing in the world too high for him.

On January 13, 1882, the jury rendered its verdict. They found Charles Guiteau guilty of the murder of President Garfield. Guiteau leaped to his feet and screamed at the jurors, "You are all low, consummate jackasses." Guards took Guiteau back to his cell to await execution. On June 30, 1882, Guiteau went to the scaffold, ranting about the Almighty as he went to his death at the end of a rope. Guiteau had been given the benefit of a new and more liberal legal definition of insanity, but like many criminal defendants to come, he found out that public opinion influences judges and juries alike.

—Stephen G. Christianson

Suggestions for Further Reading

Gray, John Purdue. *The United States v. Charles J. Guiteau. Review of the Trial.* Utica, N.Y.: Unknown Publisher, 1882.

Ogilvie, John Stuart. *The Life and Death of James A. Garfield From the Tow Path to the White House.* Cincinnati, Ohio: Cincinnati Publishing Co., 1881.

Porter, John Kilham. *Guiteau Trial.* New York: J. Polhemus, 1882.

Rosenberg, Charles E. *The Trial of the Assassin Guiteau: Psychiatry and Law in the Gilded Age.* Chicago: University of Chicago Press, 1968.

The United States v. Charles J. Guiteau. New York: Arno Press, 1973.

Yick Wo v. Hopkins: 1886

Appellant: Yick Wo **Defendant:** Sheriff Peter Hopkins, San Francisco, California **Appellant Claim:** That San Francisco was enforcing an ordinance in an unlawfully discriminatory manner against the defendant and other Chinese persons **Chief Defense Lawyers:** Alfred Clarke and H. G. Sieberst **Chief Lawyers for Appellant:** Hall McAllister, D.L. Smoot, and L.H. Van Schaick **Justices:** Samuel Blatchford, Joseph P. Bradley, Stephen J. Field, Horace Gray, John Marshall Harlan, Stanley Matthews, Samuel F. Miller, Morrison Waite, and William B. Woods **Place:** Washington, D.C. **Date of Decision:** May 10, 1886 **Decision:** That Yick Wo's conviction for violating the ordinance was unconstitutional

SIGNIFICANCE

In *Yick Wo,* the Supreme Court proclaimed that even if a law was non-discriminatory, enforcing the law in a discriminatory manner was unconstitutional.

On May 26, 1880, the City of San Francisco, California enacted an ordinance requiring all commercial laundries to be in brick or stone buildings. Wooden buildings were permissible, but only with the Board of Supervisors' approval. The ordinance made no distinction between laundries run by Chinese immigrants and those run by whites. However, the ordinance was enforced in a blatantly racist manner. The board rubber-stamped its approval of white petitions to run laundries in wooden buildings, but denied every one of the nearly 200 Chinese petitions.

Sheriff Peter Hopkins enforced the ordinance, arresting Yick Wo and over 150 other Chinese persons who continued to run laundries in wooden buildings without board approval. Yick Wo was convicted and ordered to pay a fine of $10 or spend 10 days in jail. The California Supreme Court upheld his conviction, and he appealed to the U.S. Supreme Court for an order preventing San Francisco in the person of Sheriff Hopkins from carrying out the sentence. Hopkins was represented by Alfred Clarke and H.G. Sieberst and Yick Wo was represented by Hall McAllister, D.L. Smoot and L. H. Van Schaick. The Supreme Court heard both sides' arguments on April 14, 1886 and issued its decision on May 10, 1886.

The Court reversed Yick Wo's conviction, holding that the ordinance was being unfairly administered:

> Though the law itself be fair on its face and impartial in appearance, yet, if it is applied and administered by public authority with an evil eye and an unequal hand, so as practically to make unjust and illegal discriminations between persons in similar circumstances, material to their rights, the denial of equal justice is still within the prohibition of the Constitution. . . .

And while this consent of the supervisors is withheld from [Yick Wo] and from two hundred others who have also petitioned, all of whom happen to be Chinese subjects, eighty others, not Chinese subjects, are permitted to carry on the same business under similar conditions. The fact of this discrimination is admitted. No reason for it is shown, and the conclusion cannot be resisted, that no reason for it exists except hostility to the race and nationality to which the petitioners belong.

The significance of the *Yick Wo* decision is that, even if a law is non-discriminatory, enforcing the law in a discriminatory manner is unconstitutional.

—Stephen G. Christianson

Suggestions for Further Reading

Nelson, William Edward. *The Fourteenth Amendment: From Political Principle to Judicial Doctrine.* Cambridge, Mass.: Harvard University Press, 1988.

Pole, J. R. *The Pursuit of Equality in American History.* Berkeley: University of California Press, 1978.

Haymarket Trial: 1886

Defendants: George Engel, Samuel Fielden, Adolph Fischer, Louis Lingg, Oscar Neebe, Albert Parsons, Michael Schwab, and August Spies
Crime Charged: Murder   **Chief Defense Lawyers:** William P. Black, William A. Foster, Moses Salomon, and Sigismund Zeisler   **Chief Prosecutor:** Julius S. Grinnell   **Judge:** Joseph E. Gary   **Place:** Chicago, Illinois
Dates of Trial: June 21–August 20, 1886   **Verdict:** Guilty
Sentence: Death by hanging for all but Neebe, who was sentenced to prison for 15 years

SIGNIFICANCE
The Haymarket Riot was one of the most famous confrontations between the growing labor movement and the conservative forces of industry and government. Eight police officers were killed in a bomb explosion during the Haymarket affair. The resulting public backlash against the labor movement was a serious setback for the unions and their efforts to improve industrial working conditions.

After the Civil War, the United States experienced a period of unparalleled industrial growth that lasted for decades. It was a time when men became famous building new industries and businesses, establishing great corporate empires in the process. Among them were John D. Rockefeller's Standard Oil, which dominated the new petroleum industry; Andrew Carnegie's Carnegie Steel (later U.S. Steel), which revolutionized open-hearth steel technology and became the industry leader; and Marshall Field, named for its founder, which changed retailing from a multitude of mom-and-pop operations into an industry dominated by a handful of giants. However, the wealthy few who controlled this industrial development and its riches did not share their gains with the workers who made their terrific success possible.

By the 1880s, America's rapid industrialization had not yet produced any significant change in the legal relationship between workers and employers. Under the common law, inherited from England, any worker or laborer was free to negotiate individually with his employer concerning his wages, working hours and conditions, and other benefits. This may have been fine for the medieval English guilds whose practices shaped this aspect of the common law, but it was hopelessly out of touch with the realities of the modern industrial workplace. By the 1880s, American business was dominated by companies that employed large numbers of workers in factories, stores, mills, and other workplaces.

An individual worker's right to "negotiate" his wages was thus meaningless. Immigrants from abroad and American migration from the farms to the cities swelled the labor force available to industrial employers. Any worker who complained about his or her wages, sought better hours, or wanted benefits such as sick leave or compensation for on-the-job injuries could be easily replaced.

Police, U.S. military soldiers and firefighters attempting to control the chaos brought on by the Haymarket riots. (Courtesy, Illinois State Historical Library)

The only way for workers to improve their lives was to band together, "to unionize," so that one organization representing the combined workforce could compel management to make concessions. Naturally, companies resisted, and relations between the budding union movement and management became strained and often violent. Because unionists saw the government as an ally of big business in oppressing workers, many unionists were attracted to the political ideology of anarchism, which sought to do away with government.

Chicago: Hotbed of Radicalism

Little more than a village when it was founded in the 1830s, by the 1880s, Chicago was one of America's industrial hubs. Jobs brought immigrants from central and eastern Europe to the city. Many of these same immigrants, dissatisfied with their lot, joined the labor movement and embraced anarchism. One of the most vocal members of the labor movement was August Spies, the editor of a German-language newspaper who was deeply involved in the union and anarchist movements.

In 1886, the efforts of unions in general, and Spies in particular, were focused on the struggle to enforce an eight-hour workday. Most businesses insisted on a 10-hour workday, and even longer shifts were common. Labor demanded that management reduce the workday to eight hours, while keeping the daily wage the same. On the great holiday of labor, May 1, or May Day, unions staged nationwide demonstrations in favor of the eight-hour workday. Two days later, on May 3, Spies spoke before the striking workers of the McCormick farm machinery works. Fights broke out between the strikers and the "scab" workers hired to replace them. The police intervened, firing into the crowd of strikers, killing two and wounding many.

Spies promptly publicized the incident in his newspaper, and called for a rally against police brutality at Chicago's Haymarket Square the next day. At first, the meeting proceeded peacefully. Chicago's Mayor, Carter Harrison, showed up briefly so that he would be seen by working-class voters. After Spies spoke and Harrison had left, however, the situation rapidly deteriorated. Two of Spies' fellow anarchists, Samuel Fielden and Albert Parsons, spoke to the gathered workers and lashed out at business, government, and the Chicago police.

Intending to end the meeting and disperse the crowd, Chicago police Captain John Bonfield, who was present with nearly 200 men, ordered his officers to advance toward the crowd. Suddenly, someone in the crowd threw a bomb made of dynamite at the police. The powerful explosion killed eight policemen and wounded 67 others. Furious, the police retaliated. They fired into the crowd, killing or wounding dozens of people.

Police Arrest Eight Anarchists

Both the police and labor had been responsible for loss of life since the May Day rallies. After the Haymarket bomb explosion, however, public reaction was overwhelmingly against the unions. A major Chicago newspaper ran the headline, "NOW IT IS BLOOD!" and yellow journalism fanned public fears of anarchist-, socialist-, and communist-inspired union violence. Despite widespread searches and raids of working-class neighborhoods, however, the police never found the bomber.

Prosecutor Julius S. Grinnell, the Illinois state's attorney charged with finding Haymarket culprits, needed people to prosecute. When the police started to arrest known anarchists in the labor movement, beginning with Samuel Fielden, Michael Schwab, and August Spies the day after the riot, Grinnell supported the arrests. Encouraged by Grinnell, the police arrested five more labor anarchists: George Engel, Adolph Fischer, Louis Lingg, Oscar Neebe, and Albert Parsons. On May 27, 1886, all eight men were charged with murder.

Because of the public outcry, at first the defendants had trouble finding attorneys to represent them. Although Chicago's Central Labor Union arranged for their attorneys, Moses Salomon, and Sigismund Zeisler, to represent the defendants, neither man was an experienced criminal lawyer. Eventually, however, the experienced lawyers William P. Black and William A. Foster joined the defense team. Judge Joseph E. Gary was assigned to preside over the case, which opened June 21, 1886.

Jury selection occupied the first three weeks of the trial. A total of 981 potential jurors were questioned until 12 were finally selected. There have been accusations that Judge Gary used his influence to ensure the jury favored the prosecution. Since none of the jurors worked in a factory, they were not expected to be sympathetic to the union cause, which was really on trial.

Prosecutor Grinnell's tactic was to try to prove that the defendants had conspired not only to attack the police during the Haymarket rally, but also had conspired to create anarchy by overthrowing all government authority. Grinnell's courtroom rhetoric was as expansive as his accusations:

> For the first time in the history of our country are people on trial for endeavoring to make anarchy the rule, and in that attempt for ruthlessly and awfully destroying human life. I hope that while the youngest of us lives this in memory will be the last and only time in our country when such a trial will take place.

Grinnell brought forward several witnesses, all of whom gave poor testimony. They could only testify that the defendants at various times had made inflammatory, pro-anarchist, pro-union statements. Damning as this testimony was to some sectors of the public, it did not prove conspiracy, much less murder. Zeisler for the defense attempted to expose the weakness of the prosecution's evidence:

> It is not only necessary to establish that the defendants were parties to a conspiracy, but it is also necessary to show that somebody who was a party to that conspiracy had committed an act in pursuance of that conspiracy. Besides, it is essential that the State should identify the principal. . . . If the principal is not identified, then no one could be held as accessory.

Judge Gary ruled, however, that if the jury believed the defendants were guilty *beyond a reasonable doubt* of conspiracy to attack the police or overthrow the government, then the jury could also find the defendants guilty of murder. Also, the jury merely had to find *beyond a reasonable doubt* that the defendants arranged

Attention Workingmen!

----------- GREAT -----------

MASS-MEETING

TO-NIGHT, at 7.30 o'clock,

----------- AT THE -----------

HAYMARKET, Randolph St., Bet. Desplaines and Halsted.

Good Speakers will be present to denounce the latest atrocious act of the police, the shooting of our fellow-workmen yesterday afternoon.

THE EXECUTIVE COMMITTEE.

Poster calling for a workers to attend a meeting following the previous day's violence. (Courtesy, Illinois State Historical Library)

for someone to throw the bomb. According to Judge Gary's instructions to the jury, it did not matter that no one had found the bomb thrower.

Judge Gary's interpretation of the law was the final blow. On August 20, 1886, the jury pronounced its verdict. The jury found all eight defendants guilty and gave each the death penalty, except for Neebe, who was sentenced to 15 years in jail. The public and press applauded, and most papers carried glowing accounts of Grinnell's successful prosecution. Despite the efforts of amnesty groups, assisted by a young but soon-to-be-famous lawyer named Clarence Darrow, on September 14, 1887, the Illinois Supreme Court upheld the death sentence. A final appeal to the U. S. Supreme Court was also unsuccessful: on November 2, 1887, the Supreme Court held that because no principle of federal law was involved, it could not rule on the case.

The convicted men had thus exhausted all their conventional legal avenues of appeal. Lingg committed suicide before his scheduled execution. On November 11, 1887, Engel, Fischer, Parsons, and Spies were hung. Fielden, Neebe, and Schwab sat in jail, Neebe serving out his sentence and the others awaiting execution. Luckily for the condemned men, their stay in prison lasted for years. In the interim, the liberal politician John Peter Altgeld was elected governor of Illinois. On June 26, 1893, Altgeld pardoned Fielden, Neebe, and Schwab. The three left prison as free men.

The Haymarket Riot began with a political confrontation and ended with another political confrontation. Altgeld's pardon made him a political pariah, and in the next gubernatorial election he was soundly defeated. Nevertheless, Altgeld's pardon helped to legitimize labor's claim that the trial had been unfair from start to finish and that Judge Gary had been biased.

—Stephen G. Christianson

Suggestions for Further Reading

Avrich, Paul. *The Haymarket Tragedy*. Princeton, N.J.: Princeton University Press, 1984.

David, Henry. *The History of the Haymarket Affair*. NewYork:Russell & Russell, 1958.

Foner, Philip S. *The Autobiographies of the Haymarket Martyrs*. New York: Anchor Foundation, 1978.

Ginger, Ray. *Altgeld's America*. Chicago: Quadrangle Books, 1958.

Haymarket Remembered Project Staff. *Mob Action Against the State: The Haymarket Remembered. . .an Anarchist Convention*. Seattle: Left Bank Books, 1987.

Nelson, Bruce C. *Beyond the Martyrs: A Social History of Chicago's Anarchists, 1870–1900*. New Brunswick, N.J.: Rutgers University Press, 1988.

Roediger, David and Franklin Rosemont, eds. *Haymarket Scrapbook: A Centennial Anthology*. Chicago: C.H. Kerr, 1986.

The New Orleans "Mafia" Trial: 1891

Defendants: Antonio Bagnetto, James Caruso, John Caruso, Loretto Comitz, Rocco Geraci, Bastian Incardona, Joseph P. Macheca, Antonio Marchesi, Gasperi Marchesi, Charles Matranga, Pietro Monasterio, Pietro Natali, Charles Patorno, Charles Pietzo, Emmanuelle Polizzi, Frank Romero, Antonio Scaffidi, Salvatore Sunzeri, and Charles Traina   **Crimes Charged:** Shooting with intent to murder, lying in wait to murder   **Chief Defense Lawyers:** Lionel Adams, Charles Butler, John Q. Flynn, Arthur Gastinel, A.D. Henriques, Thomas J. Semmes, and Charles Theard   **Chief Prosecutors:** W.L. Evans, Charles H. Luzenberg, and James C. Walker   **Judge:** Joshua G. Baker
Place: New Orleans, Louisiana
Dates of Trial: February 16–March 13, 1891   **Verdicts:** Scaffidi, Polizzi, and Monasterio: mistrials; Macheca, Matranga, Bagnetto, Incardona, and Antonio and Gasperi Marchesi: not guilty; Natali, Pietzo, Patorno, Sunzeri, and John and James Caruso: charges dismissed

SIGNIFICANCE

The acquittals and mistrial verdicts provoked the worst mass lynching in U.S. history and made the word "Mafia" part of the American vernacular.

On the misty night of October 15, 1890, New Orleans, Louisiana, Police Superintendent David Hennessy was fatally shot in an ambush a block from his home. The dying man's whispers would cause the most controversial trial ever held in New Orleans courts and provoke the most notorious international political incident of the Gilded Age. They would also make "Mafia" a household word in America for the very first time.

Who Killed the Chief?

In May 1890, stevedores of the Matranga & Locasio fruit importing company were ambushed at midnight on their way home from the New Orleans docks. Information was rarely volunteered by crime victims in the Italian immigrant community and, at first, this shooting was no different. However, after first denying that they had recognized their attackers, the stevedores fingered six men. The accused included members of the Provenzano family, who had lost the fruit-unloading work to Matranga & Locasio.

When the "midnight vendetta" trial came to court "Chief" Hennessy's men were strangely absent from the prosecution's case. In fact, most police witnesses were called by the inept defense lawyers. Two Provenzano brothers and the other four defendants were convicted and sentenced to life in prison. Yet Judge Joshua Baker ordered a retrial when affidavits surfaced from witnesses who heard the wounded stevedores say at the ambush scene that they had no idea who had shot them. Baker also ruled that "disinterested" testimony by police officers proved that two of the accused were elsewhere when the shooting occurred.

Popular interest in the "midnight vendetta" faded, but those watching the case closely believed that Chief Hennessy himself would take the stand on the Provenzanos' behalf in late October. When he was gunned down a few days before the retrial date, many people assumed that he had been silenced by the Matrangas. Little attention was given to the fact that the coming trial was no secret, giving anyone with a grudge against the chief a perfect opportunity to throw the blame on the city's Italians and Italian-Americans.

At the crime scene and at the hospital Hennessy gasped that "dagoes" had shot him. Friends repeatedly asked him to identify or describe his attackers, but he lived until the next morning without doing so. The dying man was taken at his word. Mass arrests, forced searches, and beatings shook the immigrant community.

Nineteen men were ultimately charged with planning or executing Hennessy's murder. Charles Matranga and Joseph P. Macheca were well-to-do fruit importers. James and John Caruso belonged to Matranga's dock crew, as did Rocco Geraci and Bastian Incardona, two of the men ambushed the previous spring. Most of the accused were poor men whose arrests were based on circumstantial evidence or outright hysteria. Pietro Monasterio, a shoemaker, was clubbed and arrested because Hennessy's killers had fired from a gateway beside his shack. Pietro Natali was arrested at the railway station "on suspicion" because his suit fit him badly.

To reduce the number of pretrial challenges, two successive trials were planned. The first nine defendants were Macheca, Matranga, Monasterio, Incardona, Antonio Scaffidi, Antonio Bagnetto, Emmanuelle Polizzi, Antonio Marchesi, and Marchesi's 14-year-old son, Gasperi. With the exception of Charles Patorno, who hired his own counsel, the accused were collectively represented by Adams & Henriques, the same law firm the district attorney's office had allowed to help prosecute the Provenzanos in the "midnight vendetta" shooting.

Absent Conspiracy, Missing Witnesses

Lionel Adams was a brilliant former New Orleans district attorney. Ironically, he had once successfully defended David Hennessy on the charge of killing the chief of detectives when Hennessy was a young cop. Ten years later, Adams was hired by the men accused of murdering Hennessy.

Adams tangled the state's case with challenges throughout the winter of 1890. He successfully had all 19 murder indictments thrown out by charging that an unauthorized stenographer was allowed into the grand-jury room during the questioning of witnesses. New indictments were quickly drawn, but Adams immediately submitted a motion to quash them, too. He argued that the grand jury was biased because it contained two members of a "Committee of Fifty" appointed by the mayor to investigate the Hennessy killing. Adams unsuccessfully subpoenaed the mayor and the entire Committee of Fifty, as well as their confidential minutes and affidavits. Officials interviewed 780 "talesmen," or potential jurors before an acceptable jury was found. Prosecutors were expected to present a clear case when testimony began February 28. Things went less smoothly in the courtroom. None of the State's witnesses could agree on whether the streetlight at the scene was burning brightly or nearly extinct when the shooting began in the misty darkness.

Laborer Zachary Foster swore that Scaffidi, Polizzi, Monasterio, and Antonio Marchesi were "like the ones" he saw shooting at Hennessy. The chief's neighbors agreed that the gun battle was brief, but a young bartender named John Daure claimed to have run four blocks in time to see Scaffidi, Bagnetto, and Antonio Marchesi firing. House painter M.L. Peeler said he saw the shooting from an upstairs gallery. Peeler identified Scaffidi, but testimony suggested painter was drunk at the time. A police officer claimed to have recognized Emmanuelle Polizzi by the back of his head from over a block away.

The courtroom tension was too much for the man newspapers called "Manuel Politz." Polizzi became hysterical, causing attorney Charles Theard to quit the case. Judge Baker replaced Theard with John Q. Flynn, who applied himself to the case more diligently than his predecessor. Four days later, however, Polizzi tried to dive through the sheriff's office window. The press theorized that Polizzi had confessed and was deathly afraid of the other defendants.

District Attorney Charles Luzenberg claimed he would prove a conspiracy in which Chief Hennessy was killed for meddling in the Matranga-Provenzano feud. Joseph Macheca was accused of renting the shack where Monasterio lived, thus arranging an ambush to be carried out by hired assassins. Witnesses of varying degrees of reliability identified Scaffidi, Monasterio, Polizzi, Bagnetto, and the elder Marches as the shooters. Yet spectators waiting for details of the alleged plot were disappointed.

In the months after Hennessy's murder, newspapers remained well stocked with stories about cruel Sicilian brigands, the Committee of Fifty's mandate to "root out foreign murder societies," and unsolved killings in the immigrant community. Violence once vaguely blamed on "stiletto societies" and "the practice of the vendetta" was now attributed to "the Mafia," a single shadowy organization devoted to murder and extortion. Much of the information the press used to accuse the Matrangas of leading a New Orleans Mafia came from their enemies, the Provenzanos, who had unsuccessfully attributed a series of extortion letters to Charles Matranga during their own trial.

Expectations of a plot being proven were high in such a climate. Yet no actual evidence of the Mafia conspiracy sketched by the daily press—or any conspiracy at all, for that matter—was offered by the prosecution during the trial.

The defense insinuated that prosecution witnesses were more interested in city-appropriated reward money than in telling the truth. Lionel Adams produced alibis—called "the felon's defense" by cynics—for all of the accused. The defense also pointed out the absence of two expected witnesses. Hennessy had been walking home with a former cop named Billy O'Connor, from whom he parted just before the shooting. Private security guard J.C. Roe was on duty at Hennessy's house that night and had been superficially wounded by the gunfire. Neither O'Connor nor Roe was called by the state. The defense claimed that their testimony would have destroyed the credibility of prosecution witnesses like John Daure.

When final arguments ended after two weeks of testimony, Judge Baker ordered the jury to find Charles Matranga and Bastian Incardona innocent. The state had introduced no evidence against them.

The First, the Best, and Even the Most Law-Abiding

The March 13 verdicts shocked the city. Monasterio, Bagnetto, and Scaffidi got mistrials on the murder charge. The other six defendants were acquitted. All nine were returned to the Orleans Parish prison, expecting the redundant "lying in wait" charge to be dismissed the next day. On the morning of March 14, however, an armed committee headed by two politically prominent New Orleans attorneys and a newspaper editor led a mob of over 6,000 people to the prison and smashed their way in. Macheca, Scaffidi, Monasterio, and Antonio Marchesi were shot to death. So were Geraci, Romero, Traina, Comitz, and James Caruso, none of whom had been tried. Polizzi was dragged out to the street, where a crowd hung him from a lamp post and emptied pistols into him. Bagnetto's broken body was strung up from a tree.

The surviving defendants were soon released by District Attorney Luzenberg, who denied the existence of Polizzi's "confession." A Grand Jury cleared the lynch mob's leaders, saying that "the first, the best and even the most law-abiding" citizens of New Orleans were driven to act because justice had been subverted by jury bribers, a jab at Adams & Henriques' slippery detective associate, Dominick O'Malley.

The Hennessy case jurors denied being bribed. The acquittals, they said, resulted from impatience in the jury room, the absence of Billy O'Connor and Officer Roe, and other holes in the state's case. Two men later got short prison terms for making suggestive comments to potential jurors, but no link between the defense and the chosen jury was unearthed.

Several of the lynched men were Italian subjects. A war scare swept America as the enraged Italian government broke off diplomatic relations. Two years later, the U.S. government paid Italy a $25,000 indemnity, and diplomacy was restored. Yet a national pattern of indiscriminately blaming violent crime in Italian-American communities on a single entity known as the Mafia had been set, helping to fuel anti-immigration sentiment. The anti-Italian insult "Who killa d' Chief?" lived on in New Orleans for decades. To this day, no one has proven who killed Chief David Hennessy.

—Thomas C. Smith

Suggestions for Further Reading

Asbury, Herbert J. *The French Quarter.* New York: Alfred A. Knopf, 1936.

Coxe, John E. "The New Orleans Mafia Incident," *Louisiana Historical Quarterly*, Vol. 20 (1937) 1067–1110.

Gambino, Richard. *Vendetta: A true story of the worst lynching in America, the mass-murder of Italian-Americans in New Orleans in 1891, the vicious motivation behind it, and the tragic repercussions that linger to this day.* Garden City, N.Y.: Doubleday, & Co. 1977.

Karlin, J. Alexander. "New Orleans Lynchings in 1891 and the American Press," *Louisiana Historical Quarterly*, Vol. 24 (1941): 187–204.

Kendall, John S. "Who Killa de Chief?" *Louisiana Historical Quarterly*, Vol. 22 (1939): 492–530.

"The Mafia and What Led to the Lynching," *Harper's Weekly*, Vol. 35 (March 28, 1891): 602–612.

Saxon, Lyle, et al. *Gumbo Ya-Ya.* Boston: Houghton Mifflin, 1945.

Lizzie Borden Trial: 1893

Defendant: Lizzie Borden   **Crime Charged:** Murder
Chief Defense Lawyers: Andrew Jennings and George D. Robinson
Chief Prosecutors: Hosea Knowlton and William H. Moody   **Judges:** Caleb
Blodget, Justin Dewey, and Albert Mason   **Place:** Fall River, Massachusetts
Dates of Trial: June 5–20, 1893   **Verdict:** Not guilty

SIGNIFICANCE

On the basis of circumstantial evidence, prosecutors accused Lizzie Borden of murdering her father and stepmother. In an attempt to circumvent its lack of direct evidence, the prosecution appealed to popular stereotypes about the slyness and cleverness of women. Lizzie nonetheless was acquitted. The acquittal was significant in that it represented the triumph of the rule of law over common prejudice.

Born in 1860 and never married, Lizzie Borden lived in quiet obscurity in the small town of Fall River, Massachusetts, until August 4, 1892. On that day an ax-murderer killed her father, Andrew J. Borden, and her stepmother, Abby Durfee Gray Borden. The police arrested Lizzie for the crime, and her trial made her a figure of national notoriety.

Lizzie's birth mother, Sarah M. Borden, died when Lizzie was a small child. Lizzie lived in her parents' house together with the family maid, her uncle, and her older sister, Emma Borden, who was, like Lizzie, a spinster. The Bordens' family life was quite ordinary and unremarkable until the morning of August 4, 1892, when a neighbor looked out of her window and noticed Lizzie, visibly upset, clinging to the screen door that opened onto the Bordens' yard. When the neighbor, Adelaide Churchill, asked Lizzie what the problem was, she replied, "Oh, Mrs. Churchill, do come over. Someone has killed father."

Churchill immediately notified the police. When a policeman, followed by a doctor, arrived at the Borden house, they found Andrew Borden's body in the family living room. Someone had come upon him, apparently while he was napping, and brutally and repeatedly attacked him with an ax. Although blood splattered the furniture, there were no signs that he had fought with an intruder. Churchill and another neighbor, Alice Russell, had accompanied the policeman and doctor into the Borden house. Churchill went upstairs with the maid to look for Abby Borden. They found her in a guest room, murdered in the same terrible fashion. Like Andrew, Abby's morning routine had been unremarkable and there was no sign of resistance to an intruder. Apparently Abby had been making the bed at the time of her murder.

Lizzie Charged with Murder

The police began an investigation and questioned Lizzie on the events of the morning of the murder. Whether out of shock or deliberate evasiveness, her answers were rambling and inconsistent. The police asked her where she had been at the time of the murders, and she answered at different times with different versions. Lizzie at various times told the police that she had been getting a piece of fishing gear from the family barn, or that she had been in the yard, or that she had been picking pears.

Turn-of-the-century-police questioning tactics, particularly those used on a murder suspect, were often less than sensitive to the effect of trauma upon a suspect's answers. It is difficult to determine, therefore, whether Fall River Mayor John Coughlin was justified in ordering the police to arrest Lizzie on the basis of their investigation and her inconsistent answers. The local coroner conducted a formal inquest, and Lizzie's answers were just as confused.

The police charged Lizzie with the murder of her father and stepmother. They suspected that Lizzie's motive was either a deep-rooted resentment related to her natural mother's death, or a desire to collect her father's sizable fortune. The police did not, however, attempt to implicate Lizzie's older sister Emma in the murders. Logically, Emma could have had the same motives as Lizzie and have committed the murders herself. With this question hanging in the air, the state of Massachusetts opened Lizzie Borden's trial on June 5, 1893.

Judges Caleb Blodget, Justin Dewey, and Albert Mason presided over the trial. The prosecutors were Hosea Knowlton and William H. Moody. Knowlton was the more experienced attorney, but because he was feeling ill he had brought Moody along as co-counsel. Lizzie's defense lawyers were Andrew Jennings and George D. Robinson. Robinson was a particularly distinguished lawyer, having once been the governor of Massachusetts.

Moody opened the prosecution's case by describing the facts to the jury and preparing them to accept the idea that a woman could have committed such horrible crimes:

> Upon the fourth day of August of the last year an old man and woman, husband and wife, each without a known enemy in the world, in their own home, upon a frequented street in the most populous city in this County under the light of day and in the midst of its activities, were, first one, then, after an interval of an hour, another, severally killed by unlawful human agency. Today a woman of good social position, of hitherto unquestioned character, a member of a Christian church and active in good works, the own daughter of one of the victims, is at the bar of this Court, accused by the Grand Jury of this County of these crimes.

The prosecution's case rested in large part on circumstantial evidence. For example, Moody made a point of emphasizing that Emma Borden had seen

Lizzie burning a dress after the murders. Implying that Lizzie had burnt the bloodstained dress she wore while murdering her parents, Moody said to the jury:

> Now, gentlemen, it will appear that about the two rooms in which the homicides were committed there was blood spattering in various directions, so that it would make it probable that one or more spatters of blood would be upon the person or upon the clothing of the assailant.

The prosecution went on to present four axes and hatchets found in the Borden house. None of these implements had any bloodstains on them, however.

Andrew Jennings, who had been the Borden family's attorney for many years, opened Lizzie's defense with a direct attack on the prosecutors' reliance on circumstantial evidence:

> They have either got to produce the weapon which did the deed . . . or else they have got to account in some reasonable way for its disappearance. . . . There are two kinds of evidence: direct evidence and circumstantial evidence. Direct evidence is the testimony of persons who have seen, heard or felt the thing or things about which they are testifying. . . . [T]here is not one particle of direct evidence in this case, from beginning to end, against Lizzie Andrew Borden. There is not a spot of blood: there is not a weapon connected with her.

Jennings and Robinson went on to challenge the prosecution's assertion that Lizzie's dress-burning was an implication of guilt. They brought Emma Borden to the witness stand and were able to elicit testimony, favorable to Lizzie, that the dress had in fact been very old, faded and stained and thus was legitimately destroyed. After nearly two days, the defense concluded its case.

Attorneys Wrap Up

Robinson made the closing argument for the defense. Of course, he could not dispute that a particularly heinous crime had occurred:

> One of the most dastardly and diabolical of crimes that was ever committed in Massachusetts was perpetrated in August, 1892, in the city of Fall River, . . . the terror of those scenes no language can portray.

Robinson went on, however, to stress how close Lizzie and Andrew Borden had been. Many years ago, Lizzie gave her father a ring to symbolize her love for and fidelity to him. Robinson used this fact to emphasize how unlikely it would be that Lizzie would murder her father:

> Here was a man that wore nothing in the way of ornament, of jewelry but one ring, and that ring was Lizzie's. It had been put on many years ago when Lizzie was a little girl and the old man wore it and it lies buried with him in the cemetery. He liked Lizzie, did he not? He loved her as a child: and the ring that stands as the pledge of plighted faith and love, that typifies and symbolizes the dearest relation that is ever created in life, that ring was the bond of union between the father and the daughter.

When the prosecutors' turn came to make their closing argument, Knowlton and Moody knew that their principal weakness was their heavy reliance on circumstantial evidence. They deliberately appealed to the all-male jury to decide the case on the basis of prevailing attitudes toward women:

> If they lack in strength and coarseness and vigor, they make up for it in cunning, in dispatch, in celerity, in ferocity. If their loves are stronger and more enduring than those of men, on the other hand, their hates are more undying, more unyielding, more persistent.

In the hope that the jurors would accept at face value this assessment of the female psyche, prosecutor Knowlton went on to dismiss the prosecutors' failure to find any bloodstained clothing belonging to Lizzie:

> How could she have avoided the spattering of her dress with blood if she was the author of these crimes? . . . I cannot answer it. You cannot answer it. You are neither murderers nor women. You have neither the craft of the assassin nor the cunning and deftness of the sex. . . . You are merciful men. The wells of mercy, I hope, are not dried up in any of us. But this is not the time nor the place for the exercise of it!

The end of the prosecutors' closing argument marked the end of the trial. All that remained were the judges' final instructions to the jury. Before the judges adjourned the court, however, they gave Lizzie the opportunity to make a statement to the jury. Under Massachusetts law, she had not been required to testify at the trial. Thus, the following words were the first that the jury had heard from Lizzie: "I am innocent. I leave it to my counsel to speak for me."

If she were convicted, the state of Massachusetts would execute her in a newly invented machine, popularly known as the electric chair.

Judges' Instructions Favor Lizzie

Judge Dewey spoke for the three judges when he gave the jury their instructions concerning the law and evidence in the case. First, he reiterated the defense's point that the prosecutors had relied on circumstantial evidence. Second, he dismissed her inconsistent statements to the police after the murders as being normal under the circumstances. Having thus effectively challenged the basis of the prosecution's case, Judge Dewey went on to remind the jury members of their duty to Lizzie:

> If the evidence falls short of providing such conviction in your minds, although it may raise a suspicion of guilt, or even a strong probability of guilt, it would be your plain duty to return a verdict of not guilty. . . . [S]eeking only the truth, you will lift this case above the range of passion and prejudice and excited feeling, into the clear atmosphere of reason and law.

On June 20, 1893, the jury left the courtroom to deliberate. Perhaps Judge Dewey's instructions had swayed the jury, or perhaps the jury was truly convinced of her innocence. In either event, after little more than an hour of deliberation the jury returned to the courtroom with its verdict. It found Lizzie Borden not guilty of the murder charges.

After two long weeks of what was one of the nation's most widely publicized trials, Lizzie left the courtroom a free woman. To this day, historians have speculated that she had been covering up for sister Emma. It is possible that Emma committed the murders, or hired someone to enter the Borden house and murder her parents. There were conflicting accounts, not fully explored by the prosecutors or Lizzie's attorneys, that a hired assassin had been seen fleeing Fall River. Other accounts about visits that Emma had made to a nearby town, visits that could have related to the murders, were also left unexplored.

Her trial over, Lizzie left the old Borden residence and moved into a new house. Collecting her inheritance from her father's estate, Lizzie could live a comfortable life. She invested this money wisely, and became a prominent local benefactor of worthwhile charities, particularly animal shelters. By all accounts, she led a respectable life for nearly 35 years until her death in 1927. The infamy of her trial, however, has outlived her death.

Despite her acquittal, to this day Lizzie is still popularly regarded as one of America's most famous murderesses. In fact, her acquittal was really a triumph for women, because the jury refused to bend the rules of law that protect defendants when the prosecution played upon popular stereotypes about the "sly sex."

—Stephen G. Christianson

Suggestions for Further Reading

Brown, Arnold R. *Lizzie Borden.* Nashville, Tenn.: Rutledge Hill Press, 1991.

Hunter, Evan. *Lizzie.* New York: Arbor House, 1984.

Lincoln, Victoria. *A Private Disgrace.* New York: G.P. Putnam's Sons, 1967.

Porter, Edwin H. *The Fall River Tragedy.* Portland, Maine: King Philip Pub. Co., 1985.

Radin, Edward D. *Lizzie Borden.* New York: Simon & Schuster, 1961.

Satterthwait, Walter. *Miss Lizzie.* New York: St. Martin's Press, 1989.

Spiering, Frank. *Lizzie.* New York: Random House, 1984.

Sullivan, Robert. *Goodbye Lizzie Borden.* Brattleboro, VT: Greene Press, 1974.

In Re Debs: 1895

Defendant: Eugene V. Debs **Crimes Charged:** Contempt of court and conspiracy **Chief Defense Lawyers:** Clarence Darrow, S. Gregory, and Lyman Trumbull **Chief Prosecutors:** John C. Black, T. M. Milchrist, and Edwin Walker **Judges:** Peter Grosscup and William A. Woods
Place: Chicago, Illinois **Dates of Trial:** January 26–February 12, 1895
Verdict: Guilty of contempt, no verdict on conspiracy **Sentence:** 6 Months imprisonment for contempt of court (a pretrial conviction)

SIGNIFICANCE

In one of the most egregious cases of the courts siding with industry against labor, a federal judge issued an injunction ordering the American Railway Union to stop a strike against the Pullman Company and sentenced the strike's leader, Eugene Debs, to six months in jail for violating the injunction. The government then put Debs on trial for conspiracy but dropped the case in mid-trial. The Supreme Court upheld Debs' sentence for contempt of court in a major confirmation of federal judges' power to enforce their orders.

In the late 19th century, as heavy industry grew and railroads spread across the country, commercial centers like Chicago and other cities mushroomed. With this industrial growth, however, came growing abuses. Ownership of industry was concentrated in a handful of wealthy men, while the factory workers and others who made industrialization possible were not protected by the government. Companies were able to get away with paying workers low wages for long hours. Further, most companies did not give workers benefits such as sick leave or disability pay. To make matters worse, there were many "company towns" where workers rented their houses and bought food from stores all owned by the very company that employed them.

The city of Chicago, where the famous Haymarket Riot occurred, was home to one of the most flagrant abusers of industrial power. George M. Pullman's Pullman Palace Car Company manufactured the world-famous railroad cars. The company operated its own company town just outside of Chicago. Not surprisingly, it was named Pullman, Illinois.

The company charged workers higher than average rents to live in company-owned housing while paying substandard hourly wages. Further, in 1893 the company responded to an economic depression by cutting wages 25 percent. In the winter of 1893, conditions were grim in Pullman, Illinois.

The "Debs Rebellion"

Eugene Debs was born in 1855 to a blue-collar Midwestern family. He began his career as a lowly railroad worker. However, he soon discovered that his real gift was in politics, and he rose quickly in the budding union movement. By 1893 Debs was president of the American Railway Union. Although the ARU was primarily a railroad-track workers union, in the spring of 1894 many Pullman employees joined. On May 11, 1894, the smoldering discontent in Pullman ignited and all 3,300 workers went on strike. Although it is likely that the strike was a spontaneous local event not called by the ARU, Debs quickly went to Pullman and assumed leadership of the strike. Because the ARU represented workers in nearly every railroad system in the United States, and the railroads threw their support behind Pullman, the strike soon became a nationwide railway work stoppage. The resulting paralysis of the American rail network was dubbed the "Debs Rebellion."

President Grover Cleveland was alarmed by the strike and sided with Pullman and the railroads. His attorney general, Richard Olney, went to federal judges Peter Grosscup and William A. Woods to ask for a court order stopping the strike. Ironically, one of Olney's arguments in asking for the injunction was that the ARU strike violated the Sherman Antitrust Act of 1890. The Sherman Act was intended to break up large corporate monopolies and gave federal judges broad powers to issue orders stopping actions they deemed harmful to interstate commerce. At Olney's suggestion, Grosscup and Woods twisted the act's meaning and on July 2, 1894 used their power to order Debs and the other ARU leaders to abandon the strike. The order even made answering a telegram from the strikers a violation of the terms of the injunction.

Furious, Debs and the ARU leadership resolved to ignore the injunction. Because violating a court order constitutes contempt of court, Judge Woods had Debs hauled into court and sentenced him to six months in jail. Contempt of court is the traditional means by which judges enforce their authority, requiring no trial or jury. The government also charged Debs with conspiracy to block the federal mail: the ARU's nationwide railroad work stoppage had halted a Rock Island Railroad train carrying mail for the post office. In the meantime, the federal government's actions were not limited to the legal system. President Cleveland sent federal troops to Chicago to crush the strike.

Debs Tried for Conspiracy

Unlike the contempt charge, the government had to try Debs for conspiracy before a jury. The ARU retained the famous lawyer Clarence Darrow, who was assisted by S. Gregory and former Illinois Supreme Court Judge Lyman

Trumbull. The prosecutors were John C. Black, T. M. Milchrist, and Edwin Walker.

When the trial opened January 26, 1895, from the start Darrow made it clear to the jury that the issue at trial was not Debs' guilt but the government's desire to crush the union movement. Referring to an executive committee of the railroads called the General Managers' Association, Darrow said:

> This is an historic case which will count much for liberty or against liberty. . . . Conspiracy, from the days of tyranny in England down to the day the General Managers' Association used it as a club, has been the favorite weapon of every tyrant. It is an effort to punish the crime of thought.

Darrow cleverly decided to subpoena George Pullman and the members of the General Managers' Association to testify at the trial. While the real opposition to the "Debs Rebellion" was being served with legal process, the prosecutors grilled Debs. They hoped to provoke him into a socialist tirade against American industry and thus alienate the jury. Prosecutor Walker asked Debs how he defined the word "strike." Debs, however, merely responded in a detached manner:

> A strike is a stoppage of work at a given time by men acting in concert in order to redress some real or imaginary grievance.

> Walker: Mr. Debs, will you define the meaning of the word "scab"?

> A scab in labor unions means the same as a traitor to his country. It means a man who betrays his fellow men by taking their places when they go on strike for a principle. It does not apply to non-union men who refuse to quit work.

Petition to release Eugene V. Debs from prison. (Courtesy, Illinois State Historical Library)

After Debs' testimony, events took a surprising turn. Judge Grosscup, probably influenced by George Pullman and the General Managers' Association, who were reluctant to testify in open court, stated on the day after Debs's testimony that:

> Owing to the sickness of a juror and the certificate of his physician that he will not be able to get out for two or three days, I think it will be necessary to adjourn the further taking of testimony in this case.

Grosscup then adjourned the case. In a remarkable turn of events, the trial never reconvened. In effect, the government dropped the conspiracy charge. It has never been conclusively determined whether this decision was the result of Pullman's influence or the weakness of the government's case.

Darrow and Debs' other lawyers appealed the still-valid contempt conviction. However, on May 27, 1895, the U.S. Supreme Court rejected their pleas and refused to overturn Woods' decision. Debs served his six-month sentence in Illinois' Woodstock Prison with other ARU leaders jailed for contempt. *In Re Debs* has been cited many times since to demonstrate the sweeping powers of federal judges to punish those who violate court orders.

Debs leaving prison in December, 1921. (Courtesy, Library of Congress)

Debs' Political Career Continued

Although his strike was crushed, Debs left prison with his political reputation intact. He became the leading spokesman for the American left, and was the presidential candidate for the American Socialist Party in every election (except 1916) from 1900 to 1920. He lost every election.

When the United States entered World War I, Debs was outraged. He criticized President Woodrow Wilson in the harshest terms, and in *U.S. v. Debs* was charged with treason. For the most part, the charges against Debs were the result of his support of the International Workers of the World, known as the "Wobblies." This time, however, a court found Debs guilty. Debs' appeals to the Supreme Court were unsuccessful. While in prison, Debs ran for the fifth and final time as the Socialist Party's candidate for president. Again, he was unsuccessful in his bid to become the nation's chief executive.

Stung by Debs' criticism, President Wilson refused to pardon him. Among Debs' choicer comments about Wilson were such gems as:

> No man in public life in American history ever retired so thoroughly discredited, so scathingly rebuked, so overwhelmingly impeached and repudiated as Woodrow Wilson.

Warren G. Harding, who won the 1920 presidential election, was more charitable. Harding pardoned Debs in December 1921 and even invited him to the White House on Christmas Day. But Debs found that the Socialist Party had lost its political force. He spent his final years with his wife in quiet retirement and died in 1926.

—Stephen G. Christianson

Suggestions for Further Reading

Coleman, McAlister. *Eugene V. Debs, a Man Unafraid.* New York: Greenberg, 1930.

Ginger, Ray. *The Bending Cross.* New Brunswick, N.J.: Rutgers University Press, 1949.

McHugh, Clare. "Why Has Socialism Never Caught on in the U.S.?" *Scholastic Update* (September 1986): 12.

Noble, Iris. *Labor's Advocate.* New York: Julian Messner, 1966.

Selvin, David F. *Eugene Debs.* New York: Lothrop, Lee & Shepard, 1966.

Theo Durrant Trial: 1895

Defendant: William Henry Theodore Durrant   **Crime Charged:** Murder
Chief Defense Lawyers: Eugene N. Deuprey and John H. Dickinson
Chief Prosecutors: W.H. Anderson, William S. Barnes, W.F. Fitzgerald, and
Edgar D. Peixotto   **Judge:** D.J. Murphy   **Place:** San Francisco, California
Dates of Trial: April 15–November 1, 1895   **Verdict:** Guilty
Sentence: Death by hanging

SIGNIFICANCE
"Theo" Durrant was tried, convicted, and executed for murdering two girls despite the fact that the prosecution never proved any motive for the murders.

William Henry Theodore Durrant, known as "Theo," was probably the last person the people of San Francisco, California, would have suspected as being capable of the "Crime of the Century," as San Francisco newspapers described the murders Durrant committed in the Emanuel Baptist Church in 1895.

Durrant was a 21-year-old medical student at the Cooper Medical College. He also belonged to the Emanuel Baptist Church, where he taught Sunday school, assisted with church services, and helped out with various repair jobs in his spare time. He was liked and well respected in the community. In April of 1895, however, he revealed a different side to his personality.

On the afternoon of April 3, Durrant took his fiancée, a high-school girl named Blanche Lamont, into the church. The church was empty, and Durrant grabbed Blanche and proceeded to strangle her to death. He then dragged her corpse to the church belfry where he committed necrophilia with the body. Afterwards he left the church, leaving Lamont's body in the belfry.

That evening, Lamont's parents contacted the police and reported that their daughter was missing. The police went to Durrant's house and questioned him. He feigned ignorance and suggested that Lamont had been kidnapped by one of the white slavery gangs then common in San Francisco. While the police investigated this possibility, Durrant murdered another girl.

On Good Friday, April 12, Durrant lured young Minnie Williams into the Church late at night. He raped and killed her, then dismembered her body in the church library. Durrant made no effort to clean up the bloodstained library or dispose of Williams' body, and once he was finished, he simply left. Some members of the congregation entered the church the next morning and discovered the scene of butchery. They summoned the police, who searched the Church and discovered Lamont's body in the belfry as well. The police promptly arrested Durrant and began the inquests that were the prelude to Durrant's trial on April 15.

Durrant Tried for Murder

The case attracted considerable publicity, with the San Francisco newspapers trumpeting that it was the "Crime of the Century." The prosecutors were W.H. Anderson, William S. Barnes, W.F. Fitzgerald and Edgar D. Peixotto. Durrant was represented by Eugene N. Deuprey and John H. Dickinson. Presiding was Judge D.J. Murphy.

The evidence against Durrant was overwhelming, except for the motive behind the murders. Why did Durrant kill the two girls? There was no inheritance that he stood to collect, no personal possessions worth stealing. In fact, there were no rational reasons for the murders. Durrant's lawyers relied on the lack of motive as their primary defense during the trial. In response, Peixotto stated for the prosecution that:

> The brilliant counsel for the defendant in his opening statement challenged the prosecution to answer the questions where Blanche Lamont was murdered, when she was murdered, by whom she was murdered, and what the motive was. We are now ready to answer these questions. . . . "What was the motive?"; unbridled passion, that same motive that has ruled and governed the world, made nations totter and decay, brought men from the highest pinnacles in life down to brutish beasts; that same motive that has filled our histories with black pages; that gave to the Roman Empire such characters as Nero, Tiberius and Caracalla.

In other words, Durrant's only motive was an inexplicable impulse to vent his sexual urges through murder. A modern court would have little difficulty accepting this, but in a 19th-century murder prosecution, the lack of a rational motive was still something of a novelty. The defense retorted that Durrant's good character and outstanding reputation in the community made it implausible that he could have acted out of such a twisted motive. It was not a terribly strong argument, but the defense had little else to go with. There was always the hope that the prosecution could be prevented from meeting its burden of proving Durrant's guilt beyond a reasonable doubt.

Dickinson presented the defense's argument to the jury:

> Now, gentlemen, in leaving this case with you, I ask you to consider carefully the good character of the defendant, which stands before you today unimpeached except by the suspicions which this testimony has thrown upon it. His character has been good these many years and there is not a particle of evidence that his character was not at all times uniformly good. His conduct has been entirely natural throughout this entire trial and since the day of his

arrest. What motive could he have had for doing such an act? What motive had he for wrecking his home and his life and his future?

By the fall of 1895, the Durrant trial was the sensation of the West Coast. The courtroom was filled to capacity with spectators every day. Despite the gruesome crimes Durrant was accused of committing, many of these spectators were young women attracted by Durrant's dark good looks. When the attorneys for the prosecution and the defense had rested their cases, Judge Murphy read his instructions to the jury. In particular, he instructed them on the law concerning proof of motive for murder:

> Motive for the killing is an important essential fact in the trial for murder . . . If upon a review of the whole evidence, no motive is apparent or can be fairly imputed to the accused in the commission of the crime charged against him, then this is a circumstance in favor of innocence, and should be so considered by you. The motive may not be apparent in many cases of homicide; there may be no motive discernible, except what arises at or near the time of the commission of the act, and yet the killing is not without a motive. . . . With regard to the grounds from which motive may be inferred, the law has never limited them; therefore it is immaterial whether the motive be hatred, wealth, or *the gratification of desires or passions.*

Judge Murphy offered the jury an illustration, to which they could compare the Durrant case:

> To illustrate this principle: If a man, being of sane mind, and in the absence of a sudden impulse, without any quarrel or word of explanation or warning, should draw his pistol, and take aim and deliberately fire its contents into the breast of another, and death should immediately follow such shooting, and upon his arrest, and ever after, he should refuse to give any explanation or excuse for his criminal act; upon the trial of such a man under such circumstances, it is certainly clear that the prosecution would not be called upon to prove by affirmative testimony what motive, or that any motive, impelled the accused to commit homicide, for the reason that the law will presume that he acted from motive, and that his actions were prompted by reason and was the result of causes acting upon his mind, and deemed sufficient by him to inspire his action.

Therefore, in a restrained manner befitting contemporary morality, Judge Murphy had told the jury that if they believed that Durrant committed the murders to satisfy some twisted sexual urge, then that would constitute a sufficient motive. On November 1, 1895, the jury returned a verdict of guilty against Durrant. Under California law, Durrant faced the death penalty.

Durrant sat in prison for more than a year following the trial while Deuprey and Dickinson filed a series of appeals challenging the verdict. On March 3, 1897, the Supreme Court of California upheld the verdict and denied the defense's appeals. Justice Henshaw (historical records do not indicate first name) spoke for California's highest court when he said that the trial court had acted properly:

> Appellant further urges that the evidence fails to disclose any motive for the crime; that proof of motive is essential to support a conviction; and that, therefore, the judgment must be reversed. If by this is meant that proof of a

particular motive must be as clear and cogent as proof of the crime, the proposition finds no support in either reason or authority. To the act of every rational human being pre-exists a motive. In every criminal case proof of the moving cause is permissible, and oftentimes is valuable; but it is never essential. . . . *Proof of motive is never indispensable to a conviction.*

In essence, the court was telling judges and juries that they were not required to speculate as to the cause of irrational crimes such as Durrant's:

The wellsprings of human conduct are infinite, and infinitely obscure. An act may owe its performance to complex and multitudinous promptings. Who:

Knows each cord its various tone,
Each spring its various bias?

After some further delays, Durrant's execution was set for January 7, 1898. He asked to say some final words, but he was hung from the scaffold before he had the chance.

Durrant's execution put an end to the story of the Crime of the Century. In a sense, it also put an end to a certain amount of judicial innocence concerning proof of motive in a murder case. It was recognized that some people of apparently good character with no prior history of violence can commit bizarre, brutal crimes for no rational reason. Although motive was still a relevant issue, the prosecution's inability to explain such behavior would not stand in the way of the guilty party's punishment.

—*Stephen G. Christianson*

Suggestions for Further Reading

Churchill, Allen. *A Pictorial History of American Crime, 1849–1929.* New York: Holt, Rinehart and Winston, 1964.

Durrant, William Henry Theodore. *Report of the Trial of William Henry Theodore Durrant, Indicted for the Murder of Blanche Lamont.* Detroit: The Collector Publishing Co., 1899.

Jackson, Joseph Henry. *San Francisco Murders.* New York: Duell, Sloan and Pearce, 1947.

Leach, Harold. *The Crime of a Century.* San Francisco: Yosemite Publishing Co., 1895.

Scott, Harold Richard. *The Concise Encyclopedia of Crime and Criminals.* London: A. Deutsch, 1961.

Plessy v. Ferguson: 1896

Appellant: Homer A. Plessy **Respondent:** New Orleans Criminal District Court Judge J.H. Ferguson **Appellant's Claim:** That Louisiana's law requiring blacks to ride in separate railroad cars violated Plessy's right to equal protection under the law **Chief Defense Lawyer:** M.J. Cunningham **Chief Lawyers for Appellant:** F.D. McKenney and S.F. Phillips **Justices:** Supreme Court Justices David J. Brewer, Henry B. Brown, Stephen J. Field, Melville W. Fuller, Horace Gray, John Marshall Harlan, Rufus W. Peckham, George Shiras and Edward D. White **Place:** Washington, D.C. **Date of Decision:** May 18, 1896 **Decision:** That laws providing for "separate but equal" treatment of blacks and whites were constitutional

SIGNIFICANCE

The Supreme Court's decision effectively sanctioned discriminatory state legislation. *Plessy* was not fully overruled until the 1950s and 1960s, beginning with *Brown v. Board of Education* in 1954.

In the years following the Supreme Court's 1875 decision in *U.S. v. Cruikshank* (see separate entry), which limited the federal government's ability to protect blacks' civil rights, many states in the South and elsewhere enacted laws discriminating against blacks. These laws ranged from restrictions on voting, such as literacy tests and the poll tax, to requirements that blacks and whites attend separate schools and use separate public facilities.

On June 7, 1892, Homer A. Plessy bought a train ticket for travel from New Orleans to Covington, Louisiana. Plessy's ancestry was one-eighth black and the rest white, but under Louisiana law he was considered to be black and was required to ride in the blacks-only railroad car. Plessy sat in the whites-only railroad car, refused to move, and was promptly arrested and thrown into the New Orleans jail.

Judge John H. Ferguson of the District Court of Orleans parish presided over Plessy's trial for the crime of having refused to leave the whites-only car, and Plessy was found guilty. Plessy's conviction was upheld by the Louisiana Supreme Court, and Plessy appealed to the U.S. Supreme Court for an order forbidding Louisiana in the person of Judge Ferguson from carrying out the conviction.

Ferguson was represented by Louisiana Attorney General M.J. Cunningham and Plessy by F.D. McKenney and S.F. Phillips. On April 13, 1896, Plessy's lawyers argued before the Supreme Court in Washington, D.C., that Louisiana had violated Plessy's Fourteenth Amendment right to equal protection under the law. Attorney General Cunningham argued that the law merely made a distinction between blacks and whites, but didn't necessarily treat blacks as inferiors, since theoretically the law provided for "separate but equal" railroad car accommodations.

On May 18, 1896, the Court issued its decision. It upheld the Louisiana law:

> A statute which implies merely a legal distinction between the white and colored races—a distinction which is founded in the color of the two races, and which must always exist so long as white men are distinguished from the other race by color—has no tendency to destroy the legal equality of the two races.

Therefore, the Court affirmed Plessy's sentence, namely a $25 fine or 20 days in jail. Further, the Court endorsed the "separate but equal" doctrine, ignoring the fact that blacks had practically no power to make sure that their "separate" facilities were "equal" to those of whites. In the years to come, black railroad cars, schools and other facilities were rarely as good as those of whites. Only Justice John Marshall Harlan dissented from the Court's decision. Harlan's dissent was an uncannily accurate prediction of Plessy's effect:

John Marshall Harlan, the only dissenting justice, argued that, "Our Constitution is color-blind, and neither knows nor tolerates classes among citizens." (Courtesy, Library of Congress)

> Our Constitution is color-blind, and neither knows nor tolerates classes among citizens. . . . In my opinion, the judgment this day rendered will, in time, prove to be quite as pernicious as the decision made by this tribunal in the Dred Scott case. . . . The present decision, it may well be apprehended, will not only stimulate aggressions, more or less brutal and irritating, upon the admitted rights of colored citizens, but will encourage the belief that it is possible, by means of state enactments, to defeat the beneficent purposes which the people of the United States had in view when they adopted the recent amendments of the Constitution.

It was not until the 1950s and the 1960s that the Supreme Court began to reverse *Plessy*. In the landmark 1954 case of *Brown v. Board of Education*, the Court held that separate black and white schools were unconstitutional, and later cases abolished the separate but equal doctrine in other areas affecting civil rights as well.

—Stephen G. Christianson

Suggestions for Further Reading

Jackson, Donald W. *Even the Children of Strangers: Equality Under the U.S. Constitution.* Lawrence: University Press of Kansas, 1992.

Kull, Andrew. *The Color-Blind Constitution.* Cambridge, Mass.: Harvard University Press, 1992.

Olsen, Otto H. *The Thin Disguise: Turning Point in Negro History.* New York: Humanities Press, 1967.

Roland Molineux Trials: 1899

Defendant: Roland Burnham Molineux **Crime Charged:** Murder
Chief Defense Lawyers: First trial: George Gordon Battle and Bartow Weeks;
Second trial: Frank C. Black **Chief Prosecutor:** James W. Osborne, both
trials **Judge:** First trial: John Goff; Second trial: John Lambert
Place: New York, New York **Dates of Trials:** First trial:
November 14, 1899–February 11, 1900; Second trial: October 1902
Verdicts: First trial: Guilty, overturned on appeal; Second trial: Not guilty
Sentence: First trial: Death by electrocution, overturned on appeal

SIGNIFICANCE

Roland Molineux's acquittal was the result of the New York courts enforcing more
stringent limitations on the admissibility of evidence in criminal cases, which
provided increased protection for the rights of defendants.

Roland Molineux was born into a distinguished family which had become rich in the chemical dye business. Molineux's father had been a Union general in the Civil War, and Molineux was raised in the upper crust of New York society. Molineux was a handsome, muscular man who had developed a reputation as a playboy and as a snob by the time he was 30.

Molineux was extremely vain about his athletic prowess, and he belonged to the Knickerbocker Athletic Club, whose membership came exclusively from wealthy and old-line New York families. He was such a snob that he repeatedly went to the club's management to demand that people he considered socially inferior be expelled. In 1898 he also began to compete with one Henry Barnet for the affections of a young and beautiful woman named Blanche Cheeseborough.

In November, Barnet received a package in the mail containing some over-the-counter stomach medicine produced by a well-known drug company. He assumed that it was a free sample, but when he took some, he became violently sick and later died. Less than two weeks after Barnet's death, Molineux married Blanche Cheeseborough. Despite the suspicious circumstances, there were no charges against Molineux. Then, in December 1898, Molineux had a confrontation with Harry Cornish, the Knickerbocker Athletic Club's athletic director.

Cornish beat Molineux in a weight-lifting competition, and in a fit of pique, Molineux demanded that the club expel Cornish. The management refused.

In late December, Cornish received a bottle containing a popular liquid headache medicine. He gave it to his aunt, Katharine Adams, who took some on December 28 and died after a bout of violent convulsions. This time, the authorities and the club performed a thorough investigation and discovered that the bottle contained cyanide, which had killed Adams. The police uncovered some letters to various drug companies, written by the murderer to obtain medicines and poisons, which bore Barnet's and Cornish's forged signatures. The handwriting was very similar to Molineux's, and so the police charged Molineux with murder.

Molineux Is Tried for Adams' Murder

The state accused Molineux of murdering Katharine Adams but was silent with respect to Henry Barnet. The trial began November 14, 1899, with Judge John Goff presiding. The prosecutor was James W. Osborne and Molineux's lawyers were George Gordon Battle and Bartow Weeks. Osborne brought in more than a dozen expert witnesses to prove that the handwriting on the letters was Molineux's. Judge Goff repeatedly denied the defense's objections concerning the credibility of the prosecution's experts and throughout the trial clearly demonstrated his bias against Molineux. Therefore, Battle and Weeks had to restrain themselves in the hope that Osborne and Goff would commit legal blunders that could be used to overturn the verdict on appeal. After Osborne finished presenting the prosecution's case, Battle and Weeks told Judge Goff that the defense would rest without presenting its side of the case or any witnesses, stating simply that:

> We believe that the prosecution has failed to establish its charge and we rest the defense upon the People's case.

The trial then proceeded directly to the attorneys' closing arguments to the jury. Osborne's statements contained the mistake that the defense had hoped for, namely improper references to evidence concerning Barnet's death:

> You must remember that this defendant was married on November 29, 1898. You must remember that Barnet died on November 10, 1898. . . . You must remember that the defendant testified at the inquest that he had been trying to marry this woman from a time running back to January 1898. . . . The plain, cold facts are that this defendant had been trying to marry this woman and that this woman had refused him until Barnet was cold in his grave.

Osborne blatantly implored the jury to draw a connection between the deaths of Barnet and Adams:

> There have been times in this case when I began to think of poor old Mrs. Adams, stricken down, stricken down without an opportunity to make her peace with her God, stricken down while she was in the performance of her family duty, leaving alone and unprotected her daughter and her son; stricken down in the most cruel and the most brutal manner. . . . Sometimes it seems to me in the nighttime that I can almost hear the voice of Mrs.

Adams, calling to me. . . . And then Barnet, Barnet, in the vigor of his youth and manhood, stricken down in that same manner. . . . And will a jury of my countrymen quail before the honest and just verdict? I think not.

On February 11, 1900, the jury returned a verdict of guilty. Judge Goff sentenced Molineux to die in the electric chair. Battle and Weeks, however, appealed to the New York Court of Appeals in Buffalo. Although it took the Court of Appeals over a year and a half, during which time Molineux stayed in Sing Sing Prison, the court finally heard Molineux's case in June 1901. Molineux's lawyers argued that Osborne's reference to Barnet's death was improper, since Molineux had only been charged with Adams' death. On October 15, 1901, the court's seven judges unanimously ruled that Molineux's conviction had to be reversed and a new trial held.

Because the Court of Appeals had also criticized Judge Goff for being biased during the trial, Judge John Lambert presided over Molineux's second trial. It was a speedy retrial, and took only a couple of days during October of 1902. James Osborne was once again the prosecutor, but this time former Governor Frank Black led the defense team.

Lambert was more sympathetic than Goff to the defense's criticism of Osborne's handwriting experts. Further, many of the prosecution's experts, witnesses and other evidence were no longer available because nearly three years had elapsed since Adams' death. The jury this time returned a verdict of not guilty.

Roland Molineux had written a book while in Sing Sing, called *The Room With the Little Door*, which enjoyed some success. After his acquittal, Molineux lived off his income as a writer and what remained of his family fortune once the lawyers' fees were paid. Molineux did some writing for a couple of newspapers and even worked with a popular playwright. He and Blanche Cheeseborough got a divorce, and although he married again, Molineux's life never returned to normal. In 1913, Molineux suffered a nervous breakdown and was committed to an insane asylum, where he died in 1917.

Molineux owed his freedom to the New York Court of Appeals' having enforced more stringent limitations on the admissibility of evidence in criminal cases. These limitations, which provided increased protection for the rights of defendants, were part of a trend among state courts at the turn of the century. This increased concern for the rights of the accused would eventually come to fruition in Supreme Court decisions of the 1950s and 1960s that expanded the scope of Constitutional protections in criminal trials.

—*Stephen G. Christianson*

Suggestions for Further Reading

Carey, Arthur A. *Memoirs of a Murder Man*. Garden City, N.Y.: Doubleday, Doran & Co., 1939.

Crouse, Russel. *Murder Won't Out*. Garden City, N.Y.: Doubleday, Doran & Co., 1932.

LeBrun, George Petit. *It's Time to Tell.* New York: William Morrow & Co., 1962.

Pearson, Edmund Lester. *Instigation of the Devil.* New York: Charles Scribner's Sons, 1930.

Pejsa, Jane. *The Molineux Affair.* Minneapolis: Kenwood, 1986.

Leon Czolgosz Trial: 1901

Defendant: Leon F. Czolgosz   **Crime Charged:** Assassinating President
William McKinley   **Chief Defense Lawyers:** Loran L. Lewis and Robert C.
Titus   **Chief Prosecutor:** Thomas Penny   **Judge:** Truman C. White
Place: Buffalo, New York   **Dates of Trial:** September 23–24, 1901
Verdict: Guilty   **Sentence:** Death by electrocution

SIGNIFICANCE

Leon Czolgosz, an avowed anarchist, was tried and sentenced to death for his
sensational assassination of President McKinley. The trial was remarkably short.
Because the court said that the law presumed Czolgosz was sane, despite
important evidence to the contrary, the jury may well have convicted Czolgosz for
his extremely unpopular political beliefs.

Leon Czolgosz was one of eight children in a poor Michigan family. Czolgosz worked in various menial jobs from childhood, and he eventually moved to Cleveland and worked in a factory. In his late 20s, Czolgosz became fascinated with anarchism. At the time, anarchism had a certain popularity amongst radical working-class circles, but most Americans viewed it with an abhorrence.

After an Italian anarchist killed the King of Italy, Czolgosz became obsessed with assassinating President William McKinley to strike a blow for the cause. In August 1901, he went to Buffalo, New York for the Pan-American Exposition, which McKinley was planning to attend. Because McKinley was very popular, there were large crowds at the Exposition to see the President. On September 6, Czolgosz made his way through the crowds to where McKinley was greeting the public and shaking hands. Czolgosz successfully made his way past the President's security men, and pulled out a concealed pistol. He shot McKinley twice before the stunned spectators could subdue him.

One shot gave McKinley only a flesh wound, but the other pierced his midsection and tore through his stomach. Despite the best efforts of his doctors, McKinley developed complications and died September 14, 1901.

Czolgosz Trial Is Swift

The public was outraged and demanded speedy justice. Czolgosz's trial began September 23, 1901, little more than a week after President McKinley died. The trial took place in Buffalo before Judge Truman C. White, and the prosecutor was Thomas Penny. Finding attorneys to represent Czolgosz was difficult; no one wanted to be associated with such a hated defendant. After some prodding by the president of the local bar association, Loran L. Lewis and Robert C. Titus agreed to be Czolgosz's counsel.

Lewis and Titus had had practically no time to prepare a defense, and to make matters worse, Czolgosz obstinately refused to talk to them. Lewis could only argue that anyone who would kill the president in the face of an almost certain death penalty must be insane:

> Every human being . . . has a strong desire to live. Death is a spectre that we all dislike to meet, and here this defendant, . . . we find him going into this building, in the presence of these hundreds of people, and committing an act which, if he was sane, must cause his death.

The prosecutor, however, brought out Czolgosz's anarchist affiliations and called upon the jury to heed the popular demand for a quick trial and execution:

> We have shown you that he had gone to these anarchistic or socialistic meetings and that there had been embedded in his diseased heart the seeds of this awful crime. . . . What evidence is there in this

case that the man is not sane? Under the presumption of the law that he is sane . . . how brief ought to be your meditation, how brief ought to be your consultation about the responsibility and criminality of this individual?

The prosecutor had argued to the jury that the law presumed Czolgosz was sane unless he could prove otherwise. Since the defense had been able to enter practically no evidence of any kind, there could be only one verdict. At Penny's request, Judge White closed the trial with instructions to the jury that supported the prosecutor's argument:

> The law in this case presumes that the defendant was sane. . . . The burden of showing insanity is upon the person who alleges it.

Vol XLV   No 2337   10 Cents a Copy

HARPER'S WEEKLY

A JOURNAL OF   CIVILIZATION

NEW YORK   OCTOBER 5, 1901

"NO ROOM ON THIS SHIP"

The anti-anarchist sentiment during this period is evident in this somewhat overzealous cartoon of admitted anarchist and assassin Leon Czolgosz. (*Harper's Weekly*)

Even if the jury believed the defense's claim that no sane man would have killed the president in such a public and blatant manner, there was still the legal definition of insanity to be overcome. Under New York law, Czolgosz was legally insane only if he was unable to understand that what he was doing was wrong on the day he shot McKinley. This legal definition was called the "test of responsibility," and was the gist of Judge White's instruction to the jury on legal insanity:

> In other words, if he was laboring under such a defect of reason as not to know the nature and quality of the act he was doing or that it was wrong, it is your duty, gentlemen of the jury, to acquit him in this case.

Judge White's instruction was the final blow to the defense. Any chance that remained of acquitting Czolgosz on the basis of insanity was gone, since the defense had no evidence to offer that he couldn't understand the wrongness of his actions. On September 24, only one day after it began, the trial ended. After a token deliberation, the jury returned its verdict that Czolgosz was not insane and that he was guilty of murder in the first degree.

Czolgosz went to the electric chair on October 29, 1901. His final statement showed no regret:

> I killed the President because he was the enemy of the good people, the good working people. I am not sorry for my crime. . . .

Czolgosz's last words, like all his other statements, contained no reason for his hatred of McKinley other than an unsupported belief that the president was an enemy of the people. Czolgosz's irrationality strongly suggested insanity, but the issue was brushed aside due to the speed of his trial and the strength of popular feeling against him in particular and anarchists in general.

—Stephen G. Christianson

Suggestions for Further Reading

Briggs, L. Vernon. *The Manner of Man that Kills*. New York: Da Capo Press, 1983.

Glad, Paul W. *McKinley, Bryan and the People*. Chicago: T.R. Dee, 1991.

Johns, A. Wesley. *The Man Who Shot McKinley*. South Brunswick, N.J.: A.S. Barnes, 1970.

Leech, Margaret. *In the Days of McKinley*. Norwalk, Conn.: Easton Press, 1986.

Restak, Richard. "Assassin." *Science Digest*, (December 1981): 78–84.

Albert Patrick Trial: 1902

Defendant: Albert T. Patrick   **Crime Charged:** Murder
Chief Defense Lawyer: Albert T. Patrick   **Chief Prosecutor:** William Travers
Jerome   **Judge:** John William Goff   **Place:** New York, New York
Dates of Trial: January 22–March 26, 1902   **Verdict:** Guilty
Sentence: Death by electrocution, later commuted to life imprisonment, and
ultimately pardoned by the governor of New York

SIGNIFICANCE

The Albert Patrick trial illustrated the often uncertain nature of medical evidence in
proving a murder. Although the jury found Patrick guilty, lingering doubts about
the evidence eventually caused the governor of New York to pardon him.

A lbert T. Patrick was the sort of man who gives lawyers a bad name. A native of Texas, where he went to law school and then practiced law for several years, Patrick moved to New York in 1892 to escape disbarment proceedings initiated by a federal judge who was outraged by Patrick's conduct in a particular case. Once in New York, Patrick continued his shady ways. Although nothing was ever proven, there were suspicious circumstances surrounding the death of a wealthy fertilizer magnate who had sued Patrick for restitution of $5,500—a respectable sum in those days—and surrounding the death of Patrick's wife in 1896.

In 1896, Patrick also became involved in the affairs of William Marsh Rice, a multimillionaire and philanthropist. Rice was born in 1816 in Springfield, Massachusetts, and moved to Texas in the 1830s when it was still the raw frontier. Rice built a fortune in oil, retailing, and real estate, and his empire extended into Louisiana and Oklahoma as well. In his old age, Rice had returned to the East Coast to live with his second wife in Rice's Dunellen, New Jersey mansion. Rice's wife died in July 1896, and in her will left a considerable amount of her estate to her family and relatives. Under Texas law, her estate consisted of half of all property acquired by Rice during their marriage, which amounted to millions of dollars. Her will conflicted with Rice's desire to leave virtually all of his estate to the William M. Rice Institute for the Advancement of Literature, Science and Art in Houston, Texas. Rice, having a Madison Avenue apartment, asserted that he was a New York resident and therefore not subject to

Texas law. When he started legal actions against the executor of his wife's estate, O.T. Holt, Holt went to Patrick for help.

William Marsh Rice Murdered

Holt retained Patrick to obtain evidence from anyone who had ever known Rice that could be used to prove that Rice was legally still a Texan. During his investigations, Patrick met Rice's personal valet and secretary, Charles F. Jones. Patrick and Jones thought up an ambitious scheme to murder Rice, plunder his estate by cashing forged checks on his New York bank accounts, and get at the rest of Rice's assets through a forged will naming Patrick and Jones as beneficiaries. Patrick himself drafted the fake will, also deliberately inserting generous legacies to Rice's relatives at the expense of the institute in the hope that the relatives would not challenge the will.

On the night of September 23, 1900, Jones covered the sleeping Rice's face with chloroform-soaked towels. The old man died without a struggle. Patrick and Jones were unable to carry through their scheme, however. Rice's Texas lawyer demanded an autopsy and came to New York to begin an investigation. When Patrick tried to cash the forged checks at Rice's bank, the bank officials became suspicious and notified the authorities. Patrick and Jones were soon arrested for Rice's murder. After unsuccessfully trying to commit suicide, Jones confessed and agreed to testify against Patrick in return for leniency.

Patrick Tried and Convicted

Albert Patrick's trial began on January 22, 1902. Patrick defended himself. The prosecutor was District Attorney William Travers Jerome and the judge was John William Goff. The central issue of the trial was proving the *corpus delicti*, namely that a murder had occurred. Although the doctors who had performed the autopsy generally agreed that Rice had been killed by chloroform poisoning, there was enough scientific uncertainty, given Rice's advanced age, that Patrick was able to keep the trial stalled for over two months. For example, take Patrick's questioning of Dr. Edward W. Lee:

> Patrick: Doctor, assuming that a patient is eighty-four years of age, that prior to death he had dropsy of the lower limbs for several months from the knees down, and that the post-mortem findings revealed . . . the lungs congested slightly . . . the kidneys firm [with] a number of small cysts, and that on the day preceding his death the patient was troubled with his urine, and had to urinate frequently, . . . what would you say would be the cause of death?

> Lee: Congestion of the lungs and diseased kidneys [which could be caused by chloroform or by tuberculosis, pneumonia or kidney disease]

On March 26, 1902, the jury returned a guilty verdict against Patrick. Goff sentenced Patrick to death by electrocution. Luckily for Patrick, however, one of his sisters had married a wealthy man, John T. Milliken, who was convinced of Patrick's innocence. Milliken financed a team of lawyers to handle Patrick's appeals, which tied up the courts for years. In 1906, Governor Frank Higgins commuted Patrick's sentence to life imprisonment. Patrick continued to fight for total freedom, however. For the next six years, Patrick and the Milliken-financed team of lawyers pursued every avenue of appeal, including, according to accounts in the press, under-the-table payments to state legislators and officials.

On November 28, 1912, Governor John A. Dix pardoned Patrick. Dix claimed that "there has always been an air of mystery about the case." Dix's pardon was widely criticized, but there was nothing that could be done about it, especially as Dix was about to leave office anyway. Patrick left New York, never to return, and died in Tulsa, Oklahoma, in 1940. Although the Patrick case amply illustrated the fact that medical evidence is often inconclusive in proving a murder, it also demonstrated that money makes a difference in the American system of justice.

—Stephen G. Christianson

Suggestions for Further Reading

LeBrun, George Petit. *It's Time to Tell.* New York: William Morrow & Co., 1962.

Medico-Legal Society. *Medico-Legal Questions Arising in the Case of People v. Patrick.* New York: Unknown Publisher, 1905.

Nash, Jay Robert. *Murder, America: Homicide in the United States from the Revolution to the Present.* New York: Simon & Schuster, 1980.

Pearson, Edmund Lester. *Five Murders.* Garden City, N.Y.: Doubleday, Doran & Co., 1928.

Symons, Julian. *A Pictorial History of Crime.* New York: Crown Publishers, 1966.

Captain William Van Schaick Trial: 1906

Defendant: William Van Schaick **Crime Charged:** Criminal negligence and misconduct **Chief Defense Lawyers:** Terence J. McManus and William M.K. Olcott **Chief Prosecutors:** Ernest E. Baldwin and Henry I. Burnett **Judge:** Edward B. Thomas **Place:** New York, New York **Dates of Trial:** January 10–27, 1906 **Verdict:** Guilty **Sentence:** 10 years in prison pardoned after serving 4 years

SIGNIFICANCE

Captain Van William Schaick was found guilty, but his corporate employer and its board of directors, who bore at least as much responsibility for the tragic death of over 900 people, went scot-free. This trial and other trials of the period, such as the Triangle Shirtwaist fire trial (see separate entry), illustrate the extreme reluctance that the legal system has had in recognizing that corporations should be held accountable for their actions.

William Van Schaick was the captain of a steamboat, called the *General Slocum*, which for years traveled the waters of the bay and harbor of New York City. Captain Van Schaick was an experienced seaman, having been a sailor for decades, and was a trusted employee of the Knickerbocker Steamboat Company, which owned the *General Slocum*.

On June 15, 1904, the *General Slocum* was traveling New York's East River. Only six weeks previously, the *General Slocum* had passed federal inspection and gotten a renewal of its sailing permit. For reasons that never became entirely clear, a fire developed on board. The fire spread quickly, and the hundreds of passengers began to panic. They rushed to the lifeboats and life preservers, only to find that the boats were lashed to the ship with wires and couldn't be freed. The life preservers, made of cork, were so old and shoddy that they crumbled in the passengers' hands. The ship's crew couldn't put out the fire because the pumps were old and the hoses leaked. Desperate to escape the flames, over a thousand people jumped overboard and hundreds drowned because they couldn't reach the shore.

The *General Slocum* disaster shocked New York and dominated the local press for weeks as bodies were fished from the East River. The final death tally was nearly 900 people. The day after the disaster, Secretary of Commerce and

Labor George B. Cortelyou ordered a federal inquiry, to be headed by George Uhler, supervising inspector general of the Steamboat Inspection Service, and James A. Dumont and Thomas H. Barrett of the local New York Board of Steamboat Inspections. Meanwhile, Bronx Coroner Joseph Berry ordered an inquest, which was to be the precursor to a criminal trial.

Only Van Schaick Is Tried

On June 20, 1904, the inquest began. There were eight days of testimony by Captain Van Schaick, the crew of the General Slocum, surviving passengers and officers and directors of the Knickerbocker Steamboat Company. Although it was Captain Van Schaick's duty to run the ship, the company should have paid for the necessary repairs to, and upkeep of, the safety equipment. Company President Frank A. Barnaby denied that the condition of the *General Slocum* had been allowed to deteriorate, but the receipts for repairs that Barnaby presented were highly suspect.

A Dramatic photograph of the *General Slocum* sinking. (*Harper's Weekly*)

> Questions: You know of your own knowledge that these bills are for *Slocum* apparatus?
>
> Barnaby: I do.
>
> Question: You are sure all these were for the *General Slocum?*
>
> Barnaby: Yes.
>
> Question: If this is the case, how is it I find in some of these bills the name *Grand Republic* [another company steamboat] scratched out or taken out with acid and the name *Slocum* inserted?
>
> Barnaby: I suppose some bookkeeper must have done that.

On June 28, 1904, the coroner's inquest jury found Captain Van Schaick and the officers and directors of the company guilty of manslaughter in the form of criminal negligence for not having fulfilled their collective duty to see that the ship had the proper safety equipment. Only Captain Van Schaick, however, was brought to trial.

The trial began on January 10, 1906, before Judge Edward B. Thomas. Captain Van Schaick was defended by Terence J. McManus and William M.K. Olcott. The prosecutors were Ernest E. Baldwin and U.S. District Attorney Henry I. Burnett. On January 27, 1906, the jury found Van Schaick guilty of the charges of criminal negligence and misconduct. Thomas told Captain Van Schaick, "You are no ordinary criminal; I must make an example of you," and sentenced him to the maximum penalty under the law, 10 years in prison.

On February 12, 1908, Captain Van Schaick's appeal was denied. He went to New York's infamous Sing Sing prison to serve his sentence, not a pleasant prospect for a man over 70 years old. His wife, Grace Mary Van Schaick, worked for his release and got over 200,000 signatures on a petition for his pardon. President Theodore Roosevelt twice refused to pardon Captain Van Schaick, but the next president, William Howard Taft, was more receptive. On Christmas Day of 1911, Taft pardoned Captain Van Schaick, who had already served nearly four years of his sentence. After leaving Sing Sing, he retired to live on a farm in Fulton County, New York until he died at the age of 90 on December 8, 1927.

Captain Van Schaick may have been partially responsible for the *General Slocum* disaster, but there was surely no justice in letting the company, its officers and directors escape punishment for their misconduct as well. The Captain Van Schaick trial and other trials, such as the one following the Triangle Shirtwaist fire (see separate entry), illustrate the extreme reluctance that the legal system had in that period in recognizing that corporations should be held accountable for their actions.

— Stephen G. Christianson

Suggestions for Further Reading

Hanson, John Wesley. *New York's Awful Excursion Boat Horror, Told By Survivors and Rescuers.* Chicago: Unknown Publisher, 1904.

Northrop, Henry Davenport. *New York's Awful Steamboat Horror.* Philadelphia: National Publishing Company, 1904.

Ogilvie, John Stuart. *History of the General Slocum Disaster.* New York: J.S. Ogilvie Publishing Company, 1904.

Rust, Claude. *The Burning of the General Slocum.* New York: Elsevier/Nelson Books, 1981.

Werstein, Irving. *The General Slocum Incident: Story of an Ill-Fated Ship.* New York: John Day Co., 1965.

Chester Gillette Trial: 1906

Defendant: Chester Ellsworth Gillette   **Crime Charged:** Murder
Chief Defense Lawyers: Albert M. Mills and Charles D. Thomas
Chief Prosecutor: George W. Ward   **Judge:** Irving R. Devendorf
Place: Herkimer, New York   **Dates of Trial:** November 12–
December 4, 1906   **Verdict:** Guilty   **Sentence:** Death by electrocution

SIGNIFICANCE

The sordid murder of a secretary by her social-climbing boss received its share of
press attention at the time but would be long since forgotten had it not provided
Theodore Dreiser with the inspiration, the characters and the plot of arguably the
greatest novel of the literary movement known as "naturalism": *An American
Tragedy.*

Chester Ellsworth Gillette was born in 1884 to a well-to-do Christian family.
His youth gave no inclination that he would become one of the most famous
murderers of his time. As a child, Gillette did missionary work for the Salvation
Army. He went to prestigious Oberlin College, which was well-known for its
divinity school and missionary work in China. After Oberlin, Gillette went to
work for a wealthy uncle who owned a dress factory in Cortland, a town located
in upstate New York not far from Syracuse.

Gillette rose steadily in his uncle's business and soon became the factory
manager. The local business community accepted Gillette as an up-and-coming
young man. Gillette developed social ambitions as well. He was good looking
and charming, and he mingled easily with the local gentry. Soon Gillette was a
regular at the parties and other functions of Cortland society.

Still in his early 20s, Gillette had high hopes of marrying a girl from one of
the town's wealthy families. There was an obstacle to Gillette's plans, however.
Grace Brown, nicknamed "Billie," had left her parents' farm in South Otselic,
New York, for Cortland and a clerical job at Gillette's factory. Gillette had an
affair with her, and in 1906 she became pregnant. If he were to marry Brown, it
would ruin Gillette's ambitions as a social climber.

One of the characteristics of the criminal mentality is that when faced with
a difficult personal situation, a criminal will go beyond the boundaries of normal
behavior and use violence to resolve the problem. Gillette was such a man. In

July 1906, he went on vacation, taking Brown with him to a hotel on the shores of Big Moose Lake outside the little town of Herkimer, New York, roughly 60 miles from Cortland. Grace Brown never returned from this vacation.

Tragedy at Big Moose Lake

On the morning of July 11, Gillette took Brown out in a rowboat. As was reconstructed later, Gillette rowed Brown around the lake for a while, then when they were out of sight, he hit her with a tennis racquet and threw her into the lake. Whether the blows killed her instantly or she died of drowning was never made clear. At any rate, after returning to shore, Gillette buried the racquet along the shore and left for another hotel. Gillette checked in at the nearby Arrowhead Inn and later asked the desk clerk whether there had been a drowning reported at Big Moose Lake. When Brown's body was found in the lake shortly thereafter, the police quickly tracked down Gillette.

Gillette claimed that Brown committed suicide by jumping in the water after he started to talk with her about the baby. However, Gillette's behavior didn't betray grief or sorrow. Further, someone discovered the tennis racquet Gillette had buried, broken as if from striking hard blows. The police arrested Gillette, charged him with Brown's murder, and kept him in the Herkimer County jail pending his trial. The press, always eager for a juicy society scandal, made him famous. From his cell, Gillette sold pictures of himself and used the proceeds to have hotel caterers deliver meals to his cell.

On November 12, 1906, Gillette's trial began. The prosecutor was District Attorney George W. Ward, with Judge Irving R. Devendorf presiding. Gillette's defense lawyers were Albert M. Mills and Charles D. Thomas.

Chester Gillette: Murderer or Coward?

Mills and Thomas knew that the evidence of Gillette's guilt was highly persuasive. He had been on the boat with Brown, left the scene under highly suspicious circumstances, and had the stigma of having gotten Brown pregnant but having not married her. However, they believed they could make a reasonable defense, based on Gillette's story that the boat had capsized after Brown jumped in the lake. According to Gillette, after the boat tipped over, he fell into the water. He came up but could not find Brown. Could it be that he had panicked and fled? This would indicate poor judgment, in that day tantamount to cowardice. But poor judgment and cowardice are not murder.

Thomas made the defense's pitch to the jury:

Now gentlemen, there are such things as moral cowards. There are men so constituted that in the presence of a great calamity they must loose themselves, and this boy, in my opinion, in that condition, wandered to the Arrowhead and registered under his own name. He didn't try to run away. He didn't try to conceal himself at all.

Thomas then called Gillette to the stand, and asked him about the critical events immediately following what Gillette said was Brown's decision to kill herself. The following is an excerpt from Thomas' questioning of his client:

Gillette: Then she said, 'Well, I will end it here,' and she, well, jumped into the lake; stepped up onto the boat, kind of threw herself in.

Thomas: What did you do?

Gillette: I tried to reach her, I leaned back in the seat in the other end, the bow seat, I guess. I tried to reach her and, well, I was not quick enough. I went into the lake, too. The boat tipped over as I started to get up. The boat went right over then. Of course, I went into the lake.

Thomas: Go on and describe what you did.

Gillette: Then I came up. I halloed, grabbed hold of the boat. Then, as soon as I could get the water out of my eyes and see, I got hold of the boat or got to the boat.

Thomas: Did you see her?

Gillette: No, I stayed there at the boat but a minute or two. It seemed like a long time, anyway, and I didn't see her. Then I swam to shore.

District Attorney Ward, knowing the thinness of the defense's argument, pressed home his attack. Not only could the defense not explain the tennis racquet, but Ward had five doctors to testify that Brow's autopsy showed evidence of blows to the body. Further, Gillette later seemed to change his story, suggesting that the boat had tipped over first and Brown had hit her head against the side before sinking beneath the lake. This sounded like an attempt to explain away the results of the autopsy. Ward said of the defense:

> When the learned counsel made this address to you in a despairing effort to withdraw from the clutches of the law a man whom he knows and whom I know and whom you all know that this evidence condemns beyond all question, when he stands up here and says that five of these doctors, men who enter your houses day after day and have your lives and the lives of your families in their hands, are perjurers and wanton liars, it ought not to be necessary to make an argument against such a statement as that.

Ward Finishes His Closing Argument

But why had Gillette been so inept in covering his tracks? If Gillette had planned Brown's murder, why hadn't he disposed of the tennis racquet better or otherwise killed her in a less suspicious manner? After all, it had taken practically no time for the police to arrest Gillette. Ward pointed out that the arrogance of murderers is often beyond the pale of ordinary human reason:

Trial Judge Irving Devendorf sentenced Gillette to die in the electric chair. (Courtesy, Herkimer County Historical Society)

> He is bloodthirsty and brutal. He is a blunderer. He does not reason on the lines that any one of us do. He reasons on different lines. Everything looks red before him. There is nothing but one object that he is going to grasp, and that is his personal safety, his personal well-being, the possibility of an arrest. He sees nothing else. He cares for nothing else. He casts all these things behind him and says "I can do this slyly. I can get the girl on the bottom of the lake. I can do it secretly. I can do it carefully. I stand well in Cortland. I go to church. They think I am a paragon of virtue, a decent man, when in reality I am a ravisher. What I do in secret will be unknown. I can take her out there and leave her body in the lake. . . ."

On December 4, 1906, after deliberating for only a couple of hours, the jury announced its verdict: guilty. Judge Devendorf prepared to sentence Gillette to death, as prescribed by New York law. But before he pronounced sentence, the judge asked Gillette if he had anything to say. Gillette replied:

> I have. I desire to state that I am innocent of this crime and therefore ought not to be punished. I think that is all.

Judge Devendorf then sentenced Gillette to die in the electric chair. Following Gillette's trial and sentence, his execution was delayed while Mills and Thomas appealed. They based their appeals on a lengthy list of objections that they had made at trial and a trial record that was more than 3,000 thousand pages long. On February 18, 1908, the New York Court of Appeals rejected Mills' and Thomas' arguments. Chief Judge Frank A. Hiscock's opinion was terse and unequivocal:

> No controversy throws the shadow of doubt or speculation over the primary fact that about 6 o'clock in the afternoon of July 11, 1906, while she was with the defendant, Grace Brown met an unnatural death and her body sank to the bottom of Big Moose Lake.

With the legal appeals finally at an end, Gillette went to the electric chair on March 30, 1908.

Gillette's story lingered in the memory of a young muckraking novelist. In *An American Tragedy*, a novel whose plot and principal characters were closely modeled on the events and figures in the case, Theodore Dreiser resurrected Gillette as the embodiment and culmination of the money-grubbing and social climbing that Dreiser believed had corrupted the nation's moral values. The novel's critical and commercial success ensured that the sordid murderer became one of the archetypal and tragic villains in American literature.

—Stephen G. Christianson

Suggestions for Further Reading

Brandon, Craig. *Murder in the Adirondacks*. Utica, N.Y.: North Country Books, 1986.

Brown, Grace. *Grace Brown's Love Letters*. Herkimer, N.Y.: Citizen Pub. Co., 1906.

Brownell, Joseph W. *Adirondack Tragedy*. Interlaken, N.Y.: Heart of the Lakes Publishing, 1986.

Dreiser, Theodore. *An American Tragedy*. New York: Boni & Liveright, 1925.

Harry Thaw Trials: 1907–08

Defendant: Harry Kendall Thaw **Crime Charged:** Murder
Chief Defense Lawyers: First trial: Delphin M. Delmas, John B. Gleason, Clifford Hartridge, Hugh McPike, and George Peabody; Second trial: Martin W. Littleton, Daniel O'Reilly, and Russell Peabody **Chief Prosecutor:** William Travers Jerome **Judge:** First trial: James Fitzgerald; Second trial: Victor J. Dowling **Place:** New York, New York **Dates of Trials:** First trial: January 23–April 12, 1907; Second trial: January 6–February 1, 1908
Verdict: First trial: None, jury deadlocked; Second trial: Not guilty by reason of insanity

SIGNIFICANCE

Harry Thaw married the glamorous showgirl Evelyn Nesbit, who had previously been the mistress of the famous architect Stanford White. Thaw shot White during a public performance in Madison Square Garden and was subsequently tried for murder. Thaw's attorneys took the insanity defense to murder to new extremes, successfully arguing that Thaw suffered from "dementia Americana," a condition supposedly unique to American men that caused Thaw to develop an uncontrollable desire to kill White after he learned of White's previous affair with Nesbit.

Harry Thaw was born in 1872 into a family of wealthy Pennsylvania industrialists. His father made a fortune estimated at $40 million in the Pittsburgh coke business and had also invested heavily in the Pennsylvania Railroad. Thaw's mother spoiled him as a youth and indulged him throughout his life—with tragic consequences.

As a young man, Thaw went to Harvard University for his higher education, but he was expelled because he spent all of his time playing poker. Over his father's objections, Thaw's mother provided him with a substantial allowance and paid off massive gambling debts that Thaw incurred after moving to New York City. Thaw also had a taste for pleasures more decadent than gambling, such as frequent visits to a whorehouse. Although Thaw had several incidents with the police, his mother and his family's money always secured his release.

Evelyn Nesbit Comes to New York

Evelyn Nesbit's background was much more modest than Thaw's but became equally as sordid sexually. Nesbit's parents in Pittsburgh were poor and could never provide for their daughter's education. Nesbit was beautiful, however, and from an early age she also showed some skill as a singer and dancer. Nesbit's family came to rely on the money she earned as a model and in the theater. Within a short time, Nesbit's career soared and she became a "Floradora girl," joining a prestigious all-girl chorus.

During a performance of the Floradora chorus, Nesbit attracted the attention of architect Stanford White. White had made a fortune designing the homes of New York's society set and had designed several famous buildings, including Madison Square Garden. White kept a private suite of rooms for himself in the Garden's tower. The apartment was decorated with oriental furnishings, and featured a red velvet swing hung from the ceiling. White's wealth enabled him to bring young showgirls to his apartment and have them use the swing while he looked underneath their long dresses. Showered with gifts and presents, Evelyn Nesbit soon became White's mistress, and their affair lasted for three years. As Nesbit later testified at trial, White's behavior was not limited to voyeurism; he ultimately got Nesbit intoxicated and raped her when she passed out.

Nesbit left White early in 1905 for Harry Thaw, who like White had seen Nesbit on stage and for some time had been pursuing her at every opportunity. Whether out of love or a desire for another wealthy benefactor, Nesbit married Thaw April 4, 1905. Thaw took Nesbit to Europe for their honeymoon and reportedly began to whip and beat her. Thaw became obsessed with Nesbit's previous relationship with White and forced her to repeat intimate details of their affair. Thaw's obsession became a conviction that he had to avenge Nesbit's disgrace and rid the world of a human monster.

On June 25, 1906, Thaw acted on his obsessions. At Madison Square Garden, where the Thaws were attending the public performance of a new musical, Thaw spotted White. With no thought in his mind but murder, Thaw charged up to White's table and pulled out a pistol; he shot White several times while hundreds of people at the musical watched in horror. Thaw made no attempt to resist arrest, and he was promptly seized by policemen who rushed to the Garden.

Thaw Is Tried for Murder

Upon learning of his arrest, Thaw's mother rushed to his defense. Publicly declaring that she would spend the family's $40-million fortune to set Thaw free, she paid to have her son represented by one of the most formidable lawyers of the age, Delphin Delmas. Delmas, an attorney short in stature but tall in reputation before the California courts, was known as the "Napoleon of the Western bar." Delmas brought four other attorneys with him to assist in Thaw's defense when the trial opened January 23, 1907: John B. Gleason, Clifford

Hartridge, Hugh McPike, and George Peabody. Gleason would speak occasionally during the trial, but Delmas conducted the bulk of Thaw's defense.

The prosecutor was William Travers Jerome, New York's district attorney, who had once served as a judge and reportedly had ambitions to become governor one day. Jerome knew that the Thaw trial would be closely followed by the press and the public, for as the *New York Times* reported, "the Thaw trial is being reported to the ends of the civilized globe" due to:

> The eminence of the victim, the wealth of the prisoner, the dramatic circumstance of the crime, and the light it sheds not only on Broadway life, but on the doings of the fast set in every capital. . . .

Thaw and his mother not only wanted to save Thaw from the electric chair, which was the penalty for murder, but prevent him from spending the rest of his life in an insane asylum. Therefore, from the beginning of the trial, Delmas conducted the defense with the aim of proving that Thaw was and always had been sane except for that evening of June 25, 1906, when he temporarily went insane and shot White. Delmas exploited Nesbit's beauty to appeal to the jury's emotions. He called Evelyn Nesbit to the stand, and asked her to describe the events of the night on which White raped her:

> Mr. White asked me to come to see the back room and he went through some curtains, and the back room was a bedroom, and I sat down at the table, a tiny little table. There was a bottle of champagne, a small bottle and one glass. Mr. White picked up the bottle and poured the glass full of champagne. . . . Then he came to me and told me to finish my champagne, which I did, and I don't know whether it was a minute after or two minutes after, but a pounding began in my ears, then the whole room seemed to go around. Everything got very flat. . . . Then, I woke up, all my clothes were pulled off of me, and I was in bed. I sat up in the bed, and started to scream.

Prosecutor Jerome, who had produced a score of eyewitnesses testifying that Thaw shot White at point-blank range, watched in frustration while Delmas, in effect, put White's treatment of Nesbit on trial. Delmas then introduced the defense's argument of temporary insanity by asking Nesbit about Thaw's reaction upon learning of the rape incident. Delmas and Nesbit both carefully avoided the subject of Thaw's penchant for sadistic sex:

> He would get up and walk up and down the room a minute and then come and sit down and say, "Oh, God! Oh, God!" and bite his nails like that and keep sobbing.

Nesbit's acting experience complemented Delmas' legal ability: the jury was masterfully presented with the picture of a young, pretty and innocent girl relating the story of her outrage to her husband, who then flies into a murderous fury. In his closing argument, Delmas hammered the argument home to the jury:

> And if Thaw is insane, it is with a species of insanity known from the Canadian border to the Gulf. If you expert gentlemen ask me to give it a name, I suggest that you label it Dementia Americana. It is that species of insanity that inspires of every American to believe his home is sacred. It is that species of insanity that persuades an American that whoever violates the

sanctity of his home or the purity of his wife or daughter has forfeited the protection of the laws of this state or any other state.

Judge James Fitzgerald reminded the jury that they could only find Thaw not guilty by reason of insanity if Thaw could not understand at the time of the murder that his actions were wrong. Jerome urged the jury to resist Delmas' appeal to their emotions:

> Will you acquit a cold-blooded, deliberate, cowardly murderer because his lying wife has a pretty girl's face?

On April 12, 1907, the jury reported to Judge Fitzgerald that it could not reach a verdict and was deadlocked: seven jurors finding Thaw guilty of first degree murder, five jurors finding Thaw not guilty by reason of insanity. Judge Fitzgerald adjourned the court, pending a retrial of Thaw.

Thaw Is Tried Again and Found Insane

Thaw's second trial began January 6, 1908. Although Jerome was still the prosecutor, Thaw had a new team of defense lawyers: Martin W. Littleton, Daniel O'Reilly, and Russell Peabody. Further, Judge Victor J. Dowling had replaced Judge Fitzgerald. Essentially the same witnesses, including Nesbit, testified as in the first trial. Neither Jerome nor the defense, however, fought as hard as they did in the first trial over the issue of temporary insanity. Perhaps both sides had decided that they would be content with a verdict of not guilty by reason of insanity, which would put Thaw in a mental institution but prevent his execution. Accordingly, this time the jury on February 1, 1908, after a trial of less than four weeks, found Thaw not guilty by reason of insanity.

Harry Thaw's "dementia Americana" was cited as his motive for murdering architect Stanford White. (AP/Wide World Photos)

After the jury's verdict, Judge Dowling sent Thaw to the Asylum for the Criminally Insane at Matteawan, New York. Thaw's trials had taken the insanity defense to a murder charge to new heights, particularly with Delmas' "dementia Americana" argument in the first trial. This defense stratagem had first been used successfully to acquit Congressman Daniel Sickles of the murder of his wife's lover back in 1859. Further, the sensationalism surrounding Nesbit and her testimony eventually led to the famous movie, "The Girl in the Red Velvet Swing."

Thaw divorced Nesbit in 1915, and spent the rest of his life in and out of insane asylums and the courts. He escaped from Matteawan and fled to Canada, but he was soon extradited by Canadian authorities back to New York. Briefly freed from the asylums by the battery of lawyers still retained by his mother, Thaw was arrested in 1917 for kidnapping and whipping 19-year-old Frederick Gump nearly to death. Mother Thaw arranged for her son to be sent to a Pennsylvania insane asylum, where he stayed until 1924. After 1924, Thaw was periodically in the news in connection with various wild parties or lawsuits by showgirls alleging that Thaw had beaten and whipped them. Thaw died February 22, 1947, at the age of 76, having lived until his last days off his inheritance from his mother.

—Stephen G. Christianson

Suggestions for Further Reading

Abramson, Phyllis L. *Sob Sister Journalism*. Westport, Conn.: Greenwood Press, 1990.

"Beauty as Evidence." *Life* (June 1981): 10–13.

Hodge, Clifford M. "The Benefactor at Dorr's Pond." *Yankee* (December 1986): 154.

Langford, Gerald. *The Murder of Stanford White*. London: V. Gollancz, 1963.

Mooney, Michael M. *Evelyn Nesbit and Stanford White: Love and Death in the Gilded Age*. New York: William Morrow & Co., 1976.

Thaw, Harry K. *The Traitor*. Philadelphia: Dorrance Publishing Co., 1926.

William "Big Bill" Haywood Trial: 1907

Defendant: William Dudley Haywood   **Crime Charged:** Conspiracy to commit murder   **Chief Defense Lawyers:** Clarence Darrow, Fred Miller, John Nugent, Edmund Richardson, and Edgar Wilson
Chief Prosecutors: William E. Borah, James H. Hawley, Charles Koelsche, and Owen M. Van Duyn   **Judge:** Fremont Wood   **Place:** Boise, Idaho
Dates of Trial: May 9–July 28, 1907   **Verdict:** Not guilty

SIGNIFICANCE

The government used the courts and the military in a blatant attempt to discredit and destroy the left-wing labor movement during a time of civil unrest. William Haywood's acquittal was widely applauded as a victory for organized labor and a defeat for big business.

Born in 1869, William Dudley Haywood, popularly known as "Big Bill," grew up in the rough-and-tumble world of the old Wild West, where the discovery of vast deposits of valuable metals had led to the exploitation of natural resources by the big mining companies. Conditions in the mines were poor: miners performed back-breaking labor for long hours and low pay in dark, cramped, and poorly ventilated mines. During the rise of organized labor in the late 19th century, union organizers found miners a ready audience for their message of labor activism.

Haywood rose through the Western labor movement and became an executive officer of the Western Federation of Miners. He was one of organized labor's recognized radicals. Haywood belonged to the Socialist Party and actively supported the anarchist International Workers of the World, or "Wobblies." Further, Haywood publicly endorsed strikes and violence to further the workers' cause. Haywood's radicalism made him the enemy of big business and the federal government.

The Coeur d'Alene Strike

Idaho's Coeur d'Alene region is the site of some of the world's richest mineral deposits. Haywood's Western Federation of Miners led a general miners' strike against all the mining companies in the area. By 1898, when Frank

R. Steunenberg was re-elected governor of Idaho, the strike had become a full-blown struggle between labor and management. The miners fought Pinkerton guards hired by the companies and "scabs," or replacement workers, sent by the companies to break the strike. When a bomb explosion killed two men, Steunenberg feared the strike would degenerate into open warfare and begged Washington for help.

In response, President William McKinley sent federal troops to Idaho, crushing the strike. In the process, the legal rights of the strikers were trampled and hundreds of men were held without bail in stockades nicknamed "bull pens." Steunenberg, who had been considered a pro-labor politician when first elected, now was a marked man. Years later, on December 30, 1905, when his term as governor had expired, Steunenberg was killed by a bomb blast in the front yard of his house in Caldwell, Idaho.

Two days later, January 1, 1906, the police arrested Harry Orchard in Caldwell for Steunenberg's murder. Orchard confessed, telling the police that Haywood and Charles H. Moyer, another executive officer of the Western Federation, paid him to kill Steunenberg. After a controversial extradition from Colorado, Haywood, Moyer, and another union member named George Pettibone were sent to Boise, Idaho, to stand trial.

The famous criminal lawyer Clarence Darrow went to Boise to defend Haywood, assisted by Fred Miller, John Nugent, Edmund Richardson, and Edgar Wilson. On the bench was Judge Fremont Wood. The prosecution team was comprised of William E. Borah, James H. Hawley, Charles Koelsche, and Owen M. Van Duyn. Haywood's trial for conspiracy to commit murder began May 9, 1907.

Haywood's Fate Rests on Orchard's Credibility

The prosecution's star witness was Harry Orchard, the confessed assassin. Orchard had a long criminal career, however, and readily admitted that he lied many times in the past "whenever it suited my purpose." Nevertheless, Orchard stuck with his story that Haywood and Moyer wanted him to murder Steunenberg. Darrow suspected that the mining companies were Orchard's real masters and said so to the jury:

> The mine owners of Colorado and Idaho are pulling the wires to make you dance like puppets. They gathered these officers of the Western Federation of Miners and sent them here to be tried and hanged.

When the prosecutors called Haywood to take the stand, Haywood denied hiring Orchard to kill Frank Steunenberg. He admitted that he hated the former governor, but no more or less than could be expected from a union radical. Responding to the prosecution's question, Haywood said:

> I felt toward him much as I did toward you and others who were responsible for martial law and the bull pen in the Coeur d'Alene.

Darrow questioned more than 80 character witnesses who knew Orchard well and who testified that he could not be trusted to tell the truth. Most of this testimony was redundant, however, since Orchard had already admitted to a history of chronic lying. Darrow went on to declare that the real issue was big business' effort to crucify Haywood and the unions. Addressing the jury, Darrow said:

> Gentlemen, it is not for him alone that I speak. I speak for the poor, for the weak, for the weary, for that long line of men who, in darkness and despair, have borne the labors of the human race. The eyes of the world are upon you, upon you twelve men of Idaho tonight. . . . If you kill him your act will be applauded by many. If you should decree Bill Haywood's death, in the railroad offices of our great cities men will applaud your names. If you decree his death, amongst the spiders of Wall Street will go up paeans of praise for these twelve good men and true.

Because the jury was composed of Idaho farmers, Darrow deliberately appealed to their working-class roots. His lengthy closing argument made it sound as if all farmers and miners were brothers united against their corporate oppressors.

Prosecutor William Borah tried to get the jury to focus on the real issue, namely whether Haywood was a party to Steunenberg's murder as Orchard had claimed:

> [T]hat bleak winter night with the blood of my dear friend marking the white earth, I saw Idaho dishonored and disgraced. I saw murder, no, a thousand times worse, I saw anarchy unfold its red menace. . . . This trial has no other purpose or implication than conviction and punishment of the assassins of Governor Steunenberg.

Not only did Borah try to keep the jury's focus on the heinous crime of murder-by-hire, but Borah saw Darrow's political appeal to the jury as a two-edged sword and effectively wielded it against him. Borah knew that the unpopular aspect of the union movement was its connection with anarchists, Wobblies, and others trying to overthrow the government. Knowing that Haywood's connection with these elements was well publicized, Borah played on the threat of social revolution to traditional values:

> We see anarchy, that pale, restless, hungry demon from the crypts of hell, fighting for a foothold in Idaho! Should we compromise with it? Or should we crush it? . . . I only want what you want, the gates to our homes, the yard gate whose inward swing tells of the returning husband and father, shielded and guarded by the courage and manhood of Idaho juries!

Haywood Goes Free

By the end of the trial, the jury had seen one of Clarence Darrow's great performances and equally respectable oratory from the prosecution. Judge Wood, however, said very little until the time came for him to give his instructions to the jury. Unexpectedly, Wood's instructions came down heavily on William Haywood's side. Wood reminded the jury that while they might not be convinced of Haywood's innocence, under the law they must find him not guilty unless the prosecutors had proven his guilt beyond a reasonable doubt. Further, in effect, Wood's instructions to the jury attacked the prosecution's inability to bring forward other evidence in support of Orchard's accusations:

> Gentlemen, under the statutes of this state, a person cannot be convicted of a crime upon testimony of an accomplice, unless such accomplice is corroborated by other evidence.

Whether it was the result of Darrow's eloquence or Judge Wood's instructions, on July 28, 1907, the jury finished its deliberations and, before a packed courtroom, returned a verdict of not guilty.

After leaving Boise and the Steunenberg murder trial behind him, Haywood returned to his radical affiliations, keeping up his support for the Wobblies. When World War I broke out, public opinion and the government turned against the Wobblies and other leftists, who were then considered unpatriotic for promoting the cause of world labor instead of American victory. The Wobblies not only circulated posters and pamphlets denouncing the war, but maintained contacts with the communists who had seized power in the former Russian Empire.

In 1918, the government again brought Haywood to trial, this time for treason. Haywood's luck had run out. The jury found him guilty and he was sentenced to 20 years imprisonment. While out on bail, Haywood fled the United States for the Soviet Union, where the communist regime granted him asylum. Haywood lived in the Soviet Union for the rest of his life, and after his death in 1928 the Soviets honored him with a burial in the Kremlin.

Despite Haywood's colorful postscript, his earlier acquittal was an important victory for organized labor. The government brought the full weight of the courts and the military to bear against labor but was unable to taint it with the blood of Steunenberg's murder. Because the government was supported by the mining companies, Haywood's acquittal was also seen as a defeat for big business.

—Stephen G. Christianson

Suggestions for Further Reading

Archer, Jules. *Strikes, Bombs & Bullets.* New York: Julian Messner, 1972.

Carlson, Peter. *Roughneck.* New York: W.W. Norton & Co., 1983.

Conlin, Joseph Robert. *Big Bill Haywood and the Radical Union Movement.* Syracuse, N.Y.: Syracuse University Press, 1969.

Dubofsky, Melvyn. *"Big Bill" Haywood.* New York: St. Martin's Press, 1987.

Haywood, William. *Bill Haywood's Book.* Westport, Conn.: Greenwood Press, 1983.

Dr. Hyde Trial: 1910

Defendant: Dr. Bennett Clarke Hyde **Crime Charged:** Murder
Chief Defense Lawyers: R.R. Brewster, M. Cleary, and Frank Walsh
Chief Prosecutors: M. Atkinson, Virgil Conkling, Elliott W. Major, and James
A. Reed **Judge:** Ralph S. Latshaw **Place:** Kansas City, Missouri
Dates of Trial: April 16–May 16, 1910 **Verdict:** None. There were three
attempts at retrial after a conviction in the first trial was overturned, but no
verdict was ever sustained against Dr. Hyde.

SIGNIFICANCE
The Dr. Bennett Clark Hyde trial was a monument to the power of money in the
criminal justice system. Hyde's wealthy wife hired the best attorneys available to
defend him, and despite the overwhelming evidence of his guilt, he was never
convicted.

Bennett Clarke Hyde was born in 1872 in Cowper, Missouri, the son of a Baptist minister, and grew up in Lexington, Missouri. He went to medical school in Kansas City, and stayed in that city to practice medicine after graduation.

From the very start, Hyde's medical career was tainted with scandal. When Hyde was working for his alma mater as an anatomy instructor, two men were arrested for grave robbing, and they confessed that they had been working for Hyde. Charges were filed against Hyde, but were dropped in March 1899. In 1905, Hyde became the Kansas City police surgeon, but he was fired in 1907 for alleged mistreatment of a patient.

On June 21, 1905, Hyde married Frances Swope in a secret marriage that connected him with the richest family in Missouri. Hyde's wife was the niece of Thomas Hunton Swope, who was born in 1829 in Kentucky and moved to Kansas City in 1860. Swope made a fortune in Kansas City real estate, and was now known as Colonel Swope. By 1909 Colonel Swope was 80 years old, and although he was a lifelong bachelor with no children of his own, he was devoted to his many nephews and nieces, several of whom lived with him in his Kansas City mansion.

In September 1909, Colonel Swope suffered a minor injury, and Hyde came to the Swope mansion to take care of him. On October 2, Hyde gave

Colonel Swope a pill, which made him violently ill, and he died on October 3. Hyde said that the cause of death was "apoplexy," but the nurse was suspicious. Hyde stayed in the Swope mansion, supposedly to look after the other residents, but a mysterious epidemic of illnesses suddenly swept through the estate over the next few months. Nine people came down with typhoid fever, and Chrisman Swope died after being treated by Hyde. By now there were five nurses in the Swope mansion, and they became afraid that Hyde was trying to kill off the entire Swope clan to collect the family fortune. The nurses went to the authorities. After autopsies on the bodies of Colonel Swope and Chrisman Swope revealed traces of strychnine and cyanide poison, Hyde was indicted for murder on February 15, 1910.

Hyde Escapes Justice

Hyde's trial began on April 16, 1910, with Judge Ralph S. Latshaw presiding. Hyde's defense lawyers were R.R. Brewster, M. Cleary, and Frank Walsh. The prosecutors were M. Atkinson, Virgil Conkling, Elliott W. Major, and James A. Reed.

The State of Missouri had an overwhelming case against Hyde and presented numerous expert witnesses who testified as to the medical evidence of poisoning. The testimony of a Dr. Hektoen was typical:

Question: State to the jury what in your opinion that man [Colonel Swope] was suffering from and died from?

Hektoen: In my opinion, death resulted from some convulsive and paralyzing poison or combination of poisons.

On May 16, 1910, the jury found Hyde guilty of murder. Latshaw on July 5, 1910, sentenced Hyde to life imprisonment. Hyde, however, had a secret weapon: his wife Frances, who refused to listen to any suggestion that her husband was guilty. Hyde publicly stated, "This case is not closed. My wife Frances will not forsake me. Yes, Frances will know what to do."

Indeed, Frances Hyde knew what to do. She financed Hyde's defense team, which launched an aggressive appeal. On April 11, 1911, the Supreme Court of Missouri reversed Hyde's conviction and remanded the case for a retrial. Hyde's second trial ended in a mistrial, ostensibly because one juror became sick towards the conclusion of the case. There were rumors, however, that the juror was bribed by agents of Mrs. Hyde.

A third trial was commenced, but the jury could not agree on a verdict. Once again, there were unsubstantiated allegations that Frances Hyde had used her share of the Swope family's millions to bribe certain jurors. Further, there were more rumors that Mrs. Hyde was financing a smear campaign against the surviving Swope family, who hated her for her efforts to absolve Hyde.

In January 1917, Hyde was put on trial for the fourth and last time. After three trials and more than seven years after the alleged murders, the fourth trial was abruptly terminated when Hyde's lawyers correctly pointed out that, under Missouri law, Hyde could not be tried more than three times for the same criminal charges. Hyde was a free man, but he never practiced medicine again, preferring to live off his wife's money instead. Frances Hyde never recanted her faith in her husband's innocence. However, it is worth noting that more than 10 years after Hyde's acquittal, she abruptly left him and took up her own household when he offered to prepare a special remedy for her upset stomach.

Despite the lengthy proceedings and the weight of evidence against him, Hyde was never convicted. Under the law, he must therefore be deemed innocent of the Swope murders, but no law can prevent the obvious conclusion that his loyal wife's money had an impact on the outcome. Not all criminal defendants are equal under the law. Sometimes justice lifts her blindfold when the defendant waves a sufficiently large billfold.

—*Stephen G. Christianson*

Suggestions for Further Reading

Duke, Thomas Samuel. *Celebrated Criminal Cases of America.* San Francisco: James H. Barry Co., 1910.

Nash, Jay Robert. *Almanac of World Crime.* New York: Bonanza Books, 1986.

———. *Murder Among the Mighty: Celebrity Slayings That Shocked America.* New York: Delacorte Press, 1983.

McNamara Brothers Trial: 1911

Defendants: James B. McNamara and John J. McNamara
Crimes Charged: Murder, for James; dynamiting the Llewellyn Iron Works, for John   **Chief Defense Lawyers:** Clarence Darrow, LeCompte Davis, Job Harriman, Cyrus McNutt, and Joseph Scott   **Chief Prosecutors:** W. Joseph Ford and John D. Fredericks   **Judge:** Walter Bordwell   **Place:** Los Angeles, California   **Date of Trial:** December 1, 1911   **Verdict:** Guilty
Sentences: Life imprisonment for James B. McNamara and 15 years imprisonment for John J. McNamara

SIGNIFICANCE

The McNamara brothers trial, which ended just as it began with confessions of guilt by the McNamaras, set the cause of organized labor on the West Coast back by decades. It also nearly ruined the career of Clarence Darrow, one of America's leading criminal defense lawyers.

At the turn of the 20th century, the issue of labor relations divided America. The unions were fighting to organize the industrial work force and for legitimacy in the face of entrenched corporate and government opposition. Both sides frequently resorted to violence to advance their interests.

Two brothers, James B. McNamara and John J. McNamara, were active in the International Association of Bridge and Structural Iron Workers, headquartered in Indianapolis, Indiana. Both men were in their late 20s. The union represented workers in the construction industry, and was particularly active on the West Coast. Harrison Gray Otis, publisher of the *Los Angeles Times,* was the Union's arch enemy. Otis used his newspaper as a public platform for his tirades against the unions and to promote the interests of the pro-management Merchants and Manufacturers Association. On the morning of October 1, 1910, a bomb exploded in the *Los Angeles Times* building, killing 20 people and causing considerable damage to the building. Shortly thereafter, there was another bombing at the Llewellyn Iron Works in Los Angeles.

The bombings drew immediate, nationwide attention. Private detectives hired by the mayor of Los Angeles found evidence that incriminated the McNamaras. In April 1911, the detectives forcibly brought the McNamaras from Indianapolis to Los Angeles for trial by means that were legally questionable at best. Unions and labor sympathizers across the country put together a $250,000 defense fund and hired the famous criminal defense lawyer Clarence Darrow to represent the McNamaras. The pro-McNamara forces claimed that escaping gas, not a bomb, had destroyed the *Times* building. More extremist labor sympathizers charged that Otis himself had arranged the explosion.

Darrow was assisted by LeCompte Davis, Job Harriman, Cyrus McNutt, and Joseph Scott. Harriman was, in fact, the Socialist candidate for mayor in the upcoming city elections, and he joined the defense team for publicity's sake. The prosecutors were W. Joseph Ford and District Attorney John D. Fredericks, and the judge was Walter Bordwell. The trial began on December 1, 1911.

The trial lasted for one short but memorable day. When Bordwell called the case of *People v. James B. McNamara,* Davis rose to his feet and said:

> Your Honor, the defendant is in court. . . . We have concluded to withdraw the plea of not guilty, and have the defendant enter in this case a plea of guilty. A like course we intend to pursue with reference to J.J. McNamara.

Before a stunned courtroom audience, James McNamara stood and pleaded guilty to the charge of murder for bombing the *Times* building. John McNamara then confessed to dynamiting the Llewellyn Iron Works. On December 5, 1911, Bordwell sentenced James to life imprisonment and John to 15 years imprisonment.

Darrow Tried for Bribing Jurors

Darrow had suffered a humiliating defeat by being unable to rescue his clients in the face of the evidence against them. Worse was yet to come, however.

One of the people on Darrow's payroll was Bert Franklin, a former investigator for the U.S. Marshal's office. District Attorney Fredericks had learned that Franklin was trying to bribe jurors to acquit the McNamaras and had approached at least two jurors, namely Robert Bain and George Lockwood. Fredericks arranged a "sting" operation, and on November 28, 1911, three days before the McNamara trial, arrested Franklin in the act of handing money to Lockwood. In January 1912, Franklin pleaded guilty to charges of jury tampering, and on January 29, he testified that Darrow had known and approved of the bribery efforts.

Fredericks arrested Darrow and put him on trial before Judge George Howard Hutton on May 15, 1912. Fredericks was assisted by W. Joseph Ford and Arthur Keetch, while Darrow's defense attorneys were Horace Appel, Harry Dehm, Jerry Giesler and Earl Rogers. When organized labor turned its back on Darrow's request for financial assistance, Darrow had to pay all the legal costs of the 13-week trial out of his own pocket. Darrow denied the charges, and on August 14 and 15, 1912, gave an impassioned closing speech to the jurors, in which he claimed that:

I am not on trial for having sought to bribe a man named Lockwood. I am on trial because I have been a lover of the poor, a friend of the oppressed, because I have stood by Labor for all these years.

On August 15, 1912, the jury returned a verdict of not guilty after deliberating for less than an hour. Fredericks, Otis and the anti-union forces hadn't given up, however.

In October 1912, 50 members of the McNamaras' International Association of Bridge and Structural Iron Workers, primarily senior officers including the union's president, were put on trial in Indianapolis for illegally transporting dynamite. Thirty-nine of the defendants were eventually found guilty. In November 1912, Darrow was put on trial for a second time, this time for an alleged bribery attempt involving juror Robert Bain.

The jury couldn't reach a unanimous decision, although eight of the 12 jurors thought Darrow was guilty, and therefore Darrow was found not guilty a second time. The prosecutors continued to pursue Darrow, although somewhat halfheartedly after two trials, but decided to drop plans for a third trial in December 1913. Darrow returned to his practice in Chicago, and after several years of difficulty was able to revive his reputation as a great criminal defense lawyer. When Darrow died on March 13, 1938, few people remembered his disgrace at the McNamara trials.

The MacNamara brothers confession of guilt in the bombing of the *Los Angeles Times* building set back the cause of organized labor on the West Coast. (*Harper's Weekly*)

Nevertheless, the McNamara case represented a serious defeat for Clarence Darrow. It also represented a serious defeat for organized labor on the West Coast and elsewhere in America, discredited as it was by the tactics of self-confessed bombers and murderers. It took decades for the unions to recover the public trust and their former political influence.

—Stephen G. Christianson

Suggestions for Further Reading

Burns, William J. *The Masked War.* New York: Arno Press, 1969.

"Clarence Darrow: the Lawyer Who Made the Case for Lost Causes." *Life* (Fall 1990): 86–87.

Jensen, Richard J. *Clarence Darrow: the Creation of an American Myth.* New York: Greenwood Press, 1992.

Livingston, John Charles. *Clarence Darrow: the Mind of a Sentimental Rebel.* New York: Garland, 1988.

Robinson, W.W. *Bombs and Bribery.* Los Angeles: Dawson's Book Shop, 1969.

Triangle Shirtwaist Fire Trial: 1911

Defendants: Triangle Shirtwaist Company partners Max Blanck and Isaac Harris   **Crime Charged:** Manslaughter   **Chief Defense Lawyer:** Max D. Steuer   **Chief Prosecutors:** Charles S. Bostwick and J. Robert Rubin
Judge: Thomas C.T. Crain   **Place:** New York, New York
Dates of Trial: December 4–27, 1911   **Verdict:** Not guilty

SIGNIFICANCE
Despite Max Blanck's and Isaac Harris' acquittal, the death of 146 young workers in a sweatshop fire focused public attention on the problem of poor workplace safety conditions and led to the passage of legislation providing for stricter regulations and tougher enforcement.

As American industry grew through the 1800s and into the early 20th century, the number of persons employed as factory workers or in other industrial occupations soared into the millions. Always eager for the cheapest possible labor, big business had no qualms about hiring women and children to perform tasks that required minimal strength, because companies could pay them lower wages than male workers commanded. Lower wages meant bigger profits, and so did spending as little as possible on safety precautions. For example, most factories had few, if any, safeguards to prevent accidental fires, such as sprinkler systems, proper ventilation, or adequate emergency exits. There were no federal safety laws, and while there were some state laws, enforcement was spotty at best.

In 1911, an incident occurred that dramatically illustrated the need for industrial safety reform. The Triangle Shirtwaist Company, which manufactured articles of women's clothing, operated several factories or "sweatshops" in New York City. Two partners, Max Blanck and Isaac Harris, owned Triangle. As was common in the garment industry, Triangle employed mostly young women, who were usually barely in their teens, to perform the fabric cutting, stitching, and sewing that went into making the finished product. The women worked side-by-side at their cutting tables and sewing machines in cramped, dirty rooms. Further, Triangle supervisors routinely locked the door to the workplace from the outside to ensure that the employees never left their stations. Triangle factories were occasionally inspected by the lax city authorities, who took no actions to improve safety.

146 Triangle Employees Die

One of the Triangle factories was located in the ninth story of a building overlooking New York City's Washington Place. A stairway led down to Washington Place. On another side of the ninth floor, the factory overlooked Greene Street. A stairway led down to the street, and also up to the roof. On March 25, 1911, a fire began on the eighth floor and came up through the Greene Street stairwell into Triangle's ninth floor, where the employees were busy at work. As smoke and fire filled the shop from the Greene Street side, the frightened women ran to the Washington Place exit, only to discover that the door was locked. They were trapped inside a burning building.

Bodies from the Triangle Shirtwaist Company fire. (Courtesy, Library of Congress)

Although firemen rushed to the scene, they were too late to prevent scores of the women from being burnt alive. Driven by panic, many women jumped out the windows, only to fall to their death nine stories below. The impact of their bodies from such a height tore through the firemen's safety nets, and smashed holes in the pavement below. A total of 146 Triangle employees died.

The tragedy drew national attention, and the public demanded action against the parties responsible. On April 11 Max Blanck and Isaac Harris were charged with manslaughter. Blanck and Harris were represented by Max D. Steuer, one of the most celebrated and skillful lawyers of the period. The prosecutors were Assistant District Attorneys Charles S. Bostwick and J. Robert

Rubin. The judge was Thomas C.T. Crain, and the trial began on December 4, 1911.

The trial took over three weeks, and 155 witnesses testified. one of the most gripping descriptions of what had happened came from Kate Alterman, a Triangle employee who survived the fire. First, she described how, amidst the chaos, she saw one Margaret Schwartz die in the flames because no one could open the Washington Place stairway door:

> I saw Bernstein, the manager's brother, trying to open the door but he couldn't. He left; and Margaret was there, too, and she tried to open the door and she could not. I pushed her on a side. I tried to open the door, and I couldn't. . . . And then she [Margaret] screamed at the top of her voice, "Open the door! Fire! I am lost, there is fire!"

Horrified, Alterman watched the fire consume Schwartz. Alterman then described how she survived a mad dash through the fire raging through the Greene Street stairway:

> And then I turned my coat on the wrong side and put it on my head with the fur to my face, the lining on the outside, and I got hold of a bunch of dresses and covered the top of my head. I just got ready to go and somebody came and began to chase me back, pulling my dress back, and I kicked her with my foot and she disappeared.

> I tried to make my escape. I had a pocketbook with me, and that pocketbook began to burn. I pressed it to my heart to extinguish the fire, and I made my escape right through the flames: the whole door was a flame right to the roof.

Once she was on the roof, firemen eventually rescued Alterman. Despite Alterman's dramatic testimony and that of other witnesses, however, the trial turned upon the question of whether Blanck and Harris knew that the Washington Place door was locked. Judge Crain read his instructions to the jury on this point:

> You must be satisfied from the evidence, among other things, before you can find these defendants guilty of the crime of manslaughter in its first degree not merely that the door was locked, if it was locked, but that it was locked during the period mentioned under circumstances bringing knowledge of that fact to these defendants.

> But it is not sufficient that the evidence should establish that the door was locked, if it was locked, during such a period; nor yet that the defendants knew that it was locked during such a period, if it was locked. . . Was the door locked? If so, was it locked under circumstances importing knowledge on the part of these defendants that it was locked? If so, and Margaret Schwartz died because she was unable to pass through, would she have lived if the door had not been locked and she had obtained access to the Washington Place stairs and had either remained in the stairwell or gone down to the street or another floor?

Blanck and Harris Go Free

On December 27, 1911, the jury announced its verdict. It pronounced Blanck and Harris not guilty. Although the prosecution's evidence was compelling,, it was not enough to overcome the judge's instructions. As one juror stated:

> I believed that the door was locked at the time of the fire. But we couldn't find them guilty unless we believed they knew the door was locked.

A union march in memory of the victims of the Triangle Shirtwaist fire. (Courtesy, Library of Congress)

With the support of District Attorney Charles S. Whitman, the prosecutors moved for another trial. Judge Samuel Seabury presided over the retrial. Despite public outrage against the first trial's acquittal, on March 12, 1912, Judge Seabury ordered the retrial dismissed on the grounds that the defendants were being tried for the same offense. Based upon the principle of double jeopardy, Judge Seabury proclaimed:

> The court has neither the right nor the power to proceed with the present trial. These men are to be tried for the same offense again and under our constitution and laws, this cannot be done. I charge you, gentlemen of the jury, to find a verdict for the defendants.

Blanck and Harris left the courtroom free men. The impact of the Triangle fire, however, was not lost. New York City soon had a Bureau of Fire Prevention, which implemented stricter safety regulations and saw to their enforcement. Other cities and states followed suit in the years and decades to come. The federal government finally acted to ensure workplace safety during the administration of Franklin D. Roosevelt, and FDR's measures were the predecessor to such protective agencies as the Occupational Safety and Health Administration. Today, there are extensive federal and state safety regulations to protect workers from the sort of dangers that resulted in the Triangle fire.

—Stephen G. Christianson

Suggestions for Further Reading

Crute, Sheree. "The Insurance Scandal Behind the Triangle Shirtwaist Fire." *MS.* (April 1983): 81–82.

Stein, Leon. *The Triangle Fire.* Philadelphia: J.B. Lippincott, 1962.

"A Sweatshop Worker Remembers." *MS* (April 1983): 83.

Floyd Allen Trial: 1912

Defendant: Floyd Allen **Crime Charged:** Murder
Chief Defense Lawyer: J.C. Buxton **Chief Prosecutors:** J.C. Wysor and
W.S. Poage **Judge:** Walter Staples **Place:** Wytheville, Virginia
Dates of Trial: April 30–May 18, 1912 **Verdict:** Guilty **Sentence:** Death
by electrocution

SIGNIFICANCE
The Floyd Allen affair represents one of the rare incidents in American history
when a criminal defendant attempted to avoid justice by assassinating the trial
judge.

Carroll County, Virginia, is a rural county, located in the Blue Ridge Mountains and far from any major city. The Allens were the county's leading family, owning a great deal of land and dominating local politics. They ran Carroll County as their private chiefdom. In the early 1900s, the patriarch of the Allen clan was Floyd Allen.

In 1911, two of Allen's nephews, Sidna Allen and Wesley Edwards, were involved in a scuffle with some Allen opponents outside a schoolhouse where Baptist services were being held. The local prosecutor in nearby Hillsville, Commonwealth's Attorney William M. Foster, was also an Allen adversary, and he promptly charged Sidna Allen and Edwards with disturbing public worship. Foster's men arrested Sidna Allen and Edwards after tracking them down in Mount Airy, North Carolina and brought them back to Carroll County for justice. On the way back to Hillsville, Floyd Allen and his henchmen set upon the lawmen and freed their kin. Foster then charged Allen with assaulting officers of the law and had Allen arrested.

A jury found Allen guilty, and on March 14, 1912, Allen went to his sentencing hearing before Judge Thornton L. Massie in the Hillsville courthouse. Massie sentenced Allen to one year in prison. There were, however, nearly 20 Allen men among the spectators in the courtroom. Allen rose to his feet and calmly said, "Gentlemen, I ain't goin'." That was the cue. The Allen men (Floyd included) pulled out their concealed pistols and began firing. Five people were killed: Judge Massie, Commonwealth's Attorney Foster, Sheriff Lew F. Webb, a member of the jury named Augustus C. Fowler, and a witness named Betty Ayers. Floyd Allen was wounded when the deputies and guards returned fire, and he was quickly arrested. The rest of the Allens fled, and it took a manhunt of several months to round them all up.

Virginia Tries Floyd Allen for Murder

Allen's murder trial began on April 30, 1912, in Wytheville, Virginia before Judge Walter Staples. His defense lawyer was J.C. Buxton, and the prosecutors were W.S. Poage and J.C. Wysor. The other Allens were tried separately. There were scores of witnesses who had actually seen Allen fire shots in the Hillsville courthouse, and so there was no plausible defense to the charges. On May 18, 1912, the jury found Allen guilty of murder, and he was sentenced to death by electrocution.

Of the many other Allens involved in the courthouse shooting who were also tried for murder, several bear mentioning. Allen's son, Claude Allen, went to trial on May 20, 1912. It took three trials, however, before a jury could agree on a verdict. On July 17, 1912, Claude Allen was found guilty of murder and also sentenced to death. Friel Allen, who had cooperated with the authorities during the manhunt, was sentenced to 18 years in prison after his trial in August 1912, despite the fact that the authorities had promised him a sentence of only five years. Sidna Allen was tried in November 1912 and sentenced to 35 years in prison, but on April 29, 1926, Virginia Governor Harry F. Byrd pardoned him.

On March 28, 1913, Floyd and Claude Allen, father and son, were electrocuted in Richmond, Virginia, within 11 minutes of each other. The Allens were one of the few people in American history who tried to escape justice by assassinating the trial judge and the prosecutor. As Judge Staples said in his sentencing order:

> You, Floyd Allen, were in custody of the law: When ordered to jail, you uttered your defiance of its authority, such a defiance as was never before heard in Virginia court.

> —*Stephen G. Christianson*

Suggestions for Further Reading

Gardner, Rufus L. *The Courthouse Tragedy.* Hillsville, Va.: Unknown Publisher, 1962.

Parker, George Martin Nathaniel. *The Mountain Massacre.* Bluefield, WV: Country Life, 1930.

Charles Becker Trials: 1912–14

Defendant: Charles Becker   **Crime Charged:** Murder
Chief Defense Lawyers: First trial: John F. McIntyre, Lloyd B. Stryker, and George W. Whiteside; Second trial: W. Bourke Cockran, John Johnstone, and Martin Manton   **Chief Prosecutors:** First trial: Frank Moss and Charles S. Whitman; Second trial: Charles S. Whitman   **Judges:** First trial: John W. Goff; Second trial: Samuel Seabury   **Place:** New York, New York
Dates of Trials: October 7–30, 1912, May 2–22, 1914   **Verdicts:** Guilty, both trials   **Sentence:** Death by electrocution

SIGNIFICANCE

The sordid career of New York police Lieutenant Charles Becker included graft, extortion, and ultimately the murder of his former gambling hall partner. Becker's brazen operation of a personal crime syndicate from within the police department provided novelist Stephen Crane with the inspiration for his work *Maggie: A Girl of the Streets*. Becker's trial also inspired the public and the press to give more attention to big-city corruption.

C harles Becker was born in 1869 into a family of German immigrants who had taken up residence in New York City. When Becker grew into manhood in the early 1890s, New York was teeming with immigrants and a new industrial prosperity. It was also a city rife with corruption. The Tammany Hall political machine and the crime bosses openly ran New York together and had a long tradition of sharing the wealth from prostitution, gambling, extortion, and other flourishing vices. Although there were many honest policemen, plenty of officers were willing to fatten their wallets by cooperating with the crooked politicians and the bosses. Unlike the lowly cop on the beat who looks the other way every now and then, however, Becker became actively involved in the New York crime world.

Becker was a tall man weighing well over 200 pounds, all of it muscle. He was violent but also intelligent. While the thugs that he controlled took in more and more protection money from pimps and gambling houses, Becker also obtained promotion after promotion in the police department. In 1911, police Commissioner Rhinelander Waldo promoted Becker again, not only making him a lieutenant and Waldo's aide, but also the officer in charge of a special squad charged with cracking down on crime.

Becker Runs Crime Ring from within Police Department

Putting Becker in charge of such a squad was the height of irony, and Becker lost no time in turning the squad into his personal mobile hit squad. Soon, every pimp and gambler on Broadway and in Manhattan knew that failure to pay Becker the cut he demanded meant swift and sure retaliation in the form of a raid by Becker's squad. From outside the police department, Becker also recruited the cream of New York's thugs to work for him, such as "Gyp the Blood," "Dago Frank," "Whitey" Lewis, "Lefty Louie," bald "Billiard Ball" Jack Rose, Sam Schepps, Harry Vallon, "Bridgey" Webber, and "Big Jack" Zelig.

Becker's criminal enterprises included dealings with Herman Rosenthal, nicknamed "Beansie," a well-known gambler. For a while, Becker and Rosenthal jointly ran and shared the profits from a gambling house, but a dispute arose between them over who was entitled to what percentage. Becker's squad raided and shut down Rosenthal's operation. In retaliation, Rosenthal went to New York's new and squeaky-clean district attorney, Charles S. Whitman, and told him everything he knew about Becker's criminal operations. Whitman surprised

Funeral procession for Herman "Beansie" Rosenthal. (Courtesy, Library of Congress)

all of New York by attacking the powerful Becker head-on, summoning a grand jury for the purpose of bringing criminal charges against Becker.

Furious, Becker ordered his thugs to kill Rosenthal, brazenly promising them police protection. On July 21, 1911, several of Becker's men, led by Jack Rose, approached Rosenthal outside the Cafe Metropole and shot him to death. Undaunted by the murder of his star witness, Whitman was able to trace the getaway car to Rose and promptly arrested him. At first, Rose refused to talk, but when Becker failed to come to his rescue, Rose cracked and told Whitman everything about Becker ordering Rosenthal's murder. Whitman mobilized his forces and smashed Becker's ring, arresting Becker and his associates for Rosenthal's murder.

Tried Before New York's Hanging Judge

On October 7, 1912, Becker's trial opened, with Judge John W. Goff presiding. Like Whitman, Judge Goff had no tolerance for corruption and had earned a reputation for being one of the toughest judges to sit on the New York bench. Whitman and his assistant prosecutor, Frank Moss, therefore had the advantage over Becker's defense attorneys, John F. McIntyre, Lloyd B. Stryker, and George W. Whiteside. The prosecution lost no time in bringing Rose to the stand and asking him what Becker had said with respect to Rosenthal. Rose replied:

> Becker said to me: "There is only one thing to do with a fellow like Rosenthal—just stop him so that he will not bother anybody any more for all time." I said: "What do you mean?" He said: "Well, there is a fellow that ought to be put off the earth." "Why," I says, "I agree with you. He is no account." He said: "Well, no use saying he is no account, and all of that, but the idea is now to do something to him." I says: "What do you mean?" and he said: "There is a fellow I would like to have croaked."

Rose went on to relate how Becker gave the order to murder Rosenthal:

> And Becker said: "I don't want him beat up. I could do that myself. I could have a warrant for any gambling house that he frequents and make a raid on that place and beat him up for resisting arrest or anything else. No beating up will fix that fellow, a dog in the eyes of myself, you, and everybody else. Nothing for that man but taken off this earth. Have him murdered, cut his throat, dynamited, or anything."

McIntyre, Becker's lead counsel, was frustrated in his efforts to cross-examine Rose and the other prosecution witnesses by Judge Goff. Goff repeatedly cut McIntyre's questioning short and denied his motions for more time. In their private conferences during breaks in the trial, Becker railed at McIntyre for his seeming ineffectiveness, but McIntyre's strategy was to lay the groundwork for a successful appeal. Goff obliged him, giving final instructions to the jury that went overboard in their bias against Becker:

> If it be true that Becker instructed Rose to kill Rosenthal, I instruct you that Becker constituted Rose his agent and instrument in the carrying out of the design; whatever Rose did, Becker in the eyes of the law did . . . .

It is apparent from this testimony that the main witnesses against the defendant Becker are what are called accomplices. There is no doubt that Rose, Webber, and Vallon are accomplices.

The jury found Becker guilty on October 30, 1912. As McIntyre predicted, the Court of Appeals overturned the conviction and ordered a new trial, ruling that Goff committed "gross misconduct" and that Whitman's witnesses were "dangerous and degenerate."

Tried Again

Becker's second trial began May 2, 1914. This time, the judge was Samuel Seabury. McIntyre was tired of representing Becker, and Becker had a new defense team: W. Bourke Cockran, John Johnstone, and Martin Manton. Whitman continued as prosecutor, but without Frank Moss' assistance.

Whitman changed his strategy in the second trial, relying less on Rose and Becker's other thugs and more on James Marshall, a young black man who had been on Becker's payroll as an informant and who had been present when Becker ordered Rose and the others to kill Rosenthal. Unlike the other witnesses, Marshall had not participated in the actual murder and thus Whitman reasoned that if Becker was convicted again, the Court of Appeals would be less likely to criticize the prosecution. Further, Judge Seabury was more scrupulous than Goff in his instructions to the jury. In his closing argument for the defense, Manton tried to convince the jury that Marshall couldn't be trusted because he used to be an informer and because he was black:

> Remember this, gentlemen of the jury, the men who accuse Lieutenant Becker would be on trial for murder had they not accused Lieutenant Becker. And the only corroboration of their desperate testimony comes from a little coloured boy whose only motive is that he was paid, fed, clothed and housed by the district attorney; a little coloured boy who was once a police informer, a man who betrays others for pay.

The jury was not swayed, however, and on May 22, 1914, found Charles Becker guilty again. Seabury sentenced Becker to die in the electric chair. This time the conviction was upheld, although Becker's appeals postponed his execution for over a year. During that time, Whitman became a celebrity for his much-publicized victory. He capitalized on his popularity by running for governor and winning the election on November 3, 1914. Ironically, when Becker's appeals ended, he begged for a pardon from the one man who could give it, now-Governor Whitman. Becker's wife Helen even went to Whitman personally, but to no avail. On July 30, 1915, Becker was executed in the Sing Sing prison electric chair.

Becker's long criminal career included an incident when he beat a young prostitute who had been reluctant to pay protection money he demanded. Stephen Crane witnessed Becker's assault on the defenseless woman and was inspired to write his famous novel *Maggie: A Girl of the Streets*. Becker's trial and execution would also live on due to its publicity and the attention it focused on urban corruption and the efforts of people such as Whitman to combat it.

—Stephen G. Christianson

Suggestions for Further Reading

Crane, Stephen. *Maggie: A Girl of the Streets*. London: Cassell, 1966.

Delmar, Vina. *The Becker Scandal: A Time Remembered*. New York: Harcourt, Brace & World, 1968.

Logan, Andy. *Against the Evidence: the Becker-Rosenthal Affair*. New York: McCall, 1970.

Root, Jonathan. *One Night in July: the True Story of the Rosenthal-Becker Murder Case*. New York: Coward-McCann, 1961.

——. *The Life and Bad Times of Charlie Becker: The True Story of a Famous American Murder Trial*. London: Secker & Warburg, 1962.

Leo Frank Trial: 1913

Defendant: Leo Max Frank   **Crime Charged:** Murder
Chief Defense Lawyers: Reuben Arnold, Herbert Haas, Stiles Hopkins, and
Luther Z. Rosser   **Chief Prosecutors:** Hugh Dorsey, Frank Arthur Hooper,
and Edward A. Stephens   **Judge:** Leonard Strickland Roan   **Place:** Atlanta,
Georgia   **Dates of Trial:** July 28–September 26, 1913   **Verdict:** Guilty
Sentence: Death by hanging, commuted by Georgia Governor John Slaton to
life imprisonment (After his commutation, Frank died at the hands of an
angry lynch mob.)

SIGNIFICANCE

The Leo Frank trial was a national scandal, which exposed the double standard of
Southern justice: one for whites and one for minorities such as Frank, who was
Jewish. Not only was Frank hung by a lynch mob after his death sentence was
commuted, but the Ku Klux Klan experienced a period of renewed growth for
years afterward due to the racist feelings brought on by the trial.

Leo Max Frank was born in Paris, Texas, in 1884. His family moved to
Brooklyn, New York while he was still a baby. Frank's family was Jewish,
and he was raised in New York City's extensive Jewish community. Frank was a
quiet, shy man, but he had exceptional mechanical aptitude and he graduated
from Cornell University with an engineering degree. After working for brief
periods with several companies, Frank went to work for his uncle, Moses Frank,
who was the principal owner of the National Pencil Company. The National
Pencil Company had a factory in Atlanta, Georgia, and in 1907 Frank was
appointed the superintendent and moved to Atlanta.

It probably never occurred to Frank that, since he was moving to the
South, racism might be a problem. Atlanta's Jewish community was small by
New York standards but nevertheless significant and had deep roots in the city's
history. In 1911, Frank married Lucile Selig, whose family was also Jewish and
well-off. Frank spent most of his time supervising the pencil factory, avoided
politics and racial issues, and was honored by the Jewish community as one of
Atlanta's most promising young businessmen. By 1913 Frank was one of Atlanta's leading citizens and was enjoying a successful career.

Little Mary Phagan Murdered

As was common at the time, Frank's factory employed women and children, who were capable of performing the light labor necessary to manufacture pencils and who could be paid lower wages than men. One such worker was Mary Phagan, a blond 13-year-old girl who lived in nearby Marietta. She was one of several workers caught in a temporary layoff, and on April 26, 1913, she came to collect her final wages from Frank. Frank paid her and thought no more of the matter after she left. Shortly before he left for the day, Frank had another encounter with a former employee, this time with John Gantt, who asked if he could retrieve some shoes he had left in his locker. Frank allowed Gantt to get his shoes, but Frank's nervous personality made him afraid of Gantt, who had a reputation as a drunkard and who Frank had fired for stealing.

That night, Frank called the night watchman, a black man named Newt Lee, several times to ask if there was any trouble. Frank probably feared some sort of action by Gantt, but there was none. In the early hours of the morning, however, Lee discovered the bound and brutalized corpse of Mary Phagan in the basement. Someone had raped and killed her after she collected her pay that day. Afraid that he would be blamed for the crime, Lee went straight to the police and reported the crime. His honesty did him no good: After the police arrived at the factory and investigated the scene of the crime, they threw Lee in jail anyway, to be held without charges for months.

The police then went to Frank's house, took him to the scene of the crime for questioning, and then to the police station for several days of further interrogation. Meanwhile, the murder had become a local sensation, and the Atlanta newspapers were filled with lurid headlines describing the details of the crime and calling for justice. Hugh Mason Dorsey, the chief prosecutor for that portion of Atlanta, had political ambitions and seized on the meek, Jewish Frank as an easy target. On April 29, 1913, Frank was formally arrested for the murder of Mary Phagan.

Frank's lawyers were Reuben Arnold, Herbert Haas, Stiles Hopkins, and Luther Z. Rosser. In addition to Dorsey, the prosecutors were Frank Arthur Hooper and Edward A. Stephens. The judge was Leonard Strickland Roan, and the trial began on July 28, 1913.

Prosecutors Emphasize Frank's Nervousness

Newt Lee, still in prison "under suspicion," was one of the first prosecution witnesses. Frank's telephone calls to Lee on the night of the murder came back to haunt him, because the prosecutors made it look as if Frank was checking to see if the body had been discovered that Saturday night. Lee Testified:

> Mr. Frank phoned me [the first time] that night about an hour after he left, it was sometime after seven o'clock. He says, "How is everything?" and I says, "Everything is all right so far as I know," and he says, "Goodbye." No, he

did not ask anything about Gantt. Yes, that is the first time he ever phoned to me on a Saturday night.

The prosecutors then turned Frank's nervous disposition to their advantage, and using the testimony of the police officers who had taken Frank to the scene of the crime on the morning of Sunday, April 27, to create suspicion in the mind of the jury. First, officer John N. Starnes testified:

I reached the factory between five and six o'clock on April 27th. I called up the superintendent, Leo Frank, and asked him to come right away. He said he hadn't had any breakfast. He asked where the night watchman was. I told him to come, and if he would come, I would send an automobile for him. I didn't tell him what had happened, and he didn't ask me.

When Frank arrived at the factory, a few minutes later, he appeared to be nervous, he was in a trembling condition. Lee was composed at the factory, he never tried to get away.

Another officer, one who had gone to pick up Frank at Frank's home, confirmed Starnes' testimony:

Mrs. Frank came to the door; she had on a bathrobe. I stated that I would like to see Mr. Frank and about that time Mr. Frank stepped out from behind a curtain. Frank's voice was hoarse and trembling and nervous and excited. He looked to me like he was pale. He seemed nervous in handling his collar; he could not get his tie tied, and talked very rapid in asking what had happened. He kept insisting on a cup of coffee.

When we got into the automobile, Mr. Frank wanted to know what had happened at the factory, and I asked him if he knew Mary Phagan, and told him she had been found dead in the basement. Mr. Frank said he did not know any girl by the name of Mary Phagan, that he knew very few of the employees.

The implication from this testimony was that Frank's nervousness was the result of a guilty conscience. Next, the prosecutors tried to prove that Frank had deliberately planned to get Mary Phagan to come to the factory that weekend. For example, a factory employee named Helen Ferguson testified that she had been Mary Phagan's friend and had in the past picked up Phagan's pay for her, but on the day before the murder, Frank suddenly refused to let Ferguson pick up Phagan's final pay:

[I went to] Mr. Frank Friday, April 25, about seven o'clock in the evening and asked for Mary Phagan's money. Mr. Frank said, "I can't let you have it," and before he said anything else I turned around and walked out. I had gotten Mary's money before.

Prosecution Clinches Their Case

The prosecutors saved their best witness for last: Jim Conley, a large black man who was the factory janitor. Despite some very suspicious circumstances that tended to implicate Conley as the actual murderer, the prosecutors put him on the stand. It has even been written that Dorsey deliberately chose to prosecute a "Yankee Jew" rather than a "nigger" for purposes of sensationalism, regardless of Frank's innocence. The gist of Conley's lengthy testimony was that he had been at the factory on the day of the murder and that Frank had confessed to the murder:

> Mr. Frank was standing up there at the top of the steps and shivering and trembling and rubbing his hands like this. He had a little rope in his hands and a long wide piece of cord. His eyes were large and they looked right funny. He looked funny out of his eyes. His face was red. . . . After I got up to the top of the steps, he asked me, "Did you see [Mary Phagan] who passed here just a while ago?" I told him . . . she hasn't come back down, and he says, "Well, that one you say didn't come back down, she come into my office awhile ago and wanted to know something about her work in my office and I went back there to see if the little girl's work had come, and I wanted to be with the little girl, and she refused me, and I struck her and I guess I struck her too hard and she fell and hit her head against something, and I don't know how bad she got hurt. . . ."

The defense lawyers cross-examined Conley for several days but were unable to impeach his testimony. The defense lawyers also had to contend with the presence of spectators in the courtroom who constantly made catcalls and racist comments—such as "Hang the Jew!"—while the defense attempted to make its case. Although Judge Roan had once been defense lawyer Rosser's partner in private practice, he made no serious effort to curb these distractions.

At the conclusion of the defense's case, Frank himself took the stand. For nearly half a day he spoke, and unequivocally denied murdering Phagan. He explained his apparent nervousness as the natural result of being dragged out of his home so early on a Sunday morning and being confronted with such a gruesome crime:

> Now, gentlemen, I have heard a great deal, and have you, in this trial, about nervousness, about how nervous I was that morning. Gentlemen, I was nervous, I was completely unstrung, I will admit it; imagine, awakened out of my sound sleep, and a morning run down in the cool of the morning in an automobile driven at top speed, without any food or breakfast, rushing into a dark passageway, coming into a darkened room, and then suddenly an electric light flashed on, and to see that sight that was presented by that poor little child; why, it was a sight that was enough to drive a man to distraction; that was a sight that would have made a stone melt.

Further, Frank bluntly called Conley a liar:

> The statement of the Negro Conley is a tissue of lies from first to last. I know nothing whatever of the cause of the death of Mary Phagan and Conley's statement . . . that I had anything to do with her or to do with him that day, is a monstrous lie.

Frank Convicted, Commuted, and Lynched

On September 26, 1913, after one of the longest trials in Georgia history, the jury found Leo Frank guilty of the murder of Mary Phagan. Judge Roan sentenced Frank to be executed by hanging on October 10, but the execution was stayed by the defense lawyers' appeals. On February 17, 1914, the Georgia

Supreme Court upheld Frank's conviction, although two judges dissented. The defense lawyers, however, did not give up. They pursued evidence that Conley had committed the murder: Witnesses had seen Conley washing his bloody clothing at the factory after the murder, Conley's girlfriend gave testimony concerning Conley's perverted sexual tendencies, and Conley's own lawyer told Judge Roan that Conley had confessed to the murder to him.

Despite the evidence of Conley's guilt and therefore Frank's innocence, Judge Roan refused to overturn the verdict and the Georgia Supreme Court again affirmed on October 14, 1914. On December 9, 1914, Frank's execution was rescheduled for January 22, 1915, but it was again stayed, this time by the defense lawyers' *habeas corpus* petition (release from unlawful confinement) to the U.S. Supreme Court. On April 19, 1915, the Court denied the petition, despite the strong dissents of Justices Oliver Wendell Holmes and Charles Evans Hughes.

Frank's last chance was an appeal to the governor of Georgia, John Slaton, for commutation of his sentence. This appeal began with a hearing on May 31, 1915, before the Georgia Prison Commission. On June 9, 1915, the Commission voted 2–1 against recommending commutation to the governor. Slaton, however, was an independent man, and had on several occasions used his power to grant clemency when in his opinion justice demanded it, regardless of the unpopularity of his decision. On June 21, 1915, Slaton commuted Frank's sentence to life imprisonment, citing the widespread national criticism of Georgia justice and the many doubts raised over the evidence against Frank.

Governor John Slanton, who commuted Frank's sentence, hanging in effigy, as "King of the Jews." (Courtesy, Georgia Department of Archives and History)

> This case has been marked by doubt. The trial judge doubted. Two judges of the Court of Georgia doubted. Two judges of the Supreme Court of the United States doubted. One of the three Prison Commissioners doubted.

As he probably foresaw, Slaton's decision was instantly unpopular in Georgia. There were demonstrations in Atlanta and in Marietta, Phagan's home town, and sporadic acts of vandalism against Jewish homes and stores. On August 16, 1915, a vigilante group drove from Marietta to the Milledgeville Prison Farm outside Macon, Georgia. They overpowered the skeleton crew of prison guards and took Frank from his cell. The vigilantes drove back to Marietta, a seven-hour trip, with Frank. Once back in Marietta, a lynch mob of local citizens gathered and watched as Frank was hung from a tree limb on the morning of August 17, 1915. The racist hatred stirred up by the Frank trial did not end with Frank's lynching. For decades, the "vindication" of Mary Phagan was a rallying cry for the resurgent Ku Klux Klan.

In 1982, an old black man named Alonzo Mann, who had worked at Frank's pencil factory as a child, publicly declared that he had seen Jim Conley drag Mary Phagan's corpse to the basement but had kept silent because Conley had threatened to kill him. On March 11, 1986, the Georgia State Board of Pardons and Paroles posthumously pardoned Frank.

—Stephen G. Christianson

Suggestions for Further Reading

Dinnerstein, Leonard. *The Leo Frank Case.* Athens, Ga.: University of Georgia Press, 1987.

Liebman, James S. "Lesson Unlearned." *The Nation* (August 1991): 217.

Lindemann, Albert S. *The Jew Accused: Three Anti-Semitic Affairs (Dreyfus, Beilis, Frank), 1894–1915.* New York: Cambridge University Press, 1991.

MacLean, Nancy. "The Leo Frank Case Reconsidered: Gender and Sexual Politics in the Making of Reactionary Populism." *The Journal of American History* (December 1991): 917–948.

Oney, Steve. "The Lynching of Leo Frank: Two Years Ago, and Seventy Years Too Late, a Witness Came Forward to Prove That Frank's Only Crime was Being a Stranger in the Old South." *Esquire* (September 1985): 90–98.

Phagan, Mary. *The Murder of Little Mary Phagan.* Far Hills, N.J.: New Horizon Press, 1987.

Joe Hill Trial: 1914

Defendant: Joe Hill   **Crime Charged:** Murder
Chief Defense Lawyers: Soren X. Christensen, Orrin N. Hilton, E.D. McDougall, and F.B. Scott   **Chief Prosecutor:** E.O. Leatherwood
Judge: Morris L. Ritchie   **Place:** Salt Lake City, Utah   **Dates of Trial:** June 17–28, 1914   **Verdict:** Guilty   **Sentence:** Execution by firing squad

SIGNIFICANCE

The trial of Joe Hill launched the legend of Joe Hill, a lyrical spokesman for the Industrial Workers of the World. His conviction and execution made him a martyr symbolizing, in the eyes of many union workers, all the injustice of American society.

The Industrial Workers of the World (IWW, better known as the Wobblies), organized in 1905, sent its messages to laboring people through song. Its *Little Red Song Book*, which set new words to popular, often religious, tunes, enjoyed print runs of 50,000. Before World War I, the Wobblies directed or participated in 150 strikes, some as large as a 10-week holdout by 25,000 textile workers in Lawrence, Massachusetts. Songs were an important element in Wobbly tactics, for they brought a sense of solidarity to heterogeneous groups of workers.

The song book's 1911 edition introduced a writer named Joe Hill and a song—"The Preacher and the Slave"—that became one of his most famous. To the tune of "In the Sweet Bye and Bye," it sang:

> You will eat, bye and bye,
> In that glorious land above the sky;
> Work and pray, live on hay,
> You'll get pie in the sky when you die.

Hill, a native of Sweden, was soon a popular hero. He meandered across the country, playing piano, banjo, guitar, and violin in hobo jungles, migrant workers' camps, and city slums. Each edition of the songbook introduced several of his new Joe Hill songs.

Hill was staying with friends in Salt Lake City, Utah, on Saturday, January 10, 1914, when he went out for the evening. Toward midnight, he knocked at the door of Dr. Frank M. McHugh, who dressed a bullet wound that pierced

Hill's chest. Hill told the doctor, "I got into a stew with a friend who thought I had insulted his wife."

The same night, police investigated a shooting at a grocery store. Proprietor John G. Morrison and his elder son were found dead. His younger son, Merlin, 13, reported seeing two men come in carrying pistols. They shouted, "We have got you now!" and fired, then ran.

Morrison was a former policeman who had lived in constant dread of those he had previously arrested. Twice he had shot and wounded men who attacked him.

Police found Morrison's pistol, discharged. A witness reported seeing two men run from the store, one holding his hands to his chest.

After Dr. McHugh dressed Hill's wound, he read of the murders and called the police. Since Hill had been wounded the same night as the murders and he would say only that his shooting occurred during a fight over a woman, he was arrested.

Circumstantial Evidence but No Motive

As the trial opened on June 17, 1914, prosecutor E.O. Leatherwood admitted that the state had only circumstantial evidence. Thirteen-year-old Merlin Morrison could not positively identify Hill as his father's murderer.

Press interest intensified as Wobbly lawyers Orrin Hilton and Soren Christensen took over the defense. They complained that Hill would rather face death than reveal his exact whereabouts and the identity of those he was with on the night of the murder. They challenged the prosecutor to prove a motive for his killing Morrison, or even for shouting "We have got you now!" before shooting. They tried to prove that Hill was wounded by a steel bullet, while Morrison's gun fired lead.

On June 28, the jury returned a guilty verdict, and Hill was sentenced to die. Attorney Hilton appealed, citing the prosecution's failure to identify Hill as the murderer, the lack of motive, the court's disallowing testimony on previous attempts on Morrison's life, errors in the admission of expert testimony (a newsman had been accepted as a gun expert), and several critical errors by the judge. The appeal was denied.

Hill's attorneys decided that an appeal to the U.S. Supreme Court was useless because the case involved no federal considerations. While rallies were held and funds were raised nationwide, execution was set for October 1. Hill's attorneys asked the Utah Board of Pardons to commute his sentence to life imprisonment. Petitions, telegrams, and letters mounted. Hill refused an offer of freedom if he would reveal, with corroboration, where he was during the Morrison murder. The execution date was set repeatedly as the Swedish minister to the United States, American Federation Labor President Samuel Gompers, and the highly respected Helen Keller all appealed to President Woodrow Wilson, who in turn, appealed to Utah governor William Spry. But Spry refused clemency unless Hill satisfactorily explained how he was wounded.

Hours before his execution, Hill wired IWW General Secretary Bill Haywood, "I will die like a true-blue rebel. Don't waste any time in mourning—organize."

At 10:00 P.M., Hill handed a guard his last poem, titled "My Last Will":

. . . let the merry breezes blow
My dust to where some flowers grow.
Perhaps some fading flower then
Would come to life and bloom again.
This is my Last and Final Will.
Good luck to All of you
—Joe Hill

The next morning, November 19, a firing squad shot Joe Hill through the heart. Thousands attended his funeral in Salt Lake City, then another in Chicago. Cremation followed. Joe Hill's ashes, distributed in small packets, were scattered worldwide.

The song, "I Dreamed I Saw Joe Hill Last Night," soon appeared, with its verse,

The copper bosses killed you, Joe,
"They shot you, Joe," says I.
"Takes more than guns to kill a man,"
Says Joe, "I didn't die."
Says Joe, "I didn't die."

In the years following, such noted authors as Upton Sinclair, Carl Sandburg, John Dos Passos, Eugene O'Neill, and Wallace Stegner, as well as folk singers Pete Seeger and Woody Guthrie and millions of workers, have all dreamed they saw Joe Hill last night.

The last of Joe Hill's ashes were scattered in Washington, D.C., in November 1988.

—Bernard Ryan, Jr.

Suggestions for Further Reading

Hampton, Wayne. *Guerrilla Minstrels: John Lennon, Joe Hill, Woody Guthrie, and Bob Dylan.* Knoxville: University of Tennessee Press, 1986.

Smith, Gibbs M. *Labor Martyr Joe Hill.* New York: Grosset & Dunlap, 1969.

Snow, Richard F. "American Characters: Joe Hill," *American Heritage* (October 1976): 79.

Stegner, Wallace. *The Preacher and the Slave.* Boston: Houghton Mifflin, 1950.

"Wobbly," *The New Yorker* (December 19, 1988): 28.

Tom Mooney Trial: 1917

Defendant: Thomas J. Mooney   **Crime Charged:** Murder
Chief Defense Lawyers: W. Bourke Cockran and Maxwell McNutt
Chief Prosecutors: Edward A. Cunha and Charles Fickert
Judge: Franklin A. Griffin   **Place:** San Francisco, California
Dates of Trial: January 3–February 9, 1917   **Verdict:** Guilty
Sentence: Death by hanging, later commuted, then pardoned

SIGNIFICANCE

Tom Mooney's case demonstrated how America's phobia about radicals from before World War I and through the 1920s and '30s corrupted its sense of justice and even its common sense. While the improper conviction of Mooney—based on perjury, suppression and fabrication of evidence, and subornation of perjury—was established within a year after the trial, political maneuvering kept him in prison until 1939. This failure of the legal system to acknowledge that a conviction based on perjured testimony justified a new trial is demonstrated that an unpopular defendant could be denied due process in the state of California.

On "Preparedness Day," July 22, 1916, a bomb killed 10 spectators and injured 40 others during a military parade in San Francisco. Opposition to the parade had been planned and announced by radical labor leaders and anarchists who thought the march promoted militarism, and who were against American entry into the World War then raging in Europe. The bombing looked like anarchists' work.

Within hours of the bombing, District Attorney Charles Fickert was visited by Martin Swanson, a private detective employed by the Pacific Gas and Electric Company (PG&E). Swanson suspected that the insurgent responsible for the parade bombing was 34-year-old Tom Mooney, a union organizer who had drifted through at least a dozen jobs across the country as an ironworker and had earned a reputation as "a comer" with officers of his union, the International Molders. Mooney had even drifted twice to Europe, where he was strongly attracted to socialism. Back in the United States, he had been an active orator and fund-raiser in the 1908 presidential campaign of Socialist Eugene V. Debs, who liked Mooney's forceful persistence and made him his "official party literature agent."

One of 'The Blasters'

Swanson knew Mooney had been acquitted of possessing dynamite in a strike against PG&E. Swanson also implicated Warren K. Billings, another labor activist who had been convicted of transporting dynamite.

Billings, Mooney, his wife Rena and their friend Israel Weinberg, a taxi driver, were arrested immediately without warrants. Rena Mooney and Weinberg were charged with complicity; Billings and Mooney with murder.

Billings was tried first, convicted, and sentenced to life imprisonment—mainly on the testimony of John McDonald, who said he had seen Billings and Tom Mooney at the scene just before the bomb went off.

On January 3, 1917, opening the Mooney trial for the prosecution, Prosecutor Edward Cunha reviewed Mooney's earlier association with an organization called "The Blasters." Their stated goal was an uprising of California's workers, who would seize property and destroy the government. Their revolution called for violence, even the assassination of the president. For a week, Cunha presented circumstantial evidence, most of which had been seen or heard in the Billings trial.

A Surprise Witness—and a Jitney

Then Cunha came up with a surprise witness: one Frank C. Oxman, an Oregon cattleman who traveled frequently to California and Kansas, buying and selling cattle. He testified that he had arrived in San Francisco on the morning of the parade and was watching it when he saw a jitney containing five people turn from Market Street onto Stewart. As it stopped, men he identified as Mooney and Billings jumped out, put a suitcase on the sidewalk, and hopped back in the car. Oxman declared under oath that Weinberg was at the wheel, and Rena Mooney was visible in the car. Dramatically pulling a yellow envelope from his pocket, Oxman stunned the courtroom by announcing he had had the presence of mind to jot down the jitney's license number. It was Weinberg's.

The Mooney defense team, led by W. Bourke Cockran, was flustered by Oxman's sudden appearance. The defense did not ask for a recess while it could check on his credibility. It also failed to exploit the inconsistencies in the testimony of Oxman and McDonald, who had testified to seeing the defendants on foot, not in a car. It did not put on the stand any of the 18 policemen stationed along Market Street during the parade, any one of whom could have testified that they had orders to keep cars off Market Street that afternoon and that only two, with official passes, had trespassed on the parade route—neither one of which was Weinberg's jitney.

The Clock in the Photos

In his defense, Tom Mooney said he and Rena Mooney had watched the parade from atop the Eilers Music Company Building at 975 Market Street, 1.15

miles from the site of the bombing. To prove this, Cockran introduced three photographs taken from the roof by an Eilers employee. Enlargements made in the presence of two detectives revealed the time on a street clock down on Market: eight minutes, five minutes, and two minutes before the bomb went off. In each photo, Tom and Rena Mooney could be seen in the foreground, on the rooftop. In addition, 12 witnesses swore that Tom Mooney had been there throughout the parade.

The defense tried to show that Mooney was being framed. Weinberg testified that private detective Swanson had earlier tried to bribe him. Cockran asked for a directed acquittal, but Judge Franklin A. Griffin ruled that was up to the jury.

The district attorney himself, Charles Fickert, summarized for the prosecution and asked for the death penalty. His stirring words urged the jury to be fearless:

> For, with conscience satisfied with the discharge of duty, no consequence can harm you. There is no evil that we cannot face or fly from but the consciousness of duty disregarded. A sense of duty pursues us ever. It is omnipresent like the deity . . .

The D.A. went on for another minute or two in this vein, an inspiration to juryman and spectator alike. But on the front page of the *Bulletin* that evening, two reporters revealed that the same inspiration had been uttered, word for word, by Daniel Webster at a murder trial in 1830.

Defense attorney Maxwell McNutt's summation to the jury charged that Martin Swanson had devised a frame-up—an idea that prosecutor Cunha labeled absurd. Judge Griffin advised jury members they were entitled to question the trustworthiness of the prosecution if they viewed the arrest of the defendants without warrants as a violation of their rights, and he invited them to weigh the credibility of the witnesses as well.

In 6½ hours, the jury found Tom Mooney guilty of first-degree murder and recommended the death penalty.

Letters to an Old Friend

Within two months, an old friend of Frank Oxman named Ed Rigall tried to sell the prosecutors several letters that Oxman had written him soon after the bombing, inviting him to San Francisco to swear that he had been with Oxman at the parade. It turned out that Oxman had arrived in the city four hours after the bombing and later, upon learning that the reward for information leading to the conviction of the perpetrator had climbed to $15,350, had had another friend inform Cunha that he, Oxman, was available as a witness.

Mooney's defense team got hold of the letters and published them. Subsequently the juries in Weinberg's and Rena Mooney's trials for complicity in the bomb murders found them each not guilty. Oxman was tried for subornation of perjury and acquitted. Meanwhile, Mooney sat on death row in San Quentin prison. In March 1918, the California Supreme Court upheld his conviction. Execution was set for August 23. President Woodrow Wilson appealed to the California governor, William D. Stephens. Demonstrations on Mooney's behalf were being held around the world. William Randolph Hearst, reversing the support his papers had given District Attorney Fickert, announced that Mooney should not be put to death. "Mooney Day" was celebrated nationwide in July, with speeches by top labor leaders and liberals, and the governor approved a reprieve. In November, Judge Griffin proposed a pardon and retrial. Two weeks before the scheduled hanging, the governor commuted Mooney's sentence to life imprisonment.

For 20 more years, attempts were made to free Mooney through legal channels. But California had an outdated system for review of convictions, and the courts declared there was no procedure that could give him a new trial based on the evident perjury. Every governor during these two decades refused to take the political risk involved in freeing the radical. From his prison cell, Mooney himself interfered with his lawyers, passing up at least one chance to ask for parole.

In 1939, Democratic Governor C. L. Olson, five days after his inauguration, gave Mooney an unconditional pardon. San Francisco then saw another Market Street parade—a victory procession with Tom and Rena Mooney, with the mayor, and prominent labor leaders at the head.

During the 22 years Tom Mooney unjustly spent in prison, numerous demonstrations were held on his behalf. (Courtesy, National Archives)

Mooney lived only three more years. For most of that time, he was bedridden with illnesses contracted in prison.

—Bernard Ryan, Jr.

Suggestions for Further Reading

Frost, Richard H. *The Mooney Case*. Stanford, Calif.: Stanford University Press, 1968.

Gentry, Curt. *Frame-up: The Incredible Case of Tom Mooney and Warren Billings*. New York: W.W. Norton & Co., 1967.

Sifakis, Carl. *The Encyclopedia of American Crime*. New York: Facts On File, 1982.

The Trials of Alice Paul and Other National Woman's Party Members: 1917

Defendants: Gertrude Crocker, Gladys Greiner, Alice Paul, and Dr. Caroline Spencer **Crime Charged:** Obstructing a sidewalk
Chief Defense Lawyer: Dudley Field Malone **Chief Prosecutor:** Hart (first name unavailable) **Judge:** Alexander Mullowney **Date:** October 22, 1917
Verdicts: Guilty **Sentences:** Alice Paul and Caroline Spencer: 7 months in prison; Gertrude Crocker and Gladys Grenier: $5.00 fine or 30 days in prison

SIGNIFICANCE

In 1917 and 1918, almost 500 suffragists were arrested during their picketing of the White House; 168, including National Woman's Party Chairperson Alice Paul, were tried, convicted, and imprisoned for terms of up to seven months, ostensibly for blocking traffic on a sidewalk. The women believed they were actually imprisoned for their political beliefs and became the first U.S. citizens to claim that their government held them as political prisoners.

Women first organized to demand suffrage in 1848, at what became known as the Seneca Falls Convention. In 1917, despite 69 years of active campaigning, women were still without the vote. Members of Alice Paul's National Woman's Party decided to try a new tactic, and on January 10 they began picketing President Woodrow Wilson and the White House.

Prior to the United States' entrance into World War I, the women received no attention from the government. Shortly after the declaration of war, however, Alice Paul was warned by the chief of police for the District of Columbia that picketers would now have to be arrested. Paul replied that her lawyers had "assured us all along that picketing was legal," and she maintained that it was "certainly . . . as legal in June as in January." The first two picketers were nonetheless arrested on June 22, 1917. They were charged with obstructing a sidewalk but released and never tried, as were 27 other women within the next four days. This process failed to put an end to the picketing, and on June 27 six women stood trial for obstructing traffic. They were found guilty and fined $25.00. Because they refused to pay their fine, they were sentenced to three days in jail.

The picketing continued. On July 14, 16 women were arrested, including Florence Bayard Hilles, the daughter of a former American ambassador to Great Britain, and Allison Turnbull Hopkins, the wife of President Wilson's New Jersey campaign coordinator. They stood trial the same day before district court Judge Alexander Mullowney.

Mullowney had earlier consulted the U.S. Attorney about the possibility of trying the women under the Espionage Act of 1917. Passed in June, it outlawed, among other things, the making of untrue statements which interfered with the conduct of war. The women's banners, Mullowney said, contained "words . . . [that] are treasonous and seditious." As it turned out, however, the women's banners contained what they considered ironic quotations of President Wilson's own speeches, such as a line from his War Message Speech of April 2: "WE SHALL FIGHT FOR THE THINGS WHICH WE HAVE ALWAYS HELD NEAREST OUR HEARTS—FOR DEMOCRACY, FOR THE RIGHT OF THOSE WHO SUBMIT TO AUTHORITY TO HAVE A VOICE IN THEIR OWN GOVERNMENTS." Since the president's own words could not feasibly be brought up under the Espionage Act, and because—as Paul had earlier insisted—picketing was perfectly legal in the United States, the women were charged with the by-now expected "crime" of obstructing traffic. All 16 women were sentenced to 60 days in the Occoquan Workhouse.

A Wilson appointee and friend, Dudley Field Malone, collector of the Port of New York, happened to witness the women's trial. Outraged at its conclusion, he took a taxi to the White House and gave Wilson his resignation, stating that he planned to offer his legal services to the suffragists. Wilson refused to accept Malone's resignation. On July 20, the President pardoned all the suffragists imprisoned at Occoquan.

Picketing continued unabated, and arrests resumed in August. Dudley Field Malone offered his resignation again on September 7, this time forwarding copies of his letter to all the leading newspapers as well as to President Wilson, writing, "I think it is high time that men in this generation, at some cost to themselves, stood up to battle for the national enfranchisement of American women." This time, Malone's resignation was accepted.

On October 4, Alice Paul herself was arrested along with 10 other women. In court October 8, the women refused to be sworn or to recognize the legitimacy of the court. Paul said: "We do not consider ourselves subject to this Court since, as an unenfranchised class, we have nothing to do with the making of the laws which have put us in this position." Although the charge was not dismissed, the women were released without sentence.

Alice Paul was arrested again on October 20, this time in the company of Dr. Caroline Spencer, Gladys Greiner, and Gertrude Crocker. The four were tried on October 22 before Judge Mullowney.

Police Sergeant Lee testified: "I made my way through the crowd that was surrounding them, and told the ladies they were violating the law by standing at the gates, and would not they please move on."

When Assistant District Attorney Hart asked Lee about the women's response, he replied: "They did not [move on], and they did not answer either . . . [I] placed them under arrest."

Paul and Spencer, who had been carrying banners, were sentenced to seven months imprisonment. Greiner and Crocker, given the choice between $5.00 fines or 30 days imprisonment, elected to go to jail.

Lucy Burns, one of the first women arrested and released on June 22, had been arrested again in September and convicted; in Occoquan Workhouse before Paul's imprisonment, Burns organized the other incarcerated suffragists to request political prisoner status. Their petition was smuggled to the commissioners of the District of Columbia. Each of the signers was immediately placed in solitary confinement. At the end of October, Paul arrived at Occoquan with the recently sentenced Rose Winslow, and the two announced a hunger strike to "secure for [their] fellow comrades treatment accorded political prisoners in every civilized country but our own."

Paul, Winslow, and others who joined the hunger strike were force-fed. Paul was held in solitary confinement and then transferred to a psychiatric hospital, where her windows were boarded over. Dudley Field Malone, finally managed to have her released to a regular hospital on a writ of *habeas corpus*.

On November 27 and 28, 1917, all of the imprisoned suffragists were released without condition or explanation. On March 4, 1918, the District of Columbia Court of Appeals ruled on an appeal filed earlier by Malone. Each one of the suffragists had been "illegally arrested, illegally convicted, and illegally imprisoned."

The Nineteenth Amendment, enfranchising women, was adopted on August 26, 1920.

— Kathryn Cullen-DuPont

Suggestions for Further Reading

Frost, Elizabeth and Kathryn Cullen-DuPont. *Women's Suffrage in America: An Eyewitness History.* New York: Facts On File, 1992.

Irwin, Inez Hayes. *The Story of Alice Paul and the National Woman's Party.* Fairfax, VA: Denlinger's Publishers, 1964.

Lunardini, Christine A. *From Equal Suffrage to Equal Rights: Alice Paul and the National Woman's Party, 1910–1928.* New York: New York University Press, 1986.

Paul, Alice. *Conversations with Alice Paul: Woman Suffrage and the Equal Rights Amendment.* An Interview conducted by Amelia Fry. Berkeley, Calif.: Bancroft Library, Regional Oral History Office, University of California, c. 1976.

Stevens, Doris. *Jailed For Freedom.* 1920, reprint. Salem, New Hampshire: Ayer Co., 1990.

Schenck v. U.S. Appeal: 1919

Appellant & Defendant: Charles T. Schenck   **Appellee & Plaintiff:** The
United States of America   **Appellant Claim:** Not guilty, as convicted, of
conspiracy to violate the Espionage Act of 1917
Chief Defense Lawyer: John Lord O'Brian
Chief Lawyers for Appellant: Henry J. Gibbons and Henry John Nelson
Justices: Louis D. Brandeis, John H. Clarke, William R. Day, Oliver Wendell
Holmes, Charles Evans Hughes, Joseph McKenna, James C. McReynolds,
Willis Van Devanter, and Edward D. White, Chief Justice
Place: Washington, D.C.   **Date of Decision:** March 3, 1919
Decision: Guilty verdict unanimously affirmed

SIGNIFICANCE
This case marked the first time the Supreme Court ruled directly on the extent to
which the U.S. government may limit speech. It produced, in the affirmative
opinion written by Justice Oliver Wendell Holmes, two of that fabled jurist's most
memorable and oft-quoted statements on the law.

On June 15, 1917, just after the United States entered the World War,
Congress passed the Espionage Act, which made it a federal crime to
obstruct the country's war effort. The act closely followed the Conscription Act
of May 18, which enabled the government to draft men for military service.

At the Socialist Party headquarters in Philadelphia, Pennsylvania, the
executive committee quickly passed a resolution authorizing the printing of
15,000 leaflets, to be sent through the mails and otherwise distributed to men
who had been drafted. The leaflets recited the first section of the Thirteenth
Amendment to the U. S. Constitution, which states:

> Neither slavery nor involuntary servitude, except as a punishment for crime
> whereof the party shall have been duly convicted, shall exist within the
> United States or any place subject to their jurisdiction.

Advising the reader that a conscript is little better than a convict, the
leaflets described conscription as despotism in its worst form and as a monstrous
wrong against humanity in the interest of Wall Street's chosen few. "Do not
submit to intimidation," said the leaflets, urging readers to petition for repeal of
the Conscription Act.

"Largely Instrumental in Sending the Circulars About"

As general secretary of the Socialist party, Charles T. Schenck was in charge of the Philadelphia headquarters from which the leaflets were sent.

Schenck was soon arrested and indicted for sedition in conspiring to cause insubordination in the armed forces and obstruction of recruitment and enlistment. No evidence was presented to prove that he had corrupted even one draftee. Rather, the publication of the pamphlets was itself considered proof enough of his guilt.

The defense presented a simple argument: Schenck had exercised the right guaranteed him by the First Amendment—the right to speak freely on a public issue.

Found guilty, Schenck appealed through the district courts and to the Supreme Court, steadfastly insisting on his right to freedom of speech.

Schenck's defense argued that there was not enough evidence to prove that he himself was concerned with sending out the pamphlets. Reviewing the testimony, Holmes pointed out that Schenck was the general secretary of the Socialist Party and was in charge of the headquarters from which the pamphlets were sent to men who had been called and accepted for military service. The general secretary's report of August 20, 1917, Holmes noted, said, "Obtained new leaflets from printer and started work addressing envelopes." Holmes also

In this significant First Amendment case, the 1919 Court unanimously affirmed that Schenck was guilty of violating the Espionage Act of 1917. (Courtesy, Library of Congress)

pointed out that "there was a resolve that Comrade Schenck be allowed $125 for sending leaflets through the mail."

"No reasonable man," concluded Holmes, "could doubt that the defendant Schenck was largely instrumental in sending the circulars about."

Justice Holmes wrote the opinion that was shared unanimously by the court. Noting that no case had been made for the leaflets having actually caused any insurrection, he commented:

> Of course the document would not have been sent unless it had been intended to have some effect, and we do not see what effect it could be expected to have upon persons subject to the draft except to influence them to obstruct the carrying of it out.

Holmes agreed with the defense that the leaflets were entitled to First Amendment protection, but only in peacetime—not in wartime.

> We admit that in many places and in ordinary times the defendants in saying all that was said in the circular would have been within their constitutional rights. But the character of every act depends upon the circumstances in which it is done. The most stringent protection of free speech would not protect a man in falsely shouting fire in a theater and causing a panic.

It may be noted in passing that Holmes never said the theater was crowded; posterity has consistently and mistakenly ascribed that adjective to the quotation. Next came the justice's second memorable phrase:

> The question in every case is whether the words used are used in such circumstances and are of such a nature as to create a clear and present danger that they will bring about the substantive evils that Congress has a right to prevent.

The "clear and present danger," said Holmes, is a question of "proximity and degree."

> When a nation is at war many things that might be said in time of peace are such a hindrance to its effort that their utterance will not be endured so long as men fight and that no court could regard them as protected by any constitutional right.

Finally, the justice observed, it made no difference that Schenck and his compatriots had failed to obstruct recruitment. "The statute," he said, "punishes conspiracies to obstruct as well as actual obstruction."

> If the act [speaking or circulating a paper], its tendency and the intent with which it is done are the same, we perceive no ground for saying that success alone warrants making the act a crime.

With that, the judgments of the lower courts were affirmed. Charles T. Schenck, who had been sentenced to 10 years' imprisonment on each of the three counts of the indictment, but with the three terms to be served concurrently, was sent to federal prison.

The Schenck case, in establishing the "clear and present danger" criterion, marked a turning point in First Amendment thinking by the court. Until then, Chief Justice Edward White and other judges had permitted the government to suppress any speech that displayed a "dangerous tendency." Within months, moreover, Holmes refined his views on the First Amendment when seven of his colleagues found a "clear and present danger" in the *Abrams v. United States* case. A Russian-born American named Jacob Abrams had been found guilty of violating the Espionage Act when he scattered leaflets protesting the sending of American troops into Russia after the Revolution of 1917. Holmes' dissent objected that Abrams had been condemned not for what he did but for what he believed. The justice insisted that the First Amendment guaranteed one's right to freedom of *opinion*, if not (as in the Schenck case during wartime) of *action*. One may assume that Holmes would have continued to insist on the guarantee of this right during the dark days of McCarthyism and the House Un-American Activities Committee.

In 1927, Holmes again dissented when the court upheld the conviction of Socialist Benjamin Gitlow under a New York state law for advocating criminal anarchy. Holmes found that Gitlow's publications, which advocated overthrowing the government, were protected by the Fourteenth Amendment's due process clause against interference by the state. The justice saw "no present danger of an attempt to overthrow the Government by force" in Gitlow's papers.

—Bernard Ryan, Jr.

Suggestions for Further Reading

Bowen, Catherine Drinker. *Yankee from Olympus: Justice Holmes and His Family*. Boston: Little, Brown and Co., 1943.

Burton, David H. *Oliver Wendell Holmes, Jr.* Boston: Twayne Publishers, Div. of G. K. Hall & Co., 1980.

Commager, Henry Steele and Milton Cantor. *Documents of American History*. Englewood Cliffs, N.J.: Prentice Hall, 1988.

Friedman, Leon and Fred L. Israel, eds. *The Justices of the United States Supreme Court 1789–1969: Their Lives and Major Opinions*. New York: Chelsea House, 1969.

Novick, Sheldon M. *Honorable Justice: The Life of Oliver Wendell Holmes*. Boston: Little, Brown and Co., 1989.

Schnayerson, Robert. *The Illustrated History of the Supreme Court of the United States*. New York: Harry N. Abrams, 1986.

Witt, Elder, ed. *The Supreme Court and Individual Rights*. Washington: Congressional Quarterly, 1980.

Sacco–Vanzetti Trial: 1921

Defendants: Nicola Sacco and Bartolomeo Vanzetti
Crime Charged: Murder   **Chief Defense Lawyers:** William J. Callahan,
Herbert B. Ehrmann, James M. Graham, Arthur Dehon Hill, Jeremiah J.
McAnarney, Thomas F. McAnarney, Fred H. Moore, Michael Angelo
Musmanno, William G. Thompson, and John P. Vahey
Chief Prosecutors: Frederick Gunn Katzmann, Donald P. Ramsey, and Harold
P. Williams   **Judge:** Webster Thayer   **Place:** Dedham, Massachusetts
Dates of Trial: May 31–July 14, 1921   **Verdict:** Guilty   **Sentences:** Death

SIGNIFICANCE

The Sacco–Vanzetti case began as a simple trial for murder. It ended as an
international cause in which the world believed that Massachusetts had executed
two innocent men because they held radical views. A study of the trial and its
aftermath provides a superb lesson in how myths are made.

On the afternoon of April 15, 1920, as a shoe manufacturer's paymaster,
Frederick Parmenter, and his guard, Alessandro Berardelli, carried the
$15,777 cash payroll in South Braintree, Massachusetts, they were killed by two
men armed with pistols. Seizing the money, the men jumped into a car containing several other men and sped away. Eyewitnesses thought the murderers
looked like Italians.

At the time, police were investigating an attempted holdup on the preceding Christmas Eve by a gang of Italians with a car in nearby Bridgewater. Police
Chief Michael E. Stewart suspected one Mike Boda, whose car was now
awaiting repairs in Simon Johnson's garage. Stewart told Johnson to call the
police when anyone came to get Boda's car.

A Car to Move Red Literature

Stewart also was busy rounding up alien communists following raids by the
U.S. Departments of Labor and Justice. Many were being deported. In May, a
radical held on the 14th floor of the New York City offices of the Department of
Justice was found dead on the sidewalk below. His friends, including Mike

Boda, decided they had better hide a large quantity of Red literature. To move it, they needed Boda's car.

Boda and three others appeared at Johnson's garage. Mrs. Johnson called the police. Johnson refused to hand over the car because it had no up-to-date license plates. Boda and one man departed on a motorcycle. The other two boarded a street car. Arrested aboard the car minutes later were Nicola Sacco and Bartolomeo Vanzetti. Sacco carried a .32-caliber pistol loaded with nine bullets, and 23 additional bullets in his pocket. Vanzetti had a fully loaded .38-caliber revolver and four 12-gauge shotgun shells. Also found on Sacco was a notice, in Italian, of a forthcoming meeting at which Vanzetti was to speak on "the struggle for existence." The two men were active anarchists.

Grilled by District Attorney Frederick Gunn Katzmann, Sacco said he had bought the gun two years earlier for $16 or $17 and had bought a new box of cartridges. Vanzetti said his gun cost $18 or $19 four or five years earlier. Neither gun was licensed.

Vanzetti's shotgun shells put him under suspicion for the failed holdup on Christmas Eve, when a 12-gauge shotgun was fired. His alibi was that, as a fish peddler, he spent a busy Christmas Eve selling eels for traditional Italian dinners that night. At his trial, several witnesses identified him as the man with the shotgun. He did not take the stand to refute them and was convicted and sentenced to 12 to 15 years. Sacco, meantime, had a solid alibi: He had been on the job in a shoe factory when the attempted robbery occurred. But he was held for trial in the South Braintree murders, for on April 15 he had taken the day off.

Bartolomeo Vanzetti and Nicola Sacco on the day their sentence was passed. (Courtesy, National Archives)

Defense Committee Organized

Anarchist friends organized the Sacco–Vanzetti Defense Committee. For three months, it collected money. Then the committee hired Fred H. Moore, a long-haired radical labor lawyer from California. Moore, experienced in handling underdog cases for Elizabeth Gurley Flynn, founder of the Workers' Defense Union, and for the International Workers of the World (The "I.W.W."), saw the Sacco–Vanzetti case as a cause. "In saving them," he said, "we strengthen our muscles, develop our forces preparatory to the day when we save ourselves."

Moore spent a busy year writing, traveling, and organizing volunteers. The United Mine Workers, the Amalgamated Clothing Workers, the American Federation of Teamsters, and the American Civil Liberties Union were among the many organizations that responded. Pamphlets were printed in batches of 50,000. Publicity releases flooded the mail weekly to 500 newspapers. The murder charge was depicted as "a mere device to get them [Sacco and Vanzetti] out of the way."

Outdated Bullets and a Cap

Opening May 31, 1921, the trial revealed that Sacco had lied about his gun. It was several years old, and his box of "new" cartridges contained a mixture of old bullets that were all obsolete. The bullet that killed Berardelli was so outdated that the state's expert witness could locate none like it with which to test Sacco's gun—except the equally obsolete bullets from Sacco's pocket.

Vanzetti, too, had lied. Although he had said he paid $18 or $19 for it, the jury learned that his was a $5 gun, that Vanzetti had said he bought a new box of cartridges and threw it away when six remained and he put them in the revolver, but that it held only five and those in the gun were not all the same make. And it learned that Vanzetti's nickel-plated pistol was identical to that of the murdered guard, whose gun could not be found after the crime.

Then there was the cap found beside the dead guard. It was not his. Sacco's employer testified that it looked like a cap that Sacco regularly wore. When the prosecutor asked Sacco to put the cap on, the defendant, pulling it down over his ears in trying to prove it was too big, threw the courtroom into giggling hysterics—but the state also put into evidence a cap of exactly the same size, found in Sacco's home. "Some one of you who wears a seven and one-eighth," said Katzmann to the jury, "try them both on. If they are not identically the same size, then so find, so find, gentlemen."

Trial for Murder, Nothing Else

Before the trial opened, Judge Webster Thayer had told counsel on both sides that he saw no reason to bring up the issue of radicalism. It was not mentioned during the prosecution's entire presentation. But on the 29th day, Vanzetti himself, under direct examination by his attorney Jeremiah J. Mc-Anarney, was explaining why the four men sought Boda's car: "We were going to take the automobile for to carry books and newspapers," he said. Why hadn't he told the police that when he was arrested? "Because there was the deportation and the reaction was more vivid than now and more mad than now." In a word, his defense was that he lied out of fear of deportation as a radical.

Under Massachusetts law, since the defense had brought it up, the door was now open for prosecutor Katzmann to cross-examine Vanzetti about all his radical activities. But the jury heard no such questions. "Neither is Radicalism being tried here," the prosecutor told them. "This is a charge of murder and it is nothing else."

Next, Sacco explained that he, too, lied when he was arrested because he feared deportation on a radical charge. And he explained another lie. Upon arrest, he had said that he was at work all day April 15. But now his boss testified that Sacco had taken that day off to see the Italian consul in Boston about a passport for a trip to Italy. The consular clerk testified that Sacco was in his office at about 2:00 P.M. April 15, but the alibi was weak: Sacco had been turned down immediately because the passport photo he offered was too large. While the jury was being told that Sacco spent an entire day in Boston (several witnesses for the defense testified to having seen him there in the morning, at lunch, and in the afternoon), his business at the consulate had consumed only 10 minutes. Then Sacco noticed a spectator in the courtroom whom he had seen on the late afternoon train home. Sworn as a witness, the man could not remember seeing Sacco but was confident he had been on the train Sacco described.

As with Vanzetti, prosecutor Katzmann refrained from any line of questioning that might have led the jury to consider Sacco a dangerous radical.

Bullets Convince Jury

At three o'clock, July 14, the jury retired. It immediately voted 10–2 for conviction. "Then," said one juror afterward:

[W]e started discussing things, reviewed the very important evidence about the bullets, and everybody had a chance to speak his piece. There was never any argument, though. We just were convinced Sacco and Vanzetti had done what the prosecution had charged them with.

Asked later what evidence impressed him most, another juror said:

The bullets, of course. That testimony and evidence on it sticks in your mind. You can't depend on the witnesses. But the bullets, there was no getting around that evidence.

The guilty verdict brought violent reactions around the world. American consulates and embassies in Europe and South America were flooded with letters of protest. The *Communist International* urged all communists, socialists, anarchists, and trade unionists to join in rescuing Sacco and Vanzetti. Demonstrations were mounted in France, Italy, Switzerland, Belgium, Spain, Portugal, and Scandinavia. It took 10,000 police and 18,000 troops to hold back the crowd besieging the American embassy in Paris. Bombs exploded in that embassy and around the world. One destroyed the home of one of the jurors. Judge Thayer's house was put under guard.

Vehement Appeals Follow

Over the next six years, the furor raged. Motion after motion for a new trial was denied. So-called experts examined the pistols, took them apart, wrongly reassembled them. Elizabeth Gurley Flynn raised $25,000 in two days to pay the advance legal fee of Harvard Law School lecturer and Massachusetts insider William G. Thompson, who replaced Moore, the radical outsider. Imprisoned criminals volunteered confessions.

By 1926, with "Sacco–Vanzetti" a worldwide battle cry, the Massachusetts Supreme Judicial Court, the state's highest, rejected an appeal. The International Labor Defense (ILD) (later to defend the Scottsboro Boys, [See separate entry]), set up by the communists, received only some $6,000 of millions raised in the names of Sacco and Vanzetti. Harvard Law professor Felix Frankfurter (later to serve on the U.S. Supreme Court), in an *Atlantic Monthly* article, attacked the jury, witnesses, verdict, and judiciary. The state's supreme court, having already rejected Thompson's appeal, now upheld the judge: He had committed, it declared, no errors of law or abuses of discretion.

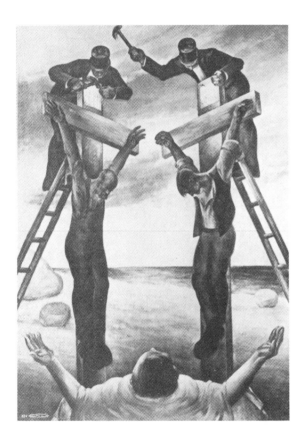

The execution of two men who held radical views provoked outrage throughout the world. (Courtesy, Library of Congress)

Lowell Committee Reviews Case

In June 1927, on Thompson's urging, Massachusetts Governor Alvan T. Fuller, who was considering an appeal for clemency, appointed an Advisory Committee headed by Harvard president Abbott Lawrence Lowell to review the entire case. After two months, and after himself interviewing 102 witnesses in addition to those from the trial, he agreed with the Lowell Committee's conclusion: Sacco and Vanzetti had a fair trial and were guilty.

Worldwide protests grew more violent. A London demonstration injured 40 people. Paris, Berlin, Warsaw, Buenos Aires, and countless other cities saw riots. Now picketers before the State House in Boston, including novelists John Dos Passos and Katherine Anne Porter, humorist Dorothy Parker, and poet Edna St. Vincent Millay, were arrested. All Boston public buildings were garrisoned by the police, who for the first time in memory permitted no meetings on Boston Common. Columnist Heywood Broun found his column suspended by the New York *World* for his violent comments on Lowell.

By now, Judge Thayer had denied a half-dozen motions for a new trial, the state superior court had denied another, and the state supreme judicial court had turned down four appeals. Several petitions for a writ of *habeas corpus*, for extensions of time, and for stay of execution were denied by the Circuit Court of Appeals for the First Circuit of the United States and by U.S. Supreme Court justices Oliver Wendell Holmes and Harlan F. Stone.

Sacco and Vanzetti were executed August 23, 1927. In 1977, their names were "cleared" when Massachusetts Governor Michael S. Dukakis signed a special proclamation.

—*Bernard Ryan, Jr.*

Suggestions for Further Reading

Ehrmann, Herbert B. *The Case That Will Not Die.* Boston: Little, Brown & Co., 1969.

Frankfurter, Felix. *The Case of Sacco and Vanzetti.* Boston: Little, Brown & Co., 1927.

Montgomery, Robert H. *Sacco–Vanzetti: The Murder and the Myth.* New York: Devin-Adair, 1960.

Porter, Katherine Anne. *The Never-Ending Wrong.* Boston: Little, Brown & Co., 1977.

Russell, Francis. *Sacco & Vanzetti: The Case Resolved.* New York: Harper & Row, 1986.

Sifakis, Carl. *The Encyclopedia of American Crime.* New York: Facts On File, 1972.

Sinclair, Upton. *Boston: A Documentary Novel.* Cambridge, Mass.: Robert Bentley, 1978.

Tragedy in Dedham. New York: McGraw-Hill, 1962.

"Why I Changed My Mind about the Sacco–Vanzetti Case," *American Heritage* (June-July 1986): 106.

"Fatty" Arbuckle Trials: 1921–22

Defendant: Roscoe Conkling "Fatty" Arbuckle
Crime Charged: Manslaughter   **Chief Defense Lawyer:** Gavin McNab
Chief Prosecutor: Matthew Brady   **Judge:** Harold Louderback   **Place:** San
Francisco, California   **Dates of Trials:** November 14–December 4, 1921;
January 11–February 3, 1922; March 13–April 12, 1922   **Verdicts:** First
and second trials: Jury deadlocked; Third trial: Not guilty

SIGNIFICANCE

The trials of "Fatty" Arbuckle, Hollywood's most popular and highest-paid come-dian, for manslaughter not only destroyed the defendant's career, they also focused America's attention on the level of morality in the movie-making king-dom. Coming just when nationwide efforts were under way to censor the film industry, the trial brought the immediate establishment of "the Hays office" and, in 1930, the Motion Picture Production Code—the industry's self-regulatory system.

In five years, "Fatty" Arbuckle had climbed from the vaudeville stage to the $1,000-a-day pinnacle of stardom in silent films. America adored his uproari-ous antics with the Keystone Kops, his deadly aim with a custard pie, his light-footed, talented dancing. He was the first movie comedian to sign a $3-million contract.

When America learned that Arbuckle had thrown a wild party in a San Francisco hotel at which he—according to a complaint sworn out by one Maude Delmont—had raped and murdered actress Virginia Rappe, it was ready for a lurid trial. The country got not one but three trials, each loaded with juicy details of the alleged sexual rampage committed by the 266-pound Arbuckle. For eight months, the Hearst newspapers fed the country a diet of three-inch headlines. But, as the jury of the third trial recognized by voting acquittal in only five minutes, the sensationalism of the newspapers and the truth were far apart.

Tabloids Conjure up Lurid Details

The indisputable facts were that 26-year-old film actress Virginia Rappe went to Arbuckle's party on Labor Day with her friend Maude Delmont, drank too much, was violently ill with severe abdominal pains for three days, and died on Friday of peritonitis brought on by a ruptured bladder. On Monday, Delmont swore out her complaint. Arbuckle was charged with murder.

The disputable "facts" or allegations were myriad and sordid. They included the charge that the comic had been alone with the actress in a bedroom for an hour during the party, at which time he raped her. "I'm hurt, I'm dying. He did it, Maudie," Rappe was reported to have yelled when Arbuckle left the room.

The doctor who examined Rappe's body just after she died on Friday issued a public statement:

> The post-mortem examination showed a ruptured bladder, the rupture being due to natural causes. There were no marks of violence on the body. There was absolutely no evidence of a criminal assault, no signs that the girl had been attacked in any way.

District Attorney Matthew Brady ignored that statement on Monday as he watched Delmont swear out her murder complaint. The tabloids that morning had already published Brady's statement that "the evidence in my possession shows conclusively that either a rape or an attempt to rape was perpetrated on Miss Rappe by Roscoe Arbuckle. The evidence discloses beyond question that her bladder was ruptured by the weight of the body of Arbuckle either in a rape assault or an attempt to commit rape." Brady's main source was Maude Delmont.

What Brady did not yet know was that on Wednesday, as Virginia Rappe lay in pain in the Arbuckle hotel suite, Delmont had sent a telegram to each of two friends: "WE HAVE ROSCOE ARBUCKLE IN A HOLE HERE. CHANCE TO MAKE SOME MONEY OUT OF HIM." Her official complaint—with its description of how Arbuckle had dragged Virginia Rappe into his bedroom saying, "I've waited five years to get you;" how Rappe had cried for help from behind the locked door and Delmont had banged on the door; how Arbuckle had at last emerged, perspiring from the struggle and she had rushed in to find Rappe naked and bruised and dying—all had been a fabrication. Delmont, the D.A. learned on Monday afternoon, had been locked in a bathroom with one Lowell Sherman for an hour when Arbuckle went to his bedroom for a few minutes and found Rappe vomiting into the toilet in that room's bathroom.

When Brady learned the truth, his extensive statement was already in newspapers around the world. He decided to proceed with the case. But he knew that if he brought Maude Delmont to the witness stand, his prosecution would fall apart. When it came to the trials, he never called on her.

The grand jury attributed the ruptured bladder to "some force which, from the evidence submitted, we believe was applied by Roscoe Arbuckle." Therefore, it charged the comedian with manslaughter. In the police court's committal proceedings, Arbuckle's lawyer established that Virginia Rappe's manager had been not only her lover but Maude Delmont's as well, and announced that the manager and Delmont had planned to extort money from Arbuckle.

"A General Lowering of the Moral Standards"

Meantime, boards of censors, mayors, and film exhibitor associations in countless cities, as well as the states of Missouri, Pennsylvania, and Kansas, banned all Arbuckle movies. The Anti-Saloon League, the Moral Efficiency League, the Women's Vigilant Committee of San Francisco, and club women everywhere agreed. Pastors in pulpits nationwide echoed the words of the

Comedian Fatty Arbuckle's lucrative career was devastated by his involvement in the murder of actress Virginia Rappe. (AP/Wide World Photos)

minister in Hollywood's Little Church Around the Corner: "The real essence of this Arbuckle matter is a general lowering of the moral standards in this country."

In this atmosphere the police judge weighing committal for trial concluded:

> I do not find any evidence that Mr. Arbuckle either committed or attempted to commit rape. The court has been presented with the merest outline. . . . The district attorney has presented barely enough facts to justify my holding the defendant on the charge which is here filed against him.

> But we are not trying Roscoe Arbuckle alone; we are not trying the screen celebrity who has given joy and pleasure to the entire world; we are actually, gentlemen, in a large sense trying ourselves.

> We are trying our present-day morals, our present-day social conditions, our present-day looseness of thought and lack of social balance. The issue here is really and truly larger than the guilt or innocence of this poor, unfortunate

man; the issue is universal and grows out of conditions which are a matter of comment and notoriety and apprehension to every true lover and protector of our American institutions.

I have decided to make a holding on the ground of manslaughter.

The first trial produced 60 witnesses, including 18 doctors. Through defense witnesses, lawyer Gavin McNab revealed Virginia Rappe's moral as well as medical history: As a young teenager, she had had five abortions in three years; at 16, she had borne an illegitimate child; since 1907, she had had a series of bladder inflammations and chronic cystitis; she liked to strip naked when she drank; the doctor who attended her in the several days before she died concluded that she had gonorrhea; when she met Arbuckle for the first time on Monday, she was pregnant and that afternoon had asked him to pay for an abortion; on Wednesday, she had asked her nurse to find an abortionist.

On the stand, "Fatty" Arbuckle was simple, direct, unflustered. He related how he had tried to help the ill actress, spending not more then 10 minutes with her before Maude Delmont dismissed him.

Medical testimony proved that Virginia Rappe's bladder was cystitic—one of the causes of rupture of the bladder.

"Until Hell Freezes Over"

The jury was out for 44 hours before Judge Harold Louderback dismissed it as hopelessly deadlocked. Members later revealed that one juror, Helen Hubbard, had announced at the start that she would vote guilty "until hell freezes over" and that she refused to discuss the evidence, look at the exhibits, or read the trial transcript. All others voted acquittal until the end, when one other joined her.

Hubbard's mother-in-law was the first California Regent of the Daughters of the American Revolution. Her husband, a lawyer, did business with the D.A.'s office. Why defense attorney Gavin McNab let Hubbard, who was clearly biased, get onto the jury remains a mystery.

Four days later, 12 of Hollywood's top leaders, including Samuel Goldwyn, Lewis J. Selznick, and Adolph Zukor, asked William Hays, chairman of the Republican National Committee and President Warren G. Harding's postmaster general, to become the czar of the film industry. His assignment, at $100,000 a year for three years, was "to have the industry accorded the consideration and dignity to which it is justly entitled." The assignment stretched into thirty years, and thus began "the Hays office" and, ultimately, the self-regulation provided by the Motion Picture Production Code.

Arbuckle Tried Again . . . and Yet Again

Trial number two brought even more defense testimony on Virginia Rappe's habit of stripping when she drank. It also discredited some major evidence: the identification of "Fatty" Arbuckle's fingerprints on the hotel bedroom door. But the defense decided not to put Arbuckle through the ordeal of testifying again, and so deprived the second jury of seeing his strongly effective manner on the witness stand. This jury came in deadlocked nine to three for conviction.

The third time around, Gavin McNab put Arbuckle on the stand and left no doubt about his version of the hotel party. He also managed to get in still more detail of Virginia Rappe's lurid past. He reviewed how the district attorney fell for the outlandish charges of Maude Delmont, "the complaining witness who never witnessed."

The jury was out and back in five minutes with its verdict: "We the jury find Roscoe Arbuckle not guilty of manslaughter." The foreman then read a statement that the jurors had spent the five minutes composing:

> Acquittal is not enough for Roscoe Arbuckle. We feel that a great injustice has been done him. We feel also that it was only our plain duty to give him this exoneration, under the evidence, for there was not the slightest proof adduced to connect him in any way with the commission of a crime.
>
> He was manly throughout the case, and told a straightforward story on the witness stand, which we all believed.
>
> The happening at the hotel was an unfortunate affair for which Arbuckle, so the evidence shows, was in no way responsible.
>
> We wish him success. . . . Roscoe Arbuckle is entirely innocent and free from all blame.

Six days later, Will Hays banned Roscoe Arbuckle from the screen. The decision, however, was not his. The heads of Paramount, Adolph Zukor and Jesse Lasky, knew that Arbuckle had become poison at the box office. If his own company banned him, Hollywood would never forgive them. So they got Hays to ban him. Based on average Arbuckle box-office draw before the trials, Paramount's projected loss was more than $100 million.

Hays lifted the ban eight months later, and "Fatty" Arbuckle started work in January 1923 on a two-reeler, *Handy Andy*. Under constant pressure from reporters, he soon quit and, under an assumed name, turned to directing. Over the next 11 years, he directed, made stage appearances, ran a popular Hollywood nightclub, and paid off debts amounting to nearly $1 million. At last, in 1932, Jack Warner invited Arbuckle to perform in a "talkie." The Hays Office permitted just one, a two-reeler, to see if the public accepted him. It did, and Arbuckle signed for six more. In June 1933, he finished the film, celebrated at dinner, and went to bed. Within minutes, his 46-year-old heart stopped beating.

—Bernard Ryan, Jr.

Suggestions for Further Reading

Olson, James S. *Historical Dictionary of the 1920s*. Westport, Conn.: Greenwood Press, 1988.

Sifakis, Carl. *The Encyclopedia of American Crime*. New York: Facts On File, 1982.

Yallop, David A. *The Day the Laughter Stopped: The True Story of Fatty Arbuckle*. New York: St. Martin's Press, 1976.

Moore et al. v. Dempsey Appeal: 1923

Appellants: Frank Moore and 11 others   **Defendant:** E.H. Dempsey
Appellants Claim: That a petition for writ of *habeas corpus* was wrongfully
dismissed   **Chief Defense Lawyers:** Elbert Godwin
Chief Lawyer for Appellant: U.S. Bratton, Scipio A. Jones, and Moorefield
Storey   **Justices:** Louis D. Brandeis, Pierce Butler, Oliver Wendell Holmes,
Joseph McKenna, James C. McReynolds, Edward T. Sanford, George
Sutherland, William Howard Taft, and Willis Van Devanter
Place: Washington, D.C.   **Date of Decision:** February 19, 1923
Decision: Order dismissing writ reversed; case remanded to district court

SIGNIFICANCE

Twelve African-Americans who had been condemned to death and had nearly
been lynched ultimately were freed from imprisonment because the U. S.
Supreme Court, led by fabled Justice Oliver Wendell Holmes, found that a
threatening mob inflamed by racial prejudice had made the trial, which lasted only
45 minutes, "absolutely void."

On the evening of September 30, 1919, a number of black people gathered in their church in the Hoop Spur neighborhood of the village of Elaine, Arkansas, near the Mississippi River and a few miles south of Helena. Their purpose in meeting was to organize so they could get legal counsel to protect them against extortion that they said was practiced on them by the landowners under the sharecropping system then prevalent in Arkansas. The meeting was attacked and fired upon by a group of white landowners. In the melee that followed, a white man was killed.

The report of the killing stirred greater excitement. Many black men were hunted down. Some were shot. By the morning of October 1, a second white man, named Clinton Lee, had been killed. Twelve black men were arrested for his murder.

A "Committee of Seven" white men was chosen to direct the operation of putting down the "insurrection" and help discover who was guilty in the two killings. Local newspapers published inflammatory articles daily. On October 7, one member of the Committee of Seven made a public statement that the trouble was "a deliberately planned insurrection of the negroes against the whites, directed by an organization known as the 'Progressive Farmers' and 'Household Union of America' established for the purpose of banding negroes together for the killing of white people."

A mob marched to the jail, ready to lynch the 12 prisoners. National Guard troops held them off. Members of the committee promised then that, if the mob would refrain, those found guilty would be executed under the law.

A grand jury was organized. It included a member of the committee and several men who had been in the posse organized to fight the blacks. It heard testimony against the defendants from two black witnesses.

In a trial that lasted 45 minutes on November 3, the courthouse neighborhood was thronged with a threatening crowd. The 12 prisoners were informed that a lawyer had been appointed their counsel. He held no preliminary consultations with them. He challenged no member of the jury, which was all white (blacks were systematically excluded from all juries). He demanded no delay or change of venue. He did not ask for separate trials for each of the accused. Although witnesses for the defense could have been produced, he called none. He did not put the defendants on the witness stand.

The jury took less than five minutes to bring in a verdict of guilty of murder in the first degree. The sentence was death for all.

Studded Straps and Strangling Drugs

The National Association for the Advancement of Colored People (NAACP) entered the case. Its appeal to the Arkansas Supreme Court for a new trial cited the riotous atmosphere in which the case was tried and the appointment of counsel at the start of the trial. It also introduced affidavits of the defendants and of the two black witnesses, who now revealed that they had been rounded up by the Committee of Seven and that, along with some of the prisoners, they had been whipped with straps studded with metal, had had "strangling drugs" forced into their nostrils, and had been made to sit in an electric chair—all until they agreed to testify against the defendants.

The appeal was denied. The NAACP then applied to the Arkansas Chancery Court for a writ of *habeas corpus* on behalf of Frank Moore et al. (one of the defendants by name, and the other 11) against E.H. Dempsey, keeper of the Arkansas State Penitentiary, claiming that the conditions in which the case was tried deprived the defendants of their lives without due process of law.

The chancery court issued the writ and an injunction against the execution of the prisoners, who were scheduled to die two days later. But the Arkansas Supreme Court then held that the chancellor had no jurisdiction. With the executions delayed, however, the NAACP then filed a petition for a writ of *habeas corpus* in the District Court of the United States for the Eastern District of Arkansas. It dismissed the writ.

"The Whole Proceeding Is a Mask"

The NAACP went to the Supreme Court of the United States. It cited testimony of two white men who had been members of the sheriff's posse and who swore that Clinton Lee had been killed by members of the posse during the confusion and that the black men had nothing to do with the murder. They also testified that they had personally whipped and drugged the two black witnesses to force from them the testimony they wanted.

The state of Arkansas argued that the Supreme Court had no jurisdiction to consider the appeal because "mere errors in point of law, however serious, committed by a criminal court in the exercise of its jurisdiction over a case properly subject to its cognizance cannot be reviewed by *habeas corpus*." Justice Oliver Wendell Holmes, writing the opinion of the court, disagreed. "The ground of the petition for the writ," he said,

One of Oliver Wendell Holmes' most famous comments, "there never was a chance for the petitioners to be acquitted," was made during the *Moore et al.v. Dempsey Appeal.* (Courtesy, Library of Congress)

302

> is that the proceedings in the State Court, although a trial in form, were only a form, and that the appellants were hurried to conviction under the pressure of a mob without any regard for their rights and without according to them due process of law.

> According to the allegations and affidavits, "there never was a chance for the petitioners to be acquitted"; no juryman could have voted for an acquittal and continued to live in Phillips County and if any prisoner by any chance had been acquitted by a jury he could not have escaped the mob.

> If the case is that the whole proceeding is a mask—that counsel, jury and judge were swept to the fatal end by an irresistible wave of public passion, and that the State Courts failed to correct the wrong, neither perfection in the machinery for correction nor the possibility that the trial court and counsel saw no other way of avoiding an immediate outbreak of the mob can prevent this Court from securing to the petitioners their constitutional rights.

> It does not seem to us sufficient to allow a Judge of the United States to escape the duty of examining the facts for himself when if true as alleged they make the trial absolutely void. Order reversed. The case to stand for hearing before the District Court.

The Supreme Court's remanding ended the case. The rehearing was never held, for shortly, under order of Governor Thomas C. McRae, the prisoners were released from the Arkansas State Penitentiary.

— Bernard Ryan, Jr.

Marcus Mosiah Garvey Trial: 1923

Defendants: Elie Garcia, Marcus Mosiah Garvey, Orlando Thompson, and George Tobias   **Crime Charged:** Using the U.S. mail to defraud
Chief Defense Lawyers: Armin Kohn, William C. Mathews, Cornelius W. McDougald, and Vernal Williams (Garvey also represented himself)
Chief Prosecutor: Maxwell S. Mattuck   **Judge:** Julian W. Mack
Place: New York, New York   **Dates of Trial:** May 18–June 19, 1923
Verdicts: Guilty (Garvey); not guilty (Garcia, Thompson, Tobias)
Sentence: 5 years' imprisonment and $1,000 fine

SIGNIFICANCE
The trial of Marcus Garvey for defrauding his followers destroyed the "Back to Africa" movement. Garvey's conviction resulted more from his unpopular concepts than from the evidence, which was slight.

Marcus Mosiah Garvey, born in Jamaica in 1887, emerged as the leader of black Americans at the end of World War I. He organized the Universal Negro Improvement Association (UNIA), a mass movement of people of African descent larger than any seen before or since. By 1922, its several million members in the United States, the West Indies, Latin America, and Africa were considered a significant threat by the European powers that controlled Africa. Garvey not only pioneered the idea that "Black is beautiful!" He set Africa's liberation from white domination as his goal.

To implement his plan to redeem Africa, Garvey established his own newspaper, *The Negro World*. Preaching the absolute separation of blacks from all forms of white domination, his eloquent speeches and articles promised hope and prosperity to black people. When he proposed a practical step—that the Black Star Steamship Line move passengers and cargo to and from African wharves—stock in the corporation was sold only to blacks. As money poured into UNIA divisions nationwide, the line bought several old freighters, none of which was entirely seaworthy (at least one sank), and paid for costly repairs.

Super Salesman in Fancy Dress

Next, Garvey organized the Negro Factories Corporation, to "build and operate factories in the big industrial cities of the United States, Central America, the West Indies, and Africa to manufacture every marketable commodity."

While Garvey succeeded as a super salesman and no one questioned his honesty and dedication, his shortcomings included a penchant for fancy dress uniforms, an ego that required he be surrounded by yes-men, and an abysmal lack of business skills—all of which made him vulnerable to enemies. By 1921, while the Black Star Line was supposedly negotiating to buy two more ships, the editor of an opposing paper revealed that the Department of Commerce said its Navigation Bureau had no record of either vessel.

Stockholders complained. Postal authorities arrested Garvey and the Black Star Line's treasurer, George Tobias, its secretary, Elie Garcia, and its vice president, Orlando M. Thompson, on charges of using the mails to defraud by selling passages on a nonexistent boat. Headlines screamed, "U.S. AGENTS SEARCH FOR 'MYTH' SHIP" and "GARVEY BUNK EXPOSED."

As the trial opened on May 18, 1923, prosecutor Maxwell S. Mattuck charged:

> While there center around Garvey other associations or corporations having for their object the uplift and advancement of the Negro race, the entire scheme of uplift was used to persuade Negroes for the most part to buy shares of stock in the Black Star Line . . . when the defendants well knew . . . that said shares were not and in all human probability never could be worth $5 each or any other sum of money.

Within two days, Garvey's lawyer, UNIA Counsel General William C. Matthews, advised the defendant to plead guilty on a technical charge and make a deal in closed chambers. Garvey fired Matthews and defended himself, making countless errors in procedure and frequently, as Judge Julian W. Mack condescendingly corrected him, producing gales of courtroom laughter.

"A Loss in Money but . . . a Gain in Soul"

Prosecution witnesses, all ex-Garveyites, testified to the defendants' wide variety of haphazard financial practices. Defense witnesses were bent on proving the value of the movement. "The Black Star Line was a loss in money but it was a gain in soul," one declared. The key prosecution witness, Benny Dancy, said he had bought 53 shares of Black Star stock, but the only evidence of mail fraud he could produce was an empty envelope from the line; he could not remember what came in the envelope.

Legal experts noted that Dancy had not been named in the indictments of the defendants as one of the persons they intended to defraud. No evidence showed when Dancy bought the stock. He did not testify that he actually received the envelope, but only that he recognized it. The envelope was offered in evidence with no other supportive testimony.

Garvey's cross-examination of some witnesses showed that the prosecution had rigged their testimony. One, who testified to working for Black Star as a mail clerk and delivering mail to the College Station post office in 1919, admitted he had not worked for the line then and didn't know where the post office was. Indeed, he conceded that the prosecutor had schooled him on dates and a postal inspector had told him the name of the post office.

Garvey was found guilty. Garcia, Thompson, and Tobias were found not guilty, on the jury's conclusion that they had merely complied with instructions from the head man. Sentenced to five years' imprisonment and a $1,000 fine, Garvey appealed. While the execution of his sentence was stayed, he organized a new shipping line.

His appeal rejected by the U.S. Circuit Court of Appeals, Garvey was immediately imprisoned in Atlanta, Georgia. President Calvin Coolidge rejected his petition for a pardon, but later, after two years and nine months, commuted his sentence to time served. Garvey then worked unsuccessfully to revive the UNIA until his death in London in 1940.

—Bernard Ryan, Jr.

Suggestions for Further Reading

Clarke, John Henrik. *Marcus Garvey and the Union of Africa*. New York: Random House, 1974.

Cronon, Edmund David. *Black Moses*. Madison: University of Wisconsin Press, 1969.

——. *Marcus Garvey*. New York: Prentice Hall, 1973.

Fax, Elton C. *Garvey*. New York: Dodd, Mead, & Co., 1972.

Foner, Eric. *America's Black Past*. New York: Harper & Row, 1970.

Garvey, Amy Jacques. *Garvey and Garveyism*. New York: Collier Books, 1970.

Stein, Judith. *The World of Marcus Garvey*. Baton Rouge: Louisiana State University Press, 1986.

Vincent, Theodore G. *Black Power and the Garvey Movement*. New York: Ramparts, 1971.

Leopold and Loeb Trial: 1924

Defendants: Nathan F. Leopold, Jr., and Richard Loeb
Crimes Charged: Murder and kidnapping
Chief Defense Lawyers: Clarence Darrow, Benjamin Bachrach, and Walter Bachrach **Chief Prosecutors:** Robert E. Crowe, Thomas Marshall, Joseph P. Savage, John Sbarbaro, and Milton Smith **Judge:** John R. Caverly
Place: Chicago, Illinois **Dates of Trial:** July 23–September 10, 1924
Verdict: Guilty **Sentences:** Life imprisonment for murder; 99 years for kidnapping

SIGNIFICANCE

Clarence Darrow, America's foremost criminal lawyer at the time, saved the defendants from execution for their "thrill murders" by changing their pleas from not guilty to guilty. The change took the case away from a jury so it was heard only by the judge, giving Darrow the opportunity to plead successfully for mitigation of punishment—life imprisonment rather than execution. The bizarre nature of the crime and the wealth of the victim and the defendants focused the nation's attention on the courtroom for nearly two months.

In May 1924, 18-year-old "Dickie" Loeb was the youngest graduate of the University of Michigan and already a postgraduate student at the University of Chicago. "Babe" Leopold, at 19 a law student at Chicago, had earned his Phi Beta Kappa key with his Bachelor of Philosophy degree. Each came from a wealthy and well-known Chicago family. Each believed his mental abilities set him apart as a genius superior to other people. Each dwelt in a fantasy world.

The Perfect Murder. . . for Its Thrill

Over several years, Leopold and Loeb had developed a homosexual relationship. In the fall of 1923, they devised a plan for the perfect murder, to be committed for the sake of its thrill. The more they detailed their plan, the stronger their compulsion to carry it out became. In March 1924, according to a report later prepared by leading psychiatrists for their defense, "they decided to get any young boy whom they knew to be of a wealthy family, knock him unconscious, take him to a certain culvert, strangle him, dispose of all his clothes, and push the body deep into this funnel-shaped culvert, through which the water flowed, expecting the body to entirely decompose and never be found."

On May 21, 1924, Leopold and Loeb rented a car. With Loeb in the back seat, Leopold drove slowly past the exclusive Harvard Preparatory School. They saw 14-year-old Bobby Franks, like them a son of a millionaire and also a cousin of Loeb, and offered him a ride. Within minutes, Loeb grabbed Franks and bashed his skull four times with a heavy chisel.

After wrapping the boy's body in Leopold's lap robe, the two drove around Chicago until dark. Then they went to the culvert, near the Pennsylvania Railroad tracks and carried out their plan. Next they buried Franks' shoes, belt buckle, jewelry, and the bloodstained lap robe, stopped off for dinner, and burned the lad's clothes in the furnace at Loeb's house. Later, they mailed a special-delivery ransom note to Franks' father and, at Leopold's house, washed the bloodstains from the car and phoned the Franks' home to say that Bobby Franks was safe, and instructions were on the way.

Unable to reach Bobby's father the next morning, they quickly learned why: Newsboys were hawking extras announcing discovery of the boy's body. A railroad workman had noticed a human foot protruding from the culvert. Another worker had found a pair of eyeglasses.

The police soon traced the glasses to Leopold. He admitted recent bird-watching near the culvert. His alibi for his whereabouts on May 21? Bird-watching with Richard Loeb, then a ride around Lincoln Park in his car with Loeb and a couple of girls. But the Leopold chauffeur said he had been repairing Leopold's car all day, and in the evening he had seen the boys washing the floor of a strange car.

Next the police pulled a beat-up Underwood typewriter from Jackson Park Harbor and proved that the ransom note had been written on it. Leopold said he owned a Hammond typewriter, but *Chicago Daily News* reporters checked with his college classmates and learned that when they borrowed "Babe's" typewriter to type their papers, it was an Underwood.

Now came the grilling. Through a day of intensive questioning, both Leopold and Loeb stuck to their story. But the next day, thinking that Leopold had betrayed him, Loeb angrily confessed.

"I Have a Hanging Case"

Now State's Attorney Robert E. Crowe tackled Leopold, surprising him with facts that could have come only from Loeb. Nathan Leopold confessed. Before noon, the confessions of each were read to them, admitting they had killed Bobby Franks for the thrill of it. Said Crowe, "I have a hanging case. The state is ready to go to trial immediately."

Clarence Darrow was already the nation's foremost criminal lawyer. (Tennessee's famous Monkey Trial, which would bring him worldwide fame, was still a year away.) He had saved some 50 accused murderers, many of whom were guilty beyond the shadow of a doubt, from execution. He told the Leopold and Loeb families he would take the case for a $100,000 fee.

Darrow threw his energy, and that of a battery of assistants, into researching the minds of his clients. Since State's Attorney Crowe had already lined up Chicago's best-known psychiatrists to examine the accused, Darrow turned to such national figures as the president of the American Psychiatric Association and the supervisor of the psychiatric clinic at Sing Sing Prison. Prominent psychiatrists Karl Bowman and Harold S. Hulbert developed profiles that revealed the defendants' mental instability and confused personalities. The doctors' extensive report came to several thousand pages and was supplemented by thousands more from the other psychiatrists.

"They Should Be Permanently Isolated from Society"

By July 23, when the trial opened, all America except Clarence Darrow and his team expected Leopold and Loeb to hang. Shocked by the idea that the sons of the rich had nothing better to do than kill younger rich kids for the thrill of it, the country wanted an eye for an eye. Darrow knew that no jury would settle for less. Standing before Chief Justice John R. Caverly, he went right to the point: "We want to state frankly here that no one believes these defendants should be released. We believe they should be permanently isolated from society. After long reflection, we have determined to make a motion for each to withdraw our plea of not guilty and enter pleas of guilty to both indictments."

Flabbergasted, the prosecution realized that Darrow had instantly wiped out the chance of a jury conviction. Now the judge alone would consider the case. Darrow went on. "We ask that the court permit us to offer evidence as to the mental condition of these young men. We wish to offer this evidence in mitigation of punishment."

The prosecution objected violently, but Judge Caverly said he would hear evidence of mitigation. "I want to give you all the leeway I can," he said. "I want to get all the doctors' testimony. There is no jury here, and I'd like to be advised as fully as possible."

"Total Lack of Appropriate Emotional Response"

At that point, Darrow had earned his fee. His job now was to convince the judge that Leopold and Loeb not only did not deserve to be executed but that justice and humanity would be served by reaching a thorough understanding of their peculiar mental states. He introduced psychiatrist witnesses who had found that Richard Loeb was a habitual liar. Since the age of 10, he had fantasized about crimes and imagined himself the "Master Mind" directing others, always outsmarting the world's best detectives; he had cheated at cards, shoplifted, stolen automobiles and liquor, thrown bricks through store windows, and only last November—with Leopold, each carrying loaded revolvers—had burglarized his own fraternity house. "The total lack of appropriate emotional response is one of the most striking features of his present condition," said the Bowman-Hulbert report, noting that Loeb felt no remorse for his actions. "He has gradually projected a world of fantasy over into the world of reality, and at times even confused the two."

Reviewing the reports on Leopold, Darrow noted that the young man had been strongly influenced by a governess who encouraged him to steal, so that she could blackmail him, and who "gave him the wrong conception about sex, about theft, about right or wrong, about selfishness, and about secrecy." To Leopold, said Darrow, "selfishness was the ideal life. Each man was a law unto himself."

Nathan Leopold's main fantasy was a king-and-slave relationship. He preferred to be the slave who could save the life of the king, then refuse the reward of freedom. Richard Loeb was his king. He had been in love with Loeb since they were 15 and 14 years old. "I felt myself less than the dust beneath his feet," Leopold had told the psychiatrists. "I'm jealous of the food and drink he takes because I cannot come as close to him as does his food and drink."

As to the kidnapping and murder, said the report, Leopold "got no pleasure from the crime. With him it was an intellectual affair devoid of any emotion. He had no feeling of guilt or remorse."

For a month, as State's Attorney Crowe's psychiatrists insisted that Leopold and Loeb were entirely sane and normal, Darrow pressed his psychiatrist witnesses to testify that the legal sanity of the defendants was undisputed, but that mental instability was not insanity and was not normal.

Finally, for 12 hours Clarence Darrow pleaded for mitigation of punishment. He noted that, while the prosecution charged the murderers with kidnapping Bobby Franks to get money to pay off gambling debts, testimony had proved that both boys had ample money and could get more from their extremely wealthy parents at any time.

"They Killed Him Because They Were Made That Way"

"Why did they kill little Bobby Franks?" asked Darrow. "They killed him as they might kill a spider or a fly, for the experience. They killed him because they were made that way. Because somewhere in the infinite processes that go to the making up of the boy or the man, something slipped. That happened, and it calls not for hate but for kindness, for charity, for consideration."

Darrow said he was astonished that the prosecution asked the judge for the death sentence. "Your Honor, if a boy of 18 and a boy of 19 should be hanged in violation of the law that places boys in reformatories instead of prisons—then we are turning our faces backward toward the barbarism which once possessed the world. Your Honor stands between the past and the future. You may hang these boys by the neck until they are dead. But you will turn your face toward the past. I am pleading for the future, for a time when hatred and cruelty will not control the hearts of men, when we can learn by reason and judgment and understanding and faith that all life is worth saving, and that mercy is the highest attribute of man."

As Darrow ended his summation, no sound was heard in the courtroom. Tears were streaming down the face of Judge Caverly.

His verdict, two days later, sentenced Leopold and Loeb each to life imprisonment for murder, plus 99 years for kidnapping. "In choosing imprisonment," he said, "the court is moved chiefly by the age of the defendants."

The prisoners were taken to the Illinois State Prison at Joliet. In 1936, Richard Loeb was slashed to death by a fellow prisoner during an argument. After World War II, Governor Adlai Stevenson reduced Nathan Leopold's original sentence, thus making him eligible for parole, in gratitude for his contribution to testing for malaria during the war. Freed in 1958, Leopold was permitted to serve out his parole in Puerto Rico, in order to avoid media attention. There he worked in hospitals and church missions, married, earned a master's degree, and taught mathematics. He died in 1971.

Clarence Darrow was forced to dun the Leopold and Loeb families repeatedly. Of the $100,000 fee agreed to, he collected $40,000 before he died in 1938.

—*Bernard Ryan, Jr.*

Leopold and Loeb were each sentenced to life for the murder of Bobby Franks and 99 years for his kidnapping. (AP/Wide World Photos)

Suggestions for Further Reading

Aymar, Brandt and Edward Sagarin. *A Pictorial History of the World's Great Trials.* New York: Bonanza Books, 1985.

Leopold, Nathan F., Jr. *Life Plus 99 Years.* Garden City, N.Y.: Doubleday & Co., Inc., 1958.

Sifakis, Carl. *The Encyclopedia of American Crime.* New York: Facts On File, 1982.

John Thomas Scopes Trial: 1925
(The "Monkey Trial")

Name of Defendant: John Thomas Scopes   **Crime Charged:** Teaching evolution   **Chief Defense Lawyers:** Clarence Darrow, Arthur Garfield Hays, and Dudley Field Malone.   **Chief Prosecutors:** William Jennings Bryan and A.T. Stewart   **Judge:** John T. Raulston   **Place:** Dayton, Tennessee   **Dates of Trial:** July 10–21, 1925   **Verdict:** Guilty; however, neither side won the case because the decision was reversed on a technicality involving the judge's error in imposing a fine that legally could only be set by the jury   **Sentence:** $100 fine

SIGNIFICANCE

The John Thomas Scopes trial checked the influence of Fundamentalism in public education and stripped William Jennings Bryan of his dignity as a key figure in American political history. It also marked the displacement of religious faith and rural values by scientific skepticism and cosmopolitanism as the dominant strains in American thought.

Rarely has the American psyche been so at odds with itself as in the early 1920s. In the cities, Americans were dancing to the opening bars of the Jazz Age, debating Sigmund Freud's theories and swigging bootleg liquor in defiance of Prohibition. In the rural heartland, particularly in the South, believers in old-fashioned values were caught up in a wave of religious revivalism. Preachers damned modern scientific rationalism in all its guises and upheld a strict and literal interpretation of the Bible as the only source of truth. A showdown between modernists and traditionalists to decide which would dominate American culture seemed inevitable. Both sides itched for a decisive battle.

Fundamentalists were particularly galled by the gains modernism had made in public schools, where the teaching of Charles Darwin's theory of evolution by natural selection had supplanted the Biblical story of creation. To them, it seemed their tax dollars were being spent to turn their own children against—even to scoff at—the religion of their parents. Led by William Jennings Bryan, the thrice-defeated presidential candidate of populism, the Fundamentalists tried to drive the Darwinian "heresy" out of the schools by legislative fiat.

In Tennessee a bill sponsored by John Washington Butler was enacted in February 1925, declaring it unlawful for a teacher in any school supported by state funds "to teach any theory that denies the story of the divine creation of man as taught in the Bible, and to teach instead that man has descended from a lower order of animals." Fearful that if the Tennessee law went unchallenged other states would soon pass similar bills, the American Civil Liberties Union (ACLU) immediately announced it would defend any teacher charged with violating the Butler Act.

A few weeks later, in the little town of Dayton, a transplanted New Yorker with Darwinian views got into a debate at the local drugstore soda fountain with two Fundamentalist lawyers. However much they fought over evolution and whether mankind and monkeys were close relatives, they quickly agreed that a trial to test the law would do wonders for Dayton's commerce. The 24-year-old science teacher of the local high school, John Thomas Scopes, was recruited that very afternoon to be the legal guinea pig. Just as quickly, the ACLU confirmed it was prepared to defend Scopes.

Using a state-approved textbook, Scopes taught a lesson on evolutionary theory on April 24 to his Rhea County High School science class. Arrested on May 7, Scopes was quickly indicted by the grand jury, setting the stage for what newspaper headline writers were already calling the "Monkey Trial."

The Circus Comes to Dayton

The legal teams fielded by both sides guaranteed the press attention they and Dayton's business leaders craved. The ACLU dispatched its chief attorney, Arthur Garfield Hays, and his partner, Dudley Field Malone, along with Clarence Darrow. Darrow, who had made his reputation by defending controversial clients, became the chief lawyer for the defense. A militant agnostic, he had long been on a personal crusade against resurgent Fundamentalism, and he saw the Scopes trial as the perfect opportunity to kick the wobbly intellectual props out from under that ideology.

Personifying the Fundamentalist world view, the star of the prosecution team was none other than William Jennings Bryan himself. No one was more holier-than-thou or more effective on the stump in defending old-fashioned rural America's Fundamentalist values than "The Great Commoner," as he liked to be called.

Pro- and anti-evolutionists alike billed the trial as a winner-take-all debate between incompatible ideologies, a forensic armageddon between religion and science, faith and reason, traditional and modern values, the forces of light and the forces of darkness. Scientists and intellectuals were horrified at the prospect of a state barring scientific knowledge from the classroom. Civil libertarians saw the case as a crucial test of academic freedom, which had to be defended regardless of the prevailing religious beliefs of the local population. Fundamentalists proclaimed the case a last-ditch battle to save the souls of their children from atheism.

Big-city editors recognized it as a circus and sent their most waspish reporters and columnists to poke fun at the hayseeds. Dozens of new telegraph lines had to be strung into Dayton to handle their cable traffic. In addition to the lawyers and reporters, the town was overrun with itinerant preachers, commercial hucksters, eccentrics of every stripe, and numerous chimpanzees accompanied by their trainers. Monkey dolls, umbrellas with monkey handles, and dozens of other souvenirs with a monkey motif were put on sale.

Despite the circus-like atmosphere, the trial was no laughing matter for Bryan. Arriving a few days early, he preached to a large audience, "The contest between evolution and Christianity is a duel to the death. . . . If evolution wins in Dayton, Christianity goes."

Evolution on Trial

The trial began Friday, July 10, 1925, with Judge John T. Raulston presiding. More than 900 spectators packed the sweltering courtroom. Because of an error in the original indictment, most of the first morning was spent selecting another grand jury and drawing up a new indictment. With that task done, a trial jury of 10 farmers, a schoolteacher and a clerk was quickly impaneled, and the court adjourned for the weekend.

On the first business day of the trial, the defense tried and failed to quash the indictment on grounds that the law violated both the Fourteenth Amendment to the U.S. Constitution, which states that no one may be deprived of rights without due process of law, and the freedom of religion clause of the First Amendment. Describing the Butler Act to be "as brazen and as bold an attempt to destroy learning as was ever made in the Middle Ages," Darrow predicted there would be a natural progression from the forbidding of the teaching of evolution in public schools to the banning of books and censoring of newspapers.

The opening statement for the prosecution was made the next day by A.T. Stewart, the attorney general of Tennessee, who charged Scopes with contradicting the Biblical story of Creation, thus violating the Butler Act. Responding for the defense, Dudley Malone insisted that for Scopes to be convicted the state had to prove two things: that he had denied the Biblical story of creation and that he had taught instead that man descended from a lower order of animals. Proving both would considerably complicate the prosecution's task. (While Scopes had admitted teaching evolution, there was no evidence he had denied the Bible's version of man's origins.) Malone conceded there was there were some apparent contradictions between the Darwinian and Biblical accounts of creation, but he noted that many people managed to reconcile the two theories. Only the Fundamentalists maintained that science and religion were totally incompatible on the subject.

The prosecution's case was presented briskly. The superintendent of the Rhea County school system testified that Scopes had admitted teaching evolution in a biology class. Stewart then offered a King James Version of the Bible as evidence of what the Butler Act described as the Biblical account of Creation. The judge accepted this as evidence over the objection of Arthur Garfield Hays, who pointed out that there were several different versions of the Bible.

Scopes' students testified that he had taught that mammals had evolved from one-cell organisms and that humans share the classification "mammal" with monkeys, cats, etc. The owner of the local drugstore where Scopes had purchased the textbook he used to teach evolution acknowledged that the state had authorized sale of the textbook. Darrow and the druggist read aloud portions on Darwin. To counter, Steward read the first two chapters of the Old Testament's Genesis into the record. With that, the prosecution rested.

The next day, Thursday, July 16, the defense started calling its witnesses, beginning with a zoologist from Johns Hopkins University. The prosecution objected, arguing the evidence was inadmissible and irrelevant since the jury did not need to understand evolutionary theory to decide whether Scopes had violated the law in teaching it.

Bryan seized this opportunity to give his major speech of the trial. Clutching the offending textbook in one hand and a palm fan in the other, he belittled the theory of evolution and ridiculed a diagram in the textbook. Bryan charged that Darwinism produced agnostics and atheists, thus weakening moral stan-

The crowded courtroom of the Scopes trial. Clarence Darrow and other members of the defense team are in the foreground. (Courtesy, Library of Congress)

dards. As evidence of this, he claimed it had inspired the German philosopher Friedrich Nietzsche, whose writings, in turn, had motivated the Chicago "thrill-killers," Nathan Leopold and Richard Loeb. Darrow, who had been the defense attorney in that case, angrily objected, stating that Bryan was misrepresenting Nietzsche's views to prejudice the jury; Judge Raulston overruled him. Bryan closed on a defiant note, assuring his audience that the Bible would survive attacks by scientists trying to reconcile it with evolution. Although some of his quips provoked appreciative laughter from spectators, observers noted that the speech lacked the eloquence and punch of Bryan's best stump performances.

Dudley Malone, presenting the defense's last argument for the admissibility of scientific evidence, charged the Fundamentalists with suppressing new ideas out of fear and claiming they had a monopoly on the truth. Malone proclaimed: "The truth always wins. . . . The truth does not need the forces of Government. The truth does not need Mr. Bryan. The truth is imperishable," Malone declared. "We feel we stand with progress. . . . We feel we stand with fundamental freedom in America. We are not afraid. Where is the fear? We defy it!" Although Malone's speech received more applause than Bryan's, it failed to persuade the judge.

The phrase "descended from a lower order of animals" was clear enough to define evolution under the law, Judge Raulston decided, ruling out the admissibility of scientific testimony.

Enraged by this decision, Arthur Hays requested the judge at least permit the expert statements to be entered into the court record, not to be heard by the jury but to be available to an appeals court. Avoiding cross-examination of its expert witnesses, the defense lawyers submitted their written statements, summaries of which went into the record.

Darrow Deflates Bryan

The trial, which had been moved to the courthouse lawn to accommodate the crowds, seemed to be winding down when defense attorney Hays dropped a bombshell: He called William Jennings Bryan to the stand as an expert on the Bible. This was an unheard-of legal tactic, but, with jaunty overconfidence, Bryan sprang up to accept the dare and the doubtful judge agreed. Darrow, whose skill at trapping witnesses with their own words was legendary, dropped his previously gentle manner when Bryan took the stand. First, he got Bryan to state every word in the Bible was literally true. He then asked how the Old Testament figure Cain got a wife if he, Adam, Eve, and Abel were the only four people on earth at the time, as the Bible said. Next, Clarence Darrow pointed out that the Book of Genesis states that the serpent who tempted Eve in the Garden of Eden was condemned by God to slither on its belly, Darrow then asked Bryan if before that, had the snake walked on its tail? The more Darrow bored in, the more entangled Bryan became in contradictions, and the more foolish he and his cause appeared.

Sweating and shaking, Bryan shocked his own supporters by admitting he didn't think the earth was made in six 24-hour days, as a literal reading of the Bible suggested. This was significant, since literalism was the cornerstone of Fundamentalist doctrine. The personal antagonism between Darrow and Bryan charged the courtroom with electricity. Bryan accused Darrow of insulting the Bible. Darrow responded, "I am examining you on your fool ideas that no Christian on earth believes."

Finally, after an hour and a half, Judge Raulston adjourned the proceedings in a transparent attempt to save Bryan further embarrassment. The next morning Bryan's testimony was described as irrelevant and removed from the record by the judge. The defense immediately rested, denying Bryan any opportunity to erase the previous day's humiliation.

Closing for the defense, Clarence Darrow stole the prosecution's lines by asking the jury to find Scopes guilty so that the case could be appealed. After nine minutes, the jury came back with a guilty verdict. In violation of Tennessee law, which required that the fine be set by the jury, Raulston advised the jury to let him fix the fine, an error that led the court of appeals to reject the original verdict. While the appeals court upheld the constitutionality of the Butler Act, it did not order a retrial for John Thomas Scopes, who by that time had given up teaching.

In a narrow sense, Scopes and the evolutionists lost the battle. But it was soon apparent that they had won the war. No attempt was made to enforce the Butler Act again, although it was not repealed until 1967. Within a few years, efforts to enforce similar laws in other states were also abandoned. The Supreme Court put the issue to rest in 1968, when it held a similar statute in Arkansas unconstitutional because it violated the separation of church and state required by the First Amendment of the Constitution.

But the Scopes trial is remembered not so much for its legal as its social and cultural significance. It marked a watershed in intellectual history; before Scopes, religious faith was the common, if not universal, premise of American thought; after Scopes, scientific skepticism prevailed. Friends and enemies alike viewed William Jennings Bryan's death just a few weeks after the trial ended as tolling the end of an era. A 1955 play and subsequent film based on the events in Dayton, Tennessee, *Inherit the Wind* by Jerome Lawrence and Robert Lee, ensured that the trial would remain among the most remembered courtroom battles in U.S. history.

—Edward W. Knappman

Suggestions for Further Reading

Allen, Leslie H., ed. *Bryan And Darrow At Dayton: The Record And Documents Of The "Bible Evolution Trial."* New York: Arthur Lee, 1925.

Coletta, Paolo E. *William Jennings Bryan.* Lincoln: University of Nebraska Press, 1969.

Darrow, Clarence. *The Story Of My Life.* New York: Charles Scribner's Sons, 1932.

De Camp, L. Sprague. *The Great Monkey Trial.* Garden City, N.Y.: Doubleday & Co., 1968.

Ginger, Raymond. *Six Days Or Forever: Tennessee v. John Thomas Scopes.* Boston: Beacon Press, 1958.

Hays, Arthur Garfield. *Let Freedom Ring.* New York: Boni & Liveright, 1928.

Koenig, Louis W. *Bryan: A Political Biography of William Jennings Bryan.* New York: G.P. Putnam's Sons, 1971.

Levine, Lawrence. *Defender of The Faith: William Jennings Bryan: The Last Decade 1915–1925.* New York: Oxford University Press, 1965.

Scopes, John. *Center of The Storm.* New York: Holt, Rinehart & Winston, 1967.

Stone, Irving. *Clarence Darrow For The Defense.* Garden City N.Y.: Doubleday & Co., 1941.

Tierney, Kevin. *Darrow: A Biography.* New York: T.Y. Crowell, 1979.

Tompkins, Jerry. *D-days at Dayton.* Baton Rouge: Louisiana State University Press, 1965.

Weinberg, Arthur, ed. *Attorney For The Damned.* New York: Simon & Schuster, 1957.

Billy Mitchell Court-Martial: 1925

Defendant: Brigadier General William Mitchell
Crime Charged: Insubordination and "conduct of a nature to bring discredit upon the military service"   **Chief Defense Lawyers:** Frank G. Plain, Frank Reid, and Colonel Herbert A. White   **Chief Prosecutors:** Major Allen W. Gullion, Lieutenant Joseph L. McMullen, and Colonel Sherman Moreland
Judges: Major General Charles P. Summerall, Chief of the U.S. Army General Staff; Major Generals William S. Graves, Robert L. Howze, Douglas MacArthur, Benjamin A. Poore, and Fred W. Sladen; Brigadier Generals Ewing E. Booth, Albert L. Bowley, George Irwin, Edward K. King, Frank R. McCoy, and Edwin B. Winans; and Colonel Blanton Winship   **Place:** Washington, D.C.
Dates of Court-Martial: October 28–December 17, 1925   **Verdict:** Guilty
Sentence: Suspension from rank, command, and duty with forfeiture of all pay and allowances for five years

SIGNIFICANCE

The Billy Mitchell court-martial demonstrated not only that a prophet is without honor in his own country but that he is particularly unwelcome in the military. The longest and most controversial court martial in U.S. history, it came to epitomize the difficulty military strategists have in adapting to changing times and technologies. The cost of the country's resultant unpreparedness for World War II lies beyond reckoning.

Nineteen-year-old William Mitchell enlisted in the Army in 1898, at the outbreak of the Spanish-American War. By World War I, he had realized the significance of the airplane, put himself through flying school at his own expense, risen to the rank of colonel, and was chief of Air Service. Seeing the Army using the airplane at first only for observation and, later, to shoot at enemy planes, he was perplexed that strafing and bombing never occurred to the men who ran the war. He proposed to General John J. Pershing that troops be dropped behind German lines by plane and parachute "in order so to surprise the enemy by taking him from the rear that it would give our infantry an opening." Pershing found the idea impossible and absurd.

By the war's end, Mitchell was convinced that "Only an air force can fight an air force." Soon he had trained the first paratrooper, used the airplane for aerial mapping, developed the turbo booster and the variable-pitch propeller, predicted high-altitude flight where the thin atmosphere would permit speeds of 300 to 400 miles per hour, and mounted cannons on planes—ordnance not flown again until, ironically, it was mounted on the B-25 Mitchell bomber (named for Billy Mitchell) for Colonel Jimmy Doolittle's daring bombing of Tokyo early in World War II.

Declaring in 1921 that "the first battles of any future war will be air battles," Mitchell became an outspoken critic of the government's failure to develop the Air Service. When the House Naval Affairs Committee refused to let him demonstrate air power by bombing former German ships that had to be destroyed under the Armistice agreement, he went public, earning so many headlines nationwide with his descriptions of Navy vessels as "sitting ducks" that the House Appropriations Committee approved his plan.

Mitchell's bombers easily sank an old American battleship and a German submarine, cruiser, destroyer, and battleship.

The Joint Board of the Army and Navy promptly announced, "The battleship is still the backbone of the fleet." A colonel from the Engineer Corps was promoted to major general in command of the Air Service. Mitchell exhausted himself appearing before clubs and organizations, prophesying the air power of Germany, Russia, Italy, and Japan. Before a Congressional inquiry, he accused Army and Navy witnesses of "deliberate falsification of facts with intent to deceive the country and Congress."

To counter Mitchell's alarms, the Navy sent the aging dirigible *Shenandoah* on a tour. It crashed. Next a Naval "publicity flight" to Hawaii crashed. Mitchell told reporters:

> My opinion is: Those accidents are the result of the incompetency, the criminal negligence, and the almost treasonable administration of our national defense by the Navy and War Departments.

Court-martial papers were served, charging the general with insubordination and conduct "to the prejudice of good order and military discipline."

For three weeks, defense counsel Frank G. Reid introduced witness after witness to prove that Mitchell, "after exhausting every usual means to safeguard the aerial defense of the United States without result, took the only way possible that would cause a study of the true conditions of the national defense to be made." Major (later General) Carl Spaatz testified on the country's numerical weakness in planes, Major (later General) "Hap" Arnold on the appalling number of deaths from worn-out equipment, former Captain Eddie Rickenbacker on the uselessness of anti-aircraft fire.

Mitchell himself testified:

> The people have placed their trust in the War and Navy Departments, to provide a proper defense for the safety of the nation. It has not been done. I consider this failure to be . . . the criminal offense of treason.

The judges, not one of whom had ever been up in an airplane, debated for three hours, found Billy Mitchell "Guilty on all counts," and sentenced him "to be suspended from rank, command, and duty with the forfeiture of all pay and allowances for five years."

Colonel Billy Mitchell (far right) at his court-martial. (Courtesy, Library of Congress)

A joint resolution of Congress immediately proposed to restore Mitchell's rank and reimburse his expenses. President Calvin Coolidge, as commander-in-chief, upheld the suspension but restored the allowances and granted the general half pay. Mitchell resigned. Congress passed no resolution.

Mitchell settled on a farm in Virginia, raising livestock, writing, speaking, and trying without success to found a University of Aviation.

Billy Mitchell died of pneumonia in 1936. Precisely as he had predicted, on December 7, 1941, the Japanese, without formally declaring war, destroyed Clark Field in the Philippines and the "sitting duck" U.S. Navy fleet at Pearl Harbor by aerial bombardment.

—Bernard Ryan, Jr.

Suggestions for Further Reading

Davis, Burke. *The Billy Mitchell Affair.* New York: Random House, 1967.

Encyclopedia Americana, Volume 19. New York: Americana Corp., 1953.

Lardner, Rex. *Ten Heroes of the Twenties*. New York: G.P. Putnam's Sons, 1966.

Mitchell, Ruth. *My Brother Bill*. New York: Harcourt, Brace and Co., 1953.

D.C. Stephenson Trial: 1925

Defendants: Earl Gentry, Earl Klinck, and David Curtis Stephenson
Crime Charged: Murder   **Chief Defense Lawyers:** Floyd Christian, Ira W.
Holmes, and "Eph" Inman   **Chief Prosecutors:** Charles E. Cox, Ralph Kane,
William H. Remy   **Judge:** Will M. Sparks   **Place:** Noblesville, Indiana
Dates of Trial: October 28–November 14, 1925   **Verdicts:** Stephenson:
guilty; Gentry and Klinck: not guilty   **Sentence:** Life imprisonment

SIGNIFICANCE

Specific events often make or break entire movements. The D.C. Stephenson case
was such an event. The defendant had been Grand Dragon—and the most
influential Northern leader—of the notorious Ku Klux Klan, dedicated to hatred
and racial and religious intolerance. The trial and conviction of Stephenson,
calling America's attention to the sinister hypocrisy of the organization, marked
the high tide of Klan membership, which dropped within three years from 10
million to a few thousand. The case also established that a defendant who
committed a criminal assault that caused the victim to commit suicide could be
tried on murder charges.

David Curtis Stephenson was a Texan who settled in Indiana in 1920 when he
was 29. There he joined the Ku Klux Klan, a fraternal organization that had
been created during Reconstruction in the South to "maintain white supremacy." Expanding nationally after World War I, the Klan had broadened its
program to include nativism, anti-Catholicism, and anti-Semitism. It grew rapidly in the North.

Stephenson worked tirelessly to expand the Klan in Indiana, recruiting
more than 300,000 fanatics in less than two years and becoming Grand Dragon of
the Realm of Indiana. Next, under contract from the Klan, he became supreme
organizer in 19 other states, was paid $4 out of every $10 initiation fee, and
pocketed $4.25 from every $6 robe and hood a Klansman bought.

"I Am the Law in Indiana"

Stephenson was less successful, however, in the in-fighting with his boss,
Hiram W. Evans, Imperial Wizard and director of the Klan. After Stephenson's

friend Ed Jackson was elected governor in 1924, along with a majority of the state's House of Representatives—all nominated and supported by the Klan—Stephenson repeatedly declared, "I am the law in Indiana." Imperial Wizard Evans decided to subject the Klan's Indiana leader to the K.K.K.'s own program. In addition to its persecution of blacks, Catholics, and Jews, the Klan preached virtue. It regularly tarred and feathered whoremongers and habitual drunkards. Now Evans let out word of Stephenson's hypocrisy: The Grand Dragon was a secret lecher and a drunkard. The Evansville Klavern tried him in secret for his many "immoralities" in several cities and "on trains and boats," found him guilty, and banished him from the Klan.

In January 1925, at a banquet honoring governor-elect Jackson, Stephenson met 28-year-old Madge Oberholtzer, manager of a public-welfare program in the state's Department of Public Instruction, who lived at home in Indianapolis with her parents. They danced together. Soon Stephenson was making dates and calling for her in his chauffeured car. He was, Oberholtzer found, always the perfect gentleman.

On Sunday, March 15, 1925, Oberholtzer came home about 10:00 P.M. from a day with young friends. Stephenson had left an urgent message. When she called back, he said he was leaving for Chicago but needed to see her first and would send an escort to get her. Thinking that Stephenson wanted to discuss some aspect of her work and expecting to return shortly, Oberholtzer left home without her purse or hat.

With a stranger later identified as Earl Gentry, she departed for Stephenson's house. In the morning, her parents, who had gone to bed soon after she went out, realized she had not come home. Distressed, they talked with a lawyer and stopped by Stephenson's house in search for her. Then came a telegram: "We are driving through to Chicago. Will be home on night train. Madge." Mrs. Oberholtzer met the train, but her daughter did not appear.

In a Pullman-Car Drawing Room

On Tuesday morning, a car arrived while Mrs. Oberholtzer was out (a roomer was the only person at home). A man later identified as Earl Klinck carried Madge Oberholtzer, who was moaning, into the house and to her bed upstairs. The man said she had been in an automobile accident, then hurriedly departed. Oberholtzer asked the roomer to call a doctor. He and her mother arrived together, and Oberholtzer, sobbing and groaning, told them how she had been taken to Stephenson's kitchen, where she found him quite drunk and where he, his chauffeur, and Gentry twice forced her (each man holding a revolver) to drain a glass of liquid that immediately made her ill and confused. When she protested that she wanted to go home, Stephenson said, "You can't go home. You are going with me to Chicago. I love you more than any woman I have ever known."

Next they took her to the railroad station and boarded a Pullman car. In a drawing room, with Gentry in the upper berth, "Stephenson [her later declaration stated] took all my clothes off and pushed me into the lower berth. He chewed me all over my body, particularly my neck and face, chewed my tongue, chewed my breasts until they bled, my back, my legs, my ankles, and mutilated me all over."

Next morning, in Hammond, Indiana, the men took Madge to a hotel, where Gentry helped bathe her wounds. Stephenson dictated the telegram and Gentry sent it. When Madge begged for a hat, Stevenson gave her $15 and sent her out with the chauffeur, who had driven to Hammond. Without his seeing her, she managed to buy bichloride-of-mercury tablets and, back at the hotel, to take six, vomiting the rest of the day. By nightfall, she had told the men she had taken the poison. She had also refused Stevenson's demands that she go to a hospital and that she marry him. The men put her in the car and headed back to Indianapolis, Madge vomiting, groaning, and screaming all the way. At Stephenson's house, they carried her to a loft over the garage at midnight, just missing her mother, who was again at Stephenson's door. In the morning, Klinck took her home.

The doctor worked for 10 days to get the poison out of Madge's system. Her wounds and bruises responded to medication—except one, the deep wound in her breast, which was infected. Soon after making a formal statement to her doctor and two lawyers, she died on April 14.

Madge's father, George Oberholtzer, a postal clerk, had already filed a criminal complaint against Stephenson, Gentry, and Klinck, and the grand jury had indicted them for assault and battery with intent to commit a criminal attack, malicious mayhem, kidnaping, and conspiracy to kidnap. The three were free on bail. Now the grand jury charged them with murder. They were arrested and held without bail.

After 11 days of interrogating 400 veniremen to get a jury that had no affiliation with or sympathy for the Klan, the trial began October 18. The prosecution quickly established the facts of Stephenson's Sunday-evening phone call and Madge's going off with Gentry for the fatal trip.

A Secondary Staphylococci Infection

Testimony in two areas established the prosecution's case. One was Madge's sworn declaration, made in the presence of four witnesses (two of them lawyers) when her doctor had told her that she could not expect to recover. The other was testimony by three pathologists that Madge had died from a secondary staphylococci infection, resulting from Stephenson's biting assault on her breast, that imposed itself on an acute nephritis, or kidney infection, caused by the poison. Cross-examination by the defense lawyers failed to shake the pathologists.

The defense itself tried to prove that Madge's infection was the residue of an attack of flu some months earlier, that she and Stephenson had been intimate and the trip with him was voluntary, and that Madge's dying statement was "a dying declaration of suicide and not of homicide, made for the justification of herself, to free herself from fault and place the blame on others."

"She Would Have Worn a Hat"

Prosecutor Ralph Kane struck the common-sense human chord during his summation:

> There are some things that you and I know. If Madge Oberholtzer had gone willingly with Stephenson that night she would have done it by prearrangement, and she would have worn a hat. If I understand anything at all about women, when they start on a 250-mile Pullman ride they take along their clothes, their hats, their cosmetics, their lingerie and other things.
>
> Another thing. Do you think she would ever have had big, pug-nosed Gentry in the same compartment if she had been conscious of what was happening? If she was a willing companion, why bring her home looking like she had been in a fight?

In six hours on November 14, the jury found Stephenson guilty of murder in the second degree and recommended life imprisonment. Gentry and Klinck were found not guilty. Stephenson immediately began a series of more than 40 proceedings to try to gain a pardon, a new trial, or release on parole. In each, an entirely different set of lawyers represented him. At last, in 1950, he gained parole but disappeared within five months. When found in November, he had failed to report to his parole officer for three months. Returned to prison, he next made disclosures to newspapers that resulted in his temporary release to produce records he had hidden. His papers resulted in the indictment of Governor Ed Jackson as well as the Republican political boss, George V. Coffin, for violation of Indiana's corrupt practices act by bribing the governor's predecessor to appoint a Klan henchman as a prosecuting attorney. Stephenson's disclosures also brought indictments against the mayor of Indianapolis and six city aldermen for accepting bribes. The governor and Coffin escaped by pleading the statute of limitations, while the mayor spent 30 days in jail and, along with the aldermen, resigned.

Stephenson's house burned soon after he went to prison. Klinck and Gentry were indicted for arson, but the case was dismissed for lack of evidence. Gentry was murdered in 1934 by a jealous rival in a love triangle. Pleading guilty and receiving a life sentence, his murderer said:

> I am not in the least sorry for the act I committed, as I feel I did a good deed for society when I killed Earl Gentry.

—Bernard Ryan, Jr.

Suggestions for Further Reading

Busch, Francis X. *Guilty or Not Guilty?* New York: Bobbs-Merrill Co., 1952.

Nash, Jay Robert. *Encyclopedia of World Crime*. Wilmette, Ill.: CrimeBooks, 1991.

Frances Hall, Henry Stevens, and William Stevens Trial: 1926

Defendants: Frances Stevens Hall, Henry Stevens, and William Stevens
Crime Charged: Murder **Chief Defense Lawyers:** Clarence E. Case, Robert H. McCarter, and Timothy N. Pfeiffer **Chief Prosecutors:** Francis L. Bergen and Alexander Simpson **Judges:** Frank L. Cleary and Charles W. Parker
Place: Somerville, New Jersey **Dates of Trial:** November 3–December 3, 1926 **Verdict:** Not guilty

SIGNIFICANCE

This trial came four years after the execution-style murders of two lovers—both adulterers—had produced sensational headlines nationwide. In what mystery writer Rex Stout called "sustained official ineptitude surely never surpassed anywhere," New Jersey authorities were unable for four years to produce an indictment. When they finally did so and the trial resulted in acquittal, *The New York Times* commented, "Jersey Justice can at least acquit the innocent if it cannot always find the guilty." The crime has never been solved.

On Saturday morning, September 16, 1922, a young couple strolling on a lovers' lane on the outskirts of New Brunswick, New Jersey, discovered two bodies. A woman's head lay on a man's right arm, her hand on his knee, a scarf over her throat. The man's business card leaned against his foot. Scattered over the bodies were pieces of paper.

The man was the Reverend Edward W. Hall, rector of the Episcopal Church of St. John the Evangelist. Handsome and popular, he had some 11 years earlier, at the age of 30 married 37-year-old Frances Noel Stevens, daughter of a well-to-do New Brunswick family.

"I Have the Greatest of All Blessings"

It was known almost instantly who the murdered woman was, for it was common knowledge that Reverend Hall was deeply involved with a member of the St. John's choir, Eleanor Mills. Her quiet and unambitious husband James served as sexton of the church. The country was titillated when the newspapers, hot on the trail of a story of torrid love, revealed that the papers scattered over the bodies were love letters such as this:

> There isn't a man who could make me smile as you did today. I know there are girls with more shapely bodies, but I do not care what they have. I have the greatest of all blessings, a noble man, deep, true, and eternal love. My heart is his, my life is his, all I have is his, poor as my body is, scrawny as they say my skin may be, but I am his forever.

The autopsies reported that the minister had been shot once and the 32-year-old choir singer three times—both in the head. Her throat had been slit from ear to ear and her voice box nearly removed.

Middlesex and Somerset county detectives and prosecutors vied for authority, for the bodies had been found almost on the line between the two counties. Soon Middlesex County prosecutor Joseph Stricker charged one Clifford Hayes with the murders. He believed a young man who said Hayes had mistaken the victims for a girlfriend and her father, whom Hayes had threatened. But Hayes was jailed in Somerset County, where its prosecutor was unable to make the mistaken-identity theory explain the slit throat or the love letters. Two days later, Hayes' accuser admitted he had lied.

Meantime, in four weeks, the police and the prosecutors had found no reason to suspect the choir singer's husband, James Mills, whom columnist Damon Runyon later described as "a harmless, dull little fellow." As for Frances Hall, she had spent the evening of the murders with her husband's visiting niece after Reverend Hall had gone out in response to a call from Eleanor Mills. At 2:30 in the morning, Frances Hall had discovered that her husband had not returned. With her brother Willie Stevens, who had been at home the entire evening, she had gone to the church to search for her husband.

The police questioned Frances Hall and her brothers extensively on October 17, even forcing her to don the gray coat she had worn on her middle-of-the-night search and submit to inspection by an unidentified woman who peered at her intently.

By now, countless eager curiosity-seekers, propelled by daily sensational newspaper stories, had traipsed through the lovers' lane property. The weekends brought hundreds of cars, police to handle traffic, and vendors to hawk peanuts, popcorn, and soft drinks.

A Mule-Riding Pig Woman

At the end of October, a 50-year-old widow named Jane Gibson, who raised hogs near the murder site, disclosed that she had mounted a mule on the night of September 14 to follow a suspected thief. In the lovers' lane, she had seen two men and two women silhouetted against the night sky, then heard screams and shots and the shouted name "Henry."

Dubbing her "The Pig Woman," the press thronged Gibson's dilapidated living room. She told them she had always wanted to talk to the police, but they wouldn't listen. When Hayes was arrested, she had forced them to pay attention. It was she who had peered intently at Frances Hall at police headquarters.

The grand jury spent five days hearing 67 witnesses, including The Pig Woman. It took no action.

Three and a half years later, a piano tuner named Arthur S. Riehl filed a petition for annulment of his 10-month marriage. His wife, he said, had withheld from him "knowledge of the doings in the well-known Hall-Mills case." He said his wife, who at the time was a maid in the Hall household, told Mrs. Hall on September 14, 1922,

> . . . that she knew Dr. Hall intended to elope with Mrs. Mills. About ten o'clock that night respondent [Mrs. Riehl], Mrs. Hall, and Willie Stevens were driven to Phillips farm. . . . Respondent told your petitioner that she got five thousand dollars for her part in the matter and for keeping quiet about it. . . . Respondent told your petitioner Willie Stevens was a good shot and that there was always a pistol in the Hall library drawer.

Mrs. Riehl denounced her husband's statement as "a pack of lies." But for the next three weeks, the New York *Daily Mirror*, a new Hearst paper eager to win a circulation war with the established *Daily News*, led the press in demanding the reopening of the Hall-Mills case. At midnight on July 28, Frances Hall was arrested and arraigned. Over the next month, several hearings, each with more than 50 witnesses, produced enough testimony to convince the grand jury to indict not only her but her brothers Willie and Henry Stevens and their cousin, Henry Carpender, for each murder. Special Prosecutor Alexander Simpson asked for a separate trial for Carpender.

The trial turned Somerville's Main Street into what one wag called "a country fair," with dozens of souvenir and refreshment stands. In the courthouse, some 300 reporters pumped their stories into 60 leased wires while 28 special operators handled a 129-position switchboard moved in from the recent Jack Dempsey-Gene Tunney prizefight in Philadelphia. In view of the intense interest, Somerset County Judge Frank L. Cleary invited New Jersey Supreme Court Justice Charles W. Parker, who had presided over some of the hearings, to help him run the trial in the murder of Eleanor Mills.

For the prosecution, a fingerprint expert testified that Reverend Hall's business card bore Willie Stevens' fingerprint, despite the fact that it had been handled by police and reporters and the curious, had developed "flyspecks," and after three years had languished in the possession of the editor of the *Daily Mirror*.

The Pig Woman provided the ultimate drama. Severely ill, she was brought by ambulance to the courthouse, where she lay flat in a bed before judges and jury and told again her story of riding her mule into the night and hearing voices. She said she had heard a woman shout, "Explain those letters." Then, she went on, "I could hear somebody's wind going out, and somebody said, 'Ugh!'" A flashlight shone, and she saw Henry Stevens. Then a woman said, "Oh, Henry," and another screamed "Oh, my; oh, my!" She heard a shot, then three shots, and she rode away.

Defense attorney Clarence Case worked to destroy The Pig Woman's credibility. Known as Mrs. Gibson, she said she was really married to a Mr. Easton—except that she couldn't remember in which church or city she married him, and at the hearings four years earlier, she had denied that marriage. Hadn't she been married in 1890 to a man who divorced her in 1898 for adultery? Had she lived with Harry Ray? Had she known "Stumpy" Gillan? She couldn't remember.

The defense produced witnesses to prove that Henry Stevens spent the night of the murders bluefishing on the Jersey shore. Three fingerprint experts could find no resemblance between the smudge on the card and Willie Stevens' prints. The detective who received the card in 1922 said he had put his initials on it then, but the card in evidence showed no initials.

"A Sort of Genius"

Cross-examining, Simpson asked Willie Stevens if it wasn't "rather fishy" to look for the missing minister in the middle of the night. Willie Stevens said, "I don't see that it is at all fishy." The prosecutor wanted to know how Stevens could prove he had been in his room during the evening of September 14. "If a person sees me go upstairs," said Stevens, "isn't that a conclusion that I was in my room?"

The press hailed Willie Stevens. The deflated prosecutor called him "a sort of genius."

Frances Hall testified that her husband was "absolutely" devoted to her. Her interest in and devotion to Eleanor Mills was demonstrated by the fact that she had taken Mills to the hospital for a kidney operation in January and paid her bills there.

Having heard 87 witnesses for the state and 70 for the defense, the jury deliberated for five hours. It found the three defendants not guilty of the murder of Eleanor Mills. The next morning, Justice Parker granted the New Jersey attorney general's motion for dismissal of all remaining charges against them. All charges against Henry Carpender were then dropped.

Willie Stevens, Henry Carpender, and Frances Hall sued the *Daily Mirror* for libel, each asking for $500,000. Later they sued William Randolph Hearst and the *Evening Journal*. All suits were settled out of court for undisclosed sums.

On the books of the Somerset County prosecutor, the Hall-Mills case continues to be unsolved.

—Bernard Ryan, Jr.

Suggestions for Further Reading

Kunstler, William M. *The Minister and the Choir Singer*. New York: William Morrow & Co., 1964.

Nash, Jay Robert. *Almanac of World Crime*. Garden City, N. Y.: Anchor Press/Doubleday, 1981.

Sifakis, Carl. *The Encyclopedia of American Crime*. New York: Facts On File, 1982.

The Teapot Dome Trials: 1926–30

Defendants: Sherman Burns: trial 3; William J. Burns: trial 3; Henry Mason Day: trial 3; Edward L. Doheny: trials 1 and 8; Albert B. Fall: trials 1, 3, and 7; Harry F. Sinclair: trials 2, 3, and 4; and Robert W. Stewart: trial 6 **Crimes Charged:** Conspiracy to defraud the U.S. government: trials 1 and 4; Contempt of the U.S. Senate: trials 2 and 5; Contempt of court for jury shadowing: trial 3; Perjury: trial 6; Accepting a bribe: trial 7; Giving a bribe: trial 8 **Chief Defense Lawyers:** Frank J. Hogan, George P. Hoover, Wilton J. Lambert, William E. Leahy, Martin W. Littleton, R.W. Ragland, G.T. Stanford, and Mark B. Thompson **Chief Prosecutors:** Neil Burkinshaw, Peyton C. Gordon, Atlee W. Pomerene, Owen J. Roberts, and Leo A. Rover **Judges:** Jennings Bailey, William Hitz, Adolph A. Hoehling, and Frederick L. Siddons **Place:** Washington, D.C. **Dates of Trials:** November 22–December 16, 1926; March 3, 1927; December 5, 1927–February 21, 1928; April 16–21, 1928; May 31–June 14, 1928; November 12–20, 1928; October 7–25, 1929; March 12–22, 1930 **Verdicts:** 1: Not guilty; 2: Guilty; 3: Guilty; 4: Not guilty; 5: Not guilty; 6: Not guilty; 7: Guilty; 8: Not guilty **Sentences:** Three months imprisonment and $500 fine: trial 2; Sinclair, six months, Day, four months, Sherman Burns, $1,000, William Burns, 15 days: trial 3; One year and $100,000: trial 7

SIGNIFICANCE

Teapot Dome in the "roaring twenties" was the largest scandal in the U.S. government since the administration of President Ulysses S. Grant. It became a permanent symbol of corruption in government. It marked the first time in U.S. history that an officer in a president's cabinet was convicted of a felony and served a prison sentence.

Oil for the U.S. Navy mixed with the greed of men in power to produce the Teapot Dome trials. American naval ships had been converted from coal to oil power before World War I. In 1909, President William Howard Taft had reserved public lands containing oil as Naval Petroleum Reserves in case of war. One such area, in Wyoming, was called Teapot Dome.

Civilian use of oil was expanding rapidly. Throughout President Woodrow Wilson's Democratic administration (1913–20), freshly made multimillionaire oil barons tried unsuccessfully to obtain leases from the government to drill the naval reserves, arguing that valuable oil was draining into private fields nearby. Finally, in 1920, Congress gave the Navy secretary broad powers to lease naval reserves, selling oil or exchanging it for supplies or construction the Navy needed.

Shortly, Republican candidate Warren G. Harding was elected president. Assembling his cabinet, Harding appointed his friend Albert Bacon Fall, with whom he had served in the U.S. Senate, as secretary of the interior.

Fall Owed Eight Years' Back Taxes

Fall had been elected as New Mexico's first senator when that state entered the Union in 1912. Born in 1861, he was a self-educated lawyer who had worked as a cowboy and prospector and, with drooping handlebar moustache and constant cigar, looked the part. He even toted a gun in the Senate. But now he owed eight years' taxes on his rundown ranch at Three Rivers, New Mexico, and had recently sold his major interest in the *Albuquerque Journal* to raise cash. Nearly broke, he was ready to quit the Senate. He took the cabinet post without hesitation.

The word "conservation" was not in Fall's vocabulary. He believed the government's lands—particularly the Naval Petroleum Reserves—should be held by private interests. He revised an executive order giving the Navy control over the reserves so that leasing did not require the approval of the Navy secretary. Next he recommended that the Navy take any royalties on oil sold from leased reserves not in cash but in oil certificates, which could be used to pay for construction done for the Navy.

By early 1922, Fall, playing on fear of drainage of the oil fields, was urging the Navy to develop Teapot Dome, build a pipeline to storage tanks on the Atlantic coast, and build storage tanks at Pearl Harbor in the Pacific. As Pacific builder, he proposed oilman Edward L. Doheny, who had prospected with him in 1886, leased profitable oil lands in California (Doheny brought in the first gusher in Los Angeles), and was currently worth $100 million.

Meantime, Harry F. Sinclair, head of the Sinclair Consolidated Oil Corporation, who had oil holdings worth $380 million, invited himself to visit Fall at his ranch. They talked about Sinclair's Mammoth Oil Company (he owned all the stock) obtaining a lease on the entire 9,481-acre Teapot Dome naval reserve.

In Washington, without competitive bidding, Fall signed the lease and locked it in his desk drawer. It gave Mammoth Oil exclusive rights to Teapot Dome oil for 20 years, with the government getting a royalty of 16 to 17 percent of the price per barrel, paid in oil certificates, which were to be used to buy fuel oil and storage tanks from Mammoth.

Word of the contract leaked. Neighbors observed sudden prosperity at Fall's ranch: A race horse and fine cattle arrived; Fall paid $100,000 to buy the ranch next-door and built a $35,000 hydroelectric plant; he also paid taxes owed since 1912.

"Sluice-way for Ninety Percent of the Corruption"

The *Albuquerque Journal* began an expose in February 1922. By April, its publisher was forced to sell the *Journal* to a bank controlled by a Harding crony. Soon Senator Robert M. La Follette of Wisconsin, saying Fall's Interior Department was "the sluice-way for ninety percent of the corruption in government," demanded an investigation. Fall resigned.

Senate Public Lands Committee, which investigated the activities of the Secretary of the Interior, Albert Fall. (Courtesy, Library of Congress)

The Senate started hearings in October 1923, soon after President Harding's sudden death. Edward Doheny testified that Fall had not profited by his Navy contracts. But he had "loaned" Fall $100,000. To show for it, however, he could produce only a note from which the signature had been torn. Secretary of the Navy Edwin Denby admitted that the contract with Mammoth Oil was his responsibility and that, having had no part in its preparation, he had not sought the competitive bids required by law. Harry Sinclair, on the stand, stonewalled so the Senate learned nothing more.

"Everything Points to Sinclair"

Called before the committee, Fall relied on the Fifth Amendment's right to not incriminate himself. President Calvin Coolidge appointed Republican Owen J. Roberts and Democrat Atlee W. Pomerene as special counsel to prosecute the oil cases. "Everything about Fall's sudden wealth points to Sinclair as the source," said Roberts.

Investigation disclosed that Fall, who had earned $12,000 a year in the Senate, had recently spent $140,000 improving his ranch and that $230,500 in Liberty Bonds deposited in his accounts bore the serial numbers of bonds distributed earlier to Sinclair and to Colonel Robert W. Stewart, chairman of the Standard Oil Company of Indiana. Indictments followed.

In 1924, Roberts brought civil suits to cancel the government's leasing contracts with Doheny and Sinclair because they were obtained fraudulently. He won against Doheny, then lost against Sinclair but won on appeal as three U.S. Circuit Court of Appeals judges agreed that:

> A trail of deceit, falsehood, subterfuge, bad faith, and corruption, at times indistinct but nevertheless discernible, runs through the transaction incident to and surrounding the making of this lease.

With the contracts proved fraudulent, Roberts tried Fall and Doheny in November 1926 for criminal conspiracy to defraud the government. Defense lawyer Frank J. Hogan dramatically compared his clients' situation to the Crucifixion and invoked the ghost of President Harding "from his sacred tomb in Marion [Ohio]" as a character witness. Debating all night, the jury acquitted both men.

In March 1927, a one-day trial found Sinclair guilty of contempt of the Senate for refusing to answer committee questions. He was sentenced to three months in jail.

Now Fall and Sinclair were tried for conspiracy to defraud the government with the Teapot Dome lease. Sinclair brazenly put 12 William J. Burns detectives to work shadowing the 12 jurors, one of whom boasted that he expected to make $150,000 to $200,000 for deadlocking the case. Judge Frederick L. Siddons declared a mistrial, then put Sinclair, his export official, Henry Mason Day, and two Burnses (father and son) on trial for criminal contempt. All were found guilty. Sinclair's six-month sentence was the stiffest.

At the fourth trial—Fall and Sinclair for conspiracy to defraud the government—in April 1928, Fall was excused, as his doctors reported him dying. Sinclair admitted giving Liberty Bonds and cash to Fall. The jury confounded the prosecution by acquitting the oil baron.

Trial five, in May, charged Colonel Robert W. Stewart with contempt of the Senate. He had told its committee he did not know where the Liberty Bonds had come from and had not profited from the deal when he helped pass them on to Fall. But he had changed his story when he made a second committee appearance, recounting the bonds' history and revealing his share in the profits. The jury said, "Not guilty."

That trial produced trial six, charging Stewart with perjury as a result of his changed story in his second Senate testimony. The jury acquitted him. Meantime, in June 1929, the U.S. Supreme Court upheld Sinclair's conviction for jury tampering, sending him to prison.

Owen Roberts was special prosecutor in the Teapot Dome scandal. (Courtesy, National Archives)

October 1929 brought Fall to trial for accepting a bribe from Doheny. In a wheelchair, frail and gasping, he heard his defense lawyer, Frank Hogan, tell the judge he should be vindicated "before he passes into the Great Beyond." The jury said, "guilty," but recommended mercy. Judge William Hitz sentenced him to one year in jail and a $100,000 fine.

When Judge Hitz held Doheny's trial in March 1930 for giving Fall the bribe, a different jury heard the same basic evidence. But Hogan dramatized Doheny's patriotism in building Navy tanks and the elderly Fall's innocent backing of a longtime friend. The jury said, "Not guilty."

Fall appealed for a year. The District of Columbia Court of Appeals upheld his bribery conviction. The U.S. Supreme Court refused to hear the case. President Herbert Hoover turned down several petitions for a pardon. On July 18, 1931, Fall went by ambulance to prison in Santa Fe, New Mexico—the first cabinet officer ever convicted of a felony and imprisoned. Parole was denied in November, but he was released in May 1932. His $100,000 fine—unpaid—remained as a judgment against him (in case he acquired the money) until he "passed into the Great Beyond" 12 years later at age 83.

As a result of cancellation of the Teapot Dome lease, the Navy recovered more than $12 million from Sinclair. The Doheny cancellation brought back nearly $35 million. The Naval Petroleum Reserves were utilized extensively in World War II and have continued to generate money, through limited exploitation, for the government.

Edward Doheny died at 79 in 1935, Harry Sinclair at age 80 in 1956. Owen J. Roberts, who persisted in the Teapot Dome prosecutions through 6½ years (much of that time without remuneration), was appointed a justice of the U.S. Supreme Court by President Hoover in 1930 and retired in 1945 after a distinguished career. He died at the age of 80 in 1955.

—Bernard Ryan, Jr.

Suggestions for Further Reading

Daniels, Jonathan. *The Time Between the Wars: Armistice to Pearl Harbor*. Garden City N.Y.: Doubleday & Co., 1966.

Henry, Laurin L. *Presidential Transitions*. Washington: Brookings Institution, 1960.

Morrison, Samuel Eliot. *The Oxford History of the American People*. New York: Oxford University Press, 1965.

Russell, Francis. *The Shadow of Blooming Grove: Warren G. Harding in His Times*. New York: McGraw-Hill Book Co., 1968.

Werner, M.R. and John Starr. *Teapot Dome*. New York: Viking Press, 1959.

Wish, Harvey. *Contemporary America: The National Scene Since 1900*. New York: Harper & Brothers, 1945.

Ruth Snyder–Judd Gray Trial: 1927

Defendants: Ruth Snyder and Judd Gray   **Crime Charged:** Murder
Chief Defense Lawyers: For Ruth Snyder: Edgar F. Hazleton and Dana
Wallace; For Judd Gray: Samuel L. Miller and William J. Millard
Chief Prosecutor: Richard E. Newcombe   **Judge:** Townsend Scudder
Place: Long Island City, Queens, New York
Dates of Trial: April 27–May 9, 1927   **Verdict:** Guilty   **Sentence:** Death
by electrocution

SIGNIFICANCE

In a macabre way, the verdict and sentence in Ruth Snyder's case was a
milestone in progress toward equality of the sexes. As a *New York Times* editorial
summed it up after Governor Al Smith denied clemency to Ruth Snyder: "Equal
suffrage has put women in a new position. If they are equal with men before the
law, they must pay the same penalties as men for transgressing it." It was also
significant that the two defendants, each of whom had confessed and tried to shift
the burden of guilt to the other, were tried together, so that each was cross-
examined by the other as well as by the State—a procedure labeled "novel and
dangerous" by Ruth Snyder's attorney.

Nine-year-old Lorraine Snyder slept late on Sunday morning, March 20, 1927.
She had gone to bed at 1:45 A.M. when she came home with her parents
from a bridge party. Long after her usual 7:30 rising time, she was awakened by
her mother, whom she found lying on the floor, her feet tied together, and her
wrists tied. Her mother said burglars had knocked her out and tied her up,
leaving her in the next room. After coming to, she had wriggled into Lorraine's
room. Lorraine's father was dead.

The police found Albert Snyder in bed, smelling of chloroform. His head
was bludgeoned, and picture wire was tied around his neck. The house had been
ransacked. Bureau drawers were empty, their contents strewn everywhere. And
Ruth Snyder claimed jewelry was missing. The house had already been robbed
three times in the past year.

"It Don't Look Right"

Within two hours, New York City's best detectives were on the job in the Snyders' fashionable home, which 44-year-old Albert Snyder, art director of *Motor Boating* magazine, had bought in the Queens suburb for his 32-year-old wife. The cops exhausted Ruth Snyder, questioning her through the day and into the night. When they told her the burglary was a fake, she indignantly replied, "What do you mean? How can you tell?"

"It don't look right," said a detective. "We see lots of burglaries. They aren't done this way."

The police explained. Mrs. Snyder said she had been hit on the head by "a tall man with a dark mustache" and knocked out for five hours, but she had no bruise or bump. Her wrists and ankles had been tied so loosely they bore no marks. Neither doors nor windows had been forced, so any intruder must have been let in. The missing jewelry had been found, under a mattress. Albert Snyder's revolver had been found on his bed, broken open at the breach but not discharged—a clumsy effort, the detectives said, to make it look as if he had resisted. And in the basement they had found a sash weight that was evidently the murder weapon.

"What About Judd Gray?"

The police did not disclose to Ruth Snyder the fact that they had found a small pin with the initials "J.G." on the bedroom floor. In Ruth Snyder's address book was an entry under "G" for the name Judd Gray. The investigators questioned her: "What about Judd Gray?"

Surprised, Ruth Snyder asked, "Has he confessed?" Bluffing, the police replied that he had, prompting Ruth Snyder's confession. For a year and a half, she and Gray had been lovers. Gray, she said, wanted her husband dead. Gray had hidden in the house while they were at the bridge party, then emerged from a closet to bludgeon Albert Snyder after he had fallen asleep. Ruth admitted she had helped to make the arrangements and ransack the house, but she said Gray had wielded the sash weight. The police later found Gray in the Syracuse, New York hotel she named.

When the Syracuse police arrested him, Gray first laughed at the accusation. "Ridiculous," he said. He had ample proof that he had been in Syracuse on Saturday night. But when he realized that Ruth Snyder had confessed, he admitted taking part in the crime. He said, however, that *he* had not wanted to kill Albert Snyder. Gray claimed he had been coerced by his lover, who threatened to tell Gray's wife about their affair.

By Tuesday, the front pages boasted pictures of Gray and Ruth Snyder, along with the full text of both their confessions. But while both had confessed, each said the other had proposed the murder. Queens District Attorney Richard Newcombe therefore obtained their indictment together as co-conspirators.

While Lorraine Was in the Elevators

The testimony—and the newspapers that eagerly reported it—brought out the inherent drama of a situation that had culminated in a crime: The older, gloomy, ill-tempered and dull husband whose idea of fun was staying home and making artistic doodads; the lively, young, party-loving, suburban housewife dutifully sewing slipcovers for the furniture and dresses for little Lorraine; the Mr.-Nice-Guy friend, a Sunday-school teacher, family man, traveling salesman for a corset-and-bra manufacturer, and member of the Orange, New Jersey, Lodge of Elks, who took an interest in Ruth and became her lover; the bribed postmen; the coded letters; the afternoon lovers' trysts at the Waldorf-Astoria, while little Lorraine was dispatched to the fun of riding up and down with the elevator operators. It all added up to the inevitable need, said prosecutor Newcombe, to get rid of Albert Snyder so Ruth Snyder and Gray could be together. But Ruth Snyder's motive was twofold: unbeknown to her husband, she had recently increased his life insurance to $100,000 and she was quietly paying the premiums.

Then, too, testimony brought out that Ruth Snyder had tried twice to asphyxiate her husband by disconnecting the gas range, had nearly succeeded in killing him with carbon monoxide by closing the garage door while the car was running inside, had poisoned his whiskey so ineptly that he dumped it out and said he must change bootleggers, and had added narcotics to his medicine when he was ill—all without Albert Snyder suspecting her.

An ironic footnote to the case was that the "J.G." pin had been a keepsake of Albert Snyder's from his long-ago engagement to one Jessie Guischard, who died before they could be married.

Judge Townsend Scudder said a jury's task, amid the conflicting stories of the confessors, was to decide who had done what. The judge reminded the jury that Gray testified Ruth Snyder "arranged the joint plan and jointly participated in the actual killing," while she testified that "Gray was determined to take the life of Albert Snyder and that she endeavored to prevent him from so doing and that she was not present at the time Gray struck the blows . . . and she testified

Ruth Snyder and Judd Gray confessed to murdering Snyder's husband and proceeded to shift the blame onto each other during this notorious trial. (AP/Wide World Photos)

she believed she had dissuaded the defendant Gray from his alleged evil purpose. . . ."

"Her Fault Is That She Has No Heart"

If the jury had much to ponder, so did the public. The tabloids were filled with colorful analyses of the characters of the defendants. The *Mirror* hired a well-known phrenologist (one who studies the conformation of the skull based on the belief that it is indicative of mental faculties and character) to study photos of Ruth Snyder. His conclusion: Her mouth was "as cold, hard, and unsympathetic as a crack in a dried lemon." Natacha Rambova, a reporter best known as Rudolph Valentino's widow, wrote, "There is lacking in her character that real thing, selflessness. She apparently doesn't possess it and never will. Her fault is that she has no heart."

In one hour and 40 minutes, the jury decided to accept Gray's version: He had struck the first blow with the sash weight, Albert Snyder had groaned and turned, and Ruth Snyder had finished him off with blows of her own, after which they together applied the strangling wire and added chloroform-soaked cotton for good measure. Both were found guilty and sentenced to death in the electric chair at Sing Sing prison.

Appeals were filed. One sought a stay of execution on the grounds that Ruth Snyder was a necessary witness in a civil suit to force three insurance companies to pay the benefits of Albert Snyder's life insurance to his daughter Lorraine. Another appeal sought a writ of *habeas corpus* (release from unlawful confinement) for Gray on the grounds that his constitutional rights had been violated by the joint trial rather than a trial of his own. Both appeals were dismissed.

Ruth Snyder went to the electric chair at 11:00 P.M. January 12, 1928. She was the eighth woman put to death for murder in New York State. As the power surged through her body, a *Daily News* photographer in the reporters' pool crossed his legs, thus triggering a forbidden concealed camera to take an unprecedented picture. When Judd Gray was executed six minutes later, no one took a snapshot.

—Bernard Ryan, Jr.

Suggestions for Further Reading

Jones, Ann. "She Had to Die." *American Heritage*, (October/November 1980): 20–31.

Sann, Paul. *The Lawless Decade.* New York: Crown Publishers, 1957.

Sifakis, Carl. *The Encyclopedia of American Crime.* New York: Facts On File, 1982.

Buck v. Bell: 1927

Plaintiff: Carrie Buck   **Defendant:** Dr. J.H. Bell   **Appellant's Claim:** That Virginia's eugenic sterilization law violated Carrie Buck's constitutional rights
Chief Defense Lawyer: Aubrey E. Strode
Chief Lawyer for Appellant: Irving Whitehead   **Justices:** Louis D. Brandeis, Pierce Butler, Willis Van Devanter, Oliver Wendell Holmes, James C. McReynolds, Edward T. Sanford, Harlan F. Stone, George Sutherland and William N. Taft   **Place:** Washington, D.C.   **Date of Decision:** May 2, 1927
Decision: Upheld as constitutional Virginia's compulsory sterilization of young women considered "unfit [to] continue their kind"

SIGNIFICANCE

Virginia's law served as a model for similar laws in 30 states, under which 50,000 U.S. citizens were sterilized without their consent. During the Nuremberg war trials, Nazi lawyers cited *Buck v. Bell* as acceptable precedent for the sterilization of 2 million people in its "Rassenhygiene" (race hygiene) program.

The Supreme Court's decision in *Buck v. Bell* resulted in only one letter of sympathy to the soon-to-be sterilized Carrie Buck and surprisingly little newspaper coverage. Oliver Wendell Holmes, who wrote the decision, had no second thoughts. As he wrote in a letter later that month, "One decision . . . gave me pleasure, establishing the constitutionality of a law permitting the sterilization of imbeciles." The decision had far-reaching and disastrous consequences, however, not only for Carrie Buck—who was not "feebleminded" or retarded— but for many other similarly sterilized individuals and the peoples involved in World War II.

Emma Buck was the widowed mother of three small children, whom she supported through prostitution and with the help of charity until they were removed from her. On April 1, 1920, she was brought before Charlottesville, Virginia Justice of the Peace Charles D. Shackleford; after a cursory interview, Shackleford committed Emma Buck to the Virginia Colony for Epileptics and Feebleminded, in Lynchburg, Virginia.

At the age of three, Emma Buck's daughter Carrie had joined the family of J.T. and Alice Dobbs. Her school records indicate a normal progression through five years, until she was withdrawn from school by the Dobbs so that she could assume more of the family's housework. The Dobbs were completely satisfied until Carrie turned 17. Then, during what Carrie claimed was a rape by the Dobbs' son, she became pregnant.

The Dobbs brought Carrie before Shackleford and asked him to commit her to the Colony for the Epileptic and Feebleminded, as he had her mother. The Dobbs and their family doctor testified that Carrie was feebleminded; a second doctor agreed. That same day, January 24, 1924, Shackleford signed the order committing the second member of the Buck family to the state colony. The Dobbs institutionalized Carrie as soon as her daughter Vivian was born; they then raised the infant as their own.

The 1927 Court upheld what Oliver Wendell Holmes later referred to as "the law permitting the sterilization of imbeciles." (Courtesy, Library of Congress)

Virginia Approaches its Courts with a "Solution"

Dr. Albert Priddy, the first superintendent of the colony, advocated eugenics—the controlled mating of humans to "improve" the species—as society's best response to the presence of those he called "mental defectives." In the seven years prior to Carrie Buck's arrival, he had sterilized 75 to 100 young women without their consent, claiming that he had operated to cure "pelvic disease." In 1924 the Virginia Assembly adopted a bill permitting the forced sterilization of "feebleminded" or "socially inadequate person[s]." It had been prepared by Aubrey Strode, a state legislator and chief administrator of the Colony for the Epileptic and Feebleminded. Strode had worked from a model

343

sterilization act drafted by American eugenicist Harry H. Laughlin, who considered compulsory sterilization to be "the practical application of those fundamental biological and social principles which determine the racial endowments and the racial health—physical, mental, and spiritual—of future generations."

Carrie Buck as a Test Case

On November 19, 1924, *Buck v. Priddy* was argued before Judge Bennett Gordon in the Circuit Court of Amherst County. Aubrey Strode represented Dr. Priddy, who had come to have Buck declared feebleminded and suitable for compulsory sterilization. Irving Whitehead, a lifelong friend to Strode and one of the first board members of the colony, represented Buck in a manner that seems to have been halfhearted. Whitehead's fee was paid by the colony.

Anne Harris, a Charlottesville district nurse, was the first witness. She testified that "Emma Buck, Carrie Buck's mother . . . was living in the worst neighborhoods, and that she was not able to, or would not, work and support her children, and that they were on the streets more or less."

Strode asked, "What about the character of her offspring?"

Harris replied, "Well, I don't know anything very definite about the children, except they don't seem to be able to do any more than their mother."

Strode pounced. "Well, that is the crux of the matter. Are they mentally normal children?"

And Harris responded, "No, sir, they are not."

Harris then admitted during Whitehead's cross examination: "I really know very little about Carrie after she left her mother [at age 3]. Before that time she was most too small."

Three teachers testified about Carrie's sister, brother, and cousin, using descriptions such as "dull in her books." There was additional testimony about several of Carrie's other relatives, one of whom was described as "right peculiar." The testimony did not relate to Carrie herself until Caroline Wilhelm—a Red Cross social worker contacted by the Dobbs family during Carrie's pregnancy, took the stand.

Strode asked Wilhelm, "From your experience as a social worker, if Carrie were discharged from the Colony still capable of child-bearing, is she likely to become the parent of deficient offspring?"

Wilhelm replied, "I should judge so. I think a girl of her mentality is more or less at the mercy of other people. . . . Her mother had three illegitimate children, and I should say that Carrie would be very likely to have illegitimate children."

Strode concluded, "So that the only way that she could likely be kept from increasing her own kind would be by either segregation or something that would stop her power to propagate."

Wilhelm next testified about Carrie's daughter, Vivian "It seems difficult to judge probabilities of child as young as that [eight months], but it seems to me not quite a normal baby."

Whitehead, on cross-examination, raised what should have been a pivotal point: "[T]he question of pregnancy is not evidence of feeblemindedness, is it? The fact that, as we say, she made a miss-step [*sic*]—went wrong—is that evidence of feeblemindedness?"

Wilhelm replied, "No, but a feebleminded girl is much more likely to go wrong."

Arthur Estabrook of the Carnegie Institute of Washington testified, discussing his 14 years of genetic research and his studies of "groups of mental defectives." Of his conclusions in *The Jukes in 1915*, a study of one family over four years, he said, "The result of the study was to show that certain definite laws of heredity were being shown by the family, in that the feeblemindedness was being inherited . . . and . . . was the basis of the antisocial conduct, showing up in the criminality and the pauperism."

Spode asked, "From what you know of Carrie Buck, would you say that by the laws of heredity she is a feebleminded person and the probably potential parent of socially inadequate offspring likewise afflicted?"

And Estabrook replied, "I would."

Dr. Priddy testified last. Carrie Buck, he said, "would cease to be a charge on society if sterilized. It would remove one potential source of the incalculable number of descendants who would be feebleminded. She would contribute to the raising of the general mental average and standard [by not reproducing]."

And, finally, Harry H. Laughlin's deposition was read into the court record. Dr. Priddy had written Laughlin, describing Carrie and asking for Laughlin's help in enforcing the sterilization law against her. The information contained in Dr. Priddy's own letter forms the basis of Laughlin's sworn testimony: Carrie, he wrote, has "a mental age of nine years, . . . a record during her life of immorality, prostitution, and untruthfulness; has never been self-sustaining; has one illegitimate child, now about six months old and supposed to be mentally defective. . . . She is . . . a potential parent of socially inadequate or defective offspring." There is no evidence that Carrie Buck was examined by Laughlin.

In February 1925, Judge Gordon upheld the Virginia sterilization law and ordered the sterilization of Carrie Buck. Irving Whitehead appealed to the Virginia Court of Appeals. (The case was now *Buck v. Bell* because Dr. Priddy had died a few weeks earlier and Dr. J.H. Bell had taken his place at the colony.) The appeals court decision upheld the circuit court decision.

Supreme Court Reviews Case

In the brief he submitted to the Supreme Court, Whitehead claimed Fourteenth Amendment protection of a person's "full bodily integrity." He also predicated the "worst kind of tyranny" if there were no "limits of the power of the state (which, in the end, is nothing more than the faction in control of the government) to rid itself of those citizens deemed undesirable." Strode, in contrast, likened compulsory sterilization to compulsory vaccination.

Justice Oliver Wendell Holmes delivered the nearly unanimous opinion on May 2, 1927:

> We have seen more than once that the public welfare may call upon the best citizens for their lives. It would be strange if it could not call upon those who already sap the strength of the state for these lesser sacrifices, often not felt to be such by those concerned, in order to prevent our being swamped with incompetence. It is better for all the world, if instead of waiting to execute offspring for crime, or to let them starve for their imbecility, society can prevent those who are manifestly unfit from continuing their kind. The principle that sustains compulsory vaccination is broad enough to cover cutting the Fallopian tubes.

Only Justice Pierce Butler dissented. Carrie Buck was sterilized by Dr. Bell on October 19, 1927. Shortly thereafter, she was paroled from the Virginia colony. She married twice: William Davis Eagle in 1932 and, after his death, Charlie Detamore. The letters she wrote to the Virginia colony seeking custody of her mother, as well as the recollections of her own minister, neighbors and health care providers, belie the notion that Carrie Buck was "feebleminded" or retarded.

Other Applications Result from *Buck v. Bell*

Laws similar to the Virginia statutes were passed in 30 other states, leading to the forcible sterilization of more than 50,000 people, including Carrie Buck's sister Doris.

Harry L. Laughlin, author of the model sterilization act adapted by Aubrey Strode for Virginia, made his draft available to state and foreign governments, and his model became Germany's Hereditary Health Law in 1933. In appreciation, he was awarded an honorary degree from Heidelberg University in 1936. After World War II, defending the forcible sterilization of 2 million people, lawyers for Nazi war criminals cited this law and pointed out that the U. S. Supreme Court, in *Buck v. Bell*, had declared such laws constitutional.

Buck v. Bell has yet to be reversed by the Supreme Court. In 1973, *Roe v. Wade* guaranteed women the right to make their own decisions concerning abortion during the first two trimesters of pregnancy. The decision, written by Justice Harry Blackmun, balances the interests of the state and the woman and finds in favor of the woman's right of privacy. Nonetheless, citing *Buck v. Bell*, Justice Blackmun specifically denies "the claim . . . that one has an unlimited right to do with one's body as one pleases."

—*Kathryn Cullen-DuPont*

Suggestions for Further Reading

Cushman, Robert F. *Cases in Constitutional Law*, 6th ed. Englewood Cliffs, N.J.: Prentice Hall, 1984.

Smith, J. David and K. Ray Nelson. *The Sterilization of Carrie Buck: Was She Feebleminded or Society's Pawn.* Far Hills, N.J.: New Horizon Press, 1989.

Alexander Pantages Trials: 1929

Defendant: Alexander Pantages **Crime Charged:** Rape
Chief Defense Lawyers: Earl M. Daniels, W. J. Ford, Jerry Giiesler, and
W. I. Gilbert **Chief Prosecutors:** Burton Fitts, and Robert P. Stewart
Judge: Charles Fricke **Place:** Los Angeles, California
Dates of Trials: First trial: October 4–27, 1929; Second trial:
November 3–27, 1931 **Verdict:** First trial: Guilty; Second trial: Not guilty
Sentence: First trial: 50 years imprisonment

SIGNIFICANCE

The Alexander Pantages case marked a turning point in California law as the
state's Supreme Court ruled on appeal that, where rape was alleged, if the girl
was under 18, evidence of her previous sexual activity was admissible to discredit
her testimony that she had been criminally attacked. The case also established a
national reputation for defense attorney Jerry Giesler, who went on to handle
many Hollywood cases.

By 1929, 54-year-old Alexander Pantages, a Greek immigrant who had never
learned to read or write any language, had put together a chain of 60
vaudeville-and-movie palaces across the western half of the United States.
Those in the know thought him worth $30 million.

On August 9, 17-year-old Eunice Irene Pringle, a well-trained dancer
hoping to book her act on the Pantages circuit, appeared at Pantages' Los
Angeles, California office, insisting, despite several previous turn-downs, on an
interview with "Alexander the Great," as he was known in Hollywood. Reluctantly, he agreed and showed her into his private office on the mezzanine level
of his theater.

Shortly, matinee moviegoers saw Eunice Pringle, her clothing disarranged,
running into the street, screaming that she had been raped. Within days, a
preliminary hearing produced an indictment and the press made Pantages the
nation's best-known "wealthy old goat" in a sordid scandal.

Pantages' defense was that the young woman had thrown herself at him
like a tigress, tearing at his shirt, suspenders, and trousers, and screaming at him.
It had taken all his strength to push the athletic young dancer from his office.

As the trial began, Hollywood law partners W.J. Ford and W.I. Gilbert asked bright junior attorney Jerry Giesler to cross-examine. He led Pringle back and forth through her story several times. Then he asked, "Did your studies in dramatic school include a course in memory training?"

"Yes."

"Were you taught to express your emotions dramatically?"

"Yes."

Giesler's thought, he said later, was that although Miss Pringle had told her pitiful tale several times to the press and to the law, she had scarcely varied a comma each time. . . . "I pointed out that her story seemed rehearsed as only a girl who was studying acting would have rehearsed it."

Schoolgirl versus "Slinky"

Next, Giesler asked Pantages' accuser, "Is that the dress you were wearing the day you say you were attacked?"

"No."

Eunice Pringle was dressed like a 13-year-old schoolgirl: blue dress, Dutch collar and cuffs, black stockings and Mary Jane shoes, small black bag and black gloves, long hair down her back and tied with a bow.

Giesler asked Judge Charles Fricke to order her to dress the next day in the same outfit and makeup she had worn to the Pantages Theatre. The jurors then saw not a schoolgirl but a well-endowed young woman in a revealing and (to use Giesler's word) "slinky" scarlet dress. Now his cross-examination tried to explore earlier acts of unchastity on her part—including a live-in affair with 40-year-old Nick Dunave, a Russian dancer. But the judge sustained the prosecution's objections and cut off the line of questioning.

The jury found "The Great God Pan" guilty. His sentence: 50 years in state prison. On appeal to the California Supreme Court, Giesler filed a three-volume, 1,200-page brief citing hundreds of cases and authorities. It pointed out that the lower court had erred in not permitting testimony on the earlier immoral conduct of the complaining witness. "There were so many new elements in that brief," Giesler later said, "that the final decision established precedent throughout the nation."

The state supreme court granted Pantages a new trial. Admitting evidence of Eunice Pringle's private life and conduct, it marked the first time in which the defense could probe the morals of an underage girl who claimed that she was criminally attacked.

Giesler even implied a conspiracy to frame Pantages. The jury found him not guilty. On her deathbed many years later, Pringle alleged that her boyfriend, Nick Dunave, had received a big payment from Joseph P. Kennedy, who had been determined to gain control over movie distribution.

In recent years, the trend in both federal and state courts has been to rule inadmissible evidence concerning the alleged victim's past sexual behavior in rape cases. Such evidence was barred from federal courts by Congress in 1978 (Rule of Evidence 412).

—Bernard Ryan, Jr.

Suggestions for Further Reading

Giesler, Jerry, as told to Pete Martin. *The Jerry Giesler Story.* New York: Simon & Schuster, 1960.

Nash, Jay Robert. *Encyclopedia of World Crime.* Wilmette, Ill.: CrimeBooks, 1990.

The Scottsboro Trials: 1931–37

Defendants: Olin Montgomery, Clarence Norris, Haywood Patterson, Ozie Powell, Willie Roberson, Charles Weems, Eugene Williams, Andy Wright, and Roy Wright **Crime Charged:** Rape **Chief Defense Lawyers:** Joseph Brodsky, George W. Chamlee, Samuel S. Leibowitz, Milo Moody, Stephen R. Roddy, and Clarence Watts **Chief Prosecutors:** H. G. Bailey, Melvin Hutson, Thomas G. Knight, Jr., Thomas Lawson, and Wade Wright **Judges:** Alfred E. Hawkins, James Edwin Horton, Jr., and William Washington Callahan **Places:** Scottsboro, Alabama; Decatur, Alabama **Dates of Trials:** April 6–9, 1931; March 27–April 9, 1933; November 20–December 6, 1933; January 20–24, 1936; July 12–24, 1937 **Verdicts:** All but Roy Wright: Guilty; Roy Wright: Mistrial **Sentences:** Death by electrocution, later reduced

SIGNIFICANCE

No one knows how many cases like Scottsboro occurred in Southern states before this one—with its large number of defendants, their youth, their brief and almost cursory trials and severe sentences—demanded national attention. The trials, and their appeals, gave America lessons in the procedures of Southern courts, the opportunism of American communists, the prejudice in the South, and the hypocrisy among Southern whites.

O n a March morning in 1931, seven bedraggled white youths appeared in a railroad station master's office in northern Alabama and announced that, while riding as hobos, they had been thrown off a freight train by a "bunch of Negroes" who picked a fight. The station master phoned ahead and, near Scottsboro, a deputy sheriff deputized every man who owned a gun. When the train stopped, the posse rounded up nine black boys and two white girls—the latter dressed in men's caps and overalls.

While the white girls chatted with townspeople, the deputy sheriff tied the blacks together and quizzed them. Five were from Georgia. At 20, Charlie Weems was the eldest. Clarence Norris was 19, Ozie Powell, 16. Olin Montgomery, 17, looked "sleepy-eyed," for he was blind in one eye and had only 10 percent vision in the other. Willie Roberson, 17, suffering from syphilis and gonorrhea, walked unsteadily with a cane. Four were from Chattanooga, Tennessee. Haywood Patterson and Andy Wright were 19. Eugene Williams was 13. And Wright's brother Roy was 12.

When the deputy sheriff had loaded his prisoners onto an open truck, one of the girls, Ruby Bates, from Huntsville, Alabama, told him that she and her friend Victoria Price had been raped by the nine blacks.

In Scottsboro, the sheriff sent the women off to be examined by two doctors. Meantime, word of the rape charge spread through Jackson County. By nightfall, a mob of several hundred, promising to lynch the prisoners, stood before the little jail. The sheriff, barricaded with 21 deputies, phoned the governor. But by the time 25 National Guardsmen arrived, the mob had cooled down and most people had drifted away.

As the trial began on April 6, 1931, 102 guardsmen held a crowd of several thousand at a distance of 100 feet from the courthouse.

Ready to appoint defense counsel, Judge Alfred E. Hawkins offered the job to any lawyer in the county who would take it. He accepted Chattanooga attorney Stephen R. Roddy, who admitted he didn't know Alabama law, when local attorney Milo Moody offered to help. Roddy, who had a jail record for drunkenness, was already inebriated at 9:00 A.M.

Circuit Solicitor H.G. Bailey tried Weems and Norris first. Victoria Price described how she and Ruby Bates had hopped freight trains to Chattanooga to look for jobs and, finding none, were returning when the black boys, after throwing the whites off the train, turned on them. She described how she was "beaten up" and "bruised up" by rape after rape, then "lost consciousness" and next found herself on her way to the jail in Scottsboro.

Dr. R.R. Bridges testified he saw no evidence of violence when he examined the girls. Victoria Price, he said, "was not lacerated at all. She was not bloody, neither was the other girl." A second doctor agreed that while both girls showed evidence of recent sexual intercourse, the semen found was "non-motile," or inactive, whereas semen is normally viable for 12 to 48 hours.

By Thursday afternoon, all defendants except 12-year-old Roy Wright had been found guilty. Because of his age, the state had asked for life imprisonment for him, but the jury was deadlocked—seven jurors insisted on death. The judge declared a mistrial for Roy Wright and sentenced the eight others to electrocution.

"Legal Lynching . . . Victims of 'Capitalist Justice'"

Liberals and radicals nationwide reacted. The Central Committee of the Communist Party of the United States called the sentences "legal lynching" of "the victims of 'capitalist justice.'" Its International Labor Defense (ILD) wing pushed the National Association for the Advancement of Colored People (NAACP) to cooperate on taking the case to the U.S. Supreme Court. In Harlem, 300,000 blacks and whites marched to the slogan "the Scottsboro Boys Shall Not Die."

The ILD hired prominent Chattanooga attorney George W. Chamlee. Requesting a new trial, he and the ILD's chief lawyer, Joseph Brodsky, produced affidavits from Chattanooga blacks stating that they had seen Victoria Price "embracing Negro men in dances in Negro houses," that Ruby Bates had bragged that she could "take five Negroes in one night," that a boarding-house operator had let Victoria use a room for prostitution, that she turned down a white man one night because it was "Negro night." The local press denounced the statements as slander, but a Huntsville detective confirmed that the girls were prostitutes.

Defendant Haywood Patterson, holding a horseshoe, with defense attorney Samuel Leibowitz. (Courtesy, Library of Congress)

"You Can't Mix Politics with Law"

The motion for a new trial was denied. The defendants switched allegiance constantly from the NAACP to the ILD and back again. Prominent attorney Clarence Darrow declined the NAACP's request that he steer the case through the Supreme Court. "You can't mix politics with law," he said, adding that the cases would have to be won in Alabama, "not in Russia or New York." The NAACP then withdrew its support.

In March, the Alabama Supreme Court upheld the convictions of all except Eugene Williams; as a juvenile, he was granted a new trial.

In November, the U.S. Supreme Court ruled that the seven boys had been denied "due process" under the Fourteenth Amendment when Judge Hawkins treated the appointment of defense counsel so casually.

As the state ordered a new trial, the ILD turned to Samuel Leibowitz, a noted criminal lawyer in New York. He argued successfully for a change of venue to Decatur, Alabama, where townspeople welcomed the reporters, and Western Union brought in extra operators.

Haywood Patterson was tried first. Leibowitz produced several revelations: Ruby Bates recanted, saying she and Price had invented the rape story to avoid arrest for vagrancy (but she damaged her credibility by testifying in smart "New York clothes" bought for her by the ILD during a trip they provided to the big city); the boys had been seized from several points all over the 42-car train; Willie Roberson's painful, raging syphilis made him incapable of sexual activity; Olin Montgomery's blindness was equally limiting; and Victoria Price, who was married, had served time for adultery and fornication.

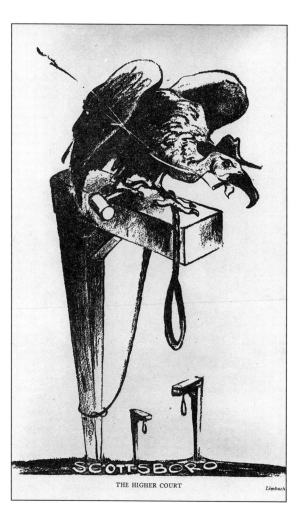

SCOTTSBORO

THE HIGHER COURT

Limbach

A poignant cartoon from the Scottsboro trials. (Courtesy, Library of Congress)

After Dr. Bridges repeated his testimony that the girls had not been raped, the second doctor—Marvin Lynch—spoke privately with Judge James Edward Horton during a recess. "I told the women they were lying, that they knew they had not been raped," said the doctor, "and they just laughed at me." But, he added, if he testified for the boys, "I'd never be able to go back into Jackson County." The judge, believing the defense would prove Patterson's innocence, said nothing.

Defense attorney Leibowitz himself now lived with National Guard protection against threats of lynching. County Solicitor Wade Wright added to the incendiary atmosphere: "Show them," he told the jury, "that Alabama justice cannot be bought and sold with Jew money from New York."

The jury found Patterson guilty. The sentence: death. When the defense filed a motion for a new trial, Judge Horton reviewed the medical testimony about the women, the lack of physical evidence of sexual activity on the part of the boys, and the unreliable testimony of Victoria Price and Ruby Bates. He set aside the jury's judgment and ordered a new trial. Then, under pressure from Attorney General Thomas Knight and the chief justice, he withdrew from the case.

"No More Picture Snappin' Around Here"

Opening the new trial, Judge William Washington Callahan, 70, dismissed the National Guard. Declaring, "There ain't going to be no more picture snappin' around here," he banned cameras inside or outside the courtroom. He dismissed Leibowitz's motion to quash the indictment because blacks had been systematically excluded from the jury lists—despite testimony by a handwriting expert that names had been fraudulently added to the jury book to make it appear that blacks were listed. He ran a 12-hour day in the courtroom. He destroyed Leibowitz's defense plan by refusing to permit testimony on Victoria Price's sexual activity during the two nights before the train ride. And when he made his charge to the jury, he told them any intercourse between a black man and a white woman was rape, but he omitted—until Leibowitz darted up to the bench and reminded him—the instructions on how to render an acquittal.

Again Patterson was found guilty and the sentence was death. Clarence Norris was next found guilty. But now Leibowitz faced an unexpected challenge: Two ILD lawyers were caught trying to bribe Victoria Price, who had hinted that money could help her change her story. Brodsky told Leibowitz the changed story would have been "good propaganda for the cause." Furious, Leibowitz announced he would withdraw "unless all Communists are removed from the defense." Brodsky capitulated.

Now the U.S. Supreme Court overturned the convictions on the evidence of exclusion of blacks from jury duty. Alabama Governor Bibb Graves responded, "We must put the names of Negroes in jury boxes in every county."

In November 1935, a grand jury of 13 whites and one black brought new indictments. At the fourth trial, in January 1936, Patterson was again found guilty, with the sentence this time 75 years' imprisonment. "I'd rather die," he said.

The next trial was delayed until July 1937. Then Clarence Norris was found guilty and sentenced to death, followed by Andy Wright (99 years) and Charlie Weems (75 years). The rape charge against Ozie Powell was dropped when he pleaded guilty to stabbing a deputy sheriff (during a jail transfer) and received 20 years. Abruptly, prosecutor Thomas Lawson, who had succeeded Knight, proposed *nol pros*, or dropping of charges, for Olin Montgomery, Roy Wright, Willie Roberson, and Eugene Williams. The Scottsboro trials were over.

"All Were Guilty or All Should Be Free"

The U.S. Supreme Court refused to review Patterson's conviction. Alabama Governor Bibb Graves listened to a clemency appeal and agreed that "all were guilty or all should be freed." He officially set a date to pardon all four, then reneged. While Graves said he changed his mind after personally interviewing the Scottsboro boys, those close to the governor said he realized public opinion had not changed and simply got cold feet.

Weems was freed in November 1943, Andy Wright and Clarence Norris in January 1944—but Wright and Norris broke parole by moving north and were sent back to prison. Wright was paroled again in 1950. Patterson escaped from prison in 1948 and was arrested in Detroit, but Michigan Governor G. Mennen Williams refused to sign extradition papers; later convicted of manslaughter, Patterson died of cancer in prison in 1952. Norris, the last surviving Scottsboro boy, was pardoned at age 64 by Alabama Governor George C. Wallace in 1976.

Victoria Price worked in a Huntsville cotton mill until it closed in 1938, then moved to nearby Flintsville, Tennessee. Ruby Bates toured briefly as an ILD speaker, then worked in a New York state spinning factory until 1938, when she returned to Huntsville. Both women died in 1961.

—Bernard Ryan, Jr.

Suggestions for Further Reading

Carter, Dan T. *Scottsboro: A Tragedy of the American South.* Baton Rouge: Louisiana State University Press, 1969.

Chalmers, Allan Knight. *They Shall Be Free.* Garden City, N.Y.: Doubleday & Co., 1951.

Crenshaw, Files and Kenneth A. Miller. *Scottsboro: The Firebrand of Communism.* Montgomery, Ala.: Brown Printing Co., 1936.

Hays, Arthur Garfield. *Trial by Prejudice.* New York: Covici, Friede Publishers, 1933.

Jordan, J. Glenn. *The Unpublished Inside Story of the Infamous Scottsboro Case.* Huntsville, Ala.: White Printing Co., 1932.

Nash, Jay Robert. *Encyclopedia of World Crime.* Wilmette, Ill.: CrimeBooks, Inc., 1990.

Patterson, Haywood. *Scottsboro Boy.* Garden City, N.Y.: Doubleday & Co., 1950.

Reynolds, Quentin. *Courtroom* (biography of Samuel Liebowitz). New York: Farrar, Straus and Cudahy, 1950.

Al Capone Trial: 1931

Defendant: Alphonse "Scarface Al" Capone   **Crime Charged:** Income tax evasion   **Chief Defense Lawyers:** Michael J. Ahern and Thomas D. Nash   **Chief Prosecutor:** George E. Q. Johnson   **Judge:** James H. Wilkerson   **Place:** Chicago, Illinois   **Dates of Trial:** October 6–24, 1931   **Verdict:** First indictment (tax liability for 1924): Not guilty; second indictment (22 counts): Guilty on five counts (tax liability for 1925, '26, '27, '28, and '29); third indictment (violation of Volstead Act): Indictment not pursued   **Sentence:** 11 years' imprisonment, $50,000 in fines, $30,000 in court costs

SIGNIFICANCE

While for 10 years the Chicago police had been unable, if not unwilling, to put the most notorious and murderous of mobsters behind bars, the federal authorities found a way to jail him: through the tax laws. Thus the head of the country's most powerful syndicate providing Americans with bootleg liquor, gambling and prostitution wound up in Alcatraz.

A Brooklyn boy who quit school in the sixth grade after beating up his teacher and getting beaten up by the principal, Al Capone earned the nickname "Scarface Al" as a teenager when his face was severely slashed in a fight. At 21, he moved to Chicago to help his uncle—the city's most powerful brothel keeper—broaden his business to include control of bootlegging. By 1925, at age 26, Capone was running an organization of 1,000 racketeers with a $300,000 weekly payroll.

By eliminating his competition (he ordered 500 deaths, while an estimated 1,000 people died on both sides in his bootleg wars), Capone built a vast network of liquor distributorship, distilleries, breweries, and brothels. To maintain control, he paid off countless politicians and police. At the same time, he made certain all his accomplices were absolutely trustworthy—a key factor in ensuring his safety. So successful was Capone that when a rival gang sent a string of cars filled with machine-gunners to pump a thousand rounds into Capone's headquarters, he remained unscathed.

The St. Valentine's Day Massacre

On St. Valentine's Day, 1929, Capone ordered his men to kill "Bugs" Moran, head of the gang that had machine-gunned the Capone headquarters. Masquerading as police officers, Capone's men massacred seven opponents in a downtown warehouse. The people of Chicago were outraged.

Colonel Frank Knox, publisher of the *Chicago Daily News*, asked newly inaugurated President Herbert Hoover for help. Reportedly, Hoover told Secretary of the Treasury Andrew Mellon, "I want that man in jail."

Federal authorities held jurisdiction over Capone's activities in only two areas: violation of the Volstead Act (i.e., Prohibition) and evasion of income taxes. The problem was proving either case: Capone had never maintained a bank account; he owned no property under his own name; he endorsed no checks; he paid cash for whatever he bought.

Nevertheless, the Internal Revenue Service sent Special Agent Frank J. Wilson to Chicago to analyze Capone's net worth and net expenditures. Over two years, Wilson compiled a list of Capone's purchases, which included custom-made suits, telephone bills, town cars and limousines, a house on Palm Island, Miami, Florida, with two new docks, a boathouse, and an extra garage.

To connect Al Capone with brothels, gambling, and bootlegging, Wilson moved Special Agent Michael F. Malone, who could be taken for an Italian, Jew, or Greek, into Capone's inner circle.

Malone supplied Wilson with inside information. But getting witnesses would not be easy because, as Wilson wrote in a memo:

> . . . all important witnesses were either hostile and ready to give perjured testimony to protect the leaders of their organization or were so filled with fear of the Capone organization . . . that they evaded, lied, left town and did all in their power to prevent the government using them as witnesses. . . . To serve them with subpoenas it was necessary to pick them up on the streets near the Capone headquarters, at Cicero hotels and at nightclubs.

Malone identified a potential witness in the Smoke Shop manager who had quarreled with Capone. Though the manager talked very little, he implied that *Chicago Tribune* reporter Jake Lingle, who knew more about Chicago's gangland than any other reporter, might have information about Capone. Colonel Robert R. McCormick, the publisher, set up a confidential meeting in the Tribune Building. On his way to it, Lingle was murdered.

By 1931, IRS agent Wilson, who had been living with round-the-clock guards after learning that Capone had brought five New York gunmen to Chicago with a contract to kill Wilson, was ready for the grand jury. It returned three indictments: the first for failure to pay 1924 income taxes; the second (with 22 counts) for not paying 1925 through 1929 taxes; the third (based on information compiled by agent Eliot Ness, citing 5,000 specific offenses) for conspiring to violate the Volstead Act. The last was reserved as an ace in the hole.

"Impossible to Bargain with a Federal Court"

If found guilty on every count, Capone would face a maximum sentence of 34 years. His lawyers negotiated with U.S. Attorney George Johnson, who, considering how tough it would be to get key witnesses to testify, agreed to 2½ years in exchange for a guilty plea. With good behavior, the time would be short. But an angry Judge James Wilkerson said, "It is time for somebody to impress upon the defendant that it is utterly impossible to bargain with a Federal court." Capone then pleaded not guilty.

Prosecutor Johnson produced witnesses who proved Capone's ownership of the extremely profitable Smoke Shop, which had brought in more than $550,000 in two years and had picked up telegrammed money orders for Capone. A parade of witnesses including decorators, contractors, jewelers, butchers, bakers, brokers who had bought his Palm Beach house and boat for him, and tailors who had sold him pea-green and mustard-brown suits, provided ample evidence of Capone's expenditures.

Capone's defense was gambling losses: He almost never won. The argument was specious, for a taxpayer must have gambling winnings to deduct gambling losses. Defense attorney Michael Ahern, without calling Capone to the stand, concluded, "The evidence in this case shows only one thing against Capone—that he was a spendthrift."

Al Capone and attorneys in a Chicago courtroom. (Courtesy, Illinois State Historical Library)

The jury found Al Capone not guilty of tax evasion in 1924, but guilty on the counts for 1925 through 1927, and guilty of failing to file returns for 1928 and 1929. He was found not guilty on 17 remaining counts of tax evasion.

Judge Wilkerson imposed sentences totaling 11 years on the various counts, with fines of $50,000 and court costs of $30,000—the strongest penalties on a tax evader to that date. Capone was put in Cook County Jail, where he had a private cell with shower, freely made phone calls and sent telegrams, and entertained visiting gangsters "Lucky" Luciano and "Dutch" Schultz.

Shortly, however, Capone was moved to Atlanta, Georgia, then to the brand-new maximum-security prison on the island of Alcatraz in San Francisco Bay, California, where he enjoyed not one special privilege. By 1938 he was hospitalized with advanced syphilis. Treatment slowed but could not stop the disease. On his release in 1939, partially paralyzed, he settled in his Miami

Beach home, where his wife and son had been waiting. There, fat and balding and haunted by imaginary killers, he lived until 1947.

—Bernard Ryan, Jr.

Suggestions for Further Reading

Kobler, John. *Capone: The Life and World of Al Capone.* New York: G.P. Putnam's Sons, 1971.

Murray, George. *The Legacy of Al Capone.* New York: G.P. Putnam's Sons, 1975.

Olson, James S. *Historical Dictionary of the 1920s.* New York: Greenwood Press, 1988.

Sifakis, Carl. *The Encyclopedia of American Crime.* New York: Facts On File, 1982.

Thomas Massie Trial: 1932

Defendants: Grace Fortescue, Albert O. Jones, Edward J. Lord, and Thomas
H. Massie   **Crime Charged:** Murder   **Chief Defense Lawyers:** Clarence
Darrow, George S. Leisure, Lieutenant L.H.C. Johnson, U.S.N., Frank
Thompson, and Montgomery Winn   **Chief Prosecutors:** John C. Kelley and
Barry S. Ulrich   **Judge:** Charles S. Davis   **Place:** Honolulu, Hawaii
Dates of Trial: April 4–29, 1932   **Verdict:** Guilty, second-degree murder
Sentences: 10 years imprisonment at hard labor, commuted to one hour in
the dock

SIGNIFICANCE

The Thomas Massie trial provides a footnote to history as the last appearance of
world-famous lawyer Clarence Darrow in a headline-making case. It provides a
penetrating glimpse into the relationship between U.S. personnel stationed in the
Hawaiian Territory before World War II and the island's natives and other
"foreigners." And it proves that it is possible for murderers sentenced to 10 years
to go free after serving only one hour.

In Honolulu, Hawaii, on September 12, 1931, 31-year-old Navy Lieutenant
Thomas H. Massie and his 21-year-old wife, Thalia, attended a Saturday
night party. Bored with her husband's boisterous U.S. Naval Academy classmates, Thalia took a stroll outdoors. Missing her toward midnight, Tom phoned
home. Thalia answered: "Come home at once. Something terrible has happened."

Tom Massie found his wife hysterical, her face bleeding and bruised. She
had been seized on the roadside by several natives, she said, driven to an
abandoned animal quarantine station, punched in the jaw when she resisted,
raped by five men of mixed race, and abandoned. She had flagged down a car
whose driver had taken her home.

Tom Massie called the police. Together they took Thalia Massie to the
hospital. Medical examination disclosed that her jaw was broken but did not
produce conclusive evidence of rape. After examination and treatment, they
went to police headquarters. There Thalia Massie suddenly remembered the
license number of the car used by her assailants—a number only one digit
different from one described earlier in the hospital's busy emergency room in

another incident. Soon the police brought in Horace Ida, who admitted that he and four friends had had an altercation with another woman that night but denied assaulting Thalia Massie. The other four—David Takai, Henry Chang, Joe Kahahawai, and Benny Ahakuelo—were equally adamant. Thalia Massie identified Kahahawai, a well-known prizefighter who had a criminal record, as the assailant who broke her jaw.

Mother-in-Law Takes Charge

A cable from Tom Massie to the mainland brought Thalia Massie's mother, Grace (Mrs. Granville) Fortescue, a domineering woman accustomed to issuing orders from her high position in the social register. She immediately took charge. While Hawaii was abuzz with doubt that Horace Ida and his friends were indeed the assailants, and with equal doubt whether rape had indeed occurred, Fortescue had no doubt. She pushed the Naval commandant, Rear Admiral Yates Stirling, to increase the Navy's already strong pressure on the authorities to prosecute the suspects.

Clarence Darrow came out of semiretirement to defend Thomas Massie. (*Harper's Weekly*)

Their trial lasted three weeks. The jury then deliberated for 97 hours but failed to reach agreement. Fortescue demanded that the defendants be held without bail for the new trial. The judge was not empowered to hold them, but he ordered them to report to the courthouse daily.

Impatient and headstrong, Grace Fortescue decided to kidnap Kahahawai and force a confession. When he reported at the courthouse on the morning of January 9, he was intercepted by Navy enlisted man Albert O. Jones, who had a fake summons prepared by Fortescue and told him that "Major Ross" of the Territorial Police wanted him. Jones and enlisted man Edward J. Lord, both of whom were Navy boxers, hustled Kahahawai into a rented car driven by Massie, who was disguised as a chauffeur.

When Kahahawai missed his courthouse appearance, the police suspected the Massies. The rented car was spotted, stopped, and searched. In it were Massie, Fortescue, sailor Lord, and, on the floor of the back seat, the body of Kahahawai, who had been shot with a .32-caliber gun. Sailor Jones, drunk, was shortly found at Fortescue's rented house.

All four were charged with murder and imprisoned aboard the decommissioned U.S.S. *Alton* in Pearl Harbor. All Navy personnel were confined to base. The native population was treated as if the rape of white women were typical behavior. Demonstrations and riots among mainland whites, island natives, and Asians broke out time and again.

Fortescue's friends advised enlisting the best legal mind from the mainland. That meant Clarence Darrow, America's most famous trial lawyer. Now 75, Darrow had been in semiretirement four years. Much of his reputation had been built on his understanding of racial minorities and on his many court fights on behalf of the National Association for the Advancement of Colored People, or NAACP. When Fortescue's friends approached him, he turned them down, writing:

> I learned that one who tried this case could scarcely avoid discussing race conflict. I had so long and decidedly fought for the Negro and all so-called "foreigners" that I could not put myself in a position where I might be compelled to take a position, even in a case, at variance with what I had felt and stood for.

Darrow's retirement savings had been severely depleted by the Great Depression. When Grace Fortescue sent word that he would have complete control of defense strategy, he changed his mind. His own friends then charged him with "selling out" to reactionaries. The lurid stories in the American press about Naval officers and socialites who took the law into their own hands had led them to believe that Tom Massie and Grace Fortescue were not the typical underdogs whom Darrow had always defended.

The trial opened on April 4, 1932. For a week, prosecutor John C. Kelley detailed the events that led to Kahahawai's death. He did not try to show who fired the shot that killed the prizefighter, however, as under Hawaiian law all four were considered equally guilty of homicide.

In the packed courtroom, Darrow launched the defense by putting Massie on the stand to describe the assault on his wife. Kelley objected: Massie's account could be relevant only if the defense planned to prove insanity. That, said Darrow, was the aim. Kelley asked which defendant was insane. Darrow said, "The one who shot the pistol," but he did not identify that one.

As tears flowed throughout the courtroom, Darrow took Tom Massie painfully through the kidnapping to the point where he remembered grilling Kahahawai in Fortescue's house while holding a .32-caliber automatic pistol provided by Jones. Kahahawai, he remembered, admitted after lengthy questioning that he and his friends had raped and beaten Thalia Massie. Then, asked Darrow, "Do you remember what you did?"

"No, sir."

"Do you know what became of the gun?"

"No, I do not, Mr. Darrow."

"Do you know what became of you?"

"No, sir."

Darrow introduced two psychiatrists who testified that, while Massie was now sane, he had been insane at the time of the kidnapping. One described his condition as "chemical insanity" brought on by changes in body chemistry resulting from the strain of the event.

"Is This Your Handwriting?"

Darrow called Thalia Massie. She sobbed through her description of the kidnapping and Jones' telling her of Kahahawai's death. The courtroom was awash in tears. Then, cross-examining, Kelley handed her a sheet of paper—a psychological self-analysis she had made while a student at the University of Hawaii—while asking, "Is this your handwriting?"

Instantly, Thalia Massie was transformed from a pathetic mass of tears to an indignant blaze of fury. "Where did you get this? Don't you know this is a confidential communication between doctor and patient?" She tore the paper into tiny bits. "I refuse to say whether that is my handwriting or not. What right have you to bring this into a public court?" To a burst of applause, she tossed the fragments aside.

"Thank you, Mrs. Massie," said Kelley. "At last you've shown yourself in your true colors."

Said Darrow to reporters afterward, "I've seen some pretty good court scenes but nothing like that one. I was pretty limp when it was all over."

It took the jury nearly 50 hours to find the four defendants guilty of manslaughter. Judge Charles S. Davis sentenced each to 10 years at hard labor. Governor Lawrence Judd then said he would grant executive clemency if the Massies and Fortescue would agree not to press for a retrial of the rape case, for the governor was determined to end the racial disturbances throughout Hawaii caused by the issue. The prosecutors agreed. Darrow got Thalia Massie to agree. The governor commuted the sentences to one hour in the courtroom dock.

Massie's naval career was destroyed by the trial. He died at 44 in 1944, 10 years after he and Thalia Massie were divorced. Thalia Massie died in 1963 after years of depression and several attempted suicides. Her mother had died years earlier.

Clarence Darrow had worked all his life toward reducing tension and conflict between races. While he lost the Massie trial in terms of the jury verdict, he was pleased to have accepted a jury of mixed races and to have avoided racial overtones in the testimony despite his clients' attitudes.

He died in 1938 without ever again handling a headline-making trial.

—Bernard Ryan, Jr.

Suggestions for Further Reading

Nash, Jay Robert. *Encyclopedia of World Crime.* Wilmette, Ill.: CrimeBooks, 1991.

Tierney, Kevin. *Darrow: A Biography.* New York: Thomas Y. Crowell, Publishers, 1979.

Weinberg, Arthur and Lila Weinberg. *Clarence Darrow: A Sentimental Rebel.* New York: G.P. Putnam's Sons, 1980.

Joseph Zangara Trial: 1933

Defendant: Joseph Zangara **Crime Charged:** Murder
Chief Defense Lawyers: James M. McCaskill, Alfred A. Raia, and Lewis
Twyman **Chief Prosecutor:** Charles A. Morehead **Judge:** Uly O.
Thompson **Place:** Miami, Florida **Date of Trial:** March 9, 1933
Verdict: Guilty **Sentence:** Death by electrocution

SIGNIFICANCE

Joseph Zangara's failed attempt to assassinate U.S. President-elect Franklin D.
Roosevelt demonstrated how the frustrations of financial misfortune in the Great
Depression could lead to desperate and mindless acts of violence.

Early in 1933, Joseph Zangara, a bricklayer who was out of work, bummed rides from Hackensack, New Jersey, to Florida in hope of finding warm weather and a job. A self-proclaimed anarchist, he carried a revolver, probably as much to protect his diminutive 5-foot frame as to protest the system.

On February 15, Franklin D. Roosevelt arrived in Miami, scheduled to make a major speech at a rally of Democrats. In November, he had won an unprecedented victory over incumbent President Herbert Hoover as the country, hoping for a savior from the economic devastation of the Great Depression, responded to his personal charm and the concern for "the forgotten man" that he had expressed in one campaign speech after another. His inauguration was set for March 4.

Huge crowds turned out to welcome Roosevelt as he rode in an open car in the official motorcade from the railroad station to his hotel. One of his escorts, seated directly behind him and Eleanor Roosevelt, was Anton J. Cermak, the mayor of Chicago, who had helped to deliver FDR's landslide vote.

At one point, the car stopped in the midst of the surging crowd. As he often did because of his relative immobility (the result of his attack of polio, or "infantile paralysis," in 1921), Roosevelt stayed in the car to deliver a short speech. Then the crowd pressed forward, eager to shake his hand. With his usual wide grin and buoyant enthusiasm, he welcomed them.

"Too Many People Starving to Death"

Amidst the tide of people pressing toward the car came Joseph Zangara. Suddenly he was eight feet away, swinging his gun toward the president-elect, shouting, "There are too many people starving to death." As he emptied his revolver, a woman seized his arm. Two shots hit Mayor Cermak. Others scattered widely, wounding four spectators.

The crowd crushed Zangara to the ground, kicking and pounding him. When the police seized him moments later, he was already bloody. Roosevelt, barely glancing at the would-be assassin, turned to help the mayor. "He was the calmest person present," said a witness. Twice, as the car moved from the fray, he had it stopped so he could help make the wounded mayor more comfortable. The whole event was Roosevelt's first national demonstration of his daring lack of fear or concern for his personal safety.

With Mayor Cermak and the wounded spectators in the hospital, Zangara was immediately tried for assault with a deadly weapon, convicted, and sentenced February 21 to 80 years in prison.

On March 6, the mayor died of his wounds. Blaming the murder of Cermak on "that woman who got in the way," Zangara said he was sorry that Cermak had died but that he had fully intended to kill the president-elect.

Dade County Solicitor Charles Morehead, who had been standing by with an indictment for murder ready, brought Zangara to trial on March 9. He pleaded guilty and was condemned to death. A few days before his execution on March 20, he told a newsman he had always hated Roosevelt. "If I got out," he said, "I would kill him at once." He sat down in the electric chair without remorse.

—Bernard Ryan, Jr.

Suggestions for Further Reading

Gunther, John. *Roosevelt in Retrospect*. New York: Harper & Brothers, 1950.

Hurd, Charles. *When the New Deal Was Young and Gay*. New York: Hawthorn Books, 1965.

Nash, Jay Robert. *Almanac of World Crime*. Garden City, N. Y.: Anchor Press/Doubleday & Co., 1981.

——. *Encyclopedia of World Crime*. Wilmette, Ill.: CrimeBooks, 1991.

"Roosevelt, Franklin D." *Encyclopedia Americana*, Vol. XXIII. New York: Americana Corp., 1953.

Ulysses Trial: 1933

Defendant: One Book Entitled *Ulysses* by James Joyce
Crime Charged: Obscenity   **Chief Defense Lawyers:** Morris L. Ernst and
Alexander Lindey   **Chief Prosecutors:** Nicholas Atlas, Samuel C. Coleman,
and Martin Conboy   **Judge:** John M. Woolsey   **Place:** New York, New York
Date of Trial: November 25–26, 1933   **Verdict:** The book was ruled not
obscene

SIGNIFICANCE

Judge John Woolsey's decision in the *Ulysses* case marked a notable change in
the policies of the courts and legislative bodies of the United States toward
obscenity. Before this decision, it was universally agreed that: a) laws prohibiting
obscenity were not in conflict with the First Amendment of the U.S. Constitution
and b) the U.S. Post Office and the U.S. Customs Service held the power to
determine obscenity. *Ulysses* became the major turning point in reducing government prohibition of obscenity.

Friends of James Joyce had warned him that *Ulysses* would run into trouble
with American postal and customs officials. As early as 1919 and 1920, when
the *Little Review* serialized some of the book, the U. S. Post Office confiscated
three issues of the magazine and burned them. The publishers were convicted
of publishing obscene material, fined $50 each, and nearly sent to prison.

After that decision, several American and British publishers backed off
from considering publishing the book in its entirety. Joyce, visiting his friend
Sylvia Beach's Parisian bookstore, Shakespeare and Company, despaired of
finding a publisher. Beach then asked if Shakespeare and Company might "have
the honor" of bringing out the book. Thus *Ulysses* was first published in 1922 in
Paris and instantly became an object of smuggling pride and a valuable collector's item when successfully transported past British and American customs
agents. By 1928, the U.S. Customs Court officially listed *Ulysses* among obscene
books to be kept from the hands and eyes of American readers.

Meantime, such literary figures as T.S. Eliot, Virginia Woolf, and Ezra
Pound had acclaimed the Joyce work as already a classic. In Paris, Bennett Cerf,
who with Donald S. Klopfer had successfully put the Random House publishing

firm on its feet by establishing the Modern Library, told Joyce he would publish the book if its publication could be legalized.

Two Percent for Life

Cerf engaged Morris L. Ernst, America's leading lawyer in obscenity cases. Ernst's fee, contingent on winning the case, was a five percent royalty on the first 10,000 published copies, then two percent for life on all subsequent printings.

Ernst and his associate, Alexander Lindey, carefully planned their strategy. Early in 1932, they had a copy of the book mailed across the sea, expecting Customs to seize it. It arrived untouched.

"So we had a friend bring a copy in," wrote Klopfer many years later, "and we went down to the dock to welcome him! The Customs man saw the book and didn't want to do anything about it, but we insisted and got his superior over, and finally they took the book and wouldn't allow us to bring it into the U. S. because it was both obscene and sacrilegious." That copy was sent by Customs to the U. S. attorney for libel proceedings. One meaning of the word "libel" is "the publication of blasphemous, treasonable, seditious, or obscene writings or pictures."

Ernst then got the U. S. attorney to agree to have the issue tried before a single judge—thus avoiding the potential pitfalls of a jury trial.

Finally, Ernst managed to keep postponing the case until it came before one particular judge: John M. Woolsey. The judge was known to Ernst as a cultivated gentleman who wrote elegant decisions and who loved old books and antique furniture.

The judge further postponed hearing the case to give himself time to read *Ulysses* and other books that had been written about it. But at last, on November 25, in a jam-packed small hearing room that seated fewer than 50 people, the hearing began. One of the prosecuting attorneys turned to Morris Ernst. "The government can't win this case," he said. Ernst asked why. "The only way to win," said the prosecutor, "is to refer to the great number of vulgar four-letter words used by Joyce. But I can't do it." Why not, asked Ernst.

"Because there is a lady in the courtroom."

"But that's my wife," said Ernst. "She's a schoolteacher. She's seen all these words on toilet walls or scribbled on sidewalks by kids who enjoy them because of their being taboo."

The government's case against Joyce's book made two distinct objections. First was the use of four-letter words not mentionable in polite company. Ernst set out to prove that standards of obscenity change, and that by the standards of 1933, Joyce's choice of words did not make the work obscene. To help make his point, Ernst traced the etymologies of a number of four-letter words. Of one particularly abhorrent word, he said, "Your Honor, it's got more honesty than phrases that modern authors use to connote the same experience."

"For example, Mr. Ernst?"

"Oh—'they slept together.' It means the same thing."

"That isn't usually even the truth," said Judge Woolsey.

At that moment, Ernst later remarked, he knew "the case was half won."

The second objection was to the frankness of the unconscious stream of thought that Joyce portrayed in such characters as Molly Bloom. This was (as Ernst later put it) Joyce's "dramatic incisive attempt to record those thoughts and desires which all mortals carry within themselves."

The judge asked Ernst if he had read through Joyce's entire book. "Yes, Judge," he replied. "I tried to read it in 1923 but could not get far into it. Last summer, I had to read it in preparation for this trial. And while lecturing in the Unitarian Church in Nantucket on the bank holiday . . . ."

"What has that to do with my question—have you read it?"

"While talking in that church I recalled after my lecture was finished that while I was thinking only about the banks and the banking laws I was in fact, at that same time, musing about the clock at the back of the church, the old woman in the front row, the tall shutters at the sides. Just as now, Judge, I have thought I was involved only in the defense of the book—I must admit at the same time I was thinking of the gold ring around your tie, the picture of George Washington behind your bench and the fact that your black judicial robe is slipping off your shoulders. This double stream of the mind is the contribution of *Ulysses*."

The judge rapped on the bench. "Now for the first time I appreciate the significance of this book. I have listened to you as intently as I know how. I am disturbed by the dream scenes at the end of the book, and still I must confess, that while listening to you I have been thinking at the same time about the Hepplewhite furniture behind you."

"Judge," said Ernst, "that's the book."

"His Locale Was Celtic and His Season Spring"

On December 6, Judge Woolsey delivered his opinion on *United States v. One Book Called Ulysses*:

I hold that *Ulysses* is a sincere and honest book, and I think that the criticisms of it are entirely disposed by its rationale. . . . The words which are criticized as dirty are old Saxon words known to almost all men, and, I venture, to many women, and are such words as would be naturally and habitually used, I believe, by the types of folk whose life, physical and mental, Joyce is seeking to describe. In respect of the recurrent emergence of the theme of sex in the minds of his characters, it must always be remembered that his locale was Celtic and his season Spring. . . .

I am quite aware that owing to some of its scenes *Ulysses* is a rather strong draught to ask some sensitive, though normal, persons to take. But my considered opinion, after long reflection, is that whilst in many places the effect of *Ulysses* on the reader undoubtedly is somewhat emetic, nowhere does it tend to be an aphrodisiac. *Ulysses* may, therefore, be admitted into the United States.

Ten minutes after the judge completed his statement, Random House had typesetters at work on *Ulysses*.

The government appealed Woolsey's decision to the Circuit Court of Appeals, where Judge Learned Hand and his cousin, Judge Augustus Hand, affirmed the judgment. Judge Martin Manton dissented.

—*Bernard Ryan, Jr.*

Suggestions for Further Reading

Esterow, Milton. "Perspective: United States of America v. One Book Called *Ulysses*." *Art News* (September 1990): 189–190.

Moscato, Michael and Leslie LeBlanc. *The United States of America v. One Book Entitled ULYSSES by James Joyce*. Frederick, MD: University Publications of America, 1984.

Oboler, Eli M. *The Fear of the Word: Censorship and Sex*. Metuchen, N.J.: Scarecrow Press, 1974.

The Obscenity Report (report to the President's Task Force on Pornography and Obscenity). New York: Stein and Day, 1970.

Berrett-Molway Trial: 1934

Defendants: Louis Berrett and Clement F. Molway **Crime Charged:** Murder
Chief Defense Lawyers: Charles W. Barrett, Charles E. Flynn, John P. Kane, and Frank Tomasello **Chief Prosecutors:** Hugh A. Cregg, Charles E. Green, and John S. Wilson **Judge:** Thomas J. Hammond **Place:** Salem, Massachusetts **Dates of Trial:** February 12–27, 1934 **Verdict:** Not guilty

SIGNIFICANCE
The Berrett-Molway trial is a classic case of mistaken identity. It proved that eight eyewitnesses who had been in close proximity to the "defendants" for two hours could all wrongly identify them, pushing them perilously close to the electric chair. The trial wiped out the jury foreman's firm belief in capital punishment.

Arriving home on Friday, January 5, 1934, Boston taxi driver Louis Berrett, 29, found a stranger in the hallway outside his apartment. The man grabbed him. Suddenly the hall was filled with strangers pointing guns at him and asking who he was. At gunpoint they backed Berrett into his kitchenette. Then one showed a police badge and Berrett recognized him. "I had seen him before," he said later. "A taxicab driver gets to know a lot of cops."

Next, the police wanted to know where Clement F. Molway was. Molway, 22, was a taxi-driver friend of Berrett. The police sought him, they said, in connection with a holdup. "I knew he was a good kid from a respectable family," said Berrett afterward. He told the cops they were crazy, that Molway "was never mixed up in any holdups," and that he would go to police headquarters with them if it would help Molway.

At headquarters, Berrett soon found himself and Molway booked. Next, handcuffed, they were driven to Lynn, Massachusetts, where the chief police inspector asked Berrett for a statement of where he had been from Sunday night to Wednesday night of the preceding week. Only after Berrett had signed a five-page statement that the chief wrote out did the chief tell him there had been a holdup and murder at the Paramount Theatre in Lynn on Tuesday morning. Berrett then insisted on writing a second statement, in his own handwriting, like the first. By the time he was locked in a cell, it was 3:00 A.M. on Saturday.

"Boys, You've Been Picked by Five People"

Morning brought more officials and more questions, while Berrett vainly asked to phone friends and the police laughed at him. Late Saturday afternoon, unwashed, unshaven, unfed, and having slept in their clothes on hard board "beds" in separate cells, Berrett and Molway found themselves in a lineup as strangers inspected them. "A girl picked me out," said Berrett later. "When she placed her hand on my shoulder, I all but passed out. I knew I had never seen her before in my life, but what could I do?"

After the lineup, the chief inspector said, "Boys, you've been picked by five people. We are changing the charge from suspicion of murder to murder."

On Sunday night, the police phoned lawyer Charles W. Barrett on Berrett's behalf, then told Berrett that Molway had cracked and "told everything." Berrett laughed at them and promised to "give them a true statement for Tuesday. When they came down, all excited, I gave them the same statement I had given them before. Gee, they were mad."

As the trial opened on Monday, February 12, the defendants challenged 19 prospective jurors to get a jury composed of laborers, mechanics, and machine operators, including a janitor, a clerk, a truck driver, and a foreman, who was made foreman of the jury. Engineers, businessmen, and professionals were excused.

In the courtroom, Berrett and Molway found themselves shackled together in a green wire cage. In front of them sat a deputy sheriff, his back to the courtroom, staring in the defendants' faces. Defense attorney Charles E. Flynn protested to the court that the prisoners' situation represented "the most prejudicial atmosphere possible" in an attempt "to impress the jury with the guilt of the defendants at the bar." Judge Thomas J. Hammond waited until the second day of the trial to have the deputy sheriff moved to the side of the prisoners' cage.

District Attorney Hugh A. Cregg opened with a description of the crime: how Berrett and Molway, with an unknown third man (named as "John Doe" in the indictment), carrying out a well-planned robbery in mid-morning at the Paramount Theatre, were interrupted by the arrival of the Paramount's bill poster, Charles F. Sumner. When Sumner turned to run, eyewitnesses would testify, he was shot down.

"That Rare Element in Murder Trials"

The state's first witness to identify Berrett and Molway was Michael Ford, a former soldier in the Irish Republican Army, who described how he was cleaning the Paramount lobby when the men came in. "Here," reported the *Boston Globe*, "was that rare element in murder trials, confident eyewitness testimony." After pointing out the defendants in the courtroom, Ford testified that upon arrival they asked for the Paramount's manager and assistant manager. When he said they wouldn't be in for two hours, the two pushed him at gunpoint into the office and warned him to make no noise. Next, they grabbed Harry Condon, an employee who came up from the basement. He broke away. "Molway said, 'Get him,'" testified Ford. "Then I saw Molway raise the gun and fire at Condon." Wounded, Condon was pushed into the office with Ford.

Next, said Ford, the men rounded up eight other Paramount employees who were in the building, tying them to chairs in the office. One was forced to phone the Paramount's manager and, on a ruse, hurry him to the office to open the safe.

"Head Him Off"

Then, testified Ford, Molway asked about two men he saw out in the parking lot. He was told they were bill posters. "We'll leave them there," said Molway. But presently Molway saw bill poster Sumner coming into the lobby. "Head him off," he ordered. Sumner was beaten with a gun butt, said Ford, then shot after he had been felled.

When assistant manager Stephen Bresnahan arrived, he was forced to open the safe. The robbers emptied it, took the manager's wallet (which contained $4), locked the 10 Paramount employees in a cloakroom, and departed.

Seven other eyewitnesses corroborated Ford's identification of Berrett and Molway as the robbers and murderers. One, Leo Donahue, pounded the rail of the witness box with his closed fist as he shouted, "I absolutely identify them as the men who held up the Paramount Theatre."

Prosecution and defense had rested and final arguments in the case were scheduled for Monday when defense attorney Flynn, in Judge Hammond's chambers, informed the court that the defense intended to show that the persons who committed the Lynn murder had committed similar holdups and murders recently in Needham and in Fitchburg, and had been convicted in Needham. The judge said he was not going to try the Needham and Fitchburg cases at this trial. Flynn pointed out that shells found at each site proved that a gun used at Lynn had been used earlier at Fitchburg.

Instead of final arguments, prosecutor Cregg asked the judge to reopen the evidence. Paramount Assistant Manager Bresnahan took the stand.

Question: Mr. Bresnahan, were you in Dedham with me today?

Answer: I was.

Question: There you were shown a defendant connected with the Needham holdup?

Answer: Yes, sir.

Question: You were shown certain statements and pictures?

Answer: Yes, sir.

Question: And as a result of what you were shown, you desire to make a statement to the jury?

Answer: I do. As a result of the pictures and statements shown me today at Dedham I feel sure that these two defendants were not at the theatre that morning.

Next, janitor Leo Donahue refuted in one minute the eyewitness testimony that, with pounding fists, he had taken nearly a full trial day to tell.

While he had taken all eight eyewitnesses to Dedham, Cregg spared the six others this moment of embarrassment. He moved for a directed verdict of not guilty. The defense made the same motion. The judge made notes for a full minute, then addressed the jury:

> It may surprise you, Mr. Foreman and jury, to learn that you have agreed
> upon your verdict. I instruct you now that as the names are read by the clerk
> you will return verdicts of not guilty.

"Not guilty," said each juror in turn. The judge then ordered the defendants released from their cage. As the taxi drivers rushed into the arms of families and friends, prosecutor Cregg released a full confession to the Lynn holdup and murder by one Abraham Faber, along with photographs of two members of his gang who could easily have been mistaken for Louis Berrett and Clement Molway.

—Bernard Ryan, Jr.

Suggestions for Further Reading

The Boston Globe. See Berrett, Louis, in *The Boston Globe* index, January 6–March 3, 1934.

Sifakis, Carl. *Encyclopedia of American Crime.* New York: Facts On File, 1982.

Gloria Vanderbilt Custody Trial: 1934

Defendant: Gertrude Vanderbilt Whitney (Mrs. Harry Payne Whitney)
Appellant: Gloria Morgan Vanderbilt (Mrs. Reginald Vanderbilt)
Appellant Claim: Custody of Gloria Laura Vanderbilt, a minor
Chief Defense Lawyer: Herbert C. Smyth
Chief Lawyer for Appellant: Nathan Burkan   **Judge:** John Francis Carew
Place: New York, New York   **Dates of Trial:** October 1–November 21, 1934
Decision: Custody awarded to Whitney

SIGNIFICANCE

The claim by her mother that Gloria Morgan Vanderbilt was unfit to have custody because of her debauched lifestyle and cold indifference to her child scandalized both society and the general public. Coming in the depths of the Great Depression, this custody battle within one of the nation's wealthiest families confirmed Americans' worst suspicions about the super-rich, while giving them two months' diversion from their own financial worries.

Gloria Laura Vanderbilt was 1 year old and her mother was 20 when her father, Reginald Vanderbilt, died at 45 in 1925. Cirrhosis of the liver, brought on by countless brandy milk punches, ended Reggie's dissipated life. By then, he had exhausted not only his own body but a $7.5-million fortune inherited at 21 and the income from a $5-million trust fund.

Once all Vanderbilt's creditors and taxes had been paid, his young widow, Gloria Morgan Vanderbilt, ended up with $130,000. But the principal in the $5-million trust fund remained to be shared between his baby daughter and her 21-year-old half-sister. Since the widow was still a minor, the fund was to be administered by New York Surrogate Court Judge James Aloysius Foley.

Shortly, little Gloria's mother petitioned the court for an allowance to cover "monthly expenses necessarily incurred for the maintenance and support of said infant and the maintenance of the home in which said infant resides." The court granted $4,000 per month.

With the allowance, Gloria Morgan Vanderbilt flitted from New York to Paris, London, Cannes, Hollywood, Monte Carlo, Biarritz, and Switzerland. She crossed the Atlantic as often as once a month. In her international set, the pace was led by the Prince of Wales, with whom Gloria's twin sister, Thelma, was having a five-year love affair (it ended when Thelma introduced her friend Wallis Warfield Simpson to the prince, who subsequently gave up the throne of England to marry the divorced Simpson).

Meanwhile, little Gloria was more than overprotected by her grandmother, Laura Kilpatrick Morgan, and by nurse Emma Keislich, who had not missed a day or night with the child since she was hired two weeks after her birth. Together the grandmother and the nurse grew to feel that little Gloria, neglected by a mother who came home intoxicated, toward dawn (if she came at all), was theirs.

"We Are Moving Again—Oh What a Life"

For almost a decade, little Gloria sometimes did not see her mother for months on end. At other times, she and nurse Keislich lived in Paris or London with her mother, who was also living with Gottfried Hohenlohe Langenburg, a destitute German prince and a great-grandson of Queen Victoria. Langenburg wanted to marry Gloria Morgan Vanderbilt, but Surrogate Judge Foley had ruled, "No part of the infant's income can be used to finance a second marriage." Little Gloria feared and hated the prince, who never spoke to her. She sent post cards from Europe to her grandmother Morgan declaring that "My mother is so bad to me I wish I could run away to New York to you," that "my mother was in Paris enjoying herself while poor me was unhappy in England [sic]," and "We are moving again oh what a life."

In June 1932, little Gloria's tonsils were removed in New York. Sailing yet again for Europe, her mother welcomed the suggestion of her sister-in-law, Gertrude Vanderbilt Whitney, that the 8-year-old recuperate over the summer at the Whitney home in Old Westbury, Long Island. That fall, the Whitney family doctor urged that she continue to live in Old Westbury. Her mother agreed. Surrogate Judge Foley, notified by Gertrude Whitney that her deceased brother's child was now living with her, cut Gloria Morgan Vanderbilt's allowance from $48,000 to $9,000 a year. Suddenly it dawned on the absent mother that, without little Gloria, she was practically a pauper.

Movie theatre magnate A. C. Blumenthal, Gloria's current lover, introduced her to lawyer Nathan Burkan. The attorney discovered that, since she was still a minor when husband Reggie Vanderbilt died, Gloria Vanderbilt had never been appointed guardian of her own child. He petitioned Surrogate Judge Foley to make her sole guardian. But a complainant appeared: Gloria Morgan Vanderbilt's mother, who said her daughter was unfit.

Lawyers and surrogate reached agreement: Little Gloria could live with Aunt Gertrude during the school year, and her mother could see her at any time. In September little Gloria went to New York City to visit with her mother. But when she arrived, Gloria Vanderbilt announced, "Little Gloria is not going back to Mrs. Whitney's."

The next morning, while her Aunt Gertrude, her Aunt Consuelo (sister of her mother) and her mother sipped sherry in the Whitney mansion, little Gloria was slipped out to the car by nurse Keislich and Gertrude Whitney's private maid. When her mother asked presently where her daughter was, Gertrude said, "Little Gloria is halfway to Westbury by now. I'm not going to let you have her."

In Old Westbury, little Gloria found guards posted throughout the house and the nurse or the maid always at her side. But that afternoon, Gertrude Vanderbilt Whitney was served court papers that commanded her to have "the body of Gloria Laura Morgan Vanderbilt by you imprisoned and detained" presented before Judge John F. Carew.

"Trial of the Century"

The opening of the trial in the "Matter of Vanderbilt" October 1, 1934, was jammed with more than 100 reporters, who dubbed it the "trial of the century," and with countless spectators. They heard nurse Keislich testify that she had seen Prince Langenburg and Mrs. Vanderbilt in bed together reading "vile" books. A chauffeur testified about Gloria Morgan Vanderbilt's several lovers. A French maid testified that she had found Lady Milford Haven at Mrs. Vanderbilt's bedside and "kissing her just like a lover." Judge Carew, who later admitted that until then he thought he had heard everything, immediately closed the courtroom to press and public.

Bedlam followed. The tabloids cried "Lesbianism." More refined papers reported Mrs. Vanderbilt's "alleged erotic interest in women." Women demonstrating outside the courthouse with placards declaring a mother's right to her child were perplexed. Meantime, testimony against Aunt Gertrude, an accomplished sculptress and founder of the Whitney Museum of Art, tried to establish her interest in the nude in art as an immoral influence on her niece.

The judge, baffled by more than five weeks of shocking public testimony, at last decided to take little Gloria, attorney Burkan, attorney Smyth, and the court stenographer into his chambers. Over 2½ hours, the stenographer recorded such questions and answers as:

How would you like to live with your mother down in the country?

No. Never. I always want to live with my aunt.

You lived a long while with your mother?

Yes, but I have hardly seen her. She has never been nice to me.

Don't you think you could learn to love her?

No. She never even kissed me good night.

On November 21, Gertrude Whitney was awarded custody of little Gloria. But the judge's decision stated that Gloria's mother could have her from Saturday morning to Sunday evening each week, for eight hours on Christmas day, and all the month of July. The *New York Journal American* summed it up:

Rockabye baby

Up on a writ,

Monday to Friday Mother's unfit.

As the week ends she rises in virtue;

Saturdays, Sundays,

Mother won't hurt you.

Little Gloria now spent quiet weekdays in Old Westbury, ignored by her Aunt Gertrude, who lost interest in her immediately after the trial, and without nurse Keislich, whom the judge had dismissed. On Saturday mornings, under guard, she traveled to her mother's suite in the Sherry-Netherland Hotel in Manhattan, where reporters mingled with detectives and curiosity-seekers to block her way and shout questions.

Lawyer Burkan tried to file an appeal to the New York State Court of Appeals. The court declined. Next, he asked the Supreme Court of the United States to review the case, on the grounds that little Gloria's constitutional rights had been violated. It, too, declined.

At 17, Gloria married Pasquale di Cicco, a Hollywood actors' agent. They divorced when, at 21, she came into her nearly $5-million estate. The next day, she married conductor Leopold Stokowski, who was 42 years older than she. The marriage produced two sons and a nervous breakdown for her, and after 10 years they parted, with Vanderbilt winning a custody fight that, ironically, awarded Stokowski permission to see the boys on weekends and for a month in the summer.

In 1956, Vanderbilt married film director Sidney Lumet. After their divorce in 1963, she married writer Wyatt Cooper, who died in 1978. They had two sons. Over the years, she had written poetry before turning to design, creating note cards, linens, china and chic blue jeans. The jeans brought her new wealth—a 3.5-percent royalty on $125 million in sales in 1979 alone—and new fame. In addition, Gloria Laura Morgan Vanderbilt di Cicco Stokowski Lumet Cooper has written two books in a projected five-volume autobiography.

— *Bernard Ryan, Jr.*

Gloria Morgan Vanderbilt, (right) and Gloria Laura Vanderbilt, (left) in a photograph of them taken after the court's decision to award custody of the child to Mrs. Whitney. (AP/Wide World Photos)

Suggestions for Further Reading

Clemons, Walter. "Poor Little Rich Girl." *Newsweek* (June 16, 1980): 43–44.

Goldsmith, Barbara. *Little Gloria . . . Happy At Last.* New York: Alfred A. Knopf, 1980.

Howard, Margo. "Gloria Vanderbilt." *People Weekly* (June 10, 1985): 122–131.

Langway, Lynn, Diane Weathers, and Lisa Whitman. "Sic Transit Gloria." *Newsweek* (June 16, 1980): 44–45.

Stasz, Clarice. *The Vanderbilt Women*. New York: St. Martin's Press, 1991.

Vanderbilt, Arthur II. *Fortune's Children*. New York: William Morrow & Co., Inc., 1989.

Vanderbilt, Gloria. *Black Knight, White Knight*. New York: Alfred A. Knopf, 1987.

——. *Once Upon A Time*. New York: Alfred A. Knopf, 1985.

Samuel Insull Trial: 1934

Defendants: Samuel Insull, Samuel Insull, Jr., Harold L. Stuart, and 13 others   **Crime Charged:** Use of the mails to defraud
Chief Defense Lawyers: Frederick Burnham, James J. Condon, Harry S. Ditchburne, William H. Haight, John J. Healy, Charles E. Lounsbury, J. Fred Reeve, and Floyd E. Thompson   **Chief Prosecutors:** Dwight H. Green and Leslie Salter   **Judge:** James H. Wilkerson   **Place:** Chicago, Illinois
Dates of Trial: October 2–November 24, 1934   **Verdict:** Not guilty

SIGNIFICANCE

Many people consider the Samuel Insull case to be the father of the Federal Securities and Exchange Act. The revelations of the trial produced immediate legislation to regulate the issuance of securities, control stock exchanges, and protect the unwary from holding companies. The trial gives insight into a time when a stock manipulator could build a pyramid of commercial wealth, making as much as a million dollars a week, at the expense of thousands of small investors doomed innocently to ruin.

Samuel Insull was a 21-year-old Englishman in 1881 when inventor Thomas Alva Edison brought him to America as his private secretary. Eleven years later, Insull was Edison's most trusted adviser, with discretion to handle all the inventor's financial matters.

In Schenectady, N.Y., the Edison General Electric Company was losing money. Edison dispatched Insull upstate: "Whatever you do, Sammy, make either a brilliant success of it or a brilliant failure. Just do something." Within a few years after Insull took charge, the company had grown from 200 employees to 6,000. Soon it was the well-established General Electric Company, or GE.

In 1892, Insull became president of Chicago Edison Company. He borrowed $250,000 from Marshall Field and began buying the independent electricity-generating plants that were proliferating in Chicago. By 1907, his Commonwealth Edison Company served the entire city, and investors had put in hundreds of millions of dollars.

Inventor of the "Power Pool"

Meantime, Insull acquired small electric companies in surrounding counties. Eventually his Public Service Company of Northern Illinois served half the state—some 6,000 square miles. Insull built the world's largest generating plants, with long transmission lines, reducing production costs and consumer rates and increasing efficiency and profits. A reliable "power pool," as he called it (it was entirely his idea), supplied the network covering all Chicago and northern and central Illinois.

By the 1920s, Insull had reorganized the near-bankrupt People's Gas Light & Coke Company (its stock rose from $20 to $400 a share). He controlled Chicago's elevated rail lines and its commuter trolleys. His utilities companies operated in 39 of the 48 states. The man was worth more than $100 million. To trusting investors, his name was magic.

In 1907, when Chicago banks refused to handle the unknown Commonwealth Edison Company securities, Insull had found Halsey, Stuart & Company. Over the years, the firm, headed by Harold L. Stuart, had sold more than 2 billion dollars of Insull properties stock.

Threatened with loss of control when the 1926–29 bull market saw new investment trusts buying up shares in his companies, Insull organized Insull Utility Investments, Inc. He and Halsey, Stuart would hold enough securities of the operating companies to keep him in command. The investment company's common stock opened at $30 a share, boomed to $147, then settled at $100.

Next, in September 1929, Insull created another investment company, Corporation Securities Company of Chicago. An offering circular was mailed to potential investors. Despite the "Black Friday" stock-market crash five days later, faith in Insull was so strong that within a year the public had bought $100 million of the new securities.

But the Great Depression steadily overpowered the Insull empire. By 1932, his holding companies were petitioning for bankruptcy. The operating companies—Commonwealth Edison, Peoples Gas, and Public Service of Northern Illinois—survived, with Insull still in charge. In June, however, he resigned, citing ill health and advanced age (he was 73). He and his wife sailed for Europe.

By September, word reached Insull in Paris: His affairs were under investigation. The Insulls moved to Greece, which had no treaty of extradition with the United States.

Accountants announced findings: Investors in Middle West Utilities had lost more than $700 million. Those in Corporation Securities had lost $85 million. Collateral had been "cross loaned" between the Insull companies. Favored creditors had been given preference. Millions in questionable brokerage fees had been taken from assets. Padded payrolls had included Insull's relatives and friends. Immense secret profits had been paid to as many as 1,600 favorites. They had bought 250,000 shares of Insull Utility Investments common stock at $12 before it opened at $30 and zoomed to $147; selling at only the opening price would have produced $4,500,000 in profits.

Arrested in Istanbul

A Cook County grand jury indicted Insull and his brother Martin for embezzlement from the Middle West Utilities Company and Mississippi Valley Utilities Investment Company. A federal grand jury indicted Insull and 16 others, including Samuel, Jr., who had joined his father's business in the 1920s, and Harold L. Stuart, for using the mails to defraud.

Insull disappeared. Congress passed a special bill allowing U.S. authorities to arrest him in any country where it had extraterritorial rights. Found aboard a ship bound for Egypt, he was arrested in Istanbul and returned under heavy guard to America.

U.S. Attorney Dwight H. Green's opening at the trial on October 2, 1934, charged that the defendants, through Utility Securities Company, fraudulently schemed to induce investors nationwide to buy the common stock of Corporation Securities Company at inflated prices. He also charged that Insull-controlled companies had maintained a fictitious market for the common stock, thus misleading prospects as to its value. To carry out the scheme, the defendants had used the mails to send circulars to those they intended to defraud.

"The Jewels of the Insull Empire"

Eighty witnesses identified books and records. Another 50 had been solicited and bought stock. As countless company names became blurs in jurors' minds, the big picture grew clear: The government was out to prove that Insull's success had been gained—repeatedly—by having one Insull electric company sell properties to another Insull electric company at a splendid profit, with the second company then selling to a third. The holding companies—the securities of which were proclaimed by a Halsey, Stuart salesman as "the jewels of the Insull empire"— and the investment companies had been created to expand the bubble . . . until the Depression deflated everything.

Samuel Insull: stock manipulator or scapegoat? (Courtesy, Illinois State Historical Library)

The specific charge against Samuel Insull and his cronies was that the circular mailed by Halsey, Stuart & Company inviting subscribers to buy stock in Corporation Securities was false and deceptive: The company, it said, would open with $80 million in assets, whereas it actually had only a bank loan of $3.5 million and 304,000 shares of Insull Utility Investments for which it had paid $7 million. And the circular failed to state that most of the stock the company intended to buy was common stock paying only a stock dividend, not cash.

Chief defense lawyer Floyd E. Thompson, a highly respected former Illinois Supreme Court justice, skillfully brought out his client's English training in business, his success with Thomas Edison and GE, the vast saving in the cost of electricity his "power pool" had generated, and his accumulation of utility companies to assure their continuing control and hold off government ownership.

Insull further testified that divisions of stock were in line with prevailing corporate practice, that stock dividends (rather than cash) were common and represented earnings plowed back to increase equity value. As to the offending circular, Insull said its statement of assets was based on completion of financing, entirely in accordance with market practice.

Next, Insull testified on the "buoyant" optimism of the financial community in March 1930, after the crash, and on how the Corporation Securities Company's portfolio depreciated some $45 million in late 1930, then appreciated $86 million in early 1932, when people thought the Depression was over. He and his associates had done nothing unusual in "supporting the market," he said; even the United States did it for government bonds. He himself had borrowed $5 million to bolster Corporation Securities Company, then borrowed a million from GE to reduce the bank loan. But by April 1932 his holding companies had gone into receivership. To avoid bankruptcy, he had given his creditors everything he had. He now owned no property, had no income, and depended on his son for food and shelter.

"We Are Trying That Age"

The gist of the Insull defense was that the government had to find someone to blame for the ills the Depression had caused. Samuel Insull, as the magic name in the era of million-dollar risks and losses, was the logical culprit. Thompson summarized:

> Gentlemen, you have had a description here of an age in American history which we hope never will be repeated. We are trying that age. There is no proof here that anyone had any wrongful motive. There is proof that these men believed implicitly in the business venture in which they were engaged, and they poured their own fortunes and their own good names into it.

The jury agreed. It found all of the defendants not guilty.

Insull faced two more trials. In March 1935, a Cook County jury found him not guilty on the charge of embezzlement. In June in federal district court, he and his son and Harold Stuart were found not guilty of illegally transferring property with intent to prefer selected creditors and defeat the purpose of the Bankruptcy Act.

Insull returned to Paris, where he dropped dead on the street at 78. It was reported that his assets then were $1,000; his debts, $14 million.

—Bernard Ryan, Jr.

Suggestions for Further Reading

Busch, Francis X. *Guilty or Not Guilty?* New York: Bobbs-Merrill Co., 1952.

Davidson, Carla. "Chicago Transit," *American Heritage* (December 1985) 33–34.

Fleming, Thomas J. "Good-bye to Everything!" *American Heritage* (August 1965) 89.

Fuhrman, Peter. "Do it big, Sammy," *Forbes* (July 13, 1987) 278–280.

Michaels, James W. "History lesson," *Forbes* (December 24, 1990) 38–40.

Phillips, Cabell. *The New York Times Chronicle of American Life from the Crash to the Blitz: 1929–1939.* New York: Macmillan Co., 1969.

Sifakis, Carl. *The Encyclopedia of American Crime.* New York: Facts On File, 1982.

Bruno Richard Hauptmann Trial: 1935

Defendant: Bruno Richard Hauptmann   **Crime Charged:** Murder
Chief Defense Lawyer: Edward J. Reilly   **Chief Prosecutor:** David T. Wilentz   **Judge:** Thomas W. Trenchard   **Place:** Flemington, New Jersey
Dates of Trial: January 2–February 13, 1935   **Verdict:** Guilty
Sentence: Death by electrocution

SIGNIFICANCE

The use of scientific crime detection, a conviction entirely on circumstantial evidence, and the circus-like atmosphere created by spectators and the press made the Lindbergh baby kidnapping trial a landmark in American history. Because of the prominence of the father of the murder victim, probably no case has ever attracted greater worldwide attention.

Influential editor and critic H.L. Mencken called Bruno Richard Hauptmann's trial "the biggest story since the Resurrection." The defendant was charged with murdering the 20-month-old son of Charles A. Lindbergh, the man who, in May 1927, had become the greatest hero of modern times by making the first solo trans-Atlantic flight, from New York to Paris. "Wild enthusiasm" understates the acclaim that had greeted Lindbergh wherever he went for five years. He belonged to America.

In 1929, Lindbergh had married Anne Morrow, daughter of the U.S. ambassador to Mexico. Charles Jr. was born June 22, 1930. Hoping to escape from the crowds they drew everywhere they went, the young family moved into a new home in remote Hopewell, New Jersey. There, on the evening of March 1, 1932, the toddler was kidnapped from his nursery. His body was found May 12 in the woods, two miles from the Lindbergh home.

Discovered Through Ransom Money

More than two years later, in September 1934, a man named Bruno Hauptmann used a $10 gold certificate to buy gasoline. Because gold notes were rare (the United States had just gone off the gold standard), the station attendant jotted down Hauptmann's license number and took the $10 bill to a bank, where it was identified as part of the $50,000 ransom paid by Lindbergh. Hauptmann was arrested. The jury would face the accused carpenter, who lived with his wife and son (now almost the same age as the Lindbergh baby when he died) in the rented second floor of a house in the Bronx, a borough of New York City. Hauptmann, who had a record of petty crime in his native Germany, had voyaged to America twice in 1923 as a stowaway. Apprehended and sent back the first time, he was successful on his second try.

Discovered behind boards in Hauptmann's garage was $14,590 in bills from the ransom. A *New York Times* compilation of his assets totaled $49,671. Written on the trim inside his bedroom closet was the address and telephone number of Dr. John F. Condon, a 71-year-old retired Bronx schoolteacher who had turned up as a self-appointed go-between when Lindbergh, not yet aware that his son had been killed, was negotiating with the kidnapper for the delivery of the ransom. Within earshot of Lindbergh, Condon had met the presumed kidnapper in the dark to hand over the money. When Lindbergh would testify, that "is the voice I heard that night," in identifying Hauptmann as the man he had heard when the ransom for his kidnapped baby was handed over, America believed him implicitly.

The Circus Comes to Town

The trial shaped up as one of the great news stories of the century. To cope with the demands of the press, the largest telephone system ever yet put together for a single event was created—adequate to serve a city of 1 million. Thousands of sightseers, 700 reporters, and hundreds of radio and telephone technicians converged upon Flemington, New Jersey. Hucksters sold models of the ladder used by the kidnapper to get into the baby's nursery, locks of "the baby's hair," and photographs of the Lindberghs, supposedly autographed by them.

On Sundays, tourists trooped through the courtroom, posed for photos in the judge's chair, carved initials in his bench, and tried to steal the witness chair. On Sunday, January 6, the invading army of curiosity-seekers was estimated at 60,000. The next weekend, the local Rotary Club took charge of protecting the courthouse from virtual demolition by the souvenir hunters.

Everything Matches

Not only would the state of New Jersey prove that Hauptmann received the money, promised the cigar-smoking 38-year-old Attorney General David T. Wilentz, it would also prove that Hauptmann had kidnapped and murdered the baby and written the ransom notes. Wilentz presented 40 examples of Hauptmann's handwriting and 15 ransom notes that Lindbergh had received. Colonel H. Norman Schwarzkopf, head of the New Jersey State Police (and father of the U. S. Army commanding general in the 1991 Persian Gulf war), testified that Hauptmann had willingly provided handwriting specimens and

Crowds lined the streets trying to witness the trial of Bruno Richard Hauptmann. (Courtesy, National Archives)

that the idiosyncratic or Germanic spellings that were found on the specimens and ransom notes were Hauptmann's own and not dictated by the police.

Next, eight different handwriting experts took the stand. Two had testified in more than 50 trials. Another had helped send Al Capone to prison. A third had been a key witness in a suit over the legitimacy of Rudolf Valentino's will. Using blowups, the experts pointed out similarities between words and letters in the ransom notes and in Hauptmann's writing specimens. By the end of their five days of testimony, Wilentz was rejoicing in a triumph of scientific investigation of evidence.

Even more damning than the handwriting evidence was the testimony on the ladder found alongside the Lindbergh driveway. Arthur Koehler, a wood technologist of the U.S. Department of Agriculture, told how he had examined the ladder microscopically to determine its North Carolina pine origin. Then he traced the distinctive marks of its machine planing through mills to conclude that it had been processed in South Carolina, sold to a Bronx lumber company, and purchased by Hauptmann in December 1931. But one ladder rail was unlike the others. It contained four nail holes that matched four holes in beams in Hauptmann's attic, and the saw-tooth marks across the rail's end grain perfectly matched marks where one attic floor board was shorter than others. When the ladder rail was positioned in the open space on the beams, nails dropped easily into place through the board and into the beams.

The Shoebox on the Shelf

At 52, Hauptmann's defense attorney, Edward J. Reilly, had tried hundreds of murder cases. A hard-drinking blusterer and one of New York's most successful trial lawyers, he had been hired to take the case by the *New York Journal,* a Hearst paper, which had made a deal with Mrs. Hauptmann: exclusive rights to her story if the *Journal* helped pay for the lawyer.

To explain how he came to have the ransom money, Hauptmann testified that he had invested in business with Isidor Fisch, who went home to Germany in December 1933, and died there of tuberculosis in March 1934. Fisch, said Hauptmann, left belongings with him—including a shoebox that Hauptmann stored on the top shelf of a kitchen broom closet.

When rain leaked into the closet, Hauptmann found the forgotten shoebox, opened it, and discovered $40,000 in gold certificates. In his garage, he divided the damp money into piles, wrapped it, and hid it. Because Fisch had owed him $7,500, Hauptmann began spending some. He felt it was his.

Reilly called Mrs. Hauptmann to corroborate the Fisch story. Cross-examining her, Wilentz proved that, while she hung her apron every day on a hook higher than the top shelf and kept her grocery coupons in a tin box on that shelf, she could not remember ever seeing a shoebox there. Later, rebuttal witnesses testified that Fisch could not have been at the scene of the crime, and that he had had no money for treatments when he was dying in Germany.

Reilly had boasted that he would introduce eight handwriting experts. He came up with one, whose authority was undermined in cross-examination. Then Reilly brought in a witness who claimed to have seen Fisch in Manhattan on the night of the crime with a woman who carried a 2-year-old blond child, and that the woman was Violet Sharpe, a maid in the Morrow home who had committed suicide after intensive interrogation (all servants in the Morrow and Lindbergh households had been questioned closely). That witness proved to be a professional who had testified for pay in dozens of trials.

Another Reilly defense witness claimed to have seen Fisch coming out of the cemetery where the ransom was passed. Prosecutor Wilentz made the witness admit he had previously been convicted of a crime and that he was with a woman on the night in question. Still another witness, who testified that he saw Fisch with a shoebox, admitted under cross-examination that he had been in and out of mental institutions five times.

Reilly talked freely with reporters. Radio listeners heard him promise that his client would be a free man within days. In one broadcast, he urged anyone with information to get in touch. During a lunch break, as Reilly sipped his third cocktail from a coffee cup, a stranger approached him and said he had information. After questioning him, Reilly, clearly frustrated by his own failure to produce a credible witness, yelled, "You've never been convicted of a crime? You've never been in a lunatic asylum? I can't use you!"

Reilly's troubles continued: To contradict the ladder testimony, he produced a general contractor as an expert on wood. After Wilentz attacked the witness' expertise, the judge allowed him to testify only as a "practical lumberman." Another carpenter said that the ladder rail had *not* been cut from the attic board, then admitted on cross-examination that he had never compared the grains of the two boards.

When the trial ended, no reliable witness had placed Hauptmann at the scene of the crime; nor had his fingerprints been found on the ladder, nor anywhere in the nursery, nor on the ransom notes. But the circumstantial evidence overwhelmed whatever doubts the jurors may have had: He had the ransom money; scientific experts said he had made the ladder—using wood from his attic for one rail; and other experts said he had written the ransom notes.

Governor Gets into the Act

When the jury found Hauptmann guilty of murder in the first degree, the crowds in and outside the courtroom cheered vigorously. The sentence was death. Execution was set for the week of March 18. Over the next year, Hauptmann's attorneys (Anna Hauptmann had fired Reilly) gained postponements by filing appeals.

New Jersey's 40-year-old governor, Harold G. Hoffman, secretly visited Hauptmann in prison, declared that he was not convinced of Hauptmann's guilt, and that the crime could not have been committed alone. In mid-January 1936, when the state's Court of Pardons denied Hauptmann clemency, the governor granted him a 30-day reprieve. The Court of Pardons turned down a second petition for clemency. By law, the governor could not give a second reprieve. On April 3, 1936, at 8:44 P.M., Hauptmann was electrocuted.

For more than half a century, book after book has re-examined and critiqued the evidence and the testimony. More than one author has described the investigation of the kidnapping and murder as incompetent or has declared Hauptmann an innocent, framed man.

In 1982, 82-year-old Anna Hauptmann sued the State of New Jersey, various former police officials, the Hearst newspapers, and David T. Wilentz (himself by then 86) for $100 million in wrongful-death damages. She claimed that newly found documents proved misconduct by the prosecution and manufacture of evidence by government agents. In 1983, the U.S. Supreme Court refused her request that the federal judge considering her case be disqualified, and in 1984 the judge dismissed her claims.

In 1985, 23,000 pages of Hauptmann-case police documents were discovered in the garage of the late Governor Hoffman. Along with 30,000 pages of FBI files not used in the trial, said Anna Hauptmann, they proved "a smorgasbord of fraud" against her husband. Again, she appealed to the Supreme Court; it let stand without comment the rulings that had dismissed her suit. In 1990, New Jersey's new governor, Jim Florio, declined her appeal for a meeting to clear Hauptmann's name.

In October 1991, Mrs. Hauptmann, now 92, called a news conference in Flemington to plead for the case to be reopened. "From the day he was arrested, he was framed, always framed," she said. Among her allegations was that the rail of the ladder taken from the attic had been planted by the state police. The ransom money, she still insisted, was left behind by Isidor Fisch.

—Bernard Ryan, Jr.

Suggestions for Further Reading

Davis, Kenneth S. *The Hero: Charles A. Lindbergh and the American Dream.* Garden City, N. Y.: Doubleday & Co., 1959.

Fisher, Jim. *The Lindbergh Case.* New Brunswick, N.J.: Rutgers University Press, 1987.

Kennedy, Ludovic. *The Airman and the Carpenter.* New York: Viking, 1985.

King, Wayne. "Defiant Widow Seeks to Reopen Lindbergh Case." *The New York Times* (October 5, 1991): 24.

"Lindbergh Kidnapping's Final Victim." *U.S. News & World Report,* (November 4, 1985): 11.

Mosley, Leonard. *Lindbergh: A Biography.* Garden City, N. Y.: Doubleday & Co., 1976.

Rein, Richard K. "Anna Hauptmann Sues a State to Absolve Her Husband of 'The Crime of the Century.'" *People Weekly* (September 6, 1982): 34–35.

Ross, Walter S. *The Last Hero: Charles A. Lindbergh.* New York: Harper & Row, 1964.

Scaduto, Anthony. *Scapegoat: The Lonesome Death of Bruno Richard Hauptmann.* New York: G.P. Putnam's Sons, 1976.

Waller, George. *Kidnap: The Story of the Lindbergh Case.* New York: Dial Press, 1961.

Vera Stretz Trial: 1936

Defendant: Vera Stretz **Crime Charged:** Murder
Chief Defense Lawyer: Samuel S. Leibowitz **Chief Prosecutor:** Miles O'Brien **Judge:** Cornelius F. Collins **Place:** New York, New York
Dates of Trial: March 20–April 3, 1936 **Verdict:** Not guilty

SIGNIFICANCE

For defense counsel Samuel S. Leibowitz, the Vera Stretz case was the 116th of 139 consecutive trials in which he saved his client from death in the electric chair. Many lawyers believe the case marked his peak as a trial lawyer before he became one of the New York courtroom's most respected judges.

Vera Stretz was 29 years old when she spent some of her $35,000 inheritance from her mother on a cruise aboard the *Vulcania* in December 1934. There she met Dr. Fritz Gebhardt, a German financier who was 42. Chatting in German (her German was better than his English), they became casual friends.

Soon after returning to New York, Stretz and the doctor dated. Witty and gallant, Dr. Gebhardt seemed determined to sweep Vera Stretz off her feet. But he had a wife and two children in Germany. The marriage, he said, had been one in name only for 10 years.

"He told me that he loved me," Stretz later said. "And then he said that he was an unusual person. Ordinary laws applied to ordinary people, but for an unusual person there must be different standards. I was fascinated by him." Stretz found herself so deeply in love that in May she traveled with him to Lake George as Mrs. Gebhardt.

Soon Stretz moved to Gebhardt's building, Beekman Towers, taking an apartment two floors below his. As he traveled often, they exchanged passionate love letters.

By November, Stretz regularly responded to late-night calls from Gebhardt, applying a heating pad to help him through stomach cramps as often as once a week. Early in November, when he returned from a European trip, he said, "I am going away again in December and you are going with me."

Stretz assumed he had decided to end his marriage. "I'd better hurry with the wedding invitations," she said. No, said Gebhardt, he knew now that he was not the type to get married. They would go on as before.

She told him she would not compromise: She wanted a home and a husband. "No one has ever left me before," he announced, "and you are not going to leave me."

Late in the night of November 11, in great stomach pain, Gebhardt called her. She put a coat on over her nightgown, slipped into shoes, and went up the back stairs.

A Revolver and Bloodstains

At 2:30 A.M., shots were heard in Beekman Towers. The police were called. They discovered Vera Stretz sitting on the stairway just below the third floor. In her large handbag they found a .32-caliber revolver, a box of bullets, two spent shells, and a crumpled silk nightgown with fresh wet bloodstains.

"Did you shoot the man upstairs?" they asked.

"Yes, I did," sobbed Stretz. "But please don't ask me why I did it." She said she was on the way to turn herself in.

The police grilled her for hours, but she would say nothing more. Her father, Frank Stretz, sent for Samuel Leibowitz, who had defended the Scottsboro boys (see separate entry) and was known as the best criminal lawyer in the country. The newspapers called Stretz "the icy blonde" because she wouldn't talk. They dug up Gebhardt's background: He had flown in World War I's famed Richtofen Squadron, was a pal of pilot Hermann Goering, held doctorates in both philosophy and political economy, had made half a million dollars in international business deals, but had made the mistake—from Nazi Germany's point of view—of marrying a non-Aryan. He had, however, moved out, leaving her with two children and no divorce.

Vera Stretz Tells What Happened

When the trial began on March 20, 1936, defense attorney Leibowitz probed each juror's knowledge of Friedrich Wilhelm Nietzsche, the German philosopher whose idea of a super-race attracted Adolf Hitler, and who said, "Man shall be trained for war and woman for the recreation of the warrior; all else is folly." Then, with Vera Stretz on the stand for 13 hours, Leibowitz carefully produced testimony on Gebhardt's attitude toward marriage and toward her. When she announced the night of November 11 that she would not continue their relationship, she testified, Gebhardt had thrown her on the bed and raped her.

Next, laughing at her and saying, "If you want to make it the last night, you will have to make it a good one," he demanded that she perform an act of sodomy so foreign to her, and so shameful, that she had been unable to tell the police. Now she recounted it, at the insistence of Judge Cornelius Collins, only through violent, uncontrollable sobbing. Recalling seeing a gun in Gebhardt's chest of drawers when she looked for his heating pad, she seized it. The doctor, crying, "You damned whore, I will kill you," grabbed at the gun, she said. It went off. He fell on the bed, got up, lunged again at her, and she shot again.

Prosecutor Miles O'Brien cross-examined her for four fours. She killed, he insisted, in a hot fever of jealousy because Gebhardt wouldn't give up his wife for her: "She is a tigress when provoked." But he was unable to produce a single contradiction in Stretz's testimony.

The judge's charge lasted five hours, defining first-degree murder, second-degree murder, first-degree manslaughter, and reasonable doubt, excusable homicide, and justifiable homicide. "If you believe her story," he finished acidly, "acquit her."

Within three hours, the jury did so. The furious judge went to his chambers without thanking the jury for its services.

Vera Stretz (center) shown with her attorney Samuel Leibowitz (right) leaving court after her arraignment on murder charges for shooting Dr. Fritz Gebhardt. (AP/Wide World Photos)

The next day, Stretz met the press. "Don't let this ruin your life," said a woman reporter.

"My life is ruined already," said Vera Stretz.

Years later, the defendant in this trial was identified only as one Laura Parr. When and how her name was changed from Vera Stretz remains a secret buried with her ruined life.

—Bernard Ryan, Jr.

Suggestions for Further Reading

The *New York Times*. *See* Stretz, Vera, in The *New York Times Index*, November 12, 1935–April 4, 1936.

Reynolds, Quentin. *Courtroom: The Story of Samuel S. Leibowitz*. New York: Farrar, Straus and Co., 1950.

Charles "Lucky" Luciano Trial: 1936

Defendant: Charles "Lucky" Luciano   **Crime Charged:** Compulsory prostitution   **Chief Defense Lawyers:** Francis W.H. Adams and George Morton Levy   **Chief Prosecutor:** Thomas E. Dewey   **Judge:** Philip J. McCook   **Dates of Trial:** May 13–June 7, 1936   **Verdict:** Guilty   **Sentence:** 30 to 50 years imprisonment

SIGNIFICANCE

The "Lucky" Luciano case is a paradox: It proves that, no matter how much money a crime boss has made or how well his lawyers and henchmen have protected him, he can be convicted and sentenced to long imprisonment. But it also proves that where there's a will, there's a way to gain release, as Luciano ultimately did.

In 1935, Charles "Lucky" Luciano was the nation's number one crime boss. He had run the national crime syndicate—later famous for its disciplinary arm dubbed "Murder, Inc."—since its organization in 1931.

A New York grand jury, briefed on the extent of vice and racketeering, asked for appointment of a special prosecutor. Governor Herbert H. Lehman appointed Thomas E. Dewey, an ambitious former chief assistant U.S. attorney.

Dewey learned that "Lucky" Luciano (so nicknamed because he usually won craps games and had survived a severe beating and throat-slitting) had expanded his operations from extortion from bordellos to complete control over them. He was taking in more than $10 million annually, with 5,000 prostitutes on the nationwide payroll.

Dewey's staff interviewed whores, pimps, loan sharks, and strong-arm men. Word reached Luciano: Many had talked. He disappeared. Dewey proclaimed him "Public Enemy Number One." The grand jury indicted Luciano on 90 counts of compulsory prostitution (later reduced to 62).

Luciano was found in Hot Springs, Arkansas, where organized crime maintained a well-protected sanctuary. He was extradited only after Dewey pictured the Arkansas governor as a protector of gangsters and 20 Arkansas Rangers removed Luciano from the protection of the Hot Springs sheriff.

"I'm Gonna Organize the Cathouses Like the A&P"

The special blue-ribbon jury heard 68 witnesses. Some 40 were prostitutes or madams who had moved up in the ranks. One, Cokey Flo Brown, testified about meetings where Luciano presided. "I'm gonna organize the cathouses like the A&P," he had told her. "We could syndicate the places on a large scale same as a chain store system."

Lucky Luciano accompanied by guards at his hearing for compulsory prostitution, 1936. (AP/Wide World Photos)

Cokey Flo also testified that strong-arm methods had brought madams and pimps into line. "First you got to step on them," she quoted Luciano as saying. "Talking won't do no good. You got to put the screws on."

Against his lawyers' advice, Luciano insisted on taking the witness stand to deny all charges and deny knowing any of the witnesses. For four hours, Dewey pummeled him with questions, proving that he was lying in answer after answer.

Dewey's seven-hour summation described Luciano's testimony as:

> . . . a shocking, disgusting display of sanctimonious perjury—at the end of which I am sure not one of you had a doubt that before you stood not a gambler, not a bookmaker, but the greatest gangster in America.

The jury agreed: guilty on all counts. Judge Philip J. McCook's sentence: 30 to 50 years—the longest ever for compulsory prostitution. On June 18, 1936, Luciano went to New York State's maximum-security prison at Dannemora.

Dewey later admitted that he had been able to convict Luciano only for "a minor racket," while:

> It is my understanding that top-ranking defendants in this case have absorbed control of the narcotics, policy, loan-shark and Italian lottery syndicates, the receipt of stolen goods and certain industrial rackets.

Aided the War Effort

World War II freed Luciano. In 1942, U.S. Navy officers, frustrated by unstable labor conditions and sabotage on the New York waterfront, visited Luciano. He ordered cooperation and gained a private cell. A year later, the Navy, planning the invasion of Sicily, asked him to enlist the help of the island's natives. A deal was struck. After the war, with the Navy citing Luciano's aid in shortening the war in Sicily and Italy and with by then-Governor Dewey's approval, he was paroled to his birthplace in Sicily.

Luciano settled in Naples, barred from Rome by the Italian government. He lived there, except for an illegal sojourn in Cuba (where he ordered the death of his syndicate associate, "Bugsy" Siegel), until he died of a heart attack in 1962.

—Bernard Ryan, Jr.

Suggestions for Further Reading

Fox, Stephen. *Blood and Power.* New York: William Morrow & Co., 1989.

Godwin, John. *Murder USA.* New York: Ballantine Books, 1978.

Gosch, Martin A. and Richard Hammer. *The Last Testament of Lucky Luciano.* Boston: Little, Brown and Co., 1974.

Nash, Jay Robert. *Almanac of World Crime.* Garden City, N.Y.: Anchor Press/Doubleday, 1981.

——. *Encyclopedia of World Crime.* Wilmette, Ill.: CrimeBooks, 1990.

Mary Astor Divorce Trial: 1936

Plaintiff: Mary Astor   **Defendant:** Franklyn Thorpe
Plaintiff Claims: Custody of child, annulment of marriage, and abrogation of property settlement in earlier divorce   **Chief Defense Lawyers:** Joseph Anderson and Michael Narlian   **Chief Lawyers for Plaintiff:** Joseph F. Rank and Roland Rich Woolley   **Judge:** Goodwin J. Knight   **Place:** Los Angeles, California   **Dates of Trial:** July 29–August 14, 1936   **Verdict:** Decree granted for plaintiff

SIGNIFICANCE

The Mary Astor case is a classic Hollywood divorce case. It entertained newspaper readers for weeks with charges, countercharges, and denials, and offered wondrous titillation and breathtaking insight into the daring illicit romances of people in show business. The case reads like the scenario of a life-in-Hollywood movie.

In 1936, actress Mary Astor was at the height of a Hollywood career that had begun in 1922 and had seen her move successfully through dozens of silent films in the 20s and into the "talkies." Her 74th film, the screen adaptation of Sinclair Lewis' novel *Dodsworth*, was in production, with Mary playing the "other woman." Over the years, she had appeared on-screen with such fabled names as George Arliss, Douglas Fairbanks, John Barrymore, William Powell, Jean Harlow, Gilbert Rowland, Dorothy Gish, Richard Barthelmess, Myrna Loy, Edward G. Robinson, Richard Dix, Frederic March, Clark Gable, and Paul Muni, in such classics as *The Man Who Played God, Don Q, Son of Zorro, Don Juan, The Lost Squadron*, and *Red Dust*.

Astor's first husband, director Kenneth Hawks, was killed in 1930 when his camera plane collided with another. In 1931, she married her doctor, Franklyn Thorpe. He sued her for divorce in April 1935, charging mental cruelty and incompatibility. Under the divorce settlement, he gained custody of their 3-year-old, Marilyn, and some $60,000 in negotiable properties and real estate. Astor could visit the child at will and have her for six months of the year if she wished.

"He'd Shake Her So Hard Her Teeth Rattled"

By the summer of 1936, Astor brought suit against Thorpe, saying she was coerced into the divorce and charging him with abusing Marilyn—"He'd shake her so hard her teeth rattled and bit her lips," she sobbed in court. Astor demanded custody of her daughter, formal annulment of the marriage, and abrogation of the property settlement. To persuade the court he was unfit to have custody of Marilyn, she produced evidence that Thorpe had been married previously but had not told her so, and that he had had four postmarital love affairs.

Thorpe's attorney, Joseph Anderson, said he would dispute Astor's contention that she was coerced. "We can prove in her own handwriting that this was not the situation at all," he announced, "but that she wilfully abandoned the child for a married man—George Kaufman."

The Diary Written in Purple

Anderson had fired a shot heard 'round the world. Headline writers outdid each other shouting that renowned playwright and director George S. Kaufman had been named in Mary Astor's diary as her lover. Thorpe had the diary, dating from 1929. According to Anderson, its presentation as evidence would prove what everyone in show business knew: that Kaufman's sexual appetite was as great as his well-known appetite for work. And the diary—written, the press reported, in purple ink—would reveal a scorecard by Mary Astor on the performance in bed of almost every well-known actor in show business.

Astor's lawyer, Roland Rich Woolley, told the court he wanted the diary produced by the defense as evidence, to prove that it was not such a compilation of titillation. Astor said the book was a forgery leaked to the press.

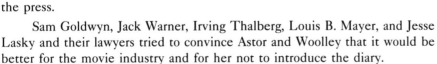

Mary Astor conferring with her attorney—Roland Rich Woolley (Hearst Newspaper Collection, University of Southern California Library)

Sam Goldwyn, Jack Warner, Irving Thalberg, Louis B. Mayer, and Jesse Lasky and their lawyers tried to convince Astor and Woolley that it would be better for the movie industry and for her not to introduce the diary.

Playwright Flees in a Laundry Basket

Judge Goodwin J. Knight examined the diary. Several pages were missing. It was a "mutilated document," not admissible as evidence. Thorpe's attorneys got Judge Knight to issue a subpoena that would force Kaufman to testify in court on his relations with Mary Astor. Irving Thalberg, for whom Kaufman was working, put Kaufman aboard his yacht, sailed him off to Catalina Island, and said the playwright had "disappeared." The judge issued a bench warrant for Kaufman's arrest. Kaufman sneaked back, hid at Moss Hart's home, then was hauled in a large laundry basket aboard a laundry truck to the San Bernardino railroad station, where he boarded a train for New York. After staying in his berth the entire trip, he said, "That's the best way to travel."

Too late, the judge issued a search warrant for Hart's home. "The bench warrant will hang over Kaufman's head always," he declared. "If he can be cited, I'll sentence him to jail."

Thorpe admitted that, before marrying Mary Astor, he had lived in Florida with another woman as man and wife, and that he also had been married earlier.

The judge negotiated with the lawyers. He ordered the diary impounded. (Later, with Mary Astor's permission, it was incinerated.) The judge awarded custody of Marilyn to Mary Astor for nine months of each year—the child could visit Thorpe during summer vacations from school—and nulled the earlier property settlement.

The bench warrant for Kaufman's arrest continued, but six months later the playwright visited the judge and paid a $500 fine, and they shook hands.

Mary Astor's career soared. Before she retired and turned to writing successful novels, she had made 109 movies, including *The Maltese Falcon, Thousands Cheer, Meet Me in St. Louis*, and *Hush, Hush, Sweet Charlotte*. She died at 81 in 1987.

—Bernard Ryan, Jr.

Suggestions for Further Reading

Astor, Mary. *A Life on Film*. New York: Delacorte Press, 1967.

——. *My Story: An Autobiography*. Garden City, N.Y.: Doubleday & Co., 1959.

Meredith, Scott. *George S. Kaufman and His Friends*. Garden City, N.Y.: Doubleday & Co., 1974.

Teichmann, Howard. *George S. Kaufman: An Intimate Portrait*. New York: Atheneum, 1972.

Martin T. Manton Trial: 1939

Appellant & Defendant: Martin T. Manton   **Appellee & Plaintiff:** United States   **Appellant Claim:** Reversal of conviction for conspiracy to obstruct the administration of justice and to defraud the United States, and dismissal of sentence   **Chief Lawyers for Plaintiff:** John T. Cahill, Mathias F. Correa, Frank H. Gordon, Silvio J. Mollo, and Robert L. Werner   **Chief Lawyers for Appellant:** William J. Hughes, William E. Leahy, John E. Mack, and E. Donald Wilson   **Judges:** Specially constituted federal court: George Sutherland (former justice, U.S. Supreme Court); Harlan F. Stone (justice, U.S. Supreme Court); Charles E. Clark (judge, U.S. Circuit Court of Appeals, Second Circuit)   **Place:** New York, New York   **Date of Decision:** December 4, 1939   **Decision:** Conviction upheld (Sentence: 2 years imprisonment and $10,000 fine)

SIGNIFICANCE

This unique appeal brought the senior judge of the country's most prominent federal appeals court before his own colleagues. With all but one of the court's judges disqualified because of their previous association with the appellant, a special federal court had to be constituted to hear the appeal. The case, involving a scandal unique in federal court history, established a landmark in the delineation of conspiracy to obstruct justice.

In 1939, Martin T. Manton was the senior circuit judge of the U.S. Circuit Court of Appeals for the Second Circuit, a position second only to the nine members of the U.S. Supreme Court. As a lawyer, Manton had made more than a million dollars before his appointment to the bench in 1916. His fortune, invested in real estate and business, had been severely depleted by the Depression.

With his friend William J. Fallon and several other men, Manton was indicted in April 1939, for conspiring to influence, obstruct and impede justice and to "defraud the United States of its right to have its legal functions exercised free from unlawful impairment."

"Without Regard to the Merits"

The indictment noted that Manton was a stockholder in, or "wholly or substantially owned or controlled" a number of corporations that had cases pending in his court between 1930 and 1939. It charged that Fallon actively proposed to those litigants that his close friendship with Manton could get them favorable action, and that such parties actively sought Fallon's help "in virtue of Manton's office, position, power and influence." Finally, the indictment charged:

> that Manton would accept and receive sums of money as gifts, loans and purported loans in return for such action, and would corruptly act in each of these cases without regard to the merits.

Harlan Stone (left) was part of a specially constituted federal court in the trial of Judge Martin Manton. (Courtesy, Library of Congress)

Manton moved to quash the indictment, claiming it charged not one conspiracy but several separate conspiracies on one count, that it did not state an offense, and that more than one crime was charged in the indictment. The motion was overruled.

The trial soon produced evidence that Manton's downfall resulted from continuing his business activities after appointment to the bench. Many suits that reached his court involved patent-infringement disputes, with the loser doomed to heavy losses. Evidence showed that Manton owned stock in companies that were litigants and in whose favor he decided.

In one case, a patent infringement suit brought by Schick Industries against Dictograph Products Company, one Archie Andrews, the principal stockholder in Dictograph, provided Fallon with $10,000 in cash through an intermediary, who gave a receipt for the money for the purchase of Dictograph stock. Fallon went off to see Manton and returned within the hour to say, "Everything is O.K. You can go and tell Archie Andrews that he is going to get the decision in his favor." The decision was against Schick.

The district court jury found Manton guilty. He received the maximum sentence: two years in federal prison and a $10,000 fine. He appealed. Paradoxically, the appeal had to land in his own court, where all his fellow judges except one disqualified themselves as his close associates. Only Judge Charles E. Clark, who had been appointed to the bench after Manton resigned while under investigation, could hear the appeal. Therefore, a special federal court was constituted. Its judges were former Supreme Court Justice George Sutherland, Supreme Court Justice Harlan F. Stone, and Judge Clark.

"Conspiracy Constitutes the Offense"

Considering Manton's claim that the indictment wrongly set forth a number of distinct conspiracies in a single count, the special court found:

> that the conspiracy constitutes the offense irrespective of the number or variety of objects which the conspiracy seeks to attain, or whether any of the ultimate objects be attained or not.

Manton's contention, it said, "confuses the conspiracy, which was one, with its aims, which were many." The offense was the single continuing agreement among Manton and his cronies to sell judicial action to all willing to pay the price.

Altogether, the court's review found, Fallon had procured some $186,146 for Manton in 28 "distinct overt acts in pursuance of the conspiracy." In conclusion, the court noted that a mass of canceled checks, promissory notes, and other accounts was "so plainly at variance with the claim of Manton's innocence as to make the verdict of the jury unassailable."

Manton requested review by the U. S. Supreme Court. It denied his petition, and he went to federal prison at Lewisburg, Pennsylvania, on March 7, 1940. While eligible for parole after eight months, he served 19 months before he was released on October 13, 1941. He died in 1946.

—Bernard Ryan, Jr.

Suggestions for Further Reading

"Ex-Judge Manton of U.S. Bench Here." (obituary) *The New York Times* (November 18, 1946): 23

"Manton Conviction in Sale of Justice Upheld on Appeal." *The New York Times* (December 5, 1939): 1.

The *New York Times. See* Courts, U.S. Federal Inferior, *New York Times Index*, January–December 1939.

Murder, Inc. Trials: 1941

Defendants: Frank "The Dasher" Abbandando, Louis "Lepke" Buchalter, Louis Capone, Martin "Buggsy" Goldstein, Harry "Happy" Malone, Harry "Pittsburgh Phil" Strauss, and Mendy Weiss   **Crime Charged:** Murder
Chief Defense Lawyers: Hyman Barshay, James L. Cuff, William Kleinman, David F. Price, Daniel M. Pryor, and Alfred I. Rosner
Chief Prosecutors: William O'Dwyer, Solomon A. Klein, and Burton B. Turkus
Judges: John J. Fitzgerald and Franklin Taylor   **Place:** Brooklyn, New York
Dates of Trials: May 8–22, 1940 (Abbandando, Malone, and Strauss, for Rudnick slaying); September 9–19, 1940 (Strauss and Goldstein, for Feinstein slaying); March 10–April 3, 1941 (Abbandando and Malone, second trial for Rudnick slaying); October 21–November 30, 1941 (Buchalter, Capone, and Weiss for Rosen slaying)   **Verdicts:** Guilty   **Sentences:** Death by electrocution

SIGNIFICANCE

These trials awakened America to the fact that crime was one of the nation's biggest businesses, so vast that the crime syndicate had established its own enforcement arm—labeled by the press "Murder, Inc." They also helped advance two political careers: Thomas E. Dewey moved from special prosecutor to district attorney to governor of New York and two unsuccessful campaigns as Republican nominee for the presidency of the United States, and Brooklyn District Attorney William O'Dwyer later became mayor of New York City.

Starting in the early 1930s, crime became organized into a national syndicate as local gangs specializing in bootlegging, prostitution, and racketeering began cooperating to produce greater wealth for themselves. Soon such bosses as Charles "Lucky" Luciano, "Dutch" Schultz, and Meyer Lansky, all of whom served on the board of directors of the syndicate, realized they needed to protect their power by eliminating any underlings caught skimming from the revenue chain, trying to seize more power than had been delegated to them, or otherwise getting out of line.

Meyer Lansky had the idea of creating a small, well-organized army of killers. In succession, the bosses put "Bugsy" Siegel, then Albert Anastasia, and finally Louis "Lepke" Buchalter in charge. Buchalter came up with the code words that eventually found their way into the American language: The murder specialists could accept a "contract" (assignment) to "hit" (kill) any "bum" (intended victim) anywhere at a price per hit that ranged from $1,000 to $6,000. Members of the force operated in secrecy and without territorial claims. The rank-and-file mobsters never knew who they were. The killers prided themselves on their ability to do their homework by studying photographs of a bum they did not otherwise know, move unrecognized into a strange city, find the miscreant, hit him by ice pick or knife or bullets (one used whatever was handy, including a fire ax grabbed from a restaurant's wall case), and quietly leave town while the perplexed police looked around among the local bad guys.

"We Only Kill Each Other"

The organization also prided itself on its businesslike outlook: Killers were provided insurance, health, and pension benefits and were kept on salary between hits. They knew that, if they were caught, the best lawyers would defend them and, if they were convicted, their families would find the take-home pay still coming in while they did time in jail. Furthermore, organization philosophy was summed up in the words of "Bugsy" Siegel to a nervous building contractor hired to make alterations in his home: "We only kill each other." Hitting police or prosecutors was strictly forbidden lest it produce intensive crackdowns by law enforcement people.

By 1935, a New York grand jury, alarmed by the path of blood left by the operations of the national crime syndicate, asked for the appointment of a special prosecutor to supersede the district attorney in investigating vice and racketeering. Governor Herbert H. Lehman appointed Thomas E. Dewey, who earlier had earned prominence as chief assistant U.S. attorney for the Southern District of New York. Within two years, Dewey had gained 72 convictions and suffered only one acquittal and had been elected district attorney of New York County (i.e., Manhattan). Meantime, the New York newspapers had invented the corporate title "Murder, Inc." to identify the hit squad that was Dewey's target. The crime syndicate began to worry.

"Dutch" Schultz told the syndicate board it was time to break the "we only kill each other" rule: A contract on Dewey should be put out, he insisted. The board tried to make the irrepressible Schultz understand what a disastrous avalanche of police pressure he was inviting. Schultz marched angrily out of the meeting, shouting, "If you guys are too yellow to go after Dewey, I'll get him myself and I'll get him in a week."

As the door slammed behind Schultz, the board consulted. Anastasia, who was commandant of the killer troop, said, "Okay, I guess the Dutchman goes." That evening, Schultz was cornered in a restaurant washroom by Charles "The Bug" Workman and Mendy Weiss and riddled with bullets.

Word reached Buchalter in 1937 that Dewey was building a case against him. His buddy Anastasia, who had himself proposed killing Dewey soon after

Schultz was eliminated, visited Lucky Luciano in Dannemora Prison (where the syndicate boss had languished since Dewey convicted him on charges of compulsory prostitution in 1936) and got permission to hide Buchalter. For two years, while Dewey offered a $25,000 reward and J. Edgar Hoover promised $5,000 to the FBI agent who turned Buchalter in, he could not be found.

Meantime, from his hiding place in Brooklyn, Buchalter became more and more belligerent, dispatching killers to eliminate every potential witness against him.

Surrender to J. Edgar Hoover and Walter Winchell

By 1939, the syndicate board knew Buchalter was a liability. He had to go. But sending him off the way Dutch Schultz was sent would inspire Dewey to even greater determination to wipe out the syndicate. From prison, Luciano masterminded a scheme to make Buchalter think a deal had been made. Trusting his pals, he came out of hiding and surrendered to J. Edgar Hoover himself in a car driven by gossip columnist Walter Winchell, then learned he had been double-crossed: There was no deal. Within a month, he was tried in federal court on a narcotics charge, convicted, and sentenced to 14 years. Next, Dewey convicted him on a charge of extortion, with a 30-years-to-life sentence.

Within a year, one of Buchalter's killers, Abe "Kid Twist" Reles, arrested on a murder charge, decided to talk in exchange for police protection and immunity from prosecution. Soon the syndicate board knew that Reles, who seemed gifted with total recall, had talked for 12 days, filling 25 stenographic notebooks.

Wanted poster for Louis "Lepke" Buchalter, leader of "Murder, Inc." (Courtesy, National Archives)

With Reles' testimony in May 1940, Brooklyn District Attorney William O'Dwyer (who later served as mayor of New York City, then resigned to become ambassador to Mexico) convicted Frank "The Dasher" Abbandando, Harry "Happy" Malone, and Harry "Pittsburgh Phil" Strauss of the murder of mobster George Rudnick. Sentenced to die, they appealed, citing an error in Judge Franklin Taylor's charge to the jury.

Meantime, O'Dwyer gained a second death sentence for Strauss in September 1940 for killing gangster Irving "Piggy" Feinstein. Convicted with

Strauss was Martin "Buggsy" Goldstein. When the New York State Court of Appeals reversed the first convictions, O'Dwyer let Strauss sit in Sing Sing Prison in March 1941 while he convicted Abbandando and Malone all over again. All three then lost appeal after appeal. Strauss and Goldstein were executed on June 12, 1941, and Abbandando and Malone on February 19, 1942.

O'Dwyer pulled Buchalter out of Federal prison in November 1941 and tried him, with Louis Capone and Mendy Weiss, for the murder of candy-store operator Joseph Rosen, whom they had forced out of business and then hit after he threatened to complain to authorities. Reles' testimony, including vivid descriptions of garrotings and ice pick stabbings, brought the first and only conviction and execution of a member of the syndicate board. (Buchalter was one of the wealthiest Americans ever lawfully executed.)

Reles was next scheduled to testify in the trial of Albert Anastasia for the murder of Teamster official Morris Diamond—another outside-the-mob murder that Luciano had cautioned Anastasia against. But early on the morning of November 12, 1941, the body of Kid Twist Reles was found lying 42 feet below the window of the hotel room where six policemen were supposedly protecting him. Deprived of his star witness, O'Dwyer withdrew the charges against Anastasia.

Buchalter, Capone, and Weiss, having exhausted all possible appeals, died at Sing Sing on March 4, 1944. With the earlier executions of Abbandando, Malone, Strauss, and Goldstein, then, a handful of men paid with their lives for the dozens upon dozens of ruthless killings by perhaps 60, perhaps as many as 100, professional killers on the "Murder, Inc." payroll over some 15 years.

—*Bernard Ryan, Jr.*

Suggestions for Further Reading

Fox, Stephen. *Blood and Power: Organized Crime in Twentieth-Century America*. New York: William Morrow & Co., 1989.

Godwin, John. *Murder USA: The Ways We Kill Each Other*. New York: Ballantine Books, 1978.

Gosch, Martin A. and Richard Hammer. *The Last Testament of Lucky Luciano*. Boston: Little, Brown and Co., 1974.

McClellan, John L. *Crime Without Punishment*. New York: Duell, Sloan and Pearce, 1962.

Messick, Hank. *The Silent Syndicate*. New York: Macmillan Co., 1967.

Nash, Jay Robert. *Almanac of World Crime*. Garden City, N.Y.: Anchor Press/Doubleday, 1981.

——. *Encyclopedia of World Crime*. Wilmette, Ill.: CrimeBooks, 1991.

Turkus, Burton B. and Sid Feder. *Murder, Inc.* New York: Farrar, Straus/Manor Books, 1951.

Errol Flynn Trial: 1943

Defendant: Errol Flynn   **Crime Charged:** Statutory Rape
Chief Defense Lawyers: Jerry Geisler and Robert Neeb
Chief Prosecutors: Thomas W. Cochran and John Hopkins   **Judge:** Leslie
E. Still   **Place:** Los Angeles, California
Dates of Trial: January 11–February 6, 1943   **Verdict:** Not guilty

SIGNIFICANCE
Despite the outcome, the Errol Flynn trial focused national attention on Hollywood's sexual mores, which both titillated and shocked many Americans. The trial also put the phrase "In like Flynn" into the American language.

In 1942, Errol Flynn was at the height of his swashbuckling Hollywood career. In 10 years, the handsome native of Australia had made 26 movies—among them such overnight classics as *Captain Blood*, *The Adventures of Robin Hood*, and *The Sea Hawk*. Flynn lived a boisterous, daring life that was also devil-may-care. He worked hard, drank hard, loved hard. Women everywhere had fallen for his splendid physique, his cleft chin, and his enticing dimples, and women everywhere were available to him.

At a party in September 1942, Flynn met 17-year-old Betty Hansen, who arrived with a studio messenger and who dreamed of moviedom fame and fortune. By dinnertime, Hansen had thrown up from too much drinking.

The next day, Hansen told her sister that Flynn had taken her upstairs to clean up, then seduced her in a bedroom. A complaint was filed with District Attorney Thomas W. Cochran, who recalled a similar complaint by one Peggy Satterlee after a voyage aboard Flynn's yacht. That charge had been dropped.

Flynn's stand-in stuntman, Buster Wiles, later said Satterlee's father had earlier approached Flynn with a demand for money, or, said Wiles, "he would lie to the police that his underage daughter had sexual relations with Flynn."

Flynn was arrested in October. He hired Hollywood's ace lawyer, Jerry Geisler.

Fans and sensation seekers thronged Flynn's neighborhood, spying through binoculars, prowling over his 11-acre property, mobbing the courthouse at his preliminary hearing, pulling at his buttons and shoes.

Selecting the jury on January 11, 1943, Geisler purposely took nine women, gambling that the females' attraction to the movie star would outweigh concern over the seduction of innocence.

Prosecutor Cochran opened with the Betty Hansen charge. Geisler's cross-examination proved that her testimony was confused and that she was currently awaiting action on a possible felony charge with her boyfriend, the studio messenger.

"J.B." and "S.Q.Q."

Now Cochran had Peggy Satterlee describe her voyage to Catalina. She said Flynn called her "J.B." (short for "jail bait") and "S.Q.Q." (short for "San Quentin quail")—evidence that he knew she was a juvenile. Nevertheless, she testified, he came to her cabin and "got into bed with me and completed an act of sexual intercourse"—an act against which, she admitted, she did not struggle. The next night, she said, he took her to his cabin to look at the moon through the porthole and there repeated the offense. This time, she said, she fought.

In cross-examination, Satterlee admitted to lying frequently about her age, then revealed that she had had extramarital relations with another man before the Flynn episode, and had undergone an abortion.

Taking the stand, Flynn denied the "jail bait" and "San Quentin quail" allegations, as well as entering Satterlee's cabin or taking her to his cabin or taking Betty Hansen upstairs after she threw up at the party or having sexual intercourse with either girl. As he finished, women were crying hysterically. Men were yelling obscenities. The bailiff had to quell a near riot.

The prosecution introduced an astronomer to back up Peggy Satterlee's description of the moon through the porthole. Geisler made him admit that, judging by the boat's course, the moon could not have been seen from Flynn's cabin.

The jury argued until the next day and found Errol Flynn not guilty. Said foreman Ruby Anderson afterward:

> We felt there had been other men in the girls' lives. Frankly, the cards were
> on the table and we couldn't believe the girls' stories.

Errol Flynn's career continued, totaling some 60 films before he died in 1959.

—Bernard Ryan, Jr.

Suggestions for Further Reading

Conrad, Earl. *Errol Flynn: A Memoir.* New York: Dodd, Mead & Co., 1978.

Flynn, Errol. *My Wicked, Wicked Ways.* New York: G.P. Putnam's Sons, 1959.

Higham, Charles. *Errol Flynn: The Untold Story.* Garden City, N.Y.: Doubleday & Co., 1980.

Thomas, Tony. *Errol Flynn: The Spy Who Never Was.* New York: Citadel Press, 1990.

Wiles, Buster with William Donati. *My Days with Errol Flynn.* Santa Monica, Calif.: Roundtable Publishing, 1988.

Eddie Slovik Court-Martial: 1944

Defendant: Private Eddie D. Slovik   **Crime Charged:** Violation of the 58th Article of War (desertion to avoid hazardous duty)
Chief Defense Lawyer: Captain Edward P. Woods
Chief Prosecutor: Captain John I. Green   **Judges:** 1st Lieutenant Bernard Altman, Captain Stanley H. French, Captain Benedict B. Kimmelman, Major Orland F. Leighty, Major Robert D. Montondo, Captain Arthur V. Patterson, Captain Clarence W. Welch, Major Herbert D. White, and Colonel Guy M. Williams.   **Place:** Rotgen, Germany   **Date of Trial:** November 11, 1944
Verdict: Guilty   **Sentence:** Execution

SIGNIFICANCE

Private Eddie Slovik was the only American executed for desertion of military duty from 1864 in the Civil War to the present. His court-martial during World War II stands as an example of the precise application of the letter of the law. It leaves disturbing questions about whether, all things considered, it was a fair trial.

In August 1944, as American forces in World War II fought across France into Germany, replacement troops, fresh off the troopship *Aquitania* and just out of basic infantry training, were moved toward combat. As one truckload of 12 soldiers neared the city of Elbeuf, some 80 miles northwest of Paris, they passed miles of bloody and charred remains of men, horses, guns, trucks, and tanks left behind by fleeing Germans. The Americans expected to join G Company of the 109th Infantry, 28th Division—Pennsylvania's famed National Guard outfit, known since World War I as the Keystone or "Bloody Bucket" division.

Toward midnight, not having found G Company and with shellfire exploding around them, the raw troops were ordered to dig in for the night. Two men, Privates Eddie Slovik and John F. Tankey, holed into side-by-side foxholes as German shells continued to pummel them. In the morning, Slovik and Tankey, saying they could not find their 10 companions or their unit, presented themselves to a Canadian unit in the vicinity and were welcomed.

A "Damn Good Guy"

Tankey wrote a letter to the 109th announcing that both men were lost. They stayed with the Canadian outfit for six weeks, roving back toward Calais as the unit posted notices explaining martial law to the natives. Eddie Slovik, 25 years old, established himself as a "damn good guy," an outstanding forager, and the creator of delicious potato pancakes, a talent grown on his Polish family tree.

Tankey noticed that Slovik quit carrying ammunition in his cartridge belt. Instead, he wadded pieces of paper, collected from the Red Cross, on which he almost constantly wrote letters to his wife in Detroit.

On October 7, Slovik and Tankey reached 109th regimental headquarters at Rocherath and were sent to Company G. No charges were placed against them, for the system of moving up rookie troops had been severely confused by the rapid movement of the outfits they were supposed to find.

"If I Leave Now, Will It Be Desertion?"

Eddie Slovik reported to his company commander, Captain Ralph O. Grotte, in a farmhouse on the afternoon of October 8. He was "too scared, too nervous," he said, to serve with a rifle company. Could he serve in a rear area? If not, he said, he would run away. The captain shook his head and assigned him to Platoon 4. Slovik reported to his platoon leader, then went back to the captain. "If I leave now, will it be desertion?" he asked. Captain Grotte said it would. Slovik disappeared.

The next morning, a cook at the Military Government Detachment, 112th Infantry, found Eddie Slovik before him, presenting a slip of green paper with handwriting and saying he had made a confession. The cook turned Slovik over to his lieutenant, who had a military policeman take him back to the 109th, where Lieutenant Colonel Ross C. Henbest read Slovik's confession:

> I Pvt. Eddie D. Slovik #36896415 confess to the Desertion of the United States Army. . . . I came to Albuff as a Replacement. They were shelling the town and we were told to dig in for the night. The following morning . . . I was so scared nerves and trembling that at the time the other Replacements moved out I couldn't move. I stayed in my foxhole till it was quiet. . . . I then walked in town. . . . I turned myself over to the Canadian Provost Corp. After six weeks I was turned over to American M.P. They turned me lose. I told my commanding officer my story. I said that if I had to go out there again I'd run away. He said their was nothing he could do for me so I ran away again AND I'LL RUN AWAY AGAIN IF I HAVE TO GO OUT THERE.

The colonel advised Slovik to take back the confession and destroy it. When Slovik refused, the colonel had him write a disclaimer on the back noting that it "can be held against me and that I made it of my own free will and that I do not have to make it."

"I've Made Up My Mind"

Eddie Slovik was then locked up in the division stockade. Charges were preferred and investigated. Lieutenant Colonel Henry P. Sommer, the division judge advocate, offered Slovik a deal: "If you will go back to your outfit and soldier," he said, "I'll ask the General if he will suspend action on your court-martial. I'll even try to get you a transfer to another regiment where nobody will know what you have done and you can make a clean start."

"I've made up my mind," said Slovik. "I'll take my court-martial."

The colonel was not surprised. He had heard many men prefer to take their court-martials. The fact was that the 28th "Bloody Bucket" Division was facing its most difficult fighting ever. Deep in the Hurtgen Forest, it was being pounded by heavy and terrifying German artillery barrages. Casualties were high, withdrawals were imperative, rookie reinforcements were inexperienced and disorganized, snow was already falling. Men who had marched exuberantly through Paris in August were ready to take dishonorable discharges and serve months or, if need be, years behind bars to escape from the front lines in November. Desertions were becoming commonplace.

The Slovik court-martial was held at 10:00 A.M. on November 11, 1944 (the anniversary of World War I's Armistice Day). Before nine officers of the court seated behind a long table, the prosecutor, Captain John I. Green, stated the charge: desertion to avoid hazardous duty. On the specific charge of desertion at Elbeuf, a single witness testified that after the rookie troops searching for Company G had dug into foxholes a subsequent order had told them to move out, and that he had heard Slovik's voice among the men. On the specific charge of desertion at Rocherath, witnesses were the MP to whom Slovik handed his confession, Captain Grotte, who told of his interview with Slovik, the cook whom Slovik first encountered at Rocherath, and the officer to whom the cook took him.

Slovik's defense counsel, Captain Edward P. Woods, announced that the accused elected to remain silent. Lieutenant Bernard Altman then read him his legal right to be sworn as a witness. Slovik conferred with Woods, then said, "I will remain silent." The defense rested.

On secret written ballots, the nine officers then found Eddie Slovik guilty on the general charge and on each specific charge. All nine then concurred, on secret written ballots, in sentencing the accused:

> To be dishonorably discharged from the service, to forfeit all pay and allowances due or to become due, and to be shot to death with musketry.

The court adjourned at 11:40 A.M.

Under military law, the sentence had to be approved by the division commander, Major General Norman D. "Dutch" Cota, after the division judge advocate prepared a comprehensive review and recommendations. The review produced an FBI check on Slovik. It disclosed that he had a prison record. After serving five years for embezzling small change and merchandise worth $59.60 from a drug store where he worked, and for automobile theft and violation of paroles, he had been paroled in 1942, had married, and had held a good job until he was drafted in 1944. The prison record, the judge advocate told the general, was a reason for not recommending clemency.

Case Reviewed Extensively

The Slovik case was also reviewed by the military justice section of the European theater judge advocate and by the branch office of the judge advocate general, which reported:

> There can be no doubt that he deliberately sought the safety and comparative comfort of the guardhouse. . . . If the death penalty is ever to be imposed for desertion it should be imposed in this case, not as a punitive measure nor as retribution, but to maintain that discipline upon which alone an army can succeed against the enemy.

General Dwight D. Eisenhower, as European theater commander, issued the order confirming the sentence and directing the execution. Eddie Slovik was executed at St. Marie aux Mines in France on January 31, 1945, by a firing squad of 12 enlisted men.

Slovik's widow received no further pay or allowances. His GI insurance was not paid because, she was told, he died under "dishonorable" circumstances. She did not learn until 1953 that her husband had been executed for desertion.

—Bernard Ryan, Jr.

Suggestions for Further Reading

Huie, William Bradford. *The Execution of Private Slovik*. New York: Dell, 1970.

Kimmelman, Benedict B. "The Example of Private Slovik." *American Heritage* (September/October 1987) 97–104.

Ex Parte Endo Trial: 1944

Appellant and Defendant: Mitsuye Endo   **Appellant Claim:** Entitlement to
habeas corpus   **Chief Lawyer for Plaintiff:** Charles Fahey
Chief Lawyer for Appellant: James C. Purcell   **Justices:** Chief Justice
Harlan F. Stone; Justices Hugo L. Black, William O. Douglas, Felix Frankfurter,
Robert H. Jackson, Frank Murphy, Stanley F. Reed, Owen J. Roberts, and
Wiley B. Rutledge   **Place:** Washington, D.C.
Date of Decision: December 18, 1944   **Decision:** Judgment reversed and
the cause remanded to district court

SIGNIFICANCE

This Supreme Court decision ended what the American Civil Liberties Union later
called "the worst single wholesale violation of civil rights of American citizens in
our history."

In February 1942, soon after the Japanese bombed Pearl Harbor in the surprise
attack that committed the United States to World War II, President Franklin
D. Roosevelt authorized the War Relocation Authority to detain persons of
Japanese ancestry living on the West Coast, many of whom were not only
American citizens but native-born.

Military commanders were authorized to designate areas from which such
persons could be excluded; if they lived within those areas, the military could
move them. Lt. General J. L. De Witt, of the Western Defense Command,
proclaimed that the entire Pacific Coast of the United States:

> [B]y its geographical location is particularly subject to attack, to attempted
> invasion by the armed forces of nations with which the United States is now
> at war, and, in connection therewith, is subject to espionage and acts of
> sabotage, thereby requiring the adoption of military measures necessary to
> establish safeguards against such enemy operations.

On those orders, 110,000 Japanese-Americans, 75,000 of whom were U. S.
citizens, were removed from their homes. Meantime, Congress enacted legislation that ratified and confirmed the president's order.

Mitsuye Endo, a native-born American whose ancestors were Japanese,
was taken from her home in Sacramento, California, to the Tule Lake War
Relocation Center at Newell, California. Endo was 22. A Methodist who had

never visited Japan and neither spoke nor read Japanese, she worked in the California Department of Motor Vehicles. At Tule, she and the others found they could not leave the center without written permission issued by the War Relocation Authority.

President Franklin Roosevelt authorized the relocation of people of Japanese ancestry after the attack on Pearl Harbor. (Courtesy, National Archives)

Petition and Appeal Stretch Over 21 Months

In July 1942, through lawyer James Purcell, who had worked with Japanese-American lawyers in Sacramento and who was appalled at the treatment the native Americans had received, Endo filed a petition for a writ of *habeas corpus* (relief from unlawful confinement) in the District Court of the United States for the Northern District of California. She asked for her liberty to be restored. One year passed. The petition was denied in July 1943. In August, Endo appealed to the U.S. Circuit Court of Appeals.

Next, Mitsuye Endo was moved to the Central Utah Relocation Center at Topaz, Utah. It took the Circuit Court of Appeals until April 22, 1944, to decide that it needed to apply to the U.S. Supreme Court for instructions on some questions of law. The Supreme Court promptly demanded the entire record of the Endo case, so that it could "proceed to a decision as if the case had been brought to the Supreme Court by appeal." Thus the case became identified as "Ex parte Endo"—ex parte being a legal way of saying that the case came from one side only (most appeals to higher courts have two sides, the appellant's and the appellee's).

Confined Under Armed Guard

The Supreme Court soon learned that Mitsuye Endo:

is a loyal and law-abiding citizen of the United States, that no charge has been made against her, that she is being unlawfully detained, and that she is confined in the Relocation Center under armed guard and held there against her will.

The court also learned, from one of General De Witt's reports, that:

Essentially, military necessity required only that the Japanese population be removed from the coastal area and dispersed in the interior. . . . That the evacuation program necessarily and ultimately developed into one of complete Federal supervision was due primarily to the fact that the interior states would not accept an uncontrolled Japanese migration.

The military's argument, noted Justice William O. Douglas in the opinion handed down December 18, 1944, was that "but for such supervision there might have been dangerously disorderly migration of unwanted people to unprepared communities" and that "although community hostility towards the evacuees has diminished, it has not disappeared and the continuing control of the Authority over the relocation process is essential to the success of the evacuation program."

Justice Douglas wrote:

We are of the view that Mitsuye Endo should be given her liberty. We conclude that, whatever power the War Relocation Authority may have to detain other classes of citizens, it has no authority to subject citizens who are concededly loyal to its leave procedure.

Loyalty is a matter of the heart and mind, not of race, creed, or color. He who is loyal is by definition not a spy or a saboteur. When the power to detain is derived from the power to protect the war effort against espionage and sabotage, detention which has no relationship to that objective is unauthorized.

If we assume (as we do) that the original evacuation was justified, its lawful character was derived from the fact that it was an espionage and sabotage measure, not that there was community hostility to this group of American citizens.

"Mitsuye Endo," concluded the Justice, "is entitled to unconditional release by the War Relocation Authority."

By this time, the War Relocation Authority, aware that no military need existed for barring Japanese Americans from the West Coast, had quietly begun permitting selected evacuees to return home. The Supreme Court decision effectively ended the detention program, as the Western Defense Command announced that "those persons of Japanese ancestry whose records have stood the test of Army scrutiny during the past two years" would be released from internment after January 2, 1945.

—Bernard Ryan, Jr.

Suggestions for Further Reading

Armor, John and Peter Wright with photographs by Ansel Adams and commentary by John Hersey. *Manzanar*. New York: Times Books division of Random House, 1988.

Burns, James MacGregor. *Roosevelt: The Soldier of Freedom*. New York: Harcourt Brace Jovanovich, 1970.

Irons, Peter. *Justice at War*. New York: Oxford University Press, 1983.

Melendy, H. Brett. *The Oriental Americans*. New York: Twayne Publishers, 1972.

Wilson, Robert A. and Bill Hosokawa. *East to America*. New York: William Morrow & Co., 1980.

Ezra Pound Trial: 1946

Defendant: Ezra Pound   **Crime Charged:** Treason
Chief Defense Lawyers: Thurman Arnold, Julien Cornell, and Robert W.
Furniss, Jr.   **Chief Prosecutors:** Isaiah Matlack, and Oliver Gasch
Judge: Bolitha J. Laws   **Place:** Washington, D.C.
Date of Trial: February 13, 1946   **Verdict:** Unsound mind; indictment
dismissed in 1958

SIGNIFICANCE

This case involved a unique combination of elements: the charge of treason, a
defendant who was widely known and respected in the literary world, the question
of insanity (never fully resolved), and the commitment of such renowned figures
as T.S. Eliot, Robert Frost, Ernest Hemingway, and Archibald MacLeish.

Ezra Pound was born in Hailey, Idaho, a town of one street, one hotel, and 47
saloons, in 1885. After unhappy college years, he moved to Europe before
World War I. There, while publishing poetry and working as secretary to Irish
poet William Butler Yeats, he helped establish such literary giants as T.S. Eliot,
Robert Frost, and James Joyce.

In Paris in the 1920s, the expatriate colony found Pound superbly confident of his own talent and outspokenly critical of all people and ideas that
earned his disdain. In the 1930s, he settled permanently in Rapallo, Italy, where
he continued to work on the long poems he called *Cantos*.

"Europe Calling! Pound Speaking!"

Hitler's war loomed. Pound had strong opinions on world politics. Turned
down when he suggested that the Italian Government put out publications that
would improve American sympathy for Italian fascism, he proposed short-wave
radio aimed at America. By January 1941, his "Europe calling! Pound speaking!
Ezra Pound speaking!" was on the air regularly. Paid for his services, he urged
America to stay out of the war and concentrated on anti-Semitism as his chief
message. "Clever Kikes," he said, were "runnin' ALL our communications
system." After Pearl Harbor, he declared (early in 1942):

America COULD have stayed out of the war. . . . IF America had stayed neutral the war would now be over. . . . For the United States to be makin' war on Italy AND on Europe is just plain damn nonsense . . . And for this state of things Franklin Roosevelt is more than any other one man responsible.

America heard Pound. Attorney General Francis Biddle had him indicted for treason, the only crime that is defined in the U.S. Constitution:

> Treason against the United States shall consist only in levying War against them, or in adhering to their Enemies, giving them Aid and Comfort. No Person shall be convicted of Treason unless on the Testimony of Two Witnesses to the same overt Act, or in Confession in open Court.

Pound was "completely surprised." He wrote Biddle:

> I do not believe that the simple fact of speaking over the radio . . . can in itself constitute treason. I think that must depend on what is said. . . .

> I obtained the concession to speak over Rome radio with the following proviso: Namely that nothing should be asked of me contrary to my conscience or contrary to my duties as an American citizen. . . .

> I have not spoken with regard to *this* war, but in protest against a system which creates one war after another. . . . I have not spoken to the troops, and have not suggested that the troops should mutiny or revolt. . . .

Treason charges against author Ezra Pound were finally dismissed based on the finding that he was unfit for trial. (Courtesy, National Archives)

Learning of the indictment, Librarian of Congress Archibald MacLeish asked if it might not "confer the paraphernalia of martyrdom upon a half-cracked and extremely foolish individual."

In Rome, after the Italian Government collapsed, Pound continued on the air under the German occupation. But the day after Italy surrendered, partisans seized him at gunpoint. He was imprisoned in Italy for six months, then flown to America.

"Poor Old Ezra Is Quite, Quite Balmy"

Said Ernest Hemingway, "He ought to go to the loony bin, which he rates and you can pick out the parts in his cantos at which he starts to rate it." MacLeish added, "It is pretty clear that poor old Ezra is quite, quite balmy."

Defense counsel Julien Cornell decided that proving clinical insanity might be the surest way to save Pound from execution. Psychiatric examinations by four doctors brought a unanimous report that Pound was not sane enough to stand trial. One said Pound suffered from delusions that he had valuable connections "in a half dozen countries" and should be "an adviser to the state department." Nevertheless, prosecutor Isaiah Matlack asked for a "public insanity hearing" before a jury.

On February 13, 1946, the jury heard that Pound:

shows a remarkable grandiosity . . . believes he has been designated to save the Constitution of the United States for the people of the United States . . . has a feeling that he has the key to the peace of the world through the writings of Confucius . . . believes that with himself as a leader a group of intellectuals could work for world order . . .

The jury was out for three minutes, then announced that Pound was of "unsound mind." He was immediately confined until he was fit for trial at the St. Elizabeth Federal Hospital for the Insane in Washington. Friends who were confident that he was *not* insane pondered how he could ever be released without facing another trial.

Pound characteristically accepted his situation, reading and writing in his room. Over the next 12 years, applications for bail and petitions of *habeas corpus* were denied. In 1948, he was awarded the prestigious $10,000 Bollingen Prize for Poetry. Congress then ordered the prize's sponsor, the Library of Congress, to give no more awards. A Presidential pardon was proposed in 1954, but was dismissed under the dubious rationale that one cannot be pardoned until after one has been found guilty.

In 1955, MacLeish began trying to get the attorney general to *nol pros*, or quash, the standing indictment for treason. Hemingway, Eliot, and Frost joined the effort. In April 1958, Judge Bolitha Laws, who had presided at the original insanity hearing in 1945, dismissed the indictment, basing his decision on an affidavit of Dr. Winfred Overholser (the superintendent of St. Elizabeth's) that Pound was still unfit for trial.

Ezra Pound was released from St Elizabeth's and promptly sailed for Italy. He died in Venice in 1972.

— Bernard Ryan, Jr.

Suggestions for Further Reading

Ackroyd, Peter. *Ezra Pound and His World*. New York: Charles Scribner's Sons, 1980.

Carpenter, Humphrey. *A Serious Character: The Life of Ezra Pound*. Boston: Houghton Mifflin, 1988.

Heymann, C. David. *Ezra Pound: The Last Rower*. New York: Viking Press, 1976.

Tytell, John. *Ezra Pound: The Solitary Volcano*. New York: Doubleday-Anchor Press, 1987.

Sally Rand Trial: 1946

Defendant: Sally Rand (Helen Gould Beck) **Crime Charged:** Indecent exposure, corrupting the morals of an audience, and conducting an obscene show **Chief Defense Lawyer:** J.W. "Jake" Ehrlich
Chief Prosecutor: Frank Brown **Judge:** Daniel R. Shoemaker
Place: San Francisco, California **Dates of Trial:** November 13–14, 1946
Verdict: Not guilty

SIGNIFICANCE

The brief trial of Sally Rand demonstrated the importance of reminding a judge of the need to see all evidence in a case with his or her own eyes. The case also provided a lighthearted, if not frivolous, moment in the usually serious calendar of court proceedings.

By 1946, Sally Rand was a nationally known entertainer whose *shtick* was unique: Synchronized to music, she waved six-foot fans while she danced nude behind them. A show-business veteran who had performed in vaudeville, movies, and Broadway chorus lines, she enjoyed an unprecedented reputation. Ever since her appearance in 1933 as a headliner, with a bevy of associated female dancers, in "The City of Paris" extravaganza at the Chicago World's Fair, the name "Sally Rand" and the term "fan dancer" had been synonymous. (Over that summer in Chicago, Illinois, her weekly pay had risen from $125 to $3,000.) Her act had played in clubs nationwide and won particular acclaim in Los Angeles, California, and Las Vegas, Nevada.

Up the Runway . . . to "Clair de Lune"

At the Golden Gate International Exposition on Treasure Island in San Francisco Bay in 1939 and 1940, "Sally Rand's Nude Ranch," featuring Sally and her troupe of females (all wearing nothing but holsters and badges), was a big hit. But one November evening in 1946, while she was appearing at the Club Savoy on O'Farrell Street in San Francisco, six members of that California city's police department watched her dance slowly and, apparently, naked up a dimly lit runway as she maneuvered a giant white fan in rhythm to Claude Debussy's romantic "Clair de Lune." Professing shock at what they viewed as an indecent performance, they arrested her. Section 311 of the Penal Code, they said, barred "indecent exposure, corrupting the morals of an audience, and conducting an obscene show."

Sally immediately called Jake Ehrlich, a leading San Francisco attorney who was well-known as the defender of celebrities and criminals. He had successfully defended singer Billie Holiday and drummer Gene Krupa against drug charges.

Prosecutor Frank Brown opened the trial by putting police Captain Joseph Walsh on the stand. The captain testified to the onerous duty his six officers had performed in watching Sally Rand disrobe, behind her fans, from full costume to a single tiny flesh-colored triangular patch—an item which, in the excitement of making the arrest, they had failed to seize as evidence. The captain was able, however, to report specific details: The patch had 10 beads sewn at each corner.

Fan dancer Sally Rand behind her ubiquitous fan. (Hearst Newspaper Collection, University of Southern California Library)

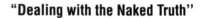

"Dealing with the Naked Truth"

Defense attorney Jake Ehrlich pointed out to Judge Daniel R. Shoemaker that nudity was "respected in the highest artistic circles and elsewhere," and reminded the court of the masterpieces of sculptors Praxiteles, Michelangelo, and Rodin. "May I suggest, Your Honor," he said, "that we adjourn until tomorrow morning, at which time my client will perform her specialty for you? Thus instead of second-hand accounts and narrow-minded criticisms, we'll be dealing with the naked truth."

The judge not only agreed but provided, at Ehrlich's request, a court order that would release Sally Rand immediately if she were arrested for the same offense again before the trial was completed. That night, with the Savoy crammed with customers and policemen, Sally Rand danced, was interrupted for arrest, and was revealed (when the lights were ordered turned up) to be wearing long flannel underwear and, instead of a triangular patch, a small card marked "CENSORED. S.F.P.D." So embarrassed they didn't know what else to do, the cops arrested the dancer even though she was fully clothed. She presented her court order for immediate release and went on with her midnight show as usual.

The next morning at the Savoy, a jam-packed crowd of court and newspaper people watched Sally Rand dance through her customary performance. When all returned to the courtroom, Judge Shoemaker said, "Anyone who could find something lewd about the dance as she puts it on has to have a perverted idea of morals." With that, the judge pronounced Sally Rand not guilty on all counts.

Sally Rand then went back to fan dancing.

—*Bernard Ryan, Jr.*

Suggestions for Further Reading

Ehrlich, J.W. *A Life in My Hands*. New York: G.P. Putnam's Sons, 1965.

Nash, Jay Robert. *Encyclopedia of World Crime*. Wilmette, Ill.: CrimeBooks, 1991.

"1933: Fifty Years Ago." *American Heritage* (April/May 1983): 9.

Bercovici v. Chaplin: 1947

Plaintiff: Konrad Bercovici   **Defendant:** Charles S. Chaplin
Plaintiff Claim: Plagiarism   **Chief Defense Lawyer:** Louis Frohlich
Chief Lawyer for Plaintiff: Louis Nizer   **Judge:** Harold P. Burke
Place: New York, New York   **Dates of Trial:** April 17–May 1, 1947
Verdict: None; suit settled for $95,000 payment by Chaplin

SIGNIFICANCE
This suit against Charlie Chaplin for plagiarism attracted international attention and tarnished the comedian's benign image. Although the plaintiff in the end settled for a modest amount of money by agreeing to a settlement, Chaplin acknowledged, in effect, that he had plagiarized another's film concept.

Silent-film star Charlie Chaplin and screenwriter Konrad Bercovici became close friends in Hollywood early in the 1920s. They continued to see each other during the 30s, when Chaplin was creating his greatest hits, *City Lights*, *Modern Times*, and *The Great Dictator*. The latter, his first sound film, was released in 1940 as Europe was already deep in World War II and the United States faced inevitable participation; the film was a powerful and caustic burlesque of Germany's Adolf Hitler.

In June 1946, a year after the war ended, the Information Control Division of the Allied Control Council, which oversaw the military administration of occupied Germany, permitted a "sneak preview" showing of *The Great Dictator* in Berlin. Replying to questionnaires, the audience said the film should not be shown throughout the nation lest it stimulate revulsion rather than mirth.

"The Little Tramp" Plays to a Full House

News of the showing brought renewed interest in the film in America. Konrad Bercovici announced a particular interest in the 7-year-old film: He was suing his old friend Chaplin for plagiarism, for, he said, he had first suggested in the mid-1930s that the "Little Tramp" play Hitler. He demanded $6,450,000.

The trial began—"before a full house," as the newspapers reported—on April 17, 1947, in U.S. District Court in New York City, with Judge Harold P. Burke presiding. Bercovici's lawyer, the renowned Louis Nizer, told the jury he would prove that Chaplin had contracted with Bercovici to collaborate in the production of a series of pictures, with the plaintiff to receive 15 percent of the gross profits. In 1938, he said, Bercovici had written a satirical scenario based on Hitler and dictatorship, but Chaplin had rejected it for political reasons. *The Great Dictator*, he charged, was based on that scenario.

A parade of witnesses ranging from actor Melvyn Douglas to producer Alexander Korda to Chaplin's ex-wife, actress Paulette Goddard, testified on Chaplin's behalf during the next two weeks.

Plaintiff Claims Oral Agreement

On the witness stand, Bercovici said that he suggested a picture on dictators while visiting Chaplin's Pebble Beach, California home in 1938, and that Chaplin orally agreed to its production but subsequently rejected the idea. Nevertheless, he insisted, *The Great Dictator*, based on his script, appeared two years later.

In a courtroom filled to capacity, the final witness was Chaplin himself. The white-haired, 58-year-old comedian spoke rapidly and clearly to the jury of nine men and three women, gesturing frequently with his head and arms. When Bercovici suggested the idea, he said, he told the writer that he had been thinking it over himself for some time, and had outlined the story he had in mind not only to Bercovici but to Melvyn Douglas and others.

On direct examination, Chaplin identified his scrapbook for 1936. It contained several stories concerning the similarity of Hitler's mustache to the one Charlie wore on the screen. Chaplin's attorney, Louis Frohlich, asked, "Had the idea of impersonating Hitler come to you for the first time from Mr. Bercovici?"

"It had not," replied the witness.

Attorney Nizer introduced Bercovici's script as evidence. Chaplin said he had never seen it before. Nor did he make oral agreements, he said. His practice was to have all contracts in written form.

The next afternoon, May 1, Judge Burke called the attorneys for both sides to his office and asked them how much longer they expected the trial to last. Then he remarked, "I don't suppose you gentlemen ever thought of settling this, did you?"

The two sides, including Chaplin and Bercovici themselves, bargained from late afternoon until 10:00 P.M. The Bercovici side dropped first to $500,000, then to $350,000. Actively negotiating on his own behalf, Chaplin said he would not consider any settlement "in six figures." They finally agreed that Chaplin would pay Bercovici $95,000, including $5,000 for his legal expenses. Bercovici agreed to deliver to Chaplin a release covering any rights he had asserted in *The Great Dictator*. Chaplin also gained worldwide motion-picture rights to two Bercovici scenarios. Judge Burke dismissed the jury.

Five years later, Charlie Chaplin departed from the United States and settled in Switzerland with his young wife, the former Oona O'Neill, and their growing family. He died there in 1977 at the age of 88. It is not known whether he ever again saw his longtime friend Konrad Bercovici.

—Bernard Ryan, Jr.

Suggestions for Further Reading

Chaplin, Charles. *My Autobiography*. New York: Simon & Schuster, 1964.

Chaplin, Charles, Jr. *My Father, Charlie Chaplin*. New York: Random House, 1960.

Epstein, Jerry. *Remembering Charlie*. Garden City, N.Y.: Doubleday & Co., 1989.

Gifford, Denis. *Chaplin*. Garden City, N.Y.: Doubleday & Co., 1960.

Haining, Peter. *The Legend of Charlie Chaplin*. Secaucus, N.J.: Castle, 1982.

McCabe, John. *Charlie Chaplin*. Garden City, N.Y.: Doubleday & Co., 1978.

McCaffrey, Donald W., ed. *Focus on Chaplin*. Englewood Cliffs, N.J.: Prentice Hall, 1971.

Manvell, Roger. *Chaplin*. Boston: Little, Brown & Co., 1974.

Robinson, David. *Chaplin, His Life and Art*. New York: McGraw-Hill, 1985.

——. *Chaplin, the Mirror of Opinion*. Bloomington: Indiana University Press, 1983.

Caryl Chessman Trial: 1948

Defendant: Caryl Whittier Chessman   **Crimes Charged:** Kidnapping, sexual perversion, and robbery   **Chief Defense Lawyers:** Caryl Chessman and Al Matthews   **Chief Prosecutor:** J. Miller Leavy   **Judge:** Charles W. Fricke
Place: Los Angeles, California   **Dates of Trial:** April 4–May 21, 1948
Verdict: Guilty   **Sentence:** Death

SIGNIFICANCE

Caryl Chessman's uniquely documented struggle against capital punishment not only aroused global sympathy for a possibly innocent man, but highlighted the imponderable sluggishness of the U.S. death penalty process.

In January 1948, a 27-year-old career criminal named Caryl Chessman was arrested after a car chase and shootout as a suspect in the armed robbery of a men's clothing store in Los Angeles, California. When police searched the stolen Ford that Chessman was driving, they found a penlight and a .45-caliber automatic pistol, items that made them suspect that Chessman might be the "Red Light Bandit," a man who had been driving up to couples in parked cars, flashing a red light to make them think it was a police car, then robbing the couples and forcing some of the women to perform sexual acts. Despite the fact that Chessman bore little physical resemblance to descriptions of the attacker, several victims identified him. The charge sheet included multiple counts of robbery, two counts of sexual perversion, and—most importantly—three counts of violating Section 209 of the California Penal Code, the so-called "Little Lindbergh Law." This covered kidnapping with intent to commit robbery: if bodily harm could also be proved, Section 209 was punishable by death.

Defends Himself

Even before the trial began April 4, 1948, Chessman, a cocky, street-smart hoodlum with an overinflated opinion of his own cleverness, created headlines by dismissing his lawyers and announcing that he intended to defend himself. It is impossible to overstate the enormity of this tactical blunder. Not only was Chessman on trial for his life, but he was facing Judge Charles W. Fricke, who in the course of his career sentenced more people to death than any other judge in California history. Right from the outset, Fricke made it plain that he regarded

Chessman as an arrogant interloper, and he did everything possible to stymie the defense. When Chessman asked Fricke that he be given a daily transcript of proceedings, Fricke denied the request, something he had never done before in a capital case. Chessman's further complaint that he had not been shown the correct way to make a motion drew an outburst from Fricke: "Mr. Chessman, the court is not engaged in conducting a law school or advising a defendant what court procedure is." (As a matter of fact, so advising the defendant was *exactly* Fricke's duty in the case of a man conducting his own defense.)

Neither did Chessman make much headway with the prosecutor, J. Miller Leavy. A 16-year veteran of capital cases, Leavy outmaneuvered his opponent at every turn. Never was this more apparent than during the jury selection process, when Chessman sat silently by and let Leavy impanel an 11-woman, one-man jury, something no experienced defense lawyer would have allowed in a sex case.

The first witness, Regina Johnson, described being taken from her car at gunpoint by a masked assailant to another vehicle where she was forced to commit a sexual act. (It was that distance between the two cars—22 feet—that made this a capital case. Technically, under California law at the time, she had been kidnapped. Those 22 feet meant the difference between a maximum sentence of 15 years for sexual perversion and death in the gas chamber.) "He told me that we would be taken away in a casket, the both of us, unless I did what he wanted." Briefly the attacker's mask had slipped, affording Johnson a glimpse of his face. She positively identified Chessman as the man.

Caryl Chessman's fight as his own attorney unarguably contributed to his demise. (Hearst Newspaper Collection, University of Southern California Library)

On cross-examination Chessman emphasized discrepancies between Johnson's description of her attacker and himself. The bandit had been of undistinguished build and 5'8" or 5'9". Chessman was close to 6' and almost 200 pounds. Johnson persisted in her identification. Then she went on the offensive. When Chessman asked, "Did this person . . . state what his intentions in taking you back to the other car was [*sic*]?" Johnson responded: "No, *you* didn't tell me until after I had gotten in your car."

"How long were you in the Ford?"

"In the car with *you?*" Johnson needled, sensing Chessman's increasing agitation. It worked. Chessman erupted, demanding of Judge Fricke that Johnson answer the questions as asked. Fricke denied the request, leaving Chessman to stew.

Another victim of the "Red Light Bandit," Mary Alice Meza, was less feisty but equally damaging. Asked by prosecutor Leavy if Chessman was her attacker, Meza replied, "There is no question. It is definitely him. I know what he looks like."

Chessman the witness was no more impressive than Chessman the lawyer. Leavy repeatedly trapped him in confusing and contradictory answers. Once, when taxed on responses made to police, Chessman replied, "Specifically, I don't remember what my answers were, because they were just fabrications."

Controversial Transcript

On May 21, 1948, Chessman was found guilty on all charges, with punishment fixed at death, and held, pending formal sentencing. Then something unusual occurred. The court reporter, Ernest Perry, an elderly man who had been ill during the trial, died from a coronary thrombosis, leaving behind his 1,800 pages of shorthand testimony. Chessman pounced. Under California law, if the court reporter died before transcribing his notes in a civil case, a new trial must be held. On June 25, 1948, Judge Fricke, pointing out that this was a criminal case, not civil, refused Chessman's request for a new trial. Then he sentenced him to death twice.

In September 1948 responsibility for transcribing the shorthand notes was given to Stanley Fraser, who just happened to be the uncle of prosecutor Leavy. (He also received $10,000 for the task, three times the going rate.) Worse than that, Fraser had several times been arrested for drunkenness—once while actually taking dictation in court. Chessman argued that the transcription which Fraser provided was hopelessly biased and inaccurate.

Over the next decade this mutilated transcript formed the bedrock of Chessman's historic struggle against his sentence. He won eight stays of execution, some within hours of the appointed time. He also wrote three books. The first, *Cell 2455, Death Row*, became a best seller and made him an international cause célèbre.

But on May 2, 1960, Chessman's ordeal ended in the San Quentin gas chamber. The circumstances of his execution were remarkably similar to those of Burton Abbott (see separate entry), three years earlier. Just seconds after guards sealed the door, a ninth stay of execution was telephoned through. Like Abbott's, it came too late. Caryl Chessman's fight was over.

No matter which side one takes regarding Chessman's guilt or innocence, few now doubt that his trial was seriously flawed. Had he been properly represented, there is every likelihood that his sentence would have been commuted. But because, in the eyes of those who mattered, he had brought the law into disrepute, he paid the ultimate price. Arrogance undid him. An old legal maxim states that anyone who defends himself has a fool for a client. Never was this more vividly demonstrated than in the trial of Caryl Chessman.

—Colin Evans

Suggestions for Further Reading

Brown, Edmund G. and Dick Adler. *Public Justice, Private Mercy*. New York: Weidenfeld & Nicolson, 1989.

Chessman, Caryl. *Cell 2455, Death Row*. Westport, Conn.: Greenwood Press, 1954.

Machlin, Milton and William Read Woodfield. *Ninth Life*. New York: G.P. Putnam's Sons, 1961.

Parker, Frank J. *Caryl Chessman, The Red Light Bandit*. Chicago: Nelson-Hall, 1975.

Hollywood Ten Trials: 1948–50

Defendants: Alvah Bessie, Herbert Biberman, Lester Cole, Edward Dmytryk, Ring Lardner, Jr., John Howard Lawson, Albert Maltz, Sam Ornitz, Robert Adrian Scott, and Dalton Trumbo **Crime Charged:** Contempt of Congress **Chief Defense Lawyers:** Bartley Crum, Charles J. Katz, Robert W. Kenny, and Martin Popper **Chief Prosecutor:** William Hitz **Judges:** Edward M. Curran, Richmond B. Keech, and David A. Pine **Place:** Washington, D.C. **Dates of Trials:** April 12–19, 1948 (Lawson); May 3–5, 1948 (Trumbo); June 22–29, 1950 (Biberman, Cole, Dmytryk, Lardner, and Scott); June 23–29, 1950 (Bessie, Maltz, and Ornitz) **Verdicts:** Guilty **Sentences:** 1 year imprisonment and $1,000 fine (Bessie, Cole, Lardner, Lawson, Maltz, Ornitz, Scott, and Trumbo); 6 months and $500 fine (Biberman, and Dmytryk)

SIGNIFICANCE

The Hollywood Ten case stands as a landmark in the history of the abuse of civil liberties. As respected author E.B. White commented, "Ten men have been convicted, not of wrong-doing but of wrong thinking; that is news in this country and if I have not misread my history, it is bad news." By setting the stage for the establishment of the blacklist, the case created a precedent for making political belief a test of employability. In refusing to accept the claims of the Ten that the First Amendment entitled them to remain silent, the House Committee for the Investigation of Un-American Activities caused future witnesses to plead the Fifth Amendment privilege against self-incrimination to avoid answering further questioning.

I n 1946 writers, producers, actors, and directors in the film industry in Hollywood who had been drawn—as "good liberals"—to the American Communist Party over the preceding decade began to sense that the party was not the liberal organization they had been told it was. The party's policy and direction—in effect during World War II, patriotic cooperation and the renunciation of revolutionary goals—were changing. Party head Earl Browder, the "good liberal" leader, was deposed and replaced by hard-liner William Z. Foster. The new policy, as described by screenwriter Albert Maltz in an essay in *New Masses*, was that "unless art is a weapon like a leaflet, serving immediate political ends, necessities and programs, it is worthless or escapist or vicious."

Hollywood Divided into Two Camps

At the same time in the film capital, several years of labor unrest had been coming to a head. Two major craft unions—the International Alliance of Theatrical Stage Employees and Motion Picture Machine Operators (IATSE) and the Conference of Studio Unions (CSU)—had been rivals in a series of jurisdictional disputes and actions. When the CSU called a strike in 1945 and were supported by Communist Party members and Communist-dominated unions, IATSE leader Roy Brewer viewed it as a concerted attempt by the Communists to take over the motion picture industry. As the strike dragged on for six months, he convinced studio heads of his conspiracy theory.

Meantime, the Hollywood Independent Citizens Committee of the Arts, Sciences and Professions, led by actor (later President) Ronald Reagan, producer Dore Schary, composer Johnny Green, actress Olivia de Havilland, and screenwriter Ernest Pascal, was becoming a militant anti-Communist unit. By 1947, the film capital seemed divided into two camps: anti-Communist and pro-Communist.

Against this background, on Capitol Hill in Washington, D.C., the House Committee for the Investigation of Un-American Activities, which had been concerned with Communist activities since the late 1930s, sent investigators from Washington to interview "key Hollywood figures," all of whom were members of the anti-Communist Motion Picture Alliance for the Preservation of American Ideals. The interviews resulted in public hearings by the House committee, mislabeled HUAC ever afterward.

"Friendly witnesses," all members of the Alliance, testified first. They included producer Jack L. Warner, novelist Ayn Rand, and actors Gary Cooper, Robert Montgomery, Ronald Reagan (then president of the Screen Actors Guild), Robert Taylor, and Adolphe Menjou. Altogether, they depicted a Hollywood virtually at the mercy of militant Communists whose orders came directly from Moscow; they described a climate all but saturated with Red propaganda.

Next, 19 people, identified by the "friendly witnesses" as suspected Communists, were subpoenaed from a list that totaled 79.

All were known as radicals. Most were writers; therefore, to HUAC, they were likely conduits for spreading Communist propaganda via the silver screen. But why these particular individuals were called has never been explained.

The Right to Remain Silent

To support them and explore strategy, the Hollywood community formed the Committee for the First Amendment. Its sponsors included four U.S. senators, author Thomas Mann, and film producer Jerry Wald. The strategy was to take the position that the First Amendment provided not only the right to free speech but the right to remain silent.

HUAC Chairman J. Parnell Thomas called 11 of the 19 subpoenaed witnesses to testify. Supporting them in the hearing room were such stars as Humphrey Bogart, Lauren Bacall, Danny Kaye, Gene Kelly, Jane Wyatt, John Huston, and Sterling Hayden. The first witness, screenwriter John Howard Lawson, proposed to read a statement, as each of the "friendly" witnesses had been permitted to do and as called for in the usual procedure of congressional committees. Chairman Thomas looked at the first line of the statement—"For a week, this Committee has conducted an illegal and indecent trial of American citizens, whom the Committee has selected to be publicly pilloried and smeared"—and denied Lawson permission to read it. The chairman then demanded an answer to the question, "Are you now, or have you ever been a member of the Communist Party of the United States?"

"The question of Communism is in no way related to the inquiry, which is an attempt," Lawson replied, "to get control of the screen and to invade the basic rights of American citizens in all fields." The chairman responded by having a nine-page single-spaced memo on Lawson's career, prepared by the committee's investigators, read into the record. Lawson was given no opportunity to respond to it. Repeatedly, as the questions and responses became a shouting match, Lawson was asked about Communist membership. Finally, the chairman, pounding his gavel for quiet, ordered the witness removed and cited him for contempt of Congress.

"I Would Hate Myself in the Morning"

In succession, writers Dalton Trumbo, Albert Maltz, Alvah Bessie, Samuel Ornitz, Herbert Biberman, producer Adrian Scott, director Edward Dmytryk, and writers Lester Cole and Ring Lardner, Jr.—all destined to be known, along with Lawson, as "The Hollywood Ten"—were treated to the same questions and the same denial of permission to read their statements. All were cited for contempt of Congress. Lardner, asked repeatedly if he were a Communist, replied at last, "I could answer, but if I did, I would hate myself in the morning."

The 11th witness was Bertolt Brecht. A successful German playwright, he had been in Hollywood for six years, had taken out first citizenship papers and announced his plan to remain permanently. To date, he had but one screen credit. "I was not a member, or am not a member," he told Chairman Thomas, "of any Communist Party." Immediately, Brecht took a plane for Europe and settled in East Germany.

Shortly, a secret conference in New York's Waldorf-Astoria Hotel brought together Hollywood's leading studio heads, including Nicholas Schenck, Joseph Schenck, Walter Wanger, Samuel Goldwyn, Louis B. Mayer, Dore Schary, Spyros Skouras, and many others, as well as Eric Johnston, president of the Motion Picture Association of America. They issued a statement:

We will forthwith discharge or suspend without compensation those in our employ and we will not re-employ any of the ten until such time as he is acquitted or has purged himself of contempt and declares under oath that he is not a Communist.

On the broader issue of alleged subversive and disloyal elements in Hollywood our members are likewise prepared to take positive action.

We will not knowingly employ a Communist or a member of any party or group which advocates the overthrow of the Government of the United States by force or by any illegal or unconstitutional methods.

The studio heads also promised not to be "swayed by hysteria or intimidation from any source"—paradoxically, the very causes of their secret meeting and public statement.

The Blacklist Is Born

Thus began the blacklist that determined who would or would not be employed not only in Hollywood films but in all of television and radio for the next several years. Institutionalized, the blacklist meant that no artist in show business who had been accused of Communist Party membership, or called to testify, could get work without naming names.

In November 1947, a special session of Congress was called to appropriate funds to resist Communist infiltration in Europe. To that session, Representative Thomas brought his 10 citations for contempt. After a handful of House members had spoken against them, they were passed, 346 to 17.

On April 12, 1948, John Howard Lawson was brought to trial, followed three weeks later by Dalton Trumbo, in U.S. District Court in Washington. In each brief trial, the jury found the defendants guilty of contempt of Congress. Judges Edward M. Curran and David A. Pine suspended their sentences—one year in jail and $1,000 fine—pending appeals. Commenting later on Lawson's and Trumbo's willingness to stand trial, Thurman Arnold, former special assistant to the U.S. attorney general, said:

To test the constitutional right of any Congressional committee to ask, 'Are you now or have you ever been a member of the Communist Party?' it was necessary for these witnesses to do three things:

1. Phrase their answers as they did.

2. Accept citations for contempt of Congress.

3. Stand trial in the Federal courts, and if convicted of contempt appeal to the Supreme Court of the United States.

Supreme Court Refuses to Review

As Lawson's and Trumbo's attorneys filed appeals, the eight others waived their rights to trial by jury, stipulating that they would stand on the records of the jury trials of the first two. However, they reserved the privilege of appealing. All 10 were confident that the Supreme Court would vindicate them. But in the summer of 1949, two liberal justices—Frank Murphy and Wiley Rutledge—died. Their successors, Tom Clark and Sherman Minton, shifted the court majority to the conservative side, and that majority refused to review the convictions of Lawson and Trumbo.

On June 9, 1950, Lawson and Trumbo began their jail terms. The trials of the remaining eight opened on June 22 before Judges Curran and Pine and Judge Richmond B. Keech. By June 29, all were found guilty. Six received one-year sentences and $1,000 fines. Dmytryk and Biberman, however, for reasons never explained, were fined $500 each and jailed for only six months.

Defense lawyers Robert W. Kenny and Martin W. Popper introduced motions for acquittal, suspension of sentence, and release on bail pending appeal. The judges denied them all. Since the eight had agreed to stand on the records of the jury trials of the first two, and the Supreme Court had denied any review, they were sentenced and jailed at once.

From their prison cells, all 10 men sued their employers for breach of contract. Negotiating together until well after the last of the Hollywood Ten had been released from prison, the studios finally settled out of court for $259,000, to be shared—but not equally—by all.

The "Hollywood Ten," May 29, 1950 (Hearst Newspaper Collection, University of Southern California Library)

Some returned to their professions but had to write in the "black market"—using pseudonyms—for years. Trumbo wrote scripts under other names for 10 years, winning an Oscar for Best Motion Picture Story in 1957 as "Robert

Rich." Lardner's blacklisting ended in 1964; he won an Oscar for *M*A*S*H* in 1971. Maltz wrote novels while blacklisted for 20 years. Cole taught screenwriting and reviewed films. Lawson moved from creating plays and films to writing about them and teaching. Bessie wrote novels.

In 1951, Dmytryk appeared before HUAC and recanted, naming 26 as Communists. Over the next 25 years, he directed a film each year. Ornitz wrote a best-selling novel. Scott wrote and produced for television. Biberman formed an independent production company and produced a semidocumentary peopled with FBI informants and right-wing fanatics that won an International Grand Prize.

In 1948, HUAC Chairman J. Parnell Thomas was convicted of conspiracy to defraud the government by taking kickbacks from his staff. By the time two of the Hollywood Ten—Cole and Lardner—were imprisoned in the federal penitentiary at Danbury, Connecticut, in 1950, Thomas was already there serving his sentence.

—Bernard Ryan, Jr.

Suggestions for Further Reading

Aaron, Daniel. *Writers on the Left.* New York: Harcourt, Brace & World, 1961.

Belfrage, Cedric. *The American Inquisition.* New York: Bobbs-Merrill Co., 1973.

Bessie, Alvah. *Inquisition in Eden.* New York: Macmillan Co., 1965.

Biberman, Herbert. *Salt of the Earth.* Boston: Beacon Press, 1965.

Cook, Bruce. *Dalton Trumbo.* New York: Charles Scribner's Sons, 1977.

Dick, Bernard F. *Radical Innocence.* Lexington: University Press of Kentucky, 1989.

Donner, Frank J. *The Un-Americans.* New York: Ballantine, 1961.

Goodman, Walter. *The Committee.* New York: Farrar, Straus & Giroux, 1969.

Kahn, Gordon. *Hollywood on Trial.* New York: Boni & Gaer, 1948.

Kanfer, Stefan. *A Journal of the Plague Years.* New York: Atheneum, 1973.

Kempton, Murray. *Part of Our Time.* New York: Simon & Schuster, 1955.

Lardner, Ring, Jr. *The Lardners.* New York: Harper & Row, 1976.

Navasky, Victor S. *Naming Names.* New York: Viking, 1989.

Taylor, Telford. *Grand Inquest.* New York: Simon & Schuster, 1955.

Vaughn, Robert. *Only Victims.* New York: G.P. Putnam's Sons, 1972.

Alger Hiss Trials: 1949–50

Defendant: Alger Hiss   **Crime Charged:** Perjury
Chief Defense Lawyers: Robert M. Benjamin, Claude B. Cross, Chester T.
Lane, Edward C. McLean, Robert von Mehren, Victor Rabinowitz, Harold
Rosenwald, Harol Shapero, and Lloyd Paul Strykr
Chief Prosecutors: Thomas J. Donegan, Myles J. Lane, Thomas F. Murphy,
and Clarke S. Ryan   **Judges:** First trial: Samuel J. Kaufman; Second trial:
Henry W. Goddard   **Place:** New York, New York   **Dates of Trials:** First trial:
May 31–July 8, 1949; Second trial: November 17, 1949–January 21, 1950.
Verdicts: First trial: Jury deadlocked; Second trial: guilty   **Sentence:** 5
years imprisonment

SIGNIFICANCE

For three years, Alger Hiss was the protagonist in a great human drama that made
headlines across America. The case polarized the country between 1948 and
1950, becoming a symbol of American policies in the onset of the Cold War. It
accelerated the rise of Richard M. Nixon. The debate about Hiss' guilt remains
endless, for either he was a traitor or he was the victim of a framing for political
advantage at the highest levels of justice.

Alger Hiss was the president of the Carnegie Endowment for International
Peace when, on August 3, 1948, reporters told him a senior editor of *Time*
magazine named Whittaker Chambers had just appeared before the Committee
for the Investigation of Un-American Activities of the House of Representatives
(consistently mislabeled HUAC). Chambers had described his 15 years' service
as a Soviet agent. In 1939, he said, two years after he had "repudiated Marx's
doctrine," he told Assistant Secretary of State Adolph A. Berle, Jr., about
Communists in the U.S. government. One, he said, was Alger Hiss, who had
been a State Department official and who later organized the U.S. representation at Yalta, as well as the conferences at Dumbarton Oaks and San Francisco,
that launched the United Nations.

Hiss telegraphed the committee, asking to appear under oath to say he did
not know Chambers.

Hiss Denies Communist Link

In Washington, Hiss told the committee the accusation was "a complete fabrication." His government service would speak for itself. But, said Karl Mundt, acting chairman of the committee, Chambers had testified that when he was breaking with the communists he had tried to persuade Hiss to break, too, and Hiss had "absolutely refused to break."

Hiss denied such an incident, repeated that the name Chambers meant nothing to him, and said he would like to see the man. Chambers was called to an executive session of a sub-committee led by U.S. Representative Richard M. Nixon of California. The witness described intimate details of the Hiss households in Baltimore, Maryland and Washington, D.C. a decade earlier.

Hiss was recalled. Nixon showed him pictures of Chambers. Hiss said they looked like a man he knew as George Crosley, a freelance writer who had interviewed him when he was counsel to a Senate committee. In June 1935, said Hiss, he and his wife Priscilla bought a house and, subletting their apartment to Crosley and his family, threw in their old Ford. But Hiss would not say that Crosley and Chambers were the same person.

In New York the next day, Congressmen Nixon and John McDowell, as a subcommittee, brought Chambers and Hiss face to face. After observing that this man's teeth were considerably improved over Crosley's, and that he looked "very different in girth and in other appearances—hair, forehead, particularly the jowls," Hiss identified Chambers as George Crosley.

Chambers denied ever going under that name, but he said Hiss was the man "who was a member of the Communist Party" at whose apartment he and his wife and child had stayed. Angry, Hiss invited Chambers "to make those same statements out of the presence of this Committee without their being privileged for suit for libel."

Chambers shortly did so on the "Meet the Press" radio program. Hiss filed a $75,000 defamation suit.

At a pretrial hearing, Hiss' attorney, William Marbury, asked Chambers if he could produce documentary proof of his assertion. Chambers went to the Brooklyn home of a nephew and, from behind a dumbwaiter, retrieved a stained manila envelope containing 43 typed copies of State Department reports, five rolls of microfilm, and four memoranda in Hiss' handwriting. He handed the documents, but not the films, to Marbury. He claimed Hiss had given them to him in 1937. Hiss, said Chambers, regularly took such classified papers home for his wife to type, returning the originals to the files the next day while Chambers transmitted the copies to a Soviet agent.

A "Bombshell," a Seaplane, a Pumpkin

Hiss told his lawyer to give the papers to the Department of Justice. The next day, Representative Nixon, who had just sailed on a vacation cruise to Panama, got a cable that a "bombshell" had exploded. He ordered a HUAC investigator to visit Chambers at his Maryland farm. Meantime, a Coast Guard seaplane picked up Nixon.

By the time Nixon was back in Washington amid flashing cameras, Chambers had led investigator Robert E. Stripling into his farm field, opened a hollowed-out pumpkin, and handed over the five rolls of microfilm that had long been hidden in the stained envelope behind the Brooklyn dumbwaiter. Three rolls, still in their aluminum cans, were undeveloped; two, developed, were in oilpaper bags. While the pumpkin held no paper, the microfilms, which contained *pictures* of documents, became known as "The Pumpkin Papers."

By one vote more than a bare majority, the New York Federal Grand Jury indicted Alger Hiss on two counts of perjury: one for denying that he had turned State Department documents over to Chambers, the second for saying he had not seen Chambers after January 1, 1937, for the jury found that he had delivered reports to Chambers in February and March 1938.

As the trial opened on May 31, 1949, prosecutor Thomas F. Murphy told the jury, "If you don't believe Mr. Chambers' story, we have no case under the Federal perjury rule." Chambers repeated the testimony given before HUAC and the grand jury on his work in the Communist underground, his close friendship with the Hisses, his 1938 break with the party.

In cross-examination, Hiss' defense counsel, Lloyd Paul Stryker, lost no time establishing Chambers' shortcomings. The witness admitted committing perjury in 1937 and 1948, using at least seven aliases between 1924 and 1938, lying to the dean of Columbia University while a student, stealing books from many libraries, living with several women (including, while a teenager, a New Orleans prostitute called "One-Eyed Annie"), and writing not only erotic poetry but an anti-religious play that got him expelled from Columbia.

A Typewriter Proves Elusive

For three weeks, the prosecution presented evidence. State Department witnesses identified the typewritten papers as cables from American diplomats around the world in 1938 and said the four memos were in Hiss' handwriting. An FBI typewriter expert testified that letters the Hisses wrote and all but one of the Chambers documents had been typed on the same machine.

The typewriter became a key piece of evidence. The Hisses said they had given it to the sons of their maid when they moved in December 1937—before the documents were typed in January and April 1938. One of the sons, Perry Catlett, testified to receiving the typewriter in December 1936 and taking it to a repair shop on K Street (where he was told it was not worth repairing), but then said, "I don't know the time" when prosecutor Murphy told him the K Street shop had not opened until September 1938.

The FBI searched unsuccessfully for the typewriter, a Woodstock built some 20 years earlier. Believing it world prove their client innocent, Hiss' own lawyers traced and found it, thus enabling a prosecution witness to demonstrate in the courtroom that it was in working order.

Before Alger Hiss took the stand for direct examination, his defense counsel introduced a parade of character witnesses—State Department officials, a former U.S. presidential candidate, a former U.S. solicitor general, a Navy admiral, a district court judge, and two associate justices of the U.S. Supreme Court. All backed Hiss' reputation "for integrity, loyalty, and veracity."

Alger Hiss arriving in the United States with the United Nations charter for delivery to President Truman. (United States Army Air Force)

On direct, examination, Hiss denied Chambers' charges and said, "I am not and never have been" a member of the Communist Party. He admitted having known one George Crosley between 1934 and 1936. Cross-examining, prosecutor Murphy tried to establish the gift of the Ford car and use of the Hisses' apartment as out-and-out fabrications.

Stryker's last witness was Dr. Carl Binger, a psychiatrist who had been observing Chambers' testimony. "Have you," asked Stryker, "an opinion within the bounds of reasonable certainty as to the mental condition of Whittaker Chambers?"

Murphy objected. Chambers' credibility, he told Judge Stanley H. Kaufman, was the case's central issue. The psychiatrist's answer would usurp the jury's function. The judge agreed.

In summation, Murphy noted that the case must stand not on Chambers' accusations but on the documents and the typewriter. Said Stryker: "The case comes down to this—who is telling the truth?"

The jury deliberated for 14 hours and 45 minutes, remained deadlocked, and was discharged.

Second Jury Reaches Guilty Verdict

The second trial began on November 17, 1949, with Judge Henry W. Goddard presiding. Most of the earlier witnesses repeated their testimony. Defense attorney Claude B. Cross, who had replaced Stryker, called Dr. Binger. Judge Goddard permitted him to testify that "Mr. Chambers is suffering from a condition known as a psychopathic personality, a disorder of character the distinguishing features of which are amoral and antisocial behavior." One important symptom was "chronic, persistent, and repetitive lying and a tendency to make false accusations."

On January 20, 1950, the jury found Hiss guilty on both counts. His sentence was five years on each, to be served concurrently. Before sentencing, Hiss again denied any guilt, promising that "in the future the full facts of how Whittaker Chambers was able to carry out forgery by typewriter will be disclosed."

Hiss was free on bail for more than a year. The Court of Appeals for the Second Circuit affirmed his conviction. The U.S. Supreme Court refused to review the case. On March 22, 1951, Hiss entered the federal penitentiary at Danbury, Connecticut.

While Hiss was in prison, his attorney of record in the appeals, Chester T. Lane, consulted experts who made exhaustive tests in document analysis, in the chemistry of paper, in metallurgy, and in the construction of typewriters. A noted typewriter engineer, working entirely from samples of typing from the machine exhibited at the trial and without seeing the trial typewriter, built another machine. It produced examples so similar that New England's leading document expert swore in an affidavit that no expert could distinguish documents typed on the two machines.

Through serial numbers and records of manufacturing, Lane also found evidence that Priscilla Hiss' typewriter had been in use in her father's real estate office in 1929—before the Woodstock in evidence in the courtroom had been built. The evidence led Lane to the conclusion that the FBI had known at the time of the trial that the typewriter put in evidence was manufactured two years after Priscilla's machine was bought by her father.

Appeal Effort Fail

Lane collected the affidavits resulting from his efforts and, arguing they provided sufficient new evidence to justify a new trial, appeared before Judge Goddard on June 4, 1952. The judge denied Lane's motion for a new trial. Lane appealed to the U. S. Court of Appeals, but the judge's opinion was affirmed. The Hiss attorneys then petitioned the U.S. Supreme Court for a writ of *certiorari*, or review of the lower courts' rulings. The petition was denied.

Alger Hiss served three years and eight months of his five-year sentence. After his release, he wrote a book about the trial, worked as a salesman for a stationery printer, and, after five years, separated (but was never divorced) from Priscilla Hiss. In 1976, the Massachusetts Bar, from which he had been automatically disbarred when convicted, readmitted him and he began work as a legal consultant.

In 1973, during the Watergate hearings, former Presidential Counsel John Dean told how President Nixon said to Charles Colson, "The typewriters are always the key. . . . We built one in the Hiss case."

At the age of 87, in 1992, Hiss asked General Dmitri A. Volkogonov, chairman of the Russian Government's military intelligence archives, to inspect all Soviet files pertaining to him, his case, and Whittaker Chambers. "Not a single document, and a great amount of materials have been studied, substantiates the allegation that Mr. A. Hiss collaborated with the intelligence services of the Soviet Union," the general reported several months later. He said the accusations were "completely groundless."

—Bernard Ryan, Jr.

Suggestions for Further Reading

Brodie, Fawn M. "I Think Hiss Is Lying." *American Heritage* (August 1981): 4–21.

Buckley, William F. "Well, What Do You Know?" *National Review* (November 19, 1990) 60.

Chambers, Whittaker. *Witness.* New York: Random House, 1952.

Cook, Fred J. *The Unfinished Story of Alger Hiss.* New York: William Morrow Co., 1958.

Cooke, Alistair. *A Generation on Trial.* New York: Alfred A. Knopf, 1950.

de Toledano, Ralph and Victor Lasky. *Seeds of Treason.* Chicago: Regnery, 1962.

Hiss, Alger. *In the Court of Public Opinion.* New York: Alfred A. Knopf, 1957.

——. *Recollections of a Life.* New York: Seaver Books/Henry Holt, 1988.

Hiss, Tony. "My Father's Honor." *The New Yorker* (November 16, 1992): 100–106.

Jowitt, William Allen. *The Strange Case of Alger Hiss.* New York: Doubleday & Co., 1953.

Levitt, Morton and Michael Levitt. *A Tissue of Lies Nixon vs. Hiss.* New York: McGraw-Hill, 1979.

Nixon, Richard M. *Six Crises.* New York: Doubleday Co., 1962.

Smith, Chabot. *Alger Hiss: The True Story.* New York: Holt, Rinehart and Winston, 1976.

Tanenhaus, Sam. "The Hiss Case Isn't Over Yet." *New York Times* (October 31, 1992): 21.

Tiger, Edith, ed. *In Re Alger Hiss.* New York: Hill and Wang, 1979.

Tyrell, R.E. "You Must Remember Hiss." *The American Spectator* (January 1991): 10.

Ward, G.C. "Unregretfully, Alger Hiss." *American Heritage* (November 1988): 18.

Weinstein, Allen. *Perjury: The Hiss-Chambers Case.* New York: Alfred A. Knopf, 1978.

Martha Beck Trial: 1949

Defendants: Martha Beck and Raymond Fernandez
Crime Charged: Murder   **Chief Defense Lawyers:** John H. Minton and
Herbert E. Rosenberg   **Chief Prosecutors:** Edward F. Breslin, James W.
Gehrig, and Edward Robinson, Jr.   **Judge:** Ferdinand Pecora
Place: New York, New York   **Dates of Trial:** June 9–August 18, 1949
Verdict: Guilty   **Sentence:** Death by electrocution

SIGNIFICANCE

This notorious "lonely hearts murders" case, in which the bizarre defendants
were tried for just one of some 20 murders committed over only two years, found
the defendants pleading insanity. The jury, however, proved that it clearly
understood the difference between the abnormal and the insane.

At 26, Martha Beck weighed 300 pounds. She had been married and divorced twice. A registered nurse, she had become superintendent of the Pensacola Crippled Children's Home in Florida. In 1947, answering an advertisement in a true-romance magazine, she spent five dollars to buy, through the mail, a membership in Mother Dinene's Friendly Club for Lonely Hearts.

A romantic letter came from one Raymond Fernandez of New York. She replied. Letters flew. Soon Fernandez stepped off a bus in Pensacola into Beck's arms and the couple began a two-day orgy. He was the Latin lover of her dreams.

After two days, however, Raymond had learned what was to him the most important fact about Beck: she had no money. He headed back to New York, where he wrote a "Dear Martha" letter that told her he just didn't love her after all.

Meantime, the overseers of the Crippled Children's Home fired Beck. She went straight to Fernandez's New York apartment and moved in. She soon discovered the nature of his business: he answered lonely-hearts ads, seduced well-to-do widows and spinsters, fleeced them of their savings, and disappeared. Undaunted, Beck proposed a partnership. She would play the role of his sister, helping to build the confidence of intended victims, but with a more sinister result than Fernandez had practiced. Rather than disappearing themselves, they would make their victims disappear.

Partnership Thrives

Time and again, lonely women naively handed their bankbooks, their jewelry, and ultimately their lives to the charming romantic who answered their lonely-hearts ads and turned up with his helpful "sister." Late in 1948, 66-year-old widow Janet Fay of Albany, New York, welcomed them, following an emotional and hopeful correspondence. By early January, she had turned over $4,000 in savings and cash, as well as jewelry and bonds, to Fernandez. Beck then skillfully packed the widow's possessions into a large trunk stolen from the most recent victim, and the three moved into a rented apartment in Valley Stream on Long Island. There Beck bashed Fay's skull with a hammer.

The murderers rented another house, buried the body in the cellar, covered it with a fresh cement floor, waited four days for the cement to harden, and departed for Grand Rapids, Michigan, and their next victim, who had already swallowed Fernandez's romance-by-mail bait and was on the hook. Soon the brother-sister act was ensconced in the home of Delphine Downing, a 41-year-old widow with a 2-year-old daughter. Wedding plans were made. But Delphine inadvertently came upon Fernandez without his toupee. Disillusioned, she rebelled: "Why, you're bald!" He shot her. Beck drowned the child in the bathtub. In the cellar, Fernandez dug a hole large enough for both bodies and poured fresh concrete.

The cement had not cured before the police, called by suspicious neighbors when they had not seen the mother and daughter for a couple of days, were at the door. Almost simultaneously, Fay's stepdaughter, unable to find her, had alerted New York police, who found the grave under the new cement floor and traced Fernandez and Beck to Michigan and the Downing home. A search of Fernandez revealed a notebook with the names of some 20 missing women.

As the couple confessed both the Fay and Downing murders, America, titillated by the image of the torrid Latin and the super-passionate fat lady, devoured the bizarre story. Spine-chilling news reports depicted the horror not only of the murders but of Martha Beck's tough, take-charge command of the weird operation.

Because New York had the death penalty for murder while Michigan did not, the two were extradited and tried for the murder of Fay.

The Kiss in the Courtroom

Opening June 9, 1949, the trial produced a torrent of sensational testimony as both defendants, apparently eager to prove their lack of sanity, burned the jurors' ears with lengthy streams of obscenity that described the intensity of their love life. What the court stenographers recorded could not be printed even by New York City's most torrid press. But the news reporters could describe how, when called to the witness stand, Martha Beck strode forward in bright green shoes, her massive body swathed in bright silks, a double-strand necklace clinking brightly, and suddenly detoured across the courtroom to Fernandez. Catching his face in her hefty hands, she pulled it toward her, kissing him on the mouth and, as the guards pulled her away, leaving him with a grin of bright red lipstick.

Following prosecutor Edward Breslin's straightforward presentation of the blood-curdling facts, the defense set out to prove insanity. Beck testified to four attempts to commit suicide, said her mind was a blank on the actual killings, and denied trying to shield Fernandez. A psychiatrist declared her mentally unsound and said that, even if she participated in the killing, she had no idea what she was doing. Defense attorney Herbert Rosenberg, contending that Beck had killed Fay in a fit of insanity inspired by jealousy, tried to prove that Fernandez had no part in the crime.

Charging the jury, Judge Ferdinand Pecora, referring to acts of perversion admitted by the defendants, said, "That kind of abnormality does not, in and of itself, constitute the kind of insanity which will excuse a person of a criminal act."

After debating for 12½ hours, the jury convicted Martha Beck and Raymond Fernandez of first-degree murder. The death sentence was mandatory. The New York State Court of Appeals denied the pair a new trial. Governor Thomas E. Dewey turned down a plea for clemency. The U.S. Supreme Court refused to review the case. Fernandez, claiming he received cruel treatment in Sing Sing Prison, was denied a *habeas corpus* order.

On March 8, 1951, the lonely-hearts murderers—Fernandez first, then Beck—died in the electric chair in Sing Sing.

—Bernard Ryan, Jr.

Suggestions for Further Reading

Brown, Wenzel. *Introduction to Murder: The Unpublished Facts Behind the Notorious Lonely Hearts Killers, Martha Beck and Raymond Fernandez.* New York: Greenberg, 1952.

Jones, Richard Glyn. *Killer Couples.* Secaucus, N.J.: Lyle Stuart, 1987.

Sifakis, Carl. *The Encyclopedia of American Crime.* New York: Facts On File, 1982.

Wilson, Colin. *A Criminal History of Mankind.* New York: G.P. Putnam's Sons, 1984.

Tokyo Rose Trial: 1949

Defendant: Iva Ikuko Toguri ("Tokyo Rose")   **Crime Charged:** Treason
Chief Defense Lawyers: Wayne M. Collins, George Olshausen, and Theodore
Tamba   **Chief Prosecutors:** Thomas DeWolfe, Frank J. Hennessy, John
Hogan, and James Knapp   **Judge:** Michael J. Roche   **Place:** San Francisco,
California   **Dates of Trial:** July 5–September 29, 1949   **Verdict:** Guilty
Sentence: 10 years in prison and a $10,000 fine

SIGNIFICANCE
The Tokyo Rose trial was one of only seven American treason trials following
World War II.

Iva Ikuko Toguri, the woman who would be labeled "Tokyo Rose" and a
traitor to the United States, ironically was born on Independence Day, 1916 in
Los Angeles, California. Her parents had migrated from Japan to California, and
Toguri grew up as an American. In July 1941, now 25 years old, Toguri went to
Japan for the first time to visit a sick aunt. Toguri stayed with relatives for several
months, attending to her sick aunt, and she was left stranded in Japan when war
broke out December 7, 1941, with the bombing of Pearl Harbor.

Toguri was hard-pressed to earn a living in wartime Japan, where food and
shelter were both expensive and scarce, and her only skill was her mastery of
English. She worked as a typist for several news agencies and foreign legations
before getting a job with Radio Tokyo. In November 1943, Toguri was forced to
become one of the several female radio announcers for Radio Tokyo. Although
Radio Tokyo broadcasts were made from many different locations throughout
the Japanese Empire, which at its height covered much of eastern Asia, the
female broadcasters were collectively termed "Tokyo Rose" by American GIs.
Toguri never used that name, and her broadcasts were limited to playing popular
American music, with a smattering of pro-Japanese propaganda written for her
by her supervisors.

Toguri Tried for Treason

Toguri was only one of an estimated 10,000 Japanese-Americans trapped
in Japan during World War II and forced to cope with the circumstances of war.

She, however, was one of the few singled out for punishment by the American authorities. She was arrested in occupied Japan on October 17, 1945, released on October 25, 1946, when the Justice Department expressed doubts on the charge of treason against her, but re-arrested on August 28, 1948, in Tokyo. She was brought back to the United States to stand trial in San Francisco, California.

In the anti-Japanese climate of postwar California, Toguri had to struggle to find lawyers to represent her, but finally Wayne M. Collins, George Olshausen, and Theodore Tamba agreed to take her case for free. The prosecutors were Thomas DeWolfe, Frank J. Hennessy, John Hogan, and James Knapp. The trial began on July 5, 1949 with Judge Michael J. Roche presiding.

Before an all-white jury, Toguri pleaded innocent to the eight treason charges against her. Despite Roche's bias in favor of the prosecution and the prevailing public sentiment against Toguri, the trial lasted for nearly three months and the jury was deadlocked. When the jury reported that it was unable to reach a verdict, Roche ordered them to continue deliberating until they had made a decision. Nine of the 12 jurors were willing to vote for a guilty verdict, and after some, time the three holdouts were cajoled to capitulate to the majority decision. One of the holdouts who reluctantly acquiesced in the guilty verdict was the jury foreman, John Mann:

> She was such an inoffensive little thing . . . . I think I know how she felt because I felt the same way when I was cut off from everybody. You ask the judge a question and he reprimands you. He definitely tells you you're out of order. The count is nine to three against you. I couldn't help feeling the isolation she must have felt in Japan.

On September 29, 1949, the jury returned a guilty verdict against Iva Ikuko Toguri. She was sentenced to 10 years in prison and a $10,000 fine. After serving just over six years in a federal women's prison in West Virginia, Toguri was released early for good behavior. On January 18, 1977, and after decades of debate over the fairness of her trial, President Gerald Ford pardoned Toguri. Toguri was thus officially exonerated, and her U.S. citizenship was finally restored. Toguri's trial was one of only seven American treason trials following World War II.

—Stephen G. Christianson

Suggestions for Further Reading

Arbus, Diane. "The Victimization of Tokyo Rose." *Esquire* (June 1983): 88–89.

Duus, Masayo. *Tokyo Rose, Orphan of the Pacific.* New York: Harper & Row, 1979.

Gunn, Rex B. *They Called Her Tokyo Rose.* Santa Monica, Calif.: Gunn, 1977.

Japanese American Citizens' League. *Iva Toguri (d'Aquino): Victim of a Legend.* San Francisco: National Committee for Iva Toguri, Japanese American Citizens' League, 1976.

Trial of Julius and Ethel Rosenberg and Morton Sobell: 1951

Defendants: Julius and Ethel Rosenberg and Morton Sobell
Crime Charged: Conspiracy to commit wartime espionage
Chief Defense Lawyers: Alexander Bloch, Emanuel H. Bloch, Fyke Farmer,
John Finerty and Daniel Marshall for the Rosenbergs; Edward Kuntz and
Harold Phillips for Sobell   **Chief Prosecutors:** Roy M. Cohn, John Foley,
James Kilsheimer III, Myles Lane, and Irving H. Saypol   **Judge:** Irving R.
Kaufman   **Place:** New York, New York   **Dates of Trial:** March 6–29, 1951
Verdict: Guilty   **Sentences:** Death by electrocution for the Rosenbergs;
30 years for Sobell

SIGNIFICANCE

The Rosenberg case, coming at the height of the anti-Communist hysteria in
America, produced the harshest result possible: the deaths of two defendants
who, as U.S. Supreme Court Justice Felix Frankfurter put it, "were tried for
conspiracy and sentenced for treason."

On September 23, 1949, four years after the United States dropped atomic
bombs on Japan to end World War II, President Harry S. Truman announced that an atomic explosion had occurred in the Soviet Union. Until then,
most Americans had been confident that the Soviets, allies in World War II but
opponents in the Cold War that developed after 1946, could not make an atom
bomb. The resulting hysteria found Americans digging basement bomb shelters
and teaching schoolchildren how to duck under classroom desks.

The following February, a German-born nuclear physicist, Dr. Klaus
Fuchs, who had worked in America's Manhattan Project developing the atom
bomb, was arrested in England. In a "voluntary confession," he said he had
transmitted atomic information to the Soviet Union. He was tried and sentenced
to 14 years' imprisonment.

Meantime in America, former Communist spy Elizabeth Bentley told a
federal grand jury that one Harry Gold had been her successor as liaison with the
Soviets. Arrested on May 24, Gold confessed that he had served as courier in the

United States between Klaus Fuchs and the Soviets' New York Vice Consul, Anatoli Yakovlev, in 1944 and 1945.

Invited to Engage in Espionage

Gold implicated David Greenglass, who operated a machine shop in New York City with his brother-in-law, Julius Rosenberg. While in the army, Greenglass had worked in the Manhattan Project in Los Alamos, New Mexico, where the atom bomb was being constructed. Arrested, Greenglass confessed that he had accepted an invitation to engage in espionage presented by Rosenberg and his wife, Ethel, and conveyed to him by his own wife, Ruth, during a visit to New Mexico in 1944.

The Federal Bureau of Investigation (FBI) figured out that two of Julius Rosenberg's college classmates, Max Elitcher and Morton Sobell, had been part of a spy ring. Elitcher confessed, implicating Rosenberg and Sobell. The FBI also learned that Rosenberg had belonged to the Communist Party but apparently had dropped out of the party when his unit was dissolved in 1944.

Julius was arrested, then Ethel. Sobell, on a vacation trip to Mexico City with his family, was abducted by Mexican secret police, "deported" across the Texas border, and arrested.

Rather than espionage itself, the Rosenbergs and Sobell were charged with conspiracy to commit wartime espionage. The distinction was important. The standards for a conviction on conspiracy to commit wartime espionage are less onerous: Each conspirator may be liable for the acts of all the others, even without specific knowledge of them, and it is necessary only to prove that they conspired toward a given end, not that they succeeded.

Prosecution Witnesses Provide Details

The trial that opened on March 6, 1951, found both Rosenbergs and Morton Sobell as defendants. Sobell, however, never took the stand. The first prosecution witness, Max Elitcher, connected him with Julius Rosenberg, and another witness testified that the Sobell family trip to Mexico was actually a flight from the United States in which they used aliases.

At the outset, prosecutor Irving H. Saypol warned defense attorney Emanuel H. Bloch, "If your clients don't confess, they are doomed." Saypol's assistant, Roy Cohn, questioned David Greenglass, the first prosecution witness against the Rosenbergs. Greenglass testified that, while stationed at Los Alamos, he gave Julius Rosenberg crude sketches of two lens molds used to focus high-pressure shock waves converging in an implosion—molds that were "new and original" in 1945 and that still merited classified status in 1951.

Greenglass further related how he had obtained a "pretty good description" of the bomb that was dropped on Nagasaki for his brother-in-law. Altogether, he had written a dozen pages of description and drawn several sketches, for which Julius paid him $200.

Prosecutor Cohn proposed to introduce one of the sketches as Exhibit 8. Defense attorney Emanuel Bloch immediately demanded that the sketch be impounded "so that it remains secret from the court, the jury and counsel." Judge Irving R. Kaufman cleared the courtroom of press and spectators—thus encouraging the jury to think it was hearing "the secret of the atom bomb." Bloch admitted later that his move was made in the desperate hope of impressing the jury with his clients' concern for national security. The impounded testimony remained under security wraps until 1966.

Ruth Greenglass testified to Ethel Rosenberg's telling her in January 1945 that she was tired from typing David's notes for Julius Rosenberg, whom she said had promised to give the Greenglasses $6,000—and actually provided $5,000—for travel.

Judge Kaufman: Who was as it coming from?

Ruth: From the Russians, for us to leave the country.

Witness Harry Gold, who already had been convicted of espionage and sentenced to 30 years, testified that he had received orders from Soviet Vice Consul Yakovlev to go to Albuquerque, New Mexico, to meet a new contact named Greenglass. On a piece of paper that Yakovlev had handed him were the words: "Recognition signal. I come from Julius." He had picked up an envelope from Greenglass, he said, and taken it back to Yakovlev in Brooklyn, New York. In addition, he revealed that Greenglass had given him a telephone number, that of his "brother-in-law Julius," where Greenglass could be reached during his next furlough in New York.

With this strong testimony on the connection between the defendants and a Soviet agent, spectators and journalists alike looked eagerly to the defense attorney. But Bloch declared, "The defendants Rosenberg have no cross-examination of this witness."

Ex-Communist Elizabeth Bentley testified that, as confidential assistant to Jacob Golos when he was chief of Soviet espionage operations in the United States, she had received several phone calls as early as 1943 from a man who said, "This is Julius," and who wanted Golos to get in touch with him.

A Jell-O Box Cut in Two

Taking the stand in his own defense, Julius Rosenberg denied a number of accusations made by prosecution witnesses. A Rosenberg console table that both Greenglasses charged had been a gift from the Russians, and which they said was adapted for microfilming, had been purchased at Macy's department store for "about $21." He testified that he had not given Ruth $150 for a New Mexico trip in November 1944, had not received information on the atom bomb from Greenglass, and had not introduced Greenglass to a man in New York who sought details of the bomb. He denied introducing a neighbor to Greenglass as an espionage courier. He had not cut a Jell-O box into two irregularly shaped pieces and given one to Ruth to be used as a recognition signal if she was succeeded by another courier, and had not said, "The simplest things are the cleverest," when David admired the idea. When Judge Kaufman asked whether he had ever belonged to "any group" that had discussed the Russian system of government, he said, "Well, your Honor, I feel at this time that I refuse to answer a question that might tend to incriminate me."

On cross-examination, Rosenberg defended his denials. But in response to questions from prosecutor Irving Saypol about his conversations with David Greenglass about money, he referred to "blackmail." Judge Kaufman asked about that word.

> Rosenberg: He threatened me to get money. I considered it blackmailing.
>
> Kaufman: Did he say he would go to the authorities and tell them you were in a conspiracy to steal the atomic bomb secret?
>
> Rosenberg: No.

The defendant's choice of words, jury members said afterward, seemed like an admission of guilt.

Ethel Rosenberg tersely denied all accusations. Like her husband, she took the Fifth Amendment when asked any questions about the Communist Party. Following cross-examination, defense attorney Bloch said no more witnesses would be called.

On rebuttal, Saypol produced a surprise witness. Found by the FBI only the day before, photographer Ben Schneider testified that in June 1950 the Rosenberg family, saying they were going to France, had him shoot a large order of passport pictures. Another rebuttal witness testified that the Rosenbergs had told her the console table was "a gift from a friend," and that, despite the fact that it was their finest piece of furniture, they had kept it in a closet. (It was not put into evidence because the Rosenbergs said they did not know where it was at that time.)

Ethel and Julius Rosenberg, separated by wire, following their conviction in March 1951. (AP/Wide World Photos)

The jury deliberated from late afternoon until nearly midnight, and for an hour the next morning, before finding both Rosenbergs and Sobell guilty as charged. A week later, on April 5, 1951, Judge Kaufman sentenced Sobell to 30 years and the couple to the electric chair.

Appeals Extended Two Years

The executions were stayed pending appeal. In February 1952, the U.S. Circuit Court of Appeals affirmed the convictions. In October, the U.S. Supreme Court refused to review the case, with Justice Hugo L. Black dissenting. December brought a motion for a new trial based on the contentions that photographer Schneider had committed perjury and Saypol had conducted an unfair trial. The motion was denied.

A motion to reduce the sentences as "cruel and excessive" because the charge was not treason and the indictments did not include "intent to injure the U.S." was denied.

In January, the executions were stayed again pending review by President Harry Truman of a petition for clemency. After Truman left office January 20, President Dwight D. Eisenhower refused clemency. Meantime, the National Committee to Secure Justice in the Rosenberg Case had mounted a worldwide effort to save them. It filled an eight-car train that took protesters from New York City to Ossining, where the Rosenbergs sat in Sing Sing's death row. Three million letters and telegrams flooded the White House. Pope Pius XII twice appealed for clemency. Albert Einstein and atomic scientist Harold C. Urey appealed.

A third execution date was stayed as appeals for clemency poured in from around the world. With Justices Black and William O. Douglas dissenting, the Supreme Court again refused to review the case. New evidence on June 8—the discovery of the missing console table in the apartment of Julius Rosenberg's mother—failed to justify a new trial or a stay of execution.

The Supreme Court again refused to review the case or stay the execution. Then, on June 17, Justice Douglas, questioning whether the defendants were correctly tried under the Espionage Act of 1917, granted a stay. The next day, Eisenhower received clemency appeals from hundreds of organizations representing millions of people in Europe, while U.S. embassies mounted police cordons to hold back the crowds, and the Supreme Court was recalled from vacation into unprecedented session. With Black, Douglas, and Felix M. Frankfurter dissenting, it vacated the Douglas stay. Eisenhower rejected another clemency plea.

The Rosenbergs ware executed precisely at sundown on June 19, 1953. That night, New York's Union Square filled with 10,000 protesters, while throngs in capitals around the world expressed their shock.

—Bernard Ryan, Jr.

Suggestions for Further Reading

De Toledano, Ralph. *The Greatest Plot in History.* New York: Duell, Sloan and Pearce, 1963.

Fineberg, S. Andhill. *The Rosenberg Case: Fact and Fiction.* New York: Oceana, 1952.

Gardner, Virginia. *The Rosenberg Story.* New York: Masses and Mainstream, 1954.

Goldstein, Alvin H. *The Unquiet Death of Julius & Ethel Rosenberg.* New York: Lawrence Hill, 1975.

Hyde, H. Montgomery. *The Atom Bomb Spies.* New York: Atheneum, 1980.

Meeropol, Robert and Michael Meeropol. *We Are Your Sons: The Legacy of Ethel and Julius Rosenberg.* New York: Houghton Mifflin, 1975.

Nizer, Louis. *The Implosion Conspiracy.* New York: Doubleday & Co., 1973.

Pilat, Oliver. *The Atom Spies.* New York: G.P. Putnam's Sons, 1952.

Radosh, Ronald and Joyce Milton. *The Rosenberg File: A Search for the Truth.* New York: Holt, Rinehart and Winston, 1983.

Reuben, William A. *The Atom Spy Hoax.* New York: Action Books, 1955.

Schneir, Walter and Miriam Schneir. *Invitation to an Inquest.* New York: Doubleday & Co., 1965.

Sharlit, Joseph H. *Fatal Error.* New York: Charles Scribner's Sons, 1989.

Sharp, Malcolm P. *Was Justice Done? The Rosenberg-Sobell Case.* New York: Monthly Review Press, 1956.

Sobell, Morton. *On Doing Time.* New York: Charles Scribner's Sons, 1974.

Wexley, John. *The Judgment of Julius and Ethel Rosenberg.* New York: Ballantine, 1977.

Whitehead, Don. *The FBI Story: A Report to the People.* New York: Random House, 1956.

Dennis v. U.S. Appeal: 1951

Appellants: Benjamin Davis, Eugene Dennis, John Gates, Gil Green, Gus Hall, Irving Potash, Jack Stachel, Robert Thompson, John Williamson, Henry Winston, and Carl Winter **Defendant:** United States
Appellants Claims: That the Smith Act, under which appellants were found guilty, violates the First Amendment and other provisions of the Bill of Rights of the U.S. Constitution **Chief Defense Lawyers:** Philip B. Perlman and Irving S. Shapiro **Chief Lawyers for Appellants:** George W. Crockett, Jr., Abraham J. Isserman, and Harry Sacher **Justices:** Hugo L. Black, Harold H. Burton, William O. Douglas, Felix Frankfurter, Robert H. Jackson, Sherman Minton; Stanley F. Reed, and Fred M. Vinson, (Tom C. Clark not participating)
Place: Washington, D.C. **Date of Decision:** June 4, 1951
Decision: Provisions of the Smith Act prohibiting willful advocacy of overthrow of government by force or violence, organization of any group for that purpose and conspiracy to violate such provisions were held not to violate the First Amendment or other provisions of the Bill of Rights in a 6-2 decision.

SIGNIFICANCE

The U.S. Supreme Court's review of this case provides a classic example of how the guarantees of the First Amendment must be balanced against the nation's need, as prescribed by Congress, to protect itself. The opinions written by the justices contain memorable expressions of this paradox.

The Alien Registration Act of 1940, known as the Smith Act, made it a crime "to knowingly or willfully advocate, abet, advise, or teach the duty, necessity, desirability, or propriety of overthrowing or destroying any government in the United States by force or violence." Publication or display of printed matter teaching or advocating overthrow of the government was forbidden, as was organizing any group that teaches, advocates, or encourages overthrow of government by force. Also against the law was "knowing" membership in any group dedicated to that end.

In July 1948, Eugene Dennis, general secretary of the Communist Party in the United States, and 10 other party leaders were indicted for violating the

Smith Act by conspiring to organize groups that taught the overthrow of the government. In a sensational trial that lasted nine months and resulted in a record 16,000 pages of testimony, the defendants argued that First Amendment freedom of speech protected them. Finding that the leaders of the Communist Party were unwilling to work within the framework of democracy but, rather, intended to initiate a violent revolution, the jury convicted them all.

"Clear and Present Danger"

They appealed. The U.S. Court of Appeals applied the "clear and present danger test" of free speech that was originated by Supreme Court Justice Oliver Wendell Holmes in *Schenck v. U.S.* (see separate entry) in 1919, when Holmes, writing the opinion of the unanimous court, said:

> The question in every case is whether the words used are used in such circumstances and are of such a nature as to create a clear and present danger that they will bring about the substantive evils that Congress has a right to prevent.

Upholding the convictions, the court of appeals applied a "sliding scale" rule for the clear and present danger test, saying it "must ask whether the gravity of the 'evil,' discounted by its improbability, justifies such invasion of free speech as is necessary to avoid the danger."

The U.S. Supreme Court agreed to review the case from the standpoint of whether the Smith Act "inherently or as construed and applied in the instant case violates the First Amendment and other provisions of the Bill of Rights."

Without Justice Tom C. Clark participating, the eight other justices showed wide disagreement over how to measure the Smith Act's restraints on the freedom of speech and association guaranteed by the First Amendment. Chief Justice Fred M. Vinson, with Justices Harold H. Burton, Sherman Minton, and Stanley F. Reed, found that:

Voting with the majority, Sherman Minton agreed that a balance must be sought between the guarantees of the First Amendment and the need to protect the country from a "clear and present danger" as defined in *Schenck*. (Courtesy, National Archives)

> Congress did not intend to eradicate the free discussion of political theories, to destroy the traditional rights of Americans to discuss and evaluate ideas without fear of governmental sanction [but] the formation of such a highly organized conspiracy, with rigidly disciplined members subject to call when the leaders felt that the time had come for action, coupled with the inflammable nature of world conditions, convince us that their convictions were justified. . . . It is the existence of the conspiracy which creates the danger. . . . If the ingredients of the reaction are present, we cannot bind the Government to wait until the catalyst is added.

Petitioners intended to overthrow the Government of the United States as speedily as the circumstances would permit. Their conspiracy . . . created a 'clear and present danger.' . . . They were properly and constitutionally convicted for violation of the Smith Act.

"Beyond These Powers We Must Not Go"

Justice Felix Frankfurter concurred, but wrote:

It is a sobering fact that in sustaining the convictions before us we can hardly escape restriction on the interchange of ideas.

Congress, not the Supreme Court, he wrote, was responsible for reconciling such a conflict of values. The Court's job was to require substantial proof before conviction and to ensure fair procedures in enforcement of the law. "Beyond these powers," he wrote, "we must not go; we must scrupulously observe the narrow limits of judicial authority."

While also concurring, Justice Robert H. Jackson wrote:

The authors of the clear and present danger test never applied it to a case like this, nor would I. As proposed here, it means that the Communist plotting is protected during its period of incubation; its preliminary stages of organization and preparation are immune from the law; the Government can move only after imminent action is manifest, when it would, of course, be too late.

Concluded Jackson: "There is no constitutional right to gang up on the Government."

Dissenters Cite Prior Censorship

Justices William O. Douglas and Hugo L. Black wrote dissenting opinions. Said Black:

The indictment is that they conspired to use speech or newspapers to teach and advocate the forcible overthrow of the Government. No matter how it is worded, this is a virulent form of prior censorship of speech and press, which I believe the First Amendment forbids.

Douglas wrote:

We deal here with speech alone, not with speech *plus* acts of sabotage or unlawful conduct. Not a single seditious act is charged.

Free speech—the glory of our system of government—should not be sacrificed on anything less than plain and objective proof of danger that the evil advocated is imminent. On the record no one can say that petitioners and their converts are in such a strategic position as to have even the slightest chance of achieving their aims.

The majority opinion concluded that the Smith Act "does not violate the First Amendment or other provisions of the Bill of Rights." As a result, not only did Dennis and his fellow appellants serve time in prison, but 121 second-rank

U.S. Communist Party officials were prosecuted for conspiracy under the Smith Act. Other individual party members also were prosecuted. In every case tried between 1951 and 1956, convictions were obtained. All were affirmed by courts of appeal. All were denied review by the Supreme Court.

—*Bernard Ryan, Jr.*

Suggestions for Further Reading

Belfrage, Cedric. *The American Inquisition, 1945–1960*. Indianapolis: Bobbs-Merrill Co., 1973.

Fast, Howard. *Being Red*. Boston: Houghton Mifflin, 1990.

Hoover, J. Edgar. *Masters of Deceit*. New York: Henry Holt, 1958.

Klehr, Harvey. *The Heyday of American Communism: The Depression Decade*. New York: Basic Books, 1984.

Mitford, Jessica. *A Fine Old Conflict*. New York: Alfred A. Knopf, 1971.

Witt, Elder. *Guide to the United States Supreme Court*. Washington: Congressional Quarterly Press, 1990.

Reynolds v. Pegler: 1954

Plaintiff: Quentin Reynolds **Defendants:** Westbrook Pegler, The Hearst Corporation, and Hearst Consolidated Publications **Plaintiff Claims:** That a certain column published by the defendants on November 29, 1949 libeled the plaintiff **Chief Defense Lawyer:** Charles Henry
Chief Lawyers for Plaintiff: Walter S. Beck, Paul Martinson, and Louis Nizer
Judge: Edward Weinfeld **Place:** New York, New York
Dates of Trial: May 10–July 22, 1954 **Verdict:** Against all defendants: Reynolds awarded $1 in compensatory damages and $175,000 in punitive damages

SIGNIFICANCE

The lopsided award of a huge amount of punitive damages in connection with an award of only nominal compensatory damages was the largest in history at the time. The decision sent a clear signal to the publishing industry that it would be held accountable for the libelous acts of its writers and reporters.

William Randolph Hearst, the publishing magnate, built an empire by publishing newspapers that had stories the public wanted to read. Hearst made sure that his papers had the best editors, writers and reporters money could buy. One of Hearst's favorite writers was Westbrook Pegler, who wrote articles for the King Features Syndicate of The Hearst Corporation, which in turn sold the articles to other Hearst papers. In particular, King Features sold Pegler articles to the *New York Journal-American*, a New York City newspaper owned by Hearst Consolidated Publications.

Hearst died in 1945, nearly 90 years old, but Pegler remained with the Hearst organization. Pegler's articles could be very vindictive and biting, and in 1949 Pegler was accused of using his writing ability to hurt an old friend. On November 20, 1949, a writer for the *New York Herald Tribune Book Review* named Quentin Reynolds wrote a review of Dale Kramer's book *The Heywood Broun His Friends Recall*. Heywood Broun, himself a writer, had once been a friend of Pegler but, during the 1930s, the two men had a falling-out. In 1939, Pegler wrote a scathing attack on Broun's works. According to Kramer, Broun was so upset by Pegler's attack that Broun was unable to recover from a minor illness and died.

Despite the fact that the events described in Kramer's book were over 10 years old, Pegler took offense at Reynolds' review. On November 29, 1949 Pegler's article, "On Heywood Broun and Quentin Reynolds," was published in the *Journal-American*. Pegler's article had little to do with any critique of Reynolds' review, and was instead a wholesale assassination of Reynolds' character. Without any substantiation, Pegler said: that Reynolds and his girlfriend made a habit of appearing nude in public; that on the way to Heywood Broun's funeral Reynolds had proposed marriage to the widow, Connie Broun; that Reynolds had been a profiteer during World War II; that while working as a war correspondent in London, Reynolds had been a coward; and so forth. Pegler also called Reynolds a degenerate who associated with communists, blacks and others Pegler regarded as undesirables.

Reynolds Sues for Libel

After the publication of Pegler's article, Reynolds sued Pegler, The Hearst Corporation and Hearst Consolidated Publications for libel. Reynolds' lawyers were Walter S. Beck, Paul Martinson, and Louis Nizer. The defendants' chief lawyer was Charles Henry, and the judge was Edward Weinfeld. The trial began on May 10, 1954.

Aware that truth was a defense to the charge of libel, Nizer showed that Pegler's allegations in the article could not possibly be true. Nizer presented witnesses who testified that Reynolds could not have proposed to Connie Broun because she had been asleep and in the company of others all the way to the funeral, that Reynolds had not been a war profiteer, that Reynolds' war record in fact showed considerable heroism rather than cowardice, and so on. Weinfeld was convinced, and he instructed the jury that they were to take it as a given that Pegler's article was libelous:

Judge Edward Weinfeld was convinced that Pegler's articles libeled Quentin Reynolds. (AP/ Wide World Photos)

> [T]hat column read in its entirety, I charge you as a matter of law, is defamatory.

Henry tried his best to present plausible justifications for Pegler's accusations, but his excuses came across sounding rather thin. For example, Henry tried to explain away Pegler's charge that Reynolds had proposed to Connie Broun as possibly referring to the same high-minded spirit as Moses's ancient laws, which in biblical times placed:

> . . . upon a brother the duty of proposing to his dead brother's widow.

The jury was not convinced. On July 22, 1954, the jurors returned a guilty verdict against all three defendants. Given the nature of Pegler's article and Weinfeld's instructions, this verdict was not surprising. What was surprising, however, was the amount of damages the jury awarded to Reynolds, which were of two types. The first type was the compensatory damages, which represented compensation to Reynolds for the damage, emotional and otherwise, caused by Pegler's vicious public attack on his character. As is common in such cases, the dollar value of the damage done was hard to determine and so the jury gave a nominal award of just one dollar. The second type of damages was punitive, which represented the punishment that the jury saw fit to impose on the defendants for having published the article.

The amount of punitive damages rocked the publishing industry, for at the time it was the largest award of its kind in American history. The jury awarded Reynolds $100,000 against Pegler, $50,000 against The Hearst Corporation, and $25,000 against Hearst Consolidated Publications, for a total of $175,000 in punitive damages. Although the size of the award was unprecedented, it was financially a drop in the bucket to the massive Hearst organization. The disturbing part, however, was that publishers could now be held financially liable for the libels and other unlawful acts of their writers. The defendants promptly appealed.

On February 16–17, 1955, the U.S. Court of Appeals for the Second Circuit heard the parties' arguments. The court issued its decision on June 7 of the same year. The court not only upheld the verdict against Pegler and the other defendants, but it reaffirmed the principle that publishers could be held accountable for the acts of their writers:

> The mere fact that there was no proof of personal ill-will or animosity on the part of any of the corporate executives toward plaintiff does not preclude an award of punitive damages. Malice may be inferred from the very violence and vituperation apparent upon the face of the libel itself, especially where, as here, officers or employees of each corporate defendant had full opportunity to and were under a duty to exercise editorial supervision for purposes of revision, but permitted the publication of the column without investigation, delay or any alteration whatever of its contents. The jury may well have found on this evidence a wanton or reckless indifference to plaintiff's rights.

Thus, the court was telling the Hearst companies in particular and the publishing industry in general that if writers like Pegler wrote vicious and personal articles, the publishers would be held liable if they did not exercise proper editorial control over potentially defamatory material. The defendants exercised their final avenue of appeal, namely a petition for a writ of *certiorari* to the Supreme Court, which was denied on October 10, 1955.

The case of *Reynolds v. Pegler*, with its stupendous award of punitive damages in relation to the nominal compensatory damages, sent a danger signal throughout the publishing industry. This new awareness of potential liability changed forever the relationship between publishers, writers, and reporters.

From this date forward, publishers and editors would take greater care to make sure that their publications were accurate and nondefamatory.

—*Stephen G. Christianson*

Suggestions for Further Reading

Farr, Finis. *Fair Enough: The Life of Westbrook Pegler*. New Rochelle, N.Y.: Arlington House Publishers, 1975.

Nizer, Louis. *My Life in Court*. Garden City, N.Y.: Doubleday & Co., 1961.

Pilat, Oliver Ramsay. *Pegler, Angry Man of the Press*. Boston: Beacon Press, 1963.

Reynolds, Quentin. *By Quentin Reynolds*. New York: McGraw-Hill, 1963.

Brown v. Board of Education: 1954

Appellants: Several parents of African-American children of elementary school age in Topeka, Kansas   **Defendant:** Board of Education of Topeka, Kansas   **Appellants Claim:** That the segregation of white and African-American children in the public schools of Topeka solely on the basis of race denied the African-American children equal protection under the law guaranteed by the Fourteenth Amendment   **Chief Defense Lawyers:** Harold R. Fatzer and Paul E. Wilson   **Chief Lawyers for Appellants:** Robert L. Carter, Thurgood Marshall, Spottswood W. Robinson, and Charles S. Scott   **Justices:** Hugo L. Black, Harold H. Burton, Thomas C. Clark, William O. Douglas, Felix Frankfurter, Robert H. Jackson, Sherman Minton, Stanley F. Reed, and Earl Warren   **Place:** Washington, D.C.   **Date of Decision:** May 17, 1954   **Decision:** Segregated schools violate the equal protection clause of the Fourteenth Amendment

SIGNIFICANCE

Brown v. Board of Education held that segregated schools were unconstitutional, overturning the "separate but equal" doctrine of *Plessy v. Ferguson* (1896).

Sometimes in history, events of great importance happen unexpectedly to modest men. Such was the case with Oliver Brown, whose desire that his children be able to attend the public school closest to their home resulted in a fundamental transformation of race relations in the United States.

Brown was born in 1919 and lived in Topeka, Kansas, where he worked as a welder for a railroad. Brown's family literally lived on the wrong side of the tracks: their house was close to Brown's place of work, and the neighborhood bordered on a major switchyard. Not only could the Brown family hear the trains day and night, but because the Topeka school system was segregated, the Brown children had to walk through the switchyard to get to the black school a mile away. There was another school only seven blocks away, but it was exclusively for white children.

In September 1950, when his daughter Linda was to enter the third grade, Brown took her to the whites-only school and tried to enroll her. Brown had no history of racial activism, and outside of work his only major activity was serving as an assistant pastor in the local church. He was simply tired of seeing his daughter being forced to go through the switchyard to go to a school far from home because she was black. The principal of the white school refused to enroll Brown's daughter. Brown sought help from McKinley Burnett, head of the local branch of the National Association for the Advancement of Colored People, or NAACP.

NAACP Takes on Topeka Board of Education

Burnett's organization had wanted to challenge segregation for quite some time, but until Brown came to them they had never had the right plaintiff at the right time. Segregation, in the public schools and elsewhere, was a fact of life in Topeka as in so many other places and few were willing to challenge it. Now that he had Brown, who was joined by several other black parents in Topeka with children in blacks-only public schools, Burnett and the NAACP decided that the time was ripe for legal action.

On March 22, 1951, Brown's NAACP lawyers filed a lawsuit in the U.S. District Court for the District of Kansas, requesting an injunction forbidding Topeka from continuing to segregate its public schools. The court tried the case June 25–26, 1951. Brown and the other black parents testified to the fact that their children were denied admission to white schools. One parent, Silas Fleming, explained why he and the other parents wanted to get their children into the white schools:

> It wasn't to cast any insinuations that our teachers are not capable of teaching our children because they are supreme, extremely intelligent and are capable of teaching my kids or white kids or black kids. But my point was that not only I and my children are craving light: the entire colored race is craving light, and the only way to reach the light is to start our children together in their infancy and they come up together.

Next, the court listened to expert witnesses who testified that segregated schools were inherently unequal because separation sent a message to black children that they were inferior. This stigma could never be eliminated from a segregated school system, as Dr. Hugh W. Speer, chairman of the University of Kansas City's department of elementary school education, testified:

> For example, if the colored children are denied the experience in school of associating with white children, who represent 90 percent of our national society in which these colored children must live, then the colored child's curriculum is being greatly curtailed. The Topeka curriculum or any school curriculum cannot be equal under segregation.

The Board of Education's lawyers retorted that since most restaurants, bathrooms and public facilities in Kansas City also were segregated, segregated schools were only preparing black children for the realities of life as black adults. Segregation pervaded every aspect of life in Topeka as in so many other places, and it was beyond the court's jurisdiction to act on anything in this one lawsuit but the legality of school segregation. The board's argument did not convince the judges. The board was assuming that segregation was a natural and desirable way of life for the races to live.

Next, the board argued that segregated schools did not necessarily result in any detrimental effect. After all, hadn't Frederick Douglass, Booker T. Washington, and George Washington Carver, among other great African-Americans, achieved so much in the face of obstacles far worse than segregated educational facilities? The fallacy in this argument was obvious, however. While some exceptional people were capable of rising above any adversity, for the majority of African-Americans the discriminatory effect of segregation meant a lessening of opportunities. Dr. Horace B. English, a psychology professor at Ohio State University, testified:

> There is a tendency for us to live up to, or perhaps I should say down to, social expectations and to learn what people say we can learn, and legal segregation definitely depresses the Negro's expectancy and is therefore prejudicial to his learning.

On August 3, 1951, the court issued its decision. The three judges noted that the leading Supreme Court opinion on public school segregation was the 1896 case *Plessy v. Ferguson.* (See separate entry.) *Plessy* legitimized the doctrine of "separate but equal" school systems for blacks and whites, and *Plessy* had not been overturned by the Supreme Court or even seriously questioned, despite some nibbling away at the doctrine's edges in a few recent cases. Therefore, regardless of the experts' testimony that separate-but-equal schools were inherently impossible, the court felt compelled to deny Brown and the other plaintiffs their request for an injunction. The court made it clear, however, that it did not relish its role in upholding Topeka's segregation:

> Segregation of white and colored children in public schools has a detrimental effect upon the colored children. The impact is greater when it has the sanction of the law; for the policy of separating the races is usually interpreted as denoting the inferiority of the Negro group. A sense of inferiority affects the motivation of a child to learn. Segregation with the sanction of law, therefore, has a tendency to [retard] the educational and mental development of Negro children and to deprive them of some of the benefits they would receive in a racial[ly] integrated school system.

Fight Goes to Supreme Court

On October 1, 1951, the plaintiffs filed a petition for appeal. Under certain special procedural rules, they were able to go directly to the U.S. Supreme Court instead of going through a federal court of appeals. On June 9, 1952, the Supreme Court put the case on its docket and consolidated it with several other cases from across the country where school segregation policies were being challenged. The Court scheduled a hearing for December 9, 1952, in Washington, D.C., during which the plaintiffs and the board of education would present their arguments.

Harold R. Fatzer and Paul E. Wilson represented the board. Brown and the other plaintiffs had a number of attorneys representing them at both the trial in the district court and now before the Supreme Court, all sponsored by the NAACP. The chief plaintiffs' lawyers were Robert L. Carter, Thurgood Marshall, Spottswood W. Robinson, and Charles S. Scott. The Supreme Court justices were Hugo L. Black, Harold H. Burton, Thomas C. Clark, William O. Douglas, Felix Frankfurter, Robert H. Jackson, Sherman Minton, Stanley F. Reed, and Earl Warren.

The December 9, 1952, hearing ended in a stalemate. After listening to both sides reiterate the arguments they had made before the district court, the Supreme Court ordered another hearing, to take place December 8, 1953. The Court directed the parties to confine their re-argument to certain specific issues that especially concerned the justices, dealing mostly with the ratification of the Fourteenth Amendment by the states in 1868. Since the plaintiffs' lawsuit rested on the equal protection clause of this amendment, the Court wanted to know more about the circumstances surrounding the Amendment's adoption. For example, the Court was interested in the debates in Congress and in the state legislatures, the views of the proponents and opponents of the amendment, and existing segregation practices. Although the NAACP, Brown and the other plaintiffs were disappointed that their case would be on hold for another year, the Court's order for re-argument signaled its willingness to reconsider the separate-but-equal doctrine of *Plessy*.

Chief Justice Earl Warren, who influenced the unanimous outcome *Brown v. Board of Education.* (Courtesy, National Archives)

Court Throws Out *Plessy;* Declares Segregation Illegal

After the December 8, 1953, re-argument, the Court announced its decision on May 17, 1954. According to the published opinion, the re-argument had not revealed anything that shed light on whether the adoption of the Fourteenth Amendment had been specifically intended to preclude segregated schools:

> Even in the North, the conditions of public education did not approximate those existing today. The curriculum was usually rudimentary; ungraded schools were common in rural areas; the school term was but three months a year in many states; and compulsory school attendance was virtually unknown. As a consequence, it is not surprising that there should be so little in the history of the Fourteenth Amendment relating to its intended effect on public education.

Instead, the Court endorsed the plaintiffs' central thesis that segregation was inherently unequal no matter how much effort the school system made to ensure that black and white schools had equivalent facilities, staffing, books, buses, and so forth. The Court reviewed some recent cases in which it had cautiously made an exception to *Plessy* where certain graduate schools were involved. In those cases, the Court said that segregation was unequal because the blacks' professional careers were hurt by the stigma of having attended schools considered to be inferior, and where they did not have the opportunity to make contacts or have intellectual discourse with their white counterparts. With this support, the Court was ready to declare that all segregation in public schools was unconstitutional:

> We conclude that in the field of public education the doctrine of "separate but equal" has no place. Separate educational facilities are inherently un-equal. Therefore, we hold that the plaintiffs and others similarly situated for whom the actions have been brought are, by reason of the segregation complained of, deprived of the equal protection of the laws guaranteed by the Fourteenth Amendment.

After nearly 60 years of legalized discrimination, the Court had thrown out *Plessy v. Ferguson.* It would take 20 years for the Court's decision to be fully implemented, however, long after Oliver Brown died in 1961. In 1955, the Court said that all American school systems must desegregate "with all deliberate speed," but most local schools in the South did nothing until they were brought to court one by one. The process dragged on throughout the rest of the 1950s, during the '60s, and into the early '70s. Meanwhile, particularly during the civil rights movement of the 1960s, the Court acted to strike down all the other forms of legal segregation in American society, from bus stations and public libraries to restrooms.

The process was painful and often violent, frequently accompanied by federal intervention and mass demonstrations. By the 1970s, however, legal desegregation was a fact. *Brown v. Board of Education* not only made it possible to demolish segregated public school systems, but it was the landmark that served as a catalyst for further antidiscrimination decision by the Supreme Court.

—Stephen G. Christianson

Suggestions for Further Reading

"The Day Race Relations Changed Forever: U.S. Supreme Court Desegregation Decision of May 17, 1954 Was Hailed by Many as the 'Second Emancipation Proclamation.'" *Ebony* (May 1985): 108–112.

Kluger, Richard. *Simple Justice: the History of Brown v. Board of Education and Black America's Struggle for Equality.* New York: Alfred A. Knopf, 1976.

Orlich, Donald C. "Brown v. Board of Education: Time for a Reassessment." *Phi Delta Kappan* (April 1991): 631–632.

Sudo, Phil. "Five Little People Who Changed U.S. History." *Scholastic Update* (January 1990): 8–10.

White, Jack E. "The Heirs of Oliver Brown." *Time* (July 6, 1987): 88–89.

Samuel Sheppard Trials: 1954 and 1966

Defendant: Samuel Sheppard   **Crime Charged:** Murder
Chief Defense Lawyers: First trial: William J. Corrigan, William Corrigan, Jr.,
Fred Garmone, and Arthur E. Petersilge; Second trial: F. Lee Bailey
Chief Prosecutors: First trial: Saul S. Danaceau, John J. Mahon, and
Thomas J. Parrino; Second trial: John Corrigan   **Judges:** First trial: Edward
C. Blythin; Second trial: Francis J. Talty   **Place:** Cleveland, Ohio
Dates of Trials: October 18–December 21, 1954; October 24–
November 16, 1966   **Verdicts:** First trial: Guilty, second-degree homicide;
Second trial: Not guilty   **Sentence:** First trial: Life imprisonment

SIGNIFICANCE

In this most sensational American murder case of the 1950s, pretrial prejudice
and adverse media publicity conspired to deprive the defendant of his constitutional rights.

Balancing First Amendment rights to free speech against a defendant's right
to a fair trial has never been easy, but in covering the Sam Sheppard trial,
Cleveland's major newspapers trampled these distinctions underfoot. The
abominations they perpetrated on a local level, radio columnist Walter Winchell
paralleled nationally, until virtually everyone in America was convinced of
Sheppard's guilt before even a word of testimony was heard. To be sure, his
story sounded unlikely, but improbability does not necessarily imply guilt. Life
is strange and so, very often, is death.

This amazing saga had its beginnings on July 3, 1954, when Dr. Samuel
Sheppard, an affluent 30-year-old osteopath, and his pregnant wife Marilyn,
invited their neighbors, the Ahearns, over for drinks at their home on the shores
of Lake Erie. While the others watched TV, Sheppard dozed on the couch. Just
after midnight the Ahearns left. Sam Sheppard remained sleeping on the couch
while Marilyn Sheppard went to bed.

Sometime later, according to his version of events, Sheppard heard a loud
moan or scream. He rushed upstairs to the bedroom and saw "a white form"
standing beside the bed. Then everything went black. When he regained
consciousness, Sheppard realized he had been clubbed on the neck. He stum-
bled across to the bed where his wife lay unmoving. A sudden noise sent him

racing downstairs. By the rear door he spotted "a man with bushy hair." He pursued the intruder onto the beach and tackled him from behind. During the struggle Sheppard blacked out again. This time when he came to, he was partially immersed in the waters of Lake Erie. Groggily, he staggered back to the house and phoned for help.

Police found Marilyn Sheppard's half-nude body lying in a pool of blood, her head and face smashed to a pulp. Downstairs, a writing desk had been ransacked and the contents of Sheppard's medical bag lay strewn across the floor. Apparently, someone had come to rob the house and ended up killing Marilyn Sheppard.

Meantime, Sam Sheppard had been whisked away by his two brothers to the hospital they owned jointly. It was this incident, more than any other, which unleashed the tidal wave of venomous press coverage that swamped this case, as circulation-hungry editors clamored that the wealthy "Sheppard Boys" had closed ranks to protect their own.

The discovery at the house of a canvas bag, containing Sheppard's wristwatch, key chain and key, and a fraternity ring, gave rise to speculation that he had faked a robbery to conceal murder. When details of an extramarital affair emerged, official suspicion heightened. Urged on by an increasingly vituperative Cleveland press, police arrested Sheppard and charged him with murder.

The Carnival Begins

Amid unprecedented ballyhoo, on Monday, October 18, the state of Ohio opened its case against Sheppard. Judge Edward Blythin set the tone early. A candidate for re-election in the upcoming November ballot, he shamelessly curried favor with the press, issuing handwritten passes for the elite like Dorothy Kilgallen and Bob Considine, even providing them their own special table at which to sit. Blythin presided over a madcap bazaar of popping flash bulbs, vindictive reporters and hideous uproar, what the *New York Times* would later describe as "a Roman circus."

Prosecutor John Mahon made the most of what was a wafer-thin case. In the absence of any direct evidence against the defendant, other than he was in the house when Marilyn Sheppard was killed, Mahon emphasized the inconsistencies in Sam Sheppard's story. Why was there no sand in his hair when he claimed to have been sprawled on the beach? Where was the T-shirt that he had been wearing? Had bloodstains received during the attack forced him to destroy it? And why would a burglar first take the belongings in the canvas bag and then ditch them? Besides which, said Mahon, "Police . . . could find no evidence that anyone had broken in." For motive, Mahon pointed to Sheppard's affair with Susan Hayes, a lab technician at the family hospital, as reason enough for him to want to be rid of his wife.

Initially, the lack of a murder weapon posed problems for the prosecution, but Cuyahoga County Coroner Samuel R. Gerber neatly circumvented this discrepancy by telling the court that a bloody imprint found on the pillow beneath Marilyn Sheppard's head was made by a "two-bladed surgical instrument with teeth on the end of each blade," probably the missing weapon. Inexplicably, the defense attorneys left this vague assertion unchallenged, an omission which caused irreparable damage to their client's case.

Morals, Not Murder

Susan Hayes, in her testimony, demurely cataloged a long-running romantic liaison. Asked where the acts of intimacy took place, she replied: "In his car, and in his apartment above the Sheppard clinic. . . . He said he loved his wife very much but not as a wife. He was thinking of divorce." Other than showing that Sheppard was unfaithful, Hayes' testimony proved nothing. But the damage had been done. Sheppard wound up being tried more for his morals than for any crime. Defense attorney Fred Garmone's final question went some way toward salvaging the loss: "Miss Hayes, during all your activities as a technician at the hospital, and your activities with Dr. Sheppard, were you always aware that he was a married man?"

"Yes," she whispered.

"That's all," Garmone said.

Arguably the most potent prosecution witness was Judge Blythin. His antipathy toward the defendant was plain and unvarnished. Early in the trial he had remarked to Dorothy Kilgallen: "Sheppard is as guilty as hell," and throughout the proceedings he had hectored and hamstrung the defense at every turn. Such an attitude on the bench ensured that Sheppard's last chance of receiving a fair trial evaporated. His own appearance on the stand was largely irrelevant. He performed well, but not well enough to overcome the atmosphere in court.

Jury deliberations lasted four days and resulted in a verdict of guilty to second-degree murder. (A rumor that some jurors were unwilling to commit Sheppard to the electric chair and might therefore acquit him, had forced Judge Blythin to dangle the second-degree carrot in front of them, and they'd gobbled it up greedily.) Blythin pronounced sentence: "It is now the judgment of this court that you be taken to the Ohio Penitentiary, there to remain for the rest of your natural life."

A Second Chance

In November 1961, attorney F. Lee Bailey, then a 29-year-old newcomer, took up Sheppard's cause. He filed a stream of motions on Sheppard's behalf and saw every one rejected. His frustration lasted until March 1964, when, by chance, Bailey attended a literary dinner. Among the other guests was Dorothy Kilgallen, and she happened to repeat Judge Blythin's off-the-record remark to her during the trial. Bailey listened intently. If he could demonstrate judicial prejudice then that would be grounds for a new trial.

Four months later a judge ordered Sheppard freed on bail, citing that the carnival conditions surrounding his trial "fell far below the minimum requirements for due process."

The following year Bailey argued his case before the Supreme Court, claiming that Blythin had displayed prejudice and that the trial had been conducted in a manner unbecoming a legal action. The Court agreed. On June 6, 1965, they handed down their decision that Sheppard's 1954 conviction be set aside, because Judge Blythin "did not fulfill his duty to protect Sheppard from inherently prejudicial publicity which saturated the county."

Ohio tried Sheppard again. Media interest remained high but this time was kept in check when the trial opened October 24, 1966, before Judge Francis J. Talty. Prosecutor John Corrigan led witnesses through essentially the same story that they had told over a decade earlier, but they now faced a defense attorney at the peak of his powers. Bailey demolished them, particularly Coroner Samuel Gerber. Referring to the elusive "surgical instrument," Gerber pompously announced that he had spent the last 12 years looking for just such an item "all over the United States."

"Please tell us what you found?" asked Bailey.

Sadly, Gerber shook his head: "I didn't find one."

Bailey scathingly dismissed the prosecution's case as "ten pounds of hogwash in a five-pound bag."

On December 16, 1966, the jury took less than 12 hours to return a verdict of not guilty: Sam Sheppard's ordeal was over.

But liberty proved brief. Sheppard died in 1970.

Journalistic irresponsibility, kindled by greedy editors, stole a decade of freedom from Sam Sheppard and probably sent him to an early grave. Sadly, trial by media is still with us, just as potent, just as pernicious as ever.

—*Colin Evans*

Suggestions for Further Reading

Bailey, F. Lee with Harvey Aronson. *The Defense Never Rests*. New York: Stein and Day Publishers, 1971.

Gaute, J.H.H. and Robin Odell. *The Murderers' Who's Who*. London: W.H. Allen, 1989.

Holmes, Paul. *The Sheppard Murder Case*. New York: David McKay, 1961.

Pollack, Jack Harrison. *Dr. Sam—An American Tragedy*. Chicago: Regnery, 1972.

Sheppard, Sam. *Endure And Conquer*. Cleveland: World, 1966.

Sheppard, Stephen with Paul Holmes. *My Brother's Keeper*. New York: David McKay, 1964.

Burton Abbott Trial: 1955

Defendant: Burton W. Abbott   **Crimes Charged:** Murder and kidnapping
Chief Defense Lawyer: Stanley D. Whitney   **Chief Prosecutors:** Frank
Coakley and Folger Emerson   **Judge:** Wade Snook   **Place:** Oakland,
California   **Dates of Trial:** November 7, 1955–January 25, 1956
Verdict: Guilty   **Sentence:** Death

SIGNIFICANCE
Shrewd advocacy and the marshaling of highly charged emotions overcame
evidential limitations in one of California's most sensational murder trials.

On April 28, 1955, 14-year-old Stephanie Bryan failed to return home after
school in Oakland, California. Apart from finding a school textbook, the
police had little to go on. A statewide search proved fruitless until July 15, when
Georgia Abbott reported that she had found some of Stephanie's personal
effects—a purse and ID card—in the basement of her Alameda home. When
police searched the basement more thoroughly the next day, they dug up yet
more books belonging to Stephanie, also her spectacles and a brassiere. Neither
Georgia Abbott nor her 27-year-old husband, Burton, an accounting student,
could explain how the effects came to be there. Burton Abbott told police that at
the time Stephanie disappeared, he was en route to the family's vacation cabin,
285 miles away in the Trinity County mountains. On July 20, the battered body
of Stephanie Bryan was found lying in a shallow grave, just 335 feet from
Abbott's cabin. Soon afterwards he was charged with murder and rape.

Emotion over Evidence

When Abbott's trial got under way November 7, 1955, his guilt seemed a
foregone conclusion. Certainly the Bay Area newspapers thought so, judging
from the virulent campaign they had waged against the defendant all summer
long, but it was soon clear that the case against Abbott was purely circumstantial:
not one direct piece of evidence existed to link him to the death of Stephanie
Bryan.

Fully aware of the shortcomings in the state's case, yet determined to
secure a death verdict, District Attorney Frank Coakley opted for emotion over

evidence. He ran into immediate opposition. Prosecution efforts to introduce a particularly gory photograph of the victim brought defense counsel Stanley D. Whitney to his feet, protesting that it was presented "for no other reason than to inflame the jury and raise prejudice against the defendant." Judge Wade Snook sided with Whitney on this point but did allow Coakley to show clothes taken from the dead girl's body. The stench from these unwashed clothes, which had been kept in a closed box, was so bad that several spectators hurriedly vacated the courtroom. The jury, denied any such opportunity, was forced to endure the ordeal, but the effect on them was palpable.

Amused Defendant

Just about the only person unaffected by these antics was the defendant himself. Throughout the trial, Abbott maintained an air of detached amusement. A man of some refinement—he played better than average chess, enjoyed crosswords and created haute cuisine dishes—Abbott didn't bother to stifle his contempt for all that was happening. He displayed that same cockiness on the witness stand, openly scoffing at prosecution charges that he had first attempted to rape Stephanie Bryan and then killed her when she resisted. It was all a "monstrous frame-up," he said, reiterating the stance he had taken from the beginning. As for the articles found in his basement, Abbott said that in May the basement served as a polling station. Dozens of people would have had access to it. Any one of them could have planted the incriminating evidence.

The subject of rape was one which Assistant District Attorney Folger Emerson pursued stridently. Sidestepping earlier pathological testimony that advanced decomposition made it impossible to determine if sexual assault had taken place, Emerson declared,

> I think it time to say from the evidence in this case that the original intent of the defendant when he kidnapped Stephanie Bryan was to commit a sex crime. . . . I think that what happened to Stephanie before she was killed was worse than death itself. . . . If ever there was a crime that fitted the punishment of death, this is it.

Emerson then concluded with one of the strangest and most garbled appeals ever to a jury:

> The state endeavors to take a life in the most humane way possible. Wouldn't it have been a blessing to Stephanie that if she had to die that she could have died that way than the way she did?

Coakley's syntax was less tangled and more effective. Brandishing the dead girl's brassiere and panties, he shouted, "You've heard the defense counsel ask 'What is the motive for this crime? What is the reason? Why? Why? Why?'" He offered the underwear in mute reply, branding Abbott a "typical psychopath and a pathological liar."

The only surprise after this was that it took the jury seven days to reach their verdict: guilty of first-degree murder. But in that delay were perhaps sown the seeds of the future doubt that would assail this case. After Judge Snook passed sentence of death, Abbott was taken to San Quentin to await execution. For more than a year his lawyers fought for commutation, but on March 15, 1957, Abbott was strapped into the gas chamber. Just minutes later a stay of execution was phoned through to the prison, but by then it was too late. The cyanide fumes were already creeping up around Abbott's face. Minutes later he was dead.

The manner and circumstances of Burton Abbott's execution sparked a renewal of the debate over whether society has the right to take life, especially on circumstantial evidence alone. It is an argument that shows no signs of abating.

—Colin Evans

Suggestions for Further Reading

Crimes And Punishment. Vol.16. England: Phoebus, 1974.

Gaute, J.H.H. and Robin Odell. *The Murderers' Who's Who.* London: W.H. Allen, 1989.

Marine, Gene. *The Nation* (May 19, 1956): 424–426.

Newsweek (February 6, 1956): 29.

Time (March 25, 1957): 25.

Cheryl Christina Crane Inquest: 1958

Defendant: Cheryl Christina Crane   **Crime Investigated:** Homicide of
Johnny Stompanato   **Chief Defense Lawyer:** Jerry Geisler
Chief Prosecutor: William B. McKesson   **Coroner:** Theodore J. Curphey
Place: Los Angeles, California   **Date of Inquest:** April 11, 1958
Verdict: Justifiable homicide

SIGNIFICANCE
The explosive plot and star-studded cast of this particular Hollywood spectacle
once again showed that the celluloid screen is no match for real life. Movie stars
and mobsters and a 14-year-old girl facing possible charges of murder kept
America hanging on the verdict of a Los Angeles coroner's inquest.

Late on Good Friday, April 4, 1958, police were summoned to 730 North Bedford Drive, the Beverly Hills, California home of screen goddess Lana Turner. The report said that someone had died. Lights blazed in the Moorish mansion as two detectives entered. In the bedroom they came across a small group of people trying to pump some life back into the unreceptive body of Johnny Stompanato, latest in a long line of Turner's lovers and bodyguard to notorious gambler Mickey Cohen. All of their efforts were in vain. A single stab wound had severed the aorta. Police Chief Clinton B. Anderson was irked to see Jerry Giesler, the "attorney to the stars," already in attendance. Giesler's reputation as a high-priced lawyer with a knack for winning difficult cases was legendary around Hollywood. Anderson asked to see Turner. Clearly distraught, her first words to him were, "Can I take the blame for this horrible thing?"

"No, not unless you have committed the act, Miss Turner," said Anderson. After more soul-searching she mumbled, "Okay, it was my daughter."

Fourteen-year-old Cheryl Crane, Turner's daughter by a previous marriage, was taken down to the police station. The next day District Attorney William B. McKesson proclaimed himself dissatisfied with Turner's version of events and announced an inquest for the following week, to determine if Cheryl Crane should be charged with murder. Although still a minor, Cheryl faced life imprisonment if found guilty of murder.

Later, Mickey Cohen, looking every inch the mobster in a felt hat and wide-lapeled suit, provided a bizarre interlude when he was asked to identify the body of his former bodyguard. Chewing on a mouthful of gum, the gambler drawled, "I refuse to answer on the grounds I may be accused of this murder," an odd response that nobody understood and nobody bothered to question.

Tale of Star-Crossed Lovers

Cameras from ABC and CBS lined the Los Angeles courtroom on April 11, 1958, ready to film what promised to be the TV event of the year. The radio networks went one better, broadcasting live when Coroner Theodore J. Curphey gaveled the proceedings to order at 9:00 A.M. After the introduction of the autopsy report and other formalities, it was time for Turner to testify.

Turner had played many roles in her life but none more important than this. She walked steadily to the stand. By now all of America was aware of her tempestuous affair with Stompanato, a third-rate hoodlum and professional gigolo. Their relationship had lasted a little over a year, 12 months of roller-coaster emotion and bruising physical battles.

They had been fighting again on the night of Good Friday. "He started shaking me badly," she told the court in a tremulous voice. "He said that if he said for me to jump, I would jump . . . he would even cut my face or cripple me." Under Jerry Giesler's gentle prompting, Turner went on: "As I broke away from his holding me [*sic*] and I turned around to face the door . . . my daughter was standing there . . . I said, 'Please, Cheryl, please don't listen to any of this. Please go back to your room.'"

When Turner broke down once during her testimony, clicking cameras recorded every emotion on her tear-stained face. Gathering her composure, she described how Stompanato had grabbed a hanger from the closet and made as if to strike her with it. "I said, 'Don't ever touch me again. I am absolutely finished. This is the end. I want you out.'"

What happened next, she said, was a blur. Cheryl came rushing into the bedroom and seemed to punch Stompanato in the stomach. He collapsed onto his back. Only then did Turner realize that he had been stabbed. While Cheryl stood sobbing, her mother ran to the bathroom for a towel. "I didn't know what to do and then I put the towel there [on the wound] and Mr. Stompanato was making dreadful sounds in his throat . . . gasping, terrible sounds."

At this point a deputy sheriff showed Turner the eight-inch kitchen knife that Cheryl had used to stab Stompanato. She stared at it grimly for a second, then looked away.

As Turner left the stand an unidentified man in the public gallery stood up and shouted, "Lies, lies, all lies! This mother and daughter were both in love with Stompanato. . . . All you Hollywood people are no good." Still yelling, the stranger strode from the court and was never seen again.

Cheryl's Statement Introduced

Because of her age Cheryl was not present at the inquest, but part of her statement made to Chief Anderson on the night of the stabbing was read into the record as follows:

Chief Anderson: Tell us what happened.

Cheryl: They had an argument . . . he was threatening Mother.

Chief Anderson: Where was this argument taking place?

Cheryl: First in my bedroom, then in mother's room.

Chief Anderson: Did you go downstairs and pick up a knife in the kitchen?

Cheryl: Yes.

Chief Anderson: Then you took it into the room?

Cheryl: Yes, in case he tried to hurt Mommy.

Chief Anderson: Then you thought your mother's life was in danger?

Cheryl: He kept threatening her and I thought he was going to hurt her, so I went into the room and stuck him with the knife. He screamed and asked me what I was doing. I ran out of the room. Mother called me back into the bedroom to help her again . . . I called Daddy before I went back into the room and told him to get over here fast.

Shortly before noon the 10 men and 2 women of the coroner's jury returned a verdict of justifiable homicide. Afterward, District Attorney McKesson, who had attended the inquest, announced to reporters: "After what I have heard today, and unless some new facts are uncovered, it would not be my inclination to prosecute her [Cheryl] on criminal charges."

Although this concluded the criminal proceedings, Stompanato's family filed a $752,250 civil suit against Lana Turner and Cheryl's father, alleging that parental neglect had caused the death of Johnny Stompanato. Jerry Giesler arranged a settlement of the suit for about $20,000.

Both mother and daughter survived the ordeal well. Oddly enough, the incident revived Lana Turner's flagging movie career. Her next film "Imitation Of Life" was a great box-office success and led to several more. Cheryl Crane, after further but minor skirmishes with authority, settled down and joined her father in his restaurant business.

The inquest into Stompanato's death afforded instructive as well as compelling viewing. For the majority of Americans, Lana Turner's torment yielded a unique opportunity to glimpse an absorbing and critical stage of the judicial process that is rarely reported by the press or understood by the public.

—Colin Evans

Suggestions for Further Reading

Crane, Cheryl and Cliff Jahr. *Detour.* New York: Arbor House, 1988.

Crimes And Punishment. Vol. 14. England: Phoebus, 1974.

Munn, Michael. *The Hollywood Murder Casebook.* New York: St. Martin's Press, 1987.

Turner, Lana. *Lana: The Lady, The Legend, The Truth.* New York: E.P. Dutton, 1982.

1958

Cheryl Christina

Crane Inquest

Raymond Bernard Finch and Carole Tregoff Trials: 1960 & 1961

Defendants: Raymond Bernard Finch and Carole Tregoff
Crime Charged: Murder   **Chief Defense Lawyers:** Don Bruggold, Grant
Cooper, Rexford Egan, and Robert A. Neeb, Jr   **Chief Prosecutors:** First
trial: Clifford C. Crail, William H. McKesson, and Fred N. Whichello; Second
trial: Clifford C. Crail; Third trial: Clifford C. Crail   **Judges:** First trial: Walter
R. Evans; Second trial: LeRoy Dawson; Third trial: David Coleman
Place: Los Angeles, California   **Dates of Trials:** January 4–March 12, 1960;
June 27–November 7, 1960; January 3–March 27, 1961   **Verdict:** First
trial: Mistrial; Second trial: Mistrial; Third trial: Guilty—Finch, first degree;
Tregoff, second degree   **Sentences:** Both received life imprisonment

SIGNIFICANCE

Despite overwhelming evidence in favor of conviction, a jury deadlocked, primarily because racial tension had pervaded the jury room.

Rampant greed, sex, and a considerable dose of comedy ensured that this trial of a wealthy doctor and his mistress as joint defendants on charges of murder dominated newspaper headlines for months.

By 1959, Finch, 42, a wealthy Los Angeles, California physician, yearned to elevate his affair with 20-year-old Carole Tregoff to something more permanent. Standing directly in the path of this ambition was Finch's wife, Barbara, backed by the formidable California community property laws. Divorce would entitle Barbara Finch to half of Finch's estimated $750,000 fortune. Furthermore, if Barbara Finch could prove adultery—and there was every indication that she intended to do just that—Finch faced financial ruin, since the court could then apportion any percentage of the community property it deemed fit to the aggrieved party.

Unwilling to accept such a calamity, Finch and Tregoff schemed. In Las Vegas, Nevada, where Tregoff had gone to work, they attempted to hire someone, anyone, to seduce Barbara Finch, and thereby provide Finch with evidence for a countersuit of adultery. This notion brought them into contact with self-confessed gigolo John Patrick Cody, a seedy ex-convict entirely untroubled by matters of conscience. Talk of seduction soon turned to plans of murder. Cody assured the couple that homicide was also high on his list of accomplishments. After accepting a down payment of $350 and an airline ticket, Cody departed, ostensibly to kill Barbara Finch in Los Angeles. (Actually he spent the weekend with one of his several girlfriends.) A few days later he resurfaced and told Tregoff that the matter had been taken care of. She paid him the agreed balance of $850, only to learn later that Barbara Finch was still very much alive. Cody professed astonishment, then explained that he must have killed the wrong woman. For another couple of hundred dollars he promised to rectify the error. With this payment in hand, Cody disappeared, leaving Finch and Tregoff sadder, wiser, and infinitely more desperate.

At 10:00 P.M. on July 18, 1959, the couple arrived at Finch's opulent house on Lark Hill Drive in suburban West Covina. Barbara Finch was not at home. Just over an hour later, she drove up in her red Chrysler. Finch went across to talk to her. A struggle broke out. At some point in the dispute, Barbara Finch was shot dead by a .38-caliber bullet. For reasons never fully explained, Finch and Tregoff somehow became separated. Finch, after stealing two cars, made his way back to Las Vegas, where he was joined early the next morning by Tregoff. That same day, Finch was arrested and charged with murder. Eleven days later Tregoff was similarly charged.

Fatal Struggle

Their trial began at the Los Angeles County Courthouse on January 4, 1960. Prosecutor Fred Whichello called his first

Carole Tregoff with Bernard Finch in the foreground. (Hearst Newspaper Collection, University of Southern California Library)

witness, Marie Anne Lindholm, the Finch maid. She told of running to the garage after hearing Barbara Finch scream and seeing Dr. Finch, gun in hand, standing over his semiconscious wife. Finch had then banged Lindholm's head against the garage wall, apparently in an effort to stun her. He'd ordered both women into the car but Barbara Finch had broken free and run. The doctor gave chase. Moments later Lindholm heard a shot, whereupon she ran to the house and called the police.

Equally damaging were Lindholm's allegations that Finch had regularly abused and threatened his wife. Over strenuous defense objections, a letter

Lindholm had written to her mother in Sweden before the murder was admitted into evidence. In it she described a beating that Finch had given Barbara Finch, and also his oft-repeated threats that he had hired "someone in Las Vegas" to kill her.

When Cody took the stand, defense lawyers must have felt confident of demolishing his testimony. If so, it was confidence misplaced. Cody's cheerful admissions to just about every form of reprehensible conduct imaginable—he had been a thief, a sponger, and an occasional swindler—gave his testimony a curious verisimilitude, an honesty, that the defense could never quite shake. Attorney Grant Cooper tried hard but it was useless:

Question: What did you do?

Answer: I loafed.

Question: How did you support yourself?

Answer: By my wit.

Question: (Later in reference to one of Cody's girlfriends): Did she support you?

Answer: Yes.

Defense attorney Rexford Egan fared no better:

Question: Would you lie for money?

Answer: (After a long, thoughtful pause) It looks like I have.

Cody also told the court of a homily that he had delivered to Finch in an effort to dissuade him from murder:

Killing your wife for money alone isn't worth it. . . . Let her have every penny. . . . Take Carole . . . up on a mountaintop and live off the wild. If the girl loves you, she's going to stick with you.

But by far the deadliest thing that Cody had to say detailed a conversation with Carole Tregoff, in which she had snapped: "Jack, you can back out. But if you don't kill her, the doctor will; and if he doesn't, I will."

When the prosecution rested, things looked bleak indeed for the doctor and the redhead.

Dying Words

Rumors that the defense had a surprise in store guaranteed a packed courtroom when Finch took the stand. The doctor didn't disappoint. He described how his wife had pulled a gun on him. Regrettably, in his efforts to take the gun away, he had been forced to club her with it, inflicting two skull fractures. At that moment, the maid Lindholm had entered the garage. Finch's misconstrued attempts to placate the maid's obvious distress—already referred to—gave Barbara Finch the chance to snatch up the gun and take off. Finch went in pursuit. Some way up the drive he saw Barbara Finch taking dead aim at Tregoff with the pistol. A further struggle ensued. Finch grabbed the gun. Barbara Finch began running again. Inexplicably, as Finch attempted to toss the gun away, it went off, neatly drilling his fleeing wife between the shoulder blades. Claiming ignorance of this fact, Finch ran across to his prone wife.

"What happened, Barb?" he cried. "Where are you hurt?"

"Shot . . . in . . . chest," she gasped.

"Don't move a thing. . . . I've got to get an ambulance for you and get you to [the] hospital."

Barbara held up a restraining hand. "Wait. . . . I'm sorry, I should have listened."

"Barb, don't talk about it now. I've got to get you to [the] hospital."

"Don't leave me. Take care of the kids."

As Finch described feeling for a pulse and finding none, his voice broke: "She was dead." He wiped away a tear. Sobs could also be heard in the public gallery. Others preferred to concentrate on the likelihood of a murder victim actually apologizing for being killed, and found the story a little thin, to say the least.

Under cross-examination the doctor regained his normal buoyancy. When prosecutor Whichello, referring to numerous affairs with other women before Carole Tregoff, asked him: "Did you tell these women that you loved them?" the doctor responded jauntily: "I think under the circumstances that would be routine."

Seven days on the stand did little to undermine Finch. His story sounded implausible, but he stuck to it and yielded nothing to the prosecution.

They made more headway against Tregoff, whose own account of events bordered on the fantastic. She told of watching the scene unfold, then cowering for five or six hours behind some bougainvillea plants, paralyzed with fear, while police turned the house upside down. Later, she had driven back to Las Vegas, alone. Allegedly, her first knowledge of Barbara Finch's death came via the car radio, information which she passed on to Finch himself. He reportedly shrugged the news off and Tregoff went to work.

Prosecutor Clifford Crail succeeded in making Tregoff look very bad, intent only on saving herself at the expense of Finch. (Since their arrest, Tregoff had spurned all of Finch's letters and advances.) Crail highlighted her leading role in the solicitation of Cody, also her conflicting stories of why the couple had gone to Lark Hill Drive that night. Originally, Tregoff told police that the intention was to talk Barbara Finch out of divorce proceedings. On the stand that evolved into an attempt to convince her to obtain a "quickie" Nevada divorce.

Stunning Verdict

Courtroom observers thought that, at a minimum, Tregoff's performance had guaranteed a berth for Finch in the gas chamber. But after eight days of wrangling, the jury members announced that they were unable to agree on a verdict and a mistrial was declared. It later transpired that racial tension—one jury member was black, another Hispanic—had led to ugly scenes in the jury room, when neither minority juror would yield to pressure exerted by the white jurors.

A second trial began June 27, 1960, and again ended in deadlock November 7, 1960, despite an extraordinary admonition to the jury by Judge LeRoy Dawson, who told them, in no uncertain terms, that they ought not to believe the evidence of either defendant.

The State of California tried for a third time, opening its case January 3, 1961 before Superior Judge David Coleman. By now much of the earlier sensational coverage had dissipated, leaving a noticeably calmer courtroom atmosphere. It showed in the jury deliberations. On March 27 they convicted Finch of first-degree murder, while Tregoff was found guilty in the second degree. Both were sentenced to life imprisonment.

In 1969 Tregoff was paroled. She changed her name and found work at a hospital in the Pasadena area.

Finch, released two years later, practiced medicine in Missouri for a decade before returning to West Covina in 1984.

Given the lurid ingredients, it was hardly surprising that the trials of Finch and Tregoff assumed national prominence. And yet two juries deadlocked over what was almost surely premeditated murder. How much their indecision was prompted by the defendants' attractive appearance and social standing will remain a matter of conjecture.

—*Colin Evans*

Suggestions for Further Reading

Ambler, Eric. *The Ability To Kill.* New York: The Mysterious Press, 1987.

Gaute, J.H.H. and Robin Odell. *The Murderers' Who's Who.* London: W.H. Allen, 1989.

Kilgallen, Dorothy. *Murder One.* New York: Random House, 1967.

Wolf, Marvin J. and Katherine Mader. *Fallen Angels.* New York: Ballantine, 1986.

Richard Hickock And Perry Smith Trial: 1960

Defendants: Richard E. Hickock and Perry E. Smith
Crime Charged: Murder **Chief Defense Lawyers:** Arthur Fleming and
Harrison Smith **Chief Prosecutors:** Logan Greene and Duane West
Judge: Roland H. Tate **Place:** Garden City, Kansas
Dates of Trial: March 22–29, 1960 **Verdict:** Guilty
Sentence: Death by hanging

SIGNIFICANCE

The case provided a classic example of the limitations of the M'Naghten Test by which defendants are judged mentally fit to stand trial. Truman Capote's book about the case, *In Cold Blood,* further cemented the author's literary reputation and brought the debate over capital punishment into focus for millions of readers worldwide.

The people of Holcomb, Kansas, had not forgotten them, but the trial and punishment of Richard Hickock and Perry Smith came and went unnoticed by most Americans. Within months of their execution, however, Smith and Hickock became two of the most famous murderers in history.

On Sunday morning, November 15, 1959, a successful, respected, and well-liked Kansas farmer named Herbert Clutter was found in the basement of his home with his throat cut and his head blown open by a shotgun blast. His wife Bonnie and their teenaged children, Kenyon and Nancy, were found bound, gagged, and shot to death elsewhere in the house. There were no clues nor any apparent motive. "This is apparently the work of a psychopathic killer," declared the local sheriff.

The bloody slayings might have remained unsolved without the help of a convicted thief, who had once shared a cell with a small-time check kiter named Richard Hickock. The thief had worked on the Clutter farm and described it to Hickock, who asked if the Clutters had a safe. The thief thought they did. Hickock declared that he would find the farm, rob the Clutters, and kill all witnesses, adding that his former cellmate Perry Smith would be just the man to help. Herb Clutter's former hired hand dismissed Hickock's plan as a fantasy, but he came forward when he heard of the murders.

Hickock and Smith were soon arrested in Las Vegas, Nevada, for parole violation and passing bad checks. The Kansas Bureau of Investigation dispatched agents to Nevada, where they questioned the suspects separately. Hickock denied any knowledge of the slayings, but a clever interrogation led Smith to confess to having shot the Clutters. Hickock confessed his part in the slayings the next day and the two men were returned to Kansas for trial.

The gruesome confessions and physical evidence made it clear that the accused men were responsible for the killings. Arguing for the death penalty, prosecutor Logan Greene said, "some of our most enormous crimes only happen because once upon a time a pack of chicken-hearted jurors refused to do their duty." The jury deliberated for only 40 minutes before returning a guilty verdict, ironically about a minute for each dollar Smith and Hickock had found in the Clutter home—there was no safe. "No chicken-hearted jurors, they," Smith joked as he and Hickock were led laughing from the courtroom. Judge Roland Tate sentenced the defendants to death by hanging.

Trial Leaves Questions Over Sanity

Yet the way the trial was conducted left lingering questions. A defense motion to have Smith and Hickock undergo comprehensive psychological testing before the trial had been denied by Judge Tate, who appointed three local general practitioners, not psychiatrists, to make the required examination. After a brief interview, the doctors judged the defendants sane.

The case of Perry Smith (left) and Richard Hickock brought the debate over capital punishment into focus. (AP/Wide World Photos)

Defense lawyers had sought the opinion of a more experienced psychiatrist from the state mental hospital, who diagnosed definite signs of mental illness in Smith and felt that Hickock's head injuries in a past auto mishap might possibly have affected his behavior. Yet the diagnosis was never heard in the Finney County courthouse.

Under the M'Naghten Test a defendant is ruled to be sane if he has sufficient mental capacity to know and understand what he is doing at the time he commits a crime, that it is wrong, and that it violates the victim's rights. The M'Naghten Test was applied strictly in the Hickock-Smith trial. By Kansas law, the psychiatrist was allowed only to give his opinion about the defendants' sanity or lack thereof at the time they were in the Clutter house. Under this constraint, the psychiatrist could only answer "yes" when asked if he thought Hickock was sane by the M'Naghten definition and "no" when asked if he could surmise what Smith's state of mind was at the time of the killings. No comment was allowed on the question of whether Perry Smith was mentally able to control his actions, regardless of his knowledge that, they were unlawful.

Appeals Fail to Overturn Conviction

Richard Hickock's complaints to the Kansas Bar Association about the fairness of the trial prompted an investigation. The arguable mishandling of the case by the defense lawyers, failure to move the trial venue outside of Finney County, and the acceptance of a juror who had made questionable statements about the suitability of capital punishment in the case opened the way for four appeals and postponements of the death sentence. Court-appointed federal lawyers tried three times to have the Hickock-Smith case heard by the U.S. Supreme Court, but each time the court declined without comment. Hickock and Smith were hanged at the Kansas State Penitentiary on April 14, 1965, five years after their conviction.

The hangings provided an ending for a book Truman Capote had been working on since the weeks when the Clutter murders were still unsolved. A brief notice of the crime in the *New York Times* had inspired Capote to choose it as the subject for what he called a "nonfiction novel," a factually correct work written with techniques usually employed in writing fiction.

Capote interviewed everyone connected with the case, from the Clutters' neighbors to Hickock and Smith themselves. After the killers were captured, he followed their trials and became their confidant. When his book, *In Cold Blood*, appeared at the end of 1965, the lives and deaths of the Clutters and their killers became intimately known to millions of Americans. *In Cold Blood* was an international best-seller and the basis for a 1967 film.

Capote's experience left him opposed to capital punishment. Instead, he favored the federal imposition of mandatory life sentences for murder. By the time the Supreme Court issued the famous "Miranda Ruling" (see separate entry) in 1966, the writer's celebrity as an authority on criminal matters was such that he was called upon by a U.S. Senate subcommittee examining the court's decision. Capote criticized the high court's opinion that arrested suspects were to be advised of their rights to silence, legal counsel, and the presence of an attorney during police questioning.

Hickock and Smith would have gone "scot-free" under such circumstances because of the lack of clues in the Clutter murders, Capote said. "Any lawyer worth his salt would have advised the boys to say nothing. Had they said nothing, they would not have been brought to trial, much less convicted." Special Agent Alvin Dewey, who had elicited Perry Smith's confession, agreed. Dewey told the subcommittee that investigators abiding by the Miranda rule would be "talking the defendant out of telling us anything."

— Thomas C. Smith

Suggestions for Further Reading

Capote, Truman. *In Cold Blood*. New York: Random House, 1965.

Clarke, Gerald. *Capote: A Biography*. New York: Simon & Schuster, 1986.

Marshall, James. *Intention—In Law and Society*. New York: Funk & Wagnalls, 1968.

Menninger, Karl, M.D. *The Crime of Punishment*. New York: Viking Press, 1966.

Plimpton, George. "The Story Behind a Nonfiction Novel." *New York Times Book Review* (January 16, 1966): 2–3.

Boynton v. Virginia: 1960

Appellant: Bruce Boynton.   **Defendant:** Commonwealth of Virginia
Appellant Claim: Unlawful arrest   **Chief Defense Lawyer:** Walter E. Rogers
Chief Lawyer for Appellant: Thurgood Marshall   **Justices:** Hugo L. Black,
William J. Brennan, Jr., Tom C. Clark, William O. Douglas, Felix Frankfurter,
John Marshall Harlan, Potter Stewart, Earl Warren, Charles E. Whittaker.
Place: Washington, D.C.   **Date of Decision:** December 5, 1960
Decision: Court upheld appellant's claim

SIGNIFICANCE

In the often acrimonious battle between the federal government and individual
states over racial segregation, Bruce Boynton's suit marked a major break-
through. For the first time, Washington sent a clear message that interstate
facilities were for the use of all citizens, irrespective of color.

In 1958, Bruce Boynton, a black student at Howard University Law School in
Washington, D.C., took a Trailways bus from Washington to his home in
Montgomery, Alabama. On a 40-minute layover at the Trailways Bus Terminal
in Richmond, Virginia, the passengers went inside to eat. Boynton entered the
segregated restaurant, sat in the white section and ordered a sandwich and tea.
When asked to move to the colored section he refused, saying that as an
interstate passenger he was protected by federal anti-segregation laws. Declining to leave, he was arrested by local police, charged with trespass, and fined $10.

The Commonwealth of Virginia conceded that the conviction could not
stand if anything in federal law or the Constitution gave Boynton a right to
service in the restaurant. But it found no such right. Lawyers for the National
Association for the Advancement of Colored People (NAACP) petitioned the
Supreme Court on grounds that Boynton *was* entitled to such protection under
the Constitution.

Pleading that case before the Supreme Court on October 12, 1960, was
Thurgood Marshall, who later became the first black Supreme Court Justice. He
maintained that Boynton's arrest placed an unreasonable burden on commerce
and denied him the equal protection of the law, both points with far-reaching
implications. However, the Supreme Court chose not to address this petition
from a constitutional standpoint after the Justice Department, intervening as a

friend of the court, raised the issue of the Interstate Commerce Act, which expressly forbade "unjust discrimination."

For the act to apply, the relationship between restaurant and terminal had to be clarified. When Trailways built the terminal in 1953 it contracted with Bus Terminal Restaurant of Richmond, Inc. for the latter to provide dining facilities for passengers on Trailways buses. The only interest that Trailways had in the restaurant came in the form of the annual rental, $30,000, plus a percentage of the gross profits. So was the restaurant subject to the same federal provisions as Trailways?

Associate Justice Whittaker (left) joined the dissent in *Boynton v. Virginia,* a landmark case, which linked the future of the civil rights movement with the federal government. (Courtesy, National Archives)

No, argued Walter E. Rogers, attorney for Virginia. He contended that the restaurant, as private property, fell outside the scope of the Interstate Commerce Act. Boynton, he said, had been justly convicted.

Court Splits, but for Boynton

On December 5, 1960, the Supreme Court decided 7-2 in favor of Boynton, the first time since 1946 it had divided on a matter of racial segregation. A strong factor in the Court's decision had been the earlier testimony of the restaurant manager who conceded that, although the restaurant received "quite a bit of business" from local people, it was primarily for the service of Trailways passengers. Describing this as "much of an understatement," Justice Hugo L. Black, in writing the majority verdict, added:

> Interstate passengers have to eat, and they have a right to expect that this essential transportation food service . . . would be rendered without discrimination prohibited by the Interstate Commerce Act. We are not holding that every time a bus stops at a wholly independent roadside restaurant the act applies . . . [but] where circumstances show that the terminal and restaurant operate as an integral part of the bus carrier's transportation service . . . an interstate passenger need not inquire into documents of title or contractual agreements in order to determine whether he has a right to be served without discrimination.

Anticipating the Supreme Court's decision, Bus Terminal Restaurants, Inc. of Raleigh, North Carolina announced that, as of August 1960, none of its establishments would be racially segregated.

The impact of this case was immense. For the first time a bridge was built between the federal government and the civil rights movement. While many obstacles remained to be conquered in the fight for racial equality, henceforth it would be a struggle fought together.

—Colin Evans

Suggestions for Further Reading

The Negro History Bulletin Vol. 26, 15. New York: Associated Publishers, 1972.

Wasby, Stephen L., Anthony A. D'Amato, and Rosemary Metrailer. *Desegregation From Brown To Alexander.* Carbondale, Ill.: South Illinois University Press, 1977.

Witt, Elder. *Guide To The Supreme Court.* Washington: Congressional Quarterly, 1990.

Clarence Earl Gideon Trials: 1961 & 1963

Defendant: Clarence Earl Gideon   **Crime Charged:** Breaking and entering
Chief Defense Lawyers: First trial: None; Second trial: W. Fred Turner
Chief Prosecutor: First trial: William E. Harris; Second trial: J. Frank Adams,
J. Paul Griffith, and William E. Harris   **Judge:** Robert L. McCrary, Jr.
Place: Panama City, Florida   **Dates of Trials:** First trial: August 4, 1961;
Second trial: August 5, 1963   **Verdict:** First trial: Guilty;
Second trial: Not guilty   **Sentence:** First trial: 5 years imprisonment

SIGNIFICANCE

One man, without benefit of wealth, privilege, or education, went up against the entire legal establishment, arguing that his constitutional rights had been violated. In doing so, he brought about an historic change in American trial procedure: all felony defendants are entitled to legal representation, irrespective of the crime charged, and courts are to appoint an attorney if a defendant is too poor to hire one.

At eight o'clock on the morning of June 3, 1961, a patrolling police officer in Panama City, Florida, noticed that the door of the Bay Harbor Poolroom was open. Stepping inside, he saw that a cigarette machine and jukebox had been burglarized. Eyewitness testimony led to the arrest of Clarence Gideon, a 51-year-old drifter who occasionally helped out at the poolroom. He vehemently protested his innocence but two months later was placed on trial at the Panama City Courthouse. No one present had any inkling that they were about to witness history in the making.

As the law then stood, Gideon, although indigent, was not automatically entitled to the services of a court-appointed defense lawyer. A 1942 Supreme Court decision, *Betts v. Brady*, extended this right only to those defendants facing a capital charge. Many states did, in fact, exceed the legal requirements and provide all felony defendants with counsel, but not Florida. Judge Robert L. McCrary, Jr. did his best to protect Gideon's interests when the trial opened August 4, 1961, but he clearly could not assume the role of advocate; that task was left to Gideon himself. Under the circumstances Gideon, a man of limited education but immense resourcefulness, performed as well as could be expected, but he was hardly the courtroom equal of Assistant State Attorney William E. Harris, who scored heavily with the testimony of Henry Cook.

This young man claimed to have seen Gideon inside the poolroom at 5:30 on the morning of the crime. After watching Gideon for a few minutes through the window, Cook said, the defendant came out clutching a pint of wine in his hand, then made a telephone call from a nearby booth. Soon afterward a cab arrived and Gideon left.

In cross-examination Gideon sought to impugn Cook's reasons for being outside the bar at that time of the morning. Cook replied that he had "just come from a dance, down in Apalachicola—stayed out all night." A more experienced cross-examiner might have explored this potentially fruitful line of questioning, but Gideon let it pass and lapsed into a vague and argumentative discourse.

Eight witnesses testified on the defendant's behalf. None proved helpful and Clarence Gideon was found guilty. The whole trial had lasted less than one day. Three weeks later Judge McCrary sentenced Gideon to the maximum: five years imprisonment.

Gideon Appeals

Gideon was outraged by the verdict, particularly the fact that he had been denied counsel. He applied to the Florida Supreme Court for a writ of *habeas corpus*, an order freeing him on the ground that he was illegally imprisoned. When this application was denied Gideon penciled a five-page document entitled "Petition for a Writ of *Certiorari* Directed to the Supreme Court." (A writ of *certiorari* is an order ·by an appellate court to hear a particular appeal.) In other words, Gideon was asking the U.S. Supreme Court to hear his case. The suit was placed on the docket under the title *Gideon v. H.G. Cochran, Jr.,* who happened to be the director of Florida's Division of Corrections.

Clarence Earl Gideon argued that his constitutional rights were denied when he was refused an attorney. (AP/ Wide World Photos)

Each year the Supreme Court receives thousands of petitions. Most are meritless and don't get heard. Sheer weight of numbers militates against the deserving remainder, and yet, against all odds, the Supreme Court decided to hear Gideon's petition. Abe Fortas, who would himself later sit on the bench, was appointed to plead Gideon's case. Responding for Cochran were Bruce R. Jacob and George Mentz. The date for oral argument was set for January 14, 1963, but before that date Mr. Cochran resigned his position with the Florida

Division of Corrections. He was replaced by Louie L. Wainwright—earning for that man an enduring and wholly unwanted place in judicial history—and the case was renamed *Gideon v. Wainwright*.

Fortas, arguing that the restrictive nature of *Betts v. Brady* had treated Gideon unfairly, drew a poignant analogy: "I was reminded the other night, as I was pondering this case, of Clarence Darrow when he was prosecuted for trying to fix a jury. The first thing he realized was that he needed a lawyer—he, one of the country's greatest criminal lawyers." It was time, said Fortas, for the law to change.

Needless to say, Jacob and Mentz stridently disagreed, but the mood of the times was against them, and, on March 18, 1963, the Supreme Court unanimously overruled *Betts v. Brady*, saying that all felony defendants were entitled to legal representation, irrespective of the crime charged. Justice Hugo L. Black wrote the opinion that set aside Gideon's conviction:

> [R]eason and reflection requires us to recognize that in our adversary system of criminal justice, any person haled into court, who is too poor to hire a lawyer, cannot be assured a fair trial unless counsel is provided for him. This seems to us to be an obvious truth.

Clarence Earl Gideon's petition to the Supreme Court. (Courtesy, United States Supreme Court)

On August 5, 1963, Clarence Gideon again appeared before Judge Robert L. McCrary in the Panama City Courthouse, and this time he had an experienced trial lawyer, W. Fred Turner, to defend him. All of the publicity resulted in a heavily bolstered prosecution team. In addition to William Harris, State Attorney J. Frank Adams and J. Paul Griffith were on hand to uphold the validity of the first conviction. Henry Cook was again the main prosecution witness but fared badly under Turner's incisive questioning. Particularly damaging was his admission that he had withheld details of his criminal record at the previous trial. Due in large part to Cook's poor showing, the jury acquitted Gideon of all charges.

He died in 1972 at age 61.

Because one man sat down and wrote a letter, no felony defendant need ever fear facing a court alone. *Gideon v. Wainwright* extended the law's protection to all. More than that, it gave justice a better name.

—*Colin Evans*

Suggestions for Further Reading

The Guide To American Law. St. Paul, Minn.: West Publishing Co., 1984.

Lewis, Anthony. *Gideon's Trumpet.* New York: Random House, 1964.

Schwartz, Bernard. *History Of The Law In America.* New York: American Heritage, 1974.

John Henry Faulk v. Aware, Inc., et al.: 1962

Plaintiff: John Henry Faulk   **Defendants:** Aware, Inc., Vincent Hartnett, and Laurence A. Johnson   **Plaintiff Claim:** Damages for libel and conspiracy
Chief Defense Lawyer: Thomas A. Bolan   **Chief Lawyer for Plaintiff:** Louis Nizer   **Judge:** Abraham N. Geller   **Place:** New York, New York
Dates: April 23–July 29, 1962   **Verdict:** Award for compensatory damages in the amount of $1 million, plus $2.5 million in punitive damages (at the time, the largest judgment ever returned in a libel suit)

SIGNIFICANCE

The verdict put an end to institutional blacklisting by private groups and individuals who claimed to be experts on Communism, "cleared" artists, and excluded artists from employment in the mass media.

In 1957, radio and television performer John Henry Faulk, a Texan with a penchant for folklore, fought back against blacklisting in the American work place by suing Aware, Inc. and two individuals for libel. In the tense Cold War years following World War II, fear of Communist subversion led to pressure on the movie and broadcasting industries to blacklist anyone suspected of the slightest past or present sympathy with Communist or leftist causes. Afraid of advertiser boycotts, the broadcasting companies buckled under the pressure from self-styled experts on Communism who insisted on their right to screen performers. Hundreds of careers were jeopardized or ruined and some victims of the practice were so distraught they committed suicide.

Despite bankruptcy and humiliation, Faulk persisted in his suit against the blacklisters through six years of pretrial motions, a dramatic trial, and numerous appeals that reached the U.S. Supreme Court.

The Cold War Climate

With the onset of the Cold War in 1946, the federal government and other sectors of American life were purged of those suspected of sympathy with the Soviet Union's Communist government. Blacklists containing the names of anyone who had refused to appear before the House Un-American Activities Committee (HUAC) were circulated to intimidate offending individuals and organizations. By the 1950s, the blacklisters, motivated as much by the desire to make a buck as anti-Communist ideology, had begun to intimidate the private sector—business, higher education, radio, and television.

Performers were systematically "cleared" through paid security consultants. Encouraged and provided with information by the continuing HUAC hearings, they researched a performer's political history. The evidence was often slight or ambiguous. A $5 donation to the "wrong" cause was sometimes sufficient to add a name to a blacklist and jeopardize the "sinner's" livelihood. By 1955, the practice was an integral part of the broadcast industry's hiring procedure.

Faulk Leads Fight Against Blacklisting

John Henry Faulk, who was all Texas charm and folksy humor, was born and reared in Austin and went on to earn a Master's degree in English at the University of Texas, where he lectured on American folklore and English while studying for a doctorate. After the war, during which he served in the Merchant Marine, the American Red Cross, and the U.S. Army, Faulk began appearing on radio and television. By 1953, he was starring in his own talk show, playing popular music and commenting in his distinctive drawl on the news of the day.

His daily afternoon radio program on WCBS, in New York City, had high ratings and solid sponsors such as Libby's Frozen Foods by 1955. Faulk was well-liked by his colleagues and substituted regularly as a panelist on television game shows. He was, in fact, planning a full-time television career.

Like all broadcast performers, he was a member of the American Federation of Television and Radio Artists, known as AFTRA. Formed in 1938, AFTRA's New York local was the largest in the country. It was governed by a 35-member board of directors, elected by the membership every year. In the mid-1950s the board was dominated by an anti-Communist faction supporting Aware, Inc., a political group organized to fight "the Communist conspiracy in entertainment communications." In fact, Vinton Hayworth, the president of AFTRA in 1955, was also an officer of Aware, Inc.

Any performer who found his name in one of Aware's regularly issued bulletins was blacklisted and rendered unemployable in the industry. Sponsors, worried that their products would be linked to those accused of Communist sympathies, canceled advertising spots. Without explanation, performers were denied all opportunities, even 10-minute guest appearances. Careers and lives were quickly ruined. Victims disappeared into obscurity, including Jean Muir, the popular mother on "The Aldrich Family." Others, like Mady Christians and Philip Loeb, committed suicide.

Alarmed by the growing practice of blacklisting, several members of AFTRA, including Faulk, recommended that Aware, Inc. be condemned by the union membership. The vote was carried, 982 to 514, and a new slate was put up for election: Charles Collingwood, a former Rhodes Scholar and then a CBS news commentator; Gary Moore, popular on radio and television; and John Henry Faulk, among others. They called themselves "the middle of the road slate" to oppose Communism and blacklisting alike, to "oppose denial of employment by discriminatory and intimidating practices, especially by outside organizations."

The bitterly fought election brought an overwhelming victory for the "middlers." The highest number of votes went to Faulk, and with it the full force of an Aware assault. In the no-holds-barred, poison-pen campaign that followed, Aware sent letters to CBS executives warning that Faulk had "a significant Communist Front record."

Faulk vehemently denied the allegations. At the urging of CBS executives, he signed an affidavit saying so. Despite the assault behind the scenes, Faulk's show continued to register high ratings. He openly discussed the continued assault on his sponsors and their ad agencies with CBS executives, even urging them to sue sponsors who canceled advertising because of the unfounded accusations. When they refused, Faulk himself filed suit on June 26, 1956. CBS renewed Faulk's contract in December 1956, and in the year that followed, Faulk's earnings were the highest ever and his show was number two in the Nielsen ratings. His friend and manager Sam Slate assured him his job was secure. But in 1957, CBS fired Faulk while he vacationed with his family in Jamaica. The network told him it needed to make format changes and would substitute Arthur Godfrey in his time slot. From that time on, with the exception of a guest appearance on Jack Paar's talk show, Faulk could not get a job. In 1959 he moved his destitute family back to Texas.

The evidence that banished Faulk from the entertainment industry and left him unemployed for 6½ years began with a list of speaking engagements Faulk had made from 1946 to 1949. It stated, "According to the *Daily Worker* (the Communist newspaper) of April 22, 1946, Jack Faulk was to appear at Club 65, 13 Astor Place, N.Y.C.—a favorite site of pro-Communist affairs."

Unlike other Aware victims, Faulk fought back with the help of Louis Nizer, the most respected civil liberties lawyer of the day. Nizer determined first that Faulk's was a case of libel, but Nizer suspected a conspiracy, too. The suit was an opportunity to attack the blacklisting techniques that permeated the industry. To prove the case, Nizer would show how a few private citizens forced the entertainment industry, the fifth-largest industry in the United States, to secretly and illegally boycott its own employees.

The defendants in the case, representing Aware, Inc., were Vincent Hartnett and Laurence Johnson. Johnson, in his 70s, was the prosperous owner of a chain of New York state supermarkets. His criticism of a program or a performer brought anxious network executives to his Syracuse headquarters seeking absolution. Johnson's attack on Faulk took him to the Madison Avenue advertising agencies representing Faulk's sponsors. There he threatened that every supermarket in the country would boycott any product sold on Faulk's show.

Vincent Hartnett was also an entrepreneur, cashing in on the anti-Communist zeal as the principal contributor to *Red Channels*, a book citing the political activities of performers. It became the desktop reference during every casting call. In 1952, Hartnett, with Paul Milton, had formed Aware, Inc., a private consulting firm to screen artists. A former network employee himself, Hartnett charged broadcast networks and ad agencies $5 a head to research a performer's background. Hartnett's alliance with Laurence Johnson added economic muscle to back up the accusations. To deny or protest only brought more controversy for the victim, more letters, more threats. Almost without exception the accused slipped quietly away.

To win the libel suit, Nizer would have to overcome the obvious defense that what was written in the bulletin was true, Nizer had to show that Faulk, as a public figure, was maliciously attacked outside the bounds of fair comment. Although the truth of the speaking engagements was proven, the claim Faulk was a Communist sympathizer was not provable by a mere newspaper listing. Nizer established in pretrial testimony that Aware, Inc., Hartnett and Johnson could not verify any of the accusations against Faulk contained in the lengthy documents they had published and distributed.

In one dramatic pretrial session, Hartnett, in front of his attorney, Godfrey Schmidt, admitted to Nizer that his research consisted of "being sold a barrel of goods." Soon after, Schmidt was replaced by Roy Cohn as the chief defense attorney.

John Henry Faulk fought back when Aware blacklisted him and sought to destroy his television career. (AP/ Wide World Photos)

Trial Witnesses Hard to Find

When the trial finally opened on April 23, 1962, New York Supreme Court Justice Abraham N. Geller immediately impressed upon the members of the jury their right to judge the facts in the case without prejudice and without fear.

The fear of blacklisting was still so great when the trial opened that witnesses whose testimony Nizer needed were hard to find. Both Faulk and Nizer implored individuals to come forward, and those who did were an impressive lot: successful performers, advertising executives, and producers who had had their fill of blacklisting.

Nizer led each one through testimony that described for the court how people were labeled Communists because they were linked to Communist Front activities, often simply because they had made small financial donations to obscure political causes. There were stories of mistaken identity and of guilt by insinuation. Rarely would someone be given the opportunity to deny an allegation, but one witness testified a victim could, if he paid a fee to the consultant, receive a "full report" and concede the wrongdoing.

Actress Kim Hunter told how she couldn't get a job in broadcasting for three years after she'd won an Academy Award in 1949. Her name had not appeared in Aware, Inc. bulletins or on any lists that she knew of, but no one in television would hire her.

Finally in 1956, she traced her lack of employment to Hartnett and sought him out. He told her that his investigation had linked her name with assorted Communist Front activities and she could have a full report for $200.

The actress' former "acts of disloyalty" now valued at $200 were: purchasing for $5 a reprint of the New York Post series entitled, "Blacklist—The Panic in Radio and Television"; lending her name to the "problem of world peace" under the auspices of the National Council of Arts, Sciences and Professions; and signing a petition for the fair trial in Mississippi of Willie McGee, "a Negro."

David Susskind, an experienced producer, testified he had to submit all the names of all the people involved in a production to the ad agency Young and Rubicam for political clearance. No one was hired until approved. In one year alone, Susskind testified he had submitted 5,000 names for approval. One-third were rejected.

Nizer tied this testimony to Hartnett by producing an agreement Hartnett had with Young and Rubicam. For $5 each, Hartnett would check the names of artists submitted to him for Susskind's program. An advertising executive corroborated this by testifying that he came to view Hartnett as a racketeer selling protection.

Apparently no performer had been excluded from the screening process. Nizer produced Hartnett's records in which one entry read, "Santa Claus, $5."

It wasn't Faulk's political sins that got him fired, argued defense attorney Thomas Bolan, who had replaced his associate Roy Cohn. It was Faulk's lack of talent and his loss of popularity. Bolan pointed out that Faulk kept his show for one year after the Aware bulletin was issued—evidence, he said, that it was Faulk's loss of popularity and his own incompetence that cost him his job.

Bolan then accused Faulk of attending Communist Party meetings in the 1940s and associating with known Communists. Faulk denied this on the stand and it gave Nizer an opening to get his client's views before the jury.

"Have you . . . ever been sympathetic to any Communist ideology, directly or indirectly?" Nizer asked. In a tremulous voice, Faulk answered, "No, sir, I have not."

It was Aware, Inc., and the defendants themselves who proved to be the most effective witnesses for the plaintiff. Paul Milton, one of Aware's founders but not included in the suit against the organization, testified for the defense. Under Nizer's questioning, Milton moved from resistance to a reluctant confession, conceding that Faulk's only wrongdoing was opposing Aware, Inc. Nizer also attacked the language of the Aware, Inc. bulletin, which Milton had helped draft. The phrase "according to the *Daily Worker*" made it appear that the Communist newspaper supported Faulk's candidacy. Nizer pointedly asked if news of Faulk's opposition in the union to Aware hadn't appeared in all the daily papers? Milton admitted he had deliberately omitted this fact.

When Hartnett took the stand, Bolan began to lead his client through an impressive-looking pile of documents on which Hartnett claimed he had relied when compiling evidence of Faulk's disloyalty.

Ordinarily notes of this sort are inadmissible, as they cannot be independently verified, but in a libel case an exception is made to permit the defendant to demonstrate a research effort had been made unmotivated by malice. Hartnett began citing the records of the House Un-American Activities Committee hearings, but he was interrupted. These congressional hearings were not admissible in a court of law, Justice Geller told the astonished defense attorney. They did not constitute a judicial finding, and their truth had not been established. With the HUAC hearing records excluded, all that was left of Hartnett's "research" were 13 notes on a file card when Nizer began cross-examination. Of these, only two mentioned Faulk's name, and both were positive references to Faulk's career.

Nizer also proved that Hartnett had attributed a story about Faulk and the "middlers" to the *Daily Worker*, though it had appeared in the *New York Herald Tribune*.

While he was under cross-examination, Hartnett was asked if he could identify Faulk's wife among the spectators. When Hartnett pointed to the wrong woman, Nizer bellowed: "Sir, is that an example of the accuracy with which you have identified your victims for the past ten years?"

Hartnett told the court he investigated individuals only at the request of a client. But no one—not the ad agency Young and Rubicam, not the sponsors, not the network, Nizer showed—had requested a report about John Henry Faulk or the middle-of-the-road slate of officers. This research Hartnett had thrown in for free.

Laurence Johnson never appeared in court to defend himself. Newspaper columnists called him "sick-call Larry," as he traveled from doctor to doctor for exemption. Nizer charged that if Johnson could withstand this many medical examinations, he was sturdy enough to appear in court. The court agreed. But as the trial reached its final days, Johnson checked into a Bronx, New York, motel, where he was found dead of a barbiturate overdose. The news was kept from the jury until both sides finished their summation.

The issue in the trial, Nizer told the jury, was not Communism at all, but private vigilantism and individuals who took the law into their own hands. When a self-appointed group fabricates information about a man, then goes behind his back to deprive him of his livelihood, Nizer declared, it could only be described as a concerted conspiracy. Nizer urged the jury to give by its verdict a "clarion call to the world" that this practice had to stop.

Bolan's defense attacked Faulk's integrity. Faulk, he told the jury, was a liar.

Justice Geller sequestered the jury for the night. The next day he substituted the estate of Laurence Johnson in place of the deceased Laurence Johnson as defendant. One day later, on July 29, 1962, the jury returned a verdict for Faulk along with the largest award in a libel suit to that date. It awarded damages of $1 million against Aware, Inc., Hartnett, and the estate of Laurence Johnson. Finding malice on the part of the defendants, it added $1.25 million in punitive damages against Aware, Inc., and the same amount against Hartnett.

In 1963, an appellate court reduced the damages from $3.5 million to $550,000, deciding that this amount was in line with Faulk's estimated earnings. The decision was upheld the next year in the New York State Court of Appeals.

Hartnett and Aware, Inc. then claimed the verdict violated their First Amendment freedoms and petitioned the Supreme Court for *certiorari*— permission to appeal the constitutional question. The request to be heard was denied with only Justices Hugo Black and William O. Douglas voting to grant it. In one last petition to the Supreme Court, the defendants argued that libel law came from the ecclesiastical law of England and violated the First Amendment separation of church and state. It was unanimously denied. Finally the blacklist and the blacklisters were finished.

—Elizabeth Gwillim

Suggestions for Further Reading

Caute, David. *The Great Fear: The Anti-Communist Purge Under Truman and Eisenhower.* New York: Simon & Schuster, 1978.

Faulk, John Henry. *Fear On Trial.* New York: Simon & Schuster, 1964.

——. "Awareness and Aware, Inc." *Bill of Rights Journal* (December, 1985): 26.

Kanfer, Stefan. *A Journal of the Plague Years.* New York: Atheneum, 1973.

Nizer, Louis. *The Jury Returns.* Garden City, N.Y.: Doubleday & Co., 1966.

Ernesto Miranda Trials: 1963 & 1967

Defendant: Ernesto Miranda   **Crimes Charged:** Kidnapping and rape
Chief Defense Lawyers: First trial: Alvin Moore; second trial: John Flynn
Chief Prosecutors: First trial: Laurence Turoff; second trial: Robert Corbin
Judges: First trial: Yale McFate; second trial: Lawrence K. Wren
Place: Phoenix, Arizona   **Dates of Trials:** June 20–27, 1963;
February 15–March 1, 1967   **Verdict:** Guilty, both trials   **Sentences:** 20–
30 years, both trials

SIGNIFICANCE

Few events have altered the course of American jurisprudence more than the 1963 rape conviction of Ernesto Miranda. The primary evidence against him was a confession he made while in police custody. How that confession was obtained exercised the conscience of a nation and prompted a landmark U.S. Supreme Court decision.

In the early hours of March 3, 1963, an 18-year-old Phoenix, Arizona, movie theater attendant was accosted by a stranger while on her way home from work. He dragged her into his car, drove out to the desert, and raped her. Afterwards he dropped the girl off near her home. The story she told police, often vague and contradictory, described her attacker as a bespectacled Mexican, late 20s, who was driving an early fifties car, either a Ford or Chevrolet.

By chance, one week later, the girl and her brother-in-law saw what she believed was the car, a 1953 Packard, license plate DFL-312. Records showed that this plate was actually registered to a late model Oldsmobile, but DFL-317 was a Packard, registered to a Twila N. Hoffman; and her boyfriend, Ernesto Miranda, 23, fit the attacker's description almost exactly.

Miranda had a long history of emotional instability and criminal behavior, including a one-year jail term for attempted rape. At police headquarters he was placed in a line-up with three other Mexicans of similar height and build, though none wore glasses. The victim did not positively identify Miranda but said that he bore the closest resemblance to her attacker. Detectives Carroll Cooley and Wilfred Young then took Miranda into an interrogation room. He was told, inaccurately, that he had been identified, and did he want to make a statement? Two hours later Miranda signed a written confession. There had been no blatant coercion or brutality, and included in the confession was a section stating that he understood his rights. When the detectives left interrogation room 2, they were pleased, not realizing the legal repercussions that would result from their efforts.

Tainted Evidence

As an indigent, Miranda was granted a court-appointed defender, Alvin Moore. Moore studied the evidence. The state had an apparently unassailable case, buttressed by Miranda's confession. And yet there was something about that confession that Moore found troubling. Convinced it had been obtained improperly, he intended to move for its inadmissibility.

Only four witnesses appeared for the prosecution: the victim, her sister, and Detectives Cooley and Young. After their testimony, Deputy County Attorney Laurence Turoff told the jury that the victim "did not enter into this act of intercourse with him [Miranda] willfully, but in fact she was forced to, by his own force and violence, directed against her."

Moore responded by highlighting inconsistencies in the victim's story. She claimed to have been a virgin prior to the attack, an assertion discounted by medical examiners, and could not remember the exact chronology of the night's events. Neither did she exhibit any bruising or abrasions after the attack; reason enough for Moore to thunder to the jury, "You have in this case a sorrowful case, but you don't have the facts to require that you send a man to prison for rape of a woman who should have resisted and resisted and resisted, until her resistance was at least overcome by the force and violence of the defendant" (an essential requirement under Arizona law at that time; anything less was regarded as compliance.)

But it wasn't until cross-examination of Carroll Cooley that Moore struck:

Question: Officer Cooley, in the taking of this statement, what did you say to the defendant to get him to make this statement?

Answer: I asked the defendant if he would . . . write the same story that he just told me, and he said that he would.

Question: Did you warn him of his rights?

Answer: Yes, sir, at the heading of the statement is a paragraph typed out, and I read this paragraph to him out loud.

Question: I don't see in the statement that it says where he is entitled to the advice of an attorney before he made it.

Answer: No, sir.

Question: Is it not your practice to advise people you arrest that they are entitled to the services of an attorney before they make a statement?

Answer: No, sir.

This admission prompted Moore to object to the confession as evidence, but he was overruled by Judge Yale McFate, who favored the jury with a well-balanced and eminently fair account of the law as it stood at the time. In 1963, the constitutional right to silence was not thought to extend to the jailhouse.

Consequently, on June 27, 1963, Ernesto Miranda was convicted and sentenced to two concurrent terms of 20-30 years imprisonment.

But Alvin Moore's arguments about the confession had touched off a legal firestorm. Miranda's conviction was appealed all the way to the U.S. Supreme Court. On June 13, 1966, Chief Justice Earl Warren, speaking for a 5-4 majority, for the first time established unequivocal guidelines about what is and what is not permissible in the interrogation room:

> Prior to any questioning, the person must be warned that he has a right to remain silent, that any statement he does make may be used as evidence against him, and that he has a right to the presence of an attorney, either retained or appointed. . .

Conviction Overturned

With Miranda's conviction overturned, Arizona glumly faced the prospect of having to free its most celebrated prison inmate. Without the confession, the chances of winning a retrial were negligible. Ironically, it was Miranda himself who brought about his own downfall. Expecting to be released after retrial, he had begun a custody battle with his common-law wife, Twila Hoffman, over their daughter. Hoffman, angry and fearful, approached the authorities and revealed to them the content of a conversation she had had with Miranda after his arrest, in which he had admitted the rape.

This fresh evidence was all Arizona needed.

Miranda's second trial began February 15, 1967. Much of the case was argued in the judge's chambers. At issue: Could a common-law wife testify against her husband? Yes, said County Attorney Robert Corbin. Defense counsel John Flynn, who had pleaded Miranda's case before the Supreme Court, bitterly disagreed. After considerable legal wrangling, Judge Lawrence K. Wren ruled such evidence admissible, and Twila Hoffman was allowed to tell her story to the jury. It proved decisive. Miranda was again found guilty and sentenced to a 20-to-30-year jail term.

The Miranda warning ensures that the accused is informed of certain rights after being arrested. (Connecticut State Police)

On January 31, 1976, four years after being paroled, Ernesto Miranda was stabbed to death in a Phoenix bar fight. The killer fled but his accomplice was caught. Before taking him to police headquarters, the arresting officers read the suspect his rights. In police vernacular, he had been "Mirandized."

The importance of this case cannot be overstated. Denounced by presidents from Richard Nixon to Ronald Reagan, the Miranda decision has withstood all attempts to overturn it. Framed originally to protect the indigent and the ignorant, the practice of "reading the defendant his rights" has become standard operating procedure in every police department in the country. The practice is seen so frequently in television police dramas that today the words of the so-called "Miranda Warning" are as familiar to most Americans as those of the Pledge of Allegiance.

—Colin Evans

Suggestions for Further Reading

Baker, Liva. *Miranda: Crime, Law and Politics.* New York: Atheneum, 1983.

Graham, Fred P. *The Self-Inflicted Wound.* New York: Macmillan Co., 1970.

Skene, Neil. "The Miranda Ruling." *Congressional Quarterly* (June 6, 1991): 164.

Tucker, William. "The Long Road Back." *National Review* (October 18, 1985): 28–35.

Georgetown College v. Jones: 1963

Plaintiff: Georgetown College, now known as Georgetown University
Defendant: Jesse E. Jones **Plaintiff Claim:** That the courts should overrule Jones' refusal to permit a blood transfusion for his wife, who was being treated in the school's hospital **Chief Defense Lawyers:** Ralph H. Deckelbaum and Bernard Margolius **Chief Lawyers for Plaintiff:** Peter R. Taft, Harold Ungar, and Edward Bennett Williams **Judge:** J. Skelly Wright
Place: Washington, D.C. **Date of Hearing:** September 17, 1963
Decision: That the hospital should be allowed to give all necessary blood transfusions

SIGNIFICANCE

Despite the expansion of civil liberties by the courts in the 1960s, the judicial system refused to recognize any right to refuse medical treatment for purely religious reasons.

One of the many Christian religious sects is a group called the Jehovah's Witnesses, which is several centuries old. Followers of the sect believe in the imminent end of the world, and in strictly following the literal words and commands of the Bible. One of these biblical commands is contained in Genesis chapter nine, which states that the consumption of blood is forbidden:

> And God went on to bless Noah and his sons and to say to them: "Be fruitful and become many and fill the earth. And a fear of you and a terror of you will continue upon every living creature of the earth and upon every flying creature of the heavens, upon everything that goes moving on the ground, and upon all the fishes of the sea. Into your hand they are now given. Every moving animal that is alive may serve as food for you. As in the case of the green vegetation, I do give it all to you. Only flesh with its soul—its blood— you must not eat."

In keeping with their literalist approach, the Jehovah's Witnesses traditionally would not eat blood sausages or blood puddings. They never had any serious conflicts with the medical profession until the 1940s, when blood transfusions and the technology of blood storage in blood banks became standardized and commonplace. In 1945, a Jehovah's Witness publication called *The Watchtower* stated that blood transfusions were akin to consuming blood.

Crisis Develops at Georgetown Hospital

In September 1963, a young man named Jessie E. Jones brought his wife into the hospital operated by Georgetown College in Washington, D.C. Georgetown College is now Georgetown University, whose hospital is a world-famous institution. Mrs. Jones, age 25 and mother of a 7-month-old child, had suffered a ruptured ulcer and lost two-thirds of her blood. The Joneses were both Jehovah's Witnesses. When Dr. Edwin Westura, the chief medical resident, said that Mrs. Jones (first name unavailable) would die unless given a blood transfusion, Jones refused to permit it.

Responsible for Mrs. Jones' life, Georgetown had its lawyers, Peter R. Taft, Harold Ungar and the famous Edward Bennett Williams, go to the courts for permission to give the necessary blood transfusions without Jones' consent. On September 17, 1963, the attorneys went to Judge Edward A. Tamm's chambers at the U.S. District Court for the District of Columbia and asked for an emergency order allowing the hospital to save Mrs. Jones' life. Judge Tamm refused. At 4:00 P.M. on the same day, the attorneys went to the chambers of Judge J. Skelly Wright of the U.S. Court of Appeals for the District of Columbia Circuit, asking for an immediate review of Tamm's decision.

Judge Wright telephoned the hospital, and Dr. Westura confirmed that Mrs. Jones would die without a blood transfusion. Wright then went to the hospital with the attorneys, where he met Jones. Jones remained firm in his refusal to grant consent. Father Bunn, Georgetown's president, even came to plead with Jones, to no avail. Westura and the other doctors assigned to the case tried without success to explain that a transfusion is completely different from drinking blood. At 5:20 P.M., Wright signed the orders prepared by the attorneys, and Mrs. Jones was given blood transfusions that saved her life.

On September 19, 1963, Wright filed a memorandum concerning his actions, which recited various legal precedents permitting courts to act in preservation of human life, and ended by stating:

> The final, and compelling, reason for granting the emergency writ was that a life hung in the balance. There was no time for research and reflection. Death could have mooted the cause in a matter of minutes, if action were not taken to preserve the status quo. To refuse to act, only to find later that the law required action, was a risk I was unwilling to accept. I determined to act on the side of life.

On October 14, 1963, Jones' attorneys, Ralph H. Deckelbaum and Bernard Margolius, filed a petition for rehearing before the full court of appeals to quash Wright's September 17 order. On February 3, 1964, the Court of Appeals denied Jones's petition because Mrs. Jones had long since recovered and left the hospital. There was a spirited dissent, however, by Circuit Judge Warren Burger, who subsequently became chief justice of the U.S. Supreme Court. Burger felt that the fact that Jones had signed a release upon bringing his wife to the hospital took the case out of the court's jurisdiction: in effect, the college had to rely on the release for legal protection without court help. Jones appealed to the

U.S. Supreme Court, but his attorneys' petition was denied without comment on June 15, 1964.

Even though the 1960s was an era of increasing civil liberties, the Supreme Court under Chief Justice Earl Warren refused to overturn the court of appeals' *de facto* approval of Judge Wright's actions to save Mrs. Jones' life. Although the Supreme Court and the judicial system were increasingly sensitive to the rights of religious minorities, they drew the line when religious sensibilities meant that modern medical technology would be denied to a person in need.

—Stephen G. Christianson

Suggestions for Further Reading

Evan, Thomas. *The Man to See: Edward Bennett Williams.* New York: Simon & Schuster, 1991.

Kelly, David F. *Critical Care Ethics: Treatment Decisions in American Hospitals.* Kansas City, Mo.: Sheed & Ward, 1991.

Marty, Martin E. and Kenneth L. Vaux. *Health/Medicine and the Faith Traditions: an Inquiry Into Religion and Medicine.* Philadelphia: Fortress Press, 1982.

Penton, M. James. *Apocalypse Delayed: the Story of Jehovah's Witnesses.* Buffalo, N.Y.: University of Toronto Press, 1985.

Rosenthal, Elisabeth. "Blinded by the Light." *Discover* (August 1988): 28–30.

U.S. v. Hoffa: 1964

Defendants: James R. Hoffa   **Crimes Charged:** First trial: jury tampering;
Second trial: mail and wire fraud, conspiracy   **Chief Defense Lawyers:** First
trial: Harry Berke, James Haggerty, Jacques Schiffer, and Harvey Silets;
Second trial: Daniel Ahearn, James Haggerty, and Maurice Walsh.
Chief Prosecutors: First trial: John Hooker and James Neal; Second trial:
William Bittman and Charles Smith   **Judges:** First trial: Frank W. Wilson;
Second trial: Richard B. Austin   **Places:** First trial: Chattanooga, Tennessee;
Second trial: Chicago, Illinois   **Dates of Trial:** First trial: January 20–
March 12, 1964; second trial: May 11–August 17, 1964.   **Verdicts:** Guilty,
both trials   **Sentences:** First trial: 8 years imprisonment and $10,000 fine;
second trial: four concurrent five-year terms

SIGNIFICANCE

U.S. Department of Justice prosecutions of union leader Jimmy Hoffa gave the
nation a series of sensational corruption trials and a debate over the acceptable
limits to which the government should investigate an individual.

The U.S. government's attempts to curtail the influence of organized crime in labor unions by prosecuting International Brotherhood of Teamsters president Jimmy Hoffa failed for nearly a decade. By the time Hoffa finally went to prison, numerous trials had cost both sides a great deal of money and arguments over the ethics of the government's pursuit of Hoffa were commonplace.

The genesis of the Hoffa trials lay in the investigative work of the U.S. Senate Select Committee on Improper Activities in the Labor or Management Field. During the late 1950s, the so-called McClellan Committee (chaired by Arkansas Senator John G. McClellan) put crooked union leaders, crime bosses, common thugs, and their victims before the public in televised hearings. Many of the most contentious exchanges took place between the committee's chief counsel, Robert F. Kennedy, and the feisty Hoffa, who was in line for the presidency of the powerful Teamsters union.

Even as the hearings began, Hoffa was indicted for illegal possession of McClellan Committee documents. Hoffa had allegedly handed attorney John Cye Cheasty $1,000 and promised thousands more if he would infiltrate the committee to obtain information. Instead, Cheasty revealed the bribery attempt to committee counsel Kennedy, who arranged to have Cheasty pass a list of witnesses to Hoffa while FBI cameras rolled.

A reporter asked Kennedy what he would do if Hoffa was not convicted. "I'll jump off the Capital dome," replied Kennedy, who was convinced that the filmed transaction gave the Justice Department a perfect case. When the trial ended with a hung jury, Teamsters attorney Edward Bennett Williams offered to send Kennedy a parachute. The growth of a mutual animosity between Kennedy and Hoffa was clear to an entire nation watching their public feud.

"Get-Hoffa Squad" Assembled

Robert Kennedy was appointed U.S. attorney general in 1960 by the newly elected president, his brother John F. Kennedy. Indicting Jimmy Hoffa was a high priority with the new attorney general, who claimed that Hoffa used extortion, bribery, and physical violence to rule the Teamsters. Robert Kennedy was equally sure that Hoffa used the threat of labor trouble to bully employers for personal profit. A small Justice Department unit of lawyers and investigators, informally known as the "Get-Hoffa Squad," was assembled to uncover and prosecute any unlawful activity within organized labor. By the time they disbanded, their conviction rate was impressive.

Yet Robert Kennedy's campaign against union corruption, and Hoffa in particular, raised questions about the role of an attorney general in prosecuting crimes. The constant investigations resembled a vendetta to those who suspected Kennedy's motives. Some thought the attorney general was dogging Hoffa out of personal spite. Others questioned the ethics of the nation's chief law enforcement officer aggressively investigating an individual before evidence of wrongdoing presented itself.

Civil libertarians were concerned by Hoffa's never-proven but steady protests that he was a victim of illegal surveillance and paid government perjurers. The debate also included his union cronies, politicians under his control, and enemies of the Kennedys, all of whom exploited the situation.

One of the first major indictments against Hoffa focused on a Florida real estate development called Sun Valley. Federal prosecutors knew that Hoffa and others had secretly loaned union money to finance the project and secured further loans from local banks by promising them large union accounts. Sun Valley was promoted as a sunny retirement community for union members. In fact, Hoffa and his associate Owen Bert Brennan held an option to buy 45 percent of the development. By risking union funds, Hoffa and Brennan stood to make personal fortunes if the development proved successful.

Instead, Sun Valley remained an undeveloped disaster area. Hoffa was indicted for mail fraud and conspiracy, but the indictments were dismissed in 1961 when a Florida judge ruled that the grand jury issuing them had been improperly impaneled (a second set of indictments was approved but dropped as investigators incorporated their evidence into Hoffa's 1964 Chicago fraud trial).

Hoffa was next indicted for violating the Taft-Hartley Act, which prohibits employee representatives from accepting illegal payoffs from employers. The government charged that a Michigan trucking firm, Commercial Carriers, had organized a Nashville, Tennessee, business called Test Fleet for the sole purpose of avoiding labor trouble with Hoffa's union. As soon as the new business was incorporated—in the maiden names of Hoffa's and Brennan's wives—Commercial Carriers leased all of Test Fleet's trucks and assumed all of their operating expenses, making the venture's income a pure profit for its "owners."

Hoffa claimed that putting the business in his wife's name was a legal tax move. The 1962 case ended with a mistrial when jurors could not agree on a verdict. Yet Hoffa and five others were immediately indicted for tampering with the jury. The new case was moved to Chattanooga, Tennessee, in early 1964 when Hoffa's attorney was arrested (and ultimately convicted) for trying to bribe a police officer into offering a prospective juror $10,000 to ensure another hung jury.

Government Succeeds

The most damaging witness in the Chattanooga trial was Ed Partin, a Teamster officer and government informant. Partin had secretly told investigators that Hoffa had spoken to him about killing Robert Kennedy. Prosecutors were wary of Partin's motives and credibility, for he was under indictment for embezzlement in Louisiana. They nevertheless decided to trust him after he passed a lie detector test.

Partin's presence in Chattanooga was kept a secret until the moment he walked to the witness stand. As Hoffa visibly paled, Partin recalled the union president speaking in detail about how the Nashville jury had been tainted.

The defense protested that the government had placed Partin in the midst of the Hoffa camp to violate Hoffa's rights by spying for prosecutors in the Test Fleet case. The government noted that Hoffa himself had invited Partin to Nashville and that Partin's information has prompted investigations that led to the present trial only. "That son-of-a-bitch is killing us!" Hoffa shouted at his lawyers outside the courtroom.

Hoffa's lawyers fiercely cross-examined Partin about his own criminal record and tried to suppress his testimony, accusing him of being a paid government informer (prosecutors denied this). The defense grew abrasive, accusing the Justice Department of stealing union documents and accusing Judge Frank W. Wilson of bias in favor of the government. The judge kept his composure in spite of apparent attempts to prod him into losing his temper and forcing a mistrial.

Federal prosecutor James Neal called the bribery conspiracy "one of the greatest assaults on the jury system the country has ever known." Neal might have said the same thing about the current trial, for amazing stratagems were being used to force a mistrial. Defense lawyers eavesdropped on the jury room. Bribed bellhops falsely swore that the sequestered jurors were drunk.

Hoffa's attorney, James Haggerty, called the government's case "a foul and filthy frame-up" designed by the "Get-Hoffa Squad." Defense attorney Jacques Schiffer threw a handful of coins at government prosecutors. "Take these thirty pieces of silver and share them—you have earned them."

A solemn Jimmy Hoffa informs the media that he will appeal his jury tampering conviction. (AP/ Wide World Photos)

While two of his co-defendants were acquitted, Hoffa and three others were found guilty. "You stand here convicted of seeking to corrupt the administration of justice itself," Judge Wilson told Hoffa before sentencing him to eight years in prison and fining him $10,000. Defense attorney Schiffer was sentenced to 60 days in prison for contempt.

Two months later, Hoffa went on trial in Chicago, Illinois, for fraud and conspiracy. Prosecutors charged that he and seven co-defendants had approved $20 million in loans from the Teamsters pension fund to real-estate developers. In returns, the developers paid $1.7 million in kickbacks when the loans were approved. The scheme was originated to pay off Sun Valley's creditors. The Chicago trial, however, revealed that Hoffa and the others had not restricted their activity to repaying the union's hidden loss in the Florida fiasco.

After 13 weeks of complex testimony, Hoffa was found guilty on four of the 20 counts against him. Judge Richard B. Austin sentenced him to five years imprisonment on each count, to run concurrently after he finished the eight-year jury-tampering sentence.

Hoffa appealed all the way to the Supreme Court without success. He entered a federal penitentiary in 1967 and served five years before President Richard Nixon commuted his sentence in 1972.

Hoffa paid minimal attention to a condition of his parole forbidding involvement in any union activities until 1980. He disappeared in Detroit, Michigan, on July 30, 1975, and was presumed to have been murdered. His body has never been found.

— *Thomas C. Smith*

Suggestions for Further Reading

Hutchinson, John. *The Imperfect Union: A History of Corruption In American Trade Unions*. New York: E.P. Dutton, 1970.

Kennedy, Robert F. *The Enemy Within*. New York: Harper & Brothers, 1960.

Navasky, Victor S. *Kennedy Justice*. New York: Atheneum, 1971.

Sheridan, Walter. *The Fall And Rise of Jimmy Hoffa*. New York: Saturday Review Books, 1972.

New York Times Company v. Sullivan: 1964

Appellant: The New York Times Company   **Appellee:** L. B. Sullivan
Appellant Claims: That the Supreme Court of Alabama's affirmation of a
libel judgment against the *Times* violated the free speech and due process
rights as defined by the First and Fourteenth Amendments of the Constitution
and certain Supreme Court decisions; also, that an advertisement published in
the *Times* was not libelous and the Supreme Court should reverse the
decision of the Alabama trial court.   **Chief Defense Lawyers:** Sam Rice
Baker, M. Roland Nachman, Jr., and Robert E. Steiner III
Chief Lawyers for Appellant: Herbert Brownell, Thomas F. Daly, and Herbert
Wechsler   **Justices:** Hugo L. Black, William J. Brennan, Jr., Tom C. Clark,
William O. Douglas, Arthur J. Goldberg, John M. Harlan, Potter Stewart, Earl
Warren, and Byron R. White   **Place:** Washington, D.C.
Date of Decision: March 9, 1964   **Decision:** The Alabama courts' decisions
were reversed.

SIGNIFICANCE

The U.S. Supreme Court limited for the first time states' authority to award libel
damages based on individual state laws and defined "actual malice" as a national
standard for determining libel cases involving public figures.

On March 23, 1960, an organization calling itself the "Committee to Defend
Martin Luther King and the Struggle for Freedom in the South" paid the
New York Times to publish a certain advertisement. The ad took up one full page
and was a call for public support and money to defend Rev. Martin Luther King,
Jr. and the civil rights struggle in the South. Bearing the caption "Heed Their
Rising Voices" in large, bold print, the ad was published in the March 29, 1960,
edition of the *Times*.

The ad criticized several Southern jurisdictions, including the city of
Montgomery, Alabama, for breaking up various civil rights demonstrations. No
individual was mentioned by name. Further, the ad declared that "Southern
violators of the Constitution" were determined to destroy King and his move-

ment. The reference was to the entire South, not just Montgomery and other localities, and again no individual was mentioned by name.

Over 600,000 copies of the March 29, 1960, *Times* edition carrying the ad were printed. Only a couple hundred went to Alabama subscribers. Montgomery City Commissioner L.B. Sullivan learned of the ad through an editorial in a local newspaper. Incensed, on April 19, 1960, Sullivan sued the *Times* for libel in the Circuit Court of Montgomery County, Alabama. Sullivan claimed that the ad's reference to Montgomery and to "Southern violators of the Constitution" had the effect of defaming him, and he demanded $500,000 in compensation.

On November 3, 1960, the Circuit Court found the *Times* guilty and awarded Sullivan the full $500,000 in damages. The Alabama Supreme Court affirmed the Circuit Court judgment on August 30, 1962. In its opinion, the Alabama Supreme Court gave an extremely broad definition of libel:

> Where the words published tend to injure a person libeled by them in his reputation, profession, trade or business, or charge him with an indictable offense, or tends to bring the individual into public contempt [they] are libelous per se. . . . We hold that the matter complained of [by Sullivan] is, under the above doctrine, libelous per se.

Supreme Court Protects the Press

The *Times*'s chief lawyers, Herbert Brownell, Thomas F. Daly, and Herbert Wechsler, took the case to the U.S. Supreme Court. Sullivan's chief lawyers were Sam Rice Baker, M. Roland Nachman, Jr., and Robert E. Steiner III. On January 6, 1964 the two sides appeared at a hearing in Washington, D.C., before Supreme Court Justices Hugo L. Black, William J. Brennan, Jr., Tom C. Clark, William O. Douglas, Arthur J. Goldberg, John M. Harlan, Potter Stewart, Earl Warren, and Byron R. White.

On March 9, 1964, the Supreme Court unanimously reversed the Alabama courts' decisions, holding that Alabama libel law violated the *Times*'s First Amendment rights. Justice Brennan stated for the Court that:

> We hold that the rule of law applied by the Alabama courts is constitutionally deficient for failure to provide the safeguards for freedom of speech and of the press that are required by the First [Amendment] in a libel action brought by a public official against critics of his official conduct.

The Court was in fact only recognizing what Alabama's own newspapers had been saying, namely that Alabama's libel law was a powerful tool in the hands of anti-civil rights officials. The *Montgomery Advertiser* had even printed an edition (before the Sullivan case went to the Court) with the headline "STATE FINDS FORMIDABLE LEGAL CLUB TO SWING AT OUT-OF-STATE PRESS," reporting that "State and city authorities have found a formidable legal bludgeon to swing at out-of-state newspapers whose reporters cover racial incidents in Alabama." The Court's decision invalidated Alabama's overly broad libel law so that it couldn't be used anymore to threaten freedom of the press.

Next, Justice Brennan stated what the Court had determined was the proper basis of libel law under the First Amendment in cases involving publications concerning public officials:

> The constitutional guarantees require, we think, a federal rule that prohibits a public official from recovering damages for a defamatory falsehood relating to his official conduct unless he proves that the statement was made with "actual malice."

Sullivan hadn't proven that the *Times* acted with actual malice, so even if Alabama's libel law wasn't unconstitutional, his lawsuit still had to be rejected. What constitutes actual malice? The Court defined it as:

> knowledge that it was false or with reckless disregard of whether it was false or not.

In certain libel lawsuits after *New York Times Company v. Sullivan*, the Court expanded the First Amendment's protection. For any "public figure" to sue for libel, he or she would have to prove actual malice. The Court has said that public figures include anyone widely known in the community, not just public officials. Further, anyone accused of libel is protected by this actual malice requirement, not just newspapers like the *Times*. The *Sullivan* case was a tremendous advance for personal as well as press freedom of speech, and it prevented legitimate criticism and social commentary from being suppressed by the threat of damaging libel lawsuits. *Sullivan* has not, however, become a license to print anything that the papers see fit: as in *Reynolds v. Pegler* (see separate entry), defendants who do act with actual malice are subject to severe penalties.

—*Stephen G. Christianson*

Associate Justice Brennan defined actual malice as "knowledge that it was false or with reckless disregard of whether it was false or not." (Courtesy, National Archives)

Suggestions for Further Reading

Bain, George. "A Question of Honor, Malice and Rights." *Maclean's* (October 1984): 64.

Friedman, Robert. "Freedom of the Press: How Far Can it Go?" *American Heritage* (October–November 1982): 16–22.

Hopkins, W. Wat. *Actual Malice: Twenty-Five Years After Times v. Sullivan*. New York: Praeger, 1989.

Lewis, Anthony. *Make No Law: the Sullivan Case and the First Amendment*. New York: Random House, 1991.

Winfield, Richard N. *New York Times v. Sullivan : the Next Twenty Years*. New York: Practicing Law Institute, 1984.

Griswold v. Connecticut: 1964

Appellants: Charles Lee Buxton and Estelle Griswold   **Defendant:** State of Connecticut   **Appellants Claim:** That Connecticut's birth-control laws violated its citizens' constitutional rights   **Chief Defense Lawyer:** Joseph B. Clark   **Chief Lawyers for Appellants:** Tom Emerson, Fowler Harper, Harriet Pilpel, and Catherine Roraback   **Justices:** Hugo L. Black, William J. Brennan, Jr., Tom C. Clark, William Douglas, Arthur J. Goldberg, John M. Harlan, Potter Stewart, Earl Warren, and Byron R. White   **Place:** Washington, D.C.   **Date of Decision:** May 11, 1964   **Decision:** Reversed Griswold's and Buxton's lower court convictions for providing contraceptive information to married couples and struck down all state laws forbidding the use of contraceptives by such couples

SIGNIFICANCE

The decision articulated a constitutional "right to privacy," which would later be interpreted as protecting the right of unmarried persons to use birth control (*Eisenstadt v. Baird,* 1972) and the right of women to terminate their pregnancies (*Roe v. Wade,* 1973).

Connecticut's anticontraceptive law, passed in 1879, was simple and unambiguous:

> Any person who uses any drug, medicinal article or instrument for the purpose of preventing conception shall be fined not less than fifty dollars or imprisoned not less than sixty days nor more than one year or be both fined and imprisoned. (General Statutes of Connecticut, Section 53–32.)

> Any person who assists, abets, counsels, causes, hires or commands another to commit any offense may be prosecuted and punished as if he were the principal offender. (Section 54–196.)

The Planned Parenthood League of Connecticut first brought the law before the U.S. Supreme Court in 1942, with a physician as plaintiff. The court ruled that the doctor lacked standing to sue, since his patients—and not he—suffered injury due to his inability to legally prescribe birth control. In June 1961, declining to rule in a suit brought by several women, the Supreme Court called the normally unenforced law "dead words" and "harmless empty shadows." Estelle T. Griswold, executive director of the Planned Parenthood

League of Connecticut, and Dr. C. Led Buxton, chairman of Yale University's obstetrics department, decided to test the "death" of the 1879 law: On November 1, 1961, they opened a birth-control clinic in New Haven. Dr. Buxton cited the June decision and explained to the press: "This leads me to believe that all doctors in Connecticut may now prescribe child spacing techniques to married women when it is medically indicated."

1879 Law Alive and Well

Griswold and Buxton were arrested and their center closed on November 10, 1961. On December 8, 1961, the opening day of the Sixth Circuit Court trial, defense attorney Catherine G. Roraback argued that Connecticut's birth-control law violated their clients' constitutional right to freedom of speech. Judge J. Robert Lacey, saying he wished to study the defense's brief, continued the case indefinitely.

On January 2, 1962, the trial took place. It lasted only six hours. Julius Martez was the Sixth Circuit Court prosecutor who had requested warrants for Griswold's and Buxton's arrests. He now called his witnesses. John A. Blasi, a New Haven police detective who had entered the clinic on its third day of operation, testified that six women were in the waiting room at the time; that Estelle Griswold freely told him that the facility was, indeed, a birth-control clinic; and that Griswold had offered him contraceptive information and devices. Another detective offered similar testimony.

Dr. Buxton testified that he and his medical colleagues believed that "this type of advice" played a crucial part in women's health care.

Prosecutor Martez said that Griswold and Buxton had broken the law and that the Connecticut legislature, not the court, was the proper forum for anyone objecting to the 82-year-old statute.

Judge Lacey agreed with Martez. He described the statute as "absolute," and he emphasized that it had been upheld three times by the Connecticut Supreme Court of Errors. Rejecting defense attorney Catherine Roraback's free speech argument, he characterized the prohibition of a physician's prescription of birth-control devices as a "constitutional exercise of the police powers of the State of Connecticut." Griswold and Buxton were then convicted of violating Connecticut's birth control law, and each was fined $100.00.

Ten days later, defense attorneys Roraback and Harriet Pilpel filed their clients' appeal with the Appellate Division of the Sixth Connecticut Circuit Court. A three-judge panel heard the case October 19, 1962, and upheld Griswold's and Buxton's convictions on January 18, 1963. However, citing questions "of great public importance," it certified the case for a review by the State Supreme Court of Errors.

That court upheld the convictions on May 11, 1964. Associate Justice John Comley's opinion declared: "We adhere to the principle that courts may not interfere with the exercise by a state of the police power to conserve the public safety and welfare, including health and morals."

On to the Supreme Court

The first action Planned Parenthood took in preparing *Griswold v. Connecticut* for the U.S. Supreme Court was to replace its female attorneys, Roraback and Pilpel, with two male attorneys: Fowler Harper and, upon his death, Thomas I. Emerson, both professors at Yale Law School.

Justice Douglas wrote the majority opinion in *Griswold v. Connecticut* that articulated the constitutional "right to privacy." (Courtesy, National Archives)

Oral argument began before the Supreme Court on March 29, 1964. Emerson argued that Connecticut's birth-control law deprived his clients and their clinic's patients of the First Amendment right to free speech and of their right to liberty, which according to the Fourteenth Amendment, could not be abridged without "due process of law." Moreover, he claimed that his clients had a right to privacy, which was guaranteed by the Ninth Amendment to the Constitution: "The enumeration in the Constitution, of certain rights, shall not be construed to deny or disparage others retained by the people."

Emerson characterized the Connecticut law as an effort to erect "a principle of morality" by declaring it "immoral to use contraceptives even within the married relationship." This was, he continued, a "moral judgment" that did not "conform to current community standards."

Both Emerson and Connecticut's attorney, Thomas Clark, were questioned about the presumed "under-the-counter" availability of birth-control devices in Connecticut. Clark classified it with clandestine bookmaking on racehorses—available, but not in the open. Emerson said the devices were simply termed "feminine hygiene" items. Clark was then asked whether it was permissible to prescribe contraceptives to prevent the spread of disease. Clark called this a "ludicrous argument" and explained that sexually transmitted disease was not present in married couples, who were claimed as clients of the Planned Parenthood clinic. As the *New York Times* summarized Clark's reasoning, "Connecticut requires applicants for marriage licenses to take venereal disease tests, and . . . Connecticut also has laws against fornication and adultery. Thus, [Clark] indicated, there would be no reason to believe that any such disease would spread."

The next day, Justice Potter Stewart asked Clark to explain the purpose of the statute. "To reduce the chances of immorality," he said. "To act as a deterrent to sexual intercourse outside marriage."

Justice Stewart replied, "The trouble with that argument is that on this record it [the clinic] involves only married women."

A little later in the questioning, Clark declared that Connecticut had the right to guarantee its own "continuity" by prohibiting contraceptives.

Justice Arthur J. Goldberg returned to the statute's alleged role in preventing intercourse outside of marriage, and he asked why Connecticut's laws banning fornication and adultery were not sufficient. Clark replied that "it's easier to control the problem" with the addition of anti-birth control laws.

Decision Reverses Convictions

The Supreme Court, in a 7–2 ruling, reversed Griswold's and Buxton's convictions, invalidated the 1879 law, and enunciated a constitutional "right to privacy." The majority opinion, written by Justice William O. Douglas, declared that the "specific guarantees in the Bill of Rights have penumbras, formed by emanations from those guarantees that help give them life and substance" and cited the Constitution's First, Third, Fourth, Fifth, Ninth, and Fourteenth Amendments. The Ninth Amendment, Douglas quoted in its entirety: "The enumeration in the Constitution, of certain rights, shall not be construed to deny or disparage others retained by the people." The enforcement of the Connecticut birth-control law would require gross violation of privacy, which was presumably a right "retained by the people." "Would we allow the police to search the sacred precincts of marital bedrooms for telltale signs of the use of contraceptives?" Douglas asked. He characterized such action as "repulsive to the notions of privacy surrounding the marriage relationship" and reversed the lower court convictions.

Justices Black and Stewart issued dissenting opinions. Black wrote:

> The Court talks about a constitutional "right of privacy" as though there is some constitutional provision or provisions forbidding any law ever to be passed which might abridge the "privacy" of individuals. But there is not. . . . I cannot rely on the Due Process Clause [of the Fourteenth Amendment] or the Ninth Amendment or any mysterious and uncertain natural law concept as a reason for striking down this state law.

Griswold, Applied Outside the Marital Bedroom

Before *Griswold,* the Ninth Amendment had usually been interpreted as reserving to the state government any right not specifically granted to the federal government; Douglas' literal interpretation, that the Ninth Amendment reserved such rights *to the people,* formed the basis of two other successful challenges to state reproduction laws.

In *Eisenstadt v. Baird* (1972), single people won the right to purchase and use contraceptives. Justice William J. Brennan, a concurring justice in Griswold, delivered the majority opinion:

> If under *Griswold* the distribution of contraceptives to married persons cannot be prohibited, a ban on distribution to unmarried persons would be equally impermissible. It is true that in *Griswold* the right of privacy in question inhered in the marital relationship. Yet the marital couple is not an independent entity with a mind and heart of its own, but an association of two individuals each with a separate intellectual and emotional makeup. If the right of privacy means anything, it is the right of the *individual*, married or single, to be free from unwarranted governmental intrusion into matters so fundamentally affecting a person as the decision whether to bear or beget a child.

The following year, in its controversial *Roe v. Wade* (see separate entry) decision, the Court held that the "right of privacy . . . is broad enough to encompass a woman's decision whether or not to terminate her pregnancy."

— *Kathryn Cullen-DuPont*

Suggestions for Further Reading

Carey, Eve and Kathleen Willert Peratis. *Woman and the Law.* Skokie, Ill.: National Textbook Co. in conjunction with the American Civil Liberties Union, New York, 1977.

Countryman, Vern, ed. *The Douglas Opinions.* New York: Random House, 1977.

Cushman, Robert F. *Cases in Constitutional Law*, 6th ed. Englewood Cliffs, N.J.: Prentice Hall, 1984.

Davis, Flora. *Moving the Mountain: The Women's Movement in America Since 1960.* New York: Simon & Schuster, 1991.

Faux, Marian. *Roe v. Wade.* New York: Macmillan Co., 1988.

The *New York Times.* October 27, 1961; November 3, 1961; November 4, 1961; November 11, 1961; November 13, 1961; November 25, 1961; December 2, 1961; December 9, 1961; January 3, 1962; January 13, 1962; October 20, 1962; January 18, 1963; May 17, 1963; May 19, 1963; May 12, 1964; December 9, 1964; March 30, 1965; March 31, 1965; June 8, 1965; June 9, 1965; June 10, 1965; June 13, 1965; and June 15, 1965.

Lenny Bruce Trial: 1964

Defendants: Lenny Bruce, Ella Solomon, and Howard L. Solomon
Crime Charged: Obscenity **Chief Defense Lawyers:** Martin Garbus and
Efraim London **Chief Prosecutor:** Richard H. Kuh **Judges:** J. Randall
Creel, John M. Murtagh, and Kenneth M. Phipps **Place:** New York, New
York **Dates of Trial:** June 16–December 21, 1964 **Verdict:** Lenny Bruce:
Guilty; Howard L. Solomon: Guilty; Ella Solomon: not Guilty
Sentence: Lenny Bruce: 4 months imprisonment; Howard L. Solomon:
$1,000 fine or 60 Days Jail

SIGNIFICANCE

Freedom of speech is a cherished right. But just how far should that right extend?
For many, comedian Lenny Bruce stepped way beyond any reasonable interpretation of free speech. That belief resulted in the costliest, and certainly the most
controversial obscenity trial in American history.

On April Fool's Day, 1964, two plainclothes New York City police officers
mingled with the audience at the Cafe Au Go Go, a Greenwich Village
coffeehouse, and watched comedian Lenny Bruce at work. It was a typical Bruce
performance, funny, scatological, bitingly accurate, laced with Anglo-Saxonisms,
and all recorded for posterity on a concealed wiretap worn by one of the officers.
Two nights later, April 3, just before he was due on stage, Bruce was arrested and
charged with using obscene language. Also arrested was club owner Howard
Solomon.

Bruce was no stranger to controversy. He had several times been cited for
obscenity and twice convicted, but this was easily his highest profile arrest yet.
He continued his engagement at the Cafe Au Go Go after posting bail. Four
nights later, he and Solomon were arrested again. This time police also took
Solomon's wife Ella into custody and charged all three with obscenity.

Just days before their trial commenced, a statement signed by more than
one hundred prominent members of the arts community was issued to the
media. In it, the signatories pledged support for the beleaguered Bruce, but
more especially for the principle of free speech.

Herbert S. Rune, an inspector with the NYC Department of Licenses, was
the final witness called to testify. He had watched Bruce perform, jotting down

surreptitious notes. Over defense objections, he read out an edited version of Bruce's act that highlighted the language used and virtually ignored the context. Worst of all was Rune's assertion, bitterly denied by the defense, that Bruce had fondled the microphone in an obvious and suggestive manner.

This allegation was reiterated by the next witness, Patrolman Robert Lane, who with his partner, William O'Neal, had recorded Bruce. That tape, scratchy, hissing and difficult to make out, was played in court. Wherever the original words were inaudible, a prosecution transcript provided damaging substitutions.

Adjournment for Illness

Two days into the trial, Bruce had to be hospitalized with pleurisy. When the trial resumed June 30, his chief attorney, Efraim London, a veteran of more than 250 censorship and obscenity cases, including notable victories on behalf of *Lady Chatterly's Lover* and *Tropic of Cancer*, moved for a dismissal, arguing that the prosecution had not proved a *prima facie* case having sufficient evidence obscenity. This stimulated a vigorous counter-assault by Assistant District Attorney Richard Kuh. Fulminating against Bruce's "anthology of filth," Kuh demanded that the trial continue. The three-member panel of judges agreed.

London had assembled an all-star cast of witnesses to plead Bruce's cause, including jazz critic, Nat Hentoff. Calling the defendant a brilliant social commentator, Hentoff hinted darkly of "a national movement to harass Lenny Bruce." Further support came from Dr. Daniel B. Dodson, associate professor of English at Columbia University, who compared Bruce favorably to Jonathan Swift and François Rabelais.

The star defense witness was supposed to be columnist Dorothy Kilgallen. She started off well enough, saying, "He [Bruce] goes from one subject to another, but there is always the thread of the world around . . . whether he's talking about war or peace or religion or Russia or New York." But Kilgallen faltered under Kuh's relentless questioning. After praising Norman Mailer and Jim Jones, writers who both employed earthy language, she slipped badly by blasting another recent book *Naked Lunch*, "which I couldn't even finish reading. . . . I think the author should be in jail."

Prosecutor Kuh grasped this gift with both hands, purring, "Unfortunately we can't do everything at once."

Adjourned for Vacation

Yet another adjournment—this time so that Judge John Murtagh could take his summer vacation—gave the prosecutor ample time to line up his own witnesses. When the trial reopened, John Fischer, editor of *Harper's* magazine, and the Reverend Daniel Potter, executive director of the Protestant Council, both opined that Bruce's work was obscene. Testimony concluded July 28, after

One year before his obscenity trial in New York, comedian Lenny Bruce is denied entrance to England "in the public interest." (AP/Wide World Photos)

which Judge Murtagh instructed counsel that the bench would consider written briefs instead of the customary oral closing arguments.

On November 4, the court reconvened to deliver its verdict. Bruce, who had remained silent throughout, chose this moment to dismiss his lawyers and belligerently insist that he be allowed to conduct his own defense. Judge Murtagh denied the request and read the verdict. "The court, Judge Creel dissenting, finds the defendants Lenny Bruce and Howard Solomon guilty. The court by unanimous vote finds the defendant Ella Solomon not guilty." Sentencing was deferred until December 21, 1964, at which time Bruce received four months Solomon was fined.

The verdict seemed to unhinge Bruce. He became obsessed with appellate litigation. Those legal wheels were still grinding when, on August 3, 1966, he was found dead in his Hollywood home, a hypodermic syringe nearby. An autopsy revealed the presence of morphine. Death was recorded as accidental.

Lenny Bruce's trial attracted immense publicity, a torrent of self-righteous indignation from protagonists on either side of the debate, and still no firm understanding of what constitutes obscenity. At its conclusion, Bruce's life and career were in shambles—vivid proof that free speech is never free, and often costly beyond measure.

—Colin Evans

Suggestions for Further Reading

Bruce, Honey and Dana Benenson. *Honey.* Chicago: Playboy, 1976.

Goldman, Albert. *Ladies And Gentlemen—Lenny Bruce!!* New York: Random House, 1974.

Moretti, Daniel S. *Obscenity And Pornography.* New York: Oceana, 1984.

Morgenstern, Joe. "Lenny Lives!" *Playboy,* (August 1991): 82ff.

Thomas, William Karl. *Lenny Bruce,* Hamden Conn: Archon, 1989.

The Whitmore Confessions and Richard Robles Trial: 1965

Defendant: Richard Robles   **Crime Charged:** Murder
Chief Defense Attorneys: Frederick H. Block and Jack S. Hoffinger
Chief Prosecutor: John F. Keenan   **Judge:** Irwin D. Davidson
Place: New York, New York   **Dates of Trial:** October 18–
December 1, 1965   **Verdict:** Guilty   **Sentence:** Life imprisonment

SIGNIFICANCE

The notoriety of two murders for which Robles was eventually convicted contributed to the legal problems of George Whitmore, Jr., who was initially arrested for the crimes. Whitmore's arrest had a profound effect upon the nature of police interrogations, earning it a mention in the U.S. Supreme Court's Miranda decision.

In the early morning of April 23, 1964, a police patrolman chased away a man assaulting Elba Borrero on a dark Brooklyn, New York, street. When the officer returned to the scene later, he found George Whitmore, Jr., standing in a doorway. The young black man asked if the officer had been the same one shooting at the woman's attacker earlier and volunteered a description of the fleeing suspect.

Similarities between the assault on Borrero and the recent murder of Minnie Edmonds in the same neighborhood convinced detectives that they should have another talk with Whitmore. He was brought to the 73rd precinct on April 24. After questioning him for 22 hours without the presence of an attorney, detectives announced that Whitmore had confessed to both the Borrero assault and the Edmonds killing.

Whitmore also signed a more spectacular confession. Eight months before, Janice Wylie and Emily Hoffert were found tied together and stabbed to death in their Manhattan apartment. A Brooklyn detective familiar with the case thought that a photo of an attractive blonde found in Whitmore's wallet resembled Wylie and had begun the interrogation leading to the confession. The police announced to the press that the bloody "Career Girls Murder" was now solved beyond a doubt.

Confessions Discredited

Brooklyn authorities immediately charged Whitmore with the Borrero and Edmonds crimes. Manhattan District Attorney Frank Hogan's office, however, was slow to indict Whitmore in the Wylie-Hoffert murders. Manhattan prosecutors noticed that every detail in Whitmore's lengthy confession was known to police beforehand. Investigators quietly collected evidence showing the confession to be false. The blonde in the photo was located alive in southern New Jersey, not far from the garbage dump where Whitmore initially claimed to have found the picture.

After Whitmore's confession was discredited, Hogan's office did not immediately dismiss the indictment against him, even though the prosecutors secretly knew that police had a new suspect. With Brooklyn authorities, the public, and even the jury still assuming that Whitmore was a confessed murderer, he was tried in November 1964 for attempting to rape Elba Borrero. She identified Whitmore as her attacker, although she acknowledged that he was the only suspect police had shown her. She also admitted that she had discussed a $10,000 reward offered for the conviction of Janice Wylie's killer with a lawyer. Brandishing Whitmore's ragged raincoat and a leather button Borrero had torn from her attacker's coat, the prosecutor asked the jury, "Haven't we nailed George Whitmore right on the button in the truest sense of the word?"

Whitmore was found guilty, but he was granted a new trial because racial prejudice and knowledge of the Wylie-Hoffert indictment had swayed the jury. The prosecutor also admitted to withholding an FBI report stating that the threads on Whitmore's coat did not match those on the celebrated button.

Richard Robles Arrested

On January 26, a man named Richard Robles was arrested for the Wylie-Hoffert murders. Upon Robles' arrest, District Attorney Hogan petitioned the courts to release Whitmore from the murder indictment on his own recognizance. Despite Robles' arrest, however, Hogan did not request complete dismissal of the Whitmore indictment. This controversial technicality allowed other prosecutors to rebuff defense claims that Whitmore's confessions to the Edmonds murder and Borrero assault were as unsound as his invalid Wylie-Hoffert confession.

In May 1965, the New York State Legislature outlawed capital punishment. Their decision was influenced by public concern over the false confession that nearly electrocuted George Whitmore. Yet Whitmore's legal troubles were far from over. With the Manhattan district attorney still refusing to clear him entirely in the Wylie-Hoffert case, Whitmore went to trial for murdering Minnie Edmonds, solely on the evidence of his "confession."

After a stormy trial marked by Whitmore's accusation that his confessions had been beaten out of him, police denials, and open feuding between the judge and the defense attorney, the jury could not agree on a verdict. Several days after the Edmonds mistrial was declared, Whitmore was finally cleared in the Wylie-Hoffert case.

Nevertheless, when Robles was tried in the autumn of 1965, his attorneys attempted to buoy the credibility of Whitmore's Wylie-Hoffert confession to create a reasonable doubt that their own client had committed the crime.

Prosecutor John F. Keenan replied by summoning Whitmore and the detectives who had arrested him. Whitmore's testimony was erratic, but Keenan's grueling questioning of the detectives illuminated the sloppy analysis of physical evidence that had put Whitmore under suspicion. Whitmore's claims of physical abuse remained in dispute, but threats and trickery had clearly helped elicit his "confession." His guilt was assumed on racist grounds like one detective's belief that "you can always tell when a Negro is lying by watching his stomach, because it moves in and out when he lies."

Robles' attorneys were unable to translate doubts about police interrogation methods to their own client's advantage, despite testimony that Robles had confessed to the Wylie-Hoffert murders while suffering from heroin withdrawal and without his attorney present. He was found guilty, largely on the basis of secretly tape-recorded conversations about the murder. Observers debated the verdict because Robles' self-incriminating statements were made to a fellow junkie, who became an informant and testified in return for immunity in an unrelated homicide.

Whitmore Retried in Assault Case

George Whitmore was retried for attempted rape in March 1966. Borrero's shaky but impassioned identification and Whitmore's confession were the prosecution's only evidence. Whitmore's attorney argued vehemently to introduce the Wylie-Hoffert episode in court, attempting to illustrate the tainted atmosphere in which the confession was obtained. When the judge agreed with the prosecution that past charges against the defendant should not be discussed before the jury—ironically reversing the protective nature of this rule to Whitmore's disadvantage—the defense attorney remained mute in protest for the rest of the trial. Whitmore was found guilty.

On June 13, 1966, the U.S. Supreme Court handed down the Miranda decision regarding the rights of crime suspects. The court acknowledged that coercive interrogations could produce false confessions. "The most conspicuous example occurred in New York in 1964," stated a footnote, "when a Negro of limited intelligence confessed to two brutal murders and a rape which he had not committed. When this was discovered, the prosecutor was reported as saying: 'Call it what you want—brain-washing, hypnosis, fright. The only thing I don't believe is that Whitmore was beaten.'"

The Miranda decision eliminated Whitmore's retrial for the Edmonds murder because his confession was the only evidence against him. When the high court voted not to apply the Miranda rule retroactively, however, Whitmore's attempted rape conviction stood. It was later overturned when an appellate court decided that preventing testimony about the Wylie-Hoffert "confession" had put the defense at a disadvantage.

Whitmore Convicted Again, Then Released

On the sole evidence of Borrero's persistent accusations, Whitmore was tried and convicted a third time in May 1967. He returned to prison, sentenced to maximum sentences for attempted rape and assault. An attempt to seek a fourth trial faltered when his conviction was upheld in July 1970.

Meanwhile, Whitmore's defenders located Borrero's sister-in-law Celeste Viruet in Puerto Rico and returned with an affidavit stating that Borrero's courtroom testimony was contradicted by what she told her family shortly after the attack. Viruet had seen the attacker from her window, but police had never asked her to look at Whitmore. Borrero also had identified a different man in a "mug shot" notebook before police had shown her Whitmore.

On April 10, 1973, after four years in prison and nine years of trials, Whitmore was released and all charges against him were dismissed. He attempted to sue the city for $10 million for improper arrest and malicious prosecution. The suits were dismissed on technicalities. "They wrecked my life," Whitmore said bitterly, "and they still won't admit they did anything wrong."

— *Thomas C. Smith*

Suggestion Further Reading

Cunningham, Barry with Mike Pearl. *Mr. District Attorney: The Story of Frank S. Hogan and the Manhattan D.A.'s Office.* New York: Mason/Charter, 1977.

Lefkowitz, Bernard and Kenneth G. Gross. *The Victims.* New York: G.P. Putnam's Sons, 1969.

Raab, Selwyn. "Justice vs. George Whitmore." *The Nation* (July 2, 1973): 10–13.

Shapiro, Fred C. *Whitmore.* Indianapolis: Bobbs-Merrill Co., 1969.

——. "Department of Amplification." *The New Yorker* (June 9, 1973): 80.

Collie Leroy Wilkins Trial: 1965

Defendants: William Orville Eaton, Eugene Thomas, and Collie Leroy Wilkins, Jr. **Crime Charged:** Felony conspiracy to deny a citizen's constitutional rights **Chief Defense Lawyer:** Arthur Hanes **Chief Prosecutor:** John Doar
Judge: Frank M. Johnson, Jr. **Place:** Montgomery, Alabama
Dates of Trial: November 29–December 3, 1965 **Verdict:** Guilty
Sentence: 10 years imprisonment

SIGNIFICANCE

Twice frustrated in attempts to convict Collie Leroy Wilkins for the murder of Viola Liuzzo, federal prosecutors successfully prosecuted Wilkins with an 1870 law for depriving Liuzzo of her civil rights.

On March 25, 1965, thousands of civil rights marchers converged on the Alabama state capitol in Montgomery, demanding an end to obstacles to black voter registration. The day of speeches ended a 54-mile march from Selma, where civil rights protesters had been gassed and beaten by police, arrested, and murdered during the previous three months.

That evening, a white volunteer from Michigan named Viola Liuzzo and LeRoy Moton, a black teenaged civil rights worker, ferried marchers back to Selma, then headed toward Montgomery for another carload. Near the rural town of Hayneville, a car traveling at nearly 100 miles per hour overtook them. As Liuzzo looked at the men in the car speeding alongside her, one of them shot her in the face, killing her. Her Oldsmobile drifted off the road into a ditch. Terrified but unharmed, LeRoy Moton saved his life by pretending to be dead when the attackers returned to look for survivors.

Gary Thomas Rowe Jr., Eugene Thomas, William Orville Eaton, and 21-old Collie LeRoy Wilkins, Jr., were quickly arrested. All four were members of the Ku Klux Klan. Unbeknownst to the others, Rowe was also a paid FBI informer, a fact which hastened their arrest and was to figure prominently in their trials.

Wilkins was tried first on a state murder charge. His attorney was Matt J. Murphy, Jr., a Klan lawyer or "Imperial Klonsel." Robert Shelton, "Imperial Wizard" of the United Klans of America, sat at the defense table until the judge ordered him to move to a spectator's seat.

LeRoy Moton quietly described the high-speed chase. Interrupted by laughter from Klansmen in the Hayneville court, he endured a cross-examination in which Murphy implied that Moton had shot Liuzzo to rob her. Prosecutors replied with an FBI ballistics report linking the bullet that killed Liuzzo to a revolver found in Eugene Thomas' house.

Gary Rowe described how the four Klansmen had noticed Liuzzo and Moton at a traffic light. Thomas, who was driving, suggested that they "get 'em." As their car gained on Liuzzo's on a desolate stretch of highway, Thomas handed his pistol to Wilkins. Wilkins said that forcing the other car off the road was too risky, for telltale paint scrapes could land them in jail. He told Thomas to speed up. When the cars were even, Wilkins fired twice.

"Shoot the hell out of it," Thomas ordered. Rowe claimed he stuck his weapon out the window, but only pretended to fire with Wilkins and Eaton.

Murphy cross-examined Rowe angrily. He recited part of the oath in which Klansmen swore to die rather than divulge secrets, resisting any "bribe, flattery, threats, passion, punishment, persecution, persuasion, [or] any other enticements."

"Did you hold up your hand before God and swear to these matters?" Murphy said.

"Yes, I believe I did," Rowe replied.

Murphy did not call Wilkins to testify. He did, however, give a vitriolic hour-long summation mingling Old Testament references with Klan doctrine. Murphy raged against blacks, Jews, Catholics, Communists, miscegenation, President Lyndon Johnson, and the National Association for the Advancement of Colored People. He called Rowe a perjurer, "a pimp," and "a white nigger."

Prosecutors told jurors that regardless of how they felt about the civil rights movement, this was a case of cold-blooded murder. Alabama Assistant Attorney General Joseph Gantt quoted segregationist Governor George Wallace, who had called Liuzzo's murder "a cowardly act that should not go unpunished."

The jury returned deadlocked, with 10 members voting for conviction. Some had stared at their hands in embarrassment during Murphy's closing speech. "He must have thought we were very, very ignorant to have been taken in by that act," said one juror. The two holdouts belonged to the white racist Citizens Council. One would not accept Rowe's testimony because the Klansman "swore before God and broke his oath" by becoming a paid informer.

When Wilkins' retrial convened, Alabama Attorney General Richmond Flowers took over the prosecution. He questioned potential jurors about their racial attitudes. Of 30 white males called for jury duty, 11 believed that white civil rights workers like Liuzzo were inferior to other whites.

Alabama law allowed Flowers to disqualify only six jurors with peremptory challenges. Because he was allowed limitless challenges "for cause-removal based on a distinct reason affecting a juror's fitness to serve;" Flowers declared that racial bias was a reason to disallow jurors. "How can the State of Alabama expect a fair and just verdict in this case from men who have already sat in judgment on the victim and pronounced her inferior to themselves?"

The Alabama Supreme Court rejected Flowers' argument. Wilkins' retrial proceeded with former Birmingham mayor Arthur Hanes replacing Murphy, who had been killed in a traffic accident. The testimony echoed the first trial. The jury, which included 10 present or former Citizens Council members, found Wilkins innocent in less than two hours.

The U.S. Justice Department then pressed an indictment against Wilkins, Thomas, and Eaton, using a Reconstruction-era law. The 1870 statute made it a felony "to conspire, to injure, oppress, threaten, or intimidate any citizen in the free exercise or enjoyment of any privilege secured to him by the Constitution or laws of the United States."

Federal prosecutor John Doar argued that the law applied to Viola Liuzzo because the Selma-to-Montgomery Freedom March had been sanctioned by a federal court order after state officials tried to prevent it. Ironically, the court order had been signed by U.S. District Judge Frank M. Johnson, Jr. who would preside over the conspiracy trial.

Gary Rowe testified that he and the defendants had spent March 25 looking for marchers to harass upon orders from their Klan superiors. Defense attorney Hanes accused Rowe of fabricating his story for money and repeated the strategy of reading portions of the Klan's secrecy vow aloud.

Ku Klux Klansman, Collie Leroy Wilkins (center) arriving at court. (AP/Wide World Photos)

535

When Rowe agreed that the words were "part of the oath" he had taken, Judge Johnson instructed Hanes to read the rest of the oath. Hanes unwillingly read the entire pledge, in which "knowledge of rape, treason against the United States, [or] malicious murder" voided the vow of silence, enjoining Klansmen to "help, aid, and assist" law enforcement officers.

After a day of deliberations, the jury told Judge Johnson that they were "hopelessly deadlocked."

"You haven't commenced to deliberate long enough to be hopelessly deadlocked," the judge replied. He lectured the jurors on the cost and serious-ness of the case, adding that it had to be decided eventually. He then delivered an "Allen charge"—also known as a "dynamite" or "shotgun" charge—asking minority-decision jurors to examine the reasoning by which they arrived at a decision contrary to the majority.

Four hours later, the jury returned with a guilty verdict. "If it's worth anything to you," Judge Johnson said, "in my opinion, that was the only verdict you could possibly reach in this case and reach a fair and honest verdict. I couldn't tell you that before. It wasn't my job." Johnson ordered the defendants to be imprisoned for 10 years, the maximum sentence.

William Eaton died of a heart attack three months later. After Wilkins and Thomas served their sentences, they appeared before a 1978 grand jury investi-gating Rowe's involvement in other violence against civil rights workers in the 1960s . They accused Rowe of shooting Viola Liuzzo. Testimony by the two convicted Klansmen and others resulted in Rowe's indictment for first-degree murder. In 1980, however, the indictment was overturned and Rowe remained in the federal witness protection plan.

— Thomas C. Smith

Suggestions for Further Reading

Dees, Morris with Steve Fiffer. *A Season For Justice: The Life and Times of Civil Rights Lawyer Morris Dees*. New York: Charles Scribner's Sons, 1991.

Kempton, Murray. "Trial of the Klansman." *New Republic* (May 22, 1965): 10–13.

Kennedy, Robert F., Jr. *Judge Frank M. Johnson, Jr*. New York: G.P. Putnam's Sons, 1978.

"Liuzzo Case Jury Retires for Night Without A Verdict" and "The Imperial Klonsel." *New York Times* (May 7, 1965): 1, 25.

O'Reilly, Kenneth. *"Racial Matters"—The FBI's Secret File On Black America, 1960–1972*. New York: Free Press, 1989.

"Pictorial Summation of a Tragicomic Mistrial." *LIFE* (May 21, 1965): 32–39.

Wade, Wyn Craig. *The Fiery Cross: The Ku Klux Klan In America*. New York: Simon & Schuster, 1987.

Candace Mossler and Melvin Lane Powers Trial: 1966

Defendants: Candace Mossler and Melvin Lane Powers
Crime Charged: Murder **Chief Defense Lawyers:** Henry Carr, Percy Foreman, Walter E. McGwinn, Marian Rosen, Harvey St. Jean, and Clyde Woody **Chief Prosecutors:** Richard E. Gerstein, Arthur E. Huttoe, and Gerald Kogan **Judge:** George E. Schulz **Dates of Trial:** January 17– March 6, 1966 **Verdict:** Not guilty

SIGNIFICANCE

Millions of dollars were at stake in this trial, one of the most sensational in years. There was talk of sexual variations, suspected contract-killers, and police corruption in this tale of greed and brutal murder.

For 12 years Candace and Jacques Mossler lived together in seeming harmony. Mossler, a multimillionaire Houston, Texas, businessman, lavished attention and money on his beautiful wife and was rewarded with her apparent devotion, until 1961. In that year, Melvin Powers, Candy Mossler's 20-year-old nephew, came to live with the couple. Not long afterwards, according to Mrs. Mossler's testimony, Jacques Mossler was struck down by a mysterious illness that left him a homosexual. Shattered by this discovery, Candy Mossler turned to her sister's son for companionship, despite their 21-year age difference. When Jacques Mossler found out, he fired Powers from the company and moved to Miami, Florida.

Candy Mossler and Melvin Powers remained in Houston until the summer of 1964, when she took her four adopted children to visit her husband in Florida. Once there, she began chauffeuring the children on a series of suspicious midnight car rides. On June at 1:30 A.M. she drove them to a nearby hospital emergency room. Just minutes later, someone broke into the Mossler household, struck Jacques Mossler over the head and stabbed him 39 times. The murder time was established by neighbors who heard loud barking from the Mossler's dog, and cries of "Don't! Don't do that to me!" A "dark-haired man in dark clothing" was also seen fleeing. Police believed that man was Melvin Powers, acting in collusion with Candy Mossler. The couple was charged with murder 12 months later.

Jury selection began January 17, 1966, and took several days. At its conclusion Arthur E. Huttoe presented the state's case against Candy Mossler and Melvin Powers, detailing a "sordid, illicit, love affair." The motive, Huttoe said, was money: with her husband out of the way, Candy Mossler would inherit millions plus control of his business.

Sexual Perversions

A fortune of that magnitude meant that Mossler and Powers were able to afford the very best in legal talent. Legendary Texas attorney Percy Foreman was imported to head the powerful defense team. He maintained that Jacques Mossler's sexual appetites—"transvestitism, homosexuality, voyeurism and every conceivable type of perversion, masochism, sadism,"—had caused his own death; he was murdered, said Foreman, by a slighted homosexual lover. In support of this claim, Foreman referred to a human hair found on Mossler's body, which, despite exhaustive investigation, had never been identified. Foreman later broadened his scope of potential killers to include disaffected business partners, saying that as "mastermind" of a great financial empire, Mossler was hated by "thousands of people."

Prosecutors believed otherwise. Their version had Powers flying into Miami on the night of the murder, killing Mossler, then leaving at eight o'clock next morning. And they had plenty of witnesses to back up the claim. Mary Alice Domick, a National Airlines ticketing agent in Houston, recalled selling Powers a ticket to Miami on June 29, 1964. Stewardess Barbara Ann Barrer confirmed that Powers was aboard, carrying just a brief case; and the manager of a lounge near Mossler's home placed Powers in his bar between 7:00 and 8:30 P.M. on the night of the killing.

At Miami International Airport, police found Candy Mossler's abandoned 1960 Chevrolet. Fingerprint expert Robert Worsham testified that of 55 prints found in the car, six belonged to Powers. Foreman wasn't impressed. "You do not know whether Melvin Powers drove that car in June, May, or April in Miami, do you?" he asked.

"No," admitted Worsham.

Another fingerprint specialist, David Plowden, wasn't so easily dismissed. He had located Powers' palm print on the kitchen counter in the murdered man's home. Mossler's handyman Roscoe Brown testified that he had wiped that counter down just hours before the killing. Brown also disclosed a telephone conversation with Candy Mossler after the murder, in which she said, "You've got to say you didn't clean that sink . . . remember, a man's life is at stake, anything you say can hurt him."

Defense attorney Clyde Woody struggled to salvage the situation. "Didn't Mrs. Mossler tell you, 'Don't let them put words in your mouth?' "

"Right," said Brown.

"Didn't she say, 'I would do the same for you if I thought you were innocent?' "

"That's right," Brown answered.

Earlier in the trial, Freddie Duhart, a colorful ex-convict from Houston, testified that Powers had offered him $10,000 to find a hired killer. "I told him you could get someone from Mexico and put the body in the trunk of the car—nobody checks the trunk of a car at the border—and give a man $50 to $100 to take the body back up in the mountains and throw if off a volcano."

Galveston, Texas, resident Edward Diehl also swore that Powers had solicited him to kill Jacques Mossler, with the promise that "there's $5,000 in it for you."

Yet another convicted felon, Billy Frank Mulvey, pointed the finger of suspicion at both defendants. After stating that, in a jailhouse confession, Powers had admitted murdering Mossler to him, Mulvey further claimed that two years earlier Candy Mossler had paid him "seven grand" as a down payment to kill her husband. At this, Candy Mossler cried out across the courtroom, "I've never seen or heard of this man," an outburst that brought a stern rebuke from Judge George E. Schulz.

Mulvey continued: "I told her it wasn't enough."

"What did you do with the $7,000," asked Foreman.

"I stashed it." Mulvey replied, adding, "I'm a thief—not a burglar." According to several defense witnesses, Mulvey was also a heroin junkie,

Candace Mossler, wearing a neck brace, was accused of murdering her husband with the help of her nephew, Melvin Powers. (AP/Wide World Photos)

pathologically incapable of telling the truth, and a police informant willing to say anything to beat an upcoming habitual criminal rap and possible life sentence.

Preparing an Alibi

In closing arguments prosecutor Gerald Kogan submitted that Candy Mossler's strange nocturnal visits to the hospital, all between the hours of midnight and 7:00 A.M., were undertaken to establish an alibi. He further submitted that the evidence, although circumstantial, could lead to only one reasonable conclusion: Powers and Candy Mossler had conspired to kill Jacques Mossler.

From among the several of defense lawyers, it was Percy Foreman who commanded center stage. In his closing 6½ hour speech Foreman laid the blame for Mossler's death everywhere except at the door of Melvin Powers. He blamed the police for entering into a "monetary conspiracy" with the dead man's daughter; he blamed "Dade County justice"; he accused police of buying testimony from "a lifetime thief and other ex-convicts"; he recited passages from the Scripture and Shakespeare. He concluded the masterly, if somewhat discursive, oration by thundering, "Let him among you without sin cast the first stone." Then Foreman sat down, smiling, confident he had won over the all-male jury.

And so it proved. After 16 hours and 44 minutes of deliberation on March 6, 1966, they returned a verdict of not guilty. State Attorney Richard Gerstein received the news in grim silence. Later, watching Candy first embrace Powers, then several of the jurors, he remarked, "I don't agree with the verdict, but this is the American system."

More Unsolved Mysteries

Following the trial, Melvin Powers returned to Houston and became a successful real estate developer. Candace Mossler continued to attract controversy. In 1971, she married Barnett Garrison, 19 years her junior. The following year Garrison suffered brain damage in a fall from the roof of the Mossler mansion in Houston. Apparently Mr. Garrison, wearing a pistol in his belt, had tried to gain access to his wife's third floor balcony window when he lost his footing and plunged 40 feet onto a concrete patio. Police ruled the fall accidental. Three months later the couple divorced.

In May 1974, Candy Mossler told police that a masked intruder had broken into her home, chloroformed her, then made off with $396,000 in jewelry and money. She had reported a similar theft in Miami Beach two weeks earlier. On that occasion a thief "with soft hands" had taken $200,000 in gems. Carelessly, Mrs. Mossler reported the same item—a $160,000 diamond—stolen in each robbery. Neither case was solved.

On October 26, 1976, Candace Mossler died in her sleep at the Fontainbleau Hotel in Miami Beach. She was 55 years old.

Florida's rush to prosecute Candy Mossler and Powers highlights the weakness of any case based solely on instinct and suspicion. At no time did the circumstantial evidence ever approach the degree of cogency necessary for conviction.

—*Colin Evans*

Suggestions for Further Reading

Axthelm, Pete. *Newsweek* (November 8, 1976).

Crimes and Punishment. Vol. 12. England: Phoebus, 1974.

Taylor, Gary. *National Law Journal* (May 22, 1989): 29ff.

Carl Anthony Coppolino Trials: 1966 & 1967

Defendant: Carl Anthony Coppolino   **Crime Charged:** Murder
Chief Defense Lawyers: Joseph Afflitto, F. Lee Bailey, and Joseph Mattice
Chief Prosecutors: First trial: Vincent Keuper; second trial: Frank Schaub
Judges: First trial: Elvin R. Simmill; second trial: Lynn Silvertooth
Places: First trial: Monmouth County, New Jersey; second trial: Naples,
Florida   **Dates of Trials:** First trial: December 5–15, 1966; second trial:
April 3–28, 1967   **Verdicts:** First trial: Not guilty; second trial: Guilty,
second-degree homicide

SIGNIFICANCE

The two trials of Dr. Carl Anthony Coppolino are case studies in the importance
juries attach to an ostensibly discredited witness. In the first trial they chose to
disbelieve a self-confessed accessory to murder and were swayed instead by the
welter of contradictory forensic evidence. A second jury, confronted by much the
same forensic testimony alone, arrived at a very different verdict.

In 1966 a conversation between two women in Florida sparked one of the most
hotly contested debates in American legal history: Did Dr. Carl Coppolino
murder his wife and his ex-lover's husband, or was he merely the hapless victim
of jealous revenge? Two trials, in two states, arrived at very different answers.

At age 30, Coppolino, a New Jersey anesthesiologist, had been declared
medically unfit for work because of a heart condition. Supported by a disability
benefit, royalties from writing, and the salary of his wife Carmela, also a
physician, Coppolino began a torrid affair with 48-year-old housewife Marjorie
Farber, a vivacious woman who looked much younger than her years. Marjorie
Farber's husband William Farber, at first tolerated the liaison, then grew
resentful.

On the evening of July 30, 1963, Marjorie Farber telephoned the
Coppolinos in a state of panic. William Farber was unconscious in the bedroom.
Could Carl come over immediately? Coppolino, wary of losing his benefits if
caught practicing, sent Carmela Coppolino instead. She found Farber dead.
Apart from being "all blue down one side," there was no outward sign of distress

to the body. At Coppolino's urging, she signed the death certificate, citing coronary thrombosis as the cause.

Over the next 18 months Coppolino's affair with Farber waned, and, in April 1965, the Coppolinos moved to Longboat Key, Florida. Disaster struck when Carmela Coppolino failed the Florida medical examination. Coppolino, in desperate need of money, began dating a wealthy divorcee named Mary Gibson.

At 6:00 A.M. August 28, 1965, the Coppolino family physician, Dr. Juliette Karow, was awakened by a phone call. She heard Coppolino tearfully describe how he had just found his wife dead, ostensibly from a heart attack. Karow was puzzled when she arrived at the house—young women in their 30s rarely suffer coronary failure—but she found no evidence of foul play and duly signed the certificate. Forty-one days later Coppolino married Mary Gibson.

Marjorie Farber, who had pursued Coppolino to Florida in hopes of resurrecting their romance, was incensed by this turn of events. She went to Dr. Karow and unburdened her soul. It was a sensational tale, one that would fill front pages across the nation for months: how she had been hypnotized into attempting murder, then stood by, a helpless onlooker, as her husband was smothered to death by Dr. Carl Coppolino.

Both New Jersey and Florida ordered exhumations. The autopsies were performed by Dr. Milton Helpern, New York's chief medical examiner. He found evidence of succinylcholine chloride, an artificial form of curare used by anesthesiologists, in both bodies. Also, Farber's cricoid—a cartilage in the larynx—was fractured, indicating that he had been strangled. These findings led to dual charges of homicide being filed against Coppolino.

Round One

After considerable interstate wrangling, Coppolino stood trial in New Jersey for the murder of William Farber. Prosecutor Vincent Keuper declared that Coppolino had not only broken the commandment "Thou shalt not covet thy neighbor's wife," but also "Thou shalt not covet thy neighbor's life."

Defense attorney F. Lee Bailey knew his only hope lay in totally discrediting Marjorie Farber. Break her testimony and Helpern's words would fall on deaf ears. His opening address contained a ringing indictment:

> This woman drips with venom on the inside, and I hope before we are through you will see it drip on the outside. She wants this man so badly that she would sit on his lap in the electric chair while somebody pulled the switch, just to make sure that he dies. This is not a murder case at all. This is monumental and shameful proof that hell hath no fury like a woman scorned.

When Bailey sat down, the battle lines had been drawn. Now it was time for the first prosecution witness: Marjorie Farber.

She told of being under Coppolino's spell ever since he had first hypnotized her to get rid of a smoking habit. She was powerless to deny him anything, especially when he told her repeatedly, "... that bastard [Farber] has got to go." Coppolino had given her a syringe filled with some deadly solution and instructions to inject Farber when he was asleep. At the last moment her nerve failed, but not until she had injected a minute amount of the fluid into Farber's leg. When he became ill she summoned Coppolino to the house. He first administered a sedative, then attempted to suffocate Farber by wrapping a plastic bag around his head. As the two men struggled, Marjorie begged Coppolino to stop. Instead, he smothered Farber with a pillow.

Devastating Cross-Examination

Bailey rose to face the witness. What followed was brutal and at times belligerent. It also remains a classic of cross-examination. Bailey began sarcastically. There had been no murder at all; everything she said had been a lie, a figment of her malicious imagination, instigated by an evil desire for revenge on the man who had ditched her. Wasn't that right? Over a torrent of prosecution objections, Bailey pressed on: "This whole story is a cock-and-bull story, isn't it?"

Sustained.

"Didn't you make this all up, Mrs. Farber?"

Sustained.

"Did you fabricate this story?"

Sustained.

Shifting tactics, Bailey ridiculed Farber's claim of having been an unwilling but helpless participant in the murder, saying he would produce medical testimony to prove such obeisance impossible. He hacked away, constantly reminding the jury of her adulterous and jealous behavior and, most of all, her age. "This 52-two year-old woman . . ." was a repeated theme, as if this were reason enough to explain Farber's vitriolic accusations. Perceptibly, the mood of the court swung against her. At the end of a two-day ordeal, she limped from the stand, her credibility in tatters.

She was replaced by Milton Helpern. Even this seasoned courtroom veteran reeled under the Bailey bludgeon. At issue was whether William Farber had suffered from terminal heart disease, and if the cricoid fracture had occurred before or after death. Helpern was emphatic on both points, although Bailey drew from him the grudging admission that there was no bruising about the neck, as would normally have been present if strangulation had occurred. Bailey speculated that rough handling of the body during disinterment, in particular a clumsy grave-digger's shovel, had caused the cricoid fracture. Helpern scoffed at such an idea. But Bailey had his own expert witnesses and they thought otherwise.

Doctors Joseph Spelman and Richard Ford, both experienced medical examiners, expressed the view that, not only was the cricoid fracture caused postmortem, but that William Farber's heart showed clear signs of advanced coronary disease, certainly enough to have killed him.

With the verdict still very much up in the air, Bailey called his star witness, Carl Anthony Coppolino. Slim and sleekly groomed, he answered his accusers well and without any noticeable guile. Coppolino came across as confident without seeming cocky, helpful but not obsequious.

Summing up, Judge Elvin Simmill commented on the vast array of conflicting medical evidence and stressed to the jury that they must be satisfied of Coppolino's guilt "beyond a reasonable doubt." It was an admonition that they took to heart. After deliberating for less than five hours they returned a verdict of not guilty.

Florida Fights Back

Coppolino's second trial opened in Naples, Florida before Justice Lynn Silvertooth on April 3, 1967. State Attorney Frank Schaub, recognizing that there was no direct evidence to link Carl Coppolino with the death of Carmela Coppolino, piled up a mountain of inconsistencies and motives for murder that the defense couldn't counter. High on the list was money. Schaub leaned heavily on the fact that Coppolino was running short of cash. He portrayed the doctor as a heartless philanderer, determined to wed Mary Gibson for her considerable fortune. But Carmela Coppolino's refusal to grant him a divorce had blown that idea sky-high. Instead, Coppolino began eying his wife's life insurance policy, $65,000. With that and Gibson's bank account, he would be set for life. "There's your motive," Schaub trumpeted.

Persuasive as Schaub's case was, other, perhaps more significant, forces were at work on his behalf. Coppolino's reputation had preceded him. Nothing was said, of course, but this particular jury gave Milton Helpern a far more favorable hearing than their New Jersey counterpart. His task was much the same as before, to explain the presence of succinylcholine chloride in Carmela Coppolino's body, and this he did in lucid terms that anyone could understand.

Marjorie Farber testified to overhearing Coppolino on the phone after his wife's death, saying, "They have started the arterial work and that won't show anything." Further questioning clarified that this referred to the fluid used by embalmers to replace the blood. It was damning stuff.

Once again F. Lee Bailey performed brilliantly, but each witness stood firm. And this time he received no assistance from the defendant. Unaccountably, Coppolino refused to testify on his own behalf. Bailey was stunned, later calling it "a terrible mistake."

Certainly the jury thought so. On April 28, 1967, they found Coppolino guilty of second-degree murder, a curious verdict that has never been fully explained; under Florida law, murder in the second degree implies a lack of premeditation on the part of the killer, and anything more calculated than willful poisoning is hard to imagine. Whatever the reasoning, their decision saved Coppolino from Death Row. Instead, the slender ex-doctor who thought he had carried out the perfect murder was led away to begin a life sentence at the state prison at Raiford, Florida.

After serving 12½ years, Carl Coppolino was paroled in 1979. Coppolino holds a unique position as the only person ever charged with two entirely separate "love triangle" murders. Either case, taken on its own, might have resulted in acquittal, but coming in such quick succession, the two proved insurmountable. Juries are not prepared to extend coincidences quite that far.

—Colin Evans

Suggestions for Further Reading

Baden, Michael M. *Unnatural Death*. New York: Random House, 1989.

Bailey, F. Lee with Harvey Aronson. *The Defense Never Rests*. New York: Stein and Day Publishers, 1971.

Block, Eugene. *Fabric of Guilt*. New York: Doubleday & Co., 1968.

Coppolino, Carl A. *The Crime That Never Was*. Tampa, Fla.: Justice Press, 1980.

Holmes, Paul. *The Trials Of Dr. Coppolino*. New York: New American Library, 1968.

MacDonald, John D. *No Deadly Drug*. New York: Doubleday & Co., 1968.

Wilson, Colin and Donald Seaman. *Encyclopedia of Modern Murder*. New York: G.P. Putnam's Sons, 1983.

Albert Henry DeSalvo Trial: 1967

Defendant: Albert Henry DeSalvo   **Crimes Charged:** Armed Robbery, Sex Offenses   **Chief Defense Lawyer:** F. Lee Bailey   **Chief Prosecutor:** Donald L. Conn   **Judge:** Cornelius J. Moynihan   **Place:** Cambridge, Massachusetts   **Date of Trial:** January 11–18, 1967   **Verdict:** Guilty   **Sentence:** Life Imprisonment

SIGNIFICANCE

When Albert DeSalvo stood trial in Massachusetts courtroom for armed robbery and sexual assault, everyone present knew they were looking at the self-confessed "Boston Strangler." Aware that legal complexities prevented DeSalvo's indictment as the Strangler, his lawyers used the enormity of those crimes to bolster their claim that DeSalvo was insane and therefore not culpable on the present charges.

Boston, Massachusetts, was a city under siege in January 1964. A reign of terror had left 13 women, ranging in age from 19 to 85, dead at the hands of a killer known as the "Boston Strangler." All of the victims were slain in their own homes by a person who seemed able to gain entrance to strange apartments at will and was possessed of an ability to elude his pursuers. And then as abruptly as they began, the killings stopped.

Fears of the Strangler were beginning to fade when, on October 27, 1964, a young Cambridge housewife called police to complain of a knife-wielding intruder who had bound and molested her. Afterwards he had loosened her bonds, mumbled, "I'm sorry," and fled the apartment. Detectives recognized the victim's description of her attacker as that of 32-year-old Albert DeSalvo, known as the "Measuring Man" from his habit of coaxing women into letting him take their measurements with a tailor's tape, under pretext of working for a modeling agency.

Following DeSalvo's arrest, it came to light that he was also the "Green Man," a mass rapist so-called because of the green slacks he wore. Psychiatrists diagnosed DeSalvo as "potentially suicidal and quite clearly overtly schizophrenic," and on February 4, 1965, he was committed to Bridgewater State Hospital "until further order of the court."

It was while in Bridgewater that DeSalvo first began hinting that he was the Boston Strangler. A fellow inmate contacted attorney F. Lee Bailey and asked him to visit DeSalvo. What Bailey heard convinced him that DeSalvo was truthful. Under hypnosis and a promise of immunity from prosecution, DeSalvo made a series of tape-recorded confessions in which he gave graphic accounts of the Strangler murder scenes, including details that only the killer could have known.

These confessions posed an awkward legal problem. Because they were uncorroborated, and because DeSalvo had already been adjudged mentally incompetent, the state was reluctant to proceed against him on the stranglings. Instead, a compromise was worked out. DeSalvo would stand trial for his "Green Man" offenses and receive a mandatory life sentence. Bailey, determined those years should be spent receiving treatment, set out to prove DeSalvo insane.

Sanity Hearing

At a pretrial competency hearing on January 10, 1967, DeSalvo declared that he was not seeking his freedom and would "go anywhere necessary to receive proper treatment." Asked by the prosecutor, Assistant District Attorney Donald L. Conn, why he had retained F. Lee Bailey, DeSalvo answered:

> To defend me, to bring out the truth, rather than let me be buried somewhere where they'd never get at the truth. . . . I'd like, myself, to know what happened. . . to bring out what's inside of me that I couldn't understand.

Albert DeSalvo, the self-proclaimed "Boston Strangler," on his way to court in Boston, January 1968. (AP/Wide World Photos.)

At the end of the day-long hearing. Judge Cornelius J. Moynihan found DeSalvo competent and announced that his trial would commence the next day.

It began with testimony from four women, all of whom had been attacked by DeSalvo in their homes. Two spoke of awakening to find DeSalvo, an experienced burglar, in their bedroom. One said he had pretended to be a detective before tying her up and committing the offense. As he was leaving, she said, "he asked me to forgive him and not to tell his mother."

Dr. James A. Brussel, associate commissioner of the New York State Department of Mental Hygiene, recounted DeSalvo's grim upbringing. His father had beaten the children repeatedly and often forced his wife to have sexual relations in front of them. The experience left DeSalvo morbidly preoccupied with sex, and with his own wife unable or unwilling to satisfy his voracious appetite, he looked elsewhere. Molestation led to rape, and ultimately to murder.

Prosecutor Conn, who had argued unsuccessfully to have all mention of murder excluded from this case, disputed Dr. Brussel's diagnosis of DeSalvo as a man reacting to an "irresistible drive." What did that mean? After much thought, Brussel replied, "He thought he was God in his own self-created world."

Conn wasn't so sure. He produced another Bridgewater inmate, Stanley Setterland, who said that DeSalvo had bragged of a cunning strategy: he would make a lot of money from his confession, then hire a good lawyer. The lawyer would have him placed in a hospital for a brain operation, after which he would be declared sane and freed.

Conn pushed Setterland hard, determined to expose DeSalvo as a schemer, perfectly aware of his actions. "What did he [tell you he did] after the killings?"

"He wiped everything . . . so he wouldn't leave fingerprints."

When Dr. Ames Robey, medical director of Bridgewater, took the stand, Bailey grilled him about several contradictory diagnoses of DeSalvo. First, Robey had declared DeSalvo sane, then changed his mind, then reverted to his original opinion.

"Why did you change the diagnosis?" asked Bailey.

"I felt I had been taken in."

"Are you saying Albert conned you?"

"I'm afraid so," the doctor conceded.

Robey also admitted that his latest change of heart had been inspired in part by Setterland's own performance on the stand. Bailey looked askance and produced Bridgewater records showing that Robey had once diagnosed Setterland as a patient capable of "a considerable degree of lying on an enormous amount of issues."

"When did you decide Setterland was a man of truth?" he asked with sarcasm.

Flustered, Dr. Robey said that Setterland was "looking a great deal better" after his recent discharge from Bridgewater, and that his testimony given just days previously confirmed Robey's current belief that DeSalvo was manipulative and an "attention grabber," a patient with an "extensive need to prove what a big man he was."

Final Arguments

Bailey closed with an impassioned plea on DeSalvo's behalf. He wasn't asking for freedom for this "dangerous uncontrollable beast" indeed "DeSalvo wants society to be protected from him," but he demanded a verdict of insanity so that DeSalvo could receive proper treatment instead of being locked away.

Prosecutor Conn saw things quite differently. He saw DeSalvo as just one more cunning criminal who had feigned the symptoms of mental illness to avoid the consequences of his actions. He told the jury:

> It's my duty to my wife, to your wife, to every woman who might conceivably be a victim of this man, to stamp his conduct for what it is—vicious, criminal conduct. Don't let this man con you right out of your shoes!

In his final charge to the jury, Judge Moynihan reminded them they were to purge all thoughts of the Boston Strangler from their minds and decide this case on its merits alone.

On January 18, 1967, they did just that, finding Albert DeSalvo sane and guilty on all 10 counts. He was sentenced to life imprisonment.

To reporters later, Bailey commented, "Massachusetts has burned another witch. No fault of the jury's, of course. It's the fault of the law."

On February 24, 1967, Albert DeSalvo and two other inmates escaped from Bridgewater. Murderer Frederick E. Erickson, 40, and armed robber George W. Harrisson, 35, were recaptured that same day, but for 24 hours the city of Boston cringed, waiting for the Strangler to strike again. It didn't happen. The next day DeSalvo was arrested in a clothing store in Lynn, Massachusetts, claiming to have escaped only to draw attention to his case. Nervous authorities decided that in the future DeSalvo would be housed in the maximum-security Walpole State Prison.

Eight months later Albert DeSalvo received an additional 7–10 years for escaping. His brothers, Richard, 32, and Joseph, 37, were each given one-year suspended sentences for aiding in the escape.

On November 26, 1973, Albert DeSalvo was stabbed to death by another inmate at Walpole State Prison. His killer was never apprehended.

Despite his many confessions, Albert DeSalvo was never tried as the Boston Strangler. Some feel that he fabricated the whole story, relying on his contact with the actual killer (allegedly another Bridgewater inmate) for the details of the crimes. Oddly enough, none of the eyewitnesses who saw the Boston Strangler identified DeSalvo as the killer, but one fact is undeniable: Boston's reign of terror ended with the incarceration of this strange and troubled man.

—*Colin Evans*

Suggestions for Further Reading

Banks, Harold K. *The Strangler!* New York: Avon, 1967.

Brussel, James A. *Casebook Of A Crime Psychologist*. New York: Grove, 1968.

Frank, Gerald. *The Boston Strangler*. New York: New American Library, 1966.

Gaute, J.H.H.and Robin Odell. *The Murderers' Who's Who*. London: W.H. Allen, 1989.

Richard Franklin Speck Trial: 1967

Defendant: Richard Franklin Speck   **Crime Charged:** Murder
Chief Defense Lawyers: Gerald Getty, James Gramenos, and Jerome Wexler
Chief Prosecutor: William Martin   **Judge:** Herbert C. Paschen
Place: Peoria, Illinois   **Dates of Trial:** February 20–April 15, 1967
Verdict: Guilty   **Sentence:** Death, later commuted to 8 life terms
imprisonment

SIGNIFICANCE
Nothing like the testimony of Corazon Amurao had ever graced an American courtroom. Witnesses to murder are rare enough; witnesses to the kind of wholesale slaughter she described were unheard of. Richard Speck's killing spree sent shockwaves around the world.

At 6:00 A.M. on July 14, 1966, the early morning calm of Jeffrey Manor, a middle-class South Chicago, Illinois, suburb, was shattered by screaming. Neighbors tracked the disturbance to a two-story townhouse occupied by nurses who worked at the nearby community hospital. They found Corazon Amurao, a diminutive Filipino nurse, perched on a second-floor window ledge, in tears and hysterical. "My friends are all dead, all dead," she cried. "I am the only one alive." Investigation of the townhouse confirmed the grim truth. Someone had turned the place into an abattoir. Eight nurses lay dead—stabbed, strangled, and mutilated.

Amurao told detectives of an armed stranger, smelling strongly of alcohol, who had forced his way in the previous night, ostensibly looking for money. Then he began systematically killing everyone present. Only by hiding beneath a bed and remaining silent was she able to avoid the carnage. She described the killer as tall and blond, and having a "Born to raise hell" tattoo on one arm.

Because of the unusual knots used to tie the victims, police theorized that they were looking for someone with nautical connections. This led them to a nearby branch of the seaman's union. Mention of the killer's tattoo produced a name: Richard Speck, a 24-year-old sailor and habitual criminal, with a long record of drug abuse and drunken violence. A photo and description were circulated throughout the Chicago area.

In the early hours of July 17, a man who unsuccessfully attempted suicide was admitted to Cook County Hospital with slashed wrists. When doctors wiped away the blood, they saw the distinctive tattoo and called police.

Trial Moved

Because of the intense local media coverage, Richard Speck's chief attorney, Gerald Getty, requested a change of trial venue. When the trial opened in the morning of February 20, 1967, it was in Peoria, Illinois, some 140 miles from Chicago. Getty also won another important victory by having all eight murder charges consolidated into one trial with one verdict and one sentence. Assistant State Attorney William Martin had wanted the cases tried individually. That way, even if Speck was acquitted on one count, there were still seven others to trap him. Despite this setback, Martin remained confident that the state had sufficient evidence for conviction.

For two days he carefully laid the groundwork of his case. His first witnesses, sailors Dante Bargellini and George Mackey, both placed Speck in the vicinity of the nurses' house just before the murder and also confirmed his expressed desire to return to New Orleans. Other witnesses testified to seeing Speck on a day-long drinking binge, brandishing a gun and a knife.

It wasn't until the third day of testimony that Martin produced the prosecution's prime witness: Corazon Amurao. She described being awakened by four knocks at her bedroom door. "I went to the door, . . . I unlocked it, . . . then I saw a man . . . with a gun in his right hand pointed towards me and I noticed that he had marks on his face . . . and his hair was blond."

The atmosphere was electric as Martin asked, "Now, Miss Amurao, if you see that same man in the courtroom today, . . . would you please step down and point him out." Amurao didn't hesitate. She crossed to the defense table, raised her hand and pointed directly at Speck. "This is the man."

Next, Amurao told how Speck herded all six girls present in the townhouse into the bedroom, then tore strips off a sheet and tied them up. Later, when three other nurses returned home, they too were made captive. She described Speck's peculiar ambivalence towards his prisoners, smiling a lot, almost friendly. "Don't be afraid," he said while tying one of the girls, "I'm not going to kill you."

Minutes later he began doing just that.

Using a scale model of the townhouse and eight wooden blocks to represent the murder victims, Martin asked Corazon Amurao to describe the events. Richard Speck, she said, went across to Patricia Wilkening, untied her ankles, and led her from the room.

"After Speck had taken Wilkening from the south bedroom, did you hear anything?" asked Martin.

"After about one minute I heard Miss Wilkening say 'Ah.' It was like a sigh."

"Did you hear anything after the noise you just described?"

"No."

But after the next two victims were removed from the bedroom, Amurao *did* hear something: "water running in the bathroom, as if Speck was washing his hands."

The macabre process continued. Speck would enter the bedroom, lead one of the girls away with him, then return several minutes later for his next victim. When the girls tried to hide, Speck found them all—except Corazon Amurao. Eventually, only she and Gloria Davy were left.

Frozen with fear in her hiding place beneath the bed, Amurao could only watch in horror as Speck stripped Gloria Davy and raped her. It later transpired that Davy, the only victim of sexual assault, was very similar to Speck's estranged wife, whom he hated and had threatened on several occasions to kill.

"Was your head down at that time?" asked Martin.

"Yes."

"When did you next look up?"

"About five minutes after the bedsprings stopped. I looked up and saw that Davy and Speck was [*sic*] not there anymore."

Amurao's account of her five-hour ordeal, made all the more poignant by her faltering English, was devastating. When Public Defender Gerald Getty rose to cross-examine, he faced the toughest task of his career. Not once had he lost a client to the electric chair; no one present in court expected that record to survive.

Richard Speck (right), with his lawyer, public defender Gerald Getty (left). (AP/Wide World Photos)

Mistaken Identity?

It had been Getty's contention throughout that Richard Speck was completely innocent, that Corazon Amurao, in her traumatized and hysterical state, had identified the wrong man. But he had to tread carefully. Amurao had obviously impressed the jury and won their sympathy as well, any suggestion of bullying could backfire badly. But no matter how he tried, Getty could not shake the young Filipino nurse. She steadfastly continued to insist that Richard Speck was the killer.

There was plenty of other evidence to support her claim. Two T-shirts found at the crime scene were of the type that Speck was known to wear. And then there were the fingerprints. Three experts testified that prints found in the townhouse matched Speck's, a pronouncement hotly disputed by assistant defense counsel James Gramenos. He avowed that the prints were too smudged for positive identification. The experts disagreed. Gramenos persisted, though he was conspicuously unable to provide his own expert to back up this claim.

But the defense was not finished yet. Murrill and Gerdena Farmer, both workers at Kay's Pilot House, a tavern several blocks away from the townhouse, swore that Speck was in the bar until 12:30 A.M. on the night in question. Prosecutor Martin sought to demonstrate that the couple had made an honest mistake, but he could not budge them.

Richard Speck remained a spectator to all of this, choosing not to testify on his own behalf. Earlier he had told his attorneys that the events of July 13–14, 1966, were a blur of drugs and alcohol; he could remember nothing.

On April 15, 1967, after just 49 minutes of deliberation, the jury found Speck guilty and recommended death. Confirmation came June 6, 1967, when Judge Herbert C. Paschen sentenced Speck to the electric chair. When U.S. Supreme Court rulings in other cases called into question all death sentences recommended by trial juries, Speck's sentence was commuted to eight terms of life imprisonment.

Speck maintained his innocence until 1978 when he was quoted as telling a newspaper, "Yeah, I killed them. I stabbed them and choked them." After spending 24 years in prison, Richard Speck died of a heart attack on December 5, 1991. He was 49 years old.

—Colin Evans

Suggestions for Further Reading

Altman, Jack and Marvin Ziporyn. *Born to Raise Hell.* New York; Grove Press, 1967.

Crimes And Punishment. Vol. 13. England: Phoebus, 1974.

Felsher, Howard and Michael Rosen. *Justice, U.S.A.* New York: Crowell, Collier & Macmillan, 1967.

Wilson, Colin and Donald Seaman. *Encyclopedia of Modern Murder.* New York: G.P. Putnam's Sons, 1983.

Price and Bowers Trial: 1967

Defendants: Cecil Price and Sam Bowers, Jr. **Crimes Charged:** Conspiracy to violate civil rights **Chief Defense Lawyers:** Clayton Lewis, H.C. Watkins, and Laurel Weir **Chief prosecutors:** John Doar, Robert Hauberg, and Robert Owen **Judge:** William Harold Cox **Place:** Meridian, Mississippi **Dates of trial:** October 7–20, 1967 **Verdict:** Guilty **Sentence:** Bowers, 10 years imprisonment; Price, 6 years imprisonment

SIGNIFICANCE

This trial's historic outcome marked a turning point in the long and often bloody struggle for civil rights that bedeviled Mississippi in the 1960s.

On the morning of June 21, 1964, two committed civil rights campaigners, Michael Schwerner and James Chayney, drove into Neshoba county, Mississippi, to investigate the burning of a church. With them was Andrew Goodman, an anthropology major who had arrived from New York the previous day. That afternoon the trio was arrested for speeding just outside the small town of Philadelphia by local sheriff's deputy Cecil Price. Around 10:00 P.M., after paying a $25 fine, they were released. All three then disappeared. Forty-four days later, following massive federal intervention, their murdered bodies were recovered from beneath a dam.

It soon became clear that a gang made up of local police officers and Ku Klux Klan members had carried out the killings. Equally obvious was the fact that chances of obtaining murder convictions were nonexistent. For this reason the federal government chose to proceed against those implicated on lesser charges of violation of civil rights. When the trial finally came to court 17 men were under indictment, but public attention had concentrated on just two:, Deputy Sheriff Cecil Price and local KKK Imperial Wizard Sam Bowers, Jr.

After three years of delays, the trial opened on October 7, 1967. The prosecution team led by the U.S. Justice Department's head civil rights attorney, John Doar, looked positively skimpy when arrayed against no less than a dozen defense attorneys, but the Justice Department case was damning. Doar contended that, while the three men were still in his custody, Price had contacted local KKK members under Bowers' leadership, and that a carefully orchestrated ambush was put into effect. After their release, Schwerner,

Chayney and Goodman were again stopped on the highway by Price, who then delivered them into the hands of his co-conspirators. One of those present, James Jordan, testifying for the prosecution, described how all three men were gunned down, then dumped into a prepared grave, which was bulldozed over.

Defense Tactics Fail

The defense's key strategy, made plain from the outset, centered around an attempt to enlist the sympathy of Judge William Cox, whose record on civil rights was less than exemplary. Their constant maneuvering for a postponement or mistrial, however, drew this stern rebuke from the judge: "I don't want this to be a pattern for this trial, gentlemen, because we are not going to have a big show out of this case. I don't run a court like that. We are going to try this case, we are going to get rid of it. It's not going to be interminable, so you can just get that out of your minds." Judge Cox's words sent a chill across the defense table as, perhaps for the first time, the accused realized that they might actually be convicted.

Another major miscalculation came when defense attorney Laurel Weir, cross-examining a prosecution witness, the Reverend Charles Johnson, asked if it was true that he [Johnson] and Schwerner had tried to "get young Negro males to sign statements that they would rape one white woman a week during the hot summer of 1964 here in Mississippi." Cox angrily interrupted, saying he found the question "highly improper—I'm not going to allow a farce to be made of this trial and everybody might as well get that through heads, including every one of the defendants."

Delmar Dennis, another renegade Klansman, testified that Bowers bragged to other Klan members of his involvement in the Neshoba killings, crowing: "It was the first time that Christians had planned and carried out the execution of a Jew." Dennis also provided details of a loosely coded letter written by Bowers, in which he had attempted to cover up details of the killings. But perhaps Dennis' most startling revelation came when he identified one of the defense attorneys, Clayton Lewis, as a Klan sympathizer. Laurel Weir's vociferous demands for a mistrial were overruled by Judge Cox.

In closing arguments Doar assured the jurors that "the federal government is not invading Philadelphia or Neshoba Country [but rather] these defendants are tried for a crime under federal law in a Mississippi city, before a Mississippi federal judge, in Mississippi courtroom, before twelve men and women from the state of Mississippi." This was a shrewd move on Doar's part. Throughout the trial he had wisely avoided turning this case into an indictment of the state: he knew his best chance of victory lay in appealing to sound common sense. Then he reminded the jurors:

> This was a calculated, cold blooded plot. Three men, hardly more than boys, were the victims. The plot was executed with a degree of self-possession and steadiness equal to the wickedness with which it was planned.

Answering defense complaints that the turncoat Klansmen had been paid sums of money by the government to testify, Doar commented that such actions were necessary on occasion. As he put it, "Midnight murder in the rural area of Neshoba County provides few witnesses."

By contrast, defense attorney, H.C. Watkins excoriated the paid informers, then attempted to blacken the character and intentions of Schwerner, Chayney and Goodman:

> It well be that these young men were sacrificed by their own kin for publicity. So far as I have been able to determine, they had no authority to be in Neshoba County. They broke the laws of that county by speeding and they violated the American Constitution by messing in local affairs in a local community. Mississippians rightfully resent some hairy beatnik from another state visiting our state with hate and defying our people.

Jury Reaches Tough Decision

On October 18 the case went to the jury. After a day they declared themselves deadlocked, but Judge Cox refused to declare a mistrial and ordered a return to deliberations, reminding them of the expense of another trial and the necessity for them to reach a verdict. The admonishment worked. On October 20 the jury found Price and Bowers and five other defendants guilty. They could reach no verdict against four other defendants; the remainder were acquitted.

Announcing himself in complete agreement with the verdicts, Judge Cox set December 29 as sentencing day. At that time he imposed a 10-year jail term on Bowers, and six years for Price. The other convicted men received sentences of 3–10 years.

History had been made. For the first time a Mississippi jury had convicted white officials and Klansmen of crimes against black people or civil rights workers. In 1988, these events were captured in the movie *Mississippi Burning*. While the factual accuracy of the film was often called into question, few doubted that its searing portrayal of bigotry and blind hatred was anything other than authentic.

—Colin Evans

Suggestions for Further Reading

Blaustein, Albert P. and Robert L. Zangrando. *Civil Rights And The American Negro.* New York: Trident, 1968.

Cagin, Seth and Philip Dray. *We Are Not Afraid.* New York: Bantam, 1988.

Huie, William Bradford. *Three Lives For Mississipppi.* New York:

Kornbluth, Jesse, "The Struggle Continues." *New York Times Magazine* (July 23, 1989): 16ff.

Alice Crimmins Trials: 1968 & 1971

Defendant: Alice Crimmins   **Crimes Charged:** First trial, murder; Second trial, murder and manslaughter   **Chief Defense Attorneys:** First trial: Marty Baron and Harold Harrison; Second trial: William Erlbaum and Herbert Lyon.   **Chief Prosecutors:** First trial: Anthony Lombardino and James Mosely; Second trial: Thomas Demakos and Vincent Nicolosi.   **Judges:** First trial: Peter Farrell; second trial: George Balbach   **Place:** New York, New York   **Dates of Trials:** First trial: May 9–27, 1968; second trial: March 15–April 23, 1971   **Verdicts:** Guilty   **Sentences:** First trial: 5 to 20 years; second trial: life plus five to 20 years.

SIGNIFICANCE

Appeals in this sensational New York case led to a ruling that courtroom errors are only prejudicial when there is a strong probability they have influenced a jury's verdict.

To millions of New Yorkers, Alice Crimmins was a tramp responsible for an unspeakable crime. To others, Crimmins was a victim of what one of her lawyers called "trial by innuendo," a woman persecuted for her defiant anger at a justice system more concerned with her social behavior than in solving the murder of her children.

On the morning of July 14, 1965, Edmund Crimmins reported that his two children were missing from the Queens apartment where they lived with his estranged wife Alice. Police searched the neighborhood, hoping to find 5-year-old Eddie Crimmins, Jr., and 4-year-old Alice Marie "Missy" Crimmins alive. In early afternoon, Missy's dead body was found in a vacant lot.

The ground-floor window of the children's room was open, but police were more interested in Alice Crimmins' reputation as a "swinger." Faced with a dearth of physical evidence, detectives felt that her sexual affairs and her failure to break into tears immediately upon viewing her daughter's body made her a suspect.

Both parents endured intense police questioning about their broken marriage. A court hearing over custody of the children was to have started on July 19. Instead, the badly decomposed body of Eddie Jr. was found that day in scrub near the busy Van Wyck Expressway.

Trial Begins Three Years Later

Mutual resentment grew between Alice Crimmins and the police who suspected her. She angrily accused them of not working to find the real killers and stopped cooperating. Detectives and district attorneys viewed her hostility as evidence of guilt. Wiretaps, electronic surveillance, and hundreds of interviews with her neighbors and friends failed to produce any evidence. The district attorney's office tried twice to convince grand juries to indict her. Secret testimony made a third attempt successful. Alice Crimmins was accused of murdering Missy—there was not enough left of Eddie Jr.'s body to support a murder charge.

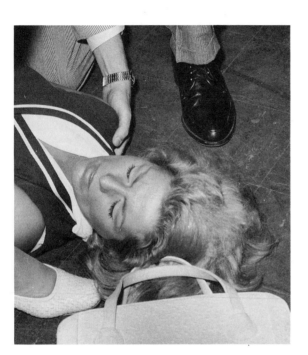

Her trial began in May 1968, nearly three years after the Crimmins children disappeared. Prosecutors called Dr. Milton Helpern to the stand. The renowned forensic pathologist testified that Missy Crimmins was strangled. He held that food in the child's stomach could not have been ingested more than two hours before her death. Helpern's testimony was irreconcilable with Alice Crimmins' insistence that she fed both children at 7:30 P.M., two hours before she put them to bed, and over four hours before midnight when she last saw them alive.

One of Alice Crimmins' lovers, a contractor named Joe Rorech remembered her telling him a month before the expected custody battle that "she would rather see the children dead" than allow her husband to take them. The night of the disappearance, Rorech claimed to have called her apartment twice, receiving no answer at 2:00 A.M.

Alice Crimmins fainted at the Queens Police Station where she faced charges of killing her two children. (AP/Wide World)

More damaging was Rorech's claim of a tearful admission in a Long Island restaurant 14 months after the children were found. "She said there was no reason for them to be killed, it was senseless," Rorech uneasily told the prosecutor. "I said Missy and Eddie are dead," and she said, "Joseph, please forgive me, I killed her."

"Joseph, that isn't true!" Crimmins cried from the defense table. When Judge Peter Farrell restored order, Rorech said that his conscience had later moved him to testify. He admitted to drinking heavily the day he called the apartment, opening the possibility that he might have dialed a wrong number. Rorech was a married man with seven children. The defense attacked him as a spiteful rejected lover, a perjurer whose marital and business problems were being exploited by the district attorney's office.

Observed from Above

The second surprise witness was housewife Sophie Earominski, whom police had discovered to be the author of an anonymous letter offering information. From her third-floor window, Earominski claimed to have seen a woman outside at 2:00 A.M., about the time Rorech supposedly phoned the Crimmins apartment. The woman carried a bundle of blankets and was walking with a man and a little boy. The man tried to hurry the woman, who had a dog on a leash. Earominski said the woman replied that the dog was pregnant and protested when the man threw the bundle into the back of a car. "Does she know the difference now?" the man said.

"Don't say that," said the woman, whom Earominski identified as Alice Crimmins. "There was agony in her voice. She was nervous, she sounded frightened." Earominski said the man snapped, "Now you're sorry!"

Alice Crimmins screamed in the courtroom, "You liar!"

The defense portrayed Earominski as a pathetic individual with an overactive imagination who enjoyed the celebrity of being a witness, adding that no one knew the Crimmins dog was pregnant until well after the killings.

Alice Crimmins' cold attitude broke when she was questioned about her children. She sobbed uncontrollably on the stand. The next day she returned to face prosecutor Anthony Lombardino. As Lombardino sarcastically questioned her about the whereabouts of her children during her numerous affairs, Crimmins' anger flared. The histrionics of the lawyers were so loud that a juror twice told Judge Farrell that the proceedings were inaudible because of the shouting. Noise from spectators was no less distracting. When Judge Farrell finally instructed the jury, he warned them, "We are not trying here a case involving sex morals. We are trying a homicide case."

On May 27, an all-male jury found Alice Crimmins guilty. As Judge Farrell prepared to sentence her, Crimmins turned her wrath on the district attorneys. "You want to close your books! You don't give a damn who killed my children!"

A New Trial

An unauthorized visit to Earominski's building by three jurors during the trial and the judge's disallowance of evidence that might have cast doubt on Rorech's and Earominski's testimony led an appeals court to overturn Crimmins' conviction in December 1969.

Six months later, she was indicted again. Under the double-jeopardy rule preventing defendants from being tried more than once for the same crime, she could not be charged twice with murdering Missy. She was charged instead with manslaughter and indicted for murdering Eddie, largely Rorech's new claim that she had "agreed to" her son's death.

The second trial revealed how sloppily detectives had handled the investigation. Potential evidence from the Crimmins apartment was not kept. Psychiatric doubts about Sophie Earominski's mental fitness were introduced. Joe

Rorech expanded his testimony, saying that Crimmins told him that a convicted bank robber named Vinnie Colabella had killed Eddie Jr. for her. Prosecutors took Colabella out of prison and put him on the stand. He denied ever seeing Crimmins before. The prosecutor from the first trial, Anthony Lombardino, was called as a witness and admitted that he had once offered Colabella "a deal" in return for testimony.

The defense attacked the only motive prosecutors gave for Crimmins having her children killed, the custody battle with her husband (who stood by her during both trials). Her divorce lawyer testified that he had advised her that she would never lose her children under New York law, regardless of allegations about her moral reputation.

A new prosecution witness, Tina DeVita, remembered glimpsing a woman, a man with a bundle, a boy, and a dog on the night the Crimmins children disappeared, echoing Sophie Earominski's scenario without identifying anyone. After DeVita's testimony, Alice Crimmins appealed to the public for help. A man named Marvin Weinstein came forward and testified that he had been walking in the neighborhood with his dog, his young son, and his wife, who was carrying their daughter in a blanket. Mrs. Weinstein came to court. She resembled Alice Crimmins. When a former business associate testified that the Weinsteins did not visit his home on the night in question, the Weinsteins retorted that the man was a liar. Mr. Weinstein said he had not come forward during the first trial because he had not realized the case depended so much on Earominski's testimony.

The state's case seemed so shaky that shock and weeping filled the courtroom when Alice Crimmins was again found guilty. In May 1971, she was sentenced to life imprisonment, for murder, with a concurrent five to 20 years for manslaughter.

The murder charge was overturned two years later by an appellate division of the New York Supreme Court, which ruled that Eddie's death had not been proven beyond a reasonable doubt to have resulted from a criminal act. The manslaughter conviction was also overturned. The court ruled that allowing errors like Joe Rorech's testimony that he had taken "truth serum" and a prosecutor's declaration that Crimmins did not "have the courage to stand up and tell the whole world she killed her daughter" were "grossly prejudicial." The court ordered her to be tried again, but only on the manslaughter charge.

In February 1975, however, the New York State Court of Appeals reinstated the manslaughter verdict. Noting that two juries had found Alice Crimmins "criminally responsible for the death of her daughter," the court ruled that the conviction was fair because there was no "significant probability, rather than only a rational possibility that the jury would have acquitted the defendant had it not been for the error or errors which occurred." Dissenting justices wrote that this decision changed the definition of prejudicial conduct, "dangerously diluting the time-honored standard of proof beyond a reasonable doubt, which has been a cornerstone of Anglo-Saxon jurisprudence."

Alice Crimmins was ordered to finish her sentence. She was paroled in 1977, quietly ending one of the most emotional and troubling cases ever heard in New York courts.

— Thomas C. Smith

Suggestions for Further Reading

Goldstein, Tom. "Appeals Court Finds 'Overwhelming Proof' Mrs. Crimmins Killed Her Daughter." The *New York Times* (February 26, 1975): 34.

Gross, Kenneth. *The Alice Crimmins Case*. New York: Alfred A. Knopf, 1975.

Helpern, Milton with Bernard Knight. *Autopsy: The Memoirs of Milton Helpern, The World's Greatest Medical Detective*. New York: St. Martin's Press, 1977.

Mills, James. *The Prosecutor*. New York: Farrar, Straus and Giroux, 1969.

John Marshall Branion Trial: 1968

Name of Defendant: John Marshall Branion, Jr. **Crime Charged:** Murder
Chief Defense Lawyer: Maurice Scott **Chief Prosecutor:** Patrick A. Tuite
Judge: Reginald J. Holzer **Place:** Chicago, Illinois
Dates of Trial: May 15–28, 1968 **Verdict:** Guilty **Sentence:** 20-30 years

SIGNIFICANCE

The murder conviction of John Marshall Branion, Jr., a prominent black doctor
and confidant of Martin Luther King, Jr., was achieved without a single scrap of
direct proof, demonstrating that, occasionally, circumstantial evidence is the best
evidence of all.

The case of John Branion reads like a best-selling mystery thriller. First there
was the crime itself, tortuous, full of twists, and ultimately hinging on one
issue: Did the defendant's alibi allow him sufficient time to carry out a murder?
And then came the trial, riddled with allegations of racial prejudice and possible
judicial corruption. Most extraordinary of all was Branion's flight after conviction. Was he, as some claim, an innocent man escaping injustice, or was this
rather the tale of a pitiless killer, desperately fleeing the consequences of his
actions?

At 11:30 A.M. on December 22, 1967, Dr. John Branion set off in his car
from the Ida Mae Scott Hospital on Chicago's South Side. Five minutes later—
after passing his home—he picked up his 4-year-old son from outside a nursery
school, then called on a Maxine Brown, who was to have lunch with Branion and
his wife. When Brown explained that she was unable to keep the engagement,
Branion drove to his apartment at 5054 S. Woodlawn Avenue. His story was that
he had arrived at 11:57 A.M. and found his wife Donna lying on the floor of the
utility room. She had been shot four times by a .38-caliber automatic pistol.
Branion immediately summoned help.

Police treated Branion's story with palpable disdain; already witnesses
were coming forward to dispute his version of events. Another factor was
Branion's unpalatable detachment. Just two days after his wife's murder he flew
to Vail, Colorado, for a Christmas break.

One month later, armed with a search warrant, police recovered two boxes
of Geco brand .38-caliber ammunition from a closet in Branion's apartment. One

full box contained 25 shells. The other box had 4 shells missing, the same number that had killed Donna Branion. Shortly afterwards Branion was arrested for murder.

Imperfect Alibi

According to prosecutor Patrick Tuite, the story that Branion had told police was correct in every respect save one: chronology. Yes, Tuite said, Branion had gone to pick up his son, then on to Maxine Brown's, but first he had sneaked home and shot his wife, before hastening to establish an alibi. This theory was borne out by Joyce Kelly, a teacher at the nursery school. She testified that Branion had entered the school between 11:45 A.M. and 11:50 A.M., some 10 minutes later than he had claimed. Furthermore, she said that Branion's young son was waiting inside the school, again contradicting the defendant's story.

Detective Michael Boyle described for the court a series of tests that he and another officer had performed, driving the route allegedly taken by Branion. They had covered the 2.8-mile journey in a minimum of six minutes and a maximum of 12 minutes. Time enough, said the prosecution, for Branion to have committed the murder and then gone to pick up his son. Oddly enough, this assertion was never seriously challenged by the defense.

A ballistics expert, Officer Burt Nielsen, stated that the bullets which had killed Donna Branion could only have been fired from a Walther PPK .38-caliber automatic pistol, a very rare make. The prosecution pointed out that Branion, an avid gun collector, had at first denied ever having owned a Walther, until it was shown that he had received just such a gun in February 1967 as a belated birthday present. This had prompted Branion to change his original statement in which he claimed that nothing was stolen from his apartment; now he said that the Walther must have been taken by the intruders who killed his wife. The murder weapon was never found.

Much was made of Branion's peculiar indifference toward the discovery of his wife's body. He admitted not bothering to examine it because he could tell from the lividity that she was dead. (Lividity is the tendency of blood to sink to the lowest extremities in a corpse.) But Dr. Helen Payne testified that when she examined the body at 12:20 P.M. lividity was not present. Branion again altered his story, saying that he had really meant 'cyanosis,' a blue discoloration of the skin caused by de-oxygenated blood.

Illicit Love

To establish motive, the state argued that Branion was conducting an affair with nurse Shirley Hudson and wanted to be rid of his wife. Questioning of Maxine Brown, who had allegedly overheard a compromising conversation between Hudson and Branion one day after the murder, produced the following, seemingly fruitless, exchange:

Prosecutor: Who is Shirley Hudson?

Defense Counsel: Objection.

The Court: Sustained.

Prosecutor: Do you know what, if any, relationship Shirley Hudson bore to the defendant?

Defense Counsel: Objection.

The Court: Sustained.

And so it went: an endless string of improper questions, countered by an equal number of objections, all of which were upheld by the court. But the damage was immense. By such tactics the prosecution was able to establish the likelihood of an illicit relationship, if not the certainty.

Declining to testify on his own behalf, Branion remained mute while the jury convicted him of murder and Judge Reginald Holzer passed sentence of 20–30 years imprisonment. Defense counsel Maurice Scott immediately argued that the trial had been prejudiced by Chicago's recent racial disturbances and vowed to appeal.

Released by Judge Holzer on an unusually low bond of $5,000, Branion took his case to the Illinois Supreme Court. On December 3, 1970, while conceding that the evidence against Branion was wholly circumstantial, the court held that it was sufficient to uphold the guilty verdict, stating:

> To support a conviction based on circumstantial evidence it is essential that facts proved be not only consistent with defendant's guilt, but they must be inconsistent with any reasonable hypothesis of innocence; but the People are not required to establish guilt beyond any possible doubt.

On the Run

In 1971, Branion, sensing that the end was nigh, fled the country. After an amazing jaunt across Africa he found asylum in Uganda, occasionally acting as personal physician to Idi Amin, that country's dictator. Upon Amin's ouster, Branion was arrested and returned to the United States in October 1983.

Yet another stunning twist came in 1986, when Judge Reginald Holzer received an 18-year jail sentence for extortion and racketeering. Branion's lawyers seized this opportunity to charge that Holzer had received a $10,000 bribe during the 1968 trial, paid by the defendant's brother-in-law, Nelson Brown. Prosecutor Patrick Tuite admitted that he had heard rumors of Holzer's intention to overturn Branion's conviction and had gone to see him, urging that the law be allowed to take its course. The speculation is that Holzer, unnerved by Tuite's visit, swindled those who allegedly paid the bribe, then sought to placate them by substituting a ludicrously low bail of $5,000, allowing Branion to escape. Because there was no way of corroborating the story—Brown had himself been stabbed to death in 1983—this final effort to overturn Branion's conviction met with the same fate as its predecessors.

After serving just seven years of his sentence, Branion was released from prison in August 1990 on health grounds. One month later, at age 64, he died of a brain tumor and heart ailment.

Branion's conviction stunned Chicago's black community. Initial outrage over a perceived lack of police effort in apprehending the killer quickly turned to fury when the verdict of the jury was announced.

—Colin Evans

Suggestions for Further Reading

Jet. (October 22, 1990): 18.

Sanders, Charles L. "A Man On The Run." *Ebony* (July 1984): 112–119.

Tuohy, James and Rob Warden. *Greylord*. New York: G.P. Putnam's Sons, 1989.

265 North Eastern Reporter, 2nd Series. St. Paul, Minn.: West Publishing. 1971.

Huey P. Newton Trial: 1968

Defendant: Huey P. Newton   **Crimes Charged:** First-degree murder,
felonious assault, and kidnapping   **Chief Defense Lawyer:** Charles R. Garry
Chief Prosecutor: Lowell Jensen   **Judge:** Monroe Friedman
Place: Oakland, California   **Dates of Trial:** July 15–September 8, 1968
Verdict: Guilty of voluntary manslaughter; not guilty of felonious assault;
kidnapping charge dismissed   **Sentences:** 2–15 years

SIGNIFICANCE
While Huey P. Newton's 1968 case was technically a murder trial, it was also one
of the most politically charged trials of its era. Defense attorney Charles Garry's
use of the *voir dire* provided a model for choosing juries for racially and politically
sensitive trials.

Before any evidence was heard, many Americans believed that Huey P. Newton, co-founder and "minister of defense" of the Black Panther Party, had murdered a police officer in cold blood. Others were equally certain that the charge was a trumped-up attempt to crush the militant Black Panther Party.

No group brought the racial tensions of the late 1960s into sharper focus than the Black Panther Party For Self Defense. The Panthers' political rhetoric and advocacy of armed self-defense against police brutality alarmed many citizens and brought down the aggressive wrath of police departments across the nation.

Just before dawn on October 28, 1967, Oakland police Officer John Frey radioed that he was about to stop a "known Black Panther vehicle," a van occupied by two men. A second officer, Herbert Heanes arrived on the scene. Minutes later, officers responding to a distress call found Frey bleeding to death and Heanes slumped in his car, seriously wounded. Police found Huey Newton at a nearby hospital with a bullet wound in his abdomen.

Newton was charged with murdering Frey, assaulting Heanes, and kidnapping a man whose car was commandeered for the dash to the hospital. While Newton recovered from his wound, his attorney, Charles Garry, began his defense with a systematic assault on the grand jury system.

Grand Jury Becomes Issue

Garry's pretrial motions argued that the Alameda County grand jury system was unconstitutional, secretive, and prejudiced against minorities and the poor. He pointed out that black citizens were seldom chosen to serve. Garry argued that trial juries also were unfair. Since blacks were disproportionately under-represented on the county voter registration lists from which jury rolls were compiled, he proposed that providing Newton's constitutional right to a trial by his peers was impossible. Garry's pretrial strategy was unsuccessful but thorough, consuming nine months.

Newton's trial began in July 1968 under massive security. During the *voir dire* questioning of prospective jurors, Garry rigorously probed attitudes about race, the Black Panther Party, the Vietnam War, and the police. Prosecutor D. Lowell Jensen frequently objected that such issues were irrelevant to the case. Garry stubbornly held to the strategy, trying to imply that Newton could not get a fair trial or, at least, to sensitize acceptable jurors to racial problems. Both sides fought hard to determine the final composition of the jury, which ultimately was composed of 11 whites and 1 black.

Prosecutor Jensen claimed that Newton was a convicted felon on probation for a 1964 assault conviction. Newton would claim that he was sentenced for committing a misdemeanor, not a felony, and that he was actually coming home from celebrating the end of his probation when Frey stopped him.

Black Panther party leader Huey P. Newton (left) after a judge dismissed a manslaughter charge against him. The man on the right is his bodyguard, Robert Leonard Bay. (AP/Wide World Photos)

Jensen held that Newton's probation was still in effect when officer Frey decided to arrest him for falsely identifying himself as the owner of the van. Two matchboxes of marijuana were allegedly found later in the vehicle. Although he was not charged with drug possession, nor was any concealable weapon produced, Newton was portrayed as a felon with both a motive and the nerve to kill a police officer rather than face additional felony charges and a guaranteed return to prison. The prosecution's motive theory thus hinged on Newton's disputed probation status.

Officer Herbert Heanes testified that he had been guarding Newton's still unnamed passenger by the van when Newton and Frey began to "tussle." As they struggled on the hood of Frey's car, Heanes was struck in the arm by a bullet. Heanes fired at Newton before blacking out. Yet Heanes did not recall seeing any weapon in Newton's hands. Garry raised the possibility that Heanes had shot fellow officer Frey. A ballistics expert testified that both officers had been struck by bullets from police revolvers.

The prosecution summoned a black bus driver named Henry Grier, who testified that his headlights allowed him to clearly see Newton pull a gun from his jacket and shoot Frey repeatedly. Yet the defense exposed more than a dozen points where Grier's testimony contradicted his initial statement to police. Newton's clothing and physique did not match the description Grier had initially given. When Garry tried to fit a pistol into the pocket of the jacket Newton wore on October 28, the gun kept falling out, weakening the claim that Newton had a concealed weapon.

The prosecution called Dell Ross, who had told a grand jury that Newton and another man had forced him to drive them to a hospital at gunpoint. At the Newton trial, however, Ross refused to answer any questions, citing the Fifth Amendment protection against self-incrimination. Despite a grant of immunity and Judge Monroe Friedman's explanation that Ross was a witness, not a defendant, Ross would not talk.

As the judge prepared to jail Ross for contempt, the prosecutor suggested that if Ross did not remember what had happened on October 28, he should say so. Ross replied that he remembered nothing. Jensen nevertheless had Ross' grand jury testimony about his alleged abduction read before the jury. Garry destroyed the effect of this maneuver by playing a taped conversation in which Ross admitted lying to the grand jury because he was afraid of being arrested for outstanding parking tickets. Judge Friedman dismissed the kidnapping charge.

The closure of Newton's probation remained in dispute. His parole officer could not remember what date he gave Newton as the end of his probation period, leaving the motive for shooting Frey unresolved. The matchboxes of marijuana, which Newton claimed were planted by police, had no fingerprints on them.

After moving unsuccessfully for a mistrial because of death threats mailed to the defense, Garry explored officer Frey's reputation. Several black witnesses recalled Frey's physically abusive and verbally insulting behavior. A white high-school teacher who had taught Frey and later invited him back to speak to students recalled the officer's classroom lecture about "niggers" in the district he was responsible for patroling.

Surprise Witness Surfaces

Garry's next witness stunned the courtroom. Gene McKinney was the man riding with Newton on October 28, but police had never learned his identity. After establishing that McKinney was Newton's passenger, Garry asked, "Did you by chance or otherwise shoot officer John Frey?"

McKinney refused to answer, citing the Fifth Amendment. Prosecutor Jensen furiously demanded that McKinney be forced to reply. Garry had skillfully managed to offer the jury a "reasonable doubt" that Newton had killed Frey. As Newton noted later, if Judge Friedman had then granted McKinney immunity, McKinney could have accepted the blame for Frey's death, freeing both himself and Newton without punishment. Instead, Judge Friedman cited McKinney for contempt and sent him immediately to jail.

When Newton took the stand, he calmly denied shooting Frey or Heanes. For nearly a full day, Garry's questions drew full descriptions of the aims of the Black Panther Party, the historical oppression of black Americans, and police brutality in the Oakland ghetto. The prosecution repeatedly objected that the lengthy answers were irrelevant.

Newton admitted using his own trial as a political forum, but the defense was also trying to establish a context in which to view Frey's harassment of Newton as typical police practice in the Oakland ghetto, particularly employed against members of the Black Panther Party.

Newton testified that he had correctly identified himself to officer Frey, who abusively ordered him out of the van. After searching Newton, Frey pushed him down the street to the parked police cars. When they stopped, Newton protested that the officer had no reasonable cause to arrest him, opening a lawbook he habitually carried. Newton claimed that Frey replied with a racial insult and a punch in the face. Newton fell. As he started to rise, Frey shot him in the stomach. Newton remembered little else after that.

Prosecutor Jensen read Newton's arrest records and political declarations, trying to portray the Black Panther minister of defense as a man fond of violence and guns. Newton responded by contending that police harassment had precipitated each arrest and expounded on the political theories in his writings.

In his summation, Jensen soberly concluded that the evidence showed Newton to be a violent man and, in this case, a murderer. Garry's summation was a broad, impassioned indictment of white racism, characterizing the trial as part of an attempt by the Oakland police to destroy Newton and the Black Panthers.

One day after the jurors began their deliberations, they asked to see the transcript of Henry Grier's initial statement to police. Garry noticed that someone had incorrectly transcribed that Grier "did" see Newton at the shooting, when Grier's voice on the police tape said that he "didn't." After a lengthy confrontation between the attorneys, Judge Friedman ordered the transcript corrected and sent into the jury room without any attached comment on the mistake.

Jury Disappoints All

The jury's verdict was a disappointment to both sides. Newton was acquitted of assaulting officer Heanes. Instead of convicting Newton on the more serious charge of murder, the jury found him guilty of voluntary manslaughter. Because the jury also decided that Newton was still on felony probation at the time of the shooting, the manslaughter conviction carried an automatic sentence of 2–15 years.

The defense appealed with a new concerted attack on the jury systems and an assortment of misrulings by the judge. On May 29, 1970, the California

Court of Appeals reversed Newton's conviction because of Judge Friedman's incomplete instructions to the jury. The judge erred by not giving jurors the option of convicting Newton of involuntary manslaughter, a charge consistent with his claim that he was disoriented and unconscious after Frey shot him.

Two More Trials, Then a Dismissal

Newton was tried again in August 1971. The charge was changed to manslaughter, but the prosecution presented an identical case. A deadlocked jury produced a mistrial.

When Newton was tried a third time in November 1971, the judge ruled that the disputed 1964 conviction should not be included in the indictment. The prosecution's court case was also weaker, despite reappearances by all of the principal witnesses. Officer Heanes, who had maintained that only Newton and McKinney were present during the 1968 incident, now remembered an unknown third man.

Garry also discredited the testimony of Henry Grier, who claimed to have seen the shooting in his bus headlights. Grier's supervisor explained that the bus schedule placed Grier's vehicle well over a mile from the incident. A hung jury delivered a second mistrial. District Attorney Jensen reluctantly dropped the charges against Newton in December 1970 .

Newton was freed, but neither he nor the Black Panther Party fared well in the ensuing years. Decimated by police shootings and internal strife, the Panthers membership swiftly declined. In 1978, Newton was convicted of possessing an illegal weapon but acquitted of assault after allegedly pistol-whipping his tailor. Charges that he murdered a prostitute were dismissed in 1979 after two mistrials. His studies in social philosophy earned him a doctorate in 1980, but his problems with alcohol and drugs persisted. In 1989, he pleaded no contest to misappropriating $15,000 from a public grant to a Black Panther Party-operated school.

Huey Newton was shot to death by an Oakland drug dealer on August 22, 1989.

—Thomas C. Smith

Suggestions for Further Reading

Frazier, Thomas R., ed. *Afro-American History: Primary Sources*. New York: Harcourt Brace Jovanovich, 1971.

Garry, Charles R. *Minimizing Racism In Jury Trials*. Berkeley, Calif.: National Lawyers Guild, 1969.

Hevesi, Dennis. "Huey Newton Symbolized the Rising Black Anger of a Generation." *New York Times* (August 23, 1989): B7.

Moore, Gilbert. *A Special Rage*. New York: Harper & Row, 1971.

Newton, Huey P. *Revolutionary Suicide*. New York: Harcourt Brace Jovanovich, 1973.

Wood, Wilbur. "Oversupply of Doubt." *The Nation* (September 30, 1968): 300–303.

U.S. v. Berrigan: 1968

Defendants: Philip Berrigan, Daniel Berrigan, and others
Crimes Charged: Willfully injuring government property, mutilating public records, and hindering the operation Selective Service System
Chief Defense Lawyers: Harrop Freeman and William Kunstler
Chief Prosecutors: Stephen H. Sachs and Barnet D. Skolnik
Judge: Roszel C. Thomsen   **Place:** Baltimore, Maryland
Dates of Trial: October 7–10, 1968   **Verdict:** Guilty   **Sentence:** 3½ years in prison for Philip Berrigan and 3 years in prison for Daniel Berrigan

SIGNIFICANCE

The courts refused to recognize moral opposition to the Vietnam War as a legal defense to prosecution for criminal acts of defiance, such as the Berrigans' raid on a Selective Service office.

The Roman Catholic Church is usually considered a conservative institution, one that doesn't get involved in American politics except in unusual circumstances. During the late 1960s, however, certain Catholic priests began to take an active role in the protest movement against the increasingly unpopular Vietnam War. Two priests in particular, the Berrigan brothers Philip and Daniel, went so far as to organize acts of disobedience that got them into serious trouble with the authorities.

On October 26, 1967, Philip, Daniel, and three other people entered the Customs House in Baltimore, Maryland, where the federal Selective Service Administration kept some draft records. The Berrigans had planned a media event, and several reporters were present when the Berrigans arrived. Philip, Daniel, and the others proceeded to break into the file area, past the minimal clerical staff, and emptied vials of blood into the file cabinets. They waited peacefully for the police to arrive.

The federal authorities charged the Berrigans and the others with criminal violation of laws against willfully destroying United States property, mutilating public records, and hindering the administration of the Selective Service Act. After having been found guilty of these charges at trial and while awaiting sentencing, the Berrigans instigated another anti-war escapade. On May 17, 1968, they led seven other people into the Selective Service office in

Catonsville, Maryland, seized nearly 400 files, and burnt them in the parking lot with homemade napalm.

Philip and Daniel Berrigan Stand Trial

The Berrigans were promptly arrested, and once again they were charged with violations of federal law. The Catonsville incident, however, sparked a nationwide wave of sympathetic anti-Vietnam demonstrations unlike anything generated by the Baltimore Customs House affair. For example, in Milwaukee, Wisconsin a group of Catholic activists stormed a Selective Service office and burnt over 10,000 files.

The trial began on October 7, 1968 before Judge Roszel C. Thomsen in Baltimore, Maryland. The Berrigans' lawyers were Harrop Freeman and William Kunstler, and the federal prosecutors were Stephen H. Sachs and Barnet D. Skolnik. Philip Berrigan testified that his moral opposition to the Vietnam War led him to participate in the Catonsville incident:

> We have been accused of arrogance, but what of the fantastic arrogance of our leaders? What of their crimes against the people, the poor and the powerless? Still, no court will try them, no jail will receive them. They live in righteousness. They will die in honor. For them we have one message, for those in whose manicured hands the power of the land lies. We say to them: lead us. Lead us in justice and there will be no need to break the law.

The Rev. Philip Berrigan pouring blood on draft records at Selective Service headquarters to protest the "pitiful waste of American and Vietnamese blood" in Southeast Asia. (AP/Wide World Photos.)

Daniel Berrigan's testimony and that of the rest of the "Catonsville Nine" was similar to Philip Berrigan's. They had all entered the Selective Service office and burnt the files because of their belief that America's involvement in Vietnam was wrong. All of the defendants understood that they were breaking the law, but they asserted that their higher purpose in attempting to save human lives justified their actions. The prosecutors scornfully replied in their closing argument that:

> Our problems are not going to be solved by people who deliberately violate our laws, the foundation and support for an ordered, just, and civilized society.

Before the jury retired to deliberate, Daniel Berrigan made an impassioned plea to Judge Thomsen to interpret the law not according to its technical requirements, but according to the dictates of human morality. Berrigan argued that the judge and the jury were responsible to a higher authority than the law, and that if they believed as he did that the Vietnam War was wrong, they could acquit him and the others.

Thomsen was clearly sympathetic to these antiwar sentiments, but he knew that his office as judge was to uphold the law. Thomsen replied to Daniel Berrigan that:

> You speak to me as a man and as a judge. I would be a funny sort if I were not moved by your sincerity on the stand, and by your views. I agree with you completely, as a person. We can never accomplish, or give a better life to people, if we are going to keep on giving so much money to war. It is very unfortunate but the issue of war cannot be presented as clearly as you would like. The basic principle of the law is that we do things in an orderly fashion. People cannot take the law into their own hands.

On October 10, 1968, after less than two hours of deliberation, the jury returned a verdict of guilty against the nine defendants. Philip Berrigan and another defendant were sentenced to 3½ years in prison, Daniel Berrigan and two other defendants were sentenced to three years in prison, and the remaining four defendants received two-year sentences.

The Berrigans' lawyers appealed the convictions to the United States Court of Appeals for the Fourth Circuit, whose jurisdiction includes Maryland. On June 10, 1969, both sides made their case to the court of appeals, which issued its decision on October 15, 1969. One of the most interesting issues that the court had to consider was the defense's argument that the jury should have been free to acquit the defendants if they chose to do so regardless of the defendants' obvious guilt:

> Concededly, this power of the jury is not always contrary to the interests of justice. For example, freedom of the press was immeasurably strengthened by the jury's acquittal of John Peter Zenger of seditious libel, a violation of which, under the law as it then existed and the facts, he was clearly guilty. In that case Andrew Hamilton was allowed to urge the jury, in the face of the judge's charge, to see with their own eyes, to hear with their own ears, and to make use of their consciences and understanding in judging of the lives, liberties, or estates of their fellow subjects.

However, the court affirmed the Berrigans' convictions, noting that the jury's freedom to do as it pleased had been greatly curtailed in modern times. No matter how noble the Berrigans' cause, the law could not sanction their criminal acts, because the alternative was to permit every group with a particular political viewpoint to do as it pleased:

> If these defendants are to be absolved from guilt because of their moral certainty that the war in Vietnam is wrong, would not others who might commit breaches of the law to demonstrate their sincere belief that the country is not prosecuting the war vigorously enough be entitled to acquittal?

The Berrigans and the rest of the Catonsville Nine went to prison. Their defense, which rested on their moral opposition to the Vietnam War, was not recognized by the courts as a legal defense to criminal conduct. In essence, Judge Thomsen and the judges of the Fourth Circuit had held that there was no place in the law for the belief that "extremism in the defense of liberty is no vice."

1968

U.S. v. Berrigan

—*Stephen G. Christianson*

Suggestions for Further Reading

Berrigan, Daniel. *No Bars to Manhood*. Garden City, N.Y.: Doubleday & Co., 1970.

Casey, William Van Etten. *The Berrigans*. New York: Avon, 1971.

Curtis, Richard. *The Berrigan Brothers: the Story of Daniel and Philip Berrigan*. New York: Hawthorn Books, 1974.

Halpert, Stephen. *Witness of the Berrigans*. Garden City, N.Y.: Doubleday & Co., 1972.

Lockwood, Lee. *Daniel Berrigan: Absurd Convictions, Modest Hopes*. New York: Random House, 1972.

Sirhan Bishara Sirhan Trial: 1969

Defendant: Sirhan Bishara Sirhan   **Crime Charged:** Murder
Chief Defense Lawyers: Grant Cooper, Russell Parsons, Emile Berman, and
Michael A. McCowan   **Chief Prosecutors:** Lynn D. Compton, John Howard,
and David Fitts   **Judge:** Herbert V. Walker   **Place:** Los Angeles, California
Dates of Trial: January 13–April 23, 1969   **Verdict:** Guilty
Sentence: Death, later commuted to life imprisonment

SIGNIFICANCE

The stature and prominence of Robert Kennedy guaranteed that the trial of his
killer, Sirhan Bishara Sirhan, would be of historic importance. And yet, had it been
left to the prosecution and defense attorneys, there would have been no trial at all.
Their negotiated plea bargain failed because a judge decided that full disclosure
mattered more than legal expediency.

Flushed with triumph, Senator Robert Kennedy stepped down from the po-
dium at the Ambassador Hotel in Los Angeles on June 5, 1968, having just
claimed victory in the California primary election. He was seemingly destined
for the White House in November. As he moved through the crowded hotel
kitchen, on his way to meet reporters in another room, a young man emerged
from the throng and began firing an eight-shot Iver-Johnson .22-caliber pistol.
Three bullets struck Kennedy, one in the head. The gunman continued shooting, injuring five bystanders, until he was subdued and taken into custody. His
name was Sirhan Bishara Sirhan, a 24-year-old Jordanian incensed by Kennedy's
support of Israel. The next day the senator died from his wounds.

That Sirhan murdered Robert Kennedy was beyond dispute—a roomful
of witnesses saw him do it—but many doubted that the diminutive Arab would
ever stand trial. District Attorney Evelle Younger, armed with a psychiatric
evaluation of Sirhan that provided clear indications of mental disorder, readily
accepted the defense plea of guilty to first-degree murder in return for a promise
of life imprisonment. It was the kind of deal worked out daily in the county court
system, vital if the system is to avoid legal gridlock. But this was not an everyday
case.

Dominating all else was the specter of President John F. Kennedy's
assassination in 1963. The alleged killer, Lee Harvey Oswald, had himself been

gunned down before standing trial, leaving forever a labyrinth of doubt and suspicion. Determined to avoid such a recurrence, the judge appointed to try the Sirhan case, Herbert Walker, rejected the plea bargain in favor of trial by jury. This ruling left the defense with no alternative but to plead Sirhan not guilty and hope that they could prove his mental insufficiency.

A Murder Plan

The prosecution's opening statement, delivered by David Fitts on February 12, 1979, was packed with examples of Sirhan's devious and deliberate preparations for murder. Just two nights before the attack, he was seen at the Ambassador Hotel, apparently attempting to learn the building's layout, and he visited a gun range on June 4 to polish his already considerable skills with the pistol. However, the testimony of one prosecution eyewitness to the attack, author George Plimpton, backfired when he described Sirhan as looking, ". . . enormously composed. He seemed—purged," a statement which dovetailed neatly with the defense assertion that Sirhan had shot Kennedy while in some kind of trance. More on track was the testimony of Alvin Clark, Sirhan's garbage collector, who claimed that Sirhan had told him a month before the attack of his intention to shoot Kennedy.

Defense hopes of proving that this killing had been the spontaneous act of a deranged mind received a severe setback when Judge Walker admitted into testimony pages from three notebooks that Sirhan had kept. They revealed a mind seriously troubled, but quite calculating and willful. One entry written May 18, 1968, read: "My determination to eliminate R.F.K. is becoming the more and more [*sic*] of an unshakable obsession. . . . Robert F. Kennedy must be assassinated before June 5, 1968."

Sirhan's behavior throughout the trial, always bizarre, reached a self-destructive zenith during some unwelcome testimony about his childhood. He raged: "I . . . withdraw my original pleas of not guilty and submit the plea of guilty as charged on all counts. I also request that my counsel disassociate themselves from this case completely."

Sirhan Sirhan in custody the day after he shot Senator Robert F. Kennedy. Despite his admission of guilt, a lengthy trial followed. (AP/ Wide World Photos)

Bemused, Judge Walker asked, "What do you want to do about the penalty?"

"I will ask to be executed," Sirhan replied coolly, an announcement which prompted a cavalry charge of reporters for the exits. Judge Walker continued, "This court will not accept the plea. Proceed with the trial." When Sirhan's counsel then attempted to withdraw of their own volition, Walker denied this also. It was all very confusing. Ultimately, order was restored and Sirhan took the stand.

Defense lawyer Grant Cooper didn't mince any words. "Did you shoot Robert F. Kennedy?"

"Yes, sir."

"Did you bear any ill will towards Senator Kennedy?"

"No."

"Do you doubt you shot him?"

"No, sir, I don't."

Cooper then steered Sirhan into the reasons for his attack on Kennedy, a vicious diatribe about the Middle East conflict between Arab and Jew. So impassioned was Sirhan's anti-Zionist rhetoric that one of his own lawyers, Emile Berman, a Jew, felt compelled to offer his resignation from the defense team. Only soothing words from Cooper made him stay.

Cynical Performance

It took cross-examination by Chief Deputy District Attorney Lynn Compton to expose Sirhan for what he was: self-absorbed and arrogant, a master manipulator.

"Do you think that the killing of Senator Kennedy helped the Arab cause?" asked Compton.

"Sir, I'm not even aware that I killed Mr. Kennedy."

"Well, you know he's dead."

". . . I've been told that."

"Are you glad he's dead?"

"No, sir, I'm not glad."

As an exercise in cynicism it was hard to beat. Certainly the jury thought so. On April 17, 1969, they returned a guilty verdict.

During the penalty phase, Prosecutor John Howard demanded death for Sirhan: "In resolving the question of this defendant's guilt," he told the jury, "you have found him lacking in honesty, in integrity, and even in the courage of his own convictions. You could not have failed to see the smirk . . . when he declared 'I don't know who killed Senator Kennedy.'" Howard ended strongly: "Have the courage to write an end to this trial and to apply the only proper penalty for political assassination in the United States of America."

In pleading for his client's life, Grant Cooper quoted from several of Robert Kennedy's own speeches on compassion, but all to no avail. After 12 hours of deliberation the jury decided that Sirhan would die in the gas chamber.

As it transpired, all of the argument was academic. The U.S. Supreme Court's rulings on capital punishment in other cases resulted in Sirhan's sentence being commuted to life imprisonment. He remains in prison, where he regularly applies for parole and is just as regularly denied.

Interestingly, while Sirhan was being tried, in Memphis, Tennessee, another admitted assassin, James Earl Ray, pleaded guilty to the murder of Martin Luther King, Jr., and was quietly dispatched without trial to prison for 99 years.

—Colin Evans

Suggestions for Further Reading

Christian, John and William Turner. *The Assassination Of Robert Kennedy.* New York: Random House, 1978.

Goode, Stephen. *Assassination! Kennedy, King, Kennedy.* New York: Watts, 1979.

Jansen, Godfrey. *Why Robert Kennedy Was Killed.* New York: Third Press, 1970.

Kaiser, Robert Blair. *R.F.K. Must Die!* New York: Dutton & Co., 1970.

Scheim, David E. *Contract On America.* Silver Spring, MD: Argyle Press, 1983.

Clay Shaw Trial: 1969

Defendant: Clay L. Shaw   **Crime Charged:** Conspiracy to assassinate John F. Kennedy   **Chief Defense Lawyers:** Irvin Dymond, Salvatore Panzeca, Edward F. Wegmann, and William J. Wegmann   **Chief Prosecutors:** James Alcock, William Alford, Jim Garrison, Alvin Oser, and Andrew Sciambra   **Judge:** Edward A. Haggerty   **Place:** New Orleans, Louisiana   **Dates of Trial:** January 31–March 1, 1969   **Verdict:** Not guilty

SIGNIFICANCE

The assassination of President John F. Kennedy has become the most analyzed and dissected murder in history. And yet from all the millions of words and countless feet of celluloid speculation—most recently the film *JFK*—just this one trial emerged.

By late 1966, public confidence in the Warren Commission's report on the assassination of President John F. Kennedy was undergoing a serious crisis. With each new inconsistency, both real and imagined, suspicion grew that, far from being the work of a lone gunman, the killing in Dealey Plaza had been a well-engineered conspiracy. The most vocal proponent of this view was Jim Garrison, the charismatic district attorney in New Orleans, Louisiana. In March 1967, Garrison stunned the world when he announced the arrest of local businessman Clay L. Shaw on charges of conspiring to assassinate the President of the United States.

Almost two years later, on January 31, 1969, Garrison finally got to make these charges in a courtroom. Before Judge Edward A. Haggerty, he fleshed out the bare bones of his theory in a 42-minute address that dealt with alleged presidential assassin Lee Harvey Oswald and the time he spent in Louisiana prior to the Dallas tragedy. According to Garrison, Oswald and the late David Ferrie, an eccentric ex-pilot, had met with a shadowy figure named Clay Bertrand. Between them, these three men plotted Kennedy's assassination. It was Garrison's contention that Clay Bertrand was really the defendant Clay Shaw, who, Garrison noted, had flown to the West Coast on November 15, 1963, where he remained until after the shooting, thereby establishing an alibi for himself. Following the assassination, said Garrison, FBI agents undertook a "systematic and thorough search for Clay Bertrand" in New Orleans but were unsuccessful. Garrison would produce conclusive evidence, he said, that the person they should have been looking for was Clay Shaw.

Garrison: Hands Over the Reins

Oddly enough, after making the opening address, Garrison took virtually no further part in the trial. The task of presenting the state's case was left in the hands of his deputy, James Alcock. Although several witnesses confirmed Oswald's presence in Louisiana—a fact never in dispute—not until the testimony of Vernon Bundy, 30, was a connection between Shaw and Oswald established. Bundy, a heroin addict, told of a trip he had taken to Lake Pontchartrain in June 1963. "I was beginning to use my drugs . . . [when] behind me I noticed a black limousine approaching. A gentleman got out of the car and walked behind me." Concerned that the newcomer might be a narcotics agent, Bundy remained watchful. "I saw a man with a towel approaching from the white section of the beach." Alcock asked Bundy if he saw either one of these men in the courtroom. "I can see one," he replied and pointed to Shaw. When shown a photograph of Oswald, Bundy identified him as the man with the towel.

Next to testify was Charles Spiesel, a New York accountant. He spoke of attending a party in New Orleans in May 1963 at which both Ferrie and Shaw were present. When conversation turned to President Kennedy, Spiesel said that Shaw had laughed when somebody remarked, "Someone should kill that son of a bitch!" Talk of "a high-powered rifle" prompted Shaw to suggest that the gunman could escape in a plane flown by Ferrie.

Taken at face value, Spiesel's testimony was devastating, until chief defense lawyer Irvin Dymond began questioning him. After raising doubts about whether Spiesel had ever actually seen Ferrie (a man of remarkably memorable appearance, with glued-on orange hair and huge, painted eyebrows), Dymond asked: "Isn't it true you filed a suit with New York in 1964 . . . claiming that over a period of several years the police and others had constantly hypnotized you and finally harassed you out of business?"

"That's right," Spiesel said, adding proudly that the suit was for $16 million. When asked how many different people had hypnotized him, Spiesel had to think for a moment: "It's hard to say. Possibly fifty or sixty."

With his next question Dymond drove a stake through the heart of the prosecution. "When you conferred with the District Attorney's office about testifying in this case, did you tell them about these lawsuits and having been under hypnosis?"

Spiesel grinned: "Yes, I mentioned it."

Focus Shifts to Zapruder Film

Without exception, every prosecution witness failed the litmus test of cross-examination. Memories grew vague, identifications less sure. Not until the prosecutors came to the main thrust of their case—a full frontal attack on the

Warren report's single-gunman theory—did they catch fire. In grim silence the jury watched Abraham Zapruder's film of the Dallas tragedy. Then the prosecution, supported by various ballistics experts, pursued its efforts to prove a triangulation of gunfire. During all of this, Clay Shaw became a forgotten man. And he remained that way until it came time for him to testify.

Those awaiting the much-anticipated duel between Garrison and Shaw suffered a grave disappointment. Again the district attorney was noticeably absent. James Alcock handled the cross-examination, though anything less confrontational was hard to imagine. Apart from admitting that he had seen Oswald once in New Orleans while Oswald was distributing political leaflets, Shaw denied all other contact with him. He also denied virtually everything that the prosecution witnesses had said about him. Alcock handled Shaw with kid gloves, declining to even quiz him on whether he had participated in a deadly conspiracy. About the best that Alcock could manage was in the following exchange:

> "Do you recall a press conference after your arrest where you called Lee Harvey Oswald 'Harvey Lee Oswald'?"
>
> "I recall the conference."
>
> "Was there any particular reason why you would call Oswald 'Harvey Lee'?"
>
> "No, it was purely a mistake."

With everyone poised for the *coup de grâce* that they were sure the prosecution had in store, Alcock stunned court-watchers by abruptly turning to Judge Haggerty after just 65 minutes and saying, "No further questions."

Jim Garrison reappeared to make the state's closing argument. Again it degenerated into an attack on the Warren Commission, full of complaints that the American public had been lied to, duped, kept in the dark. Once, just once, he mentioned the defendant Clay Shaw almost as an afterthought, and then in his final admonition to the jury, Garrison evoked the dead president's memory: "Ask not what your country can do for you, but what you can do for your country."

At six minutes past midnight on March 1, 1969, the jury retired. An hour later they were back. When the verdict of "Not Guilty" was read out, a huge roar of approval swept the courtroom.

Establishing his innocence cost Clay Shaw all of his money and most of his reputation. Many believe the ordeal hastened his death from cancer in August 1974. In all probability, he will remain the only person ever charged with complicity in the death of John F. Kennedy. But that won't stop the discussion, and it won't stop the "conspiracists," as they theorize about what really happened on that afternoon in Dallas.

—Colin Evans

Suggestions for Further Reading

Bethell, T. "Conspiracy to End Conspiracies." *National Review*. (December 16, 1991): 48ff.

Garrison, Jim. *On the Trail of the Assassins*. New York: Sheridan Press, 1988.

Gates, D. and H. Manly. "Bottom Line: How Crazy Is It?" *Newsweek* (December 23, 1991): 52ff.

Kirkwood, James. *American Grotesque*. New York: Simon & Schuster, 1970.

Chicago Seven Trial: 1969

Defendants: Rennard C. Davis, David Dellinger, John R. Froines, Thomas H. Hayden, Abbott Hoffman, Jerry C. Rubin, Bobby G. Seale and Lee Weiner
Crimes Charged: Incitement to riot and conspiracy
Chief Defense Lawyers: William Kunstler and Leonard Weinglass
Chief Prosecutors: Roger Cubbage, Thomas A. Foran, and Richard G. Shultz
Judge: Julius J. Hoffman   **Place:** Chicago, Illinois
Dates of Trial: September 24, 1969–February 20, 1970   **Verdict:** Dellinger, Davis, Hayden, Hoffman, Rubin: Guilty; Froines and Weiner: Not guilty; Seale: Mistrial   **Sentence:** 5 years imprisonment, $5,000 fine

SIGNIFICANCE

This was possibly the most divisive—certainly the most chaotic—political trial in American history.

The 1968 Democratic National Convention marked a watershed in American social unrest, as anti-Vietnam War protesters of every political hue descended on Chicago, Illinois, determined to undermine the convention and provoke a confrontation with authorities. They succeeded beyond their wildest expectations. Pitched battles in the streets led to grand jury indictments against eight conspicuously left-wing radicals: Rennie Davis, David Dellinger, John Froines, Tom Hayden, Abbie Hoffman, Jerry Rubin, Bobby Seale, and Lee Weiner. Each was charged with having crossed state lines to incite a riot, an offense that had been on the statute book less than nine months. Collusion between the accused was clearly not an issue—Seale did not even meet his co-defendants until the trial. More important was the government's resolve to quash antiwar protest with what amounted to an attack on the entire spectrum of political dissent.

Rarely does a member of the bench achieve or desire the celebrity that this trial afforded to Judge Julius Hoffman, who right from day one, September 24, 1969, displayed a pugnacious combativeness that was both ill-considered and wholly unjudicial. Seventy-three years old, humorless, and with a reputation for rulings sympathetic to the government, Hoffman's hostility toward the defendants was all too apparent.

On opening day, when U.S. Attorney Thomas Foran angrily objected because four lawyers listed for the defense were not present in court—all had withdrawn from the case by telegram—Hoffman immediately issued warrants for the arrest of the offending attorneys, then poured oil on troubled waters by temporarily jailing two of them for contempt of court. Such a firestorm of protest from the legal community greeted this action that Hoffman was obliged to rescind the order and allow the lawyers to withdraw.

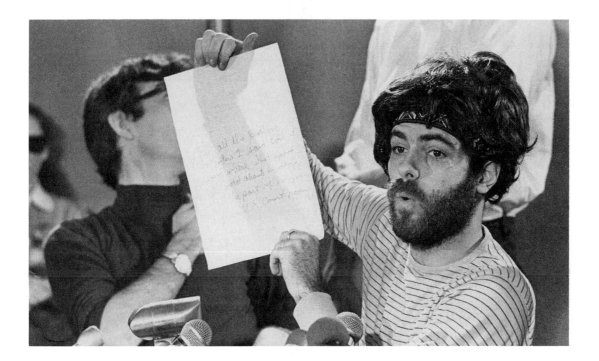

Jerry Rubin holds up a note from fellow defendant Bobby Seale who had been gagged during the previous day's trial session. (AP/Wide World Photos)

Defense attorney duties were shared by William Kunstler and Leonard Weinglass. Neither had an easy task. Besides battling the bench, they had Bobby Seale to contend with. Seale, a militant black activist, refused to accept either one as his attorney and on September 26 submitted a handwritten note to the court: "I submit to Judge Julius Hoffman that the trial be postponed until a later date when I, Bobby G. Seale, can have the 'legal council [*sic*] of choice who is effective,' Attorney Charles R. Garry, and if my constitutional rights are not respected by this court then other lawyers on record here . . . do not speak for me . . . I fire them now." Judge Hoffman, taking exception to being characterized in the note as "a blatant racist," angrily denied the motion.

Seale Bound and Gagged

Seale wouldn't be stifled. He continued to disrupt the proceedings, yelling such epithets as "pig" and "fascist" at Hoffman, likening him to a plantation slave owner. Finally, on October 29, Hoffman's thin reserve of patience ran out and he ordered Seale gagged and bound to a chair. As Seale struggled to free himself, court attendants roughly manhandled him, an action that brought Kunstler to his feet in loud protest: "Your Honor, are we going to stop this medieval torture that is going on in this courtroom? I think this is a disgrace."

With the situation fast getting out of hand, Judge Hoffman declared a mistrial as to Seale, thus severing his case from the other seven defendants. Simultaneously he found Seale guilty of 16 counts of contempt and jailed him for four years.

Virtually overshadowed by this extracurricular mayhem was the fact that the prosecution had amassed a formidable case against the remaining accused. Its main witnesses were police officers, each of whom testified to examples of incendiary behavior on the part of the accused.

Robert Murray, an undercover police sergeant, described being in Lincoln Park, scene of one particularly violent clash between police and demonstrators, and seeing defendant Jerry Rubin in conversation with a television newsman. When the reporter had intimated that he was about to leave, Murray claimed that Rubin had called him back, saying, "Wait, don't go right now. We're going out in the ball field. We want to see what these pigs [police officers] are going to do about it."

Prosecutor Foran asked, "How many police officers were standing there?"

"Ten policemen," said Murray, "and one sergeant."

Murray had carefully monitored Rubin's behavior throughout the night.

I saw him walking through the park, walking up to small groups, having a conversation with them and leaving . . . I heard him say that 'we have to fight the pigs in the park tonight. . . . we're not going to let them take the park.'

Crucial evidence of intent to riot came with the testimony of newspaper reporter Dwayne Oklepek, who spoke of attending a meeting August 9, 1968, at which defendants Hayden, Davis, and Froines were present. Oklepek told how Davis produced a street map of Chicago and plans for a march on August 28, 1968: "Mr. Davis felt that the separate groups should form up and then attempt to move their way south to the Loop area. . . . He went on to say that he thought these groups should try to disrupt traffic, should smash windows, run through stores and through the streets."

"Do you recall anything else that was discussed?" asked Foran.

"Someone asked Mr. Davis what would occur if it were impossible for the demonstrators to get out of Lincoln Park . . . and Mr. Davis said, 'That's easy, we just riot.' "

In this fashion the prosecution was able to mount a strong case of incitement to riot, at least against some of the defendants, but whether that incitement fell within the provisions of the recent law, with its proviso that a state line had to be traversed, remained in doubt.

Star-Studded Witnesses Appear

To combat allegations of malicious intent, defense attorney William Kunstler had assembled a prodigious list of eminent character witnesses. The roll call included Norman Mailer, Reverend Jesse Jackson, Allen Ginsburg, William Styron, Arlo Guthrie, Country Joe McDonald, Judy Collins, Phil Ochs, Mark Lane, Timothy Leary, even a British Member of Parliament, Anne Kerr.

Apart from their eloquence and name value, there was little that these witnesses could offer the court in the way of direct evidence. Neither did the defendants help themselves. All seemed more interested in advancing their political agenda. Abbie Hoffman's opening remarks set the tone. Asked to identify himself for the record, he said, "My name is Abbie. I am an orphan of America. . . . I live in Woodstock Nation." When defense counsel Leonard Weinglass requested clarification, Hoffman eagerly seized his opportunity. "It is a nation of alienated young people. We carry it around with us as a state of mind." Weinglass concluded his direct examination with a simple question:

> "Prior to coming to Chicago, from April 1968 on to the week of the Convention, did you enter into an agreement with [the other defendants] to come to the city of Chicago for the purpose of encouraging and promoting violence during the Convention week?"

> "An agreement?"

> "Yes."

> "We couldn't agree on lunch!"

Cross-examination by prosecutor Richard Schultz was less conciliatory but equally frivolous, as Hoffman and his fellow defendants refused to recognize the court's legitimacy. Their crude, often childish antics exacted a heavy toll from Judge Hoffman, whose exasperation found ventilation in a litany of unfortunate remarks directed toward the defendants and their counsel.

After months of confusion and much rambling testimony, closing arguments began on February 10, 1970. The final word was left with prosecutor Thomas Foran. Describing the defendants, he said, "They are not kids. Davis, the youngest one, took the witness stand. He is twenty-nine. These are highly sophisticated, educated men and they are evil men." Uproarious laughter greeted this remark. In trying to paint a picture of latent villainy, Foran succeeded only in generating humor.

All things considered, Judge Hoffman's final charge to the jurors was remarkably subdued, and on February 14 they retired to consider their verdict.

Guilty Verdicts Multiply

Judge Hoffman used the hiatus to deal with the numerous contempt of court citations that had accrued throughout the trial. He found all seven defendants and their attorneys guilty of no less than 159 counts. Sentences varied from 2 ½ months for Weiner, to four years for Kunstler.

Speculation that the jury would be unable to reach a decision proved unfounded. On February 18, 1970, they adjudged Davis, Dellinger, Hayden, Hoffman, and Rubin guilty, while acquitting Froines and Weiner. Two days later Judge Hoffman passed sentence. Each defendant received the maximum penalty of five years in prison and a $5,000 fine.

A long round of appellate action ensued. It began with the contempt verdicts. On May 11, 1972, the Seventh Circuit Court of Appeals reversed all of these convictions on grounds that, because Judge Hoffman had been targeted by the attack, due process dictated that he should not sit in judgment on the contempt charges.

In November 1972 the appellate court overturned all five incitement to riot convictions, citing numerous errors by Judge Hoffman and the prosecution attorneys. In particular, they denounced Judge Hoffman's "deprecatory and often antagonistic attitude toward the defense." Seale, too, had his conviction overturned.

The government elected not to retry the incitement case, but did proceed on the contempt charges, with the result that in November 1973, Dellinger, Kunstler, Hoffman, and Rubin were again convicted. However, Judge Edward Gignoux signaled an end to the whole unsavory affair by deciding that the imposition of further jail sentences was unwarranted.

By any reckoning the Chicago Conspiracy trial has to be considered a low-water mark in American jurisprudence. Nobody emerged from the conflict untarnished. Ironically, the only victor was the legal system itself. Mocked and derided by the defendants, it bent and on occasion threatened to break, but ultimately it came to the assistance of those who decried it most.

—Colin Evans

Suggestions for Further Reading

Belknap, Michael P. *American Political Trials.* Westport, Conn.: Greenwood Press, 1981.

Clavir, Judy and John Spitzer. *The Conspiracy Trial.* Indianapolis: Bobbs-Merrill Co., 1970.

Epstein, Jason. *The Great Conspiracy Trial.* New York: Random House, 1970.

Goldberg, Stephanie Benson. "Lessons of the 60's." *ABA Journal.* (May 15, 1987): 32ff.

Shultz, John. *Motion Will Be Denied.* New York: William Morrow & Co., 1972.

Charles Manson Trial: 1970–71

Defendants: Charles Manson, Susan Atkins, Patricia Krenwinkel, Leslie Van Houten **Crimes Charged:** First-degree murder and conspiracy to commit murder **Chief Defense Lawyers:** Irving Kanarek (for Manson), Daye Shinn (for Atkins), Paul Fitzgerald (for Krenwinkel), Maxwell Keith, Ronald Hughes, and Ira Reiner (for Van Houten) **Chief Prosecutor:** Vincent Bugliosi and Aaron Stovitz **Judge:** Charles H. Older **Place:** Los Angeles, California **Dates of Trial:** June 15, 1970–March 29, 1971 **Verdict:** Guilty **Sentence:** Death, later transmuted to life imprisonment

SIGNIFICANCE

The killings for which Charles Manson and his followers were convicted made him one of the century's most infamous murderers. The prosecution's case provided an example of how the U.S. Supreme Court's *Aranda* ruling is applied in cases involving multiple defendants. The trial was one of the longest and costliest in California history.

On August 9, 1969, police in Los Angeles, California, responded to a hysterical call from actress Sharon Tate's housekeeper. When officers arrived at the house rented by Tate and her husband, film director Roman Polanski, they found the corpses of the pregnant actress and three house guests: Jay Sebring, Abigail Folger, and Voyteck Frykowski. All had been stabbed repeatedly. Steven Parent, a friend of the groundskeeper, was found shot to death outside in his car. A day later in another part of the city, Leno and Rosemary LaBianca were found violently stabbed to death in their suburban home. All seven deaths were eventually linked to a scheme whose savagery was surpassed only by the peculiarity of its motive.

The first tips came from motorcycle gang members, who told police about a commune of young people called the "Family" living in the desolate California hills. The commune was led by an ex-convict named Charles Manson, who had bragged of committing murders that resembled the Tate killings. Two prison inmates similarly told authorities that their cellmate Susan Atkins had described to them in horrifying detail how she and fellow members of the "Family" had killed Tate and her guests, the LaBiancas, and others.

In return for a promise of immunity, Atkins repeated her story to a grand jury in December 1969, implicating Manson and others in the Tate-LaBianca killings. Ironically, Manson was already in jail. He had been arrested in October and charged with receiving stolen property. "Family" members Patricia Krenwinkel and Leslie Van Houten were indicted on murder charges and arrested. Charles "Tex" Watson, whose bloody fingerprint was found at the Tate house, was arrested at his parents' home in Texas. Watson's attorney forestalled his extradition for nine months, arguing that pretrial publicity made it impossible for Watson to get a fair trial in California. The Los Angeles district attorney decided to prosecute the others charged in the Tate-LaBianca slayings without waiting for Watson's arrival.

Atkins Reverses Course

Prosecutors lost Atkins' cooperation in March 1970, three months before the case came to trial. After a short meeting with Manson in jail, she retracted her confession and declared that she had invented the story implicating him, Krenwinkel, and Van Houten before the grand jury.

Although the four "Family" members were to be tried together, the prosecution was required to abide by the rules of the U.S. Supreme Court's 1965 *Aranda* decision. Statements made by one defendant, such as the stories Atkins told her cellmates about the "Family's" bloody deeds, could not be introduced as evidence against her co-defendants. The prosecution's task was further complicated by the fact that Manson had not been present at the Tate house the night of the slayings. Deputy District Attorneys Aaron Stovitz and Vincent Bugliosi had to try to convict Manson on the seven murder counts based on the theory that the cult leader had ordered the killings.

Manson on his way to court for his trial for the murder of Sharon Tate and six others. (AP/Wide World Photos)

Manson's request to be allowed to represent himself was denied. At first angered by this refusal, Manson then accepted Irving Kanarek as his attorney. Kanarek had a reputation in legal circles as an "obstructionist," accused of lengthening trials with pointless or improper courtroom tactics. The prosecution formally protested Kanarek's involvement with prophetic warnings that the complicated trial might last much longer than necessary if he were allowed to participate. Kanarek nevertheless became Manson's attorney. By the end of the trial, even Manson grew annoyed with Kanarek's behavior, which earned the verbose attorney numerous contempt citations.

Worldwide publicity about the case made finding an unbiased jury unusually difficult. When Judge Charles H. Older read a press account of a conference in his chambers, the infuriated judge moved to limit public speculation, about the case. He imposed a "gag order" barring the lawyers and witnesses from speaking to the press about matters not entered as evidence. Stenographers and other court officials were forbidden from giving or selling transcripts of the case to the press.

When testimony began July 24, 1970, Manson arrived in court with an "X" scratched on his forehead. He considered the trial a "game" in which he was being judged by a society unworthy and incapable of understanding him. In protest, he had symbolically "X'd" himself from the world. Atkins, Krenwinkel, and Van Houten followed Manson's example by burning an X into each of their foreheads.

The most damning prosecution witness was Linda Kasabian, a former "Family" member who was granted immunity in return for her testimony. Over protests by the defense, who held that Kasabian's use of LSD and other drugs had made her incapable of distinguishing fact from fantasy, she described sex orgies, drug use, and Manson's domination of all facets of "Family" life. Like other "Manson girls," Kasabian had once believed that Manson was Jesus Christ.

A "Helter Skelter" Scheme

Kasabian explained Manson's bizarre scenario for "Helter Skelter," a scheme to capitalize on a race war between black and white Americans, which he believed was imminent. Manson expected blacks to win, find themselves incapable of governing, and ultimately turn to him for leadership. The Tate and LaBianca murders were committed to provoke the Helter Skelter holocaust.

"Now is the time for Helter Skelter," Kasabian recalled Manson announcing on August 8, 1969. That night he told her to go with Atkins, Krenwinkel, and Watson. The foursome drove to the Tate house, where Watson cut the phone lines and ordered the others to climb over the fence. Watson stopped Parent's car and shot him before ordering Kasabian back to the "Family" car to guard it. As she waited in shock, Kasabian heard screams coming from the house. She ran toward the cries and found Watson stabbing Frykowski on the lawn. When she saw Krenwinkel chasing Folger with a knife, she fled back to the car in horror.

Out of fear for herself and her child, Kasabian drove to the LaBianca home with Manson and other "Family" members the following night. Manson parked and disappeared with Watson. When Manson returned, he said that he had tied up two people in the nearby house. "Don't let them know that you are going to kill them," Kasabian thought she heard him say before he got back into the car and drove away, leaving Watson, Krenwinkel, and Van Houten behind. Kasabian escaped from the "Family" soon thereafter.

Case Draws Presidential Remark

Kanarek's interruptions of Kasabian's testimony were so incessant that Judge Older sentenced him to a night in jail for contempt. Kasabian was about to be cross-examined when the trial was shaken by comment from an unexpected source. President Richard M. Nixon told reporters in Denver, Colorado, Manson was "guilty, directly or indirectly of eight murders." Nixon's remarks were meant to criticize what he perceived as a tendency of the media to glorify criminals, and the White House quickly issued a statement denying any intent to prejudice the case. Nevertheless, Manson's defense, arguing that such a statement by the president made a fair trial impossible, motioned for a mistrial and demanded that the charges against him be dropped. Judge Older denied the motion.

The next day in court, Manson stood and displayed a newspaper with the headline, "Manson Guilty, Nixon Declares." Judge Older questioned the jurors about their reaction to the headline. Satisfied that they would remain impartial, he ordered the trial to resume and sentenced Atkins' attorney, Daye Shinn, to three nights in jail for leaving the newspaper within Manson's reach.

Former "Family" members and visitors to the Manson commune at the isolated Spahn Movie Ranch testified for the prosecution. Danny De Carlo, one of the motorcycle gang members who furnished police with tips, said that Manson had frequently spoken to him of starting a race war. Once again, Judge Older ordered Kanarek jailed for contempt because of his frequent interruptions.

Former "Family" member Barbara Hoyt testified that she had overheard Atkins describing the murders. Juan Flynn, a Spahn Ranch worker, told the court that Manson had tried to frighten him by holding a knife to his throat and saying, "You son of a bitch, don't you know I'm the one who's doing all of these killings?"

On October 5, Manson demanded to be allowed to cross-examine a detective who had just testified. When Judge Older refused, Manson began to argue. Manson leaped toward the judge with a pencil clutched in his hand, screaming, "In the name of Christian justice, someone should cut your head off!" Atkins, Krenwinkel, and Van Houten chanted as bailiffs struggled to subdue Manson. When the trial resumed, the prosecution called Atkins' former cellmates, who described her bloody account of the Tate murders. Under the *Aranda* rule, their testimony was limited to Atkins' participation in the killings.

After nearly four months of testimony by prosecution witnesses, the state rested. Attorney Paul Fitzgerald stunned the court by resting the collective defense without calling a single witness. The three "Manson girls" suddenly announced that they wanted to testify on their own behalf, apparently to free Manson by taking sole responsibility for the murders. Fearing their clients would incriminate themselves, the defense attorneys threatened to quit if the judge allowed the testimony. Judge Older accused the defense of trying to wreck the trial.

Manson Speaks

The impasse was broken when Manson was allowed to speak without the jury present. He gave an angry hour-long statement proclaiming his innocence and condemning society for persecuting him. When he was finished, he told "the girls" not to testify.

As both sides prepared their summations during a Thanksgiving recess, Leslie Van Houten's attorney, Ronald Hughes, disappeared while camping (he was later found dead). The trial was postponed for two weeks to allow Van Houten's new attorney time to study the case. When the trial resumed with final arguments, the prosecution reviewed the abundant testimony about Manson's control over his followers and his messianic "lust for death."

The defense declared that the state had produced no evidence against Manson. Kanarek claimed that Manson was being prosecuted for having a counterculture lifestyle and attacked Kasabian and Watson as the real instigators and murderers. As Kanarek's argument began to consume entire days, Judge Older warned him against using "filibuster" tactics. Kanarek's summation lasted seven days. Van Houten's new attorney, Maxwell Keith, argued more succinctly that the three women should not be convicted if the state's portrayal of them as Manson's "mindless robots" was accurate.

Jury Convicts All Defendants

Manson and his co-defendants were found guilty on January 25, 1971. Under California law, a second trial or "penalty phase" before the same jury then began to determine sentencing. Atkins took the stand and accused Kasabian, not Manson, of ordering the murders. Van Houten and Krenwinkel admitted taking part in the slayings but denied Manson's involvement. After two months of tumultuous testimony, the jury agreed with the prosecution's argument for the death penalty on March 29, 1971.

When the first sentence was pronounced on Manson, he began shouting that he had not been allowed to defend himself. "Better lock your doors and watch your own kids," warned Atkins. "Your whole system is a game," Van

Houten exclaimed. The judge ordered all the defendants removed from the courtroom so that the judgments could be read without disruption.

Manson and the others were sentenced to die in the gas chamber. When Tex Watson was tried separately, he also was found guilty and sentenced to death. Yet no Manson case defendants were executed. Their sentences were transmuted to life imprisonment when the state of California abolished its death penalty on February 18, 1972. The U.S. Supreme Court ruled the death penalty unconstitutional under most circumstances later that year.

Long after the Manson case was over, it continued to create legal problems for William Farr, a Los Angeles newspaper reporter. Early in the trial, Farr wrote a story revealing Atkins' tales to her cellmates of "Family" plans to murder celebrities like Frank Sinatra and Elizabeth Taylor. Judge Older summoned Farr to his chambers and demanded to know who had released the confidential information. Farr refused to answer, citing a state law protecting journalists from being forced to reveal their sources.

After the trial, however, the judge learned that Farr was between jobs as a reporter and ordered him back into court to reveal his source or face a contempt charge. Farr said that two of the attorneys had provided the information, but declined to name them. All of the attorneys involved in the case swore under oath that they had not violated the "gag order." The judge ordered Farr to jail to serve an indefinite sentence for contempt. He was confined for 46 days before he was released to appeal the sentence.

The widely debated case was not resolved until 1976, when an appeals court threw out Judge Older's contempt sentence, ending Farr's numerous trips to court and massive legal bills. California laws were amended to protect former reporters as well as currently working journalists.

Leslie Van Houten was granted a new trial on grounds that Ronald Hughes' disappearance had denied her effective representation, but she was convicted again in 1978. Manson continued to charge that President Nixon's statement had tainted the fairness of his trial. Manson also cited a 1975 U.S. Supreme Court decision giving defendants the right to act as their own counsel, but the high court refused to hear Manson's appeal in 1977. In 1985 he was transferred from a state psychiatric prison to the San Quentin penitentiary, where he continues to apply unsuccessfully for parole.

— Thomas C. Smith

Suggestions for Further Reading

Bishop, George. *Witness To Evil.* Los Angeles: Nash Publishing, 1971.

Bugliosi, Vincent with Curt Gentry. *Helter Skelter: The True Story of the Manson Murders.* New York. W.W. Norton & Co., 1974.

Caldwell, Earl. "Manson Co-Defendants Allowed to Testify After Defense Rests." *New York Times* (November 20, 1970): 22.

Watson, Tex. *Will You Die For Me?* Old Tappan, N.J.: Fleming H. Revell Co., 1978.

Wright, Robert A. "Coast Reporter Ordered to Jail For Refusing to Disclose Source." *New York Times* (November 28, 1972): 36.

William Calley Court-Martial: 1970

Defendant: William L. Calley   **Crime Charged:** Murder
Chief Defense Lawyers: Brookes S. Doyle, Jr., Richard B. Kay, George W. Latimer, and Kenneth A. Raby   **Chief Prosecutors:** Aubrey Daniel and John Partin   **Judge:** Reid W. Kennedy   **Place:** Fort Benning, Georgia
Dates of Court-Martial: November 17, 1970–March 29, 1971
Verdict: Guilty   **Sentence:** Life imprisonment

SIGNIFICANCE

The trial of Lt. William Calley for war crimes is unique in American military history. It provides a unique insight into the horrors of combat and the reaction of ordinary people to extraordinary circumstances.

At first light on the morning of March 16, 1968, 105 soldiers of Charlie Company, a unit of the U.S. 11th Light Infantry Brigade, moved unopposed into the Vietnamese hamlet of My Lai. By midday almost 500 inhabitants had been massacred. All of the victims were unarmed civilians, women, babies, and elderly men. By chance, the scenes of carnage were recorded by an Army cameraman, and it was his pictures that revealed the horror of My Lai to the world. An Army inquiry into the incident resulted in charges of murder against several participants, but evidence suggested that the majority of blame for the tragedy could be laid at the door of a single platoon commander: Lieutenant William Calley.

When the court-martial began on November 17, 1970, Calley was charged with murdering 109 "Oriental human beings." It was the prosecution's contention that Calley, in defiance of U.S. Military Rules of Engagement, ordered his men to deliberately murder innocent civilians. In presenting his case, lead military prosecutor Aubrey Daniel was hamstrung by the reluctance of many soldiers to testify against Calley. Some refused point-blank, citing the Fifth Amendment privilege against self-incrimination. Perhaps the strangest of the holdouts was Paul Meadlo. It had been his televised interview, coupled with Ronald Haeberle's photographs, that had largely inflamed public opinion about My Lai. Yet only after having been ordered into custody by Judge Reid Kennedy, who scathingly derided "the nauseous detail" that Meadlo had provided for television, and being granted immunity from prosecution, would

Meadlo describe that day's tragic events. He told of standing guard over dozens of villagers when Lieutenant Calley arrived. "He said 'How come they're not dead?' I said, 'I didn't know we were supposed to kill them.' He said, 'I want them dead. He backed off twenty or thirty feet and started shooting into the people." Meadlo joined him.

"Were you crying?" asked Daniel.

"I imagine I was," replied Meadlo, confirming other testimony that had the enlisted man with tears in his eyes and a rifle in his hands. Between them, Calley and Meadlo mowed down a hundred villagers.

Barbarous Action Described

Piece by agonizing piece, Daniel painted an almost unimaginable picture of murder, rape, and wholesale devastation. He described how Calley tossed a baby into a ditch and shot it, before opening fire with an M-16, first killing a monk, then cutting a swathe through dozens of villagers cowering in an irrigation channel.

An eyewitness, Dennis Conti, described the bloodbath:

They were pretty much messed-up. There was a lot of heads had been shot off, pieces of head . . . fleshy parts of the body. . . . I seen the recoil of the rifle and the muzzle flashes and as I looked down, I seen a woman try to get up. As she got up I saw Lt. Calley fire and hit the side of her head and blow the side of her head off.

The madness was infectious. One man who had refused to participate in the slaughter, Leonard Gonzalez, told of seeing another soldier herd some women together and order them to strip. When they refused to have sex with him, the enraged soldier fired a single round from his grenade launcher into the group, killing everyone.

Originally it was the defense position that the devastation of My Lai had been caused by helicopters and aerial bombardment. Clearly the prosecution witnesses had proven that premise to be untrue. Calley's only recourse was to fall back on the defense of soldiers since time immemorial: that he was merely acting on orders.

Under the prompting of civilian attorney George Latimer, Calley told his side of the story. He outlined a briefing given one day before the operation by his commanding officer, Captain Ernest Medina, at which, he said, it was made plain that everyone in the village was to be shot. Twenty-one other members of Charlie Company present at the briefing corroborated Calley's story; others denied that any such order was given. Yet more testified that, while unstated, the intent of the order was plain.

Calley:

I was ordered to go in there and destroy the enemy. That was my job that day. That was the mission I was given. I did not sit down and think in terms of men, women, and children. They were all classified the same, and that was the classification that we dealt with, just as enemy. . . . I felt then and I still do that I acted as I was directed, and I carried out the orders that I was given and I do not feel wrong in doing so.

Some Refused Orders

But not everyone at My Lai that day blindly followed such outrageous orders. Robert Maples told of entering the village and seeing Calley and Meadlo firing into a ditch full of civilians. "[Calley] asked me to use my machine gun."

"What did you say?" Daniel inquired.

"I refused," was the reply.

Another soldier who listened to the dictates of his conscience was James Dursi.

"Did Lt. Calley order you to fire?" asked Daniel.

"Yes, sir."

"Why did you not fire?"

"Because I could not go through with it."

In his final address to the jury, Daniel said, "The defense would ask you to legalize murder," then he invoked the memory of Abraham Lincoln's order to Union troops during the Civil War: "Men who take up arms against one another in public do not cease on this account to be moral human beings, responsible to one another and to God."

On March 29, 1971, after almost 80 hours of deliberation, the six-officer jury—five of whom had served in Vietnam—found Calley guilty of the premeditated murder of 22 villagers at My Lai.

Next came the penalty phase; under military law, Calley faced possible execution by hanging. Latimer pleaded for the life of his client, saying Calley had been a "good boy until he got into that Oriental situation." Latimer reminded the jury of their isolation from the media during the long months of the court-martial. "You'll find there's been no case in the history of military justice that has torn this country apart as this one."

The defendant made an impassioned plea on his own behalf.

I'm not going to stand here and plead for my life or my freedom. I've never known a soldier, nor did I ever myself, wantonly kill a human being. . . . Yesterday, you stripped me of all my honor. Please, by your actions that you take here today, don't strip future soldiers of their honor—I beg of you.

Daniel was on his feet immediately, reminding the jury, "You did not strip him of his honor. What he did stripped him of his honor. It is not honor, and never can be considered honor, to kill men, women, and children."

The jury mandated that Calley should be sent to prison for life. Three days later he was freed from Fort Leavenworth by President Richard Nixon and returned to Fort Benning where he was held under house arrest pending appeal. On August 20, 1971, the sentence was reduced to 20 years. Calley remained at Fort Benning until February 27, 1974, when he was released on bail. On November 9, 1974, the Army announced that Lieutenant Calley had been paroled.

Following his release, Calley remained in Columbus, Georgia, and as of this writing was a successful jeweler, well-respected in the community.

Four people were tried for war crimes arising out of the My Lai Massacre. Apart from Calley, the most notable was his commanding officer, Captain Ernest Medina. In August 1971 he faced charges of murdering 175 Vietnamese civilians, only to be acquitted after a month-long trial. Calley remains the only man ever convicted for what happened on that morning in Vietnam.

Nothing in its history had prepared the United States for the appalling slaughter at My Lai, and yet the nation's initial revulsion became strangely muted during Calley 's protracted trial. Many came to view him as a scapegoat, even a hero, desperately waging the battle against Communism. Time and distance may have dulled the magnitude of his crimes, but not their historical importance.

—Colin Evans

Suggestions for Further Reading

Bilton, Michael and Kevin Sim. *Four Hours At My Lai*. New York: Viking Press, 1992.

Goldstein, Joseph, Burkr Marshall, and Jack Schwartz. *The My Lai Massacre And Its Cover-Up*. New York: Free Press, 1976.

Hammer, Richard. *The Court-Martial Of Lt. Calley*. New York: Coward, McCann & Geoghegan, 1971.

Unger, Craig and Bill Hewitt. *People Weekly* (November 20, 1989): 152–158.

John Hill Trial: 1971

Defendant: John Robert Hill   **Crime Charged:** Murder
Chief Defense Lawyers: Donald Fullenweider and Richard Haynes
Chief Prosecutors: Erwin Ernst and I. D. McMaster   **Judge:** Frederick
Hooey   **Place:** Houston, Texas   **Dates of Trial:** February 15–26, 1971
Verdict: Mistrial

SIGNIFICANCE
Sensational trials are not uncommon in Texas, but the extraordinary sequence of events that followed the death of Joan Hill made this a case without equal.

O n Tuesday, March 18, 1969, Joan Hill, a 38-year-old Houston, Texas, socialite, became violently ill for no readily apparent reason. Her husband, Dr. John Hill, at first indifferent, later drove her at a leisurely pace several miles to a hospital in which he had a financial interest, passing many other medical facilities on the way. When checked by admitting physicians, Joan's blood pressure was dangerously low, 60/40. Attempts to stabilize her failed and the next morning she died. The cause of death was uncertain. Some thought pancreatitis; others opted for hepatitis.

Joan's father, Ash Robinson, a crusty and extremely wealthy oilman, remained convinced that his daughter had been murdered. Neither was he reticent about naming the culprit: John Hill. When, just three months after Joan's death, Hill married long-time lover Ann Kurth, Robinson threw thousands of dollars into a crusade to persuade the authorities that his son-in-law was a killer. Noted pathologist Dr. Milton Helpern, hired to conduct a second autopsy, cautiously volunteered his opinion that Joan Hill *might* have been poisoned.

Under Robinson's relentless badgering, prosecutors scoured legal textbooks, searching for a way to indict Hill. They came up with the extremely rare charge of "murder by omission," in effect, killing someone by deliberate neglect. Assistance came in the unexpected form of Ann Kurth. Hill had ditched her after just nine months of marriage. What Kurth told the district attorney bolstered their decision to indict Hill.

Jury selection began on February 15, 1971. Because of the defendant's undeniably handsome appearance, Assistant District Attorney I.D. McMaster aimed for a predominantly male, middle-class panel, one he thought likely to frown on a wealthy philandering physician. His opponent, chief defense counsel Richard Haynes, quite naturally did his best to sit jurors that he thought would favor his client. In this first battle McMaster emerged a clear victor, securing a jury made up of eleven men and one woman. Haynes wasn't that perturbed. In a long and eventful career he'd overcome bigger obstacles, earning a statewide reputation second to none for tenacity and legal acumen. Not for nothing had he acquired the nickname "Racehorse." It promised to be a memorable contest.

Motive: Failed Divorce

Although not required to do so, prosecutors are generally happiest if they can demonstrate to the jury that the accused had a clear motive for committing the crime. McMaster did just this.

> We expect to prove that problems arose in the course of this marriage which resulted in the filing of a divorce petition on December 3, 1968, by the defendant Dr. John Hill. An answer to said petition for divorce was filed by Joan Hill, making the divorce a contested matter which could have resulted in a court trial. . . . Realizing that he had insufficient grounds for divorce and in fear of the adverse publicity in regard to his extramarital activities which might result from a court trial, Dr. John Hill dismissed his divorce case and agreed to a so-called reconciliation with Joan Hill. . . . Having failed to terminate the marriage legally, the defendant began to formulate a plan to rid himself of an unwanted wife.

After detailing Joan Hill's sudden and violent illness, McMaster went on:

> The state expects to show that the defendant, realizing his wife's . . . condition, intentionally and with malice aforethought failed to properly treat Joan Hill and failed to provide timely hospitalization for her in order that she would die.

Haynes listened to all of this, expressionless. He knew that the case, as presented by McMaster was wafer-thin and that, ultimately, everything would hinge on the word of Ann Kurth. But first came Vann Maxwell, a neighbor of the Hills. She testified that, on the weekend before her illness, Joan was planning to reinstitute divorce proceedings against her husband: "The final thing she said about it was . . . would I go with her?"

"How did she appear to you?" Haynes asked casually on cross-examination.

"She seemed in good health," answered Maxwell.

Haynes sat down, pleased. Now it would be up to the prosecution to explain how a healthy, physically fit woman had become a hopelessly sick patient in less than 48 hours.

Effie Brown had worked as a maid for the Hills only a matter of weeks but was well aware of their marital difficulties. "Did anyone tell you that Mrs. Hill was ill . . . that she was sick on Monday?" asked McMaster.

The 69-year-old woman nodded. "I can't recall now who told me . . . but someone did tell that she was ill and not to go into the room."

McMaster turned knowingly to the jury, letting the point sink in of a sick, helpless woman being left deliberately alone. Without actually mentioning John Hill, the inference was clear. But in this statement Haynes saw a chance. His encyclopedic memory recalled something from a deposition that Effie Brown had made, just weeks after Joan Hill's death.

Haynes was courteous as he began cross-examination of the witness. "You went up to her room, didn't you?" he asked. "And you saw Mrs. Hill sitting in the chair, didn't you, ma'am?"

"No," Brown stated positively. At which point Haynes produced the deposition, made two years earlier, and read out a question posed at that time, "On that Monday did you go up and see her? And your answer, 'I went up there one time . . . she's sitting in a big chair'."

Effie Brown shook her head. "Somebody must have put that there. I didn't say nothing."

Haynes paused. At a stroke he had managed to impugn the witness' memory, not implying perjury, just the hazy recollection of an elderly woman caught up in a situation far removed from any other in her experience. He also scored heavily with his last question to Brown. "I suppose you wouldn't hesitate in going back to work for Dr. Hill today?"

"I wouldn't mind going back if he needed me . . . I like him."

On balance this prosecution witness' testimony had been a marginal plus for the defense. Slowly they were managing to chip away at McMaster's depiction of John Hill as a cold and calculating schemer.

Outburst Leads to Mistrial

If Haynes had been discomfited by some of what Effie Brown had to say, then he wanted nothing at all to do with the testimony of Ann Kurth. Indeed, he believed that under Texas law she should not even be allowed to take the stand against her former husband. But his strident and lengthy objections on this point were overridden by Judge Frederick Hooey after the prosecutors had unearthed yet another obscure precedent, this time a case in which a wife had been permitted to testify against her husband. Judge Hooey let it be known, however, that he was uneasy with his own ruling, and had agreed only to Kurth taking the witness stand on condition that he might stop her testimony at any time.

McMaster first led Kurth through her relationship with Hill, then he asked if she had seen anything "unusual" at Hill's apartment during the week of Joan Hill's illness. She told of entering the bathroom and finding three petri dishes— the kind used in laboratories—with "something red in them." Hill had come in and angrily shooed her from the room, saying that it was "just an experiment." The next day she also spotted some unusual pastries in the refrigerator. Hill, again annoyed, told her not to eat them.

But the main thrust of Kurth's testimony was given over to a vivid account of an incident in which, she said, Hill had attempted to kill her. It came just one month into their marriage. They were out driving when, Kurth claimed, Hill deliberately smashed her side of the car into a bridge.

"What happened next?" asked McMaster.

"He pulled a syringe from his pocket and . . . tried to get it into me." Kurth said that she managed to knock the syringe from Hill's hand, but that he then produced another hypodermic needle.

"And what did he do with that one, if anything?" queried McMaster.

Kurth, who several times had to be admonished by the judge for her overly theatrical presentation, crescendoed, "He tried to get that syringe into me!"

Here the prosecutor speculated. "Was he attempting to treat you? Or harm you? Do you know?"

"Yes, I knew." Kurth hesitated, as if unsure what to say next, then blurted out, "Because he told me how he had killed Joan with a needle."

Haynes leapt to his feet, demanding a mistrial on grounds that the defense had not been given an opportunity to prepare themselves against a direct accusation of murder. (This was the first that Haynes had heard of any syringes). Judge Hooey, plainly worried by this turn of events, at first denied the request but did order a recess. During the adjournment, however, Hooey had second thoughts. The tenuous legal precedent by which Kurth had been allowed to testify, and then her foolhardy outburst, convinced him that if he allowed the trial to continue there were clear and palpable grounds for appeal. Accordingly, 11 days into the hearing, he granted the mistrial.

Interestingly enough, the jurors, when polled afterward, indicated that they were inclined to believe John Hill innocent. Ann Kurth's story hadn't impressed them at all.

Retrial Unnecessary

The retrial was set and adjourned another three times until finally being put on the docket for November 1972. But before this could happen, on September 24, 1972, John Hill, by now married for a third time, was gunned down at his mansion in the exclusive Houston suburb of River Oaks, in what had all the hallmarks of a contract killing. After several months of investigation, police arrested three people in connection with the case.

Bobby Vandiver and girlfriend Marcia McKittrick admitted complicity, but claimed that they had been hired by a notorious Houston brothel madam, Lilla Paulus. When Vandiver was shot by police in an unrelated incident, McKittrick, promised a 10-year sentence, agreed to testify against Paulus. Additional testimony was provided by Paulus' own daughter. She told the court of overhearing her mother say, "Ash Robinson is looking for somebody to kill John Hill." Eventually Paulus was convicted and sentenced to 35 years imprisonment in 1975.

This extraordinary case reached its conclusion in 1977 when Hill's surviving wife, Connie, and son, Robert, brought a civil suit against Ash Robinson alleging that he had caused John Hill's wrongful death. On this occasion Lilla Paulus' daughter declined to testify, leaving Marcia McKittrick as the main witness against Robinson. A polygraph examination indicated that she was being truthful in saying that Robinson had caused the death of John Hill. A similar test suggested that Robinson was being truthful when he said he hadn't. Given this welter of confusion, the jury acquitted Robinson of collusion in the death of his son-in-law, and the suit was quashed.

Three trials failed to establish Dr. John Hill's guilt or innocence but did provide one of the most remarkable legal sagas of the 20th century. Had a jury been given the opportunity to hear all of the available evidence against Hill, including his sudden and ominous predilection for plying his wife with unaccustomed pastries in the weeks before her death, in all likelihood he would have been convicted of murder. Whether that verdict would have survived the Texas Court of Appeals is something we shall never know.

—Colin Evans

Suggestions for Further Reading

Kurth, Ann. *Prescription: Murder*. New York: New American, 1976.

Thompson, Thomas. *Blood And Money*. New York: Doubleday & Co., 1976.

Wilson, Kirk. *Unsolved*. New York: Carroll & Graf, 1989.

New York Times Company v. U.S.: 1971

Appellant: The United States   **Defendant:** The New York Times Company

Appellant's Claim: That the government's efforts to prevent the *New York Times* from publishing certain Vietnam War documents known as the "Pentagon Papers" were justified because of the interests of national security

Chief Defense Lawyers: Alexander M. Bickel and William E. Hegarty

Chief Lawyers for Appellant : Daniel M. Friedman, Erwin N. Griswold, and Robert C. Mardian   **Justices:** Hugo L. Black, Harry A. Blackmun, William J. Brennan Jr., Warren E. Burger, William O. Douglas, John M. Harlan, Thurgood Marshall, Potter Stewart, and Byron R. White   **Place:** Washington, D.C.

Date of Decision: June 30, 1971   **Decision:** The government cannot restrain the *New York Times* from publishing the Pentagon Papers.

SIGNIFICANCE

In *New York Times Company v. U.S.,* the Supreme Court held that the government must meet a heavy burden of justification before it can restrain the press from exercising its First Amendment right to publish.

In the Spring of 1971, the Vietnam War was still raging despite the fact that popular opinion was against President Richard Nixon's administration's efforts to keep the United States in the conflict. Opposition to the war spread throughout the armed forces themselves and into what has been called the military-industrial complex. This opposition sentiment affected one man in particular, a former employee of the U.S. Department of Defense who had also worked for the Rand Corporation, an important military contractor. His name was Daniel Ellsberg.

Ellsberg and a friend, Anthony Russo, Jr., stole a copy of a massive, 47-volume study prepared by the Department of Defense titled "History of U.S. Decision-Making Process on Vietnam Policy." The study had more than 3,000 pages, supplemented with 4,000 more pages of source documents. Ellsberg and Russo also stole a one-volume study titled "Command and Control Study of the Gulf of Tonkin Incident," prepared in 1965. These studies were essentially a massive history of American involvement in Vietnam since World War II, and were classified "TOP SECRET-SENSITIVE" and "TOP SECRET" respectively.

Ellsberg and Russo passed these studies on to two newspapers, the *New York Times* in New York City and the *Washington Post* in Washington, D.C. Neither paper was involved in the theft of government documents. In its Sunday, June 13, 1971, edition, the *Times* began a series of articles containing excerpts from the studies, which were dubbed the "Pentagon Papers." The *Times* published more articles on June 14 and 15.

The Government Moves to Stop the Leak

On June 15, 1971, the government asked the U.S. District Court for the Southern District of New York to restrain the *Times* from publishing any more of the Pentagon Papers. The court refused to issue an injunction against the *Times* but did grant a temporary restraining order against the *Times* while the government prepared its case. On June 18, the *Post* also published portions of the Pentagon Papers, and the government promptly began proceedings in the District of Columbia to restrain that paper as well. The focus of the Pentagon Papers dispute, however, remained with the legal proceedings against the *Times* in New York City.

On June 18, 1971, the district court held a hearing. The government presented five experts on national security, who testified that publication of the Pentagon Papers would compromise the war effort. The next day, district court Judge Murray I. Gurfein issued his decision, in which he again refused to issue an injunction against the *Times*:

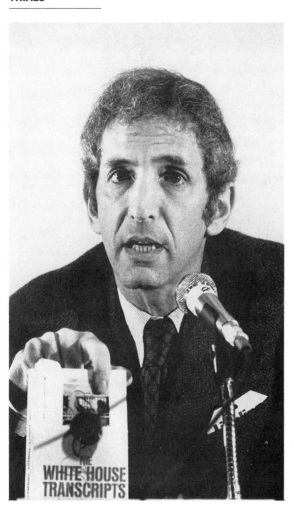

Daniel Ellsberg released the highly confidential "Pentagon Papers" to the *New York Times* and the *Washington Post,* thus setting in motion an important freedom of the press decision. (Bettye-Lane)

I am constrained to find as a fact that the . . . proceedings at which representatives of the Department of State, Department of Defense and the Joint Chiefs of Staff testified, did not convince this Court that the publication of these historical documents would seriously breach the national security. It is true, of course, that any breach of security will cause the jitters in the security agencies themselves and indeed in foreign governments who deal with us. . . . Without revealing the content of the testimony, suffice it to say that no cogent reasons were advanced as to why these documents except in the general framework of embarrassment previously mentioned, would vitally affect the security of the Nation.

Gurfein did, however, prevent the *Times* from publishing any more of the Pentagon Papers while the government hurried to file its appeal with the U.S. Court of Appeals for the Second Circuit (which covers New York). Once the appeal was filed, Circuit Judge Irving R. Kaufman continued the temporary restraint against the *Times* until the government could argue its case, which happened June 22, 1971. Usually, only three circuit judges hear an appeal, but in an unusual procedure all eight second circuit judges were on the bench that day. They listened to the government's claim that the Pentagon Papers' release would hurt national security, and the *Times*' defense that the First Amendment protected its publication of the excerpts.

The next day, June 23, the appeals court refused to give the government the injunction it wanted. On June 24, the government filed a petition with the Supreme Court. On June 25, the Court ordered the government and the *Times* to appear before the Court in Washington on the 26th for a hearing.

The *Times*' lawyers were Alexander M. Bickel and William E. Hegarty. The government's lawyers were Daniel M. Friedman, U.S. Solicitor General Erwin N. Griswold, and Robert C. Mardian. The two sides argued their positions before Justices Hugo L. Black, Harry A. Blackmun, William J. Brennan, Jr., Warren E. Burger, William O. Douglas, John M. Harlan, Thurgood Marshall, Potter Stewart, and Byron R. White.

Supreme Court Throws Out Government's Case

The Pentagon Papers case was a litigation whirlwind, beginning on June 15, 1971, and ending just over two weeks later, after having traveled through three courts, when the Supreme Court issued its decision on June 30, 1971. By a 6–3 vote, the Court slammed the door shut on the government's attempt to stop the *Times* from publishing the Pentagon Papers, with Justice Black stating:

> In seeking injunctions against these newspapers and in its presentation to the Court, the Executive Branch seems to have forgotten the essential purpose and history of the First Amendment. . . .
>
> Yet the Solicitor General argues . . . that the general powers of the Government adopted in the original Constitution should be interpreted to limit and restrict the specific and emphatic guarantees of the Bill of Rights. . . . I can imagine no greater perversion of history. Madison and the other Framers of the First Amendment, able men that they were, wrote in language they earnestly believed could never be misunderstood: "Congress shall make no law . . . abridging the freedom . . . of the press. . . ." Both the history and language of the First Amendment support the view that the press must be left free to publish news, whatever the source, without censorship, injunctions, or prior restraints."

Not only did the Court reject the government's national security argument, but it criticized in no uncertain terms the Nixon administration's attempt to subvert the First Amendment. The role of the federal courts in the division of powers set up by the Constitution, namely as the judicial branch of government charged with the responsibility of protecting individual rights, was also reaffirmed:

> Our Government was launched in 1789 with the adoption of the Constitution. The Bill of Rights, including the First Amendment, followed in 1791. Now, for the first time in the 182 years since the founding of the Republic, the federal courts are asked to hold that the First Amendment does not mean what it says, but rather means that the government can halt the publication of current news of vital importance to the people of this country.

Chief Justice Burger and Justices Blackmun and Harlan dissented, arguing that the Court should defer to the executive branch's conclusion that the Pentagon Papers leak threatened national security.

The Court also dismissed the government's legal actions against the *Post.* The Pentagon Papers proceedings were not over yet, however. The government obtained a preliminary indictment against Ellsberg on June 28, 1971 for violating criminal laws against the theft of federal property. More formal indictments came against Ellsberg, and Russo as well, on December 30, 1971. In addition to theft, the government charged Ellsberg and Russo with violations of the federal Espionage Act.

Government Thwarts Own Prosecution of Ellsberg

The criminal prosecution involved 15 counts of theft and espionage against Ellsberg and Russo. Ellsberg faced a possible 105 years in prison and $110,000 in fines if convicted. Russo faced a possible 25 years in prison and $30,000 in fines if convicted. The two men were tried in the U.S District Court for the Central District of California, which includes Los Angeles, where they were alleged to have stolen the Pentagon Papers.

The judge was William Matthew Byrne, Jr. The case was stalled for over five months with pretrial procedural activities, but jury selection finally began in June 1972. It took until July 1972 for a jury to be formed and the trial to begin, but the trial was halted almost immediately after it began when it was revealed that the government had been secretly taping the defendants' confidential communications. Supreme Court Justice Douglas, who was responsible for hearing emergency appeals from the Ninth Circuit, which includes Los Angeles, ordered the trial halted until October.

In fact, it was not until January 17, 1973, that the Ellsberg and Russo trial resumed. A whole new jury had to be selected. Further, the case was now overshadowed by the Watergate scandal. On September 3, 1971, G. Gordon Liddy and E. Howard Hunt, Jr., led a group of Cuban exiles in a break-in of the offices of Dr. Lewis Fielding, which were located in Beverly Hills, California. Fielding was Ellsberg's psychoanalyst, and the White House-sponsored break-in team was hoping to discover the identity of other Ellsberg accomplices from Fielding's files. The break-in was a total failure: there was nothing in Fielding's files.

When news of the government-sponsored bugging of the Democratic Party's headquarters in the Watergate hotel and office complex in Washington broke sometime later, it was only a matter of time before the special Watergate prosecutors learned of the Fielding break-in. This information was publicly revealed April 26, 1973, after the Ellsberg and Russo trial had been dragging on for months without any sign of an imminent conclusion.

At first, Byrne didn't want to consider dismissing the charges against Ellsberg and Russo. The government had invested a great deal of time and money in the prosecution. Then, after April 26, there were further revelations that the government had been conducting more illegal wiretaps of Ellsberg's conversations than had previously been admitted. In disgust, Byrne dismissed the entire criminal prosecution against Ellsberg and Russo on May 11, 1973.

Byrne's final dismissal of the charges against Ellsberg and Russo ended the Pentagon Papers affair. The significance of the entire episode is embodied in the Supreme Court's rejection of the government's attempt to prohibit the *Times* from publishing the news. Although the government will not necessarily always lose a case based on the alleged interests of national security, under *New York Times v. U.S.* it must meet a heavy burden of justification before it can restrain the press from exercising First Amendment rights.

—Stephen G. Christianson

Suggestions for Further Reading

Meiklejohn Civil Liberties Institute. *Pentagon Papers Case Collection: Annotated Procedural Guide and Index*. Berkeley, Calif.: Meiklejohn Civil Liberties Institute, 1975.

Salter, Kenneth W. *The Pentagon Papers Trial*. Berkeley, Calif.: Editorial Justa Publications, 1975.

Schrag, Peter. *Test of Loyalty: Daniel Ellsberg and the Rituals of Secret Government*. New York: Simon & Schuster, 1974.

Ungar, Sanford J. *The Papers & the Papers: an Account of the Legal and Political Battle Over the Pentagon Paper*. New York: Columbia University Press, 1989.

Angela Davis Trial: 1972

Defendant: Angela Y. Davis **Crimes Charged:** Murder, kidnapping, and conspiracy **Chief Defense Lawyers:** Leo Branton, Jr., Margaret Burnham, Howard Moore, Jr., Sheldon Otis, and Dorris Brin Walker
Chief Prosecutor: Albert Harris **Judge:** Richard E. Arnason
Place: San Jose, California **Dates of Trial:** February 28–June 4, 1972
Verdict: Not guilty

SIGNIFICANCE
A unique mix of murder, race, and politics ensured that this trial could never be anything but memorable.

At 10:45 A.M. on August 7, 1970, a gunman interrupted the Marin County trial of San Quentin inmate James McClains, who was facing a charge of attempted murder. The gunman, Jonathan Jackson, younger brother of George Jackson, one of the so-called "Soleded Brothers," distributed weapons to McClain and two other men, Ruchell Magee and William Christmas. Together, they took Judge Harold Haleys prosecutor Gary Thomas, and three women jurors hostages then attempted to flee in a van. When guards opened fire, Haley, Jackson, McClain, and Christmas were killed. Thomas and Magee sustained serious injuries.

Suspicion that the plot had been connected to the Soleded Brothers, three radical black Soleded Prison inmates, hardened with the abrupt disappearance of Angela Davis, a controversial professor and Soleded supporter, recently fired from the University of California at Los Angeles for her Communist sympathies. She remained at large until her discovery in New York on October 13. Following extradition she was arraigned on charges of murder, conspiracy, and kidnapping, as prosecutors sought to prove that Davis had engineered the escape attempt in a bid to barter hostages for the freedom of her lover, George Jackson.

The task of selecting a jury began before Judge Richard E. Arnason on February 28, 1972. The racial/political overtones made this an especially sensitive issue, but eventually an all-white jury was impaneled, and prosecutor Albert Harris was able to make his opening address. He outlined four elements necessary to establishing guilt through circumstantial evidence: motive, means, opportunity, and consciousness of guilt. "The evidence will show," he said, "that her [Davis'] basic motive was not to free political prisoners, but to free the one prisoner that she loved." The means came on August 5, 1970, when, in the company of Jonathan Jackson, "she purchased the shotgun that was used in the commission of the crime." Harris felt that those days preceding the crime, many of which Davis spent in the company of Jonathan Jackson, provided the opportunity to commit the crime; and finally consciousness of guilt was evidenced by the fact that just hours after the shooting, Davis boarded a flight at San Francisco and went into hiding.

Davis Ridicules Case

Despite having assembled an imposing team of attorneys, Davis chose to make the opening defense address herself. Wisely, she kept the political rhetoric to a minimum, preferring to underscore serious flaws in the prosecution's case—the fact that she had bought the shotgun quite openly in her own name, and, more importantly, her insistence that the Marin shooting had nothing to do with George Jackson. "The evidence will show that there's absolutely no credible proof of what the precise purpose of August 7 was."

This argument was countered by a prosecution witness, news photographer James Kean. He had taken several photographs of the incident and testified to hearing McClain say, "Tell them we want the Soleded Brothers released by twelve o'clock."

Chief defense attorney, Leo Branton cross-examined: "This remark that was made about freeing the Soleded Brothers—it was the last thing that was said just as the group got on the elevator . . . is that a fact?"

"Yes. That's right."

"You never heard Jonathan Jackson say anything about free the Soleded Brothers, did you?"

"No, I did not."

"You didn't hear anybody say it other than McClain and it was the last thing he said as he headed down the elevator; is that right?"

"Yes"

"As though it were a parting gesture, is that correct?"

"That's right."

Angela Davis, escorted by two FBI agents, October 1970. (AP/Wide World Photos)

Branton must have been satisfied, and even more so when Deputy Sheriff Theodore Hughes testified that he had heard some of the escapees shout clearly,

"Free our brothers at Folsom, free all our brothers." Again, no reference to Soleded.

Less easy to dispose of was the prosecution's star witness, Gary Thomas. Permanently paralyzed by his bullet wound, he was brought into court in a wheelchair. The key part of his testimony was an insistence that he had seen Magee shoot Judge Haley with the shotgun. Thomas recalled that he "watched the right side of the judge's face pull slowly away from his skull."

Branton had the unenviable task of attempting to prove how Thomas' recollection might have been clouded by the trauma he had suffered. "Isn't it a fact, sir, that the first fusillade of shots that came into the van killed both Jonathan Jackson and McClain, and that you thereupon grabbed the gun that McClain was holding . . . and that you turned around and began firing into the back of the van . . . and that you hit Christmas and you hit Magee, and you possibly even hit Judge Haley?"

Thomas angrily refuted the assertion and Branton had to back down. He made little headway with Thomas, apart from getting the witness to agree that at no time did he ever hear anyone mention the Soleded Brothers.

Mysterious Telephone Number Surfaces

Prosecutor Harris next turned his attention to a piece of paper found on the body of Jonathan Jackson. On it was written a telephone number that corresponded to a public telephone at San Francisco International Airport. Harris contended that this clearly demonstrated a predisposition on the part of Jonathan Jackson to telephone Angela Davis at the airport, and that once Davis didn't receive the call she panicked and took the next available flight out to Los Angeles.

All of this sounded fine but did not bear close inspection. First of all, Branton established that the telephone was in the South Terminal, near the Western Airlines counter. Why, he speculated, had nobody seen Davis waiting by the phone? And why had she left the Western Airlines counter, which operated a convenient hourly shuttle to Los Angeles, and then walked over to the Central Terminal to catch a flight on Pacific Southwest Airlines? It didn't make sense.

In one last desperate effort to salvage their case, the prosecutors fought to introduce into evidence an 18-page "diary" that Davis had kept. While the diary clearly documented the intense love that Davis felt for George Jackson, it did not provide any evidence to support the indictment.

Such a lackluster prosecution hardly merited much of a response. Branton called just 12 witnesses to support his assertion that Angela Davis was entirely innocent, a mere victim of her own notoriety. The case went to the jury on June 2, 1972. They came back two days later with not-guilty verdicts on all three charges.

But for Angela Davis it was a Pyrrhic victory. Six months before she faced her accusers, George Jackson was himself shot to death in an alleged prison break.

Before the trial many, including some on her own defense team, doubted Angela Davis' chances of receiving a fair hearing from an all-white jury. That the jurors were able to separate politics and race from the essential facts of the case speaks volumes for their integrity, making this one of the legal system's finer moments.

—Colin Evans

Suggestions for Further Reading

Aptheker, Bettina. *The Morning Breaks*. New York: International, 1975.

Davis, Angela. *Angela Davis*. New York: International, 1988.

Major, Reginald. *Justice in the Round*. New York: Third Press, 1973.

Mitchell, Charlene. *The Fight to Free Angela Davis*. New York: Outlook, 1972.

Timothy, Mary. *Jury Woman*. San Francisco: Glide, 1975.

Furman v. Georgia: 1972

Appellant & Defendant: William Henry Furman   **Appellee & Plaintiff:** State of Georgia   **Appellant Claim:** That the Georgia death penalty constituted cruel and unusual punishment in violation of the Eight and Fourteenth Amendments   **Chief Defense Lawyers:** Dorothy T. Beasley, Arthur K. Bolton, Harold N. Hill, Jr., Andrew J. Ryan, Jr., Andrew J. Ryan III, and Courtney Wilder Stanton   **Chief Lawyers for Plaintiff:** Anthony G. Amsterdam, Elizabeth B. Dubois, Jack Greenberg, Jack Himmelstein, B. Clarence Mayfield, and Michael Meltsner   **Justices:** Harry A. Blackmun, William J. Brennan, Jr., Warren E. Burger, William O. Douglas, Thurgood Marshall, Lewis F. Powell, Jr., William H. Rehnquist, Potter Stewart, and Byron R. White   **Place:** Washington, D.C.   **Date of Decision:** June 29, 1972   **Decision:** Georgia death penalty statute declared unconstitutional

SIGNIFICANCE

Although *Furman v. Georgia* did not completely abolish the death penalty, it placed stringent requirements on death penalty statutes.

O n the night of August 11, 1967, 29-year-old William Joseph Micke, Jr., came home from work to his wife and five children in the city of Savannah, Georgia. He went to bed around midnight. Two hours later, the Mickes were awakened by strange noises in the kitchen. Thinking that one of his children was sleepwalking, William Micke went into the kitchen to investigate. He found William Henry Furman there, a 26-year-old black man who had broken into the house and was carrying a gun. Furman fled the house, shooting Micke as he left. The bullet hit Micke in the chest and he died instantly. Micke's family promptly called the police, who arrived on the scene within minutes. The police searched the neighborhood and found Furman, who was still carrying the murder weapon.

Furman was charged with murder and was tried in the Superior Court of Chatham County, Georgia, on September 20, 1968. Furman was a poor man, and he got a poor man's trial. His court-appointed lawyer, B. Clarence Mayfield, received the court-approved standard retainer for murder cases: $150, which did not include costs. The trial lasted just one day: the jury was selected at 10:00

A.M., the evidence was presented and the judge's instructions to the jury given by 3:30 P.M., and the jury's guilty verdict was returned at 5:00 P.M.

Long before the trial, the court committed Furman to the Georgia Central State Hospital at Milledgeville for psychological examination. Furman had dropped out of school after the sixth grade, and he tested in the lowest 4 percent of the test's intelligence range. The hospital diagnosed Furman as being mentally deficient and subject to psychotic episodes. Nevertheless, the court denied Furman's insanity plea at trial.

Furman Sentenced to Death

Under Georgia law, Furman faced the death penalty. This was despite the fact that Furman had testified that his shooting of Micke was accidental:

> I admit going to these folks' home and they did caught me in there and I was coming back out, backing up and there was a wire down there on the floor. I was coming out backwards and fell back and I didn't intend to kill nobody. . . . The gun went off and I didn't know nothing about no murder until they arrested me, and when the gun went off I was down on the floor and I got up and ran. That's all to it.

Georgia's death penalty statute, however, permitted executions even for unintended killings. So long as Furman had broken into the Micke house illegally, it was irrelevant that his shooting was accidental since that shooting had caused Micke's death while Furman was committing a criminal act. The judge's instructions to the jury made this clear:

> If you believe beyond a reasonable doubt that the defendant broke and entered the dwelling of the deceased with intent to commit a felony or a larceny and that after so breaking and entering with such intent, the defendant killed the deceased in the manner set forth in the indictment, and if you find that such killing was the natural, reasonable and probable consequence of such breaking and entering, then I instruct you that under such circumstances, you would be authorized to convict the defendant of murder and this you would be authorized to do whether the defendant intended to kill the deceased or not.

The Georgia Supreme Court affirmed Furman's conviction and death sentence on April 24, 1969, but on May 3, 1969, Chief Justice W.H. Duckworth stayed the execution so that Furman could file a petition with the U.S. Supreme Court. Furman was no longer represented solely by court-appointed counsel: his case had generated some publicity, and several lawyers were now handling his appeal. Furman's chief lawyers were Anthony G. Amsterdam, Elizabeth B. Dubois, Jack Greenberg, Jack Himmelstein, B. Clarence Mayfield, and Michael Meltsner. The State of Georgia's chief lawyers were Dorothy T. Beasley, Arthur K. Bolton, Harold N. Hill, Jr., Andrew J. Ryan, Jr., Andrew J. Ryan III, and Courtney Wilder Stanton.

On January 17, 1972, the parties argued their case before the U.S. Supreme Court in Washington, D.C. The Court had agreed to hear the case to answer the legal question of whether the death penalty violates the Eighth Amendment to the U.S. Constitution, which states that 'Excessive bail shall not be required, nor excessive fines imposed, nor cruel and unusual punishments inflicted."

The Court issued its decision June 29, 1972. By a narrow five-to-four majority, the justices voted to overturn Furman's conviction on the grounds that in his case the death penalty constituted cruel and unusual punishment. The justices were deeply divided over how to interpret the Eighth Amendment, however. All nine justices filed separate opinions stating their legal reasoning, which is highly unusual. For the most part, Justice William O. Douglas' opinion spoke for the five-member majority.

Court Severely Restricts Death Penalty

Douglas reviewed the history of capital punishment under the English common law, from the Norman Conquest in 1066 through the American colonial period and up to the ratification of the Constitution. He noted that English law had evolved to consider the death penalty unfair when applied selectively to minorities, outcasts, and unpopular groups. In America, the Court had already held that discriminatory enforcement of the law violates the equal protection clause of the Fourteenth Amendment. Therefore, if a death penalty statute was applied in a discriminatory manner, it was unfair and constituted cruel and unusual punishment. For Furman, the death penalty was unfair because there had not been enough protection for him at trial. He had gotten a quick one-day trial and he was black, poor, uneducated, and mentally ill:

Justice Harry Blackmun opposed abolition of the death penalty in *Furman v. Georgia.* (Courtesy, Library of Congress)

> The generality of a law inflicting capital punishment is one thing. What may be said of the validity of a law on the books and what may be done with the law in its application do, or may, lead to quite different conclusions.

> It would seem to be incontestable that the death penalty inflicted on one defendant is "unusual" if it discriminates against him by reason of his race, religion, wealth, social position, or class, or if it is imposed under a procedure that gives room for the play of such prejudices.

The rest of Douglas' opinion reads almost like a professional case study of prisoner treatment throughout the United States. Based on surveys and statistics drawn from a variety of sources, Douglas concluded that the death penalty was disproportionately applied to blacks, the poor, and other groups who are at a disadvantage in society:

> Former Attorney General Ramsey Clark has said, "It is the poor, the sick, the ignorant, the powerless and the hated who are executed." One searches

our chronicles in vain for the execution of any member of the affluent strata of this society.

Justices William J. Brennan, Jr., and Thurgood Marshall, who had voted with Douglas, wrote opinions that called for the complete abolition of the death penalty for all crimes and under any circumstances. They were in the minority, however, and so Douglas' opinion embodied the impact of the Court's decision: the death penalty could still be imposed, but only if the law bent over backwards to make sure that people like Furman were protected.

While *Furman v. Georgia* was hailed as a landmark decision protecting minorities and other historically oppressed groups, it didn't give the states much guidance on what they had to do to make their death penalty statutes comply with the Eighth Amendment. In the 1976 case of *Gregg v. Georgia*, the Court upheld the death penalty imposed on a convicted murderer under a revamped Georgia statute that required sentencing hearings and other protective procedures. Most states with death penalty statutes have followed *Gregg* and modified their laws so there are procedures to protect the poor, minorities, the mentally ill, and other groups. Further, most states have repealed the death penalty for accidental killings and other crimes less serious than cold-blooded intentional murder.

Furman v. Georgia did not forbid capital punishment, but it did place strict requirements on death penalty statutes, at both the state and federal levels, based on the Eighth Amendment.

—*Stephen G. Christianson*

Furman v. Georgia

Suggestions for Further Reading

Aguirre, Adalberto. *Race, Racism, and the Death Penalty in the United States.* Berrien Spring, Mich.: Vande Vere, 1991.

Congregation of the Condemned: Voices Against the Death Penalty. Buffalo, N.Y.: Prometheus Books, 1991.

Horwitz, Elinor Lander. *Capital Punishment, U.S.A.* Philadelphia: J.B. Lippincott Co., 1973.

Masur, Louis P. *Rites of Execution: Capital Punishment and the Transformation Of American Culture.* New York: Oxford University Press, 1989.

Radelet, Michael L. *In Spite of Innocence: Erroneous Convictions in Capital Cases.* Boston: Northeastern University Press, 1992.

Trombley, Stephen. *The Execution Protocol: Inside America's Capital Punishment Industry.* New York: Crown Publishers, 1992.

Roe et al. v. Wade: 1973

Plaintiff: Norma McCorvey, using "Jane Roe" as an alias and representing all pregnant women in a class-action suit   **Defendant:** Texas District Attorney Henry B. Wade   **Plaintiff's Claim:** That Texas' abortion laws violated McCorvey's and other women's constitutional rights
Chief Defense Lawyers: Jay Floyd and Robert Flowers
Chief Lawyers for Plaintiff: Sarah Weddington and Linda Coffee
Justices: Harry Blackmun, William Brennan, Warren Burger, William Douglas, Thurgood Marshall, Lewis Powell, William Rehnquist, Potter Stewart, and Byron White   **Place:** Washington, D.C.
Date of Decision: January 22, 1973   **Decision:** Overturned all state laws restricting women's access to abortions during the first trimester of pregnancy and let stand second-trimester restrictions only insofar as they were designed to protect the health of pregnant women

SIGNIFICANCE

The case was the first to establish that a woman, rather than her physician, might be the party injured by a state's criminalization of abortion. Moreover, the decision was in large measure based on an implied "right to privacy" in the U.S. Constitution, which the majority held was violated by state laws restricting a woman's right to abort a fetus prior to its viability outside her womb.

The Supreme Court's landmark decision legalizing abortion in *Roe v. Wade* aroused more passion than perhaps any other in the Court's history. One segment of the population, energized by Catholic and fundamentalist religious beliefs, held that aborting the unborn was no less than murder. Another segment of the American people was just as convinced and just as adamant that denying a woman's "right to choose" whether or not to bear a child was an intolerable governmental restriction of her freedom and privacy. The decision in 1973 triggered a 20-year battle between its opponents, the self-described "Right to Life" movement who sought to overturn it, and proponents, the "Pro-Choice" advocates who worked to prevent it from being reversed or whittled away. Justice Harry Blackmun, who wrote the majority opinion, had his life threatened and his mailbox filled with letters calling him "Butcher of Dachau, murderer,

Pontius Pilate, [and] Adolph Hitler." Each of the other justices received thousands of letters of condemnation as well.

Support for abortion rights had been growing steadily in the years prior to the decision and continued to increase afterward. In 1968, for example, less than 15 percent of the participants in a Gallup Poll approved "of liberalizing the abortion laws," while 40 percent of Gallup Poll respondents approved in the following year. By mid-1972, the Gallup Poll reported 73 percent of all participants and 56 percent of Catholic participants believed "that the decision to undergo an abortion is a matter that should be left solely to the woman and her physician."

Although they appear to be in a minority, those who object to *Roe v. Wade* do so with a seemingly undying passion; nearly 20 years later, as this is written, their opposition is well organized, well funded and at times even violent. It also has been partially successful: The basic decision still stands, but the high court has narrowed it somewhat by permitting states to regulate abortion for minors and abortions performed in tax-supported institutions.

Norma McCorvey Tests the Law

The "Jane Roe" whose name would be attached to this national divide was actually 21-year-old Norma McCorvey. McCorvey's marriage had ended, and her daughter, age 5, was being reared by McCorvey's mother and stepfather. In the summer of 1969, McCorvey was working as a ticket seller for a traveling carnival; by early autumn she had lost her job and had become pregnant. McCorvey wanted to end her pregnancy, but abortion was illegal in Texas except in cases where it was deemed necessary to save a woman's life. McCorvey's search for an illegal abortionist was unsuccessful.

However, it led her to two young attorneys, both women and both interested in challenging the existing abortion laws: Linda Coffee and Sarah Weddington. Although there was virtually no chance that McCorvey herself would be helped if Coffee and Weddington succeeded in overturning the abortion laws (one could count on pregnancy coming to a conclusion well before any lawsuit simultaneously began), McCorvey agreed to become Coffee's and Weddington's plaintiff in a test case.

Texas had passed its anti-abortion law in 1859. Like other such laws in the United States, it punished only the persons performing or "furnishing the means for" an abortion. This posed a problem for Coffee and Weddington: They knew it could be argued that a pregnant woman, presumably *not* the target of a law restricting medical practice, "lacked standing to sue" regarding that law's supposed unconstitutionality. And if they passed this hurdle with McCorvey's case, they knew they'd face another: When McCorvey gave birth or at least passed the point where an abortion could be safely performed, her case—having resolved itself—might be declared moot and thrown out of court. Linda Coffee prepared and filed the pleading anyway.

Constitutional Issues

Coffee and Weddington decided to attack the constitutionality of the Texas abortion law on the grounds that it violated the Fourteenth and Ninth Amendments to the U.S. Constitution. The due process clause of the Fourteenth Amendment guaranteed equal protection under the law to all citizens and, in particular, required that laws be clearly written. Physicians accused of performing illegal abortions usually cited the Fourteenth Amendment in their defense, claiming that the law was not specific enough with regard to when a woman's life might be considered threatened by pregnancy and childbirth. However, since Coffee and Weddington wanted a decision that rested on a pregnant woman's right to decide for herself whether or not an abortion was necessary, they based their argument first and foremost on the Ninth Amendment, which states: "The enumeration in the Constitution, of certain rights, shall not be construed to deny or disparage others retained by the people." Until 1965, this had usually been interpreted to mean that rights not specifically granted to the federal government were retained by the states. In 1965, however, *Griswold v. Connecticut* reached the Supreme Court and prompted a different interpretation of the amendment.

Chief Justice Burger voted with the majority in the *Roe v. Wade* decision which affirmed a woman's "fundamental right" to privacy in the area of choosing whether or not to have an abortion. (Bettye-Lane)

Estelle Griswold, Planned Parenthood League of Connecticut's executive director, and Dr. Charles Lee Burton had been arrested for providing birth-control information and contraceptives, actions then illegal under Connecticut law. Found guilty in the Connecticut courts, the two appealed to the Supreme Court, which overturned their convictions and ruled the Connecticut law unconstitutional. Of particular note to Coffee and Weddington was Justice William O. Douglas' discussion of the Ninth Amendment in his majority opinion. Rights not specifically listed in the Constitution were retained by *the people*, Douglas emphasized, and one of these rights was the right to privacy. This right to privacy, Coffee and Weddington would argue, should certainly protect the right of a woman to decide whether or not to become a mother.

John Tolles was the assistant district attorney chosen by District Attorney Henry Wade to defend his enforcement of the Texas abortion law. Attorney General Crawford Martin chose Robert Flowers, head of the enforcement division, to defend the Texas law itself, and Flowers passed this task on to his assistant chief, Jay Floyd. The state prepared its case primarily on the basis that a fetus had legal rights, which ought to be protected.

State Court Favors Plaintiff

The Three-Judge Court Act of 1910 had created courts in which a panel of three judges drawn from a single appellate circuit might resolve interstate commerce disputes between the federal and state governments. Another act, passed in 1937, required that such a panel hear any case questioning the constitutionality of a state law. On May 23, 1970, Coffee, Weddington, Tolles and Floyd appeared in the Fifth Circuit Court in Dallas, Texas, before Judges Irving S. Goldberg, William McLaughlin Taylor, and Sarah Tigham Hughes, for whom Coffee had once clerked. The courtroom was jammed with concerned women and reporters. Norma McCorvey, or "Jane Roe," not required to be present, stayed home.

Coffee and Weddington had amended their case to a class-action suit so that McCorvey would represent not just herself but all pregnant women. They had also been joined in their suit by an "intervenor," Dr. James Hallford, who had been arrested for performing abortions. Hallford's attorneys, Fred Bruner and Roy Merrill, planned to use the traditional physician's defense, the Fourteenth Amendment.

Coffee spoke first. She had to establish that McCorvey did, indeed, have "standing to sue" and that the question was a serious, constitutional one on which the three judges should rule. At one point she said: "I think the [abortion] statute is so bad that the court is just really going to have to strike it all down. I don't think it's worth salvaging."

Weddington approached the bench next. This was her courtroom debut, and she knew it was an important case. She said she disagreed with the "justification which the state alleges for the state abortion statute, that is, the protection of the life of the child. . . .

"[L]ife is an ongoing process. It is almost impossible," Weddington continued, "to define a point at which life begins or perhaps even at which life ends."

Asked by Judge Goldberg whether the legalization of abortion would promote promiscuity, Weddington said that young women "are already promiscuous when the statute is in effect, and in fact, these are some of the girls who need this right and who have the most socially compelling arguments why they should be allowed abortions—the young still in school, those unable to shoulder the responsibility of a child—these girls should not be put through the pregnancy and should be entitled to an abortion."

Before Weddington stepped down to listen to Fred Bruner's Fourteenth Amendment defense of his physician client, Judge Goldberg asked her one more question. Did she, he wanted to know, think the abortion law was weaker in terms of the Ninth or Fourteenth Amendment? Weddington gave her answer immediately: "I believe it is more vulnerable on the Ninth Amendment basis."

After Bruner addressed the judges, Floyd rose to speak for the state. He claimed that "Roe" must certainly have reached the point in her pregnancy where an abortion would be considered unsafe and therefore had no case. Judge Goldberg flatly disagreed.

Tolles followed for the state, and argued strenuously against a woman's having the right to choose an abortion. "I personally think," he said, "and I think the state's position will be and is, that the right of the child to life is superior to that woman's right to privacy."

The judges did not agree. On June 17, 1970, they issued their opinion: "[T]he Texas abortion laws must be declared unconstitutional because they deprive single women and married couples, of their right, secured by the Ninth Amendment, to choose whether to have children."

Supreme Court Hears the Case

The fifth circuit court had issued *declarative relief*, that is, it had declared the challenged law unconstitutional. It had not, however, issued *injunctive relief*, which would have been an order for Texas to end its enforcement of that law. For this reason, Weddington and Coffee were entitled to appeal directly to the U.S. Supreme Court, which agreed to hear their case.

Forty-two *amici curiae*, or "friend of the court" briefs, were filed in support of a woman's right to choose an abortion from organizations as varied as the New York Academy of Medicine, the American College of Gynecologists and Obstetricians, Planned Parenthood and the California chapter of the National Organization for Women. There was also a "woman's brief," signed by such noteworthy women as anthropologist Margaret Mead; Barnard College President Millicent McIntosh; Oregon's past U.S. senator, Maurine Nuebuerger; and feminist theologian Mary Daly. This brief stated, as Marian Faux summarizes it, "that even if a fetus were found to be a legal person, a woman still could not be compelled to nurture it in her body against her will."

On December 13, 1971, Weddington stood before the Supreme Court and contended the state's ability to compel women to bear children left women without any control over their lives. Then she argued against Tolles' claim that a fetus was entitled to protection. "[T]he Constitution, as I read it . . . attaches protection to the person at the time of birth. Those persons born are citizens."

When Floyd's turn came, he said that "Roe" must surely have given birth by now and thus could not represent pregnant women in a class-action suit. Asked how any pregnant woman could hope to challenge Texas' abortion laws, Floyd replied: "There are situations in which . . . no remedy is provided. Now, I think she makes her choice prior to the time she becomes pregnant. That is the time of the choice. . . . Once a child is born, a woman no longer has a choice; and I think pregnancy makes her make that choice as well."

Floyd was then questioned as to why, if abortion was equivalent to murder, no state had ever punished the women involved. He was also questioned about the fact that doctors who performed abortions were not charged with premeditated murder but "ordinary felony murder," a lesser charge. Finally, he was asked to clarify when life began according to the state of Texas. After several attempts to answer the question, Floyd could only say: "I don't—Mr. Justice—there are unanswerable questions in this field."

Since there had been only seven sitting justices when *Roe v. Wade* was argued, the justices decided such an important case should be re-argued when two newly appointed justices—William Rehnquist and Lewis Powell—joined the Court, restoring the number of justices to nine. Weddington, Coffee, Tolles, and Floyd did so October 10, 1972, repeating their basic arguments.

Landmark Decision

On January 22, 1973, Justice Harry Blackmun read his majority opinion to a room filled with reporters. Reviewing the history of abortion in the United States, he pointed out that "The restrictive criminal abortion laws in effect in a majority of states today . . . are not of ancient or even of common law origin." Instead, he said they seemed to have been passed to protect women from a procedure that was, in the 19th century, likely to endanger their health. That rationale no longer existed, Justice Blackmun declared, since medical advances had made abortion as safe or safer than childbirth for women.

Justice Blackmun next discussed the high court's acknowledgment of a "right of personal privacy" in various decisions, including the recent *Griswold* birth control case. Then he delivered the crux of his decision:

> This right of privacy, whether it be founded in the Fourteenth Amendment's concept of personal liberty and restrictions on state action . . . or . . . in the Ninth Amendment's reservation of rights to the people, is broad enough to encompass a woman's decision to terminate her pregnancy.

Continuing, Justice Blackmun disagreed with Texas' claim that it had the right to "infringe Roe's rights" to protect "prenatal life." He discussed the use of the word "person" in the U.S. Constitution and found that no such use had "any possible prenatal application," and he specifically found that "the word 'person,' as used in the Fourteenth Amendment, does not include the unborn."

However, Justice Blackmun said, neither the woman's right to privacy nor the fetus' lack of a right to the state's protection was absolute:

> [T]he State does have an important and legitimate interest in preserving and protecting the health of the pregnant woman . . . and . . . it has still *another* important and legitimate interest in protecting the potentiality of human life. These interests are separate and distinct. Each grows in substantiality as the woman approaches term and, at a point during the pregnancy, each becomes "compelling."

Finally, Justice Blackmun's decision in *Roe v. Wade* provided the states with a formula to balance these competing interests. During the first trimester of pregnancy, the abortion decision would be "left to the medical judgment of the pregnant woman's attending physician." During the second trimester, a state might "regulate the abortion procedure in ways that are reasonably related to maternal health." From the end of the second trimester "subsequent to viability," a state might "regulate, and even proscribe, abortion except where it is necessary, in appropriate legal judgment, for the preservation of the life or health of the mother."

Justices William Rehnquist and Byron White dissented. Justice Rehnquist, in his brief, said:

> I have difficulty in concluding, as the Court does, that the right of "privacy" is involved in this case. Texas by the statute here challenged bars the performance of a medical abortion by a licensed physician on a plaintiff such as Roe. A transaction resulting in an operation such as this is not "private" in the ordinary usage of that word.
>
> . . . I agree with the statement . . . that . . . "liberty," embraces more than the rights found in the Bill of Rights. But that liberty is not guaranteed absolutely against deprivation, but only against deprivation without due process of law.

Justice White wrote in his dissent:

> At the heart of the controversy in these cases are those recurring pregnancies that pose no danger whatsoever to the life or health of the mother but are nevertheless unwanted for any one or more of a variety of reasons— convenience, family planning, economics, dislike of children, the embarrassment of illegitimacy, etc.
>
> The common claim before us is that for any one of such reasons, or for no reason at all . . . any woman is entitled to an abortion at her request if she is able to find a medical advisor willing to undertake the procedure.
>
> The Court for the most part sustains this position: . . . during the period prior to the time the fetus becomes viable, the Constitution of the United States values the convenience, whim or caprice of the putative mother more than life or potential life of the fetus.

Every state was affected. New York, which had previously permitted abortion until the 24th week of pregnancy, had to extend that period by several weeks, and the laws of Alaska, Hawaii, and Washington required similar amendment. Fifteen states needed a complete overhaul of their abortion laws, while 31 states—including Texas—had strict anti-abortion laws which became immediately and entirely invalid.

In the spring of 1973, with support from the Catholic church, a Committee of Ten Million began a petition drive demanding a "human rights amendment," to ban abortion in the United States. Several proposed constitutional amendments were introduced and discussed in Congress, including proposals for amendments that prohibited abortions even when required to save a mother's life. These attempts failed, and *Roe*'s opponents tried to organize the legislatures of 34 states to call for a constitutional convention; in the mid-1980s, this strategy was abandoned as well.

The Republican party has since adopted the "pro-life" position as part of its party platform, gaining Catholic and fundamentalist members and losing enough support among women to create a 24 percent "gender gap" in the 1988 elections. The Democratic Party—which supports *Roe v. Wade*—also benefitted from the women's vote in the 1992 presidential election, in which Bill Clinton, a supporter of a woman's right to an abortion, was elected president.

Subsequent Developments

Many of the Supreme Court's most liberal members have retired since *Roe v. Wade* was decided in 1973, and their conservative successors have indicated a willingness to re-examine the decision and its implications. On June 30, 1980, in *Harris v. McRae,* the high court ruled that neither the federal nor local government was obligated to pay for abortions for women on welfare, even if their abortions were medically necessary. More recently, *Webster v. Reproductive Health Care,* July 3, 1989, granted states new authority to restrict abortions in tax-supported institutions, and *Rust v. Sullivan,* May 23, 1991, upheld federal regulations that denied government financial aid to family planning clinics that provided information about abortion. Yet, for the time being, the effect of the decision remains intact: A state may not prohibit a woman from aborting a fetus during the first three months of pregnancy and may only regulate abortions during the second three months in the interest of the pregnant woman's health.

— Kathryn Cullen-DuPont

Suggestions for Further Reading

Abraham, Henry J. *The Judicial Process,* 4th ed. New York: Oxford University Press, 1980.

Cary, Eve and Kathleen Willert Peratis. *Woman and the Law.* Skokie, Ill.: National Textbook Co. in conjunction with the American Civil Liberties Union, New York, 1977.

Cushman, Robert F. *Cases in Constitutional Law,* 6th ed. Englewood Cliffs, N.J.: Prentice Hall, 1984.

Davis, Flora. *Moving the Mountain: The Women's Movement in America Since 1960.* New York: Simon & Schuster, 1991.

Ehrenreich, Barbara and Deirdre English. *For Her Own Good: 150 Years of the Experts's Advice to Women.* New York: Doubleday, 1979.

Faux, Marian. *Roe V. Wade.* New York: Macmillan Co., 1988.

Faludi, Susan. *Backlash: The Undeclared War Against American Women.* New York: Crown Publishers, 1991.

Petchesky, Rosalind Pollack. *Abortion and Woman's Choice.* Boston: Northeastern University Press, 1984, revised 1990.

Rosten, Leo. *Religions of America: Ferment and Faith in an Age of Crisis.* New York: Simon & Schuster, 1975.

Tony Boyle Trial: 1974

Defendant: W.A. Boyle   **Crime Charged:** First-degree murder
Chief Defense Attorney: Charles F. Moses   **Chief Prosecutor:** Richard A.
Sprague   **Judge:** Francis J. Catania   **Place:** Media, Pennsylvania
Dates of Trial: March 25–April 11, 1974   **Verdict:** Guilty
Sentence: 3 consecutive terms of life imprisonment

SIGNIFICANCE

Successful prosecutions of those responsible for the death of Jock Yablonski revealed that his murder had been ordered by the president of his own union and paid for with union funds.

No one assumed that the struggle for leadership of the United Mine Workers of America ended when incumbent President W.A. "Tony" Boyle defeated Joseph "Jock" Yablonski in the bitter December 1969 union election. The reform-minded Yablonski planned to take evidence of massive election fraud to the U.S. Secretary of Labor. Although he would later claim that the challenger was his "very close friend," Boyle and the hierarchy of the powerful union openly hated Yablonski.

In the New Year's Eve darkness of December 31, 1969, Yablonski, his wife, and their daughter were shot to death in their Clarksville, Pennsylvania home. The Federal Bureau of Investigation (FBI) entered the case on the premise that the killings might be related to Yablonski's union activity, thus making the murders a federal crime. A tip led them quickly to the gunmen: Paul Gilly, Claude Vealey, and Aubran "Buddy" Martin. Gilly's wife Annette was arrested soon. So was her father, Silous Huddleston, the president of a UMW district local.

There was no initial evidence to support a hunch that higher union officials were involved. State prosecutor Richard A. Sprague methodically tried the captured killers one by one, allowing the pressure to mount as each of the conspirators tried to escape the death sentence. In June 1971, Claude Vealey pleaded guilty to three counts of murder. Awaiting sentencing, Vealey was summoned as a prosecution witness at Buddy Martin's trial and implicated his fellow gunman. Both Martin and Paul Gilly, who was tried in February 1972, were convicted and faced three death sentences for murdering the Yablonskis in their beds.

Annette Gilly Confesses

Bargaining her way out of the electric chair, Annette Gilly pleaded guilty and confessed that she and her father had arranged Jock Yablonski's murder at the request of UMW officer William Prater. The ailing Silous Huddleston also confessed and pleaded guilty. Huddleston told the FBI that he and Prater were told to kill Yablonski by Albert Pass, secretary-treasurer of the UMW and a member of the union's national executive board.

As the conspiracy unfolded, the evidence began to point toward the union leadership. But Tony Boyle had more immediate legal problems. In March 1972, he was found guilty of making illegal political contributions with union funds. In May, the results of the 1969 union election were overturned. Boyle lost his bid for re-election. In June, the same month that the U.S. Supreme Court declared the death penalty unconstitutional as it was then applied in most states, Boyle was sentenced to two concurrent five-year prison terms and fined heavily. A month later, as Boyle planned his appeal, Prater and Pass were indicted for murder.

William Prater came to trial in March 1973. Still unsentenced and facing three life terms, gunman Paul Gilley testified for the prosecution. He said that Prater had arranged and paid for Yablonski's murder, allegedly on Boyle's orders. Retired miners testified that they had kicked back their pay from a nonexistent union "Research & Information" committee to Prater. The jury was convinced that this $20,000 was used to pay for Yablonski's death. William Prater was convicted on three counts of murder.

Former UMW head Tony Boyle en route to a pre-trial hearing on murder charges in the death of Jock Yablonski. (AP/Wide World Photos)

Albert Pass was tried two months later. In addition to the prosecution's array of forensics experts, manipulated pensioners, confessed killers, and handlers of the blood money, prosecutor Sprague called Prater, who had decided to confess at the urging of his family. The witness implicated Pass, who had told Prater to organize the killing and had paid Silous Huddleston when the plot was in motion. The jury found Albert Pass guilty on three counts of murder.

Unlike other conspirators, Pass did not aid investigators after his conviction, but the case was not dead. On September 6, 1973, Tony Boyle was arrested for instigating the Yablonski murders. Before he could be extradited to Pennsylvania for trial, however, Boyle swallowed an overdose of sedatives. and nearly died. He recovered in the protective custody of a District of Columbia prison hospital, charged with the federal crime of violating Yablonski's civil rights, but still unarraigned on Pennsylvania's charge of murder.

Boyle Balks on Arraignment

On December 20, U.S. marshals attempted to bring Boyle to Pennsylvania for arraignment. Boyle refused to leave his bed and fainted when the marshals tried to force him to his feet. The marshals returned the next day and physically removed the furious old man from his bed. They flew him to Pennsylvania, where he was formally charged, sitting in a wheelchair and still wearing his hospital pajamas. Boyle pleaded not guilty and was sent on his way to a Missouri federal prison to begin his sentence for election fraud.

A change of venue brought Boyle's trial into an eastern Pennsylvania court, far from the coal field region where the Yablonskis had lived, with Judge Francis J. Catania presiding. When the trial began in the spring of 1974, Boyle's attorney, Charles F. Moses, tried to stanch the testimony creeping toward his client by suggesting that Prater and Huddleston had killed Yablonski to hide their embezzlement of union funds.

Testimony by the same witnesses who had appeared at earlier trials laid out the prosecution's case. The chain now extended from the triggermen to Prater, who said that Boyle had visited him in prison and told him to "stick to your story, even if you are convicted."

Even more striking than the now-familiar machinery of the plot was a new witness directly linking Boyle to the murders. The FBI had arrested and secured the cooperation of UMW official William Turnblazer, who recalled standing in a hallway outside the UMW, executive boardroom with Boyle and Pass on June 23, 1969, six months before the union election.

"We're in a fight," Turnblazer quoted Boyle as saying. "We've got to kill Yablonski or take care of him."

Pass, Turnblazer testified, accepted the job. Turnblazer also explained that Pass gave him printed minutes of an executive board meeting at which the "R&I" group was discussed, thus fraudulently documenting the existence of the bogus committee formed to pay for the murders.

On the stand, Tony Boyle protested that he had authorized the union to offer a $50,000 reward for the conviction of the killers of his "very close friend" Yablonski. Boyle claimed that he had seen Prater in prison only at the urging of Prater's attorney, H. David Rothman, who was concerned about his client's health. Boyle recalled that both his own lawyer and Rothman were present during the encounter, which took place outside Prater's cell and lasted less than 10 minutes.

Boyle denied ever seeing the minutes discussing the R&I committee. He denied meeting Turnblazer and Pass in the corridor outside the executive board room after the June 23 meeting, when the order to kill was allegedly given. When Boyle stepped down, three former UMW board members testified that Boyle left the meeting by a side door that night and had never even entered the hallway.

Boyle's Secretary Spoils Defense

Boyle's defense was gutted by the final prosecution witnesses. Boyle's secretary testified that the union reward for Yablonski's killers was her idea. She had proposed a $100,000 sum, but Boyle cut the amount in half. The secretary also explained that there was no side door by which the union president could have avoided the corridor after the June 23 conference.

Attorney Rothman testified that the prison meeting with his client, William Prater, was Boyle's idea. Rothman recalled Boyle and Prater talking for about 20 minutes, alone. Finally, prosecutor Sprague called Charles Groenthal, an FBI fingerprint expert. Sprague handed the agent the minutes discussing the R&I committee and asked if Groenthal had identified a print found on one of its pages.

"Yes, sir, I did," answered the FBI expert. "It was the thumbprint of Mr. Boyle."

Like the conspirators who had carried out his wishes, Tony Boyle was found guilty on three counts of murder. His sentence was the final blow to the corrupt union hierarchy he had sought to preserve by having Jock Yablonski murdered. Boyle died in 1985 while serving three consecutive life terms in a Pennsylvania prison.

— Thomas C. Smith

Suggestions for Further Reading

Armbrister, Trevor. *Act of Vengeance*. New York: E.P. Dutton, 1975.

Finley, Joseph E. *The Corrupt Kingdom*. New York: Simon & Schuster, 1972.

Franklin, Ben A. "Case of the Persistent Prosecutor." *New York Times* (September 9, 1973): 2.

Lewis, Arthur H. *Murder By Contract*. New York: Macmillan, 1975.

U.S. v. Nixon: 1974

Plaintiff: United States   **Defendant:** President Richard M. Nixon
Plaintiff Claims: That the president had to obey a subpoena ordering him to turn over tape recordings and documents relating to his conversations with aides and advisers concerning the Watergate break-in
Chief Defense Lawyer: James D. St. Clair
Chief Lawyers for Plaintiff: Leon Jaworski and Philip A. Lacovara
Justices: Harry A. Blackmun, William J. Brennan, Warren E. Burger, William O. Douglas, Thurgood Marshall, Lewis F. Powell, Jr., Potter Stewart, and Byron R. White. William A. Rehnquist recused himself from the case.
Place: Washington, D.C.   **Date of Decision:** July 24, 1974
Decision: President Nixon was ordered to turn over the tapes and other documents to the prosecutors

SIGNIFICANCE

The President is not immune from judicial process, and must turn over evidence subpoenaed by the courts. The doctrine of executive privilege entitles the president to a high degree of confidentiality if the evidence involves matters of national security or other sensitive information, but the President cannot withhold evidence.

By the Spring of 1974, the government investigation into the Watergate break-in and the subsequent coverup was moving fullsteam ahead. Despite President Richard M. Nixon's repeated denials, it was becoming increasingly clear to Congress and the public that senior Nixon administration officials, and probably Nixon himself, had been actively involved in the coverup. On March 1, 1974, a 19-person federal grand jury indicted Attorney General John N. Mitchell for conspiracy to obstruct justice, and the proceeding was entitled *U.S. v. Mitchell.* Six other persons, all senior Nixon administration officials employed in the White House or the Committee to Re-Elect the President (CREEP), were indicted as co-conspirators: Charles W. Colson, John D. Ehrlichman, H.R. Haldeman, Robert C. Mardian, Kenneth W. Parkinson, and Gordon Strachan. Nixon also was included but as an unindicted co-conspirator.

On April 18, 1974, Special Prosecutor Leon Jaworski, charged with the responsibility of conducting the Watergate investigation for the government, went to Judge John Sirica of the U.S. District Court for the District of Columbia. In response to Jaworski's request, Sirica issued a subpoena ordering Nixon to produce "certain tapes, memoranda, papers, transcripts, or other writings" related to the specific meetings and conversations detailed in the subpoena. The material was to be turned over by May 2, 1974, for use in the trial, scheduled for September 9, 1974. Jaworski was able to identify the time, place, and persons present at these discussions because he already possessed the White House daily logs and appointment records.

Nixon Fights Subpoena

Nixon turned over edited transcripts of 43 conversations, which included portions of 20 conversations named in the subpoena, on April 30, 1974. On May 1, however, Nixon's attorney, James D. St. Clair, went to Sirica and asked that the subpoena be quashed. Nixon had hoped that the transcripts, which had been publicly released, would satisfy the court's and the public's demand for information without turning over the tapes. Nixon was wrong: Sirica denied St. Clair's motion on May 20, 1974. Sirica ordered "the President or any subordinate officer, official, or employee with custody or control of the documents or objects subpoenaed" to turn them over to the court by May 31, 1974.

On May 24, 1974, a week before Sirica's deadline, St. Clair filed an appeal to the U.S. Court of Appeals for the District of Columbia Circuit. Both sides realized, however, that the critical legal issue of whether the courts could subject the President to subpoenas and other forms of judicial process would ultimately have to be decided by the U.S. Supreme Court. Further, both sides were acutely aware of the political stakes and were anxious to avoid lengthy litigation. Therefore, on May 24, 1974, Jaworski took the highly unusual step of asking the Supreme Court to grant *"certiorari* before judgment," namely to take the case without waiting for the court of appeals to make a decision. The effect of bypassing the court of appeals would be to get a fast and final decision from the Supreme Court, and on June 6, 1974, St. Clair also requested *certiorari* before judgment.

On June 15, 1974, the Supreme Court granted Jaworski's and St. Clair's requests and decided to take the case from the court of appeals. St. Clair represented Nixon, and Jaworski was assisted by Philip A. Lacovara for the government. The case was argued before Supreme Court Justices Harry A. Blackmun, William J. Brennan, Warren E. Burger, William O. Douglas, Thurgood Marshall, Lewis F. Powell, Jr., Potter Stewart, and Byron R. White in Washington, D.C. on July 8, 1974. Justice William A. Rehnquist, a Nixon appointee to the court, recused himself from the case.

There is a popular notion that the judicial system, especially the Supreme Court, is above politics. This is a myth. When Jaworski and Lacovara went into the Supreme Court building on July 8, there were hundreds of cheering spectators on the steps. The justices themselves were obviously very involved as well, and grilled both sides during the oral argument. Justice Lewis Powell questioned Nixon's claim that the tapes had to be kept secret to protect the public interest:

> Mr. St. Clair, what public interest is there in preserving secrecy with respect to a criminal conspiracy?

St. Clair responded lamely:

> The answer, sir, is that a criminal conspiracy is criminal only after it's proven to be criminal.

The government's attorneys were questioned thoroughly as well, particularly on the issue of whether the grand jury set a dangerous precedent by naming the president as a co-conspirator when the prosecutors hadn't even requested an indictment. In response to Justice Powell's concerns, Lacovara stated:

> Grand Juries usually are not malicious. Even prosecutors cannot be assumed to be malicious. . . . I submit to you, sir, that just as in this case a Grand Jury would not lightly accuse the President of a crime, so, too, the fear that, perhaps without basis, some Grand Jury somewhere might maliciously accuse a President of a crime is not necessarily a reason for saying that a Grand Jury has no power to do that.

The Supreme Court issued its decision on July 24, 1974, less than three weeks later. During the intervening time, the justices struggled to write an opinion on which all eight of them could agree. Although Supreme Court justices are free to dissent as they see fit, they wanted a unanimous decision in this case because of the important issues at stake concerning the relationship between the executive and the judiciary. A split decision would weaken the impact of the Court's decision. Although Burger was the chief justice and nominally in charge of writing the opinion, in fact, all eight justices wrote or contributed to portions of the decision.

Nixon Ordered to Release Tapes

After dispensing with some initial procedural issues, the court went to the main issue, namely whether the president was cloaked with immunity from judicial process under the doctrine called "executive privilege." First, the Court restated the principle of *Marbury v. Madison* (see separate entry) that "it is emphatically the province and duty of the judicial department to say what the law is:"

> [Notwithstanding] the deference each branch must accord the others, the judicial power of the United States vested in the federal courts by Article III, section 1, of the Constitution can no more be shared with the Executive Branch than the Chief Executive, for example, can share with the Judiciary the veto power, or the Congress share with the Judiciary the power to override a Presidential veto. Any other conclusions would be contrary to the basic concept of separation of powers and the checks and balances that flow from the scheme of a tripartite government. We therefore reaffirm that it is the province and the duty of this Court to say what the law is with respect to the claim of privilege presented in this case.

Richard Nixon leaving the White House after his resignation. (Official White House photo.)

Next, the court addressed Nixon's two principal arguments in favor of executive privilege. First, St. Clair argued that for the presidency to function, conversations and other communications between high government officials and their advisors had to be kept confidential. Otherwise, if every statement could be made public, advisors would be reluctant to speak freely, and the decision-making process would suffer. Second, St. Clair argued that the very nature of the doctrine of separation of powers gave the President judicial immunity. In rejecting both arguments, the Court stated that while confidentiality was important, it could be maintained by letting a judge review evidence *in camera*, namely alone in his or her chambers:

> The President's need for complete candor and objectivity from advisers calls for great deference from the courts. However, when the privilege depends solely on the broad, undifferentiated claim of public interest in the confidentiality of such conversations, a confrontation with other values arises. Absent a claim of need to protect military, diplomatic, or sensitive national security secrets, we find it difficult to accept the argument that even the very important interest in confidentiality of Presidential communications is significantly diminished by production of such material for in camera inspection with all the protection that a District Court will be obliged to provide.

Further, the court stressed that recognizing Nixon's broad claim of executive privilege could seriously compromise the judicial system's obligation to assure the dispensation of justice in criminal trials:

> The impediment that an absolute, unqualified privilege would place in the way of the primary constitutional duty of the Judicial Branch to do justice in criminal prosecutions would plainly conflict with the function of the courts under Article III [of the Constitution]. . . . In this case the President challenges a subpoena served on him as a third party requiring the production of materials for use in a criminal prosecution; he does so on the claim that he has a privilege against disclosure of confidential communications. He does not place his claim of privilege on the ground they are military or diplomatic secrets.

Given that Nixon had not asserted any specific reason why the courts should not have the tapes in the *U.S. v. Mitchell* trial, the justices ordered Nixon to turn them over to Judge Sirica for in camera inspection.

Ordering a president to do something is one thing; enforcing that order is another. The judicial branch is a co-equal branch of government, but as one of the framers of the Constitution commented, it "possesses neither sword nor purse," meaning that it is without the military power of the executive branch or the taxing power of the legislative branch. The judiciary depends ultimately on its stature and public respect for the democratic system for enforcement of its orders. During oral argument, St. Clair had hinted darkly that Nixon "had his obligations under the Constitution," leaving it unclear whether Nixon would obey the Court's order to turn over the tapes to Sirica.

Nixon was in San Clemente, California, when he received word of the Supreme Court's unanimous decision from his aide, Alexander Haig. Within a day, however, Nixon issued a public statement that he would comply with the Court's order. The relevant part of Nixon's statement was:

While I am, of course, disappointed in the result, I respect and accept the court's decision, and I have instructed Mr. St. Clair to take whatever measures are necessary to comply with that decision in all respects.

Nixon turned over 64 tapes to Sirica, some of which included highly incriminating conversations between Nixon and his aides shortly after the Watergate break-in. Congress was ready to impeach him, and Nixon realized that his presidency was doomed. On August 8, 1974, Nixon announced his resignation and Vice President, Gerald Ford became president at noon on August 9, the effective date of the resignation. Because Ford later exercised his power to pardon Nixon, Nixon never stood trial. Nevertheless, the case established an important precedent, namely that if there is any executive privilege, it does not permit the president to withhold evidence needed by the courts. Finally, the case sounded the death knell for the political career of Richard Nixon, who had formerly been one of America's most popular and successful presidents.

—*Stephen G. Christianson*

Suggestions for Further Reading

Ball, Howard. *"We Have a Duty": the Supreme Court and the Watergate Tapes Litigation.* New York: Greenwood Press, 1990.

Berger, Raoul. *Executive Privilege: a Constitutional Myth.* Cambridge, Mass.: Harvard University Press, 1974.

Carlson, Margaret. "Notes from Underground: a Fresh Batch of White House Tapes Reminds a Forgiving and Forgetful America Why Richard Nixon Resigned in Disgrace." *Time* (June 17, 1991): 27–28.

Doyle, James. *Not Above the Law: the Battles of Watergate Prosecutors Cox and Jaworski: a Behind the Scenes Account.* New York: William Morrow & Co., 1977.

Friedman, Leon. *United States v. Nixon: the President Before the Supreme Court.* New York: Chelsea House Publishers, 1974.

Jaworski, Leon. *The Right and the Power: the Prosecution of Watergate.* New York: Reader's Digest Press, 1976.

Woodward, Bob. *The Brethren: Inside the Supreme Court.* New York: Simon & Schuster, 1979.

Joan Little Trial: 1975

Defendant: Joan Little   **Crime Charged:** Murder
Chief Defense Lawyers: Jerry Paul, Morris Dees, Marvin Miller, Karen Galloway, James Gillespie, and Milton Williamson
Chief Prosecutors: William Griffin, John Wilkinson, and Lester Chalmers
Judge: Hamilton Hobgood   **Place:** Raleigh, North Carolina
Dates of Trial: July 14–August 15, 1975   **Verdict:** Not guilty

SIGNIFICANCE
A mix of sex, race, murder, and unprecedented support for the defendant made this a trial of international notoriety. The trial was also one of the first in which "scientific" jury selection was used by defense lawyers to try to insure a favorable outcome.

At 4:00 A.M. on August 27, 1974, officers at the Beaufort County Jail in Washington, North Carolina discovered the body of guard Clarence Alligood in a cell. Nude from the waist down, he had been stabbed 11 times. His trousers were bunched up in his right hand. The fingers of his left hand enclosed an ice pick. The cell's occupant, Joan Little, age 20, had been serving a seven-year sentence for robbery; now she was gone. One week later she surrendered to authorities. The story she told made headlines. Little, a black woman, claimed that the 62-year-old white jailer had forced her into performing a sexual act, and that she had killed him in self-defense.

Even before her trial began July 14, 1975, Joan Little had achieved global celebrity. More than $60,000 in donations flooded in from around the world, enough to mount a prodigious defense. The leader of that six-person team was lawyer Jerry Paul. He was a believer in scientific jury selection and spent much of that hefty defense fund on psychological profiles to determine which juror was likely to be sympathetic and which wasn't. A revolutionary concept at that time, it only heightened public interest in the case, but as the process dragged on into its second week, Judge Hamilton Hobgood's impatience began to show. Paul protested:

> I don't intend to sit or stand here and see an innocent person go to jail. . . .
> You can threaten me with contempt or anything else, but it does not worry
> me.

Advised that his outburst could result in a jail term, Paul attempted to soft-pedal his rhetoric during the remainder of proceedings. To no avail. At trial's end, he was given 14 days for contempt.

Sexual Advance Prompts Killing

When the state commenced its case, prosecutor William Griffin argued that Little had deliberately instigated the incident, seducing Alligood, then killing him when she saw her chance to escape. When jail employee Beverly King testified that nothing in Alligood's demeanor that night indicated that he had sex in mind, deputy defense counsel Morris Dees became belligerent. Over repeated warnings from the bench, Dees pressed King on this issue. During a lunch recess he even approached her. The two were seen in earnest conversation. When court resumed, Judge Hobgood demanded to know the nature of this conversation. Sheepishly, Dees admitted exhorting King to repudiate her testimony, a flagrant impropriety that resulted in his expulsion from the trial.

Why Dees felt the need to adopt such tactics is unfathomable: the defense had a strong case. Three former inmates of Beaufort County Jail testified that Alligood often sexually molested the female prisoners. One, Rosa Robertson, claimed to have attempted suicide rather than yield to Alligood's advances, although it was later established that the suicide bid was half-hearted, to say the least.

Next came Joan Little's testimony.

In the 12 months between crime and trial she had been entirely reshaped by her lawyers. Gone was the promiscuous, streetwise tough girl. In her place was a well-groomed and demure young woman. She told how Alligood had come to her cell. "He said that he had been nice to me and that it was time that I be nice to him." Under guidance from Paul, Little described what happened next.

> He started to take off his shoes outside the corridor . . . he started in towards the cell and I backed off to the back wall . . . he just started taking off his pants . . . I told him no, I wasn't going to do nothing like that . . . he tried to force me towards him . . . that's when I noticed that he had a ice pick in his hand.

Joan Little received unprecedented support during her trial. Here attorney William Kunstler speaks on her behalf at a press conference. (Bettye-Lane)

Then, Little claimed, Alligood forced her to her knees and made her commit a sexual act. During this act Alligood let go of the ice pick. A struggle broke out. "I got to the pick first," said Little. She struck Alligood several unthinking, unaimed blows with the pick, then ran from the cell.

A Quick Acquittal

It didn't take long for prosecutor Griffin to isolate the weak spots in Little's testimony. How had the ice pick, an item normally kept in an outer office, suddenly materialized in Alligood's hand? She didn't know. How was she able to fight off Alligood? "He was a big man, wasn't he?"

"Yes," admitted Little.

Griffin pushed harder. Why had she not screamed? Why no attempt to fight back? Why, when Alligood was removing his trousers, had she not attempted to escape his clutches then? Little's answers were inconclusive but not incriminating. Nothing she said was inconsistent with her version of events in the cell.

One of the jurors, when the verdict was in, commented, "I thought about it . . . and I decided that these people [the prosecution] hadn't shown me anything to convict her," a sentiment echoed by fellow jurors. After less than 90 minutes of reflection, they found Little not guilty.

Following acquittal, Little was returned to prison to finish her seven-year robbery sentence. On October 15, 1977, she again escaped, but was recaptured and finished out her term. She resurfaced briefly in 1989 when she spent a night in jail on stolen property charges which were later dropped.

There was something in this case for everyone: civil rights activists, church groups, feminists. All made capital from what was a unique situation.

—Colin Evans

Joan Little following her acquittal, August 15, 1975. (News and Observer Company, North Carolina Division of Archives and History)

Suggestions for Further Reading

Harwell, Fred. *A True Deliverance*. New York: Alfred A. Knopf, 1979.

Jet (March 20, 1989): 37.

Reston, James, Jr. *The Innocence of Joan Little*. New York: Bantam, 1977.

In the Matter of Karen Ann Quinlan: 1975

Plaintiff: Joseph T. Quinlan   **Defendant:** St. Clare's Hospital
Plaintiff Claim: That doctors at St. Clare's Hospital should obey Mr. Quinlan's instructions to disconnect his comatose daughter from her respirator and allow her to die   **Chief Defense Lawyers:** Ralph Porzio (for Karen Quinlan's physicians), Theodore Einhorn (for the hospital), New Jersey State Attorney General William F. Hyland, and Morris County Prosecutor Donald G. Collester, Jr.   **Chief Lawyers for Plaintiff:** Paul W. Armstrong and James Crowley   **Judge:** Robert Muir, Jr.   **Place:** Morristown, New Jersey   **Date of Decision:** November 10, 1975   **Decision:** Denied Mr. Quinlan the right to authorize termination of "life-assisting apparatus" and granted Karen Quinlan's physicians the right to continue medical treatment over the objections of the Quinlan family. Overturned by the New Jersey Supreme Court, which, on March 31, 1976, ruled that Karen's "right of privacy" included a right to refuse medical treatment and that her father, under the circumstances, could assume this right in her stead.

SIGNIFICANCE

This case prompted the adoption of "brain death" as the legal definition of death in some states and the adoption of laws recognizing "living wills" and the "right to die" in other states, as well as the formation of "bioethics" committees in many hospitals. In 1985, the New Jersey Supreme Court ruled that *all* life-sustaining medical treatment—including artificial feeding—could be withheld from incompetent, terminally ill patients, provided such action was shown to be consistent with the afflicted person's past wishes.

O n April 15, 1975, 21-year-old Karen Ann Quinlan passed out and lapsed into a coma after sustaining bruises which were never satisfactorily explained and ingesting tranquilizers "in the therapeutic range" with alcohol. Unable to breathe on her own, she was placed on a respirator.

By the following autumn, Quinlan's family and doctors had given up hope of recovery. Her parents, Julia and Joseph Quinlan, were devout Roman Catholics. The Quinlans consulted their parish priest, Father Thomas Trapasso, and were told that they could, in good conscience, request that Karen be removed from the respirator. The request was made, but Karen's primary physician, Dr. Robert Morse, refused to end the artificial support. Joseph Quinlan went to court.

By the time the trial began on October 20, 1975, a lawyer, Daniel R. Coburn, had become the court-appointed guardian for Karen Quinlan and both Morris County Prosecutor Donald G. Collester, Jr., and State Attorney General William F. Hyland had intervened, or joined the case, in an attempt to uphold New Jersey's homicide statutes. During pretrial interviews, Attorney General Hyland had portrayed the case as a challenge to New Jersey's long-standing definition of death as the "cessation of vital signs" and one which could result in a new definition based on "cerebral" or "brain death."

The week before the trial, however, it was disclosed that Karen Quinlan did not have a "flat" electroencephalograph, a medical test which would have been evidence of a complete absence of brain-wave activity. She also was capable of breathing on her own for short, irregular periods and had occasionally shown muscle activity which some doctors had described as voluntary. It immediately became clear that the trial would not center on New Jersey's definition of death but on an even more complicated question of whether Karen Quinlan had a "right to die."

Accepted Standards vs. Right to Die

Karen Quinlan's neurologist, Dr. Robert Morse, was the first person to testify. He acknowledged that there was virtually no chance that Quinlan would resume a "cognitive, functional existence." However, he said he saw no medical precedent for disconnecting Quinlan from her respirator and said he would not obey a court order to do so. Dr. Arshad Jarved, Quinlan's pulmonary internist, also had refused to act on Joseph Quinlan's request; he also testified that accepted standards of medical practice did not permit the removal of the respirator.

The Quinlans' attorney, Paul Armstrong, argued that the rights of privacy and religious freedom included a right to die. He explained his clients' religious view that the respirator was keeping their daughter from God and heaven: "[T]he earthly phase of Karen Quinlan's life has drawn to a close and she should not be held back from enjoyment of a better, more perfect life."

Karen Quinlan's court-appointed guardian, Daniel Coburn, saw the matter differently: "This isn't a terminal cancer case where someone is going to die. Where there is hope, you cannot just extinguish a life because it becomes an eyesore."

The following day, Armstrong called as an expert witness Dr. Julius Korein, a neurologist at Bellevue hospital and New York University Medical School. He described Karen Quinlan—by now weighing only 75 pounds—as having signs of severe higher brain disfunction. He testified that she had only "stereotyped" responses, such as blinking or rolling her eyes, to stimuli. "This pattern of reactions," he said, "could, in no way, in my opinion, be related to conscious activity." Dr. Korein also described "an accepted but not spoken-of law," according to which physicians withheld aggressive, invasive treatment from patients who were, for example, "riddled with cancer and in pain." He added: "That is the unwritten law and one of the purposes of this trial is to make it the written law."

Then an emotional Joseph Quinlan then took the stand and asked the court: "Take her from the machine and the tubes and let her pass into the hands of the Lord."

On the third day, Karen's mother, Julia Ann Quinlan, testified that Karen had made her wishes known on three occasions, saying, "Mommy, please don't ever let them keep me alive by extraordinary means." The statements were made, Mrs. Quinlan said, when two of Karen's friends and an aunt finally died after long battles with cancer. "Karen loved life, and if there was any way that she could not live life to the fullest she wanted to be able to die in her own surroundings, instead of being kept alive for months or years. I visit her every day and as I see her in her present condition I know in my heart as a mother she would not want to be there. We discussed this many times."

Although the defense lawyers objected to such hearsay evidence, Judge Robert Muir, Jr., permitted Karen's sister and one of her friends to give similar testimony. Judge Muir declined, however, to permit a Roman Catholic priest to

Julia and Joseph Quinlan (center)–with their lawyer, Paul Armstrong, and family pastor, Thomas Trapasso, hold a press conference after the court decided the fate of their daughter. (AP/Wide World Photos)

give expert testimony regarding the church's view of extraordinary medical intervention. "It is not my role to weigh the merits of what a person believes," he explained. "It is enough that I am convinced he has these beliefs."

On October 23, three neurologists—Dr. Fred Plum of the American Association of Neurologists, Dr. Sidney Diamond of Mount Sinai Hospital, and Dr. Stuart Cook of the New Jersey College of Medicine and Dentistry—gave expert medical testimony. The three concurred that Karen Quinlan's lack of higher brain function was "irreversible" and "irreparable." However, all three agreed that Quinlan was alive by both legal and medical definitions and that it would be improper to remove the respirator.

Decision Is Appealed

On November 10, 1975, Judge Muir rendered his decision. He refused permission for the removal of the respirator and appointed Daniel R. Coburn to continue acting as the guardian of Karen's "person." Joseph Quinlan was appointed guardian of his daughter's property. Rejecting the Quinlans' plea that their daughter be allowed to pass into life after death, Muir wrote that disconnecting the respirator "is not something in her best interest, in a temporal sense, and it is in a temporal sense that I must operate, whether I believe in life after death or not. The single most important temporal quality that Karen Ann Quinlan has is life," he continued. "This Court will not authorize that life to be taken away from her."

On November 17, 1975, the Quinlans filed an appeal, which the New Jersey Supreme agreed to hear on an "accelerated schedule."

On January 26, 1976, during a three-hour session, the case was argued before the seven justices of New Jersey's highest court. Their unanimous decision-naming Joseph Quinlan guardian and authorizing him to order removal of the respirator—was rendered on March 31. Chief Justice Richard J. Hughes wrote the opinion. He specifically stated that the ruling was not based on the freedom of religion argument favored by the Quinlans: "Simply stated, the right to religious beliefs is absolute but conduct in pursuance therefore is not wholly immune from governmental restraint."

Instead, Chief Justice Hughes cited the Supreme Court's decision in the *Griswold v. Connecticut* birth-control case and based the decision on "Karen's right to privacy." It was a right, he continued, that could "be asserted on her behalf by her guardian under the peculiar circumstances here present."

Lastly, Justice Hughes dismissed the attorney general's and the Morris County prosecutor's contentions that the person removing Quinlan's respirator should be charged with homicide upon her death:

> [T]he exercise of a constitutional right, such as we here find, is protected from criminal prosecution. We do not question the state's undoubted power to punish the taking of human life, but that power does not encompass individuals terminating medical treatment pursuant to their right of privacy.

Neither the hospital, Karen Quinlan's physicians, nor the State of New Jersey chose to appeal the decision to the Supreme Court. Quinlan's respirator was removed in May 1976. She managed to breathe on her own and remained in a coma for 10 more years. She died on June 11, 1985.

— *Kathryn Cullen-DuPont*

Suggestions for Further Reading

Colen, B.D. *Karen Ann Quinlan*. New York: Nash, 1976.

New York Times: September 14, 16, 17, 20, 22, 23, 24, 25, 26, 28, 1975; October 1, 3, 8, 10, 11, 12, 13, 14, 15, 18, 19, 20, 21, 22, 23, 24, 25, 26, 27, 28, 1975; November 2, 5, 8, 9, 11, 12, 16, 18, 21, 23, 25, 26, 28, 29, 1975; December 7, 12, 17, 18, 19, 22, 1975; January 19, 26, 27, 1976; February 25, 1976; March 9, 1976; April 1, 2, 7, 8, 9, 10, 12, 13, 1976; May 2, 6, 7, 22, 24, 25, 26, 27, 28, 29, 30, 1976; June 12, 1985.

Quinlan, Joseph. *Karen Ann: The Quinlans Tell Their Story*. Garden City, N.Y.: Doubleday & Co., 1977.

Patty Hearst Trial: 1976

Defendant: Patricia C. Hearst   **Crimes Charged:** Bank robbery and use of a firearm in the commission of a felony   **Chief Defense Attorneys:** F. Lee Bailey and J. Albert Johnson   **Chief Prosecutor:** James L. Browning, Jr.
Judge: Oliver J. Carter   **Place:** San Francisco, California
Dates of Trial: February 4—March 20, 1976   **Verdict:** Guilty
Sentence: 7 years imprisonment

SIGNIFICANCE

Observers expected Patty Hearst's trial to illuminate how—or if—a young woman from one of America's wealthiest families was transformed by her own kidnappers into a gun-wielding revolutionary dedicated to provoking a violent class war. Shifting public sympathies resulted in a campaign to obtain a presidential commutation of her sentence.

February 4, 1974, Patricia Hearst was a wealthy apolitical college student living with her fiancé in Berkeley, California. That night she was abducted screaming from their apartment at gunpoint, dressed in her bathrobe. Three days later her abductors released a tape in which Hearst told her parents she was being well-treated. It was accompanied by a message from "General Field Marshall-Cinque" of the Symbionese Liberation Army (SLA).

Before the Hearst kidnapping, little was known about the SLA, a small but violent group on the fringe of radical leftist politics. In November 1973, they killed Dr. Marcus Foster, the superintendent of schools for Oakland, California. The SLA declared that Hearst was a "prisoner of war" to be ransomed for the release of Joseph Remiro and Russell Little, who were charged with murdering Foster. "Field Marshall Cinque"—an escaped convict named Donald De Freeze—demanded their release. As a gesture of "good faith," the SLA demanded that the Hearst family first distribute $70 worth of food to every needy person in California.

Remiro and Little would not be released. Hearst's father, Randolph, chairman of the Hearst media empire, offered to distribute $2 million worth of food to the poor, with another $4 million to follow his daughter's safe release. The first distribution resulted in a near riot as crowds fought to get food from trucks.

Patty Becomes Tania

Two months after her abduction, Patty Hearst announced in a new tape that she had joined the SLA and taken the name "Tania." The message was accompanied by a photograph of Hearst posing with a gun before a poster of the SLA symbol, a seven-headed cobra. Her parents skeptically replied that all the tapes were made under duress.

On April 15, two bystanders were wounded during an armed robbery of the Hibernia Bank in San Francisco. One robber announced to the terrified customers and automatic bank cameras that she was "Tania . . . Patricia Hearst." In a tape released a week later, she said that she had willingly taken part in the robbery.

Federal arrest warrants were issued for eight SLA members. The FBI chose to seek Hearst's capture only as a "material witness" to the holdup. Yet suspicion that she had indeed joined her captors was voiced by U.S. Attorney General William Saxbe, who declared that Hearst "was not a reluctant participant" in the robbery and was thus "a common criminal."

The Hearst family was outraged by Saxbe's comments, but the transformation of Patty Hearst from victim to outlaw in the public mind had begun. It was bolstered May 16 when she fired an automatic weapon from a van, enabling SLA members Bill and Emily Harris to escape a security guard at Mel's Sporting Goods store in Los Angeles. Teenager Tom Matthews told police that his van was then hijacked by the escaping Harrises and Hearst, who told him openly of her part in the bank holdup.

The "wanted" poster for Patty Hearst. (Courtesy of the FBI)

The next day Los Angeles police surrounded a small house commandeered by SLA members. As viewers watched on live television, the ensuing gun battle turned the cottage into an inferno. Patricia Hearst was not among the six bodies found when the fire expired. Three weeks later, another Hearst tape surfaced in which she spoke of her love for Willie Wolfe, one of the dead SLA members. Nothing more was heard of her for 17 months.

Captured and Arrested

On September 18, 1975, FBI agents captured Hearst in San Francisco. Instead of being freed, she was arrested for the Hibernia Bank robbery and hustled off to jail to undergo the first of many psychiatric examinations.

Hearst's parents hired F. Lee Bailey, a Boston, Massachusetts, attorney renowned for winning acquittals for the alleged "Boston Strangler" and accused wife-murderer Dr. Sam Sheppard. Bailey declared that for 20 months, Patty Hearst had been via "prisoner of war" whose actions were entirely governed by her desire to stay alive.

Hearst's trial began February 4, 1976, two years to the day after she had been kidnapped. No one disputed her presence at the Hibernia Bank heist. The jury's real task was to decide whether she had acted willingly. Bailey hoped to confine the trial to the circumstances of her kidnapping, her mistreatment by the SLA, and the robbery itself.

Prosecutor James Browning, Jr., was equally intent on establishing that Hearst's behavior before and after the holdup reflected her voluntary participation in the crime. When Browning began to question her about the "missing year"—the 17 months preceding her capture—Bailey objected. The jury was sent from the courtroom.

Bailey argued that Hearst's claims of willful participation in the robbery were made under duress and should not be admitted. Judge Oliver Carter denied the motion to suppress the government's intended evidence, ruling that "the statements made by the defendant after the happening of the bank robbery, whether by tape recording, or oral communication, or in writing, were made voluntarily." The ruling entitled the prosecution to introduce all the tapes, testimony by Tom Matthews and Mel's Sporting Goods employees, and a confiscated manuscript known as "The Tania Interview," in which Hearst spoke of her conversion to the SLA and denied being brainwashed.

Defendant Takes the Stand

The jury returned to the courtroom. Over her private objections, Bailey put his client on the stand to counter the coming flood of damaging testimony. Hearst described her violent abduction. For nearly two months, she had been bound, blindfolded, and confined in a dark closet, where she was sexually molested by Wolfe and De Freeze. She was constantly threatened, hectored with revolutionary rhetoric, and told that her parents had abandoned her by refusing the SLA's demands. After seeing the May 16 incident on television, she accepted her captors' claims that the FBI would kill her if they discovered her in a SLA hideout.

Hearst explained that SLA member Angela Atwood had written the text of the tape in which "Tania" declared her willing participation in the robbery. Bill Harris had ordered her to tell Tom Matthews about the Hibernia robbery. The Harrises, she said, also dictated the text of the "Tania Interview," which was to have been published to raise funds for the SLA.

Bailey argued that Hearst's actions and words resulted from a constant threat of death. Prosecutor Browning pressed her to explain why she had not taken advantage of numerous chances to escape, particularly during Bill Harris' botched shoplifting attempt at Mel's. She replied that she feared both the SLA and the FBI. Covering the Harrises' escape was a "reflex action" triggered by incessant drilling and the SLA's "codes of war," which stated that anyone who failed to use a weapon to help comrades escape was to be shot.

When Browning insisted that Hearst testify about her actions in "the missing year," the jury was sent from the room again. Bailey accused the prosecution of prodding Hearst to incriminate herself and leave herself open to prosecution in another case. Her only alternative would be to invoke the Fifth Amendment, possibly implying guilt. Browning replied that the Fifth Amendment was applicable only in discussing a crime. He had not suggested a crime had occurred.

Without speaking of it openly in court, each side was well aware of what the other was pursuing. A woman had been killed in a SLA bank robbery in Sacramento during the "missing year." Hearst had not been involved, but Bailey wanted the jury to hear no mention of it.

When Judge Carter allowed Hearst to claim the privilege against self-incrimination, it seemed as though Bailey had won the point. The victory turned out to apply only to the closed hearing. In his formal decision several days later, Judge Carter declared that he would allow questions about the "missing year." Over Bailey's loud objections, the judge ruled that Hearst had waived her right not to testify about the period by taking the stand and talking about events at both ends of the disputed 17 months.

The jury returned to the courtroom. As Browning's questions began, Bailey stood beside Hearst, instructing her not to answer. The Sacramento robbery was not mentioned, but the jury heard Hearst refuse to answer 42 prosecution questions implying her intimate involvement with the SLA. Judge Carter instructed the jurors that they could draw inferences from her silence if they so wished.

Psychiatrists Testify of Brainwashing

Even Judge Carter appeared to doze off during the weeks of psychiatric analysis that followed. Bailey produced three psychiatric experts, who testified that Hearst's behavior was the result of brainwashing or "coercive persuasion" techniques like those used by Chinese Communists on American prisoners of war during the Korean War. Hearst's behavior was diagnosed to be consistent with the traumas she had suffered. The government called its own experts. One felt that Hearst had cooperated with the SLA voluntarily because she enjoyed her new-found notoriety. Another described her as a "rebel in search of a cause" before her kidnapping.

In his summation, Browning methodically cataloged every action that might indicate Hearst's sympathy with the SLA, from the gunfire at the sporting goods store to her possession of a Mexican trinket given to her by Willie Wolfe. The prosecutor found it incredible that she had not tried to escape during all of her time with the SLA. Bailey's final argument was brief and rambling by comparison.

The jury found Hearst guilty of robbery and use of a firearm in the commission of a felony. Judge Carter imposed preliminary maximum sentences for each crime, with a review contingent on the results of yet another psychiatric report. Before it began, Hearst's lung collapsed. The examinations resumed after her recovery. Psychiatrists pressed Hearst to state some remorse for her involvement in the robbery, but she refused, saying that her agreement to accompany the SLA to the bank was the only thing that stopped them from killing her. Under such circumstances, she maintained, she would do the same thing again. Ironically, the government sought and received Hearst's help in gathering information about the SLA, even as it was prosecuting her. She agreed to testify against the Harrises.

On September 24, 1976, after already serving more than a year in jail, Hearst was finally sentenced to seven years imprisonment. She was freed in November on $1.5 million bail pending the appeal of her robbery conviction. She pleaded "no contest" to charges of assault and robbery in the Mel's Sporting Goods incident and was released on probation because she posed no threat to the community.

She returned to prison more than a year later when the U.S. Supreme Court refused to hear her appeal. She changed lawyers. Her new attorney, George C. Martinez, filed motions in federal court, urging that her sentence be reduced to time served and that her conviction be overturned on the grounds that her former attorneys did not defend her adequately. Hearst accused Bailey of being preoccupied with his plans to write a lucrative book about her case.

Hearst Has Groundswell of Support

A "Committee For the Release of Patricia Hearst" sent thousands of letters to President Jimmy Carter urging him to commute her sentence. U.S. Representative Leo Ryan of California circulated a petition on her behalf in Congress. It was signed by 48 members, who agreed that "never before in the history of our country has such a bizarre set of circumstances led to such a tragic result: a victim of a violent kidnapping participated in a bank robbery under the direction and motivation of her abductors."

In November 1978, all motions to reduce Hearst's sentence or to set aside the verdict on grounds of insufficiency of counsel were denied. Hearst remained in prison, maintaining her innocence and refusing to discuss parole because of its imputation of guilt.

President Jimmy Carter conditionally commuted Hearst's sentence on February 1, 1979. The White House declared that it was the consensus of all of those most familiar with this case that but for the extraordinary criminal and degrading experiences that the petitioner suffered as a victim of the SLA, she would not have become a participant in the criminal acts for which she stands convicted and sentenced and would not have suffered the punishment and other consequences she has endured.

—Thomas C. Smith

Suggestions for Further Reading

Alexander, Shana. *Anyone's Daughter: The Times and Trials of Patty Hearst.* New York: Viking Press, 1979.

Dershowitz, Alan M. *The Best Defense.* New York: Random House, 1982.

Hearst, Patricia Campbell with Alvin Moscow. *Every Secret Thing.* Garden City, N.Y.: Doubleday & Co., 1982.

Kohn, Howard and David Weir. "Tania's World." *Rolling Stone* (June 11, 1992): 100.

McLellan, Vin and Paul Avery. *The Voices of the Guns.* New York: G.P. Putnam's Sons, 1977.

Theodore Robert Bundy Trials: 1976 & 1979

Defendant: Theodore Robert Bundy **Crime Charged:** First Trial: Aggravated kidnapping; Second Trial: Murder **Chief Defense Lawyers:** First Trial: John O'Connell; Second trial: Robert Haggard, Edward Harvey, Margaret Good, and Lynn Thompson **Chief Prosecutors:** First Trial: David Yocum; Second Trial: Larry Simpson and Daniel McKeever **Judges:** First Trial: Stewart Hanson; Second Trial: Edward Cowart **Places:** First Trial: Salt Lake City, Utah; Second Trial: Miami, Florida **Dates of Trials:** February 23– March 1, 1976; June 25–July 31, 1979 **Verdict:** Guilty, both trials **Sentences:** First Trial: 1–15 years; Second Trial: death

SIGNIFICANCE

More than any other murderer, Ted Bundy both fascinated and horrified onlookers. Others have killed more, some killed more horribly, but for most Americans, this young man with the movie star appearance remains one of the most notorious. Often overshadowed by his grim charisma was the controversial testimony that eventually undid him. Bundy's ready smile might have been tailor-made for the cameras, but it proved lethal in the hands of those prosecutors determined to convict him.

Between 1969 and 1975 an unprecedented wave of sex-killings swept from California, through the Pacific Northwest, and into Utah and Colorado. All of the victims were strikingly similar—female, young, attractive, and generally with long hair parted in the middle. Some were found dumped in deserted areas, others were never seen again. As the various law enforcement agencies compared notes and suspects, one name kept cropping up: Ted Bundy, a handsome young Seattle, Washington, law student. But nothing could be proved.

And then on November 8, 1974, 18-year-old Salt Lake City, Utah, resident Carol DaRonch was tricked into entering a Volkswagen outside a shopping mall by a stranger claiming to be a police officer. When the man attempted to handcuff and bludgeon her, DaRonch managed to escape from the car. On August 16, 1975, a Salt Lake City police officer arrested a Volkswagen driver who had been acting suspiciously. Inside the car were a crowbar and handcuffs.

The driver turned out to be Ted Bundy. DaRonch identified him as her abductor, leading to charges of aggravated kidnapping.

Bundy Forgoes Jury

The biggest problem facing prosecutor Dave Yocum when Bundy's trial began February 23, 1976, was safeguarding against the possibility of a mistrial. By this time, speculation that Bundy was indeed a mass murderer had grown; any hint of that appearing in this case could bring about a reversal. Bundy opted to forgo trial by jury and put his fate in the hands of Judge Stewart Hanson. Virtually the entire prosecution case hinged on Carol DaRonch. Painfully shy, she gave her testimony, eyes fixed on the floor, a point not lost on Judge Hanson. By her own admission, DaRonch found it difficult to look people in the face. But when Yocum asked her, "Is that man in court today?" she answered, "Yes."

"Where is he seated?"

For the first time, DaRonch looked at Bundy, a fleeting glance. "Right there," she breathed.

On cross-examination, defense counsel John O'Connell highlighted discrepancies in DaRonch's descriptions of her attacker to police. At first she claimed he had a mustache, then he did not, then he did. He also queried her identification of the Volkswagen, drawing attention to the fact that it now looked markedly different. In a quiet voice, DaRonch conceded that her identification of the vehicle had been stimulated by police assurances that it "was supposed to be the car."

Naturally, Bundy denied everything. He was ingratiating and pugnacious by turns, but prosecutor Yocum prevailed. A series of quick-fire questions about the circumstances surrounding his arrest clearly rattled Bundy and culminated in a damaging admission that he had, on occasion, worn a false mustache.

After a troubled weekend of deliberation, Judge Hanson returned a guilty verdict, saying, "I cannot say that there weren't any doubts." Following a prolonged psychological evaluation, Bundy was sentenced to 1–15 years imprisonment.

One year later, in June 1977, after extradition to Colorado on a murder charge, Bundy escaped. He was captured after eight days of living on the run. Incredibly, on December 30, 1977, Bundy escaped again. This time he proved more elusive.

On the Run and Deadly

Two weeks and 2,000 miles later, five female students attending Florida State University (FSU) in Tallahassee were savagely attacked at the Chi Omega sorority house. Two of the girls, Lisa Levy and Margaret Bowman, died. Just a few blocks away, another student was attacked but lived. On February 16, 1978, a man using the name "Chris Hagen" was arrested for driving a stolen vehicle. Ted Bundy had been captured for the last time. Only later was it learned that just days before his arrest he had killed again: 12-year-old Kimberly Leach, of Lake City, Florida. Her body was found April 7, 1978.

Bundy—after he was recaptured outside Aspen, Colorado's city limits. (AP/Wide World Photos)

Because of local feeling, Bundy's trial for the FSU killings was moved to Miami. Earlier it had appeared likely that there would be no trial. Faced with the possibility of two lengthy trials—Bundy was scheduled to be tried for the murder of Kimberly Leach later—the prosecutors reluctantly agreed to a plea bargain. Everything was set; Bundy signed a confession, admitting that he had killed Lisa Levy, Margaret Bowman, and Kimberly Leach. In return, he expected that, "Under the terms of this negotiated plea, I will serve seventy-five (75) calendar years in prison before I become eligible for parole." But when Bundy stood in court to deliver this plea, he abruptly changed his mind and stated, "I'm not going to do it." His attorneys looked on aghast as a trial was set.

The Miami trial got under way June 25, 1979. Larry Simpson made the opening prosecution statement, a low-key, workmanlike presentation, long on fact and bereft of emotion. For theatrics, the court had to rely on the self-appointed chief defense counsel: Bundy himself. It wasn't supposed to be that way—the court had appointed a fine team to argue his case—but Bundy's ego would not allow him to leave well enough alone. His cross-examination of Roy Crew, the FSU officer first on the scene at Chi Omega, was inept. Bundy pushed

Crew hard to describe the murder scene in graphic detail, as if determined to impress upon the jury the awfulness of the crime.

Testimony That Could Kill

However, when Coral Gables dentist Dr. Richard Souviron assumed the stand, Bundy took a back seat. This was testimony that could kill him and he knew it. Lisa Levy had sustained bite marks to the buttocks. By comparing photographs of those teeth marks with an oversize photo of Bundy's mouth, Dr. Souviron was able to show undeniable similarities. Prosecutor Simpson asked, "Doctor, can you tell us, within a reasonable degree of dental certainty, whether or not the teeth . . . of Theodore Robert Bundy . . . made the bite marks?"

"Yes, sir." For the first time, there was actual physical evidence linking Bundy to a murder victim.

Defender Ed Harvey was quick to try and undermine the setback. "Analyzing bite marks is part art and part science, isn't it?" he asked the dentist.

"I think that's a fair statement."

"Your conclusions are really a matter of opinion. Is that correct?"

Dr. Souviron agreed that it was, but the damage had been done. Confirmation came from Dr. Lowell Levine, chief consultant in forensic dentistry to the New York City Medical Examiner, who told the court that dental identification had been admitted into testimony as far back as the late 19th century. This evidence dealt a body-blow to the defense lawyers, one from which they never recovered. Significantly, Bundy, so eager to play the advocate, declined to testify on his own behalf.

On July 23, 1978, Ted Bundy was found guilty on all charges. Even at the end, his personal magnetism didn't desert him. Judge Edward Cowart, after passing sentence of death, felt moved to add a few words: "You'd have made a good lawyer . . . but you went another way, partner. Take care of yourself." It was an extraordinary end to an extraordinary trial.

Bundy received a third death sentence on February 12, 1980, following his conviction for killing Kimberly Leach. After years of appellate pleas, on January 24, 1989, "the most hated man in America" was executed in Florida's electric chair.

More than anyone else, Ted Bundy shattered popular notions of how a crazed killer should look and act. He was not wild-eyed, dirty, or dissolute; on the contrary, he was incredibly charming. And in a society where such a premium is placed on appearance, he remains a reminder that things are often not what they seem, and nothing is unthinkable.

—Colin Evans

Suggestions for Further Reading

Kendall, Elizabeth. *The Phantom Prince*. Seattle: Madrona, 1981.

Larsen, Richard W. *Bundy: The Deliberate Stranger*. Englewood Cliffs, N.J.: Prentice Hall, 1980.

Michaud, Stephen G. and Hugh Aynesworth. *The Only Living Witness*. New York: Simon & Schuster, 1983.

Rule, Ann. *The Stranger Beside Me*. New York: W.W. Norton & Co., 1989.

Gary Mark Gilmore Trial: 1976

Defendant: Gary Mark Gilmore   **Crime Charged:** Murder
Chief Defense Lawyers: Michael Esplin and Craig Snyder
Chief Prosecutor: Noall T. Wootton   **Judge:** J. Robert Bullock
Place: Provo, Utah   **Dates of Trial:** October 5–7, 1976   **Verdict:** Guilty
Sentence: Death

SIGNIFICANCE
Convicted killer Gary Gilmore's craving for self-destruction fueled a re-examination of capital punishment in America and led to a best-selling book, *The Executioner's Song,* and a subsequent movie.

At age 35, Gary Gilmore had spent more than half his life behind bars. In April 1976 he was paroled from the federal penitentiary in Marion, Illinois, and went to live with family members in Utah. On July 19, 1976, he robbed and killed a gas station attendant in Orem, Utah. The next day, he held up a motel in nearby Provo, forced the manager, Ben Bushnell, to lie face down on floor, then shot him through the head. Less than 24 hours later, Gilmore was in custody. Because there were eyewitnesses to the motel killing, it was decided to try Gilmore on the Bushnell murder first.

When the trial began on October 5, 1976, the evidence against Gilmore was overwhelming. Peter Arroyo, a motel guest, described seeing Gilmore in the registration office. Prosecutor Noall Wootton asked, "How far away from him were you at the time?"

"Somewhere near ten feet."

"Did you observe anything in his possession at the time?"

"In his right hand he had a pistol with a long barrel. In his left hand he had a cash box from a cash register."

Moments later Arroyo found Ben Bushnell, shot to death in the office.

Gilmore had accidentally shot himself in the hand while escaping from the motel. When detectives traced the blood spots to some bushes, they discovered a .22-caliber pistol. Gerald F. Wilkes, an FBI ballistics expert, compared a shell casing found there with one from the murder scene. Wootton asked him, "Would you tell the jury, please, what your conclusions were?"

"Based on my examination of these two cartridges, I was able to determine that both cartridge cases were fired with this weapon and no other weapon."

No Defense

In the face of such damning testimony, Gilmore's chief counsel, Michael Esplin, declared that the defense intended to offer no evidence, a decision that did not sit well with the defendant. Gilmore loudly protested that he be allowed to testify. Judge J. Robert Bullock told him, "I want you to fully understand that if you do that then you're subject to cross-examination by the State's attorney. Do you understand that?" Gilmore replied affirmatively.

At this point Gilmore's other attorney, Craig Snyder, stepped in with an explanation of why he and Esplin had offered no defense. Essentially both felt that there *was no* defense. Snyder's argument obviously impressed the mercurial Gilmore who abruptly said, "I'll withdraw my request. Just go ahead with it like it is."

"What?" gulped Judge Bullock, stunned by this turn of events.

Gilmore said it again. "I withdraw my request."

All that was left was for both sides to make their closing arguments. At 10:13 A.M. on October 7, 1976, the jury retired to consider their verdict. Before mid-day they were back with a verdict of guilty. Later that day they unanimously recommended the death penalty. Because Utah had dual methods of capital punishment—hanging and firing squad—Gilmore was given a choice. "I prefer to be shot," he said.

When Gary Gilmore went to Death Row, nobody in America had been executed in over a decade, and nobody expected Gilmore to be the first—except Gilmore. He adamantly refused to appeal his conviction or sentence, dismissed both of his lawyers when they did, and insisted that he just wanted to be shot and be done with it. Anything, he said, was preferable to spending the rest of his life behind bars. Two failed suicide bids, on November 16 and December 16, 1977, only strengthened his resolve. Despite frantic legal wrangling by opponents of capital punishment, Gilmore got his wish.

On January 17, 1977, he was strapped to a chair in the Utah State Prison. Five marksmen took aim at the white circle pinned to Gilmore's shirt, then shot him through the heart.

—Colin Evans

Suggestions for Further Reading

McFarland, Samuel G. *Journal Of Criminal Law And Criminology* (Fall 1983): 1014–1032.

Mailer, Norman. *The Executioners's Song.* Boston: Little, Brown & Co., 1979.

White, Welsh S. *University of Pittsburgh Law Review* (Spring 1987): 853–857.

Randall Adams Trial: 1977

Defendant: Randall Dale Adams **Crime Charged:** Murder
Chief Defense Lawyers: Edith James and Dennis White
Chief Prosecutors: Douglas Mulder, Winfield Scott, and Stephen Tokely
Judge: Donald J. Metcalfe **Place:** Dallas, Texas **Dates of Trial:** March
28–May 3, 1977 **Verdict:** Guilty **Sentence:** Death

SIGNIFICANCE

The tragedy of Randall Adams, recorded in the movie, *The Thin Blue Line*, represents a withering indictment of the dangers that accompany overzealous prosecution.

In the early hours of November 29, 1976, police officer Robert Wood was gunned down on a Dallas, Texas, side street by the driver of a blue car. Car and driver made a clean getaway. Three weeks later a 16-year-old petty criminal, David Harris, was arrested in Vidor, Texas, about 250 miles from Dallas, on charges of stealing a blue Mercury Comet. Harris, who had bragged to friends about shooting a Dallas cop, led police to a swamp where they recovered the murder weapon. Harris admitted witnessing the killing but claimed that the gunman was Randall Adams, a 28-year-old hitchhiker he had picked up. Granted immunity from other charges, Harris agreed to testify against Adams.

Going into the trial on March 28, 1977, prosecutor Douglas Mulder had a 100-percent conviction record in capital murder cases. But on this occasion that record looked in serious jeopardy. Harris' disingeniousness under oath posed serious problems, even for someone of Mulder's considerable skill. When defense attorney Dennis White began cross-examination of Harris, he did so incredulously: "Now, after this murder you are saying that the defendant . . . drove right on home [to his motel] and said forget it?"

"Yes, sir," replied Harris.

"And insofar as you know he went in, went to bed and whatever?"

"Yes, sir."

Shaking his head, White turned to comments Harris made to friends in Vidor. "Is it a fact when the story of the policeman in Dallas came on the television you turned to these people and said, 'I wasted that pig'?"

"No, sir."

"What did you say?"

"I told them I was there whenever he got shot, that I did it."

"That you did it?"

"Yes, sir." Earlier, Harris had admitted saying this only to impress his friends: "I thought it was making me big to their standards."

White showed how, prior to the killing, Harris had been on a month-long crime spree and had good reason to shoot Wood. Being caught in possession of a stolen vehicle would have resulted in the revocation of his parole and subsequent return to jail. Adams, by contrast, had no police record whatsoever.

Surprise Witnesses Emerge

With Mulder unable to shake Adams' assertion that he had left Harris two hours prior to the shooting, acquittal seemed a formality. Then, at the 11th hour, three surprise eyewitnesses came forward. R.L. Miller and his wife, Emily, described driving slowly by and seeing everything. Both identified Adams as the driver of the car. (Significantly, one week later, Mrs. Miller's daughter, due to face armed robbery charges, learned that her case had been quietly dropped.)

Another motorist, Michael Randell, claimed to have seen two people in the car. The passenger was indistinct but he had no trouble recognizing Adams as the driver.

White fulminated at the unfairness of these tactics: "Mr. Mulder is trying to convict an innocent man." But his words fell on deaf ears. Judge Donald J. Metcalfe ruled the evidence admissible and, on May 3, 1977, Randall Adams was convicted and sentenced to death.

But the fight continued. In June 1980 the U.S. Supreme Court overturned the conviction on the grounds of improper jury selection. Dallas prosecutors, anxious to avoid a retrial, advised the governor that Adams' sentence be commuted to life imprisonment.

In 1985, David Harris, on Death Row for another killing, began hinting that much of his testimony against Adams had been coached into him by conviction-hungry prosecutors. In a series of taped interviews Harris obliquely admitted culpability. The three eyewitnesses also admitted that their evidence had been compromised.

Another four years would pass before an appeals court ordered Adams' release. While refusing to admit any error, prosecutors declined to retry him. Adams was freed but has still not been fully exonerated.

In 1988, Errol Morris' Oscar-nominated "docudrama," *The Thin Blue Line*, brought the name of Randall Adams to national prominence. A searching examination of Dallas justice, it did more than pave the way for Adams' ultimate release, it exposed the heartless folly of placing ambition over truth.

—*Colin Evans*

Suggestions for Further Reading

Adams, Randall, William Hoffer, and Marilyn Mona Hoffer. *Adams V. Texas*. New York: St. Martin's Press, 1991.

Bruning, F. "Why Did Randall Adams Almost Die?" *Mclean's* (March 27, 1989).

Carlson, M. "Recrossing The Thin Blue Line." *Time* (April 3, 1989): 23.

Cartwright, Gary. "The Longest Ride of His Life." *Texas Monthly* (May 1987): 124ff.

Marvin Mandel Trial: 1977

Defendant: Maryland Governor Marvin Mandel   **Crimes Charged:** Mail fraud and racketeering   **Chief Defense Lawyers:** M. Albert Figinski, Eugene Gressman, D. Christopher Ohly, and Arnold M. Weiner
Chief Prosecutors: Russell T. Baker, Jr., Daniel J. Hurson, Barnet D. Skolnik, and Elizabeth H. Trimble   **Judge:** Robert L. Taylor   **Place:** Baltimore, Maryland   **Dates of Trial:** June 1–August 21, 1977   **Verdict:** Guilty, later overturned   **Sentence:** 4 years in prison, commuted after 19 months served.

SIGNIFICANCE

The Marvin Mandel trial was a national scandal, exposing massive political corruption at the highest level of Maryland state government. The reversal of Mandel's conviction, however, signaled a limit on the ability to attack state crimes through federal statutes.

On December 31, 1971, a group of businessmen and investors purchased the Marlboro Race Track in Prince George's County, Maryland. Like all of Maryland's horse racing tracks, the Marlboro track was regulated by the state, and it was allotted 18 racing days. Eager to increase their profits, and not too concerned about the means used, the new owners approached Maryland Governor Marvin Mandel and asked for help. Mandel, formerly a strong advocate of strict horse racing regulation, suddenly dropped his opposition to a bill pending in the Maryland General Assembly that would increase Marlboro's racing days from 18 to 36. The bill passed on January 12, 1972. In March 1972, Mandel successfully lobbied the General Assembly to increase the number of racing days again, this time from 36 to 94. Further, Mandel helped the Marlboro owners acquire interests in other Maryland racetracks.

For his help, Mandel received cash and other valuables under the table from the investors. Expensive clothes and jewelry that Mandel purchased were paid for by the racetrack owners, who also gave Mandel a valuable interest in a new Maryland waterfront development called Ray's Point. Federal prosecutors discovered Mandel's activities, however, and indicted him along with racetrack investors Ernest N. Cory, Jr., W. Dale Hess, Irvin Kovens, Harry W. Rodgers III, and William A. Rodgers.

Tried, Convicted, and Ultimately Acquitted

Mandel was charged with violations of federal law and not state law, namely those federal laws which prohibit mail fraud and racketeering. Prosecutors frequently invoke "mail fraud" when anything connected with a crime goes through the U.S. mail system, such as a check mailed by one defendant to another. Mandel's lawyers were M. Albert Figinski, Eugene Gressman, D. Christopher Ohly, and Arnold M. Weiner. The chief prosecutors were Russell T. Baker, Jr., Daniel J. Hurson, Barnet D. Skolnik, and Elizabeth H. Trimble. The trial began on June 1, 1977, before Judge Robert L. Taylor in Baltimore, Maryland.

The trial lasted nearly three months, during which Mandel fought with the prosecutors over virtually every issue. For example, when Skolnik introduced telephone company records into evidence to show the existence of phone calls between Mandel and the other defendants, Mandel even denied knowledge of his own telephone number.

Jury foreman Howard Davis delivers the guilty verdict to the court clerk in the fraud and racketeering trial of Governor Marvin Mandel. (AP/Wide World Photos)

Question: Governor, who in [your personal office suite] had the phone number 267-5901?

Answer: Mrs. Grace Donald.

Question: And who else, sir?

Answer: Mrs. Grace Donald.

Question: Wasn't that your phone number, sir?

Answer: No, sir, that was Mrs. Grace Donald's phone number listed to the executive office. That was her phone. That is the way she handled it.

Exasperated, Skolnik presented a Maryland state government phone directory, which established that Mandel's telephone number was indeed 267-5901.

On August 21, 1977, the jury found Mandel guilty. He was sentenced to four years in prison. Mandel's attorneys appealed and won a brief victory when the U.S. Fourth Circuit Court of Appeals overturned Mandel's conviction. The Fourth Circuit reheard the appeal, however, and decided to uphold the conviction. Mandel went to prison and served 19 months of his sentence, but the rest was commuted. Even after he served his sentence, Mandel continued to fight the conviction to clear his name.

On November 12, 1987, Judge Frederic N. Smalkin of the U.S. District Court for the District of Maryland, where Mandel had been tried, overturned Mandel's conviction. Smalkin did not deny the strong evidence of bribery and dishonesty presented at Mandel's trial, but he insisted that the prosecutors had stretched their interpretation of federal mail fraud and racketeering laws past the breaking point to bring Mandel to trial for what were really state crimes. Thus, although Mandel remains a political pariah, the outcome of his trial was, in fact, a failure for the federal prosecutors.

—Stephen G. Christianson

Suggestions for Further Reading

Jacobs, Bradford. *Thimbleriggers: the Law v. Governor Marvin Mandel.* Baltimore, MD: Johns Hopkins University Press, 1984.

"Marvin Mandel's Life in Prison." *Newsweek* (November 24, 1980): 20–21.

"A New Verdict for Mandel." *Time* (November 23, 1987): 31.

"Parting Shots." *The Washingtonian* (July 1981): 21.

Collin v. Smith: 1977

Plaintiff: Frank Collin, on behalf of the National Socialist Party of America
Defendant: Albert Smith, as president of the Village of Skokie, Illinois
Plaintiff Claims: That Skokie had illegally prevented the American Nazis from holding a political march   **Chief Defense Lawyers:** Gilbert Gordon and Harvey Schwartz   **Chief Lawyer for Plaintiff:** David A. Goldberger
Judge: Bernard M. Decker   **Place:** Chicago, Illinois
Date of Hearing: December 2, 1977   **Decision:** That Skokie could not prevent the Nazis from marching

SIGNIFICANCE

Despite the fact that the Nazis had deliberately chosen a heavily Jewish community to march in, the courts stuck firm to the First Amendment principle that unpopular groups must be allowed to express their political opinions.

Prior to World War II, there was a small yet fairly significant Nazi movement in the United States, which grew out of the German-American Bund. After the war, the movement was discredited, and survived only due to the leadership of George Lincoln Rockwell, who was assassinated in 1967. As with other fringe groups, such as the Ku Klux Klan, hatred and prejudice kept the National Socialist Party of America alive with a small but vocal membership. In the mid-1970s, to generate publicity and attract new members, Nazi leader Frank Collin targeted the Chicago, Illinois, suburb of Skokie as a site for a series of marches and demonstrations.

Over half of Skokie's 70,000 residents were Jewish, and many were survivors of German concentration camps. Seeing Nazi marchers and the swastika was bound to bring back tragic memories. Skokie was initially successful in getting an injunction against any Nazi marches from the Illinois state courts, but the Supreme Court summarily dismissed the injunction as unconstitutionally infringing on the Nazis' First Amendment right to political expression. Determined to protect its Jewish residents, on May 2, 1977, Skokie decided to thwart the Nazis by passing a series of municipal ordinances. The ordinances required any group wishing to stage a public demonstration to obtain $350,000 in liability and property insurance, and forbade the dissemination of racist literature and the wearing of military-style uniforms by group members during such demonstrations. The Nazis promptly took Albert Smith, president of the Village of Skokie, and other municipal officials to court.

Nazis Must Be Allowed to March

Ironically, both sides were represented by Jewish attorneys. David A. Goldberger from the American Civil Liberties Union represented the Nazis; Gilbert Gordon and Harvey Schwartz represented Smith and Skokie. The case was heard before U.S. District Court Judge Bernard M. Decker in Chicago on December 2, 1977.

Collin was brutally honest about his party's beliefs. He stated that the Nazis believed blacks were inferior, and that Jews were involved in an international financial and communist conspiracy. Further, Collin testified that the Nazis deliberately copied the military uniform style of the notorious "Brownshirts" of Hitler's Third Reich:

> We wear brown shirts with a dark brown tie, a swastika pin on the tie, a leather shoulder strap, a black belt with buckle, dark brown trousers, black engineer boots, and either a steel helmet or a cloth cap, depending on the situation, plus a swastika arm band on the left arm and an American flag patch on the right arm.

On February 23, 1978, Decker issued his decision. Stating that "it is better to allow those who preach racial hate to expend their venom in rhetoric rather than to be panicked into embarking on the dangerous course of permitting the government to decide what its citizens may say and hear," Decker held that the ordinances violated the First Amendment and were unenforceable.

Skokie appealed to the U.S. Court of Appeals for the Seventh Circuit, and the case was argued on April 14, 1978. On May 22, 1978, the Seventh Circuit refused to overturn Decker's decision:

> No authorities need be cited to establish the proposition, which the Village does not dispute, that First Amendment rights are truly precious and fundamental to our national life. Nor is this truth without relevance to the saddening historical images this case inevitably arouses. It is, after all, in part the fact that our constitutional system protects minorities unpopular at a particular time or place from government harassment and intimidation, that distinguishes life in this country from life under the Third Reich.

Finally, Skokie asked the Supreme Court to review the case, a procedure called "petition for a writ of *certiorari*." On October 16, 1978, the justices of the Supreme Court voted to deny *certiorari*, and so Decker's original decision was upheld. Justices Harry Blackmun and Byron White, however, dissented. Blackmun and White felt that the court should make an official pronouncement on the important First Amendment issues in the Skokie litigation, and not just let the lower court decision stand by default:

> [We] feel that the present case affords the Court an opportunity to consider whether, in the context of the facts that this record appears to present, there is no limit whatsoever to the exercise of free speech. There indeed may be no such limit, but when citizens assert, not casually but with deep convic-

tion, that the proposed demonstration is scheduled at a place and in a manner that is taunting and overwhelmingly offensive to the citizens of that place, that assertion, uncomfortable though it may be for judges, deserves to be examined. It just might fall into the same category as one's "right" to cry "fire" in a crowded theater, for "the character of every act depends upon the circumstances in which it is done." [Quoting *Schenck v. U.S.*, see separate entry]

There was now nothing to prevent Collin and the Nazis, victorious in the courts, from marching in Skokie. Collin, however, abruptly called the march off. Declaring that his aim had been to generate "pure agitation to restore our right to free speech," Collin proclaimed the whole affair a moral victory for the Nazis and never marched in Skokie. Whether the Skokie affair was a victory for the Nazis is debatable, but it was certainly a victory for the right of every minority group, no matter how unpopular, to express its political views without government interference.

—Stephen G. Christianson

Suggestions for Further Reading

Bartlett, Jonathan. *The First Amendment in a Free Society.* New York: H.W. Wilson, 1979.

Downs, Donald Alexander. *Nazis in Skokie: Freedom, Community, and the First Amendment.* Notre Dame, Ind.: University of Notre Dame Press, 1985.

Gross, Alan. "I Remember Skokie: a Cultural Defense." *Chicago* (February 1981): 90–97.

Hamlin, David. *The Nazi/Skokie Conflict: a Civil Liberties Battle.* Boston: Beacon Press, 1980.

Neier, Aryeh. *Defending My Enemy: American Nazis, the Skokie Case, and the Risks of Freedom.* New York: E.P. Dutton, 1979.

The "Son of Sam" Trial: 1978

Defendant: David R. Berkowitz   **Crimes Charged:** Second-degree murder, attempted murder, and assault   **Chief Defense Lawyers:** Ira Jultak and Leon Stern   **Chief Prosecutors:** Eugene Gold, Mario Merola, and John Santucci   **Judges:** Joseph R. Corso, William Kapelman, and Nicholas Tsoucalas   **Place:** New York, New York   **Date of Trial:** May 8, 1978   **Verdict:** Guilty   **Sentence:** Six 25-years-to-life terms, with additional 15-and 25-year terms for assault and attempted murder

SIGNIFICANCE

While there was never any question that David Berkowitz committed the crimes with which he was charged, his case fueled debate over the difficulty of determining the sanity of defendants and the culpability of the mentally ill. He also inspired a state law preventing criminals from profiting from books or films about their crimes. The "Son of Sam Law" was overturned by the U.S. Supreme Court in 1991.

From October 1976 to August 1977, fear spread across New York City whenever night fell. Six young people were killed and seven more were wounded by an unknown gunman who seemed to be hunting young women. Hundreds of detectives were assigned to find "the .44 caliber killer," so-called because of the unusually large handgun bullets he used. When police found a bizarre note at the scene of a double murder New Yorkers came to know the killer by his own nickname, the "Son of Sam."

After the killer mortally wounded 20-year-old Stacy Moskowitz and blinded her date Robert Violante in Brooklyn on July 31, detectives got a lead. They discovered a parking ticket issued to a 24-year-old postal clerk named David Berkowitz for parking alongside a fire hydrant near the crime scene. Police located Berkowitz's car at his Yonkers apartment building and found a duffel bag full of guns behind the front seat. Berkowitz was seized when he came outside, carrying a .44-caliber revolver in a small paper bag.

Berkowitz's statement to police left no doubt that he was responsible for the attacks. He described unreleased details in the "Son of Sam" letter and claimed that "Sam" was a 6,000-year-old man inhabiting the body of a neighbor,

Sam Carr. "Sam" and other Satanic "demons" had ordered Berkowitz to kill by transmitting commands through the Carr family's Labrador Retriever.

Insanity Issue Arises

Berkowitz was arraigned in Brooklyn for the Moskowitz-Violante shooting, as prosecutors in the Bronx and Queens quickly wrote indictments against him for murders in their boroughs. The primary legal issue immediately became whether David Berkowitz was sane enough to stand trial.

A psychiatric report delivered to New York State Supreme Court justices in all three boroughs on August 30 concluded that David Berkowitz was not mentally capable of assisting in his own defense and did not understand the charges against him. Psychiatrists Daniel Schwartz and Richard Weidenbacher, Jr. felt that Berkowitz was "well aware" of the six murder charges, understood that they were criminal acts, and had "the intellectual capacity" to understand the legal process unfolding against him. Yet the doctors concluded that paranoid psychosis left Berkowitz so "emotionally dead" that he was neither capable of nor interested in assisting in his own defense.

Brooklyn District Attorney Eugene Gold challenged the report, obtaining court approval for Berkowitz's examination by prosecution psychiatrist Dr. David Abrahamsen. A month of interviews convinced Dr. Abrahamsen that Berkowitz's demons were "a conscious invention" he was able to control, not a psychotic disorder which controlled his actions. Abrahamsen declared that Berkowitz could understand the legal process and assist in his own defense if he chose to do so. Justice John R. Starkey agreed at a competency hearing on October 21. A week later, Justice Starkey withdrew from the case amidst a furor over controversial statements he had made to the press about Berkowitz's intention to blame his actions on the demons. A new competency hearing was scheduled for the following spring before a different judge.

At the second hearing, psychiatrists Schwartz and Weidenbacher reversed their original opinion. They reported that Berkowitz's mental condition was improving from treatment. While not suggesting that he was sane at the time he allegedly committed the murders, they agreed that Berkowitz was now able to participate in his defense. Their reversal helped Judge Joseph R. Corso determine that Berkowitz was mentally fit to stand trial.

Cases Consolidated

Throughout the proceedings again, David Berkowitz remained determined to plead guilty, a decision he insisted was his own in spite of the advice of his "demons." His attorneys unsuccessfully tried to persuade him to plead not guilty by reason of insanity. Expectations of a guilty plea were so high that a special agreement was reached to consolidate all of the legal proceedings to a single trial venue for security and to save court costs.

On May 8, 1978, in a Brooklyn courtroom, Judge Corso accepted Berkowitz's guilty pleas for the Moskowitz-Violante shooting. Justice Corso then signed a special administrative agreement allowing Justice William Kapelman of the Bronx to come to the bench. Justice Kapelman similarly turned the proceedings over to Queens Justice Nicholas Tsoucalas after accepting Berkowitz's guilty plea for three murders in the Bronx. Like the other judges, Justice Tsoucalas asked Berkowitz if he was making the guilty pleas of his own free will and wanted to know if the defendant had meant to cause serious injury to two young women he had wounded in Queens. "Oh, no, sir," Berkowitz replied. "I wanted to kill them." Judge Tsoucalas accepted Berkowitz's guilty pleas for two murders and five attempted murders.

David Berkowitz during an interview in Attica prison. (AP/Wide World Photos)

The three judges returned to Brooklyn on May 22, but postponed sentencing when Berkowitz struggled with deputies and screamed, "I'd kill them all again!" On June 12, 1978, he was sentenced to the maximum term of 25 years to life imprisonment for each of the six murders, plus additional terms for assault and attempted murder. The life terms were to run consecutively, but the New York state practice of "merging" sentences would make him eligible for parole as if he had committed only one murder.

Case Inspires New Law

After four months psychiatric treatment, Berkowitz was transferred to Attica State Prison, where he ordered his lawyers to drop all appeals on his behalf. Negotiations for lucrative book and film projects about the case began against his wishes. Berkowitz tried to stop the deals by telling the *New York Times* that his stories of demons were a hoax.

Ironically, even before his capture, Berkowitz had inspired a law barring him from receiving any money generated by his crimes. Anticipating that anyone committing such gruesome acts might later profit by telling his story, the New York State Legislature passed a statute popularly known as the "Son of Sam Law" in 1977. The law required that an accused or convicted criminal's income from printed or film work describing his crime be deposited in an escrow account, where it would be available to answer possible claims by crime victims for five years. Berkowitz took no interest in the money swirling around his case, but claims by his lawyers resulted in an eight-year legal battle before the New York Crime Victims Compensation Board was able to distribute royalties to his victims and their families.

The "Son of Sam Law" separated memoir royalties' from famous convicted murderers like Jack Henry Abbott, Jean Harris, and Mark David Chapman. In 1986, however, publishers Simon & Schuster contested the compensation board's demand for future royalties plus $96,000 already paid to career criminal Henry Hill for revealing his misdeeds in the book *Wiseguy* (the basis for the film *Goodfellas*). On December 10, 1991, the U.S. Supreme Court unanimously ruled that the law was an unconstitutional "content-based" suppression of the First Amendment right to free expression. The decision left New York and 41 other states searching for acceptable wording for laws meant to protect the rights of crime victims.

While his trial was the legal finale of one of the bloodiest murder sprees in American history, accepting David Berkowitz's guilty pleas meant that the issue of his sanity at the time of his crimes would never be resolved. As he began serving his time, debates over the insanity defense, the role of psychiatric testimony, and ethical questions about trying the mentally ill continued to grow.

— *Thomas C. Smith*

Suggestions for Further Reading

Abrahamsen, David. *Confessions of Son of Sam*. New York: Columbia University Press, 1985.

——. "Unmasking Son of Sam's Demons." *New York Times Magazine* (July 1, 1979): 20–22.

Goldstein, Tom. "The Berkowitz Legal Puzzle." *New York Times* (May 25, 1978): Section IV, 20.

Klausner, Lawrence D. *The Son of Sam*. New York: McGraw-Hill, 1981.

Salisbury, Stephan. ".44-Caliber Journalism." *The Nation* (May 26, 1979): 591–593.

Bakke v. University of California . . . Appeal: 1978

Appellee: Allan Bakke **Appellant:** The Medical School of the University of California **Appellee Claim:** That the California Supreme Court erred in ruling that the school's special-admissions program for minorities violated Bakke's civil rights as a white male when he was denied admission
Chief Lawyer for Appellee: Reynold H. Colvin
Chief Lawyers for Appellant: Archibald Cox, Paul J. Mishkin, Jack B. Owens, and Donald L. Reidhaar **Justices:** Harry A. Blackmun, William J. Brennan, Jr., Warren E. Burger, Thurgood Marshall, Lewis F. Powell, Jr., William H. Rehnquist, John Paul Stevens, Potter Stewart, and Byron R. White
Place: Washington, D.C. **Date of Decision:** June 28, 1978
Decision: That the school's special-admissions program was unconstitutional

SIGNIFICANCE
For the first time, the Supreme Court said there could be such a thing as reverse discrimination.

The University of California operates several campuses throughout the state, and it is one of the largest state-sponsored higher education systems. At the university's campus in Davis, California, a medical school was established in 1968 with an entering class of 50 students. Three years later, the entering class size was doubled to 100 students. Originally, there was no preferential admissions policy for minorities. From 1968 to 1970, the school implemented a special-admissions program to increase minority representation in each entering class.

The special admissions program worked separately from the regular admissions program. Sixteen percent of the entering class was reserved for minorities, and minority applicants were processed and interviewed separately from regular applicants. The grade point averages and standardized test score averages for special-admissions entrants were significantly lower than for regular-admissions entrants.

In 1973, a Caucasian male named Allan Bakke applied to the Davis Medical School. Although Bakke got a combined score of 468 out of a possible

500 from his interviewers, his application was rejected. There were 2,464 applications for the 100 positions in the 1973 entering class, and by the time Bakke's application came up for consideration the school was only taking applicants with scores of 470 or better. Four special-admissions seats were left unfilled, however, and Bakke wrote a bitter letter to Dr. George H. Lowrey, associate dean and chairman of the Admissions Committee, complaining about the injustice of the special-admissions process.

Bakke applied again in 1974. That year there was even more competition for the 100 entering class positions: the school received 3,737 applications. Lowrey was one of Bakke's interviewers and gave him a low score, which contributed to Bakke's being rejected once again. Furious, Bakke sued the University of California in the Superior Court of California.

Bakke alleged that the Medical School's special admissions program acted to exclude him on the basis of his race and violated his rights under the Equal Protection Clause of the Fourteenth Amendment to the U.S. Constitution, the California state constitution, and civil rights legislation. The trial court agreed but refused to order the school to admit Bakke as a student. Bakke appealed to the California Supreme Court, which confirmed the trial court's decision that the school's admissions programs were unconstitutional and also ordered the school to admit Bakke.

Protesters equated the Court's decision in *Bakke* as racist and sexist. (Bettye-Lane)

Reverse Discrimination Claimed

The School appealed to the U.S. Supreme Court. Its attorneys were Archibald Cox, Paul J. Mishkin, Jack B. Owens and Donald L. Reidhaar, and Bakke's chief attorney was Reynold H. Colvin. The parties argued their case before the Supreme Court on October 12, 1977. Bakke's attorney, Colvin, was making his first Supreme Court appearance, and he faced several experienced attorneys. For example, Cox was a former Harvard Law School professor and had served as Watergate Special Prosecutor. Colvin found himself immersed in an argument with Justice Thurgood Marshall, the only African-American on the court, over whether minorities should be accorded any preference in the school's admissions process:

> Marshall: You are arguing about keeping somebody out and the other side is arguing about getting somebody in.
>
> Colvin: That's right.
>
> Marshall: So it depends on which way you look at it doesn't it? . . .
>
> Colvin: If I may finish . . .
>
> Marshall: You are talking about your client's rights. Don't these underprivileged people have some rights?
>
> Colvin: They certainly have the right to . . .
>
> Marshall: To eat cake.

On June 28, 1978, Justice Lewis F. Powell, Jr., announced the decision of the majority in the 5-4 decision. It held that the school's special-admissions policy constituted reverse discrimination and was thus illegal. The court upheld the decision of the California Supreme Court, and affirmed the California court's order that Bakke be admitted to the school. Further, the Court upheld the California court's determination that the school's special-admissions program had to be scrapped. However, the Court held that schools could continue to give preference to minorities, so long as they didn't exclude whites from a specific portion of the entering class, like the school had. The Court cited Harvard University's program as a model for an acceptable admissions policy that gave consideration to racial status without violating the civil rights of whites such as Bakke:

> The experience of other university admissions programs, which take race into account in achieving the educational diversity valued by the First Amendment, demonstrates that the assignment of a fixed number of places to a minority group is not a necessary means toward that end. An illuminating example is found in the Harvard College program. . . . When the [Harvard] Committee on Admissions reviews the large middle group of applicants who are admissible and deemed capable of doing good work in their courses, the race of an applicant may tip the balance in his favor just as geographic origin or a life spent on a farm may tip the balance in other candidates' cases. A farm boy from Idaho can bring something to Harvard College that a Bostonian cannot offer. Similarly, a black student can usually bring something that a white person cannot offer.

In Harvard college admissions the Committee has not set target quotas for the number of blacks, or of musicians, football players, physicists or Californians to be admitted in a given year.

In a nutshell, the Court had ruled that while schools could give minority applicants some extra preference and consideration, they couldn't set aside a quota of positions for minority students that excluded whites. Such a program, like that at the Davis Medical School, constituted reverse discrimination. Bakke had won his case and would be admitted as a student. It was the first time that the Supreme Court applied civil rights protection to white students seeking admission to a university.

—Stephen G. Christianson

Suggestions for Further Reading

"Five Cases That Changed American Society." *Scholastic Update* (November 30, 1984): 19–20.

"Minorities Down at Davis Univ. Since Bakke Case." *Jet* (June 7, 1982): 8.

Mooney, Christopher F. *Inequality and the American Conscience: Justice Through the Judicial System*. New York: Paulist Press, 1982.

O'Neill, Timothy J. *Bakke & the Politics of Equality: Friends and Foes in the Classroom of Litigation*. Middletown, Conn.: Wesleyan University Press, 1985.

Schwartz, Bernard. *Behind Bakke: Affirmative Action and the Supreme Court*. New York: New York University Press, 1988.

The Marvin v. Marvin "Palimony" Suit: 1979

Plaintiff: Michelle Triola Marvin   **Defendant:** Lee Marvin
Plaintiff Claim: That Michelle Triola Marvin was entitled to half of Lee
Marvin's earnings during the six years they spent together as an unmarried
couple   **Chief Defense Lawyers:** Mark Goldman and A. David Kagon
Chief Lawyer for Plaintiff: Marvin Mitchelson   **Judge:** Arthur K. Marshall
Place: Los Angeles, California   **Dates of Trial:** January 9—March 28, 1979
Verdict: $104,000 for "rehabilitation" awarded to Michelle Marvin, later
rescinded

SIGNIFICANCE

The case established the right of partners in nonmarried relationships to sue for a
division of property.

When film actor Lee Marvin married in 1970, his former lover Michelle Triola was not inclined to wish him well. After all, she had lived with the rambunctious, hard-drinking actor for six years and had even legally changed her name to Marvin. At first she accepted the $833 per month he sent to support her while she tried to resume her singing and acting career. When the promised checks stopped, she decided to sue him. Her claim reverberated in divorce courts across America in a decade when the number of unmarried couples living together more than doubled.

Michelle Marvin contacted Marvin Mitchelson, a colorful Los Angeles, California divorce lawyer often hired by Hollywood celebrities. Mitchelson filed a suit charging that, apart from the lack of a $3 marriage license, Lee Marvin and Michelle Triola Marvin were essentially married from 1964 to 1970. Michelle Marvin had given up her career as a singer and an actress to serve as the actor's "cook, companion, and confidante." She claimed that she was entitled to half of what he had earned during their relationship. Her share would be $1.8 million, including $100,000 for the loss of the career she had forgone. Attorney Mitchelson announced he was demanding "palimony" for his client—alimony from a former "pal." While popular usage of the term palimony would result from the case, Mitchelson's real task was to prove that Lee Marvin had reneged on an oral or implicit contract to share his assets.

California had abolished the concept of common-law marriage in 1895. Because the circumstances of the case were so similar to the common-law concept, Michelle Marvin's suit was initially rejected by the courts. On appeal, however, the California Supreme Court endorsed the principle of seeking palimony in 1976, allowing her case to be heard and sparking similar suits in 15 other states. By the time *Marvin v. Marvin* arrived in court in 1979, more than l,000 palimony suits were pending in California courts alone.

Lee Marvin's lawyers tried to have the case dismissed, but Judge Arthur K. Marshall denied their final motion in January 1979. In Judge Marshall's opinion, only the lack of a marriage license and the absence of a clergyman made the life the two Marvins led together different from that of a married couple.

Trial Enthralls Spectators

Lee Marvin's celebrity and the legal implications for thousands of unmarried couples ensured that the courtroom was packed. Sensation-seeking spectators were not disappointed. Michelle Marvin claimed that Lee Marvin told her early in their relationship, "What I have is yours and what you have is mine." She felt that this and her six years with the actor added up to an implicit marriage contract. The pair had maintained joint bank accounts and were accepted as husband and wife in Hollywood social circles. She offered a packet of love letters from Lee Marvin as evidence and tearfully recalled having several abortions at the actor's insistence because he did not want to become a parent.

Lee Marvin testified that his declarations of love were sexual endearments and denied ever promising to share his assets with his former lover. He dismissed her name change as an act that was entirely her decision, taken in the last days of their relationship. He claimed that he had tried to talk her out of it, joking that she should take the name of a more successful Hollywood star and call herself Gary Cooper. The joint bank accounts were opened as a convenience on movie locations. He had not relinquished sole ownership of his house nor did he and Michelle Marvin co-own any property.

Lee Marvin's lawyers argued that if he had ever intended to marry Michelle Triola during their six years together, he obviously would have done so.

With dramatic flair, attorney Mitchelson unsuccessfully motioned that Lee Marvin should be forced to pay $1 million punitive damages for the fraud of telling the plaintiff he loved her without meaning it.

Career Claim Fails

The picture of a promising career Michelle Marvin claimed to have abandoned faded on the witness stand. Testimony by nightclub owners and singer Mel Torme appraised her talents as being somewhere between mediocre and "slightly better than average." She claimed that her devotion to Lee Marvin caused her to refuse a part in the Broadway musical *Flower Drum Song,* but dancer Gene Kelly denied ever offering her a role.

After 11 weeks in court, Judge Marshall ruled that Michelle Marvin had failed to prove her claim of an oral or implicit contract to share her lover's assets. Under the legal principle of "equitable remedy," however, the judge awarded her $104,000 so that she would "have the economic means to re-educate herself and learn new employable skills." The $104,000 "rehabilitation" figure represented $1,000 a week for two years, the top weekly salary she had earned as a singer before becoming the film star's companion.

Michelle Triola Marvin and celebrity attorney Marvin Mitchelson after her victory in the first "palimony" case. (AP/ Wide World Photos)

The judge stopped short of likening his decision to alimony or property division in conventional divorces. To accept the notion of equal division of property without a marriage contract, he wrote:

> would mean that the court would recognize each unmarried person living together to be automatically entitled by such living together and performing spouse-like functions, to half of the property bought with the earnings of the other nonmarital partner.

Judge Marshall felt that this would come too close to recognizing the long-abolished concept of common-law marriage.

Both sides claimed victory. The only loser appeared to be attorney Mitchelson, who had taken the case on a contingency-fee basis, agreeing to be paid a percentage of the expected million-dollar settlement. *Time* magazine calculated that the years Mitchelson had invested in the case had earned him $6.50 an hour, a miniscule fraction of his normal hourly fee.

Mitchelson attempted to have the $104,000 award increased or, at least, to have Lee Marvin pay Michelle Marvin's legal bill. Judge Marshall refused. Mitchelson's only victory was that he had established the right to file a palimony suit, testing the legal property rights of unmarried couples for the first time. "This principle," ruled the judge, "did not come at the expense of the defendant." Mitchelson tried without success to get the State of California to pay him $500,000 for his work.

Observers debated whether Judge Marshall had set forth new legal guidelines for unmarried couples or had arbitrarily awarded an alimony payment under a different name. In 1981, the California State Court of Appeals overturned the $104,000 award, ruling that there was no basis in law for arriving at such a specific figure. The court's decision related only to the sum itself. The basic precedent set by the Marvin case remained, entitling estranged unmarried partners to sue for an equal division of their assets and prompting luckier couples to have legally binding nonmarital contracts drafted to guard against unforeseen future problems.

— Thomas C. Smith

Suggestions for Further Reading

Burnett, Barbara A., ed. *Every Woman's Legal Guide*. Garden City, N.Y.: Doubleday & Co., 1983.

Couric, Emily. *The Divorce Lawyers*. New York: St. Martin's Press, 1992.

Van Gelder, Lawrence. "Lawyers Troubled By Rehabilitation Concept In Marvin Decision." *New York Times* (April 20, 1979): 18.

Weitzman, Lenore J. *The Marriage Contract: Spouses, Lovers, and the Law*. New York: The Free Press, 1981.

Zec, Donald. *Marvin: The Story of Lee Marvin*. New York: St. Martin's Press, 1980.

Silkwood v. Kerr-McGee: 1979

Plaintiff: Estate of Karen Silkwood   **Defendant:** Kerr-McGee Nuclear Company   **Plaintiff Claim:** Damages for negligence leading to the plutonium contamination of Karen Silkwood   **Chief Defense Lawyers:** Elliott Fenton, John Griffin, Jr., Larry D. Ottoway, William Paul, L.E. Stringer, and Bill J. Zimmerman   **Chief Lawyers for Plaintiff:** Gerald Spence, Arthur Angel, and James Ikard   **Judge:** Frank G. Theis   **Place:** Oklahoma City, Oklahoma   **Dates of Trial:** March 6—May 18, 1979   **Verdict:** Defendant was found negligent and was ordered to pay $505,000 actual damages, $10 million punitive damages

SIGNIFICANCE

This precedent-setting action between the estate of a dead woman and a giant industrial conglomerate sparked a public uproar about the issue of safety at nuclear facilities and held a company liable for negligence.

Karen Silkwood, a young lab technician and union activist at an Oklahoma plutonium plant operated by the Kerr-McGee Nuclear Company, uncovered evidence in 1974 of managerial wrongdoing and negligence. On November 13, three months after providing the Atomic Energy Commission (AEC) with a detailed list of violations, she was en route to deliver documents to a *New York Times* reporter when her car crashed under mysterious circumstances and she died. An autopsy revealed plutonium contamination, confirming the results of tests taken when she was alive. Speculation among her opponents at that time, was that she had deliberately contaminated herself to embarrass Kerr-McGee, an assertion that Silkwood bitterly denied. When the Silkwood estate announced its intention to sue, Kerr-McGee insisted that its Cimarron plant met federal guidelines and that any contamination Silkwood sustained must have come from elsewhere.

After more than four years of delay, on March 6, 1979, Karen Silkwood's family finally had their day in court against Kerr-McGee. Actually they had three months, the longest civil trial in Oklahoma history. Leading off for the Silkwood estate, attorney Gerry Spence put Dr. John Gofman, a physician and an outspoken critic of lax nuclear regulation, on the stand. In answer to a Spence question about the dangers of plutonium, Gofman replied, "The license to give out doses of plutonium is a legalized permit to murder."

"Was Karen in danger of dying from the plutonium inside her?" asked Spence.

"Yes, she was."

Pressed on Kerr-McGee's skimpy employee training program, Gofman responded: "My opinion is that it is clearly and unequivocally negligence."

The only member of the Kerr-McGee management team to testify against his former employers was ex-supervisor James Smith. While conceding little affection for Silkwood as a person—as a union organizer she had been prickly and combative—Smith corroborated her findings about safety violations at Kerr-McGee. Most alarming was his assertion that there were 40 pounds of Material Unaccounted For (MUF), meaning deadly plutonium that was missing. He dismissed company claims that the MUF was still at the plant. "Let me put it this way," said Smith, who had been in charge of flushing out the system pipes, "if there's 40 pounds still at Cimarron, I don't know where it is."

Another ex-Cimarron employee, now a highway patrol officer, Ron Hammock, told of defective fuel rods, packed full of plutonium pellets, knowingly being shipped to other facilities. "Who told you to ship them?" Spence asked. "My supervisor," the officer calmly replied.

Near Disaster

Three weeks into the trial something happened that raised the question of nuclear safety throughout the United States. A nuclear reactor in Pennsylvania had a near meltdown. For most Americans, the disaster at Three Mile Island was their first experience of the potential for nuclear calamity. The incident cast an inevitable pall over the Silkwood suit, enough for Kerr-McGee chief attorney Bill Paul to move for a mistrial. After careful consideration, Judge Frank Theis denied the request. On hearing this decision, the Silkwood team heaved a vast sigh of relief. Lacking the limitless financial resources of Kerr-McGee, they were fighting this action on a shoestring; any delay would only play into the hands of the $2-billion giant.

Disgruntled, Bill Paul called Kerr-McGee's star witness, Dr. George Voelz, health director at the prestigious Los Alamos Scientific Laboratory. Voelz testified that, in his opinion, the level of contamination displayed by Karen Silkwood fell within AEC standards. Spence thought otherwise. In a cross-examination lasting two days, he drew one embarrassing retraction after another from the frazzled scientist. Central to Voelz's theme was a model used to arrive at the standards. Spence showed how Karen Silkwood in no way conformed to the average person used in the model, she had been less than 100 pounds and a heavy smoker, both factors that influence the chances of contamination. Also, Spence extracted from Voelz the grudging admission that he really didn't know the level of plutonium exposure necessary to cause cancer.

In his final instructions to the jury, Judge Theis spelled out the law: "If you find that the damage to the person or property of Karen Silkwood resulted from the operation of this plant, . . . Kerr-McGee . . . is liable."

On May 18, 1979, after four days of deliberation, the jury decided that Kerr-McGee had indeed been negligent and awarded $505,000 in damages. A gasp swept the courtroom when the jury added on their assessment for punitive damages: $10 million.

It was a huge settlement, one obviously destined for the appeal courts. The litigation dragged on until August 1986, when, in an out-of-court settlement, Kerr-McGee agreed to pay the Silkwood estate $1.38 million, which amounted to less than one year's interest on the sum originally awarded.

Many regarded Karen Silkwood as a nuclear martyr. To this day, the circumstances surrounding her death remain shrouded in mystery. Was she killed to be silenced? That may never be known. What is known is that the Silkwood estate's victory, modest though it may have ultimately been, sent the nuclear industry a clear message: Dangerous sources of energy demand unusually vigilant regulation.

—Colin Evans

Suggestions for Further Reading

Kohn, Howard. *Who Killed Karen Silkwood?* New York: Summit, 1981.

Rashke, Richard. *The Killing Of Karen Silkwood*. New York: Houghton Mifflin Co., 1981.

"Silkwood Settlement." *Science News* (August 8, 1986): 134.

Spence, Gerry. *With Justice For None*. New York: Times Books, 1989.

Stein, J. "The Deepening Mystery." *Progressive* (January 1981): 14–19.

U.S. v. *The Progressive:* 1979

Plaintiff: The United States   **Defendant:** *The Progressive,* Inc.
Plaintiff Claims: That *The Progressive* magazine should be prevented from publishing an article concerning how to build a hydrogen bomb
Chief Defense Lawyer: Earl Munson, Jr.
Chief Lawyers for Plaintiff: Thomas S. Martin and Frank M. Tuerkheimer
Judge: Robert W. Warren   **Place:** Milwaukee, Wisconsin
Date of Hearing: March 26, 1979   **Decision:** Injunction forbidding *The Progressive* from publishing the article

SIGNIFICANCE
The court's injunction, constituting prior restraint on publication, was the first of its kind in American history.

In 1909, Robert LaFollette, the famous Progressive leader from Wisconsin, founded a monthly news magazine in Madison, Wisconsin called *The Progressive.* The Progressive movement enjoyed some success as a third-party movement in American politics into the 1920s, and the magazine enjoyed a wide circulation. After LaFollette's 1924 bid for the presidency, which won 16% of the popular vote, third parties such as the Progressives largely disappeared as a force in American politics until the 1992 campaign of H. Ross Perot. Today, the magazine has a small but loyal audience of approximately 50,000 subscribers.

In 1978, the magazine commissioned freelance writer Howard Morland to write an article concerning government secrecy in the area of energy and nuclear weapons. Energy and nuclear issues were Morland's specialty, and after months of extensive background research Morland wrote "The H-Bomb Secret: How We Got It, Why We're Telling It." On February 27, 1979, Samuel H. Day, Jr., the magazine's managing editor, sent a copy of Morland's draft to the Department of Energy's offices in Germantown, Maryland. Day asked the DOE to verify the technical accuracy of Morland's draft before the magazine published it.

John A. Griffin, DOE's director of classification, and Duane C. Sewell, assistant secretary of energy for defense programs, read the article with alarm. They determined that it contained sensitive material, material that constituted "restricted data" under the Atomic Energy Act. On March 1, 1979, Lynn R.

Coleman, DOE's General Counsel, phoned Day and Erwin Knoll, another editor involved in the Morland article. Coleman asked that the magazine not publish the article, stating that in addition to DOE, the State Department and the Arms Control and Disarmament Agency believed publication would damage U.S. efforts to control the worldwide spread of nuclear weapons. The next day, Sewell met with Day, Knoll, and Ronald Carbon, the magazine's publisher.

Despite the government's efforts, on March 7, 1979, the magazine informed Coleman that it would publish the Morland article. The next day, the government sued the magazine in the U.S. District Court for the Western District of Wisconsin, and asked the court to stop publication.

Government Wins Battle, Loses War

The magazine's attorney was Earl Munson, Jr., and the government was represented by Thomas S. Martin and Frank M. Tuerkheimer. On March 9, the day after the suit was filed, Judge Robert W. Warren in Milwaukee, Wisconsin issued a temporary restraining order against the magazine until a preliminary injunction hearing could be held on March 16, 1979. The hearing was delayed for 10 days, however, and took place on March 26, 1979.

At the hearing, Knoll testified that, despite the government's concerns, the article would actually benefit the United States by promoting public debate free of secrecy:

> [I am] totally convinced that publication of the article will be of substantial benefit to the United States because it will demonstrate that this country's security does not lie in an oppressive and ineffective system of secrecy and classification but in open, honest, and informed public debate about issues which the people must decide.

Judge Warren was in a bind. Under the First Amendment, the injunction that the government wanted constituted a prior restraint on publication, which is difficult to justify legally because of the principle that the law isn't broken until an illegal act is actually committed, not before. However, the government had presented very strong evidence that the Morland article would contribute to the spread of nuclear know-how. Warren balanced the two considerations, and came down on the government's side:

> A mistake in ruling against *The Progressive* will seriously infringe cherished First Amendment rights. If a preliminary injunction is issued, it will constitute the first instance of prior restraint against a publication in this fashion in the history of this country, to this Court's knowledge. Such notoriety is not to be sought . . . .

> [But] a mistake in ruling against the United States could pave the way for thermonuclear annihilation for us all. In that event, our right to life is extinguished and the right to publish becomes moot.

Therefore, Warren signed a preliminary injunction restraining the magazine, its editors, and Morland from "publishing or otherwise communicating, transmitting, or disclosing in any manner any information designated by the

Secretary of Energy as Restricted Data contained in the Morland article." The injunction would last until a full trial could be held.

Having won the first litigation battle, the government ultimately lost the legal war. Inspired by the publicity surrounding the case, other publications such as *Scientific American* began to run articles related to the H-bomb and nuclear power. Neither the Morland article nor any other article, however, contained much more than a general description of how nuclear weapons work and were devoid of the many intricate technical details necessary to design an actual weapon, much less build one. Rather than begin a massive and probably unpopular litigation against the press, the government dropped its proceedings against *The Progressive* before the trial and the Morland article was published. Nevertheless, Warren's injunction, imposing a prior restraint on the article's publication, was the first of its kind in American history.

—*Stephen G. Christianson*

Suggestions for Further Reading

Born Secret: the H-Bomb, The Progressive Case and National Security. New York: Pergamon Press, 1981.

Knoll, Erwin. "The Good it Did." *The Progressive* (February 1991): 4.

———. "Through the Looking Glass." *The Progressive* (February 1985): 4.

Morland, Howard. "The Secret Sharer." *The Progressive* (July 1984): 20–21.

———. *The Secret That Exploded.* New York: Random House, 1981.

Daniel James White Trial: 1979

Defendant: Daniel James White   **Crime Charged:** Murder
Chief Defense Lawyers: Douglas Schmidt and Stephen Scherr
Chief Prosecutor: Thomas F. Norman   **Judge:** Walter F. Calcagno
Place: San Francisco, California   **Dates of Trial:** April 25—May 21, 1979
Verdict: Guilty, Voluntary Manslaughter   **Sentence:** 7 years, 8 months.

SIGNIFICANCE

Celebrity murder trials inevitably attract massive media coverage. What made the Dan White case unique was the volatile mix of politics, revenge, and homosexual intolerance. Many wondered if that intolerance spilled over into the jury room. How else could they explain such a verdict based on a defense of impaired mental capacity resulting from eating too much "junk food?"

On November 27, 1978, 32-year-old Dan White entered the San Francisco City Hall by crawling in through a basement window. He adopted this unorthodox means of access to avoid negotiating a metal detector in the main entrance, for reasons which would soon become clear. Once inside, White breezed through the familiar corridors of power. He was on a retrieval mission. Earlier that summer, this ambitious young politician had impetuously resigned his post as a city supervisor, citing financial difficulties; now he wanted that job back. Only one man could make that possible: Mayor George Moscone. White reached Moscone's office and was invited in.

The two men talked, or rather argued, for several minutes. As the exchange heated up, Moscone made it plain that he had no intention of reappointing White, who had become a political liability, whereupon White drew a .38-caliber Smith and Wesson revolver that had been tucked into his belt and pumped four bullets into his former boss. After reloading, White hunted down long-time political foe Harvey Milk, another city supervisor. Five shots ended Milk's life. White ran from the building, only to surrender to the authorities one hour later.

Police guarded White closely, fearing possible retaliation. They had good cause for concern. Milk, one of San Francisco's most militant gay activists, had many supporters, all of whom loathed White and the homophobic attitudes he had espoused when in office. Anything was possible in such a volatile situation.

Double Execution

Prosecutor Thomas Norman sought to diffuse some of that volatility with a calm, orderly representation of the facts when the state opened its case against Dan White on May 1, 1979. He described in simple terms what amounted to a double execution, carried out deliberately and with malice aforethought. It was, he said, a crime deserving of death in the gas chamber.

Few could have envied Douglas Schmidt's task when he rose to make the opening statement on White's behalf; after all, he was representing an admitted double assassin. However, he soon went on the offensive. In a fine speech he skillfully diverted the jury's attention away from the crime itself and onto the emotional traumas that White had undergone since relinquishing his position as city supervisor. "Good people, fine people, with fine backgrounds, simply don't kill people in cold blood," said Schmidt, "it just doesn't happen, and obviously some part of him has not been presented thus far." Schmidt claimed that White's crimes had been the product of manic depression, "a vile biochemical change" over which the defendant had no control. As added insurance, just in case this line of reasoning failed to sway the jury, Schmidt rounded out his opening with some very pointed comparisons between Milk's overtly homosexual lifestyle and White's all-American background.

The prosecution responded with a parade of witnesses, each of whom recounted events leading up to and on the fateful day at City Hall. Chief among

Former policeman Dan White (right) was suspected in the killings of city Supervisor Harvey Milk (left) and Mayor George Moscone (center). (AP/Wide World Photos)

them was recently elected San Francisco Mayor Dianne Feinstein. Mayor Feinstein detailed White's frustration with the political system, his inability to make a difference, as a major source of his discontent. Schmidt scored heavily on cross-examination when he asked, "Would it be your opinion that the man you knew [White] was the type of man who would have shot two people?" Over strenuous state objections, she was allowed to respond. "No," she said. "It would not."

At this point the prosecution began to unravel. What was supposed to be the high-water mark of their case—a taped confession made by White within hours of the shootings—turned into disaster. The tape should have sealed his fate. It did no such thing. Jurors heard him whine: "Well, it's just that I've been under an awful lot of pressure lately, financial pressure, because of my job situation, family pressure . . . because of not being able to have time with my family." The killings were hardly mentioned at all, and White's only display of remorse came when describing his own predicament. And yet, several jurors wept openly as they listened to the story of a man pushed beyond his endurance. Prosecutor Norman could not believe the evidence of his own eyes and ears— Dan White had been turned into a martyr, an object of sympathy.

Unique Defense

Schmidt capitalized on what had been a lackluster prosecution by turning the trial into an examination of White's mental state. Several psychiatrists testified that the defendant had not really meant to commit murder but had been driven to it by factors beyond his control. Much was made of White's prodigious intake of junkfood and candy—what came to be known as the "Twinkies Defense"—in which an abnormally high blood sugar count was blamed for the mayhem that he had wrought. It was a novel but effective defense.

But most effective of all were Schmidt's repeated portrayals of White as an upstanding young man, an ex-fireman and ex-police officer, someone who had been defeated by a corrupt system he was powerless to change. Schmidt cunningly marshaled public resentment against both politicians and homosexuals into one neat package. He found nothing unusual in the fact that White was carrying a gun on the fateful day (As an ex-cop, could anything have been more natural?), or that he had crawled in through a window at City Hall to, as one psychiatrist stated, avoid "embarrassing the officer at the metal detector." Dan White, Schmidt said, was acting under an "irresistible impulse to kill," and as such, under California law, was entitled to a verdict of manslaughter.

The jury agreed. On May 21, 1979, they returned two verdicts of voluntary manslaughter. Judge Walter Calcagno handed down the maximum sentence, seven years, and eight months imprisonment. With time off for good behavior, Dan White was looking at freedom in five years.

When news of the verdicts hit the streets, an already incendiary situation exploded. Five thousand gays marched on City Hall to protest, and a full-scale riot ensued. Inside the jail, the target of their rage, Dan White, lay on his cell cot, ears plugged against the bedlam.

Over concerted gay protests, White was paroled in 1984. But liberty proved even more onerous than incarceration. Plagued by demons that just wouldn't leave him alone, on October 21, 1985, Dan White wrote the final chapter in this tragedy by committing suicide.

The Dan White trial became a rallying call for homosexuals all across America. In their eyes, the jury had semi-officially sanctioned gay murder. Overlooked was the fact that George Moscone was a happily married family man. Somehow that got lost in the politics. Even so, it is difficult to dispute their firmly held belief that had White killed Moscone alone, he probably would still be behind bars.

—Colin Evans

Suggestions for Further Reading

Fitzgerald, Frances. "The Castro-II." *New Yorker* (July 28, 1986): 44–63.

Robinson, P. "Gays In The Streets." *New Republic* (June 9, 1979): 9–10.

Shilts, Randy. *The Mayor of Castro Street*. New York: St. Martin's Press, 1982.

Weiss, Mike. *Double Play*. Reading, Mass.: Addison-Wesley, 1984.

Jeffrey Robert MacDonald Trial: 1979

Defendant: Jeffrey Robert MacDonald **Crime Charged:** Murder
Chief Defense Lawyers: Bernard L. Segal and Wade Smith
Chief Prosecutors: James L. Blackburn and Brian Murtagh **Judge:** Franklin
T. Dupree **Place:** Raleigh, N.C. **Dates of Trial:** July 16—
August 29, 1979 **Verdict:** Guilty **Sentence:** Life imprisonment

SIGNIFICANCE

The horror of the triple murder and the long delay between the crime and the trial alone were sufficient to make this one of the most notorious trials in recent history. The subsequent best-selling book *Fatal Vision* by Joe McGinnis, written with the cooperation of the murderer, seared the case into the memories of many Americans. Jeffrey MacDonald's suit against McGinnis for betraying his trust in writing a book that portrayed him as guilty, raised ethical and legal issues about ''checkbook'' investigative journalism.

Few murder defendants have so assiduously courted the media as Jeffrey MacDonald. Through books, television, newsprint, and even civil litigation, he made his name a household word. For more than two decades, America watched and read about this enigmatic ex-Green Beret. Most remained convinced he was guilty as charged, and yet doubts persisted.

The crime was horrible: a young pregnant mother, Colette MacDonald, and her two young daughters, hacked and battered to death at their home on Fort Bragg Army Base in Fayetteville, North Carolina, on February 17, 1970. Immediately suspicion fell on the woman's husband, Captain Jeffrey Mac-Donald, a 26-year-old medical doctor. He told of being attacked by four hippie-type intruders: two white men, one black, and a white woman with long blonde hair who wore a large floppy hat, high boots, and carried a candle. Throughout the ordeal she chanted, "acid is groovy . . . kill the pigs." To ward off blows from an ice pick, MacDonald wrapped a blue pajama jacket around his hands. Even so, he sustained multiple stab wounds.

The superficial nature of MacDonald's injuries—none required stitching—and the remarkably tidy condition of the room in which he claimed to have fought for his life, convinced military detectives that his story was false. Also, they wanted to know how fibers from his blue pajama jacket came to be found beneath Colette MacDonald's body?

On May 1 the army announced that MacDonald was being charged with three counts of murder. The preliminary hearing began July 6 and soon revealed a seriously flawed investigation into the death of Colette MacDonald and her two daughters. So embarrassing were the disclosures of official negligence that, in October 1970, the army dismissed all charges against MacDonald.

Shortly afterwards, in a remarkable display of nerve, MacDonald appeared on a national TV talk show and lambasted the army for its ineptitude. He came across as indignant about his own mistreatment and indifferent towards the fate of his family. Galvanized by the criticism, detectives resumed their inquiries. The upshot was a mammoth report in 1972, which again concluded that MacDonald was guilty of murder. In July 1974, a grand jury was impaneled and returned three murder indictments against him.

The Trial, at Last

Bringing the case to court was a laborious process, but in July 1979, 9½ years after the murders, MacDonald finally faced his accusers in a North Carolina courtroom. He came bearing defense fund contributions from many influential supporters who believed in his innocence.

Defense attorney Bernard Segal was confident when the trial opened, but right from day one things went badly. Judge Franklin Dupree refused to admit into evidence a psychiatric evaluation of MacDonald which suggested that someone of his personality type was most unlikely to have committed violent crimes. Dupree did this for the soundest of reasons. If the defense were allowed to present their side of the psychiatric argument, then the prosecution would doubtless counter with experts of their own. Because no plea of insanity had been entered, Dupree didn't want the trial bogged down by a mass of what was likely to be contradictory testimony.

Then Dupree admitted into testimony something that the MacDonald camp very much wanted left out: a copy of *Esquire* magazine, found in the MacDonald household, containing a lengthy article about the Charles Manson murders. (In 1969, Manson, a commune leader, had ordered his "disciples" on a killing binge that left seven dead in southern California.) This was a big plus for

Jeffery MacDonald after being freed of murder charges. He was found guilty of the crime nine years later (Ken Cooke, News and Observer Company, North Carolina Division of Archives and History)

the prosecution. They intended to suggest that reading this article had implanted in MacDonald's mind the idea of blaming a hippie gang for his own murderous activities.

In a sedate North Carolina courtroom, Segal's wide-open style of combative advocacy did not sit well with Judge Dupree. The two locked horns repeatedly, mostly to MacDonald's detriment. But it wasn't just a clash of personalities that hurt the defendant; there was the evidence as well.

FBI analyst Paul Stombaugh led the jury through a clear exposition of the blue pajama jacket and its relevance. He showed how all 48 holes made by the ice pick were smooth and cylindrical. In order for this to have happened the jacket would need to remain stationary, an unlikely occurrence if MacDonald had indeed wrapped the jacket around his hands to defend himself and was dodging a torrent of blows. Also, by folding the jacket in one particular way, Stombaugh demonstrated how all 48 tears could have been made by 21 thrusts of the ice pick, coincidentally the same number of wounds that Colette MacDonald had suffered. By implication, Stombaugh was saying that MacDonald's story was a tissue of lies; what really happened was that Colette MacDonald had been repeatedly stabbed through the pajama jacket by her enraged husband, who then concocted the story of four intruders to mask his actions.

Drama in Court

A moment of high drama occurred when prosecutors Brian Murtagh and James Blackburn abruptly staged an impromptu re-enactment of the alleged attack on MacDonald. Murtagh wrapped a pajama top around his hands and tried to fend off a series of ice pick blows from Blackburn. For his troubles Murtagh received a small wound to the arm, but two telling points had been made. First, all of the holes in the pajama top were rough and jagged, not smoothly cylindrical as the holes in MacDonald's pajama jacket had been; second, Murtagh was stabbed, albeit not seriously. When MacDonald had been examined at Womack Hospital he did not have a single wound on his arms. The inference was obvious and highly damaging to MacDonald.

The strongest defense witness was supposed to be Helena Stoeckley, 18 years old at the time of the murders, a known liar with a long record of drug abuse and alcoholism. Over the years, she had yielded several confessions to involvement in the slaughter and an equal number of retractions. Segal was at least hoping to establish some kind of link to a "hippie gang," but Stoeckley let him down. On this occasion she denied ever having been inside the MacDonald home. Furthermore, she denied ever having seen MacDonald before that very morning in court.

Segal was furious. He fought for the introduction of evidence from other witnesses to whom Stoeckley had confessed. But Judge Dupree, in the absence of any evidence to connect Stoeckley to the house and unimpressed by her performance on the stand, refused. When Segal persisted in arguing the point he got his comeuppance. Dupree revealed that, over the weekend, he had received two phone calls from Helena Stoeckley. She had talked about hiring a lawyer because she felt herself to be in mortal danger from none other than Bernard Segal. Upon hearing this Segal sank back into his chair and let the matter drop.

Perhaps the most decisive evidence against MacDonald was a tape made during his original 1970 interview with military investigators. Jury members got to hear a man who sounded evasive and indifferent. Worse than that, he sounded arrogant. Describing himself, MacDonald said: "I'm bright, aggressive, I work hard. . . . Christ, I was a doctor!" Later: "I had a beautiful wife who loved me and two kids who were great. . . . What could I have gained by doing this?" By way of an answer, a detective showed MacDonald the photograph of a young woman, just one of MacDonald's many sexual conquests, a side of his nature that he had desperately tried to conceal. MacDonald, rattled by this surprise revelation, said quietly, "You guys are more thorough than I thought." One juror later remarked, "Until I heard that, [tape] there was no doubt in my mind about his innocence. . . . but hearing him turned the whole thing around."

Under Segal's gentle probing, MacDonald performed well on the stand, but as soon as he was subjected to cross-examination that old cockiness began to reassert itself. Whenever asked to explain an awkward fact or statement, he would shrug indifference. In the end, his performance failed to convince those who mattered most: the jury. On August 29, 1979, they found MacDonald guilty. Judge Dupree sentenced him to the maximum allowable under federal law, three consecutive life terms.

After several appeals, in January 1983 the Supreme Court upheld all three convictions. But Jeffrey MacDonald wasn't finished yet.

Murderer Sues Writer

In 1984 one of the most extraordinary civil actions in American legal history began. The plaintiff, MacDonald, a thrice-convicted murderer, claimed breach of contract and fraud against Joe McGinnis, author of *Fatal Vision*, the definitive account of the murders. McGinnis had been contacted prior to Mac-Donald's trial. The intention, as MacDonald saw it, was for McGinnis to write an account that painted him in the most favorable light. The two had signed a contract in which MacDonald agreed to provide material in return for a handsome percentage of the book profits. As is customary, MacDonald signed a release, the third paragraph of which read:

> I realize, of course, that you do not propose to libel me. Nevertheless, in order that you may feel free to write the book in any manner that you deem best, I agree that I will not make or assert against you, the publisher, or its licensees or anyone else involved in the production or distribution of the book, any claim or demand whatsoever based on the ground that anything contained in the book defames me.

As an afterthought Bernard Segal added the following, ". . . provided that the essential integrity of my life story is maintained."

It was this addendum that proved so controversial. No one reading *Fatal Vision* could have been in any doubt that McGinnis thought Jeffrey MacDonald had slaughtered his wife and children. The book, which later became a TV movie, portrayed MacDonald not as an innocent victim but as a heartless murderer. For this perceived betrayal MacDonald cried foul, claiming that McGinnis had taken advantage of his privileged position, and filed suit.

The action was heard in Los Angeles, California in 1987 before Judge William J. Rea. At the heart of the plaintiff's case was a series of letters that passed between MacDonald and McGinnis, in which the writer, right up to the publication of the book, continued to impress on MacDonald a purported belief in his innocence. Attorney Gary Bostwick, appearing for MacDonald, asked McGinnis: "Did you consider yourself [MacDonald's] . . . friend at the end of the trial?"

"I considered myself the author," said McGinnis, "I don't know how you would define 'friend'. It was a professional relationship."

Bostwick tightened the noose.

"Would you look at Exhibit 36A [a letter] again. . . . It says, 'Goddamn it, Jeff, one of the worst things about all this is how suddenly and totally all of your friends—self included—have been deprived of the pleasure of your company.' "

"Well, that was eight years ago," McGinnis replied lamely, "And my recollections were a lot fresher." It only got worse.

You said yesterday, . . . looking at the letters of the first six to nine months after the trial, that you never intended to deceive him. . . . After the first six or nine months, did you intend to deceive him?

"Well, there certainly came a time when I was willing to let him continue to believe whatever he wanted to believe, so he wouldn't try to prevent me from finishing my book."

"Is the answer yes?"

"The answer could be interpreted that way, I suppose."

Such candor did not sit well with the six-person jury. And neither did the testimony of noted authors Joseph Wambaugh and William F. Buckley, both of whom stated that McGinnis' only obligation was to the truth as he saw it. Defense attorney Daniel Kornstein steered them through a high-minded rationale of the journalist's craft. Their testimony, given with the best of intentions, provided Bostwick with just the weapons he needed to portray MacDonald as the injured party. He extracted a painful admission from Wambaugh that duplicity and deception were everyday currency for the investigative writer, wholly acceptable so long as the ends justified the means. Bostwick, in his charge to the jury, concluded simply, "We cannot do whatever is necessary. We have to do what is right."

Undistracted by any of the murder evidence, the jury heard only Bostwick's tale of a gullible subject, duped by an unscrupulous writer. Five members of the jury agreed with his reasoning; one did not. On August 21, 1987, a mistrial was declared. Later, the parties agreed to settle for $325,000, the sum originally requested. Interestingly, afterward, each jury member revealed his or her belief that MacDonald had murdered his family. That they were able to divorce personal bias from their deliberations on a purely civil matter speaks highly of the essential integrity and impartiality of the jury system.

In July 1991, Judge Franklin T. Dupree, after hearing arguments that MacDonald should be granted a new murder trial on grounds of prosecutorial misconduct, denied the petition.

—*Colin Evans*

Suggestions for Further Reading

Garbus, Martin. "McGinnis: A Travesty Of Libel." *Publishers Weekly* (April 21, 1989): 69.

Malcolm, Janet. *The Journalist And The Murderer.* New York: Alfred A. Knopf, 1990.

McGinnis, Joe. *Fatal Vision.* New York: G.P. Putnam's Sons, 1983.

Taylor, John. "Holier Than Thou." *New York Times* (March 27, 1989): 32–35.

U.S. v. Snepp Appeal: 1980

Appellant: Frank W. Snepp III **Appellee:** The United States
Appellant Claims: That a district court erred in ruling that Snepp violated the terms of his Central Intelligence Agency employment agreement by having his book *Decent Interval* published without the agency's prior consent
Chief Lawyers for Appellee: David J. Anderson, Barbara Allen Babcock, William B. Cummings, Brook Hedge, Thomas S. Martin, Elizabeth Gere Whitaker, Glenn V. Whitaker, and George P. Williams
Chief Lawyers for Appellant: Alan M. Dershowitz, Bruce J. Ennis, Joel M. Gora, Mark H. Lynch, Jack D. Novik, John H.F. Shattuck, John Cary Sims, and Geoffrey J. Vitt **Justices:** Harry A. Blackmun, William J. Brennan, Jr., Warren E. Burger, Thurgood Marshall, Lewis F. Powell, Jr., William H. Rehnquist, John Paul Stevens, Potter Stewart, and Byron R. White
Place: Washington, D.C. **Date of Decision:** February 19, 1980
Decision: That Snepp had unlawfully breached the terms of his employment agreement

SIGNIFICANCE

Despite the strong interest in protecting First Amendment rights, the government is entitled to enforce contracts with its employees that prohibit publishing sensitive material without prior consent.

On September 16, 1968, a young man named Frank W. Snepp III took the final step necessary to begin working for the Central Intelligence Agency. The job application process with the CIA is a long one, involving extensive background checks for issuing a security clearance and other procedures. That day for Snepp culminated in signing a secrecy agreement, which obligated Snepp not to "publish or participate in the publication of" any material relating to the CIA's activities during Snepp's term of employment without "specific prior approval by the Agency."

Snepp worked for the CIA for more than seven years. He served two tours of duty with the CIA station in South Vietnam, June 2, 1969—June 21, 1971, and October 4, 1972—April 29, 1975. Snepp became disillusioned with the CIA's conduct in Vietnam, particularly with its role in the final stages of American withdrawal from Saigon. Snepp resigned from the CIA effective January 23, 1976, and was required to sign a termination secrecy agreement reiterating his obligation to obtain the "express written consent of the Director of Central Intelligence" before publishing anything about the CIA.

Snepp Sells *Decent Interval*

Despite the documents he had signed, Snepp went to the publishing company Random House with his manuscript for a book titled *Decent Interval*. The book described the American withdrawal from Vietnam and Saigon and gave unflattering details about the CIA's involvement. Snepp received a $60,000 advance from Random House, and his contract called for potentially lucrative royalties. The book was based on Snepp's experience in the CIA, and he never submitted it to the agency for approval.

Random House published the book in November 1977. On February 15, 1978, the government sued Snepp in the U.S. District Court for the Eastern District of Virginia, which covered Snepp's suburban Washington, D.C., residence. Because the book didn't contain any information that was officially designated as classified, secret or top secret, the government took a conservative approach. Instead of criminal prosecution or seeking an injunction against publication of the book, the government asked the court for all of Snepp's profits as compensation for breach of contract. Snepp stood to lose everything under his contract with Random House.

Frank Snepp III, author of *Decent Interval*, and attorneys leaving U.S. District Court. The case was ultimately heard by the Supreme Court. (AP/Wide World Photos)

The District Court ruled in the government's favor on July 7, 1978, and the U.S. Court of Appeals for the Fourth Circuit largely affirmed the District Court's actions on March 20, 1979. Snepp appealed to the Supreme Court. Both sides had extensive legal teams, because the American Civil Liberties Union and the Authors League of America came to Snepp's assistance.

In an extremely rare procedure, the Supreme Court decided to consider the case, but the Court made its decision solely on the basis of the papers filed by both sides. There was no hearing. In upholding the district court's decision to make Snepp turn over all his proceeds from book sales to the government, the court relied heavily on the testimony of CIA Director Admiral Stansfield Turner before the district court that Snepp's book had hurt CIA operations:

> Over the last six to nine months, we have had a number of sources discontinue work with us. We have had more sources tell us that they are very nervous about continuing work with us. We have had very strong complaints from a number of foreign intelligence services with whom we conduct liaison, who have questioned whether they should continue exchanging information with us, for fear it will not remain secret. I cannot estimate to you how many potential sources or liaison arrangements have never germinated because people were unwilling to enter into business with us.

Snepp's defense was based on the argument that the secrecy agreements violated his right under the Constitution's First Amendment to express himself, a right which cannot be contracted away. In rejecting Snepp's argument, the court held on February 19, 1980, that the government could use employment agreements to bind its employees to vows of secrecy:

> The Government has a compelling interest in protecting both the secrecy of information important to our national security and the appearance of confidentiality so essential to the effective operation of our foreign intelligence service. The agreement that Snepp signed is a reasonable means for protecting this vital interest.

Therefore, despite the court's historic concern for First Amendment rights, it held in a 6-3 decision that the government is entitled to enforce contracts with its employees that prohibit publishing sensitive material without prior consent.

— *Stephen G. Christianson*

Suggestions for Further Reading

Alter, Jonathan. "Slaying the Message." *Washington Monthly* (September 1981): 43–50.

Mullin, Dennis, and Robert S. Dudney. "When CIA Spies Come in From the Cold." *U.S. News and World Report* (September 28, 1981): 41–44.

Nocera, Joseph. "Finally Proof That Frank Snepp Was Framed." *Washington Monthly* (November 1980): 11–19.

Snepp, Frank. *Decent Interval: An Insider's Account of Saigaon's Indecent End Told by the CIA's Chief Strategy Analyst in Vietnam.* New York: Vintage Books, 1978.

———. "The CIA's Double Standard." *Newsweek* (January 25, 1982): 10.

ABSCAM Trials: 1980 & 1981

Defendants: First trial: Howard L. Criden, Angelo J. Errichetti, Louis C. Johanson, and Michael J. Myers; Second trial: Alexander Feinberg and Harrison A. Williams, Jr. **Crimes Charged:** Bribery and conspiracy
Chief Defense Lawyers: First trial: Richard Ben-Veniste, Ray Brown, Plato Cacheris, and John Duffy; Second trial: Harry C. Batchelder, Jr. and George J. Koelzer **Chief Prosecutors:** Edward A. McDonald and Thomas P. Puccio
Judge: George C. Pratt **Place:** New York, New York
Dates of Trials: August 11—31, 1980; March 30—May 1, 1981
Verdicts: Guilty **Sentences:** First trial: Myers: 3 years imprisonment, $20,000 fine; Errichetti: 6 years imprisonment, $40,000 fine; Johanson: 3 years imprisonment, $20,000 fine; Criden: 6 years imprisonment, $40,000 fine; Second trial: Williams: 3 years imprisonment, $50,000 fine; Feinberg: 3 years imprisonment, $40,000 fine

SIGNIFICANCE

The sting operation that became known as ABSCAM worked beyond the government's wildest expectations. No previous federal investigation had bagged so many highly placed corrupt political figures or produced so many trials.

In 1978, undercover FBI agents and convicted swindler Melvin Weinberg began posing as American representatives of wealthy Arab businessmen eager to make sizable investments in the United States. Under the auspices of a company called "Abdul Enterprises Limited" (from which the name ABSCAM derived), they let it be known that their clients were willing to pay heavily for influence and favors, especially visas from the Immigration and Naturalization Service (INS). The first politician snared was U.S. Congressman Michael J. Myers, who was videotaped accepting a $50,000 bribe.

As ABSCAM spread its tentacles and word of easy money circulated, more and more politicians fell prey, including U.S. Senator Harrison A. Williams, Jr., and five other congressmen. Geographical considerations and the sheer number of defendants necessitated several trials. The first began in Brooklyn, New York, on August 11, 1980, before Judge George C. Pratt.

In opening his case, Thomas P. Puccio, who would handle most of the ABSCAM prosecutions, brought to the stand Anthony Amorosa, a federal undercover agent. Amorosa and Weinberg had run the sting in a New York hotel room. That videotaped transaction was played to the packed, hushed courtroom. Amorosa handed Myers an envelope containing $50,000, saying, "Spend it well." Myers, who sat next to fellow defendant Mayor Angelo J. Errichetti of Camden, New Jersey, boasted of the influence he wielded in Congress. "As leader of the Philadelphia delegation, I control four and then six when we go into state matters . . . I'm going to tell you something real simple and short-money talks in this business . . . and it works the same way down in Washington."

Four-Way Conspiracy

As the tape rolled, the other two defendants, Louis C. Johanson, a Philadelphia City Councilman, and Howard L. Criden, Johanson's former law partner, watched intently. Both were charged with having conspired with Myers and having shared the money. Myers let slip the names of other prominent Washington politicians, though none was ever charged with wrongdoing. Stifled laughter in court greeted Myers' comment when, leaning across confidentially to the agents, he said, "The key is, you got to deal with the right people," adding a moment later, "I feel very comfortable here."

Next came Melvin Weinberg, a colorful character who provided detailed descriptions of the ABSCAM sting and his efforts to help federal agents. In defense estimations Weinberg was the state's weak link, and they set about undermining his credibility in a three-day grilling. John Duffy, appearing for Johanson, set the tone:

"Are you a con man?"

"I don't know. They say I am."

"Have you spent most of your adult life living by your wits?"

"That's correct."

Richard Ben-Veniste, representing Criden, quizzed Weinberg on the scam he had "franchised to con men all over the world."

"We franchised it," shrugged Weinberg, "but not to con men."

"You were like the MacDonald's of con men?"

Weinberg beamed. "That's correct."

When Congressman Michael Myers took the stand, the 37-year-old Democrat was led through some gentle questioning by his attorney, Plato Cacheris. Cacheris' theme, one adopted by most ABSCAM defense lawyers, was that because there had been no criminal intent, there had been no crime. Myers agreed: "No, it wasn't proper that I accepted this money, but I didn't do anything wrong . . . and didn't intend to do anything wrong . . . It seemed like a chance to pick up some easy money." Myers explained that he had grossly exaggerated his influence during the course of the meeting to get the money.

Less compelling were his attempts to explain away a second meeting, also captured on tape, at which he received an additional $35,000—paid because after dividing up the original payment with his co-defendants, Myers had been left with just $15,000 and felt "entitled" to more. Myers blamed this verbal indiscretion on two bourbons given him by the undercover agents, causing him to say things he didn't really mean.

Prosecutor Puccio had an easy task on cross-examination. The videotape said it all. Pouncing on Myers' assertions that he meant to take the money and then do nothing in return, he asked, "Congressman Myers, did you think it was dishonest to obtain money by false pretenses?"

"No, I didn't think that this was dishonest."

Untrustworthy Witness

In closing arguments each defense attorney fell back on attacking Weinberg's credibility. Ben-Veniste hit the hardest: "Mel Weinberg makes J.R. Ewing look like Peter Pan." He was, said Ben-Veniste, the kind of man that if you shake hands with him, "you count your fingers afterward and then look for your watch."

It was a theme easily countered by Puccio. Myers, he argued, was the man who failed on standards of honesty. "Would a man like that hesitate for one second to lie on the witness stand to get off the hook?"

On August 30, 1980, all four defendants were found guilty. Their attempts to have the convictions overturned were rejected by Judge Pratt on July 24, 1981. In a 136-page decision, he said of the accused:

> Their major defense has been that they were tricked into committing the crime on videotape. The government's need to unmask such conduct more than justifies the investigative techniques employed in these cases. Without question these convictions were reliable, and no constitutional right of any defendant has been infringed.

Sentencing was deferred until August 13, 1981, when Judge Pratt imposed jail sentences and heavy fines on each defendant. But before that, the judge had presided over yet another ABSCAM trial. Puccio was again the chief prosecutor, as the government this time sought to convict the biggest fish caught in their net.

Influential Senator Charged

At the time of his arraignment, Harrison A. Williams, Jr., 61, had been a senator for New Jersey for 22 years and was one of the most powerful men in Washington. He and an associate, 72-year-old lawyer Alexander Feinberg, were jointly accused of scheming to illegally benefit a Virginia titanium mine and processing plant. Williams had allegedly agreed to use his position to obtain government contracts to buy the output of the mine and plant, in which he was to have a secret 18 percent interest.

Assistant prosecutor Edward A. McDonald opened on March 31, 1981, by showing the jury a photograph of Williams aboard a yacht in Delray Beach, Florida, posing with Sheik Yassir Habib, actually Richard Farhart, an FBI agent. "Habib"—supposedly ready to lend $100 million to the titanium project—was also present at an Arlington, Virginia meeting with Williams, which was video-taped. When the conversation turned to matters of influence, Williams assured Habib that he could "go right to the top," and mentioned then Vice President Walter Mondale. Speaking of Mondale, he said, "We have a relationship that will make all of that possible . . . that's all I want to tell you now."

Another ABSCAM victim, Henry Williams (no relation to the senator but a longtime associate) decided to cut his losses and turn state's evidence. He described the senator's tendency and willingness to exploit his position for money. Contrary to what the defense had claimed, Williams said that the senator had been connected with the titanium company since 1976.

To counter this allegation, the defense produced ex-Secretary of the Treasury Henry H. Fowler, now an investment banker. Chief defense counsel George J. Koelzer asked, "Did you feel that Senator Williams was putting any pressure on you to help this enterprise?"

"No."

"Did he indicate. . .that his business could get government contracts?"

Again the answer was no.

Which was the line taken by Williams himself, when he gave evidence on his own behalf.

"Were you guaranteeing government contracts?" Koelzer asked.

"Absolutely not, not at all."

Warning From Bench

At Koelzer's behest, Williams repeatedly and emphatically denied all charges. So often, in fact, that Judge Pratt expressed concern to Koelzer that such repetition might backfire. "You may convince the jury of exactly the contrary of what the witness is saying, simply because he is saying so often. And it may in their view become very artificial and rehearsed." Koelzer, insisting that the technique was necessary to counteract the damaging effects of the tape, then turned to his client and a section on the videotape where the subject of influence was raised. He asked Williams,

"Why didn't you get up and walk out?"

"I respected the man [Habib]."

Prosecutor Puccio wasn't so sure.

"What did you have in mind?"

"To impress the sheik."

"Impress the sheik with what?"

"The baloney, this was the baloney session."

With this answer, Williams went right to the heart of the defense argument of entrapment. Before Habib had arrived, Williams had received coaching from another undercover FBI agent on how to flatter the sheik. None of this would have happened, Williams claimed, had he not been coerced by that instruction.

It was a line of reasoning that failed to impress the jury. On May 1, 1981, they found both defendants guilty. Judge Pratt later mandated jail sentences similar to those in the previous trial.

No Acquittals

There were six more ABSCAM trials and not one defendant was acquitted. The final tally included one senior U.S. senator; six members of Congress; one mayor, who was also a New Jersey state senator; three members of the Philadelphia City Council; an INS inspector; one lawyer; one accountant; and assorted business associates of the public officials. All of the politicians were either expelled from office or else turned out by voters at the next election. By any reckoning, ABSCAM had to be counted a major success.

—Colin Evans

Suggestions for Further Reading

Caplan, Gerald M. *ABSCAM Ethics*. Cambridge, Mass.: Ballinger, 1983.

Eubanks, Brian F. *Stetson Law Review* (Spring 1984): 691–706.

Frey, Richard G. *Criminal Justice Journal* (Summer 1984): 203–250.

Greene, Robert. *The Sting Man*. New York: Dutton, 1981.

Verrone, Patric M. *Boston College Law Review* (March 1984): 351–381.

Jean Harris Trial: 1980–81

Defendant: Jean S. Harris   **Crime Charged:** Second-degree murder
Chief Defense Lawyer: Joel Aurnou   **Chief Prosecutor:** George Bolen
Judge: Russell R. Leggett   **Place:** White Plains, New York
Dates of Trial: November 21, 1980–February 24, 1981   **Verdict:** Guilty
Sentence: 15 years to life

SIGNIFICANCE

Jean Harris' trial was initially famous for the celebrity of the lover she was accused of murdering, but the handling of her defense and the sentence pronounced were debated for years afterward. Her prison writings were among the books prompting review of New York's "Son of Sam" law by the U.S. Supreme Court.

On March 10, 1980, Jean Harris left the exclusive Virginia school for girls where she was headmistress and drove 400 miles to the Purchase, New York, home of Dr. Herman Tarnower. Harris entered the bedroom of her lover of 14 years carrying a bouquet of flowers and a loaded revolver. Her version of what happened next would be emotionally debated in one of the most widely examined trials in the history of New York state.

Bullets from Harris' gun had indisputably killed the 69-year-old Tarnower, author of the popular *The Complete Scarsdale Medical Diet.* Yet Harris' attorney, Joel Aurnou, announced that his client's intended victim had been herself. Despondent over Tarnower's rejection of her for a younger woman and depressed by the pressures of her job at the Madeira School, the 57-year-old headmistress had driven to the cardiologist's house to see him a last time before committing suicide. Harris claimed that Tarnower was accidentally wounded trying to wrest the gun from her.

The Westchester County District Attorney's office proposed that Harris' actions were hardly self-destructive. They accused her of shooting Tarnower in a jealous fury that had been building for years. From the moment her trial began in November 1980, her intent at the time she pulled the trigger was the crucial issue that would determine her fate.

The early weeks of the trial went awkwardly for the prosecution. Physical evidence had been mishandled by suburban police, who seemed unaccustomed to following proper procedures amid the novelty of such a bloody situation. Prosecutor George Bolen called Deputy Medical Examiner Dr. Louis Roh, who testified that a bullet hole in Tarnower's hand was consistent with the nature of a "defensive wound," sustained while trying to push away a gun barrel. Roh testified that one of the three bullets found in Tarnower's body had entered through the palm, passed through the hand, and lodged in the chest. Aurnou responded with forensic expert Herbert Leon MacDonnell, who explained how the bloodstains found on Tarnower's bedclothes and pajamas supported defense claims of a struggle over the gun.

Hours turned into weeks as contending medical and ballistics experts testified in numbing detail. Dr. Roh reappeared to testify that tissue found in a chest wound might have been carried from Tarnower's palm by the bullet, bolstering the theory that the victim had raised his hand defensively. Aurnou counter attacked with a succession of pathologists who disputed Roh's palm-tissue theory.

As the prosecution's case wobbled, Aurnou called numerous character witnesses, attempting to portray Harris as "a lady" whose self-control made it impossible for her to commit murder. Madeira School trustees and students testified to Harris' reputation for integrity and discipline, despite her growing signs of depression.

Harris Testifies

Aurnou decided to put Harris on the stand. The strain of Tarnower's rejection and the pressures of her career burst forth in emotional exchanges between lawyer and client. Aurnou's probing of Harris' precarious emotional state intended to show that she had been pushed to the point of suicide, not murder. Harris described in detail how she and Tarnower struggled over the gun with which she tried to kill herself.

The defense view of Harris as a stolid, sympathetic figure in control of her behavior despite intense suffering began to blur under prosecutor Bolen's cross-

Jean Harris after her second day on the witness stand in the murder trial of Dr. Herman Tarnower. She is followed by her son. (AP/Wide World Photos)

examination. Harris' responses to his questions were haughty and abrasive. She accused other witnesses of perjury. Yet Aurnou's failure to subdue his client's temper was overshadowed by an even graver miscalculation.

Harris testified that she had mailed Tarnower a registered letter on the morning of March 10. She telephoned him later, interrupting his consultation with a patient. Harris told the doctor to throw the letter away when it arrived. After Tarnower's death, the defense team had quickly retrieved the thick envelope from the post office. When the prosecution asked to examine it during the trial, Aurnou theatrically removed it from his pocket and handed it to Bolen, certain that its pleading depiction of Tarnower as a faithless philanderer would win the defense's case.

Instead, the image of a cultivated, quietly suffering headmistress vanished when Bolen read the 11-page "Scarsdale letter" aloud. Pain and bitterness, which the defense had denied was compatible with her character, raged from its page. Harris wrote of her rival for Tarnower's affections, calling her "your whore" and "your adulterous slut." The rambling letter also spoke of Tarnower removing Harris from his will.

Because Harris had voluntarily testified about her March 10 telephone call, Bolen was free to produce the doctor's patient as a rebuttal witness. Juanita Edwards testified that she was with Tarnower when his phone rang that day. The doctor took the call in his office but left the examination room phone off the hook.

"Goddammit it, Jean, I want you to stop bothering me!"

Edwards could hear Tarnower shout angrily at a woman over the open line.

"You've lied and you've cheated!"

Edwards also heard Tarnower say,

"Well, you're going to inherit $240,000!"

Aurnou objected fiercely but to no effect. After more analytical haggling over the tissue found in Tarnower's chest wound, the defense rested. Judge Russell Leggett instructed the jurors that if they found Harris had intended to kill Tarnower at the moment she pulled the trigger, they could find her guilty of second-degree murder. If they decided that she had not intended to kill him, she could be found guilty of either second-degree manslaughter or criminally negligent homicide.

Defense Goes for Broke and Loses

"Don't compromise!" Aurnou told the jury, confident that they would acquit his client completely. It was a disastrous supposition. The jury found Harris guilty of second-degree murder. When Judge Leggett pronounced the mandatory 15-years-to-life sentence, with no possibility of parole until the 15-year minimum had been served, he asked if Harris had anything to say.

"I did not murder Dr. Tarnower," she answered.

"I loved him very much and I am innocent as I stand here. You and Mr. Bolen have arranged my life in such a way that I'll be in a cage for the rest of it, and with irons on my hands every time I go out."

She held up her hands as if they were manacled.

"That is not justice. It is a travesty of justice."

Some spectators applauded when she concluded her statement.

"You have had a fair trial," Judge Leggett replied, expressing regret that "the events of March 10" had ever taken place. The judge hoped that Harris would use her teaching talents to aid fellow prisoners.

Despite her defiant protests that she had been condemned by perjury and an immoral justice system, jurors later revealed that Harris' own testimony convicted her. During eight days of deliberations, the jury tried to re-create the scene in Tarnower's bedroom as Harris described it. They found no way that Tarnower could have been shot through the palm by trying to deflect the pistol from her temple. The jury also was impressed by her lack of any explanation for the other two bullet wounds in Tarnower's body.

Attorney Aurnou appealed for a reversal of the verdict, accusing one juror of possible bias and citing the presence of a police officer during Harris' phone call to a lawyer friend after the shooting. The officer later testified to overhearing Harris say, "Oh my God, I think I've killed Hy." Aurnou also argued that international press coverage had made a fair trial impossible and that the jury's attempt to re-create the shooting during deliberations had been improper.

Westchester County District Attorney Carl Vergari retorted that the "Scarsdale letter" had convinced the jury that Harris was "a liar and that the roots of her hatred for Dr. Tarnower ran to the marrow." Vergari called the letter "an X-ray of Mrs. Harris' state of mind as it existed on March 10" and faulted Aurnou's "go for broke" pursuit of a total acquittal instead of pursuing an "arguably valid defense of extreme emotional disturbance." Many observers including Judge Leggett, agreed that Harris might have gotten a shorter sentence or been acquitted if she had agreed to plead guilty to a lesser charge.

An appeals court unanimously ruled that while Harris' trial was not perfect, it was fair. Judges noted that Aurnou himself had been lax in securing physical evidence. He had not asked for a change of venue and had participated in pretrial publicity. As to the jurors' conduct, the decision noted stonily that "the defendant would appear to be in no position to complain since, in defense counsel's summation, he twice invited the jurors to test Mrs. Harris's version in the deliberation room."

Relentless Appeals Finally Succeed

With the help of prominent sympathizers, Harris continued to appeal. In 1983 she lost a bid for a new trial on grounds that her testimony had been impaired by withdrawal from amphetamines supplied by Tarnower and that Aurnou had not properly explained the option of presenting a psychiatric defense. Appeals to the New York governor's office for clemency after serving half of her minimum sentence were rejected as premature. In 1992, a federal court ruled that the failure to raise a defense of "extreme emotional distress" was a tactical gamble on which Harris and Aurnou had agreed and lost, not a violation of her Sixth Amendment right to counsel.

Harris wrote two books about her life, her trial, and her prison experiences. She wanted the proceeds to benefit a charity for the children of convicts. The money was instead put in escrow by New York's Crime Victims Compensation Board. Under the state's "Son of Sam law," Harris was forbidden from directing profits gained by writing about her crime. Harris challenged the law. She lost her suit in New York courts, shortly before the U.S. Supreme Court's 1991 ruling that the "Son of Sam law" was unconstitutional.

In early 1993, Governor Mario M. Cuomo granted her request for clemency and she was preparing to retire to New Hampshire after undergoing heart surgery.

— *Thomas C. Smith*

Suggestions for Further Reading

Alexander, Shana. *Very Much A Lady*. Boston: Little, Brown and Co., 1983.

———. "Matter of Integrity." *People* (March 9, 1981): 90ff.

Feron, James. "Jurors In Jean Harris Trial Re-enacted Night of Murder." *New York Times* (February 26, 1981): Al, Bl.

"Graduation Day." *Time* (January 11, 1993): 55.

Harris, Jean S. *Stranger In Two Worlds*. New York: Macmillan Co., 1986.

Jones, Ann. "Why Are We So Fascinated By the Harris Case?" *New York Times* (November 8, 1981): 24.

Trilling, Diana. *Mrs. Harris*. New York: Harcourt Brace Jovanovich, 1981.

John Demjanjuk Denaturalization Trial: 1981

Defendant: John Demjanjuk   **Crime Charged:** Illegal procurement of U.S. citizenship   **Chief Defense Lawyer:** John Martin
Chief Prosecutors: Norman Moskowitz and George Parker
Judge: Frank Battisti   **Place:** Cleveland, Ohio   **Dates of Trial:** February 10–June 23, 1981   **Verdict:** Guilty   **Sentence:** U.S. naturalization revoked

SIGNIFICANCE

The denaturalization trial of accused war criminal John Demjanjuk marked the beginning of a long and acrimonious legal battle that would be fought out in courtrooms on two continents for more than a decade.

In 1975 the U.S. Immigration and Naturalization Service (INS) began investigating a list of approximately 70 war criminals allegedly living in America. High on this list was a sadistic Ukrainian guard known as "Ivan the Terrible," who had personally gassed thousands of Jews in the Nazi death camp at Treblinka in 1942–43. Evidence suggested that after the war Ivan had entered America illegally and was currently living in Cleveland, Ohio. In 1977, a 57-year-old Ford Motor Company plant mechanic named John Demjanjuk was accused of being Ivan the Terrible.

Demjanjuk arrived in America in 1952. Six years later he was granted citizenship. At this time he also Anglicized his name from Ivan to John. In 1979 INS investigators were shown a photocopied identification card purportedly issued to an "Ivan Denjanjuk" at Trawniki, a German training camp for SS elite guards in Poland. Demjanjuk denied that the card was his. When several ex-Treblinka inmates identified the person shown on the ID card as "Ivan the Terrible," the INS decided to review Demjanjuk's application to find out if he had covered up any concentration camp activities. If this turned out to be the case, his citizenship could be revoked.

The hearing began on February 10, 1981. Prosecutor Norman Moskowitz led off with the expert witnesses. It was their job to verify the disputed ID card. Professor Wolfgang Sheffler, an acknowledge Nazi expert, admitted never having seen a card exactly like it, but he thought the information shown on the

Trawniki card seemed genuine. Heinrich Schaeffer, a former paymaster at Trawniki, declared unequivocally that the card was genuine.

Holocaust Survivors Testify

Next came the victims of Ivan the Terrible's barbarism. Of more than a million prisoners who passed through the gates of Treblinka, fewer than 60 survived to tell the world of the horrors it had housed. Of that 60, only five were left. Four had flown half-way around the world, prepared to swear John Demjanjuk was indeed Ivan the Terrible.

Yehiel Reichman, 65, had seen Ivan daily at Treblinka and had no difficulty in identifying Demjanjuk. Similarly, Pinhas Epstein described Ivan "a big, thickset man" who operated the diesel engine that pumped deadly carbon monoxide into the gas chambers. He also saw Ivan beat prisoners to death with a lead pipe.

Others followed, including Eliahu Rosenberg, who had worked as corpse carrier, clearing the chambers of dead bodies, and Sonia Lewkowicz, a laundress. All had tales to tell, and all identified Demjamjuk as the demon who had murdered thousands. Try as he might, defense counsel John Martin could not budge any of them.

When it came time to testify on his own behalf, Demjanjuk did so briefly and in Ukrainian. His defense was that he had never been at Treblinka at all: it was all a case of mistaken identity. He dismissed the ID card as a KGB forgery (the card had originally surfaced in the Soviet Union). According to Demjanjuk, throughout 1942-43 he was an imprisoned Soviet soldier at a German POW camp at Chelm in Poland.

The testimony was heard by Judge Frank Battisti, sitting alone without a jury.

Demjanjuk is escorted into Israel's supreme court. (AP/Wide World)

After lengthy deliberation, in a 44-page decision delivered on June 23, 1981, Judge Battisti found that Demjanjuk had illegally obtained U.S. naturalization by concealing his wartime record and ordered the immediate revocation of his citizenship.

This opened the door for deportation proceedings. Appeals delayed the process until May 23, 1984, when Demjanjuk was given 30 days to leave the country voluntarily. He chose to stay and fight. In February 1985 the INS Board of Appeals ruled that Demjanjuk's background denied him the privilege of voluntary departure and he was imprisoned to await the results of an extradition request made by Israel. On February 27, 1986, Demjanjuk was escorted by two U.S. marshals onto an El Al 747, Israeli airlines jet, bound for Tel Aviv.

Sentenced to Death

John Demjanjuk finally faced his accusers in a Jerusalem courtroom on February 16, 1987. In a emotional trial, the same witnesses who had denounced him in Cleveland repeated their accusations. During testimony Demjanjuk seemed vague and evasive about his past. On April 18, 1988, after 14 months of testimony, Judge Dove Levin read the verdict of the three-member bench: "We determine unequivocally and without the slightest hesitation or doubt that the accused is Ivan [the Terrible]. We therefore find guilty as charged, a) of crimes against the Jewish people; b) of crimes against humanity; c) of war crimes." One week later Demjanjuk was condemned to be hanged.

In January 1992, Israel's Supreme Court announced that it would hear fresh evidence culled from Soviet archives, supporting defense claims of misidentification. The evidence is compelling: 21 former Soviet Treblinka inmates all identified Ivan the Terrible as not Demjanjuk but another Ukrainian, someone strikingly similarly, Ivan Merchanko (present whereabouts unknown). Other evidence strongly suggested that Demjanjuk was a lower-echelon guard at another Nazi camp, not Treblinka.

On July 28, 1993, the Israeli Supreme Court overturned Demjanjuk's conviction, ruling that the totality of the evidence indicated he was not Ivan the Terrible. In September, a U.S. appeals court is expected to make a decision on his petition to rescind the deportation.

Eyewitness testimony is notoriously unreliable: memories fade and sometimes fail. If John Demjanjuk is Ivan the Terrible then he is one of the 20th century's worst criminals. If not, he might still be a man with much to hide.

—Colin Evans

Suggestion for Further Reading

Loftus, Elizabeth and Katherine Ketcham. *Witness For The Defense*. New York: St. Martin's Press, 1991.

Teicholz, Tom. *The Trial Of Ivan The Terrible*. New York: St. Martin's Press, 1990.

Wagenaar, Willem A. *Identifying Ivan*. Cambridge, Mass: Harvard University Press, 1988.

Wayne Williams Trial: 1981

Defendant: Wayne B. Williams   **Crime Charged:** Murder
Chief Defense Lawyers: Alvin Binder and Mary Welcome
Chief Prosecutors: Joseph Drolat, Jack Mallard, and Lewis Slaton
Judge: Clarence Cooper   **Place:** Atlanta, Georgia
Dates of Trial: December 28, 1981–February 27, 1982   **Verdict:** Guilty
Sentence: Life imprisonment

SIGNIFICANCE
The trial of the man suspected of being America's worst child-killer was bound to generate immense attention. But did it produce a just verdict?

Beginning in 1979 an unprecedented wave of killings struck Atlanta, Georgia. Over the next two years upwards of 20 young black males were found murdered. In the early hours of May 21, 1981, police staking out the Chattahoochee River, one of the killer's favorite dumping grounds for his victims, spotted a station wagon on a bridge. The driver, Wayne Williams, was questioned but allowed to leave. Two days later, the body of Nathaniel ("Nate") Cater was dragged from the river. Although forensic evidence connected Williams, a 23-year-old black homosexual music promoter, with many of the Atlanta killings, he was charged on only two counts.

Williams' trial began December 28, 1981. Following an adjournment for the holidays, testimony got under way on January 6, 1982. District Attorney Lewis Slaton likened the Atlanta killings to a "jigsaw puzzle with a whole lot of little pieces fitting in." Chief defense counsel Alvin Binder preferred to highlight Williams' solid family background, insisting to the jury: "You don't get a killer from a boy who was raised like this."

Officer Fred Jacobs, part of the surveillance team watching the Chattahoochee River, testified to seeing a station wagon "drive very slowly" across the bridge, moments after hearing a loud splash.

The story was taken up by FBI Special Agent Gregg Gulliland. After being stopped, Williams had given conflicting reasons for being on the bridge, then blurted out, "What's all this about?. . . I know. This is about those boys, isn't it?"

Challenging the defendant's claim that he had not known either victim, Margaret Carter, an acquaintance of Cater's, stated, "I saw Nate sitting on the bench in the park. . . with another fellow." She identified Williams as that man.

Prosecutors Use Microscopic Analysis

But it was the forensic evidence that really undid Williams. Microanalyst Larry Peterson had compared fibers and dog hairs found on the bodies of Cater and second victim Jimmy Ray Payne with examples taken from Williams' house, car, and German shepherd. "In my opinion," said Peterson, "it is highly unlikely any other environment other than that present in Williams' home and car could account for the combination of fibers and hairs I recovered from Mr. Cater and Mr. Payne."

Under cross-examination from Binder, Peterson acknowledged that there was no absolute scientific means of determining the origin of any fiber, and that identification was a subjective judgment on the part of the examiner.

Evidence of Williams' aggressive homosexuality came from two young men who testified that he had made unwanted advances toward them.

Williams Takes the Stand

Other than attack the credibility of prosecution witnesses, there was little the defense could do, except present Williams himself. Describing himself as a "carefree, happy-go-lucky person," Williams went on, "I haven't killed anybody, or thought about it, or plan on thinking about killing anybody."

Assistant prosecutor Jack Mallard pressed Williams on his reasons for being out at 3:00 A.M. Williams said he was searching for the address of a singer with whom he was to meet in the morning. Mallard wondered why he had not asked for directions.

"Me being in Cobb County at three o'clock in the morning?" Williams sounded incredulous. "Sir, they've got the Ku Klux Klan up there'."

Mallard pounced. "If you're so afraid of the Ku Klux Klan, what are you doing in Cobb County at three o'clock in the morning?"

Williams hurriedly mumbled an excuse but soon recovered his composure, insisting loudly, "Sir, I haven't killed anyone!"

The expected lengthy jury deliberation actually took less than 12 hours. On February 27, 1982, Williams was convicted of double murder. That same day, Judge Clarence Cooper imposed two consecutive life terms.

Doubts still linger about Williams' guilt. Many cling to a belief that a KKK-type organization carried out the killings; others dispute the forensic evidence. Although the case against Williams was wholly circumstantial, the fact remains that with his incarceration, the Atlanta killer's reign of terror came to an end.

—Colin Evans

Suggestions for Further Reading

Baldwin, James. *The Evidence Of Things Not Seen*. New York: Holt, Rinehart & Winston, 1985.

Fischer, Mary A. "Was Wayne Williams Framed?" *Gentlemen's Quarterly* (April 1991): 228ff.

Koltz, Charles. "The Atlanta Murders." *New Jersey Law Journal* (December 3, 1981): 11ff.

Wilson, Colin and Donald Seaman. *Encyclopedia of Modern Murder*. New York: G.P. Putnam's Sons, 1983.

Jack Henry Abbott Trial: 1982

Defendant: Jack Henry Abbott   **Crime Charged:** Murder
Chief Defense Lawyer: Ivan S. Fisher   **Chief Prosecutor:** James H. Fogel
Judge: Irving Lang   **Place:** New York, New York   **Dates of Trial:** January
4–21, 1982   **Verdict:** Guilty of first-degree manslaughter
Sentence: 15 years to life imprisonment

SIGNIFICANCE
The outrage that surrounded Jack Abbott's trial was deep and understandable. Public opinion took the view that, had it not been for influential but naive intellectuals, Abbott would have remained behind bars and one young life would have been saved.

While in jail, convicted killer Jack Abbott began a correspondence with author Norman Mailer. Mailer encouraged Abbott in his writing and helped to find a publisher for these letters which were released, to great critical acclaim, under the title *In The Belly Of The Beast*. Mailer petitioned Abbott's parole board, describing Abbott as "a powerful and important American writer." They promised to review Abbott's record.

Since age 12 (he was then 35) he had spent less than six months out of jail. Minor thefts had led to more serious bank robberies. In 1966 he received an extra 14-year jail term for stabbing a fellow prisoner to death. The board decided to parole Abbott to a halfway house in New York City. Six weeks later, on July 18, 1981, he and two female companions visited an all-night diner. Abbott got into an argument with waiter Richard Adan over use of the staff lavatory. The two took their quarrel outside, where Abbott stabbed Adan once in the heart, killing him almost instantly. Abbott fled. Police traced him to a Louisiana oil field and brought him back to New York to face trial.

Book Not Admissible

Following four days of jury selection, assistant District Attorney James H. Fogel opened the state's case on January 8, 1982. He suffered an early setback when Acting Justice Irving Lang refused to admit into evidence excerpts from *In The Belly Of The Beast*, which the prosecution said demonstrated Abbott's predisposition to kill. One passage that Fogel particularly wanted read out contained detailed instructions on how to kill in a knife-fight: "You have to move into total activity from a totally inactive posture to sink a knife in as close to his heart as possible," which, said Fogel, was virtually a blueprint for what had happened to Richard Adan.

It was defense attorney Ivan S. Fisher's contention that Abbott had merely been acting in self-defense, that Adan had grabbed a knife just before the two men left the diner to settle their dispute, a point contradicted by the first witness, Roger Schwarzchild, another waiter at the diner. He said that the only weapons available to Adan were dull butter knives, but that he did not see Adan with a knife of any description. He had seen the two men step outside, then moments later Abbott re-entered the diner and said, "Let's get out of here," to his two companions.

This last statement was corroborated by one of the two women present, a Barnard College student, Susan Roxas, except that in her version Abbott added, "I just killed a man." Once outside, Abbott told the women, "You don't know me," then ran off up the street. Roxas confirmed that Abbott had been carrying a knife earlier in the evening and that all three in the party had been drinking heavily.

Just Like the Book

Another witness, Wayne Larsen, told of seeing Abbott and Adan outside the diner. After a brief dispute, Abbott had lunged at the other man with a knife. Adan staggered back, clutching his chest. Abbott screamed, "Do you still want to continue this?" Adan, bleeding profusely, replied: "God no. Are you crazy? I already told you I don't."

Earlier rumors that Norman Mailer would testify on Abbott's behalf proved erroneous. It was left to Abbott alone to give the court some insight into the rigors of prison life, rigors that he claimed had honed his paranoia to a lethal level. In the midst of tearfully recounting his brawl with Adan, Abbott was caught off guard when the victim's father-in-law, Henry Howard, suddenly leapt up and yelled, "Abbott, you scum! You useless scum! It's just like the book, Abbott, just like in the book." Still shouting, Howard was led away.

Abbott took the interruption coolly, eyes blinking through gold-rimmed spectacles, and continued with his version of events on the fateful night. Adan had approached him outside the diner. "I was going to run, but then I thought, 'You don't do that.'" Adan kept coming. Abbott claimed that Adan went for a knife (none was ever found), that he had tried to block it, and that a brief struggle ensued. "All of a sudden the knife was in his chest and it was dead still. . . . It was one of the most tragic misunderstandings I can imagine."

Abbott's culpability was never in dispute, only the degree. After more than 24 hours of deliberation, the jury adjudged him guilty of first-degree manslaughter, but not murder. On April 15, 1982, Judge Irving Lang sentenced

Abbott to 15 years to life imprisonment. He did so regretfully, blaming Abbott's behavior on "a prison system that brutalizes rather than rehabilitates."

Norman Mailer, asked for his opinion on the verdict, sounded melancholic. "What can I say—the man is used to jail. Jail, sadly enough, is his home."

This case is eerily similar to that of Edgar Smith, when another renowned literary figure, William F. Buckley, took up a murderer's cause with disastrous repercussions. But it also highlights the problem facing all parole boards: balancing humanitarian concerns for the inmate against the public's right to protection from its worst elements. One cannot escape the nagging suspicion that, in this case at least, the weight of celebrity opinion counted for more than common sense.

—Colin Evans

Suggestions for Further Reading

Abbott, Jack. *In The Belly Of The Beast*. New York: Vintage, 1981.

Gaute, J.H.H. and Robin Odell. *The Murderers' Who's Who*. London: W.H. Allen, 1989.

Wilson, Colin and Donald Seaman. *Encyclopedia of Modern Murder*. New York: G.P. Putnam's Sons, 1983.

Claus Von Bülow Trials: 1982 & 1985

Defendant: Claus Von Bülow   **Crime Charged:** Attempted murder
Chief Defense Lawyers: First trial: John Sheenan and Herold Price
Fahringer; second trial: Thomas P. Puccio and John Sheehan
Chief Prosecutors: First trial: Stephen Famiglietti and Susan McGuirl; second
trial: Marc DeSisto and Henry Gemma   **Judges:** First trial: Thomas H.
Needham; second trial: Corrine Grande   **Places:** First trial: Newport, Rhode
Island; second trial: Providence, Rhode Island   **Date of Trials:** First trial:
January 11–March 16, 1982; second trial: April 25–June 10, 1985.
Verdict: First trial: Guilty; second trial: not guilty   **Sentence:** 20 years
imprisonment

SIGNIFICANCE

A study in contrasts, the two trials of Claus Von Bülow provide a unique insight
into the excesses and foibles of the super-rich.

For 13 years Claus and Martha "Sunny" Von Bülow had been bulwarks of
Rhode Island's blueblood colony, but by 1979 their marriage was over in all
but name. Around Christmas of that year Sunny slipped into a coma at their
oceanside mansion. Claus dithered over summoning medical attention and only
prompt mouth-to-mouth resuscitation revived the ailing woman. Sunny seemed
as baffled as everyone else as to the cause. Almost exactly one year later, on
December 21, 1980, she again lapsed into a coma and was transferred to Columbia Presbyterian Hospital in New York City, where she remained comatose as of
this writing. A family-inspired investigation led to indictments against Von
Bülow, a Danish-born aristocrat, charging that he had twice attempted to murder
Sunny by injecting her with insulin.

Because of its glittering cast, the trial attracted global attention. The
courthouse in Newport, Rhode Island, jammed with reporters and TV cameras,
reflected this when testimony began February 2, 1982. Prosecutor Stephen
Famiglietti argued that with a $14-million inheritance, the house, and a beauti-
ful young mistress all at stake, Von Bülow had every reason to want Sunny dead.
Describing the delay in requesting medical help, Famiglietti said: "He generally
conducted himself in a manner not consistent with that of an innocent man."

Witness Cites Mysterious Vials

Had it not been for Maria Schrallhammer, Sunny Von Bülow's secretary, the prosecution would not have had a case. Making no attempt to conceal her loathing of the defendant, Schrallhammer first outlined the tension that existed between the Von Bülows, then told of entering a closet in February 1980 and finding a black bag that contained several prescription vials made out to the accused. This set her thinking. The preceding Thanksgiving she had found similar vials labeled insulin. Schrallhammer, puzzled because no family member had a history of diabetes, had shown the vials to Prince Alexander von Auersperg, Sunny's son by her first marriage, remarking, "Insulin. What for insulin?" There seemed to be no reason for it to be around—unless, said Famiglietti, Von Bülow wanted to murder his wife. (When doctors examined Sunny they found abnormally high amounts of insulin in her system.) Auersperg's subsequent discovery of a hypodermic needle encrusted with insulin in yet another black bag merely strengthened her story.

Dr. George Cahill, a former president of the American Diabetes Association and one of the world's top experts in blood-sugar disorders, told the court that injected insulin was the only possible explanation for Sunny's coma. Cahill testified with the air of a man unused to having his opinions questioned, shrugging off defense counsel Herald Fahringer's suggestions that the high insulin level could have resulted from other means. "No, that is not correct . . . the sugar levels alone would lead me to suspect insulin."

What was supposed to be the defense's trump card turned into a disaster. By her own account, Joy O'Neill was a close friend of Sunny's and had frequently gone to the house in her capacity as exercise coach. O'Neill testified that during one of these visits in 1978, Sunny had recommended that she try a shot of insulin as a means of losing weight, saying it enabled one to eat "sweets and everything." On rebuttal Famiglietti was able to show that O'Neill had never actually visited Sunny during 1978 and that her reputation for truthfulness was less than sterling.

Claus Von Bülow at his trial (*Providence Journal-Bulletin* Photo)

After what had been the longest trial in Rhode Island history, the jury then set a record of its own by taking the longest time ever to reach its verdict, nearly six days. Many were surprised at the delay—the case seemed so open and shut—but on March 16, 1982, Claus Von Bülow was found guilty.

Seven weeks later Judge Thomas Needham passed sentence of 20 years imprisonment.

New Trial, New Evidence

Freed on bail, Von Bülow engaged the services of noted Harvard law professor Alan M. Dershowitz to organize his appeal. Under Dershowitz's skilled probing, revelations came to light suggesting the strong likelihood that Sunny's coma was self-induced, as friends cataloged a lifetime of drug and alcohol abuse, interspersed with mammoth food binges, a potentially lethal combination for a known reactive hypoglycemic (someone who suffers from low blood sugar). Even more revealing, Maria Schrallhammer's memory was seriously flawed. Dershowitz found some notes made at the time by family attorney Richard Kuh, which unveiled grave inconsistencies in her various statements to police. These and other discrepancies convinced the Rhode Island Supreme Court, on April 27, 1984, to reverse the convictions and order a new trial.

Two days short of a year later it began. Apart from the counsel—Marc DeSisto had taken over as chief prosecutor—the state's case was essentially unchanged. But this time the defense team mounted a far more vigorous campaign. They were led by Thomas Puccio, fresh from his success as a prosecutor in the ABSCAM trials (see separate entry), and now in private practice. He went after Schrallhammer on the vials. "The first time you spoke to Mr. Kuh you didn't tell him about the insulin. Is that correct?"

"That could be. That could very well be, since I was not concerned so much about the insulin."

In fact, Puccio established that Schrallhammer had not mentioned insulin to anyone, not until hearing that doctors had found insulin in Sunny's system. Turning to the vials found at Thanksgiving, Puccio extracted a grudging admission from the witness that she had no idea what they contained because, as she had told Kuh at the time, the labels had been scraped off. It was a telling blow.

Alexander von Auersperg, locator of the insulin-encrusted needle, also came under pressure. Puccio focused on a family meeting held shortly after that discovery. "One of the thing's you discussed at that meeting was a desire on the part of some of the people present to pay your stepfather some money to have him renounce any interest in your mother's estate. Isn't that right?"

Again Kuh's contemporaneous notes gave the witness no escape. He sheepishly nodded, "That's correct," virtually admitting the existence of a family plot to usurp Von Bülow.

Blood-sugar expert, Dr. George Cahill, also was forced to recant some of his former testimony. In a three-hour grilling Cahill now admitted that his previous assertion that only injected insulin could have produced Sunny's symptoms was false; certain prescription drugs might also produce a similar reaction.

The evidence of the encrusted needle was annihilated by Dr. Leo Dal Cortivo, a forensic toxicologist. He dismissed suggestions that it could have been used to inject Sunny, then gave the jury a practical demonstration why. The hypodermic was of the type which employed a separate vial, at no time would it come into contact with any insulin except through its hollow body and tiny aperture at the point. Once the insulin was injected, any residue on the needle would be wiped off by the skin as it was being withdrawn. Dal Cortivo's testimony obviously provoked speculation as to how the needle might have become encrusted. One possible solution was that it had been deliberately dipped into insulin. This theory, raising as it did the specter of Von Bülow being framed, was not one which the defense actively pursued.

Von Bülow's accusers. Left to right (second row): Ala and Franz Kneissl, Maria Schrallhammer, Alexander von Auersperg, and their attorney Richard Kuh. (*Providence Journal-Bulletin* Photo)

They didn't need to. Earlier, with the prosecution faltering, Judge Corrine Grands had almost granted the defense a mistrial, conceding that she was "holding this case together with baling wire."

As in the first trial Claus Von Bülow maintained a lofty silence and did not take the witness stand. Furious family members angrily denounced this as an act of cowardice but other than a certain callous infidelity there was little that the defendant had to answer for. The jury members clearly thought so. On June 10, 1985, they acquitted Von Bülow on all charges.

Considerable anger greeted this verdict, generating the belief that Claus Von Bülow was a guilty man who had bought his freedom. Certainly his own wealth and that of affluent friends enabled him to employ the very best legal and forensic talent available, but it should be remembered that he was up against an equally well-endowed and very determined family, one prepared to spare no cost to see him convicted.

—Colin Evans

Suggestions for Further Reading.

Briton, Tracy. "Von Bülow's Victory." *The National Law Journal* (June 24, 1985): 24ff.

Dershowitz, Alan M. *Reversal Of Fortune.* New York: Random House, 1986.

Frey, Darcy. "Boomerang." *American Lawyer* (November 1986): 36ff.

Lapayowker, Stewart. "Evidence." *Temple Law Review* (Winter 1988): 1561–1586.

Wright, William. *The Von Bülow Affair.* New York: Delacorte Press, 1983.

John Hinckley Trial: 1982

Defendant: John W. Hinckley, Jr.   **Crime Charged:** Attempted murder
Chief Defense Lawyers: Lon Babby, Gregory Craig, Vincent Fuller, and
Judith Miller   **Chief Prosecutors:** Roger Adelman and Robert Chapman
Judge: Barrington Parker   **Place:** Washington, D.C.
Dates of Trial: April 27–June 21, 1982   **Verdict:** Not guilty by reason of
insanity

SIGNIFICANCE
The insanity plea has always been a gray area with lawyer and layperson alike,
difficult to plead, often difficult to accept. But the outrage caused by this trial
brought into question the very existence of insanity as a defense.

The facts were never in dispute. On March 30, 1981, John Hinckley, Jr., fired six shots at President Ronald Reagan and his entourage outside the Washington Hilton Hotel. The President, Press Secretary James Brady, police officer Thomas Delahanty, and Secret Service Agent Timothy McCarthy were hit. All recovered. Hinckley was arrested at the scene and later charged with attempted murder.

With the abortive assassination having been captured on videotape and replayed endlessly on television, Hinckley's trial was expected to be a foregone conclusion—until the defense attorneys announced their intention to enter a plea of not guilty by reason of insanity. In this respect they were greatly aided by Judge Barrington Parker's decision to hear the case under federal procedural rules, which meant that the prosecution would bear the burden of proving Hinckley's sanity beyond a reasonable doubt, whereas, under local rule, the onus would have fallen on the defense attorneys prove their client insane. This was an important distinction.

Stalking Gunman Fires Six Shots

Senior prosecutor Roger Adelman made his opening address on May 5, 1982. He described how Hinckley had deliberately stalked the President, and that when the time came to act, he assumed the "crouch position" used by an experienced marksman cognizant of his own actions. "With six shots, Mr.

Hinckley hit four people," said Adelman, concluding that these were "the central and critical events" of the case.

Chief defense counsel Vincent Fuller made no attempt to deny the truth of what Adelman had said, but he disputed the motivation. He traced the origins of the assassination attempt back to Hinckley's four-year obsession with movie actress Jodie Foster, an obsession that led to prolonged psychiatric treatment. Frustrated by his inability to meet Foster, Fuller said, Hinckley retreated "into this world of isolation." He began stalking President Jimmy Carter, and later President Reagan. On the morning of the shooting Hinckley checked into a Washington hotel and wrote Foster an undelivered letter, clearly outlining his intentions:

> Dear Jodie,
>
> There is a definite possibility that I will be killed in my attempt to get Reagan. It is for this reason that I am writing you this letter now. . . . I am asking you to please look into your heart and at least give me the chance, with this historical deed, to gain your respect and love.
>
> I love you forever.
>
> —John Hinckley

The accused's father, Jack Hinckley, delivered an impassioned plea from the witness stand. Referring to the rancor between himself and his psychologically troubled son—enough to compel Hinckley's banishment from the family home—Jack Hinckley cried,

> I am the cause of John's tragedy. I forced him out at a time when he simply could not cope. I wish to God that I could trade places with him right now.

Testimony, quite predictably, developed into a battle of medical opinion. Was Hinckley a helpless victim of his own neurosis, or was he, as prosecutors alleged, a willful assassin? Dipping deep into his sizable fortune, Hinckley's father paid the handsome fees of an impressive array of psychiatrists to argue the former.

Just How Mad?

Dr. David Bear of Harvard University described Hinckley's obsession with the movie *Taxi Driver*, in which Jodie Footer had starred, explaining how Hinckley identified with the leading character, Travis Bickle, and his attempt to shoot a presidential candidate. Bickle's later success with an attractive woman, said Bear, convinced Hinckley that "violence, horrible as it is, was rewarded . . . [he] felt like he was acting out a movie script."

Answering for the government, Dr. Park Dietz characterized Hinckley as a spoiled rich kid, basking in "notions of achieving success and fame in a way that would not require a great deal of effort." Settling on some sensational crime as the easiest means of gaining attention, Hinckley then "thought about a variety of potential crimes and how much publicity each would attract." While conceding Hinckley's abnormality, Dietz insisted that the defendant was never out of touch with reality—the hallmark of psychosis.

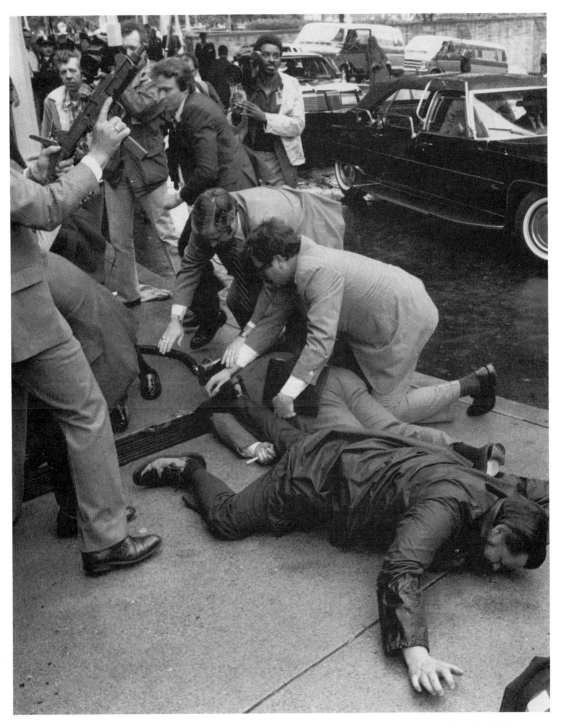

The scene immediately after John Hinckley, Jr.'s assassination attempt on President Ronald Reagan, March 30, 1981.
(Courtesy, Ronald Reagan Library)

Such contradictory and confusing testimony clearly presented enormous problems for the jurors as they retired on Friday, June 18, 1982. They returned the following Monday. Judge Barrington Parker, visibly shaken, read their verdict—not guilty by reason of insanity—to a stunned courtroom. In post-trial interviews some jurors hinted that they had been coerced into this verdict by other jurors. Following acquittal, Hinckley was detained at St. Elizabeth's mental hospital and remains there to the present day.

The most grievously injured victim of Hinckley's havoc, James Brady, lent his name to a bill designed to stiffen gun control regulation but saw his efforts fail to pass the U.S. House of Representatives in March 1992.

In September 1992 a federal judge ruled that Hinckley's insanity did not absolve him of liability for damages to the three presidential aides wounded in the shooting, all of whom had brought suit against the would-be assassin. This case is still pending.

Hinckley's acquittal sparked a vigorous and often misguided debate about the insanity defense. Many sought to curtail its use; others urged total abolition. Sadly, the swell of unrest owed more to the standing of the victims than it did to the facts of the case. John Hinckley had enough peculiarities of mind and behavior to justify the jury's decision.

—Colin Evans

Suggestions for Further Reading

Caplan, Lincoln. *The Insanity Defense*. Boston: Godine, 1984.

Hinckley, Jack and Jo Ann Hinckley. *Breaking Points*. Grand Rapids, Mich.: Zondervan, 1985.

Lindbergh, Tod. "Keep Him Out of the Public Eye." *Insight* (September 4, 1989): 64ff.

Winslade, William J. and Judith Wilson Ross. *The Insanity Plea*. New York: Charles Scribner's Sons, 1983.

Pulitzer Divorce Trial: 1982

Plaintiff: Herbert Pulitzer, Jr. **Defendant:** Roxanne D. Pulitzer
Chief Defense Lawyers: Joseph D. Farish, Jr., and Louis L. Williams
Chief Lawyers for Plaintiff: Mark T. Luttier and Robert T. Scott
Judge: Carl H. Harper **Place:** Palm Beach, Florida
Dates of Trial: September 20–November 9, 1982 **Verdict:** Divorce
granted, and custody of the children awarded to Herbert Pulitzer

SIGNIFICANCE

While the Pulitzer marriage was dissolved simply under Florida's "no-fault" divorce law, sensational allegations about Roxanne Pulitzer's conduct caused the judge to rule that the state's "tender years doctrine" awarding custody of young children to the mother should not be applied in this case. Some of the testimony at the trial was graphic enough to border on the pornographic, which ensured that the trial received more news coverage than any divorce trial in recent history.

Until it ended, the marriage of Roxanne and Herbert "Peter" Pulitzer looked like a real-life Cinderella story. The couple came from very different worlds. The divorced Pulitzer, wealthy grandson of publishing magnate Joseph Pulitzer, was considered to be one of the most eligible bachelors in the wealthy Florida enclave of Palm Beach. The recently divorced Roxanne Dixon, 21 years younger, was a former cheerleader from a small town in rural New York state. The pair met at a party, married, had twin sons, and seemed to have a happy marriage for 5½ years until things went wrong. To the discomfort of Palm Beach society and the titillation of the rest of the world, tales of what went wrong between the Pulitzers made their televised divorce extremely popular.

When Herbert Pulitzer sued his wife for divorce, he offered her a substantial financial support settlement if she would relinquish custody of their children. Roxanne Pulitzer refused and was initially granted custody of their two young sons in an emergency custody hearing. When the Pulitzers' lawyers took their proposed settlements for child custody and the financial terms of the divorce before Circuit Judge Carl Harper, the case quickly became ugly. To little effect, Judge Harper slapped a "gag order" on all parties involved to prevent the case from being tried in the press. Palm Beach seemed to empty of socialites, many of whom feared being subpoenaed to testify about the Pulitzer marriage.

Herbert Pulitzer accused his wife of wrecking their marriage with adultery and drug abuse. His lawyers called a train of witnesses—many of them Pulitzer employees—whose allegations portrayed Roxanne Pulitzer as an unfit mother by virtue of her heavy cocaine use and alleged affairs with a race car driver, a French bakery owner, and a former nanny's boyfriend, whom the lawyers characterized as a drug dealer.

Both Pulitzers claimed that they had shared in sexual encounters with Jacquie Kimberly, socialite wife of Kleenex heir James Kimberly. Herbert Pulitzer further accused the two women of carrying on a lesbian relationship, a charge which provoked Jacquie Kimberly to retort that Pulitzer was "definitely deranged." When Roxanne Pulitzer counterattacked with accusations that her husband had an incestuous relationship with a daughter by his previous marriage, Pulitzer's daughter appeared on the stand and accused Roxanne Pulitzer of propositioning her.

Several witnesses testified about Roxanne Pulitzer's active interest in the supernatural. A psychic described seances in the Pulitzer bedroom, during which a trumpet lay on the bed. Wondering aloud how it could be relevant, Judge Harper allowed the trumpet to be entered as evidence. Newspapers immediately dubbed Roxanne Pulitzer "the strumpet with the trumpet."

Judge Harper did little to disguise his contempt for what he was hearing. "It surely made me appreciate my wife," said the judge. "I go home every night and give her a big hug."

Judge Harper ultimately ruled in Herbert Pulitzer's favor with a severity that struck many observers as peculiar. Contrasting Pulitzer's "doleful eyes and aging face" with his wife's apparently unconcerned "doodling" on a notepad during the trial (she later claimed she was trying to maintain her composure), the judge proclaimed that Herbert Pulitzer was a hard worker and loving parent who deserved custody of his children.

Judge Harper's decision intimated that Roxanne Pulitzer was a gold digger intent on profiting financially from the divorce. He wrote that her "exorbitant demands shock the conscience of the court, putting the court in mind of the hit record by country singer, Jerry Reed, which laments, 'She Got the Gold Mine, I Got the Shaft.' "

Herbert Pulitzer was ordered to pay his wife's legal fees, return $7,000 she had contributed toward the purchase of his yacht, and pay her $2,000 a month in "rehabilitative alimony" for two years so that she would have a means of support until she could become gainfully employed. All other alimony and financial claims were denied. In view of her husband's wealth, his pretrial offer, and the annual $144,000 alimony payment she had requested, Roxanne Pulitzer's cash award was minuscule. She was given two weeks to vacate the house for which lawyers had fought.

In 1982, Florida's "tender years doctrine" was based on the premise that a child forms a strong emotional bond with its mother during the first three years of age. Courts customarily awarded custody to mothers in divorce suits for fear of breaking this bond and damaging the emotional development of any children involved. Judge Harper, however, declared that Roxanne Pulitzer's "flagrant adultery and other gross marital misconduct" required abandoning the doctrine in her case. He ruled that the children would live with their father. Their mother would be allowed custody two weekends per month, holidays on alternating years, and for an annual four-week vacation.

The decision left Roxanne Pulitzer emotionally shattered. She contacted Los Angeles divorce attorney Marvin Mitchelson, winner of the celebrated "palimony" suit brought against actor Lee Marvin by his former lover Michelle Triola Marvin. The flamboyant and expensive attorney offered to take Roxanne Pulitzer's case without a fee, but bowed out after the ensuing publicity faded, leaving her appeals in the hands of Florida attorneys.

Roxanne Pulitzer's three appeals of the custody ruling were unsuccessful, but she found a way to capitalize on her notoriety. Working as an aerobics instructor and occasionally lecturing in favor of joint child custody policies, she paid her legal bills with the help of $70,000 she received for posing nude in *Playboy* magazine. In 1987, she told her side of the story in *The Prize Pulitzer*, an immediate best-seller whose portrait of the Pulitzer marriage and its dissolution differed greatly from the scenario that emerged from the trial.

Roxanne Pulitzer claimed to be the victim of perjurers and a methodical character assassination that cost her custody of her children. She portrayed her ex-husband as a manipulator whose constant hints of reconciliation led her not to take his divorce action seriously until it was too late. "I had no game plan," she told the *Houston Post* during a promotional interview for the book. "I was sleeping with him right up to the trial and after the trial. And he evidently had a plan that was way beyond me. . . . I was an idiot."

—*Thomas C. Smith*

Suggestions for Further Reading

Axthelm, Peter. "The Palm Beach Fun Couple." *Newsweek* (January 10, 1983): 69.

Couric, Emily. *The Divorce Lawyers*. New York: St. Martin's Press, 1992.

Pulitzer, Roxanne with Kathleen Maxa. *The Prize Pulitzer*. New York: Random House, 1987.

Thompson, Hunter S. "A Dog Took My Place." *Rolling Stone* (July 21–August 4, 1983): 18–22.

Weatherman Brinks Trials: 1983

Defendants: First trial: Cecilio Ferguson and Edward Joseph; second trial: Kuwasi Balagoon, Judith Clark, and David Gilbert   **Crimes Charged:** First trial: Murder, robbery, racketeering, and conspiracy; second trial: Murder and robbery   **Chief Defense Lawyers:** First trial: Jesse Berman, Chowke Lumumba, and William Mogulescu; second trial: The accused
Chief Prosecutors: First trial: Robert S. Litt, Stacey J. Moritz, and Paul E. Summit; second trial: Kenneth Gribetz   **Judges:** First trial: Kevin T. Duffy; second trial: David S. Ritter   **Places:** First trial: New York, New York; second trial: Goshen, New York   **Dates of Trials:** First trial: April 13–September 3, 1983; second trial: July 11–September 15, 1983   **Verdicts:** First trial: Not guilty of murder/robbery, guilty of acting as accessories after the fact; second trial: all defendants found guilty   **Sentences:** First trial: 12½ years; second trial: 25 years to life

SIGNIFICANCE
Political dissent in America has a long, often violent history. Of all the extremist groups that sprang from the seventies, none was more prepared to continue that bloody tradition than a band of black rights activists who called themselves the Weather Underground.

Ten years of Weather Underground politico/criminal mayhem culminated in a botched robbery of a Brinks armored vehicle in October 1981. In making off with $1.6 million, robbers killed one guard and two policeman. After a chase four people were arrested. Over the next 15 months several more suspects were rounded up. The complexity of the case necessitated multiple trials.

In the first hearing, which opened April 13, 1983, Cecilio Ferguson and Edward Joseph stood trial with four other Weather Underground members, none of whom was charged with the Brinks robbery. The government, perplexed by how best to proceed against a gang which had been robbing and killing for much of the preceding decade, had decided on a catch-all federal action against this batch of Weathermen. One component of the prosecution was the Brinks robbery.

Before the trial, defense attorneys William Mogulescu and Jesse Berman won an important victory when they persuaded Judge Kevin Duffy that the prosecution should not be allowed to call two other gang members whose testimony was considered unreliable. However, they were less successful in keeping Tyrone Rison off the stand. He readily admitted his own complicity in the murderous robbery.

"You had the M-16 rifle, is that right?" asked defense attorney, Chowke Lumumba.

"That's correct."

"And you shot the gun at the guard who was on the ground?"

"That's correct."

"A man who was totally disarmed and helpless?"

"That's correct."

And so it went. Defense counsel depicted Rison as a thug who had done a deal with the government in exchange for a 12-year sentence, questioning whether such a man should escape so leniently while the defendants faced a lifetime behind bars?

The jury thought not. On September 3, 1983, they convicted Ferguson and Joseph only of being accessories after the fact, an outcome the defense team jubilantly declared "a defeat for the government."

Judge Duffy had a different view. Sentencing both defendants to 12½ years imprisonment, he commented, "I have never understood juries."

A Straightforward Case

The state trial against Kuwasi Balagoon, Judith Clark, and David Gilbert began on July 11, 1983, and was far more clear-cut. Here the charges related entirely to the Brinks robbery, allowing the jury to concentrate more fully on the facts of one case, rather than be confused by several. At least it should have been that way, until the defendants, declaring themselves "freedom fighters," refused to mount a conventional defense. When Judge David Ritter clashed with Balagoon, the prisoner said, "In that case I'm leaving," and he stormed from the courtroom accompanied by his co-defendants. Gilbert yelled, "All the oppressors will fail." Clark chimed in with, "Death to U.S. imperialism."

Their departure left prosecutor Kenneth Gribetz an open field. Over two weeks he presented 86 witnesses and some devastating evidence. Clark and Gilbert had been arrested on the day of the murder in a car with $800,000 of the stolen money, while Balagoon's palm print was found on bags of the stolen money.

When the prosecution rested, the defendants deigned to return. Their only witness, Sekou Odinga, already convicted of robbery in the preceding federal trial, justified the Brinks murders because the victims had obstructed the "expropriation" of money earmarked to create the black Republic of New Africa in five Southern U.S. states. Odinga further rationalized the theft, saying it was designed "to take back some of the wealth that was robbed through the slave labor that was forced on them and their ancestors."

Both Clark and Gilbert warmed to this theme. Gilbert said, "I just want to meet you, Comrade Odinga, and express my respect for you for twenty years of commitment . . . for the New African people, and all oppressed people." Clark sought reassurance, wondering if white persons, like herself, "have a responsibility to struggle for the rights of oppressed people, for their human rights and self-determination?" Odinga gave ready assent, then was led away to begin his own 40-year jail term.

When the jury returned its guilty verdict September 15, 1983, prosecutor Gribetz's only complaint concerned the sentencing: "We're upset, frankly, that there's no death penalty." On October 6, Judge David Ritter sentenced each defendant the maximum three consecutive life terms in prison without possibility of parole until each had served 75 years.

On June 14, 1984, yet another Weatherman, Samuel Brown, was convicted of complicity in the Brinks murders and later jailed for 75 years.

Ironically, the most notorious Weather Underground member, Kathy Boudin, never stood trial. This daughter of left-wing radicals and a lifelong extremist, plea-bargained her way to a 20-year jail sentence.

These trials reveal how, masquerading under the guise of political activism, the Weathermen slid from committed principle into heartless criminality. In doing so, they trod a well-worn path as agents of change who succeeded only in changing themselves.

—Colin Evans

Suggestions for Further Reading

Castellucci, John. *The Big Dance.* New York: Dodd, Mead & Co., 1986.

Frankfort, Ellen. *Kathy Boudin And The Dance Of Death.* New York: Stine & Day, 1983.

Tell, Larry. "Socialists Sue Over Suspect ID." *The National Law Journal* (December 7, 1981): 3ff.

New Bedford Rape Trial: 1984

Defendants: John Cordeiro, Jose M. Medeiros, Virgilio Medeiros, Victor Raposo, Daniel Silva, and Joseph Vieira **Crime Charged:** Aggravated Rape **Chief Defense Lawyers:** Edward F. Harrington, Judith Lindahl, Kenneth Sullivan, and David Waxler **Chief Prosecutors:** Ronald A. Pina and Raymond P. Veary **Judge:** William G. Young **Place:** Fall River, Massachusetts **Dates:** February 23–March 21, 1984 **Verdicts:** Cordeiro, Raposo, Silva, and Vieira, Guilty; Jose Medeiros and Virgilio Medeiros, Not guilty **Sentence:** 6 to 12 years imprisonment

SIGNIFICANCE

Reports of the crime spurred a national debate as to whether a woman's independent or (as some saw it) compromising behavior made her partially responsible for sexual crimes committed against her; the conviction of four of the men was widely hailed by feminists, who insisted that rapists, and not the character of their victims, should be tried in court.

A gang rape that took place March 6, 1983, in Big Dan's tavern, New Bedford, Massachusetts, quickly became national news. The first reports were of a 21-year-old mother of two raped by a half-dozen men over the course of two hours, while the bar's 15 other patrons cheered. Later investigation of the evidence reduced the size of the cheering squad, but confirmed the other details of the crime. According to eyewitness testimony, two men tried to force the woman to perform oral sex; two others threw her on a pool table and raped her; the bartender was physically restrained from going to a phone; and another nonparticipating man—who first ignored the bartender's instructions to call the police—dialed a wrong number and then didn't bother to try again.

Amid the outrage of women's groups and many of New Bedford's citizens, Big Dan's tavern was closed and its bar cut up with a chain saw. But many members of the town's Portuguese community just as quickly rallied behind the accused rapists, claiming, as one woman put it, "There was guilt by national origin." Throughout the trial and for years afterward, they would express resentment against the woman. "She should have been home in the first place," the *New York Times* quoted one Portuguese-American woman shouting on the day of sentencing. The paper aptly summed up the sentiment:

By their lights she wasn't raped. Rather she got herself raped, a very different crime for which they think the victim must take the blame. She did, after all, enter a bar, drink, flirt—behavior which offends a conservative community like theirs. Those demonstrators may not condone her rapists' behavior, but they are more ashamed of hers.

The New Bedford gang rape trial served as a benchmark for the feminist community characterized by Susan Brownmiller, author of the landmark book *Against Our Will: Men, Women and Rape*, as a "public morality play," the trial was broadcast live on CNN, discussed on op-ed pages and homes across America, and monitored daily by both the Coalition Against Sexist Violence and the Committee for Justice (founded to support the accused).

Who's on Trial?

Originally, David Silva (26), John Cordeiro (23), Joseph Vieira (26), and Victor Raposo (23) were charged with aggravated rape, while Jose Medeiros (22) and Virgilio Medeiros (23)—who were not related—were charged as accessories. By the time the trial began in Fall River, Massachusetts on February 23, 1984, Jose Medeiros and Virgilio Medeiros also were charged with aggravated rape. (As alleged participants in a "joint venture" crime, they could be guilty of aggravated rape if they were found to have aided in or encouraged the crime.) Because some of the men were expected to incriminate the others, the trial was split into separate morning and afternoon sessions: Silva and Vieira in the afternoon, the others in the morning. All six of the defendants and one of the witnesses, Carlos Machado, spoke in Portuguese through interpreters.

Assistant District Attorney Raymond Veary outlined the case against Silva and Vieira for Judge William Young and the jury. The rape of the young woman, he said, took place while bystanders "were cheering like at a baseball game." Defendant Silva, he continued, had pushed the woman onto the pool table, and had held her there and raped her. Then Silva and Vieira "traded places."

The woman—who requested anonymity—began her own testimony the following morning. "I was screaming—I was begging for help. I could hear people laughing and cheering, yelling." She said she had gone out to buy cigarettes after tucking her two young daughters into bed. Two stores were closed, she continued, and she had ended up in Big Dan's. She bought cigarettes from the vending machine and sat beside the only other female patron to order a drink. That woman left. When she herself headed for the door, she said, a man yanked her jacket and she complained: "What the hell do you think you're doing?" Another man took her feet. "They started dragging me across the floor. I started kicking and screaming." She told the court that the men threw her onto the pool table and removed her jeans. She said that one man raped her while another held her down; then the men switched places and she was raped again.

The defense attorneys accused the woman of fabricating a story to make money through the sale of book rights or by suing the bar's owners, charges which the woman denied. The defense lawyers then questioned the woman about her original statement to the police, accusing six men of rape, and her testimony since, which referred to four men. The woman remained calm and said, "It was told when I had not slept and was very upset."

Carlos Machado, the bartender at Big Dan's on the night of March 6, testified that he saw the woman on the floor and heard her screaming while Joseph Vieira and Daniel Silva removed her pants. Jose Medeiros and Virgilio Medeiros, he said, were shouting, "Do it! Do it! That's it! That's it!" One of them, he continued, kept him back from the phone. Victor Raposo and John Cordeiro, then attempted to force the woman to engage in sex. She was then placed on the pool table, Machado concluded, and Daniel Silva "took off his pants and went on top of her."

During cross-examination on March 2, Machado said he'd noticed the woman before the rape occurred. "I had a bad impression of the girl," he said. "She was laughing and talking with the boys, and I wanted to call the police and get her out."

Defense attorney Kenneth Sullivan asked Machado why he wanted the woman to leave. Machado explained: "A group of guys around a girl in such a tight crowd."

Sullivan asked, "That was so unusual that you thought she should be ejected?"

Machado replied, "Yes." He also testified that she had three drinks, not one.

Following the New Bedford rape, "take back the night" rallies took place throughout the country. (Bettye-Lane photo)

Before resting their case against Silva and Vieira, the prosecution called 19 additional witnesses. Among them was Detective Sandra Grace, who testified about her meeting with the woman shortly after the rape was reported. "She was hysterical and in a state of shock," the officer recalled. Another officer described finding the woman outside of the tavern. She was nude below the waist, he testified, and "said she had been repeatedly raped and abused."

Detective Kenneth Gormley testified that when John Cordeiro arrived at the police station, he "told us that he wanted to tell us what he did." Gormley continued, "He said he was sorry. He said he was drunk, but that was no excuse for what he had done." Cordeiro had admitted that "he and Victor held her legs."

On March 13, 1964, Edward Harrington, defense lawyer for Daniel Silva, offered another version of events. "He was talking to her alone," Harrington claimed. After Silva removed the woman's pants, "both fell on the floor." When Silva placed the woman on the bar, Harrington continued, "His state of mind was that he and she would do something just by themselves. But by then a lot of men came over." Harrington declared that "Whatever he was doing with that girl was between he and she. It was consensual, no screaming, crying or protest."

Harrington called four witnesses on Silva's behalf. One, Lizetta Robida, was a friend of the woman's. She testified that she had "told her she should stay home" and that the woman had consumed two drinks while in her company earlier that evening. Marie Correia was the other woman in Big Dan's on March 6, 1983. She testified that the woman "was bubbly, she was bouncing around the chair. Her pupils were large and her eyes were very glassy." The chief toxicologist for Allegheny County's coroner's office, Charles Winek, then testified that the woman was "clinically poisoned, poisoned with alcohol," according to a blood test taken several hours after the incident.

Silva also testified on his own behalf, saying, "She was, you know, willing." Silva said the woman had asked if he had drugs to share, and that he had said no but offered to "fool around" with her. "She said yes," Silva said. "She looked very happy." He testified that they had kissed and partly undressed when others interrupted them. Contradicting the bartender's testimony, Silva said he had not entered the woman.

Verdicts and Sentencing

On March 17, 1984, Daniel Silva and Joseph Vieira were convicted of aggravated rape by a jury of eight men and four women. Some people in the courtroom cried, "Shame!" When news reached the parking lot, others smashed their fists on cars and shouted obscenities. Women's groups and their supporters sponsored a candlelight march, in which 2,500 people participated.

News of the convictions was kept from the other jury, which convened as scheduled on Monday the 19th. The defense continued to characterize the woman as a drunken liar, and John Cordeiro testified that "she was enjoying herself."

On March 22, the last verdicts were rendered. Virgilio Medeiros and Jose Medeiros were acquitted; John Cordeiro and Raposo were found guilty. There was immediate upheaval in Fall River as 3,000 to 4,000 people attended a candlelight vigil in support of the victim, while 7,000 to 10,000 marchers protested the convictions. Judge Young sentenced the four men to six to 12 years in prison. He also responded to what had become an underlying question. He had not reduced the sentence because the victim had been in a bar, he said, because to do so would "virtually outlaw an entire gender for the style of their dress, the length of their skirts or their choice to enter a place of public refreshment." The four men first asked for retrials and then appealed; all attempts to overturn their convictions were unsuccessful. The woman moved to Miami with her children and was killed in an automobile accident in December 1986.

— Kathryn Cullen-DuPont

Suggestions for Further Reading:

Brownmiller, Susan. *Against Our Will: Men, Women and Rape.* New York: Simon & Schuster, 1975.

Faludi, Susan. *Backlash: The Undeclared War Against American Women.* New York: Crown Publishers, Inc., 1991.

The *New York Times.* March 11, 12, 13, 18, 19, 1983; September 1, 3, 4, 1983; February 6, 24, 25, 28, 29, 1984; March 1, 3, 4, 6, 7, 8, 9, 13, 14, 15, 16, 17, 18, 20, 22, 23, 24, 27, 28, 1984; April 11, 25, 1984; May 7, 1985; October 7, 1986; and December 18, 1986.

Westmoreland v. CBS: 1984

Plaintiff: General William C. Westmoreland   **Defendant:** CBS, Inc.
Plaintiff Claim: That a certain television documentary broadcast by CBS
concerning the conduct of the Vietnam War libeled the plaintiff
Chief Defense Lawyers: David Boies and Stuart W. Gold
Chief Lawyers for Plaintiff: Dan M. Burt and David M. Dorsen
Judge: Pierre N. Leval   **Place:** New York, New York
Dates of Trial: October 9, 1984–February 18, 1985   **Decision:** None. The
case was settled out of court before it went to the jury.

SIGNIFICANCE
The principle of *New York Times v. Sullivan* remains strong: public figures must
prove actual malice to win libel suits. Despite strong evidence of press misconduct in this and a related case, namely *Sharon v. Time, Inc.,* both plaintiffs lost.

On January 23, 1982, CBS Television ran a documentary entitled "The Uncounted Enemy: A Vietnam Deception" The narrator, Mike Wallace, took an aggressive investigative approach in preparing the documentary. The theme of the program was that the effects of infamous Tet offensive, which took American forces by surprise and caused much loss of life, could have been avoided if the actual size of North Vietnam's troop strength had been calculated accurately. The documentary placed much of the blame on the commanding general, William C. Westmoreland, who had been in command in Vietnam throughout the late 1960s and during the Tet offensive.

The CBS report took several liberties with the truth, however. For example, Wallace accused Westmoreland of juggling enemy troop figures to produce an artificially low count and please President Johnson:

> Wallace: Isn't it a possibility that the real reason for suddenly deciding in the summer of 1967 to remove an entire category of the enemy from the Order of Battle, a category that had been in that Order of Battle since 1961, was based on political considerations?
>
> Westmoreland: No, decidedly not. That—that . . .
>
> Wallace: Didn't you make this clear in your August 20th cable?
>
> Westmoreland: No, no. Yeah. No.
>
> Wallace: I have a copy of your August 20th cable.

Westmoreland: Well, sure. Okay, okay. All right, all right.

CBS had succeeded in making Westmoreland look like a liar and a fool, but in fact the cable in Wallace's possession had been sent by another officer in Saigon while Westmoreland was away, a fact known to CBS but not revealed on the program.

Incensed, after the program was televised, Westmoreland denied the allegations it raised about his conduct. The Capitol Legal Foundation offered to represent Westmoreland for free, and attorneys Dan M. Burt and David M. Dorsen filed Westmoreland's libel suit on September 13, 1982. CBS's chief attorneys were David Boies and Stuart W. Gold. Before the case went to trial, Boies and Gold succeeded in having it transferred from South Carolina, where the case was originally filed, to New York City, where it was tried before Judge Pierre N. Leval.

The trial began on October 9, 1984. On February 15, 1985, Leval ruled that under such First Amendment precedents as *New York Times Company v. Sullivan* (see separate entry), Westmoreland had to prove by "clear and convincing evidence" that CBS acted with actual malice in preparing a false documentary. Legally, this is a heavy burden of proof for the plaintiff in a libel suit, one which was invoked by Leval because Westmoreland was a famous general and thus a "public figure." Faced with the prospect of a lengthy legal battle against difficult odds, Westmoreland settled his case with CBS out of court on February 18, 1985. Both sides agreed to pay their own legal fees, and of the $120 million for which Westmoreland had sued, he got nothing.

Retired General William Westmoreland and his attorney announce his intention to sue CBS for libel. (AP/Wide World Photos)

At the same time the Westmoreland case was pending, another prominent military figure was pursuing a libel lawsuit. Israeli general Ariel Sharon sued Time, Inc., which publishes *Time* magazine, for having printed an article on February 14, 1983, that accused Sharon of encouraging certain Lebanese militia forces to massacre some Palestinians in 1982. The case was tried from November 13, 1984, to January 24, 1985, in New York City before Judge Abraham D. Sofaer. The jury found *Time* not guilty due to lack of actual malice, and Sharon dropped his case. However, jury members made a special point of stating that they thought *Time* had acted "negligently and carelessly" in preparing the article.

Generals Westmoreland and Sharon ran into the same obstacle in their cases: despite strong evidence of press misconduct, under the *New York Times*

Company v. Sullivan case's standard they couldn't make the difficult showing necessary for public figures to win libel suits.

—Stephen G. Christianson

Suggestions for Further Reading

Adler, Renata. "Annals of Law: Two Trials." (Part 1) *The New Yorker* (June 16, 1986): 42–85.

———. "Annals of Law: Two Trials." (Part 2) *The New Yorker* (June 23, 1986): 34–79.

———. *Reckless Disregard: Westmoreland v. CBS, Sharon v. Time.* New York: Vintage Books, 1988.

Benjamin, Burton. *Fair Play: CBS, General Westmoreland, and How a Television Documentary Went Wrong.* New York: Harper & Row, 1988.

Roth, M. Patricia. *The Juror and the General.* New York: William Morrow & Co., 1986.

Falwell v. Flynt: 1984

Plaintiff: Jerry Falwell **Defendant:** Larry Flynt **Plaintiff Claim:** That an ad parody published in *Hustler* magazine was libelous and intended to cause Jerry Falwell emotional distress **Chief Defense Lawyers:** David O. Carson, Alan Isaacman, and Arthur P. Strickland
Chief Lawyers for Plaintiff: Jeffrey H. Daichman, Norman Roy Grutman, and Harold H. Rhodes, Jr. **Judge:** James C. Turk **Place:** Roanoake, Virginia
Dates of Trial: December 3–8, 1984 **Verdict:** That the ad was not libelous but did inflict emotional distress, thereby entitling Falwell to $200,000 in damages

SIGNIFICANCE

This First Amendment battle between long-time adversaries culminated in an unprecedented verdict.

For several years Larry Flynt's magazine *Hustler* had published a bizarre mix of sex, religion, humor and political comment. In the November 1983 issue it spoofed a Campari vermouth ad campaign in which various celebrities were asked to recall their "first time," that is, the first time they tried Campari. *Hustler*'s version had nationally known pastor and political activist Reverend Jerry Falwell describing his "first time" as an incestuous encounter with his mother. The ad further stated that Falwell needed to be drunk to preach. At the foot of the page was a brief and barely noticeable disclaimer, "Ad parody—not to be taken seriously." Falwell, a perennial target of Flynt's irreverence, filed suit for libel, requesting $45 million in damages.

The jury was seated on December 3, 1984 and after opening statements, Falwell's attorney, Norman Roy Grutman, led off with his star witness. Falwell vehemently denied every allegation in the ad. "Have you ever taken alcoholic beverages before going into the pulpit to deliver your message?" asked Grutman.

"Never at any time," responded Falwell.

Over strident defense objections, Grutman inquired, "Mr. G. Falwell, specifically, did you and your mother ever commit incest?"

"Absolutely not."

The reason for the defense objections was simple: it had been their contention all along that the idea of Jerry Falwell enjoying an incestuous relationship with his mother was so preposterous that no one could possibly believe it. Judge James Turk's decision to allow the question dealt a body blow to that argument, as did Falwell's heartfelt comment to the jury, "It is the most hurtful, damaging, despicable, low-type personal attack that I can imagine one human being can inflict upon another."

Flynt Duels with Lawyer

When it came time for Flynt to testify, he did so from the wheelchair to which he had been confined since 1978 when a would be assassin's bullet left him paralyzed. Earlier, the defense failed in its attempt to suppress a foul-mouthed videotaped deposition that Flynt had given to Grutman. That allowed the jury to see Flynt at his worst. Now they had the opportunity to observe the publisher in a far different light. Flynt protested that pain and medication had rendered the deposition meaningless: this, he assured the court, was the real him. "What," asked chief defense attorney Alan Isaacman, "was intended to be conveyed by the ad?"

> Well, we wanted to poke fun at Campari . . . because the innuendoes that they had in their ads made you sort of confused as to if the person was talking about their first time as far as a sexual encounter or whether they were talking about their first time as far as drinking Campari . . . . They [the public] know that it was not intended to defame the Reverend Falwell, his mother, or any members of his family, because no one could take it seriously.

Isaacman explored whether Flynt had deliberately intended to damage Falwell's reputation by printing the satire.

Flynt scoffed. "If I really wanted to hurt Reverend Falwell, I would do a serious article on the inside . . . talk about his jet airplane or maybe Swiss bank accounts . . . I don't know if such accounts exist, but if you want to really hurt someone . . . you put down things that are believable. You don't put down things that are totally unbelievable."

The duel between Flynt and Grutman, neither of whom attempted to conceal their poor opinion of the other, was much awaited. They were old protagonists. Grutman had previously represented *Penthouse* magazine in an action against Flynt and lost. Here, as the two crossed swords, Judge James Turk several times had to defuse the rhetoric. But Grutman pounded away. "Mr. Flynt, have you ever said, 'Free expression is absolute?'"

"Yes, I believe free expression is absolute . . ."

"And 'absolute' means that you can say whatever you want?"

"Yes," replied Flynt, adding coolly. "You want to bait me?"

Grutman shrugged off the taunt and played a televised interview in which Flynt charged that his deposition had been a parody of Grutman's conduct in this case. "Do you deny having said what appears to have been uttered by you, as it was shown on that video monitor?"

Flynt sighed. "Yes. It's very difficult to take you seriously."

Jury Verdict Unprecedented

After clarification from Judge Turk on the complex legal issues involved, the jury retired. On December 8, 1984, they rejected the libel suit but found that Flynt *had* intended to cause Falwell emotional distress. For this reason they awarded the plaintiff $100,000 actual damages and $100,000 punitive damages.

Never before had a jury reached such a verdict. Clearly this was a decision headed for appeal, and in February 1988, the Supreme Court unanimously voted to reverse the lower court's verdict. In reaching their decision the Court made no attempt to condone the content of the *Hustler* parody, other than to say it was entitled to Constitutional protection.

Falwell v. Flynt ignited a storm of protest among America's media. Many feared an erosion of First Amendment right to free speech. In upholding this view the Supreme Court implied that while insults to public figures might be painful, denying the right to make them would be intolerable.

—Colin Evans

Suggestion for Further Reading

D'Souza, Dinesh. *Falwell, Before The Millenium*. Chicago: Regenery Gateway, 1984.

Falwell, Jerry. *Strength For The Journey*. New York: Simon & Schuster, 1987.

Martz, Larry and Ginny Carroll. *Ministry Of Greed*. New York: Wiedenfeld & Nicolson, 1988.

Smolla, Rodney A. *Jerry Falwell v. Larry Flynt*. New York: St. Martins' Press, 1988.

In the Matter of Baby M: 1987

Plaintiffs: William and Elizabeth Stern   **Defendant:** Mary Beth Whitehead
Plaintiff Claim: That Whitehead—who had entered a "Surrogate Parenting Agreement," become pregnant via artificial insemination with William Stern's sperm, and delivered his and her own biological child—ought to be forced to give up the baby   **Chief Defense Lawyers:** Harold Cassidy and Randy Wolf
Chief Lawyers for Plaintiffs: Frank Donahue and Gary Skoloff
Judge: Harvey Sorkow   **Place:** Hackensack, New Jersey
Dates of Trial: January 5–March 31, 1987   **Verdict:** The Judge terminated the parental rights of Mary Beth Whitehead and permitted Elizabeth Stern to adopt Whitehead's and William Stern's daughter. This verdict was overturned in part by the New Jersey Supreme Court which, on February 2, 1988, granted William Stern custody but invalidated Elizabeth Stern's adoption and restored Whitehead's parental rights.

SIGNIFICANCE

This was the first highly publicized trial to examine the ethical questions raised by "reproductive technology."

On February 5, 1985, three parties entered into an agreement in the offices of Noel Keane's Infertility Center of New York.

Richard Whitehead consented to the agreement's "purposes, intents, and provisions" and acknowledged that his wife, Mary Beth Whitehead, would be inseminated with William Stern's sperm. Since Richard Whitehead would be the legal father of any child born to his wife, he also agreed to "surrender immediate custody of the child" and to "terminate his parental rights." Mary Beth Whitehead agreed to be artificially inseminated, to conceive and bear a child without forming "a parent-child relationship," and to relinquish the child and her own parental rights to William Stern. She also relinquished her right to make a decision concerning an abortion. She promised not to seek one unless the fetus was deemed "physiologically abnormal" or the inseminating physician declared that it was necessary to preserve her "physical health." Moreover, she granted William Stern the right to demand that she undergo amniocentesis testing and agreed "to abort the fetus upon demand of WILLIAM STERN" if the fetus was found to be congenitally or genetically abnormal. Together, the Whiteheads "agree[d] to assume all risks, including the risk of death, which are incidental to conception, pregnancy, [and] childbirth."

William Stern agreed to pay Mary Beth Whitehead $10,000 upon her surrender of the baby. Although the contract stated that its "sole purpose . . . is to enable WILLIAM STERN and his infertile wife to have a child which is biologically related to WILLIAM STERN," it described the $10,000 as "compensation for services and expenses," which should "in no way be construed as a fee for termination of parental rights or a payment in exchange for a consent to surrender the child for adoption." Betsy Stern was neither a party to the contract nor mentioned by name; the Whiteheads did agree, however, "that the child will be placed in the custody of WILLIAM STERN'S wife" in the event of Stern's death prior to the child's birth.

Noel Keane of the Infertility Center was paid a fee of $10,000 from the Sterns.

A Child Is Born, and Plans Go Awry

Events did not go as outlined on paper. Mary Beth Whitehead gave birth to a daughter on March 27, 1986. She refused the $10,000, named the baby "Sara Elizabeth Whitehead," and took her home. The Sterns demanded the baby and took her home on Easter Sunday, March 30. Whitehead got her back on March 31 and, 12 days later, told the Sterns she could never surrender her daughter. The Sterns, determined to enforce the contract, hired attorney Gary Skoloff. The first time the police showed up, Whitehead presented a birth certificate for her daughter, Sara Elizabeth Whitehead, and the police left without "Melissa Elizabeth Stern." The next time the police knocked on the door, Mary Beth Whitehead passed the infant to her husband through an open window and begged him to run. The battle was on.

By the time the trial commenced on January 5, 1987, a *guardian ad litem*, Lorraine Abraham, had been appointed for the infant. Temporary custody of the child known as "Baby M" had been awarded to the Sterns, and Mary Beth Whitehead had been granted two-hour visits each week "strictly supervised under constant surveillance . . . in a sequestered, supervised setting to prevent flight or harm." She had also been ordered by Judge Harvey Sorkow to discontinue breast-feeding the infant.

The contract itself was considered first. The Sterns' attorney, Gary Skoloff, said: "The issue to be decided in this court is whether a promise to make the gift of life should be enforced. . . . Mary Beth Whitehead agreed to give Bill Stern a child of his own flesh and blood." He then explained that Betsy Stern's multiple sclerosis "rendered her, as a practical matter, infertile . . . because . . . she could not carry a baby without significant risk to her health."

Whitehead's attorney, Harold Cassidy, countered in his own opening remarks: "The only reason that the Sterns did not attempt to conceive a child was . . . because Mrs. Stern had a career that had to be advanced. . . . What Mrs.

Stern has is [multiple sclerosis] diagnosed as the mildest form. She was never even diagnosed until after we deposed her in this case. . . . We're here," Cassidy concluded, "not because Betsy Stern is infertile but because one woman stood up and said there are some things that money can't buy." Dr. Gerard Lehrer, a neurologist with a teaching position at Mount Sinai School of Medicine then testified that Betsy Stern had merely "a very, very, very slight case of MS, if any."

Custody was quickly raised, and Skoloff claimed that his clients were exclusively entitled to the baby, under contract law and because it would serve the child's best interests: "If there is one case in the United States, where joint custody will not work, where visitation rights will not work, where maintaining parental rights will not work, this is it." He appealed directly to Judge Sorkow: "Your Honor, under both the contract theory and the best-interest theory, you must terminate the rights of Mary Beth Whitehead and allow Betsy Stern to adopt. . . . Terminate the parental rights of Mary Beth Whitehead and allow Bill Stern and Betsy Stern to be Melissa's mother and father."

Lorraine Abraham testified that she "knew the day would come when I would have to stand before this court [as *guardian ad litem*] and present a recommendation." She explained that she had consulted three experts while trying to make her decision: Dr. Judith Brown Greif, a social worker; Dr. David Brodzinsky, a psychologist; and Marshall Schechter, a psychiatrist. The three, Abraham continued, "will . . . recommend to this court that custody be awarded to the Sterns and visitation denied at this time." As for her own opinion, Abraham concluded, "I am compelled by the overwhelming weight of their investigation to join in their recommendation."

When Betsy Stern took the stand, she was asked by one of Whitehead's lawyers, Randy Wolf: "Were you concerned about what effect taking the baby away from Mary Beth Whitehead would have on the baby?"

She replied: "I knew it would be hard on Mary Beth and in Melissa's best interest."

Wolf asked her: "Now, I believe you testified that if Mary Beth Whitehead receives custody of the baby, you don't want to visit."

Stern answered: "That is correct. I do not want to visit."

Skoloff then tried to demonstrate that Mary Beth Whitehead would be an unfit mother. Whitehead had fled to Florida and hidden there with the baby for a time. Skoloff characterized this as the action of an unstable person. Then he played a tape recording of a phone conversation between William Stern and Mary Beth Whitehead:

Stern: I want my daughter back.

Whitehead: And I want her, too, so what do we do, cut her in half?

Stern: No, No, we don't cut her in half.

Whitehead: You want me, you want me to kill myself and the baby?

Stern: No, that's why I gave her to you in the first place, because I didn't want you to kill yourself.

Whitehead: I've been breast-feeding her for four months. She's bonded to me, Bill. I sleep in the same bed with her. She won't even sleep by herself. What are you going to do when you get this kid that's screaming and carrying on for her mother?

Stern: I'll be her father. I'll be a father to her. I am her father. You made an agreement. You signed an agreement.

Whitehead: Forget it, Bill. I'll tell you right now I'd rather see me and her dead before you get her.

Mary Beth Whitehead took the stand the next day. Randy Wolf asked her, "If you don't get custody of Sara, do you want to see her?"

Whitehead answered,

Yes. I'm her mother, and whether this court only lets me see her two minutes a week, two hours a week, or two days, I'm her mother and I want to see her, no matter what.

The prominent child psychologist Dr. Lee Salk testified on behalf of the Sterns: "[T]he legal term that's been used is 'termination of parental rights,' " he said,

and I don't see that there were any 'parental rights' that existed in the first place. . . . The agreement involved the provision of an ovum by Mrs. Whitehead for artificial insemination in exchange for ten thousand dollars . . . and so my feeling is that in both structural and functional terms, Mr. and Mrs. Stern's role as parents was achieved by a surrogate uterus and not a surrogate mother.

On February 23, Marshall Schechter, one of the experts consulted by Lorraine Abraham, testified. As Abraham had earlier indicated, he thought the Sterns should be awarded custody. Schechter also said that Whitehead had a "borderline personality disorder" and said that "handing the baby out of the window to Mr. Whitehead is an unpredictable, impulsive act that falls under this category." Finally, he testified that Whitehead dyed her prematurely white hair, evidence of a "narcissistic personality disorder."

The next day, Dr. Phyllis Silverman, a Boston psychiatric social worker, defended Whitehead's flight to Florida and "crazy behavior." She testified:

Mrs. Whitehead's reaction is like that of other "birth mothers" who suffer pain, grief, and rage for as long as thirty years after giving up a child. The bond of a nursing mother with a child is very powerful.

Whitehead Gets Support

Other women organized to defend Whitehead's fitness as a mother. Children's author Vera B. Williams, actress Meryl Streep, and writers Margaret Atwood and Susan Sontag were among a group of 121 prominent women who released a letter mocking statements made by Schechter and the other "experts." The letter, entitled, "By These Standards, We Are All Unfit Mothers," demanded that "legislators and jurists . . . recognize that a mother need not be perfect to 'deserve' her child."

In his closing argument on Whitehead's behalf, Harold Cassidy pointed out again that Mrs. Stern was not, as originally represented to Whitehead, infertile. He pointed out that the law permitted a termination of parental rights only in the case "of actual abandonment or abuse of the child." And he predicted that a verdict upholding the contract would result in "one class of Americans . . . exploit[ing] another class. And it will always be the wife of the sanitation worker who must bear the children for the pediatrician."

Mary Beth Whitehead speaks to supporters outside the New Jersey Courthouse. Dr. Phyllis Chesler is at far right. (Bettye-Lane)

On March 31, 1987, Judge Sorkow announced his decision: "The parental rights of the defendant, Mary Beth Whitehead, are terminated. Mr. Stern is formally judged the father of Melissa Stern." Judge Sorkow then took Betsy Stern into his chambers and presided over her adoption of Baby M.

Supreme Court of New Jersey Overrules

On February 2, 1988, the Supreme Court of New Jersey invalidated the surrogacy contract, restored Mary Beth Whitehead's parental rights, and annulled the adoption of Baby M by Betsy Stern. "We do not know of, and cannot conceive of, any other case," Chief Justice Robert Wilentz wrote for the unanimous court, "where a perfectly fit mother was expected to surrender her newly born infant, perhaps forever, and was then told she was a bad mother because she did not." After invalidating the surrogacy contract, the justices classified the dispute as one between "the natural father and the natural mother, [both of whose claims] are entitled to equal weight." The court granted custody to William Stern and ordered the trial court to set visitation for Mary Beth Whitehead.

The decision permitted future surrogacy arrangements in New Jersey only where "the surrogate mother volunteers, without any payment, to act as a surrogate and is given the right to change her mind and to assert her parental rights."

By 1992, 16 other states had passed legislation outlawing or restricting commercial surrogacy contracts.

— Kathryn Cullen-DuPont

Suggestions for Further Reading

Chesler, Phyllis. *Sacred Bond: The Legacy of Baby M*. New York: Times Books, 1988.

Davis, Flora. *Moving the Mountain: The Women's Movement in America Since 1960*. New York: Simon & Schuster, 1991.

Evans, Sara M. *Born for Liberty: A History of Women in America*. New York: The Free Press, 1989.

Sack, Kevin, "New York is Urged to Outlaw Surrogate Parenting for Pay." *New York Times* (May 15, 1992).

Whitehead, Mary Beth with Loretta Schwartz-Nobel. *A Mother's Story: The Truth About the Baby M Case*. New York: St. Martin's Press, 1989.

Bernhard Goetz Trial: 1987

Defendant: Bernhard Hugo Goetz   **Crimes Charged:** Attempted murder, assault, reckless endangerment, and criminal possession of a gun
Chief Defense Lawyers: Mark Baker and Barry Slotnick
Chief Prosecutor: Gregory Waples   **Judge:** Stephen G. Crane
Place: New York, New York   **Dates of Trial:** March 23–June 16, 1987
Verdict: Guilty of criminal possession of a gun; not guilty of all other charges
Sentence: 1 year imprisonment, $5,075 fine, 4 years probation

SIGNIFICANCE

How far should an American citizen be allowed to go in the defense of his life and liberty? That was the question facing a jury in this, one of the most highly charged trials New York City had ever seen.

Following a 1981 beating that left him with a permanently damaged knee, Bernhard Goetz, a 36-year-old electrical engineer, took to carrying a gun everywhere he went. On December 22, 1984, while riding a New York City subway train, he was approached by four black youths, one of whom demanded $5. Goetz's response was to yank a revolver from a special quick-draw holster and begin spraying bullets. As two of the youths fled, Goetz shot them in the back. One, Darrell Cabey, fell. Goetz approached him and said, "You seem to be all right; here's another," firing a second open-nosed bullet that severed Cabey's spinal cord. Then Goetz calmly left the scene and disappeared.

Nine days later Goetz gave himself up at a police station in Concord, New Hampshire. Following several lengthy confessions he was charged with 13 various offenses, from attempted murder to criminal possession of a gun.

Bringing the case to court took time—more than two years. Selecting a jury for such an obviously volatile trial proved almost as laborious, as neither side wanted to concede any advantage in this most critical phase of the judicial process. Eventually, after one month, a jury of 10 whites and two blacks was impaneled, and on April 27, 1987, they heard Assistant District Attorney Gregory Waples make the opening presentation. He outlined the salient facts, then said: "These terribly destructive shots . . . were fired not by a typical New Yorker, not by a reasonable person such as yourselves, responding to provocation in an appropriate and limited manner, but by an emotionally troubled individual." Goetz was, said Waples, "a man with a passionate but very twisted and self-righteous sense of right and wrong . . . an emotional powder keg, one spark away from explosion." To drive home this point Waples highlighted Goetz's refusal to wear gloves, even on the coldest winter day, so that he might remain "fast on the draw" should trouble arise. Such an obsession, the prosecutor reasoned, was far more likely to lead Goetz into conflict rather than avoid it.

The Defense Attacks

Quite naturally the defense, led by Barry Slotnick, saw things in an entirely different light. His opening statement left no doubts about their intention to turn this trial into an indictment of the "aggressors . . . this gang of four." Excoriating them as "savages and vultures . . . who got what the law allowed," Slotnick launched into a vitriolic assault on the character and credibility of James Ramseur, one of the alleged assailants. Five months after the Goetz incident, Ramseur had been arrested for participating in the savage gang-rape of a pregnant woman. "And to add insult to injury," thundered Slotnick, "Mr. Ramseur and his friends took her earrings and her ring, and left her bleeding on the rooftop landing." So heavy-handed and graphic did Slotnick's depiction of this rape become that it drew a sharp rebuke from Justice Stephen Crane: "Why don't you get off this, Mr. Slotnick."

But the damage had been done. The impression of the four black youths as rampaging sadists was firmly implanted in the jury's mind. This skillful defense manipulation of proceedings went a stage further when one of the state's witnesses, Detective Michael Clark, referred to "the four victims on the train." Slotnick was on his feet immediately. "Your Honor, I would object to the characterization of the 'victim'. That's a decision the jury will have to make." Surprisingly Waples yielded the point, when there was no real need for him to do so, agreeing to the much meeker term "young men." It was another small but important victory for the defense. Slowly Bernhard Goetz was being turned into the victim in the case, not the perpetrator.

Central to the prosecution case was a taped confession that Goetz had made to police. Because Goetz would not take the stand, this was the jury's only opportunity to hear him speak. In a rambling two-hour account Goetz gave his version of the attack. It contained many damaging statements. Most incriminating of all was his clearly expressed intention "to murder them, to hurt them, to make them suffer as much as possible." Also revealed was his aversion to being "played with . . . as a cat plays with a mouse."

Several witnesses from the subway train testified. Through careful questioning Slotnick succeeded in drawing admissions that the action had happened so quickly as to impair their recollection of what actually occurred. In particular Slotnick created doubt about the actual number of shots fired. The intention here was to undermine the prosecution's claim that Goetz had cold-bloodedly stood over Cabey and fired the fifth and most damaging shot. Slotnick desperately needed to demonstrate that this injury had occurred just in random gunfire. By far the most resistant to this line of questioning was Christopher Boucher, a

San Franciscan vacationing in New York at the time of the shooting. Boucher testified that he initially heard gunfire but that his view was blocked. However, he then saw Goetz "standing, looking down at the man in the seat." Waples asked, "How far was the defendant from him [Cabey]?"

Answer: Two to three feet.

Question: Did you see the gun at any point?

Answer: Yes.

Question: And what did the person, who was sitting down, do at the moment the shot was fired?

Answer: Well, he was sitting, grasping the bench, and he just tightened.

Slotnick, aware that this was the most damaging eyewitness testimony yet, did everything in his power to discredit it. He began by implying that Boucher had been unduly influenced by media accounts of the shooting, an allegation that Boucher strenuously denied. Next, Slotnick asked Boucher, had he not been "shaken and traumatized" by the violence, perhaps enough to compromise his memory?

"Actually no," Boucher replied. "That's the funny thing."

Effective Demonstration

Slotnick fared much better with Joseph Quirk, a ballistics expert hired to recreate the crime scene in court. For the purposes of this demonstration Slotnick had engaged the services of four black youths, dressed like street toughs, to act out the parts of the attackers. Had the defense only been interested in demonstrating bullet paths, then the color of the assistants would have been immaterial, but the sight of four black teenagers jostling Quirk, a white man, was highly inflammatory. So much so, that Judge Crane ordered Slotnick to use court employees in the future should he need to carry out any further demonstrations.

Bernhard Goetz leaving court escorted by Guardian Angel Keith Johnson. The Goetz trial addressed the question of a citizen's right to defend himself. (AP/Wide World Photos)

Without meaning to be, prosecution witness James Ramseur was far and away the defense's strongest card. He entered the court in prison dungarees, pugnacious and petulant, determined to face down Slotnick. At first he refused to testify, earning for himself several citations for contempt. When he eventually condescended to take the stand, Ramseur foolishly bandied words with counsel. "When was the last time . . . that you . . . committed a crime against a human being?" asked Slotnick.

"When was the last time you got a drug dealer off?" sneered Ramseur. Three days later, in sentencing Ramseur for contempt, Judge Crane upbraided him for his stupidity:

> Your conduct has played right into the hands of Mr. Goetz's lawyer. He owes you a vote of thanks. . . . The jurors saw your contemptuous conduct. That can never be erased from their minds.

On Friday, June 12, 1987, the jury retired to consider their verdict. By the following Tuesday they had reached agreement on all 13 counts. Twelve times jury foreman, James Hurley, intoned, "Not guilty." Only once did he respond, "Guilty"—to a charge of criminal possession of a weapon in the third degree.

Three months later, on October 19, 1987, Judge Crane passed sentence: six months in jail, plus a fine and probation. Upon review in January 1989, the jail sentence was increased to one year.

The Bernhard Goetz trial opened up many old wounds and left a peculiar sense of public dissatisfaction at its outcome. Many believed that he should never have faced a court; they saw him as acting well within his rights. Others, fearful of vigilantism adding to the problem of already dangerous streets, were outraged by the jury's refusal to convict on all but the least serious charge. In the final analysis, skillful advocacy emerged as the only winner in this case. It wasn't elegant, but it was effective.

—Colin Evans

Suggestions for Further Reading

Blecker, R. "A Verdict By Their Peers." *The Nation* (October 3, 1987): 334ff.

Fletcher, George P. *A Crime Of Self-Defense*. New York: Free Press, 1988.

Jet (October 22, 1990): 22.

Lesly, Mark and Charles Shuttleworth. *Subway Gunman*. Latham, N.Y.: British American Pub., 1988.

Cipollone v. Liggett Group: 1988

Plaintiff: Estate of Rose Cipollone   **Defendant:** Liggett Group
Plaintiff Claims: That the defendant, a cigarette company, was liable for Rose Cipollone's death from cancer because it failed to warn consumers about the dangers of smoking   **Chief Defense Lawyer:** H. Bartow Farr III
Chief Lawyers for Plaintiff: Alan Darnell, Marc Z. Edell, and Cynthia Walters
Judge: H. Lee Sarokin   **Place:** Newark, New Jersey
Dates of Trial: February 1–June 13, 1988   **Decision:** Jury awarded plaintiff damages of $400,000; reversed on appeal, and lawsuit later dropped

SIGNIFICANCE
Despite encouraging early victories, the lesson of the Cipollone case is that smokers face very burdensome legal difficulties in suing cigarette companies.

Rose Cipollone of Little Ferry, New Jersey, was born in 1926. Like many people of her generation, she took up smoking at an early age, in her case, 16. Although medical studies examining evidence of a link between smoking and cancer began to appear as early as the 1920s, they' were not widely read, and the U.S. Surgeon General didn't look into the issue until 1962. In 1966 the first federal law on cigarette warning labels went into effect, and in 1969 Congress passed a stricter law requiring that the label, "Warning: The Surgeon General Has Determined That Cigarette Smoking Is Dangerous to Your Health," be printed on all cigarette packs.

Decade after decade, the cigarette industry spent billions of dollars on advertising. Newspaper, magazine, radio, and television ads extolled the pleasures of smoking. There was no mention of any risk, and the tobacco companies vigorously fought government regulation in the 1960's and 1970's with studies of their own that denied any health risk from smoking. Meanwhile, Cipollone had been smoking since 1942. Her favorite brands were Chesterfields and L&M, manufactured by Liggett Group, Inc., one of the smaller tobacco companies.

In 1981, Dr. Nathan Seriff diagnosed Cipollone as having lung cancer, caused by smoking cigarettes. Cipollone filed a lawsuit against Liggett on August 1, 1983 in the U.S. District Court for the District of New Jersey in Newark. She was represented by Alan Darnell, Marc Z. Edell, and Cynthia Walters, and the judge was H. Lee Sarokin. Of Liggett's team of defense lawyers, who worked to prevent the case from going to trial for nearly five years, the most prominent lawyer was H. Bartow Farr III . . . Early in the litigation, however, Cipollone won an important victory when Sarokin refused to dismiss the case on the grounds that Liggett's compliance with the federal warning-label law absolved Liggett from further legal liability:

> This case presents the issue of whether cigarette manufacturers can be subjected to tort liability if they have complied with the federal warning requirement. . . . In effect, the cigarette industry argues that such compliance immunizes it from liability to anyone who has chosen to smoke cigarettes notwithstanding the warning, that federal legislation has created an irrebuttable presumption that the risk of injury has been assumed by the consumer. This court rejects that contention.

Cippolone Dies, but Her Case Proceeds

Sarokin's decision was issued on September 20, 1984, and generated enormous publicity about the case. The prospect of successful smokers' litigation sent tobacco company stocks into a tailspin. Unfortunately for her, Cipollone died shortly thereafter, on October 21, 1984. Her husband, Antonio Cipollone, continued the case on behalf of her estate. After years of foot-dragging and delays by Liggett's attorneys, the Cipollone case finally went to trial on February 1, 1988. Just getting the case to trial was an accomplishment: of the 300 lawsuits on record against tobacco companies in the past 40 years, fewer than 10 have actually gone to trial.

Edell, the senior attorney in the Cipollone legal team, described Liggett's legal defenses to the jury as basically a statement to all smokers:

> If you trusted us, if you thought we would test, if you thought we would warn, if you believed our statement in the press, if you believed our advertisements, if you were stupid enough to believe us, then you deserve what you got.

Cipollone's attorneys introduced documents showing that the cigarette companies were aware of smoking-related health risks before the government took any action but failed to disclose these risks to the consumer. For example, one Liggett report from 1961 described certain ingredients in cigarettes as "(a) cancer-causing, (b) cancer-promoting, (c) poisonous, (d) stimulating, pleasurable, and flavorful."

On June 13, 1988, the jury returned its verdict. It was a very conservative finding, mostly based on Liggett's failure prior to the 1966 law to warn smokers like Cipollone about the dangers of smoking. Further, the jury found that Cipollone was 80 percent responsible for her death by smoking, and Liggett only 20 percent responsible. Nevertheless, the jury assessed $400,000 in damages against Liggett, the first such award in tobacco-litigation history.

Liggett appealed, and the case ultimately reached the U.S. Supreme Court on October 8, 1991. During the lengthy appellate process, however, Antonio Cipollone died in 1990. His son, Thomas Cipollone of Grass Valley, California, carried on the case on behalf of both his parents' estates. The Supreme Court required the parties to re-argue the case on January 13, 1992, and issued its opinion on June 24, 1992. Although the court ruled in a 6-3 decision that health warnings on cigarette packs don't shield cigarette companies like Liggett from personal-injury lawsuits, the court did impose tougher evidentiary requirements concerning the companies' advertising and promotions. The case would have to be retried.

Thomas Cipollone and the attorneys had had enough. After nine years of expensive litigation, they were back at square one, facing even more time-consuming hurdles thanks to the Supreme Court's decision. To make matters worse, Judge Sarokin had been removed from the case for comments he had made elsewhere about how he believed that the tobacco industry was hiding evidence. On November 5, 1992, the Cipollone family dropped their case against Liggett. While the initial jury verdict was the first of its kind in American legal history, the ultimate lesson is that the tobacco companies can delay and delay in court until their victims die or give up in despair.

—Stephen G. Christianson

Suggestions for Further Reading

Crudele, John. "The Smoke Clears: Tobacco Liability Suits Decline." *New York* (November 14, 1988): 28.

"For the First Time Ever." *The New Republic* (July 4, 1988): 10–11.

Gostin, Larry O. "Tobacco Liability and Public Health Policy." *Journal of the American Medical Association* (December 11, 1991): 3178–3182.

Spencer, Leslie. "Just Smoke." *Forbes* (December 23, 1991): 41–42.

"Where There's Smoke . . ." *Time* (April 8, 1991): 55.

Joel Steinberg Trial: 1988–89

Defendant: Joel Steinberg   **Crime Charged:** Murder
Chief Defense Lawyers: Ira London and Adrian DiLuzio
Chief Prosecutors: Peter Casolaro and John McCusker   **Judge:** Harold
Rothwax   **Place:** New York, New York   **Dates of Trial:** October 25, 1988–
January 30, 1989   **Verdict:** Guilty, First degree manslaughter
Sentence: 8½-25 years

SIGNIFICANCE

New York's first-ever televised murder trial held the interest of the nation with its account of chronic child abuse and obsessive love. Initial audience anger and frustration with an adoption system that could allow such a thing to happen soon coalesced into bewilderment over why a seemingly intelligent and upscale couple would resort to such atrocities.

For 12 years criminal lawyer Joel Steinberg and Hedda Nussbaum, a former editor and writer of children's books, shared a one-bedroom apartment in New York City's Greenwich Village. Theirs was a brutal relationship, fueled by cocaine and sado-masochistic sex. Violent beatings often sent Nussbaum to the hospital, but she always returned to the man she loved and their filthy apartment. One observer would later describe it as "a cave." Inexplicably, they sought to introduce children into this nightmare, but they were unable to have children themselves. Steinberg used his knowledge of legal loopholes to "adopt" two babies without filing the necessary paperwork. These loopholes cost one little girl her life.

At 6:35 A.M. on Monday, November 2, 1987, a 911 call from Nussbaum brought paramedics to the apartment. They found 6-year-old Lisa naked and emaciated, unable to breathe, covered with bruises. Steinberg, 47, his knuckles scratched and raw, told the paramedics that she had choked on some food and lapsed into a coma, and he had attempted to revive her with a combination of cardiopulmonary resuscitation and the Heimlich maneuver. Nussbaum, 46, watching from the bedroom, said nothing. Investigators later found the couple's other child, Mitchell, 16 months old, tethered to a makeshift playpen with a rope. He too showed obvious signs of neglect.

The full extent of Lisa's maltreatment became apparent at the hospital. Hardly an inch of her 43-pound-body was unmarked. Guided by the varying discoloration, doctors were able to plot a long pattern of abuse. The examination resulted in Steinberg and Nussbaum being charged with attempted murder. On November 5, when it became clear that Lisa would never recover from the coma, her life-support system was removed. The couple now faced murder charges.

Joel Steinberg conferring with his attorneys. Steinberg was convicted of murdering 6-year-old Lisa Steinberg whom he had illegally adopted. (AP/Wide World Photos)

In building their case, prosecutors realized that to secure a conviction against Joel Steinberg, they needed Hedda Nussbaum's testimony. Reluctantly they agreed to drop all charges against her if she would cooperate with their inquiries. She readily agreed.

A Deadly Relationship

The trial opened October 25, 1988, before Judge Harold Rothwax. In what promised to be an emotional hearing, a cool head on the bench was essential, and Judge Rothwax had a reputation as a jurist of unflappable demeanor. He presided over a courtroom packed with spectators and members of the media. In his opening address, Assistant District Attorney Peter Casolaro made it clear that he would be picking apart the relationship between Steinberg and Nussbaum piece by piece. By this means he hoped to convince the jury of Steinberg's guilt. But first there was the medical evidence.

Dr. Douglas Miller, a New York pathologist, told the court that Lisa had died from a brain hemorrhage caused by a blow to her right temple. He also described two other severe blows. All three, in his opinion, were administered by a large, strong person. Every eye in court fell on the powerfully built Steinberg. He remained impassive. A videotape of Nussbaum, filmed by police on the night of her arrest, showed a battered, frail woman, barely able to walk, let alone capable of beating anyone to death.

Other witnesses testified to the tragedy and traumas of Lisa's brief life, but only Hedda Nussbaum could provide the evidence that would convict Joel Steinberg. When she took the stand, the problem, as prosecutors saw it, was to build her credibility with the jury. For her testimony to be believed, she had to be presented as yet another of Steinberg's victims. Casolaro started off slowly, asking Nussbaum to describe her feelings towards her former lover.

"I thought he was probably the most wonderful man I'd ever met."

"What qualities was it that attracted you to him, Miss Nussbaum?"

"Well, he seemed to be extremely intelligent and bright, and I loved to hear him talk for hours."

Cocaine Rage

But any admiration that she felt for Steinberg soon faded. She catalogued their mutual involvement with cocaine and the fury that it provoked in him. Without any provocation he would pound her unmercifully with his fists. Five times between 1983 and 1985, she fled the house. Casolaro, anticipating the defense, asked why on each occasion she had not taken Lisa with her. Nussbaum's answer was most illuminating. "I thought she would be better off with Joel's care . . . . I thought that he had tremendous insight and ability to handle people, including children, and he was very sensitive, and that I had those problems and obviously caused problems in the house." With these few words, Hedda went to the core of what came to be known as the "Nussbaum Defense," an attempt to show the world a woman whose self-esteem had been so undermined by Steinberg as to make her feel worthless and, by extension, not wholly responsible for her actions.

In her flat voice, Nussbaum described the deadly argument. It began, like nearly all the others, over something inconsequential. Steinberg became incensed because she and Lisa had not drunk any water. From such trivia he routinely manufactured rages that would last for hours. On this occasion he insisted that they both eat slices of hot pepper, then forced them to drink several glasses of water. Later, Nussbaum was in the bathroom. "The next thing was that Joel came into the bathroom carrying Lisa in his arms." She had been beaten senseless. For an hour, Nussbaum said, she and Steinberg attempted to revive Lisa, then Steinberg left to attend a business meeting. When he returned later that night, Lisa was still unconscious. The couple used cocaine and went to bed. At six o'clock the next morning Nussbaum woke Steinberg with the news that Lisa wasn't breathing. Minutes later she dialed 911.

It took no great effort for the prosecutors to depict Steinberg as a villain, but in attempting to portray Hedda Nussbaum as a hapless and helpless victim of abuse, they had fallen short of their goal. Now it was up to defense counsel Ira London to demonstrate that this particular tragedy had more than one villain.

He began by delving into Nussbaum's background. "Do you consider yourself to have had an unhappy upbringing?"

"Not especially."

"Do you consider it to have been uneventful?"

". . . I think it was average."

Unable to make much headway with this line of questioning, London turned to an incident in 1981, when Steinberg had beaten Nussbaum so badly that her spleen had to he surgically removed. The next day, Steinberg showed up at the hospital. Nussbaum admitted that she was pleased to see him. "I was feeling very connected to him, not like he was someone who had hurt me."

London pounced. "Are you familiar with the term masochist?"

Nussbaum acknowledged that she was. London also drew from her an admission that she should have done more to help Lisa on the night of her final beating. When Nussbaum dissolved into tears, London asked who the tears were for. "Hedda," she answered, then added as an afterthought, "and Lisa."

Because Joel Steinberg chose not to testify, we only have Hedda Nussbaum's version of what happened on the night that Lisa was beaten. All Ira London could offer by way of defense was an attempt to prove that it was Nussbaum who had caused Lisa's death, not Steinberg. After 12 weeks of testimony, the jury convicted Steinberg of first degree manslaughter. Steinberg did speak at his sentencing on March 24, 1988, a rambling and incoherent address that did nothing to affect the outcome. Judge Harold Rothwax imposed a prison term of 8½-25 years.

In the wake of this case, New York State passed new legislation in 1988. Called the "Lisa Law," it was designed to seal some of the glaring loopholes in laws affecting private adoptions.

Enormous publicity surrounded the trial of Joel Steinberg. For many people, it was their first indication that child abuse knows no financial boundaries, has nothing to do with social status or income, and can prosper anywhere.

—Colin Evans

Suggestions for Further Reading.

Brownmiller, Susan. "Madly In Love." *Ms.* (April 1989): 56ff.

Johnson, Joyce. *What Lisa Knew*. New York: G.P. Putnam's Sons, 1990.

Volk, Patricia. "The Steinberg Trial." *New York Times Magazine* (January 15, 1989): 22ff.

Wulfhorst, E. and B. Goldberg. "The Steinberg File." *New York* (April 17, 1989): 42ff.

Oliver North Trial: 1989

Defendant: Oliver Laurence North   **Crimes Charged:** Obstruction of justice, corruption, and perjury   **Chief Defense Lawyers:** Barry Simon and Brendan V. Sullivan, Jr.   **Chief Prosecutors:** Michael Bromwich, John Keker, and David Zornow   **Judge:** Gerhard Gesell   **Place:** Washington, D.C. **Dates of Trial:** January 31–May 4, 1989   **Verdict:** Guilty, 3 counts; Not guilty, 9 counts   **Sentence:** $150,000 fine, 2 years probation, 1,200 hours of community service

SIGNIFICANCE
"I was only following orders" has been an excuse of soldiers facing disciplinary action since time immemorial. But the trial of Colonel Oliver North added a new dimension, as a nation wondered, "just who did issue those orders?"

In 1985 the administration of President Ronald Reagan embarked on a plan to secure the release of American hostages by illegally selling arms to Iran. Funds from those sales were channeled to the Contra guerrillas in Nicaragua who were attempting to overthrow that country's leftist government. When news of this deal broke in 1986, a Congressional hearing followed. Under promise of immunity, Oliver North, a Marine Corps lieutenant colonel and member of President Reagan's National Security Council (NSC), provided an account of the U.S. government's role. North's emotional performance captured the public imagination but left doubts about his veracity. A grand jury later charged him with having lied to Congress, obstructed justice, and received kickbacks.

Jury selection and other legal gyrations delayed opening arguments until February 21, 1988. Chief Prosecutor John Keker laid out the government's case, alleging that North had shredded documents and altered computer records, knowing them to be vital to the Iran-Contra investigation, before visiting U.S. Attorney General Edwin Meese III. There, he "met with the attorney general and some of his top assistants, and when they asked him questions about something very important to know, he lied.... The evidence in this case is going to show that these were crimes, and the reason for these crimes was that Colonel North was covering up crimes he had already committed."

Defender Brendan Sullivan's response was simple and direct. His client "never broke the law. He acted within the law at all times. He followed the instructions of the highest ranking officials of the United States of America. He protected the secrets that he was ordered to protect, to save the lives of many people, many sources, many relationships. That's what he was ordered to do, and he followed his orders as any Marine Corps officer and any officer that worked at the National Security Council [would do]." Sullivan painted a stirring portrait of North as a Vietnam war hero, whose personal valor under fire had led to the heady promotions that came his way.

Unhelpful Witnesses

The biggest problem facing prosecutors was that most of their witnesses were unswerving admirers of North, with testimony couched in such a way as to impart the facts without leaving any doubts as to which side they were really on. Contra leader Adolfo Calero was typical. "He [North] became sort of a savior. . . . The Nicaraguan people have a tremendous appreciation of this man. So much so . . . that they're going to erect a monument for him once we free Nicaragua." Rarely has a prosecution witness been more accommodating to the defense.

Former NSC advisor Robert McFarlane—North's immediate superior—took the stand, already having pleaded guilty to four separate charges of withholding information from Congress. Reluctant and evasive, McFarlane had a knack for framing his answers in language and syntax so arcane as to render them incomprehensible. One of his few unambiguous responses came when Keker

National Security briefing in the Oval Office with Oliver North at rear. (Courtesy, Ronald Reagan Library)

asked, "Do you ever recall hearing the president of the United States, Ronald Reagan, instruct you or anyone else in your presence to lie to . . . Congress?"

"No," McFarlane replied.

"About anything?"

"No."

Probably the witness more eagerly anticipated than any other was Fawn Hall, North's former secretary. A media favorite, she told of deliberately shredding papers at North's request and also smuggling documents from his office. "I . . . placed them inside the back of my skirt so they were secured there." Those reporters present hoping for elaboration on this last tantalizing tidbit were disappointed; Hall, yet another witness clearly under North's spell, said nothing further to harm him.

When North testified, he did so with the same confidence that had served him so well at the congressional hearing. The first part of his testimony comprised a condensed version of the $25,000-a-night speech that he had been making lately to boost coffers for his defense fund. In a brief geopolitical slide show, North sketched a picture of the United States under assault at every border. He explained how only the efforts of himself and other like-minded Cold War knights kept the Western world safe from communism. Asked by Sullivan how he regarded his position, the defendant replied in the tremulous voice that had become his trademark, "I felt like a pawn in a chess game being played by giants."

Missing Funds

The prosecution, determined to keep the jury's attention on the charges and not allow them to be swayed by appeals to their emotions, began by probing North about $300,000 in travelers checks, which had passed through his hands. "Where would you keep careful track of it, in what kind of book?" asked Keker.

"In a ledger."

"Is that ledger still around?"

"No . . . it was destroyed."

"Do you know who destroyed it?"

"Yes."

"Who?"

"I did," North grudgingly admitted.

Equally suspicious was the source of $15,000 in cash which North kept at his home. He insisted that it came from his pocket change, dutifully deposited in a metal box every Friday evening over the course of 20 years.

Keker was incredulous. "The change in your pocket grew to $15,000?"

"Yes."

In building their case, prosecutors had compiled a large dossier on North, detailing his occasional economies with the truth. That groundwork paid off. Over four days of cross-examination, Keker repeatedly trapped the defendant in an endless succession of contradictions and deceit, especially on matters of money. When North left the stand, the aura of selfless patriot had been replaced by one of artful dissembler.

In the wake of this mauling, Sullivan did a masterful job of damage control. He returned to and expanded on the theme of North as victim: "I draw the conclusion that the president was using Ollie North as a scapegoat" Sullivan concluded on a biblical note, " 'Greater love hath no man than he be willing to lay down his life for another.' That's Ollie North, that's the kind of man he is."

Now it was up to the jury. They retired on April 20. Twelve days of deliberation produced not guilty verdicts on every count save three. It was a long way from the clear message that the prosecutors wanted to send. Their disappointment only hardened when Judge Gerhard Gesell imposed sentence: $150,000 fine, two years probation, and 1,200 hours of community service. At the very least, the prosecution had been expecting some jail time. North supporters rushed to pay the fine but it was all academic. On July 20, 1990, the U.S. Court of Appeals, citing that evidence used against North had been obtained under immunity, overturned the convictions, wiping the stigma of 'felon' from his name.

Hero or villain? Oliver North's astonishing charisma and a carelessly enacted immunity provision pulled him through. Whether that makes his actions excusable is still open to debate.

—Colin Evans

Suggestions for Further Reading

Bradlee, Ben, Jr. *Guts and Glory*. New York: D.I. Fine, 1988.

Meyer, Peter. *Defiant Patriot*. New York: St. Martin's Press, 1987.

North, Oliver L. and William Novak. *Under Fire*. New York: HarperCollins, 1991.

Toobin, Jeffrey. *Opening Arguments*. New York: Viking Press, 1991.

Texas v. Johnson: 1989

Appellant: State of Texas   **Defendant:** Gregory Lee Johnson
Appellant Claim: That the Texas statute against "desecration of venerated objects," in this instance burning an American flag, did not violate Gregory Lee Johnson's constitutional rights   **Chief Defense Lawyer:** William M. Kunstler   **Chief Lawyer for Appellant:** Kathi Alyce Drew   **Justices:** Harry A. Blackmun, William J. Brennan, Jr., Anthony M. Kennedy, Thurgood Marshall, Sandra Day O'Connor, William H. Rehnquist, Antonin Scalia, John Paul Stevens, and Byron R. White   **Place:** Washington, D.C.
Date of Decision: June 21, 1989   **Decision:** Texas statute declared unconstitutional

SIGNIFICANCE
No matter how unpopular it is to burn an American flag, the First Amendment protects that act and other forms of political expression.

Gregory Lee Johnson, nicknamed "Joey," was a fervent supporter of an American communist movement known as the Revolutionary Communist Youth Brigade. When the Republican National Convention met in Dallas, Texas in 1984, Johnson decided to participate in a political demonstration called the "Republican War Chest Tour." The demonstration's purpose was to protest the policies of the Reagan Administration.

On August 22, 1984, Johnson, amidst a crowd of approximately 100 other demonstrators, unfurled an American flag. He splashed it with kerosene and set it on fire, while the other demonstrators chanted. "America, the red, white, and blue, we spit on you." After the flag burned, the demonstrators left, and one of the many shocked onlookers gathered the burnt remains for burial in his backyard. No one was hurt, and no property other than the flag was destroyed. Both the press and the police were at the scene of the flag burning, and when police reinforcements arrived shortly thereafter they arrested Johnson.

Johnson was prosecuted under a Texas law that made it illegal to "intentionally or knowingly desecrate . . . a state or national flag." Johnson was convicted in Dallas County Criminal Court No. 8 of desecration of a venerated object and sentenced to a year in prison and a $2,000 fine. The prosecutor blatantly asked the jury to convict Johnson for the political symbolism expressed by the flag-burning incident:

> And you know that he's also creating a lot of danger for a lot of people by what he does and the way he thinks.

The Court of Appeals of Dallas, Texas, affirmed Johnson's conviction on January 23, 1986. On April 20, 1988, the Texas Court of Criminal Appeals reversed the court of appeals and the trial court, and threw out Johnson's conviction. The court of criminal appeals rejected the state's argument that the antiflag-burning statute was a valid measure to preserve a symbol of national unity:

> Recognizing that the right to differ is the centerpiece of our First Amendment freedoms, a government cannot mandate by fiat a feeling of unity in its citizens.

The state of Texas appealed to the U.S. Supreme Court. Johnson's attorney was William M. Kunstler, and the state's attorney was Kathi Alyce Drew. The parties argued their case before the Supreme Court on March 21, 1989.

Justice William J. Brennan authored the decision for the majority of the court, which was issued on June 21, 1989. By a 6–3 vote the justices upheld the Texas Court of Criminal Appeals decision, stating that:

> The way to preserve the flag's special role is not to punish those who feel differently about these matters. It is to persuade them that they are wrong. . . . We can imagine no more appropriate response to burning a flag than waving one's own, no better way to counter a flag-burner's message than by saluting the flag that burns, no surer means of preserving the dignity even of the flag that burned than by, as one witness here did, according its remains a respectful burial. We do not consecrate the flag by punishing its desecration, for in doing so we dilute the freedom that this cherished emblem represents.

The Supreme Court's decision sparked a vigorous but brief political uproar, culminating in President George Bush proposing an antiflag-burning Constitutional amendment, which quietly died. The lasting legacy of the Johnson case was to demonstrate that the First Amendment's protection of forms of political expression, extends even to those as unpopular and provocative as burning the national flag.

—Stephen G. Christianson

Suggestions for Further Reading

"The Flag Again." *The Progressive* (February 1989): 8.

Grogan, David. "Unimpressed by the Freedom to Burn Old Glory Joey Johnson Still Wants a Revolution." *People* (July 10, 1989): 98–100.

Jacoby, Tamar. "A Fight for Old Glory." *Newsweek* (July 3, 1989): 18–20.

Simpson, Glenn. "Decision Unravels Flag's Very Fabric." *Insight* (July 24, 1989): 8–13.

"Waiving the Flag." *The New Republic* (January 23, 1989): 7–8.

U.S. v. Helmsley: 1989

Defendant: Leona Helmsley   **Crimes Charged:** 47 criminal offenses concerning conspiracy, tax evasion, filing false tax returns, mail fraud, and extortion   **Chief Defense Lawyer:** Gerald A. Feffer
Chief Prosecutors: James R. DeVita and Rudolph Giuliani   **Judge:** John M. Walker   **Place:** New York, New York   **Dates of Trial:** June 26–August 30, 1989   **Verdict:** Guilty on 33 counts   **Sentence:** 4 years in prison and more than $7 million in fines

SIGNIFICANCE
The Leona Helmsley prosecution signaled a new determination by the government to prosecute brazen tax evaders, regardless of their wealth or power.

Leona Helmsley, whose full name is Leona Mindy Rosenthal Roberts Panzirer Lubin Helmsley, married into money. Her husband, Harry Brakmann Helmsley, had been in the real estate business for decades. By the 1980s, his collection of hotels, office buildings, and other properties stretched across more than a dozen states and was worth at least $5 billion.

In 1980, Harry brought Leona into his business activities. He built the massive Helmsley Palace hotel in Manhattan, which became the flagship of the Helmsley Hotels corporation, and handed it over to Leona to manage. Leona not only managed the hotel successfully, but in short order she became the president of Helmsley Hotels, overseeing all 26 of Harry's hotels. As a reward, in 1983, Harry bought Leona an estate called Dunnellen Hall in Greenwich, Connecticut. Dunnellen Hall contained an enormous mansion situated on 26 carefully landscaped acres. Harry gave Leona carte blanche to redecorate it as she saw fit, and that's when her troubles began.

Leona had expensive tastes. She spent millions having a marble dance floor and a custom-built swimming pool installed, on antiques and art for decoration, and on everything from gardening to her personal wardrobe to make Dunnellen Hall live up to her vision of a dream house. Although the cost of remaking Dunnellen Hall was less than one percent of the value of the Helmsleys' fortune, Leona paid the bills through the various Helmsley corporations so that they could be deducted as business expenses. To help cover her tracks, Leona forced suppliers to submit their invoices with phony work descriptions on them under the threat of losing all Helmsley business.

A regional newspaper, the *New York Post*, learned about some of Leona's dubious activities and published an article about her on December 2, 1986. Assistant U.S. Attorney James R. DeVita happened to read the article and promptly initiated an investigation. For the next 2½ years, the federal prosecutors and their counterparts in the office of New York State Attorney General Robert Abrams pored over the Helmsleys' personal and business records, questioned their employees, and went to the various suppliers and contractors involved. The prosecution's efforts resulted in an indictment against Leona for 47 violations of federal law, relating to her evasion of more than $4 million in taxes from 1983 to 1986, as the result of illegally writing off the estate renovations as business expenses. Leona was even charged with extortion, for having forced suppliers to provide phony paperwork.

"We Don't Pay Taxes. Only the Little People Pay Taxes."

This notorious statement attributed to Leona may go down in history as one of the most ironic on record. For the Helmsleys did indeed pay taxes, and quite a lot of them: usually more than $50 million a year on the income from their vast holdings. Leona would go to jail and see her world shattered because she tried to cheat the government out of a fraction of that.

Leona's trial began June 26, 1989, in New York City before federal Judge John M. Walker. Her chief defense lawyer was Gerald A. Feffer, from the elite criminal defense firm of Williams and Connolly. The chief prosecutors were DeVita and Rudolph Giuliani. The evidence against Leona was overwhelming, and the public animosity toward her for her arrogant attitude on taxes was shared by the former contractors and Helmsley Hotels employees who testified against her. Feffer, who had once headed the criminal tax division of the U.S. Justice Department and was an expert on tax fraud cases, couldn't stem the avalanche. On August 30, 1989, the jury found Leona guilty on 33 of the charges against her.

All that remained was the sentencing. Leona begged the court for mercy:

I'm guilty of a serious crime. I'm more humiliated and ashamed than anybody could imagine. I feel as though I have been living through a nightmare for three years.

Walker sentenced Leona to four years in prison and a fine of more than $7 million. In his sentencing order Walker made it clear that he found Leona's expression of remorse to be too little and too late given the severity of her crimes. Walker addressed his comments directly to Leona:

You bear full responsibility for this scheme. It was carried out under your direct orders for your benefit. Unlike many defendants who come before the court, you were not driven to this crime by financial need. Rather, your conduct was the product of naked greed. Throughout its course you persisted in the arrogant belief that you were above the law. Moreover, since the indictment and the trial, you have displayed no remorse or contrition. I trust that the sentence today will make it very clear that no person, no matter how wealthy or prominent, stands above the law.

Leona hadn't given up yet, however. Helmsley hired the famous criminal defense lawyer Alan M. Dershowitz to assist Feffer in the appeal and subsequent proceedings, such as motions for retrial. Dershowitz is well-known for his role in overturning the murder conviction of socialite Claus Von Bülow and has been involved in several cases concerning wealthy and prominent people. Dershowitz began an aggressive appeal, part of which included a personal attack on Judge Walker.

Leona Helmsley arrives at Manhattan Federal Court to await a verdict. (AP/Wide World Photos)

In addition to being a highly respected judge, Walker is extremely well-connected politically. His first cousin is George Bush. Whether because of his abilities or connections, in September 1989, Walker was nominated by President Bush to an opening on the U.S. Court of Appeals for the Second Circuit, which includes New York. Moving from district court to circuit court is a significant career move upward for a federal judge. Dershowitz, however, publicly opposed Walker's nomination. Not only did Dershowitz criticize Walker in the press, but he even appeared at Walker's confirmation hearing on November 7, 1989, before the Senate Judiciary Committee. At that hearing, Dershowitz testified in opposition to Walker's appointment, to no avail.

On December 19, 1989, Walker was sworn in as a judge on the court of appeals. Walker continued to hear post-trial motions on the Helmsley case, however, because he also was still a district judge "by special designation" so that he could continue to preside over the case. On March 27, 1991, Walker denied Dershowitz's request that he disqualify himself and let another judge hear Dershowitz's various post-trial motions. Despite Dershowitz's vehement opposition to Walker's promotion, Walker claimed that he was not biased against Dershowitz. Meanwhile, of course, Leona Helmsley is still serving her term in jail.

Leona Helmsley's fall from wealth and arrogance was in many ways another signal that the excesses of the 1980s were over. No matter how rich and prominent you were, the government would prosecute you if you broke the law.

—Stephen G. Christianson

Suggestions for Further Reading

Green, Michelle. "Heartbreak Hotel." *People* (April 1992): 101–102.

Hammer, Richard. *The Helmsleys: the Rise and Fall of Harry and Leona.* New York: New American Library, 1990.

"Leona Helmsley and the Iniquitous 1980s." *Economist* (April 1992): A28.

Moss, Michael. *Palace Coup: the Inside Story of Harry and Leona Helmsley.* New York: Doubleday & Co., 1989.

Pierson, Ransdell. *The Queen of Mean: the Unauthorized Biography of Leona Helmsley.* New York: Bantam Books, 1989.

Jim Bakker Trial: 1989

Defendant: Jim Bakker **Crime Charged:** Fraud and conspiracy
Chief Defense Lawyers: Harold Bender and George T. Davis
Chief Prosecutors: Jerry Miller and Deborah Smith **Judge:** Robert D.
Potter **Place:** Charlotte, North Carolina **Dates of Trial:** August 21–
October 5, 1989 **Verdict:** Guilty **Sentence:** 45 years imprisonment and
$500,000 fine

SIGNIFICANCE
This trial marked the first prosecution of a television evangelist on charges of
duping his followers.

For years Jim Bakker's *Praise The Lord (PTL)* ministry had been the most successful television program of its type. Following the exposure in 1987 of an affair with assistant Jessica Hahn, his financial empire began to crumble. An investigation into the workings of PTL led to 24 indictments charging that Bakker had defrauded the public of millions.

Between 1984 and 1987, PTL supporters paid $158 million to obtain "lifetime partnerships" in Bakker's Heritage USA theme park, Assistant U.S. Attorney Jerry Miller alleged when testimony began August 28, 1989. Miller explained how the $1,000 partnerships were supposed to entitle the contributor to three nights' lodging a year for life at Heritage USA. But with accommodations for just 25,000 vacationers, Bakker oversold an additional 43,000 memberships, diverting $3.7 million to his own personal use. According to Miller, Bakker used PTL to "cheat people out of their money . . . [with] a disdain for all those around him."

George Davis, defending, said that Bakker admitted the facts of the case but denied any wrongdoing. "He was," argued Davis, "a creative, religious genius."

When Bakker's former personal assistant David Taggart, himself previously convicted of fraud, took the stand, he cataloged Bakker's lavish lifestyle: condominiums, houses, mink coats, diamonds, two Rolls Royces, and a Mercedes, all paid for out of donations.

Further evidence of extravagance came from Steve Nelson, an ex-PTL vice president, who also spoke of warning Bakker about the overbooked vacation deals. "I told him that I thought we had some big-time problems. I specifically said, 'Someone could go to jail for this.' He told me not to worry, that there was always room at the inn." Seconds after giving his testimony, Nelson collapsed in court. At the behest of his lawyer, Bakker prayed gently at Nelson's side while paramedics administered treatment.

The next day it was Bakker's turn to require medical attention. He had been found beneath a desk in his lawyer's office, huddled in a fetal position, apparently hallucinating. "Please don't do this to me," he sobbed, as he was led away in shackles for psychiatric evaluation.

One week later Bakker was back in court to hear former aide Richard Dortch agree with prosecution contentions that the partnerships had been a classic "pyramid scheme." Dortch quoted Bakker as saying, "There's no limit to the amount of people we can offer them to, because I can control the crowds of people as they come."

Hurricane Interrupts Trial

No sooner had Bakker's defense gotten under way than Judge Robert Potter had to suspend the trial yet again, this time because Hurricane Hugo was imminent. When testimony resumed, Heritage contributor Sam Gassaway, an Atlanta land developer, denied expecting a guarantee of lodging. "I was a partner to help build something, . . . I did not expect title or anything of that nature."

Central to the defense argument was the contention that Bakker had never actually sold anything, that all of the monies he had received were donations, not purchases.

Bakker confirmed this when he testified. He started out in control, but the longer he remained on the stand the more his composure frayed. Prosecutor Deborah Smith lashed him for continuing to receive million-dollar bonuses, despite knowing that PTL was financially troubled.

"I said to them not to give me the bonuses many, many times," insisted Bakker.

"And then you cashed the checks and used them to buy houses many, many times," Smith replied icily.

Alluding to $600,000 in bonuses received over six weeks in 1986, Bakker reiterated the Heritage board credo: "We say that by faith, God will supply the need."

"How about truth?" Smith shot back. "Did you ever tell them the truth of what the financial situation was?"

His voice dropping to a whisper, Bakker went on to blame Jerry Falwell and other evangelists for the PTL debacle. "The real conspiracy to defraud came from the group of people who took over the ministry for their own gain."

In closing, Smith told the jurors, "What you have here is a pyramid on the brink of collapse, a house of cards ready to fall." She concluded by quoting Lord

Tennyson: "A lie which is half a truth is ever the blackest of lies. Mr. Bakker is a world-class master of using half-truths."

Both defense attorneys made final addresses. George Davis, apparently pinning all his hopes on a mistrial, urged those jurors with doubts to hold out, "even if it's one versus eleven."

Fellow counsel Harold Bender adopted a more traditional tack. "He [Bakker] doesn't expect you to give him mercy. He doesn't expect mercy. But he does have the right to expect justice under the law."

On October 5, 1989, the jury returned a guilty verdict. Judge Robert Potter, as expected, came down hard. Saying, "Those of us who do have a religion are sick of being saps for money-grubbing preachers and priests," he jailed Bakker for 45 years and fined him $500,000.

Citing federal sentencing guidelines and Judge Potter's inappropriate mention of religion, an appeals court in February 1991 ordered a resentencing. On August 23, 1991, Judge George Mullen reduced Bakker's jail term to 18 years, making him eligible for parole in 1995. Mullen reduced Bakker's sentence again on December 22, 1992, to eight years, making him eligible for parole in 1993.

Those who expected Jim Bakker's trial to titillate and tantalize came away disappointed. There was hardly a mention of his affairs. Wisely, the prosecution concentrated on Bakker's greed and hubris. Measured against his indifference to those he bilked, any other diversions would have seemed irrelevant.

—Colin Evans

Suggestions for Further Reading

Fitzgerald, Frances. "Jim And Tammy." *The New Yorker* (April 23, 1990): 45ff.

Martz, Larry and Ginny Carroll. *Ministry of Greed.* New York: Weidenfeld & Nicolson, 1988.

Richardson, Michael. *The Edge of Disaster.* New York: St. Martin's Press, 1987.

Shephard, Charles E. *Forgiven.* New York: Atlantic Monthly Press, 1989.

Pete Rose Trial: 1990

Defendant: Pete Rose   **Crime Charged:** Filing false tax returns
Chief Defense Lawyers: Reuven Katz, Roger J. Makley, and Robert
Pitcairn, Jr.   **Chief Prosecutors:** G. Michael Crites and William E. Hunt
Judge: S. Arthur Spiegel   **Place:** Cincinnati, Ohio
Date of Trial: April 20, 1990   **Verdict:** Guilty   **Sentence:** 5 months'
imprisonment, 3 months in a community treatment center or halfway house,
$50,000 fine, and 1,000 hours of community service

SIGNIFICANCE

This case revealed how a spectacular career as a nationally admired, record-
breaking athlete can be ruined by an addiction to gambling. It also demonstrated
that even national heroes face prison when they stiffarm the Internal Revenue
Service.

On August 23, 1989, long-time Cincinnati Reds player-manager Pete Rose was banished forever from the game of baseball by Baseball Commissioner A. Bartlett Giamatti. Rose, who held the record for more career hits and games played than any other player in baseball history, admitted that he had bet on football and basketball games. His behavior, said the commissioner, had "stained" the game. The evidence before the commissioner led him and, almost immediately, the American public to the conclusion that Rose was a compulsive gambler.

Six months later, a federal grand jury was investigating whether Rose might owe taxes on income from cash he earned at baseball card and memorabilia shows. One newspaper quoted "sources" as saying that the beloved ballplayer had failed to report to the Internal Revenue Service at least $250,000 in income between 1985 and 1987. Witnesses were reported to have seen Rose take cash earned at baseball card shows—where he signed hundreds and hundreds of autographs at $8 each—and stuff it into suitcases and sacks. The implication was that Rose used the huge amounts of cash to support his costly gambling habit.

By mid-April, the news was confirmed. Pete Rose and his lawyers had worked out a plea bargain. He would plead guilty in U.S. District Court in Cincinnati to two felony counts of filing false federal income-tax returns. The bargain was that Rose would not be charged with failing to report income from gambling, despite the fact that one of his associates had been convicted only months earlier of conspiring to defraud the IRS by claiming one of the ballplayer's winning racetrack tickets as his own.

On April 21, Rose appeared before Judge S. Arthur Spiegel. Confirming charges that he had knowingly failed to reveal income of more than $300,000 in 1985 and 1987, he pleaded guilty to the two felony counts. The Statement of Facts, a court document signed by Rose and his attorneys, described him as a "chronic gambler during the years 1984 through 1988, betting substantial amounts of money at horse and dog racetracks, as well as with illegal bookmakers." Said Assistant U.S. Attorney William E. Hunt, who presented the government's case:

> Rose received $129,000 from an individual who purchased his '4,192' bat [the bat with which he broke Ty Cobb's record for career hits] by requesting and receiving [as partial payment] 11 checks for $9,000 and one check for $5,000. These checks were cashed at the bank on separate days in order to avoid the filing of currency transaction reports.

Even more was revealed in the courtroom. In 1987, Rose had filed amended tax returns for the years in question. But they were still false, for he failed to report $51,800 in 1984, $95,168 in 1985, $30,659 in 1986, and $171,552.60 in 1987.

Some Losses Greater than Winnings

Rose's diehard fans were astonished to learn still more. By entering into partnerships on Pick-6 horse-track bets on 10 occasions between 1984 and 1987, an activity that Rose had previously denied, he had won $136,945.30. But the irony was that, while gross income amounts as high as $59,788.40 (in 1984) were not reported, he was not liable for failure to report the figures because his losses were greater than his winnings.

In a jam-packed courtroom on July 19, Judge Spiegel handed down Rose's sentence:

> We must recognize that there are two people here: Pete Rose, the living legend, the all-time hit leader, and the idol of millions, and, Pete Rose, the individual who appears today convicted of two counts of cheating on his taxes. Today, we are not dealing with the legend. History and the tincture of time will decide his place among the all-time greats of baseball. With regard to Pete Rose, the individual, he has broken the law, admitted his guilt, and stands ready to pay the penalty.

The judge then sentenced Pete Rose to five months in a federal correctional institution, to be followed by three months in a community treatment center or halfway house. In addition, he would pay a $50,000 fine and serve 1,000 hours of community service.

Rose said he would not appeal. "I accept my punishment," he said. "I will serve my sentence, pay my debt to society, and get on with my life." The sentence did not permit any parole.

Rose served his five months at the Southern Illinois Prison Camp at Marion. His days were spent in the prison machine shop, where he earned 11 cents an hour fabricating and welding metal. "He gets in there and works just as hard as the rest of them," said the assistant warden.

Pete Rose surrounded by reporters following his conviction for failing to report income on his tax returns. (AP/Wide World Photos)

When released January 7, 1991, Rose began his 1,000 hours of community service, working as an assistant in physical-education programs in five Cincinnati public schools and at recreational centers in the city's lower-income areas.

On January 10, the board of directors of baseball's Hall of Fame voted unanimously that anyone on baseball's permanently ineligible list could not be eligible for the Hall of Fame. The rules change effectively barred Pete Rose, who would have become eligible for election into the hall by the Baseball Writers' Association of America the following December.

— Bernard Ryan, Jr.

Suggestions for Further Reading

Andrews, A.E. "Bittersweet Homecoming." *U.S. News & World Report* (January 14, 1991): 14.

Callahan, T. "Justice for a Baseball Felon." *U.S. News & World Report* (July 23, 1990): 15.

Corelli, R. "The Fall of a Titan." *Maclean's* (July 30, 1990): 38.

Goodman, M.S. "Pete Rose Longs to Rise Again." *People Weekly* (September 2, 1991): 47.

Leerhsen, C. "All is Not Lost in Cincinnati." *Newsweek* (July 30, 1990): 61–62.

Lieber, J. and S. Wulf. "Sad Ending for a Hero." *Sports Illustrated* (July 30, 1990): 22–25.

Reston, James, Jr. *Collision at Home Plate: The Lives of Pete Rose and Bart Giamatti.* New York: HarperCollins, 1991.

Rose, Pete, and Roger Kahn. *Pete Rose: My Story.* New York: Macmillan Co., 1989.

Marion Barry Trial: 1990

Defendant: Marion Barry, Jr. **Crime Charged:** Drug offenses (14 counts)
Chief Defense Lawyers: Robert Mance and Kenneth Mundy
Chief Prosecutors: Judith Retchin and Richard Roberts **Judge:** Thomas
Penfield Jackson **Place:** Washington, D.C. **Dates of Trial:** June 4–August
10, 1990 **Verdict:** Guilty on 1 count of cocaine possession; Not guilty on 1
count; Mistrial on remaining 12 counts **Sentence:** 6 months imprisonment,
$5,000 fine, 1 year probation

SIGNIFICANCE

The sensational arrest of Marion Barry guaranteed that the ensuing trial would be
high drama. But almost no one was ready for such a remarkable verdict.

For years Washington, D.C., had buzzed with rumors that Mayor Marion Barry had a drug problem. Concrete proof came January 18, 1990, when Barry entered Room 726 at the Vista International Hotel to keep an assignation with ex-girlfriend Rasheeda Moore. After rejecting Barry's sexual advance, Moore produced a pipe for smoking cocaine. (Barry had earlier given Moore $20 to buy some crack cocaine.) Seconds after Barry put the pipe to his lips, half a dozen FBI agents and other police officers rushed into the room and arrested him. The sting had worked perfectly: Every incident had been captured on videotape.

On June 19, 1990, prosecutor Richard Roberts outlined Barry's six-year involvement with drugs, emphasizing the mayor's hypocrisy:

> "During the course of this trial, you will learn that while the defendant preached 'Down with dope!' he was putting dope up his nose. . . . Every person has two sides. . . . This case is about the other side, the secret side of Marion Barry."

The star prosecution witness was Charles Lewis, a confessed drug dealer. He first met Barry in the Virgin Islands in June 1986. "He asked me if I could get some rocks [crack cocaine]. . . . I told me yes." According to Lewis, Barry's drug binge included straight cocaine and marijuana, as well.

Chief defense counsel Kenneth Mundy, deriding Lewis' claim that conscience had prompted his testimony, scoffed, "You didn't wake up and start cooperating [with the authorities] until you got convicted in the Virgin Islands, is that correct?"

"Both things happened at the same time."

"You were facing big time weren't you?"

"The reason I waited. . . ."

"Is that a yes or a no?" barked Mundy.

"Yes," Lewis admitted.

For three days Mundy kept up the attack, extracting one damaging concession after another from Lewis. It was a superb feat of advocacy, one which gave the prosecution pause for thought: Perhaps their case wasn't so airtight after all?

Mayor Marion Barry is escorted by police following his appearance before a federal magistrate. (AP/Wide World Photos)

Violent Relationship

Help was at hand—Rasheeda Moore. She detailed a three-year liaison with Barry, plagued with drugs and occasional violence, that put the prosecution back on track. It was during her testimony that the Vista videotape was played. Mundy grilled Moore about her background—hardly exemplary—portraying her as out to get Barry because he had ditched her for another woman. He also scored points with her admission that she had used drugs in April 1990, three months after the Vista sting.

"It's something I have to deal with everyday," said Moore, referring to her cocaine addiction. When Mundy suggested that the receipt of several thousand dollars from the government had loosened her tongue, Moore demurred. Her decision to set Barry up, she said, had resulted from a revival of religious belief.

Because Barry declined to testify on his own behalf, the defense comprised mainly of witnesses who placed Barry elsewhere at times when he was supposed to have participated in alleged drug deals.

On August 2, 1990, the jury began deliberations. More than a week later they announced themselves hopelessly deadlocked on all except two counts, one guilty, the other not guilty. Judge Thomas Jackson had no alternative but to declare a mistrial on the remaining 12 charges. Later, in a public attack, Judge Jackson suggested that some jurors had been less than forthcoming about their true feelings during the impanelment process, telling a Harvard Law School class that he had "never seen a stronger government case" than the one mounted against Barry.

The final act in this drama came October 26, 1990, when Judge Jackson sentenced Barry to six months imprisonment, a fine and probation.

The verdict temporarily derailed Barry's political career—reinforcing the perception in some quarters that had been the intent all along. After completing his jail term, Barry was elected in November 1992 to Washington's city council.

—Colin Evans

Suggestions for Further Reading

Agronsky, Jonathan I.Z. *Marion Barry: The Politics Of Race*. Latham, N.Y.: British American, 1991.

Morley, Jefferson. "Crack in the Washington Culture." *The Nation* (February 19, 1990): 221ff.

Puddington, Arch. *Insight* (June 3, 1991): 44–45.

Starr, Richard. *Insight* (February 5, 1990): 22ff.

Central Park Jogger Rape Trials: 1990

Defendants: First trial: Antron McCray, Yusef Salaam, Raymond Santana Jr.; second trial: Kevin Richardson and Kharey Wise **Crimes Charged:** First trial: Second-degree attempted murder, rape, sodomy, first and second-degree assault, robbery, riot; second trial: all of the above, plus sexual abuse **Chief Defense Lawyers:** First trial: Robert Burns, Michael Joseph, Peter Rivera; second trial: Howard Diller and Colin Moore **Chief Prosecutors:** Arthur Clements and Elizabeth Lederer **Judge:** Thomas B. Galligan **Place:** New York, New York **Dates of Trials:** June 13–August 18, 1990; October 22–December 11, 1990 **Verdicts:** First trial: all acquitted of attempted murder, sodomy, and one of five counts of assault, but guilty of all other charges; second trial: Richardson guilty of all charges, Wise guilty of sexual abuse, assault, and riot **Sentences:** First trial: 5–15 years imprisonment; second trial: 5–10 years imprisonment for Richardson, 5–15 years imprisonment for Wise

SIGNIFICANCE

The violent assault and rape of the woman known as "the Central Park Jogger" resulted in two tense and widely publicized trials that many New Yorkers felt were emblematic of the crime and racial problems characterizing the era.

More than 3,000 rapes were reported in New York City in 1989, but none aroused more fear and anger than an attack on a young woman who became known simply as "the Central Park jogger." The facts sometimes disappeared in chaotic arguments outside the courts—and in the spectators' seats—over the racial politics of dispensing justice in America. Yet most of the trial itself was fought over one point that horrified New Yorkers on both sides of the case: the fact that nearly all of the suspects were legally children.

On the spring evening of April 19, 1989, a loosely knit gang of about 30 adolescents roamed the northern acres of Central Park, terrorizing everyone they encountered. Police grabbed several suspects, including one who blurted, "I know who did the murder!" The confession made little sense until several hours later, when two passers-by heard moans coming from the darkness. A naked woman was discovered lying in the woods. She had been bound, raped, and beaten so severely that doctors expected her to die.

The victim was a white 28-year-old investment banker who enjoyed jogging in the park at the end of long days at a Wall Street firm. The suspects were all black or Hispanic. All but one were 14 or 15 years of age. None had an arrest record, but outrage and sadness ran through the city with reports of the young suspects' apparent indifference to human life. It was just a "wilding," one explained, a night of terror for the sake of fun.

Several suspects were released for lack of evidence or pleaded guilty to earlier assaults in the park. The rape victim remained unidentified by most of the press, who simply called her "the Central Park jogger." Despite their youth, six suspects indicted for the attack were publicly identified in the press. The indicted minors were to be tried as adults, but sentenced as juveniles if found guilty.

Confessions Prove Crucial

To abide by the U.S. Supreme Court's 1965 *Aranda* rule, which forbids testimony in which one codefendant implicates another, three trials were planned to separate youths who had implicated each other in videotaped or written confessions. These incriminating statements quickly defined the case for the defense. After unsuccessfully trying to bar the confessions for nearly a year, defense attorneys continued to challenge their legal and ethical legitimacy throughout the trials.

When defendants Antron McCray, Yusef Salaam, and Raymond Santana, Jr., came to trial in June 1990, they faced prosecutor Elizabeth Lederer, who began by methodically reconstructing the night of violence. Seven victims of earlier harassment, robberies, and beatings in the park testified, although none implicated the three defendants. Doctors who treated the jogger testified that she had lost 75 percent of her blood by the time she was discovered. Her skull had been hammered so violently that the normally wrinkled surface of her brain had been beaten flat. Yet lack of physical evidence remained the weakest part of the prosecution's case. Blood and semen tests of the jogger were inconclusive.

In spite of the seriousness of her injuries, the scarred victim had recovered enough strength to appear in court. She testified briefly about the lingering after-effects of the beating, but she could remember nothing about the assault itself.

The atmosphere changed when video monitors appeared in the courtroom. Jurors watched a half-hour videotape in which the prosecutor read McCray his Miranda rights as his parents looked on. On the tape, McCray then described how he and the gang had "charged" the jogger and beaten her to the ground. Someone, he said, hit her with a length of pipe before the gang took turns raping her. McCray admitted dropping his pants and climbing on top of the jogger but denied raping her. "I didn't do nothing to her," he said.

In his signed and videotaped confessions, Santana admitted assaulting other joggers in the park and implicated two youths who were scheduled to be tried later for rape. He confessed that he had held the jogger while Kevin Richardson raped her and Steven Lopez hit her in the head with a brick to stop her screams.

While police denied intimidating the suspects or promising them anything in return for the crucial confessions, detective Thomas McKenna testified that he had tricked a written confession out of Salaam, who denied even being in the park. When the detective falsely told Salaam that his fingerprints were found on the jogger's synthetic running tights, Salaam changed his story.

"Yes, I was there but I didn't rape her," Salaam said.

"How could you possibly do something like this?" the detective asked.

"It was just something to do," Salaam replied. "It was fun." Salaam admitted hitting the jogger twice with a metal pipe and grabbing her breasts, but he said that four others raped the woman, including Richardson and Wise.

McKenna said that Salaam's statement ended when his mother arrived and told police that her son was only 15. Minors were entitled to have a parent or guardian present during questioning, but when police took Salaam into custody, he claimed he was 16 and produced a transit authority pass to prove it. Defense witnesses claimed that the police knew Salaam was a minor and interrogated him anyway. Judge Thomas Galligan allowed the prosecution to introduce Salaam's unsigned statement and instructed jurors to decide for themselves if it was obtained fairly.

Defense Unwittingly Helps Prosecution

Without any physical evidence, the unsigned confession represented all of the prosecution's case against Salaam until his lawyer made a series of strategic blunders. When attorney Robert Burns asked McKenna why he believed the confession was true, the detective replied that he knew none of the particulars of the attack until Salaam revealed details which later turned out to be true. Burns also allowed the detective to mention that an unindicted witness placed Salaam in the park on the night of the attack.

McCray's and Santana's lawyers objected vehemently when Burns decided to put his client on the stand. Salaam denied taking part in the attack and testified that he told police he was only 15 when they questioned him. Under cross-examination, however, his confused explanation for being in the park dissolved into bickering with the prosecutor.

The defense claimed that the entire prosecution case rested on confessions coerced with lies and threats. The prosecution was accused of playing to the jury's emotions by unnecessarily putting the victim on the stand. Burns also suggested that the jogger had freely engaged in sex with an unnamed person before embarking on her run and that no rape had occurred. After 10 days of turbulent deliberations, however, the jury found the defendants guilty.

Details of the confessions had been leaked almost from the moment they were given, producing considerable press commentary that presumed the youths guilty. This bias and the absence of forensic evidence in the trial prompted some black New Yorkers to be suspicious of the verdict. A few activists, including the Reverend Al Sharpton, observed and criticized the trial, ignoring the multiracial jury's insistence that the youths were convicted by their own admissions.

When Kharey Wise and Kevin Richardson came to trial two months later, their supporters rained racial insults on prosecutors arriving at the courthouse. Richardson's attorney, Howard Diller, threatened to ask for a mistrial when Wise's lawyer announced publicly that he would cross-examine the jogger, a move the defense in the first trial had avoided for fear of alienating the jury. Richardson's family responded by trying to fire Diller for not being aggressive enough.

The tense courtroom erupted almost immediately. "That woman, she's lying!" Wise sobbed during prosecutor Lederer's opening argument. "I can't take it anymore!"

Wise's lawyer, Colin Moore, kept his promise to cross-examine the jogger vigorously. He inferred that she had been seeing more than one man and that her boyfriend had attacked her in a jealous fury. Moore's suggestive questions were buried in a hail of sustained objections.

Surprise Witness Surfaces

A subpoena forced one of Wise's friends to testify against her will as a surprise witness for the prosecution. Melody Jackson tearfully recalled Wise telephoning her from the Riker's Island detention center three months after his arrest. He denied raping the jogger, but he said that he had fondled her and helped hold her legs down.

The prosecution introduced two videotaped confessions featuring Wise. In the first, he admitted only that he had watched the rape. The second was more vivid. "It was my first rape," he said. He described how he had hit the jogger repeatedly with a rock. He recalled Salaam laughing while Santana and Lopez raped the victim. Wise claimed that he talked Lopez out of killing the woman. He also accused Richardson of rape, but his references to his codefendant were removed from the tape shown in court.

Wise's mother testified that her son had returned home at approximately the time he was accused of taking part in the rape. When the prosecutor asked if her son had not returned half an hour later, Mrs. Wise refused to cooperate and began screaming at Lederer. The judge ordered Wise's mother to be ejected from the court and told the jury to disregard her testimony.

Wise's own temper flared when he was asked to explain his admissions to police. He stalked off the stand and briefly refused to answer any questions. When he returned, his lawyer asked why he had confessed.

"The detectives told me to put myself in it," Wise replied. "They promised I could go home if I did."

Second Jury Issues Surprise

The verdict was a surprise to both sides. Jurors believed that Wise had been pressured into making the second videotape and convicted him only of sexual abuse, assault, and riot. Richardson, who had confessed to being present during the rape but denied taking part, was found guilty on all counts. The jury decided that physical evidence, including semen in Richardson's underwear and a strand of the victim's pubic hair found on his shirt, was more damning than any of the videotaped confessions. The absence of identical verdicts also disregarded the judge's instructions concerning the concept of "acting in concert," which holds that those who contribute to a major crime are liable to prosecution for its most serious aspects, even if they participate to a lesser degree.

Richardson's family shouted angry insults at prosecutors and the judge, accusing them of racism. ". . . you'll pay for this," Wise spat at Lederer as he was led away amid the uproar.

Richardson received the maximum sentence for minors. Wise, the only defendant who was not a minor when he was arrested, was sentenced as an adult to slightly less than half of the maximum sentence.

Ironically, the suspect accused by the convicted youths of raping and beating the jogger most violently never stood trial. Only Steven Lopez had not given police an incriminating statement. Prosecutors prepared to try him for rape anyway, but the accusations of his codefendants were inadmissible and other witnesses ultimately refused to testify.

A plea bargain allowed Lopez to admit his part in the earlier muggings and plead guilty to a charge of robbery. In sentencing Lopez to 1½–4½ years imprisonment for his part in the "sadistic rampage" in Central Park, Judge Galligan called the conviction "the final chapter of a cowardly attack that will continue to live in the hearts of New Yorkers."

— Thomas C. Smith

Suggestions for Further Reading

Didion, Joan. "New York: Sentimental Journeys." *New York Review of Books* (January 17, 1991): 45–56.

Glaberson, William. "Jogger Case Defense: Scattershot Approach." *New York Times* (July 13, 1990): B1, B3.

Stone, Michael. "What Really Happened In Central Park." *New York* (August 14, 1989): 30–43.

Sullivan, Ronald. "Confessions Lawyers Couldn't Undo." *New York Times* (August 20, 1990): B4.

Turque, Bill and Anne Underwood. "Judgment For the Wilders." *Newsweek* (August 27, 1990): 39.

Mapplethorpe Obscenity Trial: 1990

Defendants: Dennis Barrie and the Cincinnati Contemporary Arts Center
Crime Charged: Displaying obscene material, namely pictures by the artist Robert Mapplethorpe   **Chief Defense Lawyers:** Marc D. Mezibov and H. Louis Sirkin   **Chief Prosecutors:** Richard A. Castellini, Frank H. Prouty, Jr., and Melanie J. Reising   **Judge:** F. David J. Albanese   **Place:** Cincinnati, Ohio   **Dates of Trial:** September 24–October 5, 1990   **Verdict:** Not guilty

SIGNIFICANCE
The acquittal of the Mapplethorpe defendants was a major reaffirmation of First Amendment freedom of speech protection in the new realm of homosexual art.

In the Spring of 1990, the Contemporary Arts Center (CAC) in Cincinnati, Ohio, held an exhibit of photographs by the late artist Robert Mapplethorpe. The exhibit was controversial from the start because of the openly homosexual nature of much of Mapplethorpe's work and was well covered in the Cincinnati press. There was a great deal of negative public reaction, and rumors spread that the city of Cincinnati would attempt to close down the exhibit under Ohio's obscenity statute, which makes it illegal for any person to "Promote, . . . display . . . or exhibit . . . any obscene material."

The CAC's director, Dennis Barrie, attempted a preemptive strike aimed at heading off an obscenity prosecution. The CAC filed an action for a declaratory judgment, which is a type of civil lawsuit, on March 27, 1990, in Hamilton County (which includes Cincinnati) Municipal Court. CAC asked the court to declare the exhibit not obscene, but on April 6, 1990, the court refused and dismissed the action. The next day, the Hamilton County Grand Jury indicted CAC and Barrie for criminal violations of the Ohio obscenity statute.

Of the approximately 175 pictures in the exhibit, seven were particularly controversial and were the focus of the ensuing trial. Two pictures were of naked minors, one male and one female, with a "lewd exhibition or graphic focus on the genitals." The other five were of adult men in unusual sadomasochistic poses.

Obscenity or Art?

The trial began on September 24, 1990, before a jury of four men and four women with Judge F. David J. Albanese presiding. The lawyers for CAC and Barrie were Marc D. Mezibov and H. Louis Sirkin. The prosecutors were Richard A. Castellini, Frank H. Prouty, Jr., and Melanie J. Reising.

Following the jury's verdict of "pandering obscenity," hundreds of protesters demonstrated outside the Cincinnati Arts Center. (AP/Wide World Photos)

The prosecutors had to convince the jury that the seven pictures were legally obscene, as "obscene" was defined by the Supreme Court in the 1973 case *Miller v. California. Miller* says that material is obscene only if: (1) the average person, applying contemporary community standards, would find that the material as a whole appeals to the prurient interest; (2) the material depicts or describes sexual conduct in a patently offensive way; and (3) the material, as a whole, lacks serious literary, artistic, political or scientific value.

Both the prosecution and the defense wanted Albanese, rather than the jury, to make the decision on particular elements of the *Miller* test. Prosecutor Prouty argued that Albanese should determine what community standards were:

> We're not required to show community standards because the court [Albanese] becomes the community.

For the defense, Mezibov argued that Albanese and not the jury should decide whether the pictures had serious artistic value:

> It would be inappropriate, it would be wrong, I submit, for lay people to guess and to speculate as to what constitutes serious artistic value.

Albanese, however, decided to leave all three elements of the Miller test to the jury, holding that, "The court will not substitute its judgment for that of the jury."

To prove the defense's claim that the seven pictures had serious artistic value, therefore, Mezibov and Sirkin brought in several art experts to testify. The art experts called the pictures the work of "a brilliant artist," with "symmetry" and "classic proportions."

On October 5, 1990, the eight jurors found CAC and Barrie not guilty of the charges of displaying obscene material. Under Ohio law, the case ended then and there, because the state is prohibited from appealing a jury verdict. Although CAC and Barrie were vindicated, the victory was expensive: The trial cost CAC over $200,000 in costs and attorneys' fees.

The acquittal of the Mapplethorpe defendants reaffirmed the obscenity principles of *Miller v. California* and the protection of the First Amendment in a new area. This new area was the field of gay rights and the right of homosexual artists to express themselves. As Mezibov said after the trial:

Yes, we have a Bill of Rights. But it's meaningless unless you fight for it.

—*Stephen G. Christianson*

Suggestions for Further Reading

Cembalest, Robin. "Who Does it Shock? Why Does it Shock?" *Artnews* (March 1992): 32–33.

——. "The Obscenity Trial: How They Voted to Acquit." *Artnews* (December 1990): 136–141.

Gurstein, Rochelle. "Current Debate: High Art or Hard-Core? Misjudging Mapplethorpe: the Art Scene and the Obscene." *Tikkun* (November–December 1991): 70–80.

Light, Judy. "Jury Acquits Museum in Landmark Art Trial." *Dancemagazine* (December 1990): 12–13.

Merkel, Jayne. "Art on Trial." *Art in America* (December 1990): 41–46.

Parachini, Allan. "Year of the Censor: How Photography Became the Focus of Fear and Loathing." *American Photo* (November–December 1990): 39–42.

Carolyn Warmus Trials: 1991 & 1992

Defendant: Carolyn Warmus   **Crime Charged:** Murder
Chief Defense Lawyers: First trial: David L. Lewis; second trial: William I.
Aronwald   **Chief Prosecutors:** Douglas J. Fitzmorris and James A. McCarty
Judge: John Carey   **Place:** White Plains, New York   **Dates of Trials:** First
Trial: January 14–April 27, 1991; second trial: January 22–May 27, 1992
Verdicts: First trial: mistrial; second trial: guilty   **Sentence:** 25 years to life

SIGNIFICANCE

Obsession, deadly and destructive, was never more chillingly illustrated than in this trial resulting from one woman's determination to have the man she craved at any cost.

For several weeks following the January 15. 1989 shooting of Betty Jeanne Solomon in her Westchester County, New York, home, husband Solomon was the chief suspect. But when police learned that Solomon's longtime lover, Carolyn Warmus, had been more relentless than ever in her pursuit of the reluctant widower, official attention turned toward this 27-year-old Manhattan schoolteacher. Their investigation revealed a woman with a turbulent history of romantic fixations, most often with unavailable men. But there was other evidence, too, enough to warrant a murder indictment against Warmus. Guaranteed immunity from prosecution, Solomon agreed to testify against his former lover when her trial began January 14, 1991.

In his opening statement, chief prosecutor James A. McCarty described Warmus as driven by a "consuming passion to possess" Solomon. McCarty conceded the lack of any single piece of proof that would on its own prove Warmus guilty, but "like pieces of a puzzle," he said, circumstantial evidence would "reveal a clear picture of the killer . . . Carolyn Warmus."

David L. Lewis, lawyer for the defendant, countered that his client was the victim of a "deliberate, malicious" frame-up, reminding the jury that "love and passion are not on trial here, this is a trial about murder."

The first witness to link Warmus to a potential murder weapon was private investigator James A. Russo. In the fall of 1988, Warmus had come to him, he said, seeking protection from Betty Jeanne Solomon, who was jealous about the defendant's affair with her husband. Russo had suggested a bodyguard. "Her answer was no," he said. "I pushed her to say exactly what she wanted. She said a 'machine gun and silencer,' " I said, 'We're not arms dealers.' "

Solomon Tells of Unusual Marriage

When Paul Solomon took the stand he cataloged a bizarre marriage. While acknowledging that neither partner had been faithful—there had been "ups and downs"—he maintained that the union was basically sound. Responding to questions about his affair with Warmus, Solomon said that for some time he had been trying unsuccessfully to terminate the relationship. Even so, he admitted meeting Warmus on the night of the killing and having sex with her in a car. Afterward he had gone home and found his wife murdered. Unnerved by Warmus' subsequent and, he said, unwanted pestering, he confronted her in a bar. "Did you have anything to do with Betty Jeanne's death?" he asked. She replied, "No."

For five days Solomon underwent a battering at the hands of defense counsel Lewis, who insinuated that it was actually Solomon himself who had arranged the murder. "You told your wife you'd be home early, but you didn't come home early because you knew your wife was dead!"

Finally Solomon erupted. "You twist and turn words, manipulate facts . . . to make them what they aren't," he shouted. But Lewis scored heavily when he drew an admission from the witness that he stood to profit significantly from his wife's death, having already signed a movie contract worth $175,000.

The star prosecution witness was yet another private investigator, Vincent Parco. He testified that one week before the shooting he sold Warmus a .25-caliber pistol—the kind used to kill Betty Jeanne Solomon—equipped with a silencer. (The murder weapon was never found.) Parco claimed he had done so only after considerable badgering by the defendant. "Almost every time I'd see her she'd bring it up." The silencer had been his idea, so she could practice in a "house, woods, or garage, and no one would know."

Vigorous Defense Launched

Lewis launched an assault assault on Parco's credibility, forcing him to admit his own infatuation with Warmus and asserting, without producing evidence, that it was Parco, hired by Paul Solomon, who had shot Betty Jeanne Solomon and then framed Warmus.

Strong circumstantial evidence tying Warmus to the murder came in the form of phone company records, which showed that the defendant had called a New Jersey sporting goods shop on the day of the killing. The prosecution alleged that, using fake identification, Warmus bought some .25-caliber bullets from the store, then shot Betty Jeanne Solomon nine times before keeping her rendezvous with Paul Solomon.

In response the defense produced its own phone record. Not only did this record lack the New Jersey call, but it logged an additional 6:44 P.M. call from

Warmus' Manhattan apartment, thereby making it virtually impossible for her to have committed the murder several miles away at 7:15 P.M. But the veracity of this second record was challenged by MCI executive Thomas Sabol, who declared it a forgery.

With Warmus exercising her right to silence, the major defense witness was Joseph Lisella, a building contractor. He claimed to have overheard a conversation between "Parco" and "Solomon" in a Yonkers, New York, bowling alley bathroom less than an hour after the killing. Lisella said, "Paul" handed over $20,000 to the other man, saying, "Count it if you don't believe me." Later, "Vinnie" remarked, "Don't worry about the gun. It's in the deepest part of the river."

During cross-examination McCarty attempted to impugn Lisella's credibility by outlining several house fires connected with the witness. Lisella denied McCarty's charge that "people call you 'Toaster Joe,'" but did admit to contact with Warmus' wealthy father.

Following directions from Judge John Carey, the jurors retired to consider their verdict. Twelve days later they announced themselves irretrievably deadlocked, and a mistrial was declared.

Second Trial Results in Conviction

On January 22, 1992, the state tried again. This time Warmus' defense was in the hands of William I. Aronwald, a somewhat more understated advocate than his predecessor. In essence, he had to deal with much the same evidence, except for one vital difference. Original crime-scene photographs had shown a black bloodstained glove near the body. Somehow it had vanished, only to reappear when Paul Solomon was searching a box in his bedroom closet between trials.

From Warmus' credit card records the prosecution was able to prove that the defendant had purchased just such a pair of gloves one year before the murder. Aronwald fumed, accusing McCarty of "trial by ambush," but the evidence was in and its effect was deadly, especially when forensic expert Dr. Peter DeForest gave his opinion that stains on the glove could be human blood.

Again it was no easy matter for the jurors but after a week of consideration, they convicted Warmus of murder. On June 26, 1992, Judge Carey passed sentence—25 years to life—and the blond-haired defendant was led away without ever uttering a word in her own defense.

—Colin Evans

Suggestions for Further Reading

Brady, Diane. "Fatal Attraction." *Maclean's* (April 8, 1991): 44–45.

Colapinto, John. "By Love Obsessed." *Mademoiselle* (August 1990): 188–191.

Hammer, Joshua. "Teacher, Lover, Schemer, Killer?" *Newsweek* (February 25, 1991): 57ff.

Kunen, James S. "A Dangerous Passion." *People Weekly* (April 15, 1991): 34–39.

Pamela Smart Trial: 1991

Defendant: Pamela Smart   **Crime Charged:** Conspiracy to commit murder
Chief Defense Lawyers: Mark Sisti and Paul Twomey
Chief Prosecutors: Paul Maggiotto and Diane Nicolosi
Judge: Douglas R. Gray   **Place:** Exeter, New Hampshire
Dates of Trial: March 4–22, 1991   **Verdict:** Guilty   **Sentence:** Life
imprisonment

SIGNIFICANCE

Millions watched this trial on live television, fascinated by the sensational saga of a murderous plot hatched in high school.

Just one week before his first wedding anniversary, Gregory Smart, a 24-year-old insurance salesman, was shot dead at his New Hampshire condominium during what appeared to be a botched burglary. Six weeks later William Flynn, 16, Vance Lattime, 17, and Patrick Randall, 18, were arrested and charged with the murder. All three pleaded guilty. In return for reduced sentences the teenagers agreed to testify against the person they claimed persuaded them to carry out the killing: Pamela Smart, wife of the dead man.

When oral argument commenced March 4, 1991, Assistant Attorney General Diane Nicolosi portrayed the teenagers as naive victims of an evil woman bent on murder. Nicolosi claimed that Smart, a 22-year-old high-school teacher, seduced Flynn with the sole intent of duping him into murdering her husband, so that she might avoid an expensive divorce and benefit from a $140,000 life-insurance policy.

Graphic details of the murder were provided by Patrick Randall. He told how Flynn had enlisted his services, together with Vance Lattime, and how all three went to the Smart residence. While Lattime waited outside, Flynn and Randall ransacked the townhouse, then ambushed Greg Smart when he returned home from a sales meeting. Randall admitted holding a knife at Smart's throat as Flynn fired a .38-caliber bullet through the victim's brain. Afterward the two took some jewelry to create the impression of a robbery gone wrong.

Defense counsel Mark Sisti bitterly denounced all of Randall's allegations, noting that only in the course of pleabargaining had he implicated Pamela Smart.

"Pamela Smart didn't make you kill anybody, right?" Sisti asked.

"No," agreed Randall.

"You went to kill Greg Smart for your friend Bill [Flynn], right?"

"Yes."

"Pamela Smart had nothing to do with that, correct?"

"Correct," Randall admitted.

Payoff for Murder: Stereo Speakers and $250

Vance Lattime, driver of the getaway car, told the jury that Smart gave him a pair of stereo speakers and promised an additional $250 for his part in the slaying. He added that, prior to the murder, she asked the other gang members how she should act upon finding her husband's body. "She didn't know whether to scream, run from house to house or call the police. We told her just to act normal." About one point Lattime was adamant: Smart insisted that they shoot her husband rather than stab him, because she didn't want blood splattered all over her white furniture.

When William Flynn took the stand, he tearfully recounted how Smart seduced him, interspersing the sexual blandishments with repeated and ever more urgent stories of physical abuse inflicted by Greg Smart on his wife, especially one incident when he locked her out of the house in winter while she was clad in only her nightclothes. Flynn said, "She started crying and said the only way she could see for us to be together was if we killed Greg." At first Flynn doubted Smart's seriousness, but as her temper and threats worsened, he yielded to her demands. "I was afraid if I didn't do it, she would leave me."

Flynn described to an emotion-packed courtroom how he put the revolver to Smart's head, then uttered, "God, forgive me," before pulling the trigger.

"Why did you say 'God, forgive me'?" asked Assistant Attorney General Paul Maggiotto.

"Because I didn't want to kill Greg," said Flynn. "I wanted to be with Pam, and that's what I had to do to be with Pam."

A grieving Pamela Smart at her husband's funeral. (Himsel Photo, The Telegraph)

Of all the prosecution witnesses, none created more of an impact or did more damage than Cecelia Pierce, 16, another Winnacunnet High School student. She repeated a conversation with Smart: "I have a choice: either kill Greg or get a divorce," she quoted Smart as saying. "I told her to get a divorce," Pierce said. Asked how Smart responded, Pierce replied, "She said she couldn't, because Greg would take the dog and the furniture and she wouldn't have any money or a place to live."

Pierce did admit prior knowledge of the murder plot even to the point of aiding Smart in her search for a gun, but she claimed that conscience led her to the police afterward. At their behest she secretly taped several conversations with Smart. In one, Smart ordered Pierce to keep quiet, otherwise they would all "go to the slammer for the rest of our entire lives." On another occasion Smart boasted of committing the perfect murder.

Sisti cast a pall over much of this testimony by revealing that Pierce had sold the rights to her story to a Hollywood production company for a considerable sum of money. "What this all comes down to," he said, "is that you have a shot at $100,000 . . . and you claim to have been Pam's best friend?"

"Yes," admitted Pierce.

The Ice Melts

Throughout the proceedings Pamela Smart had maintained her composure, but contrition took over in the witness box. She claimed that her attempts to break off the affair with Flynn had been thwarted by his threats of suicide. "I was devastated," she said. While conceding the impropriety of their relationship, Smart vehemently denied any suggestion that she had planned murder. "I didn't force anybody to kill Greg!"

Then why, wondered Maggiotto, had she made those statements to Cecelia Pierce?

That had been a subterfuge, Smart said, all part of her own investigation into the murder of her husband.

"What were you going to do," asked Maggiotto, "Make a citizen's arrest?"

"No."

"Or was Pam Smart going to use her own investigation skills . . . and write a report and mail it in?"

"Yes," replied Smart, blaming some medication she was taking at the time for her apparent instability.

It was Smart's position, as it had been for the defense from the outset, that the murder was solely the work of the three teenagers, who now saw a way to ameliorate their sentences by implicating her. "They murdered Greg," she cried. "They're the ones who broke into the house. They waited for him. And they're the ones who brought him to his knees and brought a knife to his throat, before shooting him!"

The jury took 13 hours to decide Smart's fate. She stood emotionless as the guilty verdict was read. When Judge Douglas Gray imposed a life sentence without the possibility of parole, she seemed equally unaffected.

For their involvement in the murder, William Flynn and Patrick Randall each received sentences of 28 years to life. Vance Lattime received 18 years to life. Yet another student who knew of the plot, Raymond Fowler, also pleaded guilty to conspiracy and was jailed for 15 to 30 years.

In a made-for-television movie, *Murder in New Hampshire*, Pamela Smart was depicted as a scheming architect of murder. While the pertinency of that view is a matter of record, often overlooked is the ease with which her young lover was able to recruit assistants for his deadly mission. In this extraordinary case there was more than enough blame for everyone.

—Colin Evans

Suggestions for Further Reading

Case, Tony. "Trial Coverage Under The Microscope." *Editor & Publisher* (April 20, 1991): 25ff.

Diamond, John N. *Washington Journalism Review* (June 1991): 15–16.

Plummer, William and Stephen Sawicki. *People Weekly* (February 4, 1991): 105–110.

Manuel Noriega Trial: 1991

Defendant: Manuel Antonio Noriega   **Crime Charged:** Drug trafficking, racketeering, and conspiracy   **Chief Defense Lawyers:** Jon May and Frank A. Rubino   **Chief Prosecutors:** James McAdams, Myles Malman, and Michael P. Sullivan   **Judge:** William M. Hoeveler   **Place:** Miami, Florida   **Dates of Trial:** September 6, 1991–April 9, 1992   **Verdict:** Guilty   **Sentence:** 40 years imprisonment

SIGNIFICANCE
This landmark trial marked the first time that a former head of a foreign government had ever faced criminal charges in an American court of law.

At 45 minutes past midnight on December 20, 1988, U.S. armed forces began the costliest and deadliest arrest mission in history, when 25,000 troops invaded Panama, all looking for one man, General Manuel Antonio Noriega, dictator of that country and suspected conduit for the flow of cocaine into America. After holing up at the Papal Embassy for two weeks, Noriega meekly surrendered and was flown to Miami, Florida, to face charges of drug trafficking.

The five-year running battle between the U.S. Government and General Noriega entered its climactic phase when his trial began September 5, 1991. Following a week given over to the demanding process of jury selection, Michael Sullivan opened for the government. He derided Noriega as a "small man in a general's uniform," who gave his "permission, authorization, and encouragement to a scheme to transform his nation into an international cocaine trafficking and manufacturing center."

In a surprise move, defense counsel Frank Rubino waived his right to deliver an opening statement to the jury, choosing instead to wait until the prosecution had revealed its entire hand before deciding what direction the defense should take.

After various academic witnesses provided some background on Panama's geopolitical history, the prosecution really got into gear when Lieutenant Colonel Luis del Cid, a close aide to Noriega for 25 years, took the stand. Like many of the prosecution witnesses, Cid was himself facing drug charges and had agreed to testify against Noriega only in return for a lighter sentence. Describing himself as Noriega's "errand boy, bodyguard and bagman," he told of suitcases stuffed with cash arriving from Colombia, either as a payoff for Noriega or to be laundered through Panamanian banks. An extraordinary interlude came when Cid, asked to identify the defendant, leapt to attention as his former boss stood up. Those in court half expected the witness to salute.

Cartel Contacts Revealed

Floyd Carlton, Noriega's personal pilot, recounted how two prominent Medellin cartel members, Pablo Escobar and Gustave Gavira, had approached him through an intermediary to "go and talk with Noriega" about an arrangement which would allow Carlton to fly cocaine to Panama under the general's authority. Carlton said that Noriega "told me he didn't want his name involved in this type of problem, and that if something happened he would know nothing about it," but, he added later, "Nothing is to be done without notifying me." According to Carlton the cartel originally offered Noriega between $30,000 and $50,000 for each flight of cocaine. When he relayed this news to Noriega the general exploded: "Either they're crazy or you are! Not for that kind of money. I won't allow it to happen for less than $100,000 a flight." Over the years, Carlton estimated that Noriega received $5 million in kickbacks.

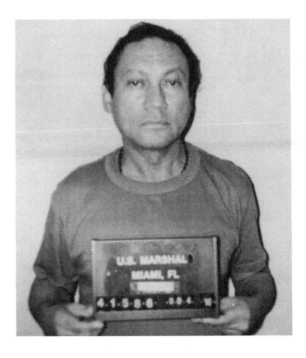

When Rubino reproved Carlton because no one else was present at these alleged meetings, the witness snapped back, "Mr. Rubino, this was a cocaine deal, we weren't talking about cookies!" Counsel fared slightly better in getting Carlton to admit that Noriega had been angered to learn of illicit money-laundering flights into Panama.

By far the most prominent witness against Noriega was Carlos Ledher Rivas, the only founding member of the Medellin cartel ever to face charges in an American court. Amid heavy security, Ledher, whose 1988 conviction for drug trafficking brought him a sentence of life plus 135 years, said Noriega offered the cartel a cocaine pipeline to the United States." In addition to paying the general $1,000 for every kilo of cocaine that passed through the country, the cartel agreed to pay Noriega 5 percent of all profits deposited in Panamanian banks—a sum that other witnesses said often amounted to $60 million a week.

Ledher explained the cartel's plight: "We were desperately looking for new routes. We had no point of transshipment for the cocaine that was piling up in Colombia." Under questioning from prosecutor Guy Lewis, Ledher elabo-

Former Panamanian dictator General Manuel Noriega being booked in Miami for charges of drug trafficking, conspiracy, and racketeering. (AP/ Wide World Photos)

rated on Noriega's alleged involvement with Fidel Castro, whom he said was also dealing with the Medellin cartel. The doubtful pertinence of much that Ledher had to say aroused defense suspicions that the witness was testifying very much out of self-interest, prepared to blacken Noriega's name at all costs in hopes of getting his own jail sentence reduced.

After establishing the existence of such a *quid pro quo*, Rubino challenged Ledher about Medellin involvement with the Nicaraguan Contras, a line of questioning that clearly unsettled the witness. With great reluctance, he said, "To the best of my recollection, there was some contribution to the Contra anticommunist movement." When Rubino pushed for an exact figure, Ledher hedged and tried to dodge, until finally saying, "It could have been around $10 million." Rubino was prevented from pursuing this source of potential embarrassment to the U.S. government, which had also been funding the Contras, on grounds that it was not relevant.

Judge Taken III

The much-awaited defense strategy had be put on hold when Judge William Hoeveler was stricken by illness and had to undergo open heart surgery. After more than a six-week delay, Noriega's team finally got its chance. The defense attorneys provided few surprises and none of the bombshells that had been predicted. Attorney Jon May portrayed Noriega as one of America's greatest allies in the fight against drugs. The level and quality of cooperation he gave the United States, May proclaimed "unprecedented among the leaders of Central and South American nations. . . . Over and over the U.S. came to General Noriega for assistance," when it served "our national interest to use that relationship in times of crisis."

Some evidence to support that contention came from Thomas Telles, former head of the Drug Enforcement Agency's Panamanian office. He said that Noriega had promised to help the United States in identifying cartel members' bank accounts, monitoring movements of their money, and seizing the chemicals needed to make cocaine.

Further confirming Noriega's ties to U.S. policy was Donald Winters, Central Intelligence Agency station chief in Panama from 1984 to 1986. Over a period of 15 years, he said, Noriega provided Washington with considerable information about Fidel Castro, information deemed so useful that then CIA Director William Casey made a personal visit in 1984 to thank the Panamanian dictator. Asked to characterize the nature of the meeting, Winters said, "I would describe it as something more substantial than a courtesy call."

Throughout the trial Noriega remained impassive and largely silent, He did not take the stand in his own defense. After almost seven months, closing arguments finally began on March 31, 1992. Describing Noriega as "nothing more than a corrupt, crooked and rotten cop [who] sold his uniform, his army and his protection to a murderous criminal gang called the Medellin cocaine cartel," Assistant U.S. Attorney Myles Malman said that Noriega had been responsible for polluting U.S. streets with "tons and tons of a deadly white powder." Malman admitted that many of the prosecution witnesses were less than model citizens, but as he put it, law enforcement officials must use "small fish" to catch "big fish" and Noriega was "the biggest fish of all."

It was an argument bitterly denounced by Frank Rubino. "This indictment stinks," he told the jurors, "It stinks like dead fish. It smells from here to Washington." The case against Noriega, he said, was predicated solely on the theory that "if you throw enough mud against a wall, some of it will stick." He zeroed in on the more than 20 prosecution witnesses already convicted of drug offenses. "They are the scum of the earth. These people are disgusting. What kind of morals do these people have?" He reserved his most acerbic condemnation for Carlos Ledher Rivas, whom he called "the Charles Manson of this case."

Over five difficult and often stormy days, the jury deliberated. At one point the recalcitrance of a single juror threatened to bring about a mistrial, but on April 9 they found Noriega guilty on eight charges, while acquitting him of two.

Two months later, Judge Hoeveler sentenced Noriega to 40 years imprisonment.

In political, criminal, and economic terms, the trial of General Manuel Noriega is without equal. By some estimates it cost $168 million to convict him. More certain is the expense in American lives: 25 killed in the invasion. What impact Noriega's incarceration has on the flow of drugs into the United States remains to be seen.

—*Colin Evans*

Suggestions for Further Reading

Booth, Cathy. "The Trial Of Manuel Noriega." *The Los Angeles Daily Journal* (April 7, 1992): 6ff.

Dinges, John. *Our Man in Panama*. New York: Random House, 1990.

Kempe, Frederick. *Divorcing the Dictator*. New York: G.P. Putnam's Sons, 1990.

Koster, R. Medellin and Guillermo Sanchez. *In the Time of the Tyrants*. New York: W.W. Norton & Co., 1990.

McDonald, Marci. "Threat Of The Beast." *Maclean's* (September 16, 1991): 22ff.

El Sayyid Nosair Trial: 1991

Defendant: El Sayyid A. Nosair **Crime Charged:** Murder, attempted murder, and assault **Chief Defense Lawyers:** William M. Kunstler and Michael Warren **Chief Prosecutor:** William Greenbaum **Judge:** Alvin Schlesinger **Place:** New York, New York **Dates of Trial:** November 4– December 21, 1991 **Verdict:** Not guilty, murder, and attempted murder; Guilty, assault with a deadly weapon **Sentence:** 7–22 years imprisonment

SIGNIFICANCE
Never has the unpredictability of juries been more idly demonstrated than in this case of such seeming straight forwardness.

Just minutes after delivering a speech at a New York City hotel in November 1990, Meir Kahane, militant conservative rabbi and former Jewish Defense League head, was shot down by a gunman. As the assassin fled, he wounded a Kahane supporter. Outside the building, El Sayyid Nosair, a 36-year-old Arab, was tackled by an armed U.S. Postal Service officer. Shots were exchanged, and both men were hit. Following treatment for his wound, Nosair was charged with murder.

Violent clashes between extremist Jews and Arabs on the steps of the courthouse marred the trial's opening day, November 4, 1991. Judge Alvin Schlesinger, plagued by death threats, commented sadly, "I have never seen so much hate. It's beyond reason, principle, and cause."

When lead prosecutor William Greenbaum led off for the state he contended that Nosair alone had fired the deadly bullets. Contrary to several pretrial statements in which he called Kahane's murder "a planned political assassination," Greenbaum neglected to attribute any motive to the accused, apparently feeling that the sheer weight of evidence obviated this customary bulwark of most prosecution cases.

Chief defense attorney William Kunstler argued that the reason for this omission was simple: his client was innocent, just someone who had fled the hotel fearing for his own life. According to Kunstler, Kahane had been murdered by a disgruntled supporter in a dispute over money. "You'll have to decide who shot Meir Kahane," he told the jury. "This case is not cut and dried."

Michael Djunaedi, a student, placed Nosair with a gun in his hand just moments after the shooting. "I heard some guys yelling, 'He's got a gun!'" Seconds later, Djunaedi said, postal worker Carlos Acosta and Nosair began firing at each other.

Positive Identification Introduced

Corroboration came from Acosta, who, without being asked, stood up from the witness chair, pointed at the defendant, and shouted, "This man shot me!" Kunstler's suggestion that Nosair Chad actually had been fleeing from armed pursuers drew a scoffing response. "My focus was on him, he had the gun."

Another spectator, Ari Gottesman, told of standing between Kahane and "a dark-skinned, dark-haired man," who fired two shots at point-blank range. Asked whether he saw the gunman in court, Gottesman picked out Nosair.

When Dr. Steven Stowe, who had attended Kahane immediately after he was shot, took the stand, Kunstler seized the chance to expand on his conspiracy theory. "Didn't you do everything in your power that night to see that Meir Kahane never reached Bellevue (Hospital]?"

"No, sir," the doctor replied. Later, though, he did concede that he and paramedics had argued over what treatment to give.

Kunstler brushed aside the testimony of a forensic expert, Detective Robert Cotter, positively identifying the Magnum found next to Nosair as the murder weapon. Kunstler claimed it had been "planted" by the real killers of Kahane.

In all, the prosecution presented 51 witnesses. By contrast Kunstler called just six, none of whom supported his vague contention that Kahane had been shot by his own followers. Nosair, exercising his right to silence, heard Kunstler depict him as a tragic victim of circumstances.

Kunstler's eloquence found a ready audience. On December 21, 1991, the jury acquitted Nosair of murder or attempted murder and convicted him only on assault and weapons charges.

Sentencing Nosair to a maximum sentence of 7–22 years, Judge Schlesinger denounced the jury's verdict as "against the overwhelming weight of evidence . . . devoid of common sense and logic." Bemoaning his inability to impose a stiffer sentence, Judge Schlesinger said: "I believe the defendant conducted a rape of this country, of our Constitution and of our laws."

The extraordinary outcome of this case provided compelling proof that the human content in a trial can never be ignored or taken for granted.

—Colin Evans

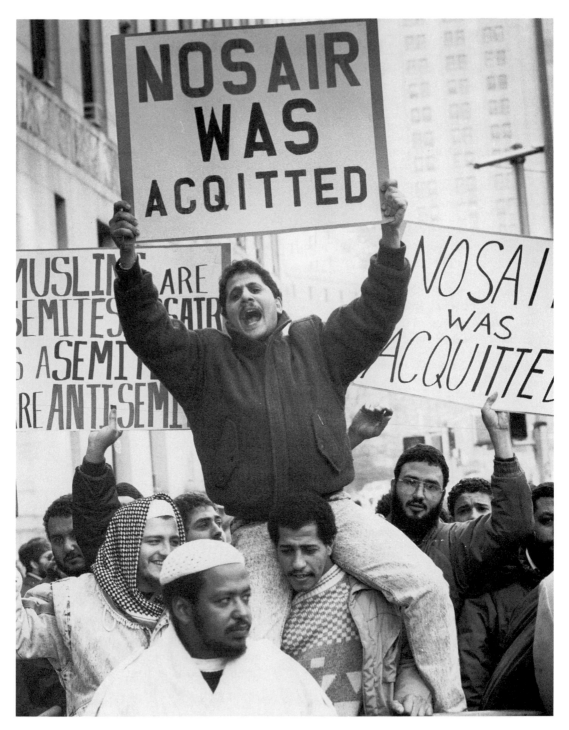

Supporters of El Sayyid Nosair after the jury's surprising verdict. (AP/Wide World Photos)

Suggestions for Further Reading

Friedman, Robert I. *The False Prophet*. New York: Lawrence Hill Books, 1990.

Hewitt, Bill. "A Career Of Preaching Hatred." *People* (November 19, 1990): 48ff.

Kotler, Ya'ir. *Heil Kahane*. New York: Adama Books, 1986.

Masland, Tom. "The High Price Of Hatred." *Newsweek* (November 19, 1990): 48ff.

Rosenbaum, Ron. "The Most Hated Man In America." *Vanity Fair* (March 1992): 68ff.

Charles Keating Trials: 1991–93

Defendant: Charles F. Keating, Jr. **Crime Charged:** Securities Fraud
Chief Defense Lawyer: Stephen C. Neal **Chief Prosecutor:** William
Hodgman **Judge:** Lance A. Ito **Place:** Los Angeles, California
Dates of Trial: November 18–December 4, 1991 **Verdict:** Guilty
Sentence: Not definite as of this writing, but potentially up to 10 years in
prison and a $250,000 fine. There may be further prison terms and fines
depending on the outcomes of additional, pending trials.

SIGNIFICANCE

Charles Keating was convicted for securities fraud in connection with the largest
savings and loan collapse in history, which cost the American taxpayers $2.6
billion. The repercussions reached the U.S. Senate, where five senators popularly
called the Keating Five were investigated for ethics violations in connection with
their helping Keating avoid federal regulators in return for large campaign
contributions.

The problems experienced by the savings and loan industry did not begin with
the spectacular wave of collapses in the late 1980s. In fact, savings and loans
have had financial problems for nearly 20 years. In the 1970s, S&Ls chafed
under federal restrictions that limited the amount of interest they could pay to
depositors, the types of investments S&Ls could make and when they could
borrow money. Many of these restrictions made the S&Ls uncompetitive with
traditional banking and finance companies.

Congress bowed to S&L lobbying, abolished the interest rate limitations
on deposits, and lifted restrictions that previously only permitted S&Ls to invest
in single-family home mortgages. Congress believed that deregulation would
bring private-sector money into S&Ls and revitalize the industry without
federal involvement. In many respects, Congress deregulated the S&Ls rather
than spend federal money to bail them out, with disastrous consequences.

Charles F. Keating, Jr., was one of many people who would treat S&L
deregulation as a license to steal. Keating was a close associate of Carl Lindner, a
wealthy businessman from Cincinnati, Ohio who owned the American Financial
Corporation. In 1976, Keating bought a subsidiary of AFC called American
Continental Homes from Lindner, which Keating later renamed American

Continental Corporation. ACC embarked on several ambitious real estate development projects, mostly in Arizona and Colorado. To finance its activities, ACC set up its own in-house mortgage company and was a pioneer in creating the type of financial package and instrument known as the "mortgage-backed security." Keating, however, had his eye on bigger game.

ACC Buys Lincoln Savings and Loan

On February 24, 1984, Keating's ACC bought Lincoln Savings and Loan for $55 million. Lincoln S&L was one of the largest S&Ls in southern California, with assets at the time of more than a billion dollars. Keating was attracted to Lincoln S&L not only because of its size, but because, in addition to federal deregulation, California state S&L regulations were very lax.

Keating and ACC installed their own management team to run Lincoln S&L and began a program of unrestricted pillaging of Lincoln S&L's assets through thinly disguised accounting gimmicks. Millions were funneled into ACC to cover ACC's losses from real estate projects that had turned sour. Further, Lincoln S&L was used as a conduit to sell hundreds of millions of dollars of ACC bonds to depositors. More than 20,000 people, many of whom were retired and were investing their pensions, bought ACC junk bonds from salesmen who told them that the bonds were federally insured. In fact, the bonds were not federally insured.

Keating surrounded himself, Lincoln S&L, and ACC with an army of lawyers and accountants who thwarted the few efforts federal and state authorities made to look at ACC's transactions with Lincoln S&L. Finally, however, the house of cards fell in. On April 14, 1989, the Federal Home Loan Bank Board (FHLBB) exercised its authority and appointed a conservator, who took over Lincoln S&L. Unable to sustain itself on Lincoln S&L's assets any longer, ACC went bankrupt in the same month, and the purchasers of ACC bonds lost all of their money. After the conservator found that Lincoln was insolvent by more than $600 million, the FHLBB (later succeeded by the Office of Thrift Supervision) put Lincoln S&L into receivership on August 2, 1990. Cleaning up Lincoln S&L would eventually cost the taxpayers $2.6 billion.

Litigation Abounds

A myriad of civil litigation and criminal prosecutions followed the collapse of ACC and Lincoln S&L, most of which was still awaiting trial or under appeal as of this writing. There were civil class action suits by the purchasers of ACC bonds against Keating, other officers and directors of ACC, and the banks, lawyers, and accountants who shielded them from regulatory scrutiny for so long. There were federal and state criminal charges against Keating and others. Finally, there were regulatory actions by the OTS against the same banks, lawyers, and accountants being sued in civil court. In March 1992, the OTS rocked the legal world when it froze the assets of the huge, 400-lawyer law firm

Kaye, Scholer, Fierman, Hays & Handler, which had represented Keating, and after bringing the firm to its knees imposed a $41 million settlement on it.

The only criminal case against Keating that has gone to trial and resulted in a verdict and sentence as of this writing, is the California state prosecution for securities fraud in connection with the sale of ACC junk bonds under the misrepresentation that they were federally insured. This trial took place in Los Angeles before Judge Lance A. Ito. The chief defense lawyer was Stephen C. Neal and the prosecutor was Deputy District Attorney William Hodgman.

The trial began on November 18, 1991. Many of the elderly investors who had purchased ACC junk bonds attended the trial, and yelled angrily at Keating both in the courtroom and to and from the trial. One spectator managed to punch Keating in the arm.

There were 18 separate securities fraud counts against Keating. Keating's lawyers argued that Keating had no control over what salesmen were telling investors about federal insurance coverage for ACC junk bonds, but the jury disagreed. On December 4, 1991, the jury returned its verdict. The jury found Keating guilty of 17 of the 18 counts.

Keating Draws Maximum Sentence

During the sentencing hearing on April 10, 1992, seven small investors testified, and begged Judge Ito to punish Keating to the extent provided by law. One of the witnesses, Harriet Chappuise, stated that "Charles Keating did not steal a loaf of bread. He stole the bread out of the mouths of thousands of old people. Try, Mr. Keating, try living on Social Security checks." Ito sentenced Keating to the statutory maximum of 10 years in prison, and to pay a $250,000 fine, but Keating's lawyers have not yet exhausted all appeals. One potential tactic for Keating's lawyers was to argue that the number of legal actions against him violated his right to due process under the Constitution. Defense attorney Neal has stated:

> You can make a pretty good case that it is overkill and a waste of taxpayers' money.

Joseph W. Cotchett, an attorney involved in the civil cases against Keating, does not concede that there is any due process violation resulting from "overkill" litigation, but he agrees that there are too many federal agencies jumping on the bandwagon too late to do any good:

> Where were all the inside-the-beltway bureaucrats when Charley Keating was riding high on the backs of the public?

Keating was involved in another criminal trial as of this writing in Los Angeles, this time for violating federal laws against fraud, conspiracy and racketeering. The case went to trial in October 1992, and on January 6, 1993 the jury returned a guilty verdict on all 73 criminal counts against Keating. When Keating goes to sentencing, he faces a theoretical total of 525 years in additional prison time. However, with delays and any subsequent appeals, it could be a long time before a final sentence is rendered.

Keating Loses in Civil Court, Too

The only civil case against Keating that has gone to trial as of this writing is a class action lawsuit filed in federal court in Tucson, Arizona. The lawsuit was filed on behalf of the more than 20,000 people who lost their money after buying ACC bonds. In addition to Keating, there were three other defendants, who had been involved in ACC's real estate schemes: a wealthy businessman in Tempe, Arizona, named Conley Wolfswinkel, Continental Southern, Inc. of Atlanta, Georgia, and the Saudi European Investment Corporation.

The trial began on April 1, 1992, before Judge Richard Bilby. Keating did not appear at the trial or have any lawyer represent him during the proceedings, claiming that he was too busy preparing for the October 1992 federal criminal trial in Los Angeles. The other defendants, however, denied that they had acted jointly with Keating in causing Lincoln S&L's collapse and dragged the case out for more than three months.

After deliberating for eight days, on July 10, 1992, the jury found Keating and the other three defendants guilty of violating federal anti-fraud laws. The plaintiffs' lawyers sought $288.7 million in compensatory damages from Keating for the class of plaintiffs, but the jury gave an award of $600 million in compensatory damages, with an additional award of $1.5 billion in punitive damages. Because the compensatory damages are tripled under federal anti-racketeering statutes to $1.8 billion, the total amount of the verdict against Keating is $3.3 billion. The jury rendered similarly large verdicts against the other three defendants as well. Of course, it is possible that part or all of the verdict against Keating will be set aside on appeal. Further, any final judgment in this case or any other civil case is only as good as Keating's ability to pay it off. Keating claims to be near bankruptcy, so the plaintiffs may collect only pennies on the dollar from him.

Shadows Fall Over Senators

Keating's downfall had repercussions at the highest levels of government. During the height of his power, Keating contributed heavily to the political campaigns and causes of U.S. Senators Alan Cranston, Dennis DeConcini, John Glenn, John McCain, and Donald W. Riegle, Jr. These senators intervened on Keating's behalf several times with federal regulators in the late 1980s to allay growing suspicions about Keating's activities. Cranston was the largest beneficiary, receiving roughly $850,000 in contributions from Keating. When Keating's empire collapsed and the senators' involvement was revealed, they were labeled the Keating Five by the press. After an investigation of several months by the Senate Ethics Committee, the committee voted on November 19, 1991, to rebuke Cranston for improper conduct, but did not recommend formal censure by the full U.S. Senate. The other Senators received nothing but minor chastisement.

Regardless of the outcome of all the criminal and civil legal actions against Keating, his fall from power and prestige is certainly final. Keating's conviction for securities fraud in connection with the Lincoln S&L collapse—the largest S&L collapse in history, which cost the American taxpayers $2.6 billion—closed the door on the go-go years of the 1980s.

—Stephen G. Christianson

Suggestions for Further Reading

Davis, Sally Ogle. "Keating's Folly." *Los Angeles* (November 1991): 58–62.

Fowler, Jack. "The Keating Fizzle." *National Review* (February 1991): 22–23.

Glassman, James K. "The Great Banks Robbery: Deconstructing the S&L Crisis." *The New Republic* (October 1990): 16–21.

"House of Ill Repute." *The New Republic* (December 1990): 7–9.

Morgenstern, Joe. "Profit Without Honor." *Playboy* (April 1992): 68–75.

United States Senate. *Preliminary Inquiry Into Allegations Regarding Senators Cranston, DeConcini, Glenn, McCain, and Riegle, and Lincoln Savings and Loan.* Washington: U.S. Government Printing Office, 1991.

William Kennedy Smith Trial: 1991

Defendant: William Kennedy Smith **Crime Charged:** Rape
Chief Defense Lawyers: Roy E. Black, Mark Schnapp, and Mark Seiden
Chief Prosecutors: Moira K. Lasch and Ellen Roberts **Judge:** Mary E. Lupo
Place: West Palm Beach, Florida **Dates of Trial:** December 2–11, 1991
Verdict: Not guilty

SIGNIFICANCE
The Kennedy family name and the concomitant glare of global media attention
made this nothing less than the most heavily scrutinized rape trial in history.

A chance encounter at a Palm Beach, Florida, nightspot between William
Kennedy Smith and Patricia Bowman led to the couple returning to the
Kennedy compound overlooking the Atlantic Ocean. From the house they
walked down to the beach. What happened next would become the subject of
worldwide headlines. According to Bowman, Smith raped her. Smith maintained
that everything which occurred had been with Bowman's consent. The state,
satisfied that Smith had a case to answer, filed rape charges against him.

When she rose to speak to a jury of four women and two men on December
2, 1991, prosecutor Moira Lasch already had lost an important battle. Judge Mary
Lupo had earlier denied the prosecution's request to admit the testimony of
three other women who claimed that Smith had assaulted them between 1983
and 1988 on grounds that it did not demonstrate the discernible pattern of
behavior required by Florida law for introduction. This meant that Lasch had to
pin virtually her entire case on the word of the accuser.

First, though, Anne Mercer, a friend of Bowman's, who had also been at
the Kennedy house on the night in question, told the court that Bowman was
"literally shaking and she looked messed up . . . she said she had been raped."
When Mercer had confronted Smith to ask him how he could have acted as he
did, his response, she said, was simply to shrug his shoulders.

Tabloid Interview Nets $40,000

In a blistering cross-examination, defense counsel Roy Black knocked gaping holes in Mercer's testimony. He forced a retreat from her earlier assertion to police that Bowman had been raped twice, and that on one of these occasions Smith's uncle, Senator Edward M. Kennedy of Massachusetts, had watched. Black also got Mercer to admit that she had failed to inform the authorities of details she subsequently revealed for the tabloid TV program "A Current Affair."

After posting a $10,000 bond, Kennedy Smith makes a statement to the press. (AP/Wide World Photos)

Gasps filled the courtroom when Mercer confessed that she had been paid $40,000 for her story. By implication, Black suggested that Mercer's tale had been heavily embellished for monetary gain. It was a stigma that the witness never fully shrugged off. Black drove home his advantage by playing Mercer a taped account she had made earlier for the police that contained several statements that disagreed with the version she had provided the court.

In a surprise move, prosecutor Lasch produced the accuser early in the trial. To protect her identity, TV cameras obscured Bowman's face with a blue dot. (Following the trial Bowman elected to abandon her anonymity for a TV interview.) Referring to the defendant first as "Mr. Smith," and later as "that man," Bowman described the alleged assault, saying, "I thought he was going to kill me."

When Black chided Bowman for several lapses of memory, she insisted, "The only thing I can remember about that week is Mr. Smith raped me."

Black wasn't impressed. "I know you've been prepared to say that."

Bowman snapped back. "I have not been prepared to say anything."

Throughout his cross-examination Black walked a fine line; how best to undermine the accuser's credibility without wishing to appear bullying or insensitive. On those occasions when his questioning provoked a tearful response, Black immediately backed off and suggested a recess. Under his deft probing, however, Bowman did acknowledge a history of problems with men, resulting, she said, from "having one-night stands."

On rebuttal, Lasch asked Bowman whether she had any ulterior motives for bringing the charge. Bowman replied, "What he did to me was wrong. I have a child and it's not right and I don't want to live the rest of my life in fear of that man. And I don't want to be responsible for him doing it to someone else."

This final comment brought Black to his feet, objecting. Judge Lupo ordered the remark stricken from the record, calling it "inappropriate."

Curiously, the prosecution called Smith's uncle, Senator Edward Kennedy, as its witness. If, as some observers believed, Lasch was attempting to visit some of the senator's perceived foibles upon his nephew, then she sorely miscalculated. For some 40 minutes Senator Kennedy managed to re-create Camelot in a Palm Beach courthouse as he evoked memories of the family's numerous tragedies. Nothing he said was remotely helpful to Lasch's case. Not for the first time the prosecution's strategy showed signs of being ill-conceived and poorly executed.

Much of the defense was built around forensic testimony. Charles M. Sieger, an architect, said that, given the house's construction, had Bowman screamed as she claimed, the sounds would have been clearly audible indoors, yet no resident admitted to hearing anything.

Rather less successful was Professor Jay Siegel's testimony. He stated that sand found in Bowman's underwear most likely came from the beach, which tallied with Smith's version of events, and not the lawn, where Bowman claimed she had been raped. Lasch bored in. "Wouldn't you agree that a 6-foot-2, 200-pound man running up a beach is going to churn up some sand?" Siegel agreed. Lasch went on: "And if the defendant was wet . . . some of that [sand] could stick to his body, couldn't it?" Besides having to concede this possibility, Siegel also was forced to admit that the lawn itself actually contained a significant amount of sand, thus rendering his testimony virtually useless.

Defendant Remains Cool

It took William Kennedy Smith just 29 minutes to tell his side of the story. Black concluded the brief account by asking if he had "at any time" raped his accuser. "No, I did not," Smith replied firmly.

Lasch went on the attack. "What are you saying, that she raped you, Mr. Smith?" Later, in reference to an alleged second sexual encounter, she leered, "What are you, some kind of sex machine?"

Smith weathered the assault coolly. He reiterated his story that the evening had turned ugly when he had inadvertently called the accuser "Kathy." She "sort of snapped . . . she got very upset." Later, he said, Bowman apologized as she was leaving the compound, "I am sorry I got upset . . . I had a wonderful night. You're a terrific guy." Minutes later, however, she was back, crying and claiming that he had raped her, repeatedly calling him "Michael."

Frustrated by Smith's matter-of-fact responses, Lasch adopted a different tack, claiming the Kennedy family was trying to engineer a cover-up. Smith would have none of it. "If you're implying that my family is lying to protect me, you are dead wrong." Someone else less than impressed with this line of questioning was Judge Lupo. "If you ask one more question along these lines," she told Lasch, "you will not get away with it. Failure to abide by this instruction will result in legal action." It was a humiliating rebuke for the prosecutor, coming as it did with Judge Lupo's oblique reference to the fact that she suspected Lasch might be angling for a deliberate mistrial, thus salvaging her case for another day.

In closing, Black said, "they want us to believe that this young man goes up there and rapes a screaming young woman under the open windows not only of his mother, but his sister, two prosecutors from New York, and the father of one of them who is a former special agent for the FBI!" Making no attempt to apologize for his client's self-confessed dishonorable behavior on the night concerned, Black still appealed to the jury to exhibit "general, human common sense."

Lasch could dwell on only inconsistencies. Referring to Bowman, "She didn't know this man. She didn't even have an opportunity to know him. . . . This woman has had a child. She's a high-risk pregnancy. If she was going to have consensual sex on March 30, 1991, she would use birth control."

On December 11, 1991, the case went to the jury. After deliberating for just 79 minutes they returned with a verdict of not guilty.

Millions of viewers watched this drama played out on their television screens. For most it was their first glimpse of the extraordinary problems that attend "date rape" cases. By its very nature this kind of rape will always remain a question of "he said, she said." In such circumstances courtroom demeanor invariably decides the day.

—Colin Evans

Suggestions for Further Reading

Dunne, Dominick. "The Verdict." *Vanity Fair* (March 1992): 210ff.

Fields, Suzanne. "Sexual Revolution Bares Its Flaws." *Insight* (January 6, 1992): 17ff.

McDonald, Marci. "Beyond The Trial." *Maclean's* (December 23, 1991): 16ff.

Stein, Harry. "It Happened One Night." *Playboy* (April 1992): 78ff.

Taylor, John. "A Theory Of The Case." *New York* (January 6, 1992): 34ff.

John Gotti Trial: 1992

Defendant: John Gotti   **Crimes Charged:** Racketeering; racketeering conspiracy; murder; Illegal gambling; obstruction of justice; and conspiracies to murder, bribe a detective, obstruct justice, commit loan sharking, and commit tax fraud   **Chief Defense Lawyer:** Albert J. Krieger
Chief Prosecutors: John Gleeson and Andrew J. Maloney   **Judge:** I. Leo Glasser   **Place:** Brooklyn, New York   **Dates of Trial:** January 21– April 2, 1992   **Verdict:** Guilty   **Sentence:** Life imprisonment without parole and $250,000 fine

SIGNIFICANCE

Fear, bribery, flawed prosecutions, and his lawyers' obstreperous courtroom behavior helped outspoken mob boss John Gotti avoid prison three times before he was successfully convicted of violating the Racketeer Influenced and Corrupt Organizations Act.

When John Gotti was indicted along with members of the Gambino organized crime "family" in New York in March 1985, law enforcement officials considered him to be a small-time hoodlum who had served short sentences for hijacking and attempted manslaughter. Everything changed December 16, 1985, when Gambino crime family leader Paul Castellano and "underboss" Thomas Bilotti were shot to death outside a midtown Manhattan restaurant.

Leadership of the powerful Gambino organization seemed to shift swiftly to Gotti. Law officers speculated that the new mob boss or "don" had murdered his predecessor before Castellano could have Gotti killed for violating a Gambino family prohibition against narcotics dealing. Gotti's violent celebrity grew quickly. Shortly after Castellano's murder, a terrified refrigerator mechanic who had accused Gotti of assaulting him in a parking dispute lost his memory in court.

Yet Gotti still faced trial for violating the federal Racketeer Influenced and Corrupt Organizations Act, popularly known as the RICO statute. Under the 1970 law, anyone found guilty of two felonies listed in a RICO indictment was considered to be engaged in a pattern of criminal activity and thus open to conviction for violating the RICO law itself. Federal prosecutors began using the statute against organized crime in the 1980's with considerable success.

The most serious charges in the 1985 Gambino RICO indictment died with Castellano and terminally ill Mafia boss Aniello Dellacroce, leaving Gotti to face lesser charges that had little to do with his sudden eminence as a mob boss. The government's case also was hampered by a bitter jurisdictional dispute between several state and federal law enforcement agencies. Each was building its own case against Gotti. None wanted to share witnesses or information for fear of jeopardizing its own chances for a successful conviction.

Gotti Eludes Conviction

Gotti's RICO trial began in August 1986. The prosecution case relied heavily on testimony by convicted felons. All were admitted liars who agreed under defense cross-examination that they hoped their testimony was buying them shorter sentences. One informer falsely denied ever working for the FBI. Another openly perjured himself, accusing the prosecution of offering him drugs in prison in return for testimony. After a long and acrimonious trial in which the defense repeatedly fired crude personal insults at the prosecutors and outshouted the judge's orders, Gotti was acquitted in March 1987.

Federal prosecutors immediately announced that Gotti would be indicted for a different set of racketeering crimes. When Gotti next appeared in court in January 1990, however, he faced assault and conspiracy charges in the wounding of John O'Connor, an officer of the United Brotherhood of Carpenters. The corrupt union officer had ordered a Manhattan restaurant wrecked for resisting his bribery demands, unaware that the restaurant had ties to the Gambino crime family. Gotti was accused of ordering O'Connor shot in retaliation. If convicted, Gotti faced a sentence of 15 years to life as a thrice-convicted, "persistent felony offender."

Witnesses Weaken Prosecution

The main witness for the prosecution was James McElroy, a former "enforcer" for the Westies, a violent gang based in the Hell's Kitchen section of Manhattan. McElroy claimed that the Westies had done the shooting as a favor to Gotti, who wanted O'Connor "whacked," or killed. Gotti's combative lawyer Bruce Cutler argued that the Westies' leader was an admitted perjurer and murderer, "a lying bum" trying to bargain his way out of a 60-year prison sentence for racketeering.

Secret tapes which purportedly showed Gotti's desire for revenge were imperfect. Cutler admitted that they reflected Gotti's involvement in Gambino family business, but he argued that his client's promise to "bust 'm up" referred to reorganizing Gambino "crews" and was not a description of what he wanted done to O'Connor. The issue was further confused when state and federal prosecutors gave jurors differing transcripts of the same secretly taped conversation between two Westies. The star defense witness was the victim himself, John O'Connor, who denied that he could identify his assailants.

Gotti's supporters and neighbors celebrated with a fireworks display at the news of his third acquittal. Media pundits transformed the stylishly dressed "Dapper Don" into "The Teflon Don," a criminal to whom charges would not stick. "He is a murderer, not a folk hero," replied U.S. Attorney Andrew J. Maloney, who handed down the long-awaited new set of RICO charges in December 1990. Gotti and his top associates Frank Locasio and Salvatore Gravano were arrested and held without bail for multiple felonies ranging from murder to tax evasion.

Tide Changes for Prosecutors

Before testimony began, federal prosecutors succeeded in having Gotti's loud but effective lawyer Bruce Cutler barred from the trial. Judge I. Leo Glasser agreed that secret tapes showed that Cutler and two other attorneys had acted as "house counsels" for the Gambino crime organization. Since playing the tapes would result in the lawyers having to testify about matters the prosecution intended to introduce as evidence, the enraged Cutler was disqualified from working on the case.

Rumors of jury tampering in Gotti's previous trials also helped prosecutors convince the judge that the jury should remain anonymous and be sequestered throughout the trial. But the hardest blow of all came in the announcement that "Sammy Bull" Gravano, Gotti's "underboss," or second in command, would plead guilty and testify as a government witness.

When the trial began in Brooklyn, New York on January 21, 1992, Gotti's new lawyer, Albert J. Kreiger, opened the defense by stating that his client's only crime was the lack of a formal education. Kreiger wasted no time in accusing the admitted murderer Gravano of being the rightful object of the prosecution's attention.

Unruffled government prosecutors had learned from past mistakes. "This is not a complex case," Maloney told the jury. "These defendants will tell you in their own words what it's about." Prosecutors played hours of secretly taped conversations in which Gotti spoke of murders and other crimes. "Anytime you got a partner who don't agree with us," Gotti told Locasio on one tape, "we kill him."

The second source of strength in the government's case was Gravano, who admitted his role in 19 murders, including 10 authorized by Gotti. The former underboss described how he and Gotti waited in a nearby car while Castellano and Bilotti were shot and then drove slowly past the bloody scene. Gravano added that a taped conversation in which Gotti falsely disavowed any part in Castellano's slaying was performed for the benefit of eavesdropping "bugs."

The defense attacked Gravano's description of the Castellano murder and characterized him as "a rat" who was willing to implicate others falsely to obtain a lighter sentence for his own violent crimes. Gravano admitted his hopes for leniency, but his testimony remained unshaken. Prosecutors also submitted evidence that Gotti had bribed a police detective for information and had failed to file income tax returns for six years during which he claimed to work as a plumbing company salesman.

The sole defense witness was a tax lawyer who had advised Gotti to exercise a "legitimate privilege of silence" by not filing returns while under indictment. As Judge Glasser ruled that appearances by all five other defense witnesses would be inappropriate for various legal reasons, Gotti's former cheery bluster eroded completely. He bickered openly with the judge, who threatened to have him removed from court.

In his summation, defense attorney Krieger accused the government of victimizing his client with a case manufactured from Gravano's lies. Prosecutor John Gleeson replied, "these defendants ranted and raved about Salvatore Gravano because he is their nightmare."

The jury agreed. On April 2, 1992, after only 13 hours of deliberations, Gotti was found guilty on all counts. Locasio was convicted of all charges, except one count of illegal gambling. Both career criminals were sentenced June 23 to life in prison without parole. Gotti's supporters protested the sentence by fighting with police and overturning cars in the streets outside the Brooklyn courthouse. Seven protesters were arrested on felony riot charges.

As Gotti was taken to a federal prison to spend the rest of his days in solitary confinement, his former confidante "Sammy Bull" Gravano continued to testify about the Gambino organization's hidden financial assets. Under the seizure provisions of the RICO statute, the FBI moved to confiscate ill-gotten properties owned by Gotti and the nation's largest Mafia family.

Prosecutor Gleeson's summation lingered as the last word. The attorney who had faced Gotti's sarcastic jibes and hateful stares during both RICO trials told the jury that there were two ways to convict mobsters: "One, catch them talking about their crimes. Figure out a way to find those secret meetings and record them. There's one other way. Get one of them to come in and tell you about the crimes. We did both."

—Thomas C. Smith

Suggestions for Further Reading

Cummings, John and Ernest Volkman. *Goombata: The Improbable Rise of John Gotti and His Gang.* Boston: Little, Brown & Co., 1990.

Dannen, Frederic. "The Untouchable? How the FBI Sabotaged Competing Prosecution Teams In the Race to Nail Mob Boss John Gotti. *Vanity Fair* (January 1992): 26–44.

Fisher, Ian. "Defending the Mob: A User's Guide." *New York Times* (March 26, 1992): Bl, B5.

McFadden, Robert D. "For Gotti Prosecutors, Hard Work Pays off With Conviction." *New York Times* (April 3, 1992): Al, B3.

Mustain, Gene and Jerry Capeci. *Mob Star: The Story of John Gotti.* New York: Franklin Watts, 1988.

Raab, Selwyn. "A Weakness in the Gotti Case." *New York Times* (March 14, 1987): A1.

Mike Tyson Trial: 1992

Defendant: Michael Gerard Tyson   **Crimes Charged:** Rape, criminal deviant conduct, and confinement   **Chief Defense Lawyers:** Kathleen I. Beggs, Vincent J. Fuller, and F. Lane Heard   **Chief Prosecutors:** David Dreyer, J. Gregory Garrison, and Barbara J. Trathen   **Judge:** Patricia J. Gifford
Place: Indianapolis, Indiana   **Dates of Trial:** January 26–February 10, 1992
Verdict: Guilty   **Sentence:** 10 years imprisonment

SIGNIFICANCE
In the ring, boxing superstar Mike Tyson had engaged in many epic struggles, but nothing to rival this trial.

At age 25, Mike Tyson had already won and lost the world heavyweight boxing championship. Seemingly on the verge of challenging to regain his crown, in July 1991 he attended the Black Expo in Indianapolis. One of the scheduled events was the Miss Black America pageant and one of the contestants was Desiree Washington, the 18-year-old Miss Rhode Island. Tyson, whose fondness for and occasional problems with attractive young women were well documented, invited Washington to his hotel room. Around 2:00 A.M. on July 19, she agreed. Three days later Washington went to the police. What she had to say resulted in Tyson facing charges of rape and related offenses.

Once the jury was impaneled on January 29, and after Judge Patricia J. Gifford had denied a request from Tyson's chief attorney, Vincent J. Fuller, that the accuser's sexual history be admitted into evidence, it was time for the opening statements.

Prosecutor J. Gregory Garrison delivered a ringing indictment of the defendant. "This man," he said, pointing at Tyson, "is guilty of pinning that 18-year-old girl to a bed and confining her . . . callously and maliciously raping her even though she cried out in pain."

Fuller, on the other hand, depicted a calculating vixen "mature beyond her 18 years," sophisticated and poised and out for money, an educated over-achiever more than a match for a high-school dropout like Tyson. To be sure, Washington's level of sophistication had unnerved prosecutors before the trial, but when it came time for her testify she did so in a childlike voice, peppering her speech with expressions like "yukky."

She described receiving a phone call from Tyson at 1:36 A.M. Minutes later, believing herself to be en route to a party, she joined Tyson in his limousine. As soon as she entered the car Tyson grabbed her: "I kind of jumped back because I was surprised that, being who he is, he acted like that and, besides, his breath smelled kind of bad."

Boxer Mike Tyson pleaded not guilty to rape and was released after posting a $30,000 bond in Indianapolis. (AP/Wide World Photos)

Instead of the expected party, they drove to Tyson's hotel. Once inside his room Tyson resumed his advances. At that point, Washington said, she told him that she was "not like the girls he must be used to hanging out with." Tyson, undeterred, pinned her down on the bed with one arm and used his free hand to undress her. All the while, she said, he mocked her efforts to resist, saying, "Don't fight me. Don't fight me."

Brutal Attack

Then the alleged rape took place. Washington described the pain as "excruciating," and that when she began to cry, "he started laughing like it was a game or something, like it was funny." Then she ran from the room, shoes in hand. Outside she saw Tyson's chauffeur who offered to drive her back to her hotel.

When cross-examined, Washington conceded that on several occasions she had the opportunity to leave the hotel room but chose not to do so. Fuller probed reports that after meeting Tyson, she had told other pageant contestants, "He's rich. Did you see what Robin Givens [Tyson's ex-wife] got out of him? Besides, he's dumb." Washington denied that any such exchange had ever taken place. Neither had she sung "Money, money, money, money, money," from the song "For the Love of Money" to a girlfriend later, as alleged.

Partial corroboration of Washington's story came from the chauffeur, Virginia Foster, 44. When Washington returned to the limousine, said Foster, "She looked like she may have been in a state of shock . . . dazed, disoriented. She seemed scared." (Earlier the defense had successfully petitioned to have disallowed as evidence Foster's claim that Tyson had been sexually aggressive toward her also. No charges were ever filed.)

Dr. Thomas Richardson, the emergency room physician who examined Washington more than 24 hours after the incident, confirmed the presence of abrasions "consistent with forced or very hard intercourse."

Earlier prosecution comparisons between Tyson's menacing bulk and Washington's slight 98-pound stature came into stark relief as the defendant took the stand. He began by saying that everything had taken place with Washington's full cooperation and consent. Asked by Fuller if he forced himself upon her, Tyson replied, "No, I didn't. I didn't violate her in any way, sir."

In graphic terms Tyson described the encounter, but denied Garrison's claims that he had willfully misled Washington, insisting she had been aware of his sexual intentions beforehand and had only become annoyed when he remained in bed afterwards and refused to accompany her downstairs. "I told her that was the way it was. I said 'The limousine is downstairs. If you don't want to use the limousine, you can walk.'"

Quizzed by Garrison on why he had urged Washington to wear loose-fitting clothes, Tyson admitted that he had planned to have sex in the limousine, and tight-fitting jeans "would have complicated it."

Ten hours of jury deliberation produced a guilty verdict. On March 26, 1992, Judge Gifford passed sentence: 10 years imprisonment, with the last four suspended. With time off for good behavior, Tyson would be eligible for parole in 1995.

Often, in trial by jury, demeanor is everything. In the words of her deputy defense counsel, Barbara Trathen, Desiree Washington made "a great victim" on the stand, demure, almost adolescent. By contrast, Tyson's untutored responses to questioning came across as brutish and arrogant.

—Colin Evans

Suggestions for Further Reading

"Boxer Mike Tyson Convicted of Rape." *Facts On File* (February 13, 1992): 97ff.

Jet (February 24, 1992): 16ff.

Oates, Joyce Carol. "Rape and the Boxing Ring." *Newsweek* (February 24, 1992): 60ff.

Steptoe, S. "A Damnable Defense." *Sports Illustrated* (February 24, 1992): 92.

Los Angeles Police Officers' Trials: 1992 & 1993

Defendants: Theodore J. Briseno, Stacey C. Koon, Laurence M. Powell, and Timothy E. Wind   **Crimes Charged:** First trial: Assault, excessive force by a police officer, and filing false report; Second trial: Violating civil rights
Chief Defense Lawyers: First trial: Paul DePasquale, Darryl Mounger, and Michael P. Stone; second trial: Harland W. Braun, Paul DePasquale, Ira M. Salzman, and Michael P. Stone   **Chief Prosecutor:** First trial: Terry L. White; second trial: Steven D. Clymer, and Barry F. Kowalski   **Judges:** First trial: Stanley M. Weisberg; second trial: John G. Davies   **Places:** First trial: Simi Valley, California; second trial: Los Angeles, California   **Dates of Trials:** First trial: March 4–April 29, 1992; second trial: February 3–April 17, 1993
Verdict: First trial: Not guilty; jury deadlocked on one charge against Powell; Second trial: Koon and Powell, guilty; Briseno and Wind, not guilty
Sentence: Koon and Powell sentenced to 30 months imprisonment each.

SIGNIFICANCE
What was already one of the highest profile cases in American legal history assumed landmark proportions when a second jury had to wrestle not only with questions of guilt or innocence, but how best to assuage outraged civic sensibilities.

In the early hours of March 3, 1991, motorist Rodney King was stopped by Los Angeles, California, police officers following a three mile high speed chase. According to arrest reports filed later, King refused orders to exit the car, then put up such a struggle that officers had to use batons and stun-guns to subdue him. However, unbeknownst to police, the entire incident had been captured on video by a nearby resident, and the resulting 81-second tape told a different story. In it King seemed to offer little resistance as several officers kicked and beat him to the ground while a dozen of their colleagues looked on. Public outrage led to a grand jury investigation and indictments against four officers for assault and use of excessive force.

Because of the extraordinary pretrial publicity, a defense motion to move the proceedings from Los Angeles succeeded, and on March 4, 1992, the trial began in suburban Simi Valley. In his opening speech, chief prosecutor Terry L. White referred to falsified reports submitted after the incident as evidence that the police had realized the illegality of their conduct and had tried to conceal it. But it was the evidence of another California Highway Patrol officer, Melanie Singer, which yielded the most prosecutorial advantage. She testified that defendant Laurence Powell had unnecessarily struck King six times with his metal baton. "He had it in a power swing and he struck the driver right across the top of the cheekbone, splitting his face from the top of his ear to his chin," she said. "Blood spurted out." Singer did say that defendants Koon and Briseno tried to restrain Powell from further beating King.

King, a tall, heavyset man and former convict, was never called to the stand by the prosecution, a decision reportedly based on prosecution fears that he would make a poor impression on jurors.

Under questioning, Briseno admitted that he did not consider King's actions to be threatening, and he repeatedly described codefendants Powell and Wind as "out of control." He further blamed Sergeant Stacey Koon, the highest ranking officer present, for not intervening.

It was the defense contention that the officers had believed King to be under the effects of PCP, a powerful hallucinogenic, and therefore extremely dangerous. (King had acknowledged that he had been drinking, but there was no evidence he had taken any drugs.) In his closing statement, defense attorney Michael P. Stone said of the tape, "We do not see an example of unprovoked police brutality. We see, rather, a controlled application of baton strikes, for the very obvious reason of getting this man into custody."

The jury clearly agreed. On April 29, 1992, they returned not-guilty verdicts for all defendants, deadlocking on only one charge against Powell.

A City in Flames

The verdict rocked Los Angeles. Within hours the city erupted in rioting that left 58 people dead and caused $1 billion in damage. In the aftermath of this tragedy the U.S. government filed charges of civil rights violations against the four officers.

Prosecutors Barry F. Kowalski and Steven D. Clymer faced an uphill task when the second trial began in Los Angeles on February 3, 1993: convincing a jury that the officers had *deliberately* intended to deprive Rodney King of his constitutional rights. But first they had to select that jury.

The absence of black jurors in the state trial had kindled a firestorm of criticism, but on this occasion a more ethnically diverse panel was selected. In his opening argument, Clymer declared "Rodney King is not on trial." "The issue of whether he was guilty or innocent that night is not the issue in this trial. What we will tell you is that while he was being beaten while he was on the ground he didn't kick a police officer, he didn't punch a police officer, he didn't grab a police officer, he didn't injure a police officer."

Confirmation of this came from Dorothy Gibson, an eyewitness. "He [King] was lying on the ground, face down with his hands stretched out like a cross shape." Another eyewitness, Robert Hill, described hearing King scream in pain as officers beat him.

Sergeant Mark Conta, an expert on police procedure with the LAPD, condemned the tactics used. "It is my opinion that it was a clear violation of Los Angeles police policy." Conta singled out Koon for special criticism. "He should have stopped this and should have taken care of his officers when they needed him most."

Following the first trial it was widely believed that the prosecution had miscalculated by not putting King on the witness stand. On this occasion he did testify and made an effective witness.

Describing his actions to Kowalski, King said, "I was just trying to stay alive, sir." King admitted that he had responded defiantly when the officers began baiting him, chanting, "What's up, nigger? How do you feel, killer?" "I didn't want them to know that what they were doing was getting to me—I didn't want them to get any satisfaction." He described the baton blows as feeling "like you would get up in the middle of the night and jam your toe . . . on a piece of metal. That's what it felt like every time I got hit."

Throughout a grueling day of cross-examination, King did much to dispel earlier defense depictions of him as a menacing brute. Even when defense attorney Michael Stone drew an admission from him that he had lied to investigators when he denied driving drunk on the night of the beating, King managed to salvage the situation, saying that, as a parolee, he had been afraid of being returned to prison.

Another defense team member, Harland W. Braun, hammered away at King's varied and contradictory versions of events that night, implying that King had appended the assertions of racial epithets to enhance his civil suit against the city of Los Angeles. "You can become a rich man," said Braun, suggesting that King stood to gain $50 million in the suit.

King did admit to a faulty memory: "Sometimes I forget things that happened and sometimes I remember things," conceding an uncertainty about whether the taunts leveled at him had actually included the word 'nigger.' "I'm not sure. I believe I did hear that." In earlier grand-jury testimony, King had made no mention of racial slurs.

Braun was incredulous. "As an Afro-American who admittedly was beaten, you would forget that police officers called you nigger? . . . The fact is that you were trying to improve your case or lawsuit and really didn't care about the impact it would have on anyone else!"

The assault was continued by Paul DePasquale, attorney for Timothy Wind, who also highlighted King's hazy recollection of events by referring to an interview in which King had erroneously claimed that he was handcuffed all through the beating. Despite these inconsistencies, Rodney King left the stand largely undiminished and having impressed the majority of those present.

In a strange turn of events, officer Melanie Singer was again called, this time for the defense, but the content and manner of her testimony yielded a bonanza for the prosecution. Defense attorneys could only stand aghast as she tearfully condemned their clients' conduct. It was a devastating setback.

Textbook Tactics

Now only the defendants could help themselves. Stacey Koon was first to take the stand. Insisting that his actions were a textbook example of how to subdue an aggressive suspect, the sergeant said, "My intent at that moment was to cripple Rodney King . . . that is a better option than going to deadly force." Koon maintained that "He [King] made all the choices. He made all the wrong choices." In a cool, confident voice, Koon continued, "This is not a boxing match. We had a tactical advantage and we keep the tactical advantage, and we do not give it up. The tactical advantage is Rodney King is on the ground and we are going to keep him on the ground."

The prosecution was denied an important line of inquiry when Judge John G. Davies barred Steven Clymer from raising allegedly racial passages included in a book written by Koon about the incident. Instead, Clymer could isolate only minor inconsistencies in Koon's testimony. "You are exaggerating, are you not, the amount of things you say happened?"

"No, sir," Koon replied firmly. "I am telling you my recollection."

To general astonishment, it was announced that none of the other defendants would testify. Which left only the closing arguments. Following these representations, Judge Davies gave the jury a careful reading of the complex law involved and they retired.

With the media, many public officials, and ordinary citizens predicting another round of riots if the four officers were acquitted, the tension built in Los Angeles as the jurors deliberated. Police officers were put on 12-hour shifts, and California Governor Pete Wilson mobilized National Guard units. Gun stores did business at breakneck speed as shopkeepers and residents set about protecting themselves. One week after jurors began deliberation on April 17, 1993, they were back. Koon and Powell were emotionless as their guilty verdicts were read out, while Briseno and Wind were acquitted. Koon and Powell were each sentenced to 30 months imprisonment on August 4, 1993.

Rodney King's civil suit against the city of Los Angeles was still pending as of this writing. Few jury decisions have so affected everyday life as the verdicts in these two trials. The first prompted violence on an appalling scale, while an entire city held its breath awaiting the second. And yet, almost unmentioned in all of the turmoil, was the question of possible double jeopardy, and whether the officers should have been retried for essentially the same crime. As puzzling as the first verdict may have been, many felt that the subsequent federal trial was predicated more on outrage than the Constitution.

—Colin Evans

Suggestions for Further Reading

Boyer, Peter J. "The Selling of Rodney King." *Vanity Fair.* (July 1992): 78–83.

Duffy, Brian and Ted Gest. "Days of Rage." *US News & World Report.* (May 11, 1992): 20–26.

Koon, Stacey and Robert Dietz. *Presumed Guilty.* Chicago, Regnery Gateway, 1992.

Prudhomme, Alex. "Police Brutality." *Time* (March 25, 1991): 16–19.

GLOSSARY

Note: References to other defined terms are set in bold type.

Accessory after the fact one who obstructs justice by giving comfort or assistance to the felon (*see* **felony**), knowing that the felon has committed a crime or is sought by authorities in connection with a serious crime

Accessory before the fact one who aids in the commission of a **felony** by ordering or encouraging it, but who is not present when the crime is perpetrated

Accomplice one who voluntarily engages with another in the commission or attempted commission of a crime

Amicus curiae literally, "friend of the court," an individual or entity not party to the lawsuit whose role is to provide the court with information, typically a legal brief, which might not otherwise be considered by the court

Annulment a nullification, as of a marriage; when a marriage is annulled, it is as if it never existed, whereas divorce terminates the legal status of the marriage from that point forward

Appellant the party appealing a decision to a higher, appellate court

Appellate jurisdiction the power of a superior court or other tribunal to review the judicial actions of lower courts, particularly for legal errors, and to revise their judgments accordingly

Appellee the party who prevailed in the court below the appellate court and who argues on appeal against setting aside the judgment of the lower court

Aranda rule a 1965 ruling by the Supreme Court that forbids testimony in which one codefendant implicates another

Arraignment the procedure by which a criminal defendant is brought before the trial court and informed of the charges against him or her and the pleas (guilty, not guilty, or no contest) he or she may enter in response

Bench warrant an order from the court empowering legal authorities to seize an individual, usually to compel attendance to answer a contempt charge or when a **subpoena** has been ignored

Change of venue the removal of a lawsuit from a county or district to another for trial, often permitted in criminal cases where the court finds that the defendant would not receive a fair trial in the first location because of adverse publicity

Circumstantial evidence indirect, secondary facts from which the existence or non-existence of a fact at issue in a case may be inferred

Claimant the party, customarily the **plaintiff**, asserting a right, usually to money or property

Clemency the act, usually by a chief executive such as a president or governor, of forgiving a criminal liability for his or her actions, as when a **pardon** is granted

Co-conspirator one who engages in a **conspiracy** with others; the acts and declarations of any one conspirator are admissible as evidence against all his or her co-conspirators

Common law principles and rules of action derived from past judicial decisions, as distinct from laws created solely through legislative enactment

Commutation alteration or substitution, such as when one criminal punishment is substituted for another, more severe one

Compensatory damages monetary damages the law awards to compensate an injured party solely for the injury sustained because of the action of another (cf. **punitive damages**)

Conspiracy the agreement of two or more individuals to commit, through their joint efforts, an unlawful act

Coroner's inquest an examination by the coroner, often with the aid of a jury, into the causes of a death occurring under suspicious circumstances

Corpus delicti objective proof that a crime has been committed, which ordinarily includes evidence of the criminal act and evidence of who is responsible for its commission

Cross-examination questioning a witness, by a party or a lawyer other than the one who is called the witness, about testimony the witness gave on **direct examination**

Court of chancery courts that follow rules of equity, or general rules of fairness, rather than strictly formulated common law; distinctions between courts of equity and courts of law have essentially disappeared at both the state and federal levels

Declarative judgment of relief a binding adjudication of the rights and status of parties that does not require any further action or relief

Defamation speech (**slander**) or writings (**libel**) that damages the reputation of another

Direct evidence testimony at trial by a witness who actually heard the words or saw the actions that, if believed by the trier of fact, conclusively establish a fact at issue

Direct examination initial questioning of a witness by the lawyer who called him or her, the purpose of which is to present testimony regarding the facts of the examining party's case

Diversity jurisdiction one basis for granting federal courts the power to hear and determine cases, applicable to controversies arising between citizens of different states or between a citizen of a state and an alien

Double jeopardy a bar against double prosecution or double punishment for the same offense, operational only in criminal cases and only if there is no appeal of a conviction

Due process applicable only to actions of state or federal governments and their officials, it guarantees procedural fairness when the state deprives an individual of property or liberty; also, substantive due process requires that all legislation be enacted solely to further legitimate governmental objectives

Ex parte literally, "on behalf of"; a judicial proceeding brought for the benefit of one party without notice to the adverse party, who does not participate

Extortion a criminal offense, usually punished as a **felony,** consisting of obtaining property from another through use or threat of force, or through illegitimate use of official power

Extradition the surrender by one state or country of an individual who is accused or convicted of an offense outside the borders of that state or country

Expert witness a witness, such as a psychological statistician or ballistics expert, with special knowledge concerning the subject he or she will testify about

Felony high crimes, such as burglary, rape, or homicide, which unlike misdemeanors, are often punishable by lengthy jail terms or death

Gag order a court order restricting dissemination, by attorneys and witnesses, of information about a case (such orders directed at the press are unconstitutional); also, an order to restrain an unruly defendant who is disrupting his or her trial

Grand jury traditionally consisting of twenty-three (as opposed to twelve- or six-member **petit juries**) individuals empaneled to determine whether the facts and accusations presented by prosecutors in criminal proceedings warrant an **indictment** and trial of the accused

Guardian *ad litem* a guardian appointed by the court to represent the interests of an infant or incompetent in legal proceedings

Habeas corpus a procedure for a judicial ruling on the legality of an individual's custody, used in a criminal context to challenge a convict's confinement and in a civil context to challenge child custody, deportation, and commitment to a mental institution

Hearsay a statement, other than one made by a witness at a hearing or trial, offered to prove the truth of a matter asserted at the hearing or trial; such statements are inadmissable as evidence except under certain circumstances

Immunity exemption from a duty or penalty; witnesses are often granted immunity from prosecution in order to compel them to respond to questions they might otherwise refuse to answer based on the Fifth Amendment's privilege against self-incrimination

Impeach to call into question the truthfulness of a witness's testimony by offering evidence of his or her lack of veracity

Impeachment criminal proceedings against a public official, such as a president or a supreme court justice, accused of wrongdoing while in office

Indictment a formal written accusation drawn up by a public prosecuting attorney and issued by a grand jury against a party charged with a crime

Injunction a judicial remedy requiring a party to cease or refrain from some specified action

In re literally, "in the matter of"; used to signify a legal proceeding where there are no adversaries, but merely a matter, such as an estate, requiring judicial action

Interspousal immunity a state common law rule, now largely abolished, prohibiting tort actions, or lawsuits concerning certain civil wrongs, between husbands and wives

Judicial notice recognition by a court during trial of certain facts that are so universally acknowledged or easily verifiable (e.g., historical facts, geographical features) that they do not require the production of evidence as proof of their existence

Judicial review review of a trial court decision by an appellate court; power and responsibility of the U.S. Supreme Court and the highest state courts to determine the constitutionality of the acts of the legislatures and executive branches of their respective jurisdictions

Jury tampering a criminal offense consisting of attempting to improperly influence one or more jurors' vote(s) by threats, bribes, etc.

Justifiable homicide the killing of another in self-defense or in the lawful defense of one's property; killing another when the law demands it, such as in execution for a capital crime

Libel a method of defamation expressed by false and malicious publication in print for the purpose of damaging the reputation of another

Libelant formerly, the party who filed a complaint in an admiralty or ecclesiastical case; a **plaintiff**

Manslaughter unlawful killing of another without malice, aforethought, or an intent to cause death, it calls for less severe penalties than murder; most jurisdictions distinguish between voluntary, or intentional manslaughter, and involuntary manslaughter, such as a death resulting from an automobile accident

Misdemeanor any criminal offense less serious than a **felony,** generally punishable by a fine or imprisonment other than in a penitentiary and for a shorter period than would be imposed for a **felony**

Mistrial a trial declared void before a verdict is returned, usually because the jury is deadlocked or because some incurable and fundamental error that is prejudicial to the defendant

M'Naghten Rule a test to be applied to the insanity defense under which the accused will be found not criminally liable if, at the time he or she committed the act in question, the accused was incapable of knowing that it was wrong

Nol. pros. (*nolle prosequi*) a formal declaration, usually by the prosecutor in a criminal case, that the state will not prosecute a given defendant or case any further

Obstruction of justice the offense of attempting to interfere with the administration of justice through such acts as **jury tampering** or attempting to influence an officer of the court

Original jurisdiction the authority to hear a case at its inception and to pass judgment on its law and facts, as opposed to **appellate jurisdiction,** which grants the power to review the decisions of lower tribunals, which can then be affirmed, reversed, or modified

Parole a conditional release of a prisoner after he or she has served part of a sentence

Pardon an act, usually of a chief executive such as a president or governor, that relieves a convicted individual from the punishment imposed for his or her crime and restores rights and privileges that have been forfeited because of it

Perjury the criminal offense of making false statements while under oath

Petit jury an ordinary trial jury, as opposed to a **grand jury,** traditionally composed of twelve (in some jurisdictions six) persons whose job it is to determine issues of fact in civil and criminal proceedings

Plaintiff the party who initiates a lawsuit, seeking a remedy for an injury to his or her rights

Police power of the state the power of state and local governments to impose upon private rights restrictions that are necessary to the general public welfare

Prima facie case a case that, because it is supported by the requisite minimum of evidence and is free of obvious defects, can go to the jury; thus the defendant is required to proceed with its case rather than move for dismissal or a directed verdict

Punitive damages compensation in excess of actual losses awarded to a successful **plaintiff** who was injured under circumstances involving malicious and willful misconduct on the part of the defendant (cf. **compensatory damages**)

Reasonable doubt the degree of certainty required for a juror to find a criminal defendant guilty, meaning that proof of guilt must be so clear that an ordinary person would have no reasonable doubt as to the guilt of the defendant

Recusation the act whereby a judge is disqualified, or disqualifies himself or herself, from a case because of the potential for bias or a conflict of interest

Reprieve a temporary relief or postponement of a criminal punishment or sentence

Remand to send a matter back to the tribunal from which it was appealed; when an appellate court reverses a judgment, the case is usually remanded to the lower court for a new trial

RICO laws "Racketeer Influenced and Corrupt Organization Act," federal statute designed to prosecute organized crime; many states have enacted similar statutes

Sedition any illegal action intended to disrupt or overthrow the government

Seditious libel publication of words intended to excite public sentiment against the government (cf. **sedition**)

Slander oral defamation; false and malicious words spoken with the intent to damage another's reputation

Statutory rape the crime of having sexual intercourse with a female under an age set by the state statute

Subornation of perjury the criminal offense of procuring another to commit **perjury**

Subpoena a written order issued under court authority compelling the appearance of a witness at a judicial proceeding

Talesman a court bystander summoned to serve as a juror

Temporary insanity a criminal defense asserting that, because the accused was legally insane at the time the crime was committed, he or she did not have the necessary mental state to commit it and is therefore not responsible for the alleged criminal conduct

Venireman one of a panel of jurors

Voir dire examination by the court or by lawyers for the parties of prospective jurors; also, a hearing by the court during trial out of the jury's presence to determine initially a question of law

Writ of certiorari a means of gaining appellate review; a written order issued by an appellate court to an inferior tribunal, commanding the latter to forward the record of the proceedings below in a particular case

Writ of habeas corpus a procedure used in criminal contexts to bring a petitioning prisoner before the court to determine the legality of his or her confinement (*see* **habeas corpus**)

Writ of mandamus an order issued by a court, usually to an inferior tribunal, commanding performance of some ministerial act or mandatory duty, or directing the restoration to the petitioner of rights and privileges that have been illegally denied

INDEX